HISTORY
OF
THE AFGHANS

HISTORY
OF
THE AFGHANS

BY J. P. FERRIER

AUTHOR OF 'CARAVAN JOURNEYS AND WANDERINGS IN PERSIA, AFGHANISTAN, ETC.'; FORMERLY OF THE CHASSEURS D' AFRIQUE, AND LATE ADJUTANT-GENERAL OF THE PERSIAN ARMY.

Translated from the Original Unpublished Manuscript
BY CAPTAIN WILLIAM JESSE

GYAN

Published by

GYAN

Gyan Publishing House
5, Ansari Road
Daryaganj, New Delhi-110002
Phone: 011-47034999, 9811692060
E-mail: books@gyanbooks.com

Distribution Network
gyanbooks.com
India, USA, Canada, UK, Australia, France

ISBN : 978-81-212-4570-8 (HB)
First Published, 1858

2nd Impression 2020

Printed at: Gyan Press, Delhi.

History of the Afghans
Author: J. P. Ferrier

HISTORY

OF

THE AFGHANS.

BY J. P. FERRIER,

AUTHOR OF 'CARAVAN JOURNEYS AND WANDERINGS IN PERSIA, AFGHANISTAN, ETC.';
FORMERLY OF THE CHASSEURS D'AFRIQUE, AND LATE ADJUTANT-GENERAL
OF THE PERSIAN ARMY.

Translated from the Original Unpublished Manuscript

BY CAPTAIN WILLIAM JESSE.

LONDON:
JOHN MURRAY, ALBEMARLE STREET.
1858.

BY THE SAME AUTHOR,

CARAVAN JOURNEYS AND WANDERINGS IN PERSIA, AFGHANISTAN, TURKISTAN, AND BELOOCHISTAN, AND THROUGH PARTS OF CENTRAL ASIA previously unvisited, THE HAZARAH COUNTRY, Gour, Helmund, Seistan, &c. Translated from the original French Manuscript, by Captain Jesse. *Second Edition,* with Original Map, 8vo. 21*s*.

This Work contains important information regarding the opening for British Manufactures through the Indus, into the heart of Central Asia.

"M. Ferrier's conclusions are those of an intelligent observer, but they concern us more especially as coming from a foreigner, and from one whom we are entitled to regard as an unprejudiced witness. It is most welcome to find that such a critic of our Indian dominion is so satisfied of its secure tenure, that he is convinced it 'will last for ages if it be not attacked by any European nation.'"—*Times.*

Dedicated

TO MY OLD COMRADES

OF

THE 2ND REGIMENT OF CARABINEERS

AND

THE 1ST REGIMENT OF CHASSEURS D'AFRIQUE.

J. P. FERRIER.

PREFACE.

The Translator, having accomplished his very interesting, though laborious, task of rendering into English the manuscripts of General Ferrier, is anxious to avail himself of this opportunity to congratulate that officer on having added these instructive volumes to the Eastern literature of this country. They can be more thoroughly appreciated here than in France; and that they must prove of real value in England is evident when we consider how great are the interests involved in the development—commercial, social, and religious—of that vast continent which Providence has permitted to fall under our rule.

As an old soldier also, the Translator wishes to mark his sense of the frank and generous manner in which General Ferrier has spoken of the arduous services of the Anglo-Indian army in Afghanistan; more especially as at the period at which he gave expression to these sentiments—1845—the *entente* between his own nation and England was by no means so cordial as happily it is now. The Author's criticisms, when unfavourable, are generally well-founded; and though, no doubt, inaccuracies are to be met with in some portions of the 'History of the Afghans,' it is evident that they proceed from defective information, and not from any ignoble desire to write disparagingly of the British Empire or our gallant soldiers. As to his comments on the Indian policy of this country, or the manner in which that policy has been carried out, the Translator cannot, agreeing as he does with the greater number of them, feel at all surprised at their severity; indeed, he considers that we ought to accept these comments with gratitude, inasmuch as they present to us a more unprejudiced view of the subject than we have yet seen.

At a very early period French travellers greatly distinguished themselves in the East, and the names of Tavernier, Bernier, and Thevenot justify the assertion; but the travels of General Ferrier are even of a more interesting character than those of these pioneers in Asiatic adventure; moreover, his sufferings were great while wending his weary way over the deserts of Central Asia, in some districts where European foot had never before left its imprint on the burning sands. The cruelty and hardships he then endured entitle him to the commiseration of every feeling mind, and the industry and perseverance that enabled him to collect and to preserve the materials for his History and Travels, under circumstances so adverse, are worthy of all admiration.

Important also are the opinions of one who is capable of giving us much sound advice, and critically examining the conduct of Great Britain, in connection with the countries which join her Indian frontiers on the north and north-west. Our information regarding these countries, their inhabitants, and their policy, has hitherto come almost exclusively from officers or civilians in the East India Company's service; it is profitable to see the same subjects treated by a foreigner and from another point of view, for reasons which must be apparent to many.

General Ferrier has pointed out, in his chapter on the invasion of India, in 'Caravan Journeys,' the probability of the Sepoys joining the Russian army, and the princes and rajahs throwing off their allegiance; opinions which, no doubt, elicited expressions of indignation from many of his readers, especially those who were the servants of the East India Company—but how fearfully has his estimate of native fidelity been justified since the publication of that volume!

The reader will do well to consult the highly interesting notes and appendices of Sir H. Rawlinson, Sir John Login, and Mr. Danby Seymour, in 'Caravan Journeys,' as they elucidate many points in the History of the Afghans.

The style of the author is rather severe, and there are several portions of the present work in which there was an opening for much touching writing and for appeals to the highest and best feelings of our nature; even a few words only here and there would have considerably increased the interest of the subject, but the translator did not consider himself at liberty to do otherwise than adhere strictly to the text. When there was a duplication of thought, or want of arrangement, he has endeavoured to remedy these defects; but otherwise the reader is in possession of General Ferrier's work in its integrity.

WILLIAM JESSE.

Maisonette, Ingatestone, March 27, 1858.

CONTENTS.

CHAPTER I.

CHAPTER II.

CHAPTER III.

CHAPTER IV.

CHAPTER V.

CHAPTER VI.

CHAPTER VII.

CHAPTER VIII.

CHAPTER IX.

CHAPTER X.

CHAPTER XI.

CHAPTER XII.

CHAPTER XIII.

CHAPTER XIV.

CHAPTER XV.

CHAPTER XVI.

CHAPTER XVII.

CHAPTER XVIII.

CHAPTER XXII.

CHAPTER XXIII.

CHAPTER XXIV.

CHAPTER XXV.

CHAPTER XXVI.

CHAPTER XXVII.

CHAPTER XXVIII.

CHAPTER XXIX.

CHAPTER XXX.

CHAPTER XXXI.

CHAPTER XXXII.

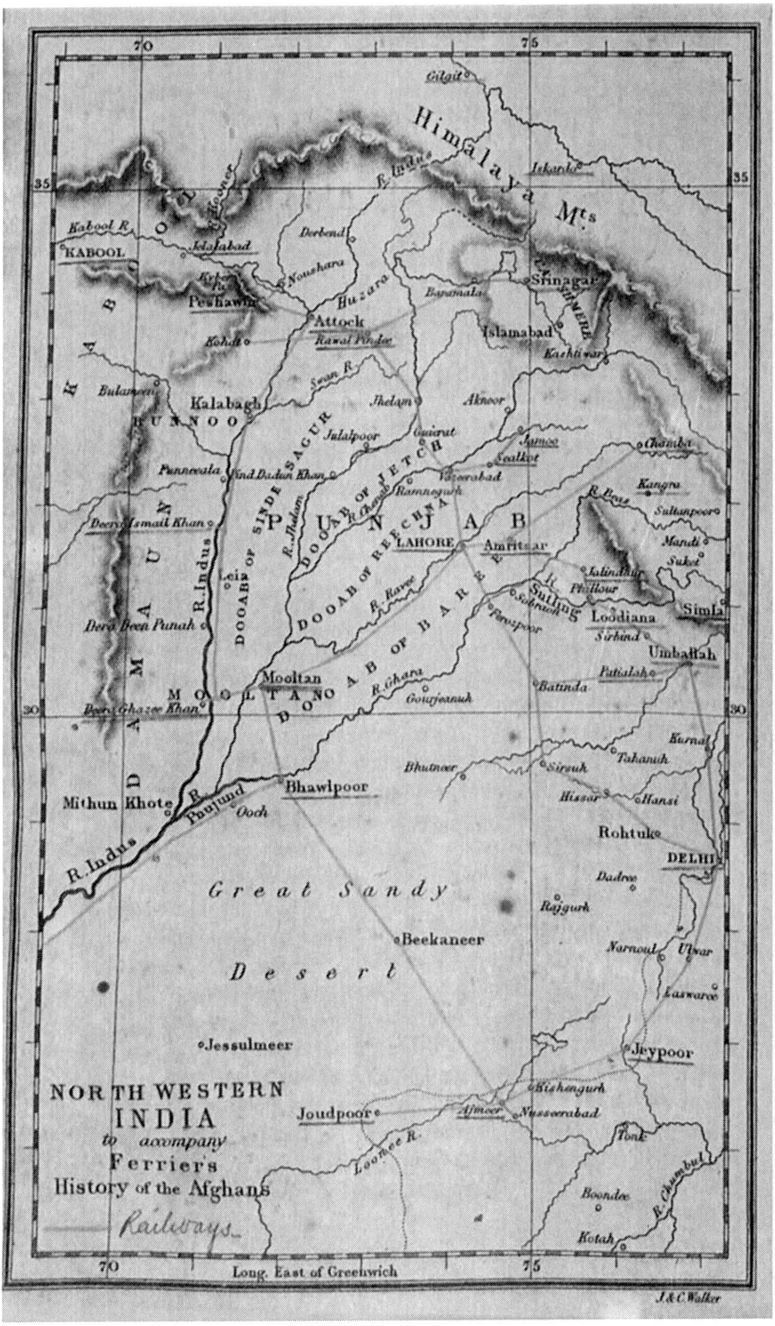
Himalaya Mts
Gilgit
Iskardo
R. Indus
Kabool R.
KABOOL
Jelalabad
Derbend
Noushara
Huzara
Peshawur
Attock
Rawul Pindee
Kohat
Srinagar
Baramula
Islamabad
Kashtiwar
Kalabagh
Swan R.
Jhelum
Aknoor
Julalpoor
Guzerat
Jumoo
Sealkot
Chamba
Punnewala
Pind Dadun Khan
Ramnugur
Kangra
Sultanpoor
R. Beas
Mandi
Suket
Deera Ismail Khan
DOOAB OF SINDE SAGUR
DOOAB OF JETCH
DOOAB OF REECHNA
DOOAB OF BAREE
P U N J A B
LAHORE
Amritsar
R. Jhelum
R. Chenab
R. Indus
Leia
Phillour
Sutlug
Sobraon
Loodiana
Simla
Ferozpoor
Sirhind
Dera Deen Punah
R. Ravee
Umballah
Mooltan
R. Ghara
Patialah
Batinda
Deera Ghazee Khan
Kurnal
Bhutneer
Sirsuh
Hissar
Hansi
Bhawlpoor
Mithun Khote
Punjund
Ooch
Rohtuk
DELHI
R. Indus
Great Sandy Desert
Dadree
Rajgurh
Beekaneer
Narnoul
Ulwar
Laswaree
Jessulmeer
Jeypoor
Kishengurh
Joudpoor
Ajmeer
Nusseerabad
Loonee R.
Tonk
R. Chumbul
Boondee
Kotah
NORTH WESTERN INDIA
to accompany
Ferrier's
History of the Afghans
Railways
70
75
35
30
Long. East of Greenwich
J.&C. Walker

HISTORY OF THE AFGHANS.

CHAPTER I.

Origin of the Afghans — Opinion of Monsieur Ruffin, Eugène Boré, and others — Opinion of Afghan authors — Afghans mentioned by Tamerlane in his Institutes — The probability of their Jewish origin — Their conversion to Islamism — A Hebrew Bible presented to Nadir Shah by the Yoosoofzyes — Afghans of Indian and Khorassian origin — Warlike and independent under Sebek-Taghee — Aborigines of Afghanistan — Afghans in India known as Patans and Rohillas — First mentioned as Afghans in the reign of Aboo Seid — Classification of Afghan tribes — The author adopts that of Abdullah Khan — Persecution of the Afghans under Ghengis Khan — The Abdalees settle in the Suleiman mountains — Yoosoofzyes established in Cashmeer — Afghanistan inhabited almost exclusively by Abdalees and Ghildjzyes — List of Afghan tribes and their branches — Schism amongst them on this subject — Makoohees and Khaouganees — A singular reason for taking offence — Subdivision of the tribes and their branches.

The origin of the Afghans, which is involved in obscurity, has given rise to a variety of opinions, and it is not easy to adopt any one in particular. Some pretend that they are descended from the soldiers of Alexander the Great, whom he left in these countries after he had conquered them; and from some Greek colonists who, under the kings that succeeded that emperor, subsequently joined these descendants of his victorious legions. Others affirm that the Copts of Egypt, the Chaldæans, and even the Armenians, were their ancestors; but the majority of Eastern writers consider them to be the descendants of one of the ten tribes of Israel—and this is the opinion of the Afghans themselves. Finally, a few authors assure us that this nation is not of Jewish origin, but that those who introduced the Mahometan religion amongst them were converted Jews.

The following is taken from the work of that celebrated orientalist, M. Ruffin: "The Afghans," he says, "had their origin from the Albanians of Asia, who, in consequence of their numerous revolts, were transported from one extremity of Persia to the other, and driven into Khorassan; they were a very warlike people, known under the name of *Aghvan* or *Avghan*, and made themselves famous in the history of Persia. Their Albanian origin is evident by the name itself, for *agvan* is the Greek word HA'ΛB."

This opinion, which has been contradicted by several authors, merits nevertheless some attention, because it is in accordance with the custom which the Persian monarchs are supposed to have followed, viz. that of removing from the shores of the Mediterranean or the Black Sea any population that gave them the least uneasiness or apprehension; also that of bestowing upon the Greeks, a considerable number of whom were at all times in the Persian armies, a certain portion of territory, where they were allowed to establish themselves, as a reward for their services. The historians of Alexander have made us acquainted with one of these colonies, and we learn from them that, when that monarch advanced into Bactria in pursuit of Bessus, he destroyed the town of the Brances, the inhabitants of which, descended from Milesian Greeks, he put to death, as a punishment for a crime committed by their ancestors —a most cruel and unjust act.

The opinion of M. Ruffin is in opposition to that of another oriental scholar, M. Eugène Boré, who, in his Letters on the East, thus explains himself on the subject of these Albanians :—

"The Aghovans," he remarks, "were an ancient and distinct people, first brought to our notice by Pompey at the time of his expedition into the Caucasus. The Greeks and Latins, by an inaccurate transcription of their name, called them Albanians; they inhabited the high mountains and the valleys bordering on the Caspian Sea, which now form the provinces of Daghestan and Shirvan. The Armenians were never able to subjugate this brave people, who were governed by feudal laws similar to those which existed in Europe during the middle ages; they were Christians before they adopted the faith of Mahomet, and it is known that they preserved their liberty up to the period of the arrival of Bouzan, general of the Sultan Seljookide Malek Shah. The language of this nation differed entirely from that of the Armenians. . . . . . In short, we may say that the people mentioned by the Greek authors under the denomination of Albanians cannot, on account of their peculiar language, be considered as of Chaldæan origin—an opinion which is in direct contradiction to that of their historian, Moses Galganderasti, who lived about the ninth century of the Christian era, and who, with Moses of Chorenus, affirms that they are descended from Sisag, of the Armenian race. We hope to clear up this point after having collected from the mountainous district in which these pretended sons of the Aghovans lived, the remains of the language they speak. It is with less reason still that some of the learned, led astray by a similarity of words, have confounded the Aghovans with the Afghans, feudal tribes dispersed over the south of Persia, and who, more than any other, recall to our minds the ancient Parthians. The language of the Afghans is analogous to that of the primitive Persian, and, in the opinion of Sir William Jones, they are neither of Jewish nor Chaldæan extraction. The supposition that they were identified with the Aghovans, once formed, has led to the conclusion that they were the descendants of Jews, because the province of Kir, to which the Assyrians transported the captive tribes of Israel, appeared to commentators to be the country watered by the Kour, the Cyrus of the Greeks."

Some persons have with reason affirmed that Tamerlane, exasperated at the depredations committed by the people inhabiting Mazanderan, south of the Caspian, transported the whole of them into the mountains situated between India and Persia. But they erred in supposing that from this population are descended the Afghans of our own day, for the posterity of the unfortunate people who were removed to these mountains by the Tartar conqueror form at the present time a small tribe of Eïmaks, known under the appellation of Firooz Kohis, after the city of that name (situated about sixty-three miles from Teheran), where they were defeated and taken captive by Tamerlane: this tribe now inhabit the country between Herat and Meimana. Besides, the Tartar warrior and legislator mentions the Afghans, in his Institutes, as a nation which had for many years inhabited the Suleiman mountains, and was much given to pillage.

The Afghan authors who admit the Jewish origin of their nation thus account for the removal of their ancestors to Central Asia: some declare that Afghana, who gave his name to the Afghans, was lineally descended from Abraham and Hagar by Ishmael; others affirm that he was the grandson of Saul; and all think that Bakht ul Nasser * must have sent some Jewish prisoners into the mountains of Gour. These prisoners would soon have considerably

* Nebuchadnezzar.

increased; and though far from their mother-country, without doubt they would have preserved their faith, which was kept alive by the periodical reception of letters from their countrymen who, more fortunate than themselves, had returned to the Holy Land. Matters remained in this state until Mahomet announced himself as the messenger of God. A Jew, by name Khaled, whom he converted, wrote at this time to his brethren in Gour to give notice of this happy event, and induce them to embrace the new faith; but they, before adopting Islamism, sent several of their chiefs to the Prophet. Amongst these was Keïs, who pretended to be descended in a direct line from Saul through forty-seven generations, and Abraham through sixty-five. Mahomet loaded him and his companions with favours, and gave him the title of Malek * Abd-ul-reshid, a rank to which he was entitled as the descendant of the Jewish king. These Afghan ambassadors, now Mussulmans, accompanied Mahomet in several of his wars, and distinguished themselves by many remarkable deeds of valour; nevertheless, with the sanction of the Prophet, and after having received his benediction, they returned to their own homes, accompanied by a few Arabs, and with their assistance succeeded, in the space of forty years, in completely converting their countrymen to Islamism.

Some authors affirm that Afghana was the son of Khaled; others say he was contemporary with Solomon, and assert that he was one of the principal officers of that monarch.

These different versions, which do not rest upon any sufficient proof, are very difficult to admit; the Afghans, however, think that they have evidence of their Jewish origin in the following tradition. When Nadir Shah, marching to the conquest of India, arrived at Peshawur, the chiefs of the tribe of the Yoosoofzyes presented him with a Bible written in Hebrew, and several articles that had been used in their ancient worship which they had preserved; these articles were at once recognised by the Jews who followed the camp. This fact, supposing it to be one, if affording evidence sufficiently convincing to some persons, can only be considered as authority with respect to the Yoosoofzyes; but it does not follow, therefore, that other Afghan tribes are branches from the same stem; on the contrary, everything leads to the conclusion that, although they all speak a common language, the Pushtoo,

* Prince.

the tribes are not all of the same origin,—they are distinguished by marked characteristics, moral as well as physical. The Afghans of Kabul consider themselves as Indian Afghans, whereas those of Herat say they are Khorassani Afghans; one tribe repudiates another, and denies its Afghan origin, and there is not the least sympathy between them. We may believe that, being enemies in bygone ages, their union, such as it was, progressed only by degrees, with a view of delivering themselves from slavery, and repulsing the common enemy. The names of Patan, Rohilla, Afghan, which serve at the present time to designate the Afghan nation, are really those of so many distinct races now confounded in one. If we could admit, as they do, their Jewish origin, we must also suppose that they would, on the spot to which they were transferred, have developed all the characteristics of an enslaved people, humble and degenerate; but such is not the case, for we find the Afghans from the very first, that is to say from the reign of Sebek-Taghee, courageous, and animated by a love of independence—always warlike and energetic, retiring to their mountain fastnesses to escape from tyranny, and leaving them whenever the smallest hope presented itself of seizing lands which they considered they had any right to—it is only a primitive race who could have remained so strongly attached to the soil.

No one has thought of the aboriginal people, nevertheless they must not be lost sight of, for, according to Quintus Curtius and Arrian, the Arians, Arrachosians, and others, were both numerous and brave. The conquests of Alexander did not lead to their extermination; and it is very natural to suppose that their race has descended to the present day through intermarriages, though in small proportions, with the Greeks who remained amongst them, and afterwards with the Tartar and Persian conquerors who invaded them. However, under all circumstances, there is little affinity between them and these two nations; it is not thus with the Beloochees, with whom they have many points of resemblance, moral as well as physical. In spite of the foreign domination which has weighed upon the Afghans for so many generations, we ought to believe them when they state that their race has never mixed with any other, for in our day they make no alliances except amongst themselves; and the Afghan who should give his daughter in marriage to a stranger would dishonour himself; this, however, is a remark which in a strict sense applies only to those tribes that inhabit Afghanistan properly so called, for those disseminated through India connect themselves without distinction with all Mahomedan nations.

The natives of India have known the Afghans for centuries under the name of Patans and Rohillas,* a designation which they now apply to them; they also call them Pushtoonees, from the language they still speak; and it is not till the reign of the Sultan Abouseid, of the race of Ghengis Khan, that certain Eastern writers speak of them under the name of Afghan, which is only the plural of the Arab word *feghan.*† This was applied to them because they were always in a disunited state amongst themselves, and continually addressing their complaints to the sovereigns on whom they were dependent; nevertheless the name was but little used till the reign of Shah Abbas the Great, who, tired with their incessant lamentations, ordered them henceforward to be called by that designation only.

There are almost as many classifications of the Afghan tribes as there are Eastern authors who have written on the subject; not only are they not agreed, but they have called each other very hard names to prove their accuracy. Being incompetent to decide which is right, we shall adopt the opinion of Abdullah Khan of Herat as the one most deserving of credit, and we will precede it by giving his view of the manner in which the Afghans were brought to Afghanistan. The following is a translation of his manuscript:—

"The word *Afghan* is derived from the Arab, that of *aoughan* from the Persian, and both one and the other are used in Hebrew.

"Malek Thalut (Saul) king of the Jews had two sons, Afghan and Djalut—the first was the father of the Afghan nation and gave his name to it. After the reigns of David and Solomon, who succeeded Saul, anarchy divided the Jewish tribes, and this continued to the period at which Bouktun Nasr ‡ took Jerusalem, massacred 70,000 Jews, and after destroying that city led the surviving inhabitants captives to Babylon. Subsequently to this disaster the Afghan tribe, struck with terror, fled from Judea and settled in Arabia: here they remained some considerable time, but as pasturage and water were scarce, and both man and beast suffered extreme privation, some of the tribe determined to emigrate to

* *Roh* in Pushtoo signifies mountain, and *Rohilla* an inhabitant of mountains.

† Noise, tumult.

‡ Nebuchadnezzar.

Hindostan. The branch of the Abdalees continued to reside in Arabia, and during the caliphat of Aboo Bekr their chiefs allied themselves to a powerful sheikh, by name Khaled ibn Velid, of the tribe of Korech. The position and condition of the Abdalees was sensibly ameliorated in consequence of the assistance which they obtained from Khaled, but at the period when the Arabs subjugated Persia the Abdalees left Arabia and settled in this new conquest, establishing themselves in the provinces of Fars and Kerman, and here they remained until Ghengis Khan invaded those districts. The tyrannical proceedings of this conqueror weighed with such terrible effect on the population, that the Abdalees quitted Persia and, passing by the Mekrane, Scinde, and Mooltan, arrived in India; but the results of this new migration were not more fortunate, for they were scarcely settled here when their neighbours made war upon, and forced them to leave the plains and inhabit the rugged mountains of Suleiman, considered as the cradle of the tribe, and called by them Kooh-Khasseh.* The whole Afghan nation was brought together by the arrival of the Abdalees in the Suleiman mountains, and then consisted of twenty-four tribes, of which, as it has been already observed, Afghan, the son of Saul, was the father: this prince had three sons, named Tsera-Bend, Argoutch, and Kerlen, and each of them was the father of eight sons, who gave their names to the twenty-four tribes.

"The following is the manner in which they are classed:—

"Sons of Tsera-Bend.	Names of the Tribes.	Sons of Argoutch.	Names of the Tribes.
Abdal	Abdalees.	Ghildj	Ghildjzyes.
Yoosoof	Yoosoofzyes.	Kauker	Kaukerees.
Baboor..	Babourees.	Djumourian	Djumourianees.
Wezir	Wezirees.	Storian	Storianees.
Lohooan	Lohooanees.	Pen	Penees.
Beritch	Beritchees.	Kass	Kassees.
Khooguian	Khooguianees.	Takan	Takanees.
Chiran	Chiranees.	Nassar	Nassarees.

"Sons of Kerlen.	Names of the Tribes.	Sons of Kerlen.	Names of the Tribes.
Khattak	Khattakees.	Zaz	Zazees.
Soor	Soorees.	Bab	Babees.
Afreed	Afreedees.	Benguech	Banguechees.
Toor	Toorees.	Lendeh-poor	Lendeh-poorees.

* Aden and the surrounding country is at the present time inhabited by an Arab tribe, which, as well as the principal Afghan tribe, is known by the name of Abdalee. Are we to conclude that they have one and the same origin, as an Afghan author has stated? I do not think we should: a similarity of name and the alliance of the Afghan Abdalees with the Arab tribe of Korech are not sufficient proofs in the affirmative.—*Ferrier.*

"The greater number of these tribes were scattered over India; but there, instead of increasing, they so diminished that scarcely a trace of any of them is to be found in these days. The only exception to this remark is the tribe of Yoosoofzyes settled in Cashmeer. Nadir Shah, desirous of ascertaining their numbers, issued a decree that each family should bring a spear to his camp, and when these were counted they were found to amount to 600,000: at the present time there would not be half that number. This tribe has for more than thirty years been under the dominion of the Sikhs. Afghanistan, properly so called, is inhabited almost exclusively by Abdalees and Ghildjzyes, and of these we shall speak more especially. The first, although inhabiting every part of Afghanistan, are principally resident in Herat and Kandahar; the Ghildjzyes are established in the last-mentioned principality and Kabul; the Kaukerees near the Bolan Pass; the Babeorees, Nassarees, Lohooanees, and Babees, in Kandahar and Scinde, where they are profitably occupied in commercial pursuits; the Beritchees are in the neighbourhood of Pisheen; the Chiranees and the Mohmunds to the north-east of Kabul; the Benguechees (Shiahs) between the last-mentioned town and the country of the Hazarahs,—these are divided into four branches, viz. the Bede-kheelee, Chaloozanee, Djajee, and Bertedjee; finally, the Chiranees are to be found everywhere, though in small numbers: the remaining tribes are in India, or have become extinct.

"Having only to consider Afghanistan Proper, I will now give more detailed information respecting the Abdalees and the Ghildjzyes, which form the bulk of the population of this country; and as the offshoots in which they are subdivided are tolerably numerous, it will be useful to give here a tabular statement, which I have endeavoured to render as accurate as possible.

"The powerful tribe of the Abdalees is known at the present time under the name of Dooranee, which was given to them by Ahmed Shah Suddozye on the occasion of his ascending the throne in 1747. When Nadir Shah ordered a census to be made of the Abdalee tribe, there were 195,000 families, and from these he raised 12,000 excellent cavalry; but the Abdalees have decreased in number since Nadir's time.

"Abdal, the son of Tsera-Bend, the founder of this tribe, had only one son, named Teryn, who had two sons, Zirek and Pindjpa: from the first originated three tribes, and from the second five.

"The tribes that descended from Zirek are,—

"1st. Koofelzye, more generally known under the name of Popolzye, divided into five branches, namely,—1st, the Hussenzalee; 2nd, Badoozye; 3rd, Kalenderzye; 4th, Ayoobzye; 5th, Suddozye. The legitimate sovereigns who have reigned over the Afghans during the 17th and 18th centuries were of the branch of the Suddozyes. The tribe of the Koofelzyes numbered 20,000 families.

"2nd. Barukyze. This was in very ancient times one of the most distinguished offshoots of the Abdalees; it is divided into six branches—1st, the Mohamedzye; 2nd, Kharzye; 3rd, Sefretzye; 4th, Inguizye; 5th, Gurjizye; 6th, Etchekzye. The actual sovereigns of Kandahar and Kabul are of the branch of Mohamedzye. The Barukzyes numbered 40,000 families.

"3rd. Alikiouzye, which is divided into three branches—1st, the Djaloozye, to which belonged the chiefs of the Alikiouzye tribe; 2nd, Melazye; 3rd, Serkanee. Yar Mohamed Khan, of Herat, is of this tribe and the Djaloozye branch. The Alikiouzyes number 20,000 families.

"The tribes descended from Pindjpa are—

"1st. Isakzye, numbering 10,000 families and divided into four branches, viz., 1st, Ahmedzye; 2nd, Avazye; 3rd, Merdinzye; 4th, Biroozye.

"2nd. Alizye, numbering 10,000 families and divided into three branches—1st, Hassanzalee, to which the chiefs of the Alizye tribe belong; 2nd, Alekzye; 3rd, Guerazye.

"3rd. Noorzye, numbering 30,000 families and divided into three branches—1st, Tchalakzye; 2nd, Bahaderzye; 3rd, Derzakee.

"4th. Khaouganee, numbering 6000 families and divided into two branches—1st, Khaouganee Kelan; 2nd, Khaouganee Kitchik.

"5th. Makoohee, numbering 10,000 families and divided into three branches—1st, Bedelzye; 2nd, Firoozye; 3rd, Sebzalee.

"The tribe of the Ghildjzyes, from which sprung Mir Weis, Mir Mahmood his son, and Mir Echreff his nephew, had Ghildj, the son of Argoutch, for its founder. Ghildj had two sons, Ibrahim and Thooran, from whom sprung the six tribes that follow, viz., 1st, Suleiman-Kheilee; 2nd, Outekee; 3rd, Tookhee—from this came the branch of the Loods, which gave India its sovereigns; 4th, Khaleelee; 5th, Toorkee; 6th, Euderee. The three first descended from Ibrahim, and the three last from Thooran.

A TABLE of the TRIBE of the ABDALEES.

Founders.	Stock.	Tribes.	Branches.
Abdal and his son Teryn founders of the Tribe.	Zirek ..	Popolzye ..	Suddozye. Hussenzalee. Badoozye. Kalenderzye. Ayoobzye.
		Barukzye ..	Mohamedzye. Kharzye. Sefretzye. Inguisye. Gurjizye. Etchekzye.
		Alikiouzye ..	Djaloozye. Melazye. Serkanee.
	Pindjpa ..	Isakzye	Ahmedzye. Avazye. Merdinzye. Biroozye. Hassanzalee.
		Alizye	Alekzye. Guerazye. Tchalakzye.
		Noorzye ..	Bahaderzye. Derzakee.
		Khaouganee	Khaouganee Kelan. Khaouganee Kitchik.
		Makoohee ..	Bedelzye. Firoozye. Sebzalee.

TRIBE of the GHILDJZYE.

Founders.	Stock.	Tribes.	Branches.
Ghildj	.. ..	Ibrahim.. ..	Suleiman-Kheilee. Outekee. Tookhee.
		Thooran ..	Khaleelee. Toorkee. Enderee."

The primitive tribe of the Afghans was called *taifeh*, a word which corresponds with that of *nation:* the first divisions of this primitive tribe are called *ferguch*, *tribe;* the subdivisions of this, *tirehs* or *branches*. Thus the families which are descended from the first generation—Tsera-Bend, Argoutch, and Kerlen—as the Abdalees, the Ghildjzyes, the Kaukerees, form the *Taifeh*, nation; those which descend from these last, such as the Popolzyes, Barukzyes, Ibrahim, Thooran, &c., are called *Ferguch*, tribes; and the subdivisions of these (see the above table) are called the *Tireh*, branches.

The Abdalees and Ghildjzyes, by reason of their numerical superiority over the others, and also from the power they have exercised, and continue to exercise, in Afghanistan at the present day, have arrogated to themselves a certain kind of supremacy over the other tribes, and consider themselves of an origin more noble than theirs: they even refuse to acknowledge their right to the title of Afghan. It is more especially the Abdalee tribe that has put forth, and in the most positive manner, this pretension. Not only do they refuse the title of Afghans—and this even to the Ghildjzyes—but also there is a schism on the subject amongst themselves, and the Zireks affirm that they are of a more noble extraction than the Pindjpas. This scornful assumption has often given rise to sanguinary conflicts between them, and is based upon the fact that the mother of Abdal was a legitimate wife, whereas the mother of Ghildj was a concubine, which is, they say, proved by the name which was given him, for Ghildj in Pushtoo signifies bastard.

On the other hand, the tribes of Makoohee and Khaouganee, though of Afghan origin, were not at the outset of the Abdalee tribe, but, by reason of the perfect friendship which always existed between them, the Abdalees adopted them and classed them amongst the Pindjpas, and they have ever since been considered as belonging to that family. After the death of Nadir Shah an occurrence took place which will give some idea of the importance the Afghans attach to their belonging to the most noble tribe.

Ahmed Shah had scarcely founded the dynasty of the Suddozyes when it was nearly overthrown by an intrigue fomented against him by the Serdar Noor Mohamed Khan. Obliged to employ severe measures to repress the evil-disposed, he ordered that ten persons of each tribe taken from amongst the most guilty should be put to death. It was the first time he had shed the blood of his subjects, and the experiment was not without danger, for the Afghans talked of avenging themselves and retaliating upon the Shah and his family; but the sovereign authority triumphed, and from that moment it was admitted by the tribes that the king had the right of shedding blood without any one having the power to question it. The Makoohees and Khaouganees had not been included in these acts of severity, on the ground that, not being Abdalees by descent, their fault was of less magnitude, and therefore it was possible to pardon them; but these tribes, affronted at the exception, withdrew from the Shah's camp. An explanation naturally followed, and Ahmed Shah, to satisfy them, ordered ten

Makoohees and ten Khaouganees to be put to death, upon which they immediately returned to their duty, for they considered themselves vilified by the exception that had been made in their favour.

Independently of the tribes and branches that we have classified, those of the Abdalees and the Ghildjzyes are again subdivided into so great a number of *tireh*, or families, and there is so much confusion in these subdivisions, that it would be impossible for an Afghan, even the best informed upon the subject, to give a perfect list of them. There would be no exaggeration in stating their numbers at more than three hundred. These have been formed from time to time when the surplus population of a tribe has been obliged to separate from it and seek a fresh district, or when an influential relative of the chief had some misunderstanding with him and withdrew from his authority, with those who were attached to his own person. At other times some successful conqueror broke up a tribe, to render it less powerful; each subdivision then took the name of the new chief whose fortunes it followed, but they always looked upon themselves as members of the original tribe, though often separated by considerable distances from each other. These separations are also to be attributed to the fear entertained by the sovereigns of the numerical force of some of the tribes. Shah Abbas the Great was the last who adopted this measure on a large scale; and to secure the permanent tranquillity and stability of the populations to which he had assigned a new territory, he carried a number of hostages with him to Ispahan.

The Abdalees, besides having the name of Dooranees, which they received from Ahmed Shah, are still called Suleimanees, from the mountains whence they came; the district they then inhabited bears the appellation of Tobeh-Maharoof.

CHAPTER II.

Afghanistan conquered by Alexander — Reconquered by the aboriginal inhabitants — Taken by the Tartars — Death of Mansoor — Success of Sebek-Taghee — Character of the Afghans at this period — Concession of territory to the Abdalee tribe — Ghildjzyes opposed to the Tartar dominion — The first sovereign of Afghanistan — His son Mahmood — Cruelty of the Tartar princes — Expulsion of Beiram — Khosroo Malek the last of the Ghaznevide dynasty — List of the monarchs of that race — Afghan princes of Gour — Mahmood Gouree — His conquests in India — Eldooz — Djellal Eddin — Afghanistan conquered by Ghengis Khan — Malek Kurt — Chems Eddin Gouree — Their suzerainty to the Tartars — Conquered by Tamerlane — Description of the Afghans by that invader — Afghan rule in India — Mahmood III. — Ibrahim Khan defeats Bellal and seizes Kabul and Kandahar — Mirza Baboor — Assisted by the Persians — Defeated by the Uzbeks, but successful in India — Fall of Ibrahim Khan — Death of Mirza Baboor — Succeeded by his son Humayoon — Protected by Shah Thamasp — Anecdote of the latter — Assists Humayoon with a Persian army — The Loods defeated — Their attempts to retake Delhi — The prophetess Kiemal Eddin — Shah Jehan drives out the Loods — Aurungzebe finally annihilates them — Kandahar ceded to Persia by Humayoon — Taken and retaken by the Persians and Moguls — Afghan deputation to Shah Abbas — Extract from Sir John Malcolm's 'History of Persia' — Afghans quiet under Shah Abbas — Tyranny of his grandson Shah Seffee — Kandahar taken by Shah Abbas II. in 1642 — Success of the Ghildjzyes — Their revolt suppressed by the Shah Hoosein — Gourguin Khan — Deputation of the Afghans to the Persian Court in 1706.

AMONGST the conquests of Alexander the Great was that of Afghanistan, and at the death of this invader his lieutenant, Seleucus, succeeded to the sovereignty of the greater portion of his dominions in Asia. It is presumed that his son and grandson followed him; but history does not inform us how or why, under the reign of the last-mentioned monarch, Afghanistan was taken from the Seleukides by the aboriginal chiefs, and soon formed, with Bactria, an independent state, which existed with some degree of splendour during one hundred and fifty years. After the lapse of that period the Tartars made themselves masters of the country, and appear to have held possession of it up to the tenth century. This blank remains in profound obscurity, and it is only from about the year A.D. 997 that we have any information which can elucidate the history of the Afghans.

At that time Mansoor reigned in Tartary, and when he died an officer of rank, named Sebek-Taghee, threw off the allegiance he owed to his successor, established his dominion over all the southern part of Afghanistan, and made Ghuznee his capital. The Afghan tribes at this period were for the most part a nomade and barbarous people, living by plunder and rapine, and under a host of chiefs very careful of their independence, who were almost always at enmity with each other, and ready to sell their services to the highest bidder. Thence it often happened that a part of the nation was to be found in one camp, while another was opposed to it in that of the enemies, and, like true Condottieri, they fought against one another without the least scruple. The disunion existing amongst the Afghan tribes in the present day may be traced back to the most remote times, and it is not surprising that with this sentiment they have so long delayed to organize themselves as a nation. Their migratory habits also contributed to this result, and they were for a long time a wild race dispersed over Persia, India, and the mountains of Afghanistan, but everywhere and at all periods turbulent and difficult to govern, adapting themselves very little to the habits of those of a different origin within whose territory they established themselves. The consequence was, that on very many occasions quarrels arose in which many of the tribes were decimated without pity, while the remainder were obliged to seek refuge in the mountains where they are to be met with in the present day. The tribe of the Abdalees, the most powerful now existing, did not fix itself in the Suleiman range till it had received authority to do so from Sebek-Taghee, who was desirous of recompensing them by this concession of territory for the support they had afforded him in his Indian campaigns. The Ghildjzyes, on the contrary, were always strongly opposed to the Tartar dominion over their country, which was so much the more dangerous for them, because their tribe was at that time exceedingly numerous. They carried their malpractices to such an extent, that Mahmood, son of Sebek-Taghee, who succeeded him on the throne of Ghuznee, was obliged almost entirely to exterminate them. But succeeding centuries have enabled the Ghildjzyes to recover from this disaster, and the tribe is now, next to that of the Abdalees, the most numerous and the most powerful in Afghanistan.

Sebek-Taghee may be considered as the first sovereign who ruled over Afghanistan properly so called; but the Afghans, in consequence of his Tartar origin, looked upon him and his descendants as tyrants and usurpers, and thought little of his good deeds and the benefits he conferred upon them. Mahmood, after the death of his father, carried his arms into Persia and India, and with the spoils of war obtained in these countries enriched Afghanistan, and made Ghuznee, his capital, one of the most beautiful cities in Asia. His death took place in 1028. His descendants, little worthy of succeeding him, soon lost the territory which he had added to the kingdom founded by Sebek-Taghee; their dominion was soon reduced to the Afghan provinces, in which their authority was not always respected; and if they preserved these during two centuries, they owed this circumstance much more to the difficulties in which their neighbours were involved than to any fear they entertained of the Tartar dynasty.

Beiram, one of these princes, seized upon an Afghan chief, of the name of Sooree, who about the year 1151 commanded in the province of Gour, and put him to a cruel death to punish him for the resolution with which he had opposed him. The barbarity of the Tartar prince on this occasion exceeded anything that can be imagined; he made him suffer a thousand tortures, and insulted him by every species of outrage.

Allah-Eddin, brother of this unfortunate Afghan and his successor in the sovereignty of Gour, determined to revenge himself by force of arms, and completely succeeded. He seized the town of Ghuznee, abandoned it during seven days to the fury and excesses of an army burning with vengeance and possessed with an inherent passion for plunder, and who carried the spirit of a savage temperament so far as to mix the blood of the vanquished with the mortar destined to repair the walls of the city.

Beiram, thus vanquished, retired beyond the Indus, and continued to reign in the Punjab, abandoning the western provinces of his kingdom to his victorious adversary.

War was declared on several other occasions between these two princes, when Beiram was less unfortunate, and his son Khosroo Shah inherited the reduced territory he had preserved; but the dynasty of the Ghaznevides was brought to a close during the lifetime of his grandson Khosroo Malek. Attacked in 1160 by Mahmood Gouree, cousin and successor of Allah Eddin, Khosroo Malek was overthrown, and his kingdom annexed to that of Afghanistan. The following is a list of the Ghaznevide princes who reigned over the last-mentioned country:—

	A.D.	Hejira.		A.D.	Hejira.
Sebek-Taghee	976	365	Ali	1049	441
Ismaël	997	387	Abd-ul-Reschid	1052	443
Mahmood	997	387	Ferakh-zad	1053	444
Mohamed	1030	421	Ibrahim	1059	450
Massood	1031	422	Massood	1098	492
Madood	1041	433	Arselane Shah	1104	508
Massood	1049	441	Beiram Shah	1108	512

The Afghan princes of Gour, from being simple chiefs of a small principality, were thus raised to the sovereign power in Afghanistan, to which they soon added divers principalities of India. Gour is a little province, well situated for defence, and in the heart of the most rugged mountains of the Paropamisus, but possessing none of those means of aggression which could enable the Afghans to hope for victory against one so powerful as that of Ghuznee. It may be supposed that Allah Eddin found a ready support in the other tribes of his nation, who submitted with regret to the dominion of the Tartars. The humiliation which the Afghans experienced in being treated as a conquered people, added to their feelings of nationality, must have excited heroic sentiments in their breasts, and made them triumph over the foreign race that oppressed them.

Mahmood Gouree carried his arms into the interior of India and seized Benares, in which city he committed a thousand atrocities. This prince left no heirs, and died in 1205. His empire, in accordance with his desire, was divided between his favourites and his freedmen. Afghanistan proper fell to Eldooz, but he was soon despoiled of it by a prince of Kharism, whose successor, Djellal Eddin, was in like manner obliged to retire before the victorious armies of Ghengis Khan. Ferishteh informs us that the descendants of this conqueror were in possession of Afghanistan up to the year 1251—the period at which an Afghan or Patan King, which is synonymous, seized upon Ghuznee and Kabul, and annexed them to the Indian empire.

Less than a century later a new dynasty, which western authors mention under the name of Malek Kurt,* established itself in the province of Gour and extended its dominion over Kandahar and Herat from A.D. 1336 (Hejira 736) to A.D. 1383 (Hejira 785).

The first sovereign of this dynasty, Chems-Eddin Gouree,

* The word *Kurt* is a corruption of the word *Gour*, which, united with that of Malek, signifies Prince of Gour. This dynasty was of the Afghan race.—*Ferrier*.

nevertheless, acknowledged the suzerainty of the Tartar monarchs; this was the case also with his sons and successors, Rookn-Eddin and Fakhr-Eddin, but the third, Ghyaz-Eddin, threw off the vassalage which had been laid upon him by the descendants of Ghengis Khan. Chems-Eddin, Malek Hafez, Moez Eddin Hoosein, and Malek Bagher, who succeeded him, preserved their independence; nevertheless the latter claimed the support of the Tartars to maintain him in the position he had usurped; but his reign was of brief duration, for his brother Moez-Eddin overthrew him, and left the reins of power to his son Ghyaz-Eddin, the ninth and last sovereign of this dynasty. This prince was made prisoner by the Emir Tamerlane, who seized his territory as well as that of Ghuznee and Kabul.

Tamerlane speaks of the Afghans in his Institutes as a barbarous people, devoted to pillage, and by no means so far advanced in civilization as the Tartars; but he limits the country they then occupied to the Suleiman mountains, from which we are left to conclude that he understood by the name Afghan or Aoughan only the tribe of the Abdalees, who, since the days of Sebek-Taghee, were in possession of the country mentioned in the Institutes. This circumstance is therefore confirmatory of the opinion we have already set forth on the uncertainty of the origin of the Afghans.

From the conquest of Afghanistan by Tamerlane up to the commencement of the sixteenth century the information respecting them is exceedingly vague, and yet this epoch ought to have been one of the most honourable in the annals of Afghan history; but a portion of the facts which relate to it occurred in India, and beyond the territory the history of which we are endeavouring to sketch: we shall therefore pass on very rapidly, and only have recourse to the manuscript from which we have already given some passages.

The Afghan rule in India commenced at the death of Mahmood Gouree, which took place in 1205; thus, as we have already stated above, the dominions of this Mahmood were, for want of a direct heir, divided between his favourites and freedmen. The Indian provinces fell to Koutoob, one of his generals of the Afghan tribe of Lood. This tribe, seeing its chief the sovereign of a vast empire, with Delhi for its capital, left Afghanistan and settled themselves in India, where, protected and favoured by the monarch, they increased rapidly. Accustomed from their infancy to a life spent in camps, and of rude and simple habits, they with little difficulty obtained an ascendancy over the natives of India, and the fear with which they inspired them resulted in their accepting with resignation the yoke of the Afghan dynasty. This dynasty still held possession of that country in 1398, when Tamerlane conquered it. Mahmood III. was then on the throne, and the invader allowed him to retain the supreme power as a recompense for the assistance which he gave him during those bloody massacres that obtained for him the title of the destroyer of humanity.

Mahmood III. died in 1450, a period at which an Afghan lord, also of the tribe of Lood, named Bellal, overthrew the reigning family. This new sovereign made Agra his capital. During his reign the empire was a prey to continual agitation; the revolts amongst the Loods were incessant, and Bellal was at length driven out and succeeded by Ibrahim Khan, another Afghan chief of the same tribe, who subdued each of his competitors in turn; he invaded successively Kandahar and Kabul, meeting with scarcely any resistance, favoured as he was by the Afghan tribes. Successes so easily obtained increased his ambition, and he resolved to march upon the Tartar kingdom of Ferghana, already attacked in the rear by Chahee Beg, king of Bokhara, with whom he concluded a treaty offensive and defensive, stipulating that the conquered countries should be divided between them. Mirza Baboor, of the tribe of Gurkani, and fifth in descent from Tamerlane,* was at this time sovereign of Ferghana, who, already despoiled of some of the best parts of his territory by Chahee Beg, and menaced on the south by Ibrahim Khan, despaired of being able to resist this combination of his enemies, fled from his kingdom, and placed himself under the protection of the King of Persia. This took place in the year 1498 (Hejira 904). Shah Ismael Seffavye received him in the most gracious manner, and soon after gave him a force of 20,000 horsemen, commanded by Mir Nadjm, with which to recover his kingdom. Mirza Baboor also took the field, and commenced operations against the Uzbeks; but he had scarcely laid siege to Bokhara when the inhabitants, reinforced by the troops which Ibrahim Khan had sent to his support, attacked the Persians during the night, routed them, and killed their leader, Mir Nadjm. This occurred in 1505 (Hejira 911).

---

* He was the son of Omar Sheikh, who was the son of Aboo Seid, who was the son of Miranshâh, who was the son of Tamerlane.—*Ferrier.*

After this disaster Mirza Baboor retreated by the way of Balkh, the road to which city remained open: he was fortunate enough to be able to take Kabul, and within a brief space he had made numerous partisans in that country, which he entirely subdued. In 1508 (Hejira 913) he seized upon Kandahar, and not long after the Punjab. The natives of India, seeing his success, wrote to him in 1511 (Hejira 916), and besought his assistance in throwing off the tyranny of Ibrahim Khan, promising to act with vigour the moment he should appear at the head of his army. This request consorted with the projects of vengeance that Mirza Baboor cherished against Ibrahim Khan, and he accepted it with readiness. He marched, therefore, against that monarch in 1525, defeated him, and took possession of the whole of the Indian territories of which Ibrahim had usurped the sovereignty.

After this brief description of the transient power which the Afghans possessed in this part of India, the manuscript of Abdullah Khan of Herat proceeds thus. The natives of India had little reason to congratulate themselves in having requested another monarch to come and govern them, for Mirza Baboor oppressed and plundered, and made them almost regret Ibrahim Khan the Lood.

At the death of Mirza Baboor, sovereign of India and Afghanistan, which took place in 1530 (Hejira 937), his eldest son succeeded to all his dominions, but his brother Kamran, and his vizier Shere Khan, an Afghan of the tribe of Lood, revolted against him, and, assisted by those devoted to their interests, obliged him to fly; the Persians, on the other hand, had some time before attacked Kandahar and taken it from the Moguls. Notwithstanding this act of hostility, Humayoon did as his father had done—he retired to the court of Persia and sought the protection of the Shah Thamasp. This monarch, having been informed that the fugitive prince was approaching his territory, sent an order to the governor of Herat to receive him with every mark of respect, and to escort him to Kasbeen, the capital, in a manner worthy of his rank and with a splendour truly regal. After their meeting the two monarchs felt a lively interest in each other. The Shah Thamasp not only acceded to the wishes of his royal guest, but did everything in his power to anticipate them, as the following anecdote will show:—

Humayoon, walking one day in the streets of Kasbeen, came to a canal, the clear and limpid waters of which ran with a rapid course between banks covered with flowers and verdure; the spot pleased him greatly, and turning to one of his officers he said, "If I had the means of doing so, I would here build a magnificent mosque." A Persian nobleman who heard these words repeated them to the Shah Thamasp, who swore that the wish of Humayoon should not remain ungratified, and his architect, having been called into his presence, was ordered to construct a magnificent mosque, and within the space of six months, upon the site indicated by the exiled prince. He also forbade any of his servants from mentioning the circumstance, and gave strict injunctions that Humayoon should never be permitted to walk near the spot until the edifice was completed. In six months the beautiful mosque was finished, and the name of the Shah's guest inscribed over the portal in the façade as having been the founder. Humayoon, to whom no intimation on the subject had been given, was conducted to it. His astonishment on seeing it was great indeed, and his gratitude to the Shah Thamasp for this delicate mark of his friendship not less. Subsequently the Shah gave him further proofs of his attachment; indeed he was prodigal of them.

Humayoon, nevertheless, became at length sensible that the state of his affairs in India would never improve if he continued to pass his time amidst the festivities of the court at Kasbeen; he therefore begged the Shah to give him some troops with which he might hope to regain his crown and punish the usurpers of his throne. The King of Persia received this new request as he had done every other, and placed 12,000 cavalry, commanded by Beyram Khan, at his disposal. This officer had resided many years in India, was well acquainted with the habits and feelings of the people of that country, and the Shah charged him to re-establish Humayoon in all his rights. The march of this army upon Delhi was soon known, and the Loods at once made every preparation for defence, but in vain. Humayoon had scarcely arrived at Kabul when his Indian subjects revolted against Shere Khan, and after having killed a large proportion of his Afghans obliged him to fly from the country. On hearing this Humayoon travelled night and day to reach his dominions, leaving Beyram Khan and his Persians, with a crowd of Tartars and Parsivans that soon joined him, to follow. This numerous and well-trained army was broken into divisions on its arrival in India, and Humayoon sent them in various directions with orders to massacre the Afghan Loods wherever they were met with and not leave one alive. These instructions were rigorously executed, and those who were fortunate enough to escape were reduced to a pitiable condition; but when they recovered from the terror into which they had been thrown, they showed themselves in arms at various points and again threatened the Emperor of the Moguls. Nevertheless they did not attempt anything in the lifetime of Humayoon, but after his death, which took place in 1555, and in the reign of his son Mohamed Akim Mirza, surnamed Djellal Eddin Akbar, Roouchen Bayazid, one of the chiefs of the Loods, who passed amongst them as inspired, in short almost a prophet, united the scattered warriors of the tribe, placed himself at their head, and declared his pretensions to the throne of Delhi. For several years he kept up a desultory warfare against the Moguls, but without obtaining any positive result, for death surprised him in the midst of it. His son, Omar Sheikh Kiemal Eddin, continued the strife, and owed the success which he obtained, as his father had done, to the co-operation of the Prince Noor Eddin Jehanghir, second son of Humayoon, who had also raised the standard of revolt against Akbar. The Loods continued to carry on this party warfare for a considerable time, but without being able to grasp a second time the Indian sceptre, for the Moguls were too powerful.*

After the death of Omar Sheikh Kiemal Eddin, a young maiden of the tribe of Lood, named Kiemal Khatoon, endeavoured to create a schism in the Mahomedan religion as professed by the Afghans, the Moguls, and a few Indian tribes; her preaching and that of her disciples was the cause of great commotions in the empire: the Loods, who were always at the head of every disturbance, suffered new misfortunes, and fresh massacres considerably reduced their numbers. These troubles were rife up to the commencement of the reign of Shah Abedin Mohamed Shah, surnamed Shah Jehan, who again persecuted the Afghan Loods, and in 1632 (Hejira 1042) drove them out of India, but the revolts, which had been excited by this religious schism, were not thoroughly put down until the close of the reign of Aurungzebe, who succeeded him. From this period the Lood tribe ceased to have any influence in India; they made no further attempts to obtain power; and we shall in future become further acquainted with their history in that of Afghanistan Proper.

Mirza Baboor, the founder of the dynasty of the Moguls, was

enabled to hold possession of Kabul, which he left to his successors; but he lost Kandahar, and this as well as the principalities of Herat and Gour fell into the hands of the Persians. Subsequently, however, he retook Kandahar, against which he sent his son Kamran Mirza, but soon after it was again in the power of the Shah Thamasp. Seffavye Humayoon, the successor to Baboor, seized upon it once more, but, to mark his gratitude for the services which he had received from the Shah of Persia, he ceded it to him by treaty in 1545; it continued in the possession of Persia during the lifetime of Humayoon, after which his son Akbar retook it. It fell, however, in 1609 (Hejira 1018), into the hands of the great Shah Abbas Seffavye, but only to revert to the Emperor Jehangir, who carried Kandahar by assault. This was the last time but one that the Moguls were enabled to take this fortress, the advantageous position of which on the frontiers of the two states made them dispute its possession with so much tenacity against the Persians. The contest for it was again renewed in 1620 by Shah Abbas, and the efforts which Aurungzebe made to retake it at a later period completely failed. The officers appointed by the Persian monarch to govern Kandahar so oppressed the Afghans that they sent two of their principal Serdars to the Shah to obtain a relaxation of the rigorous measures to which they were subjected, and requested that the governor might henceforth be chosen from the chiefs of the Afghan tribes, promising that their fidelity should be proof against every temptation. The following are the terms in which Sir John Malcolm, in his excellent work on Persia, speaks of this embassy; the information is taken from the Persian manuscript of Mirza Syud Mohamed of Ispahan:—

"In the time of the Saffavean kings of Persia the Affghans were often oppressed; and on one occasion they were so discontented with their Persian governor, that they sent a secret deputation to Ispahan to solicit his removal and the appointment of one of their own tribe. Their request was granted; and two of the tribe of Abdallee were raised to the office of Reish Saffeed, or Kutkhodah of the tribes, and their authority was confirmed by a royal patent. The name of one of these two persons was Seedoo, of the family of Bameeyehi, from whom Ahmed Shah, the founder of the present royal family of Cabul, is lineally descended. The name of the other was Ahmed, of the family of Bareekzehi, from whom the present Affghan chiefs, Serafray Khan and Futteh Khan, are descended. The Affghans were delighted with this arrangement, and granted their entire and respectful obedience to the chief appointed by the Persian Government. Time has confirmed this respect; and the superiority of the chiefs so selected has become an inheritance to their family. The race of Seedoo obtained sovereignty, while that of Ahmed has only gained high station and command. The Seedoozehis (or descendants of Seedoo) are held in such veneration, that, if one of them was to attempt the murder of an ameer, or lord of another tribe, it would be considered wrong to obtain safety by assaulting the Seedoozehis. If an Affghan acted otherwise he would be deemed an outcast in his own class or tribe. There is, however, an exception to this rule in favour of the descendants of Ahmed, and the Ahmedzehis may without sacrilege slay a Seedoozehi; but a great number of the Affghans deny this privilege, even to the Ahmedzehis. Seedoo and Ahmed (this author adds) were raised to rank by Shah Abbas the Great, and derived their fortunes from that fountain of dignity and splendour."

This respect for the Suddozyes amongst the Afghans has disappeared in our days; and since they have been dispossessed of the throne, not only those who belonged to this branch, but also all the members of the tribe of Popolzye, from which it was derived, are persecuted and often plundered by the Mohamedzyes actually in power.

So long as Shah Abbas lived the Afghans settled in Herat and Kandahar remained perfectly tranquil under his dominion; but a Persian governor, appointed by his grandson and successor Shah Seffee, having maltreated them, they revolted. This sovereign managed to keep the Heratees in check, but his governor in Kandahar, a traitor to his duty, passed over to the camp of the Mogul Emperor with the Persian troops under his orders, and gave up the fortress to the Shah in 1634.

Kandahar was taken from the Moguls by the Persians in 1642, during the reign of Shah Abbas the Second. The conquerors of Delhi subsequently made every effort, but in vain, to recapture the city, and were obliged to remain satisfied with the possession of Kabul, which had belonged to them from the time of Baber. The Persians retained Herat and Kandahar in spite of the adverse feeling of the Afghans, who were always more anxious to be under the dominion of the Great Mogul, which they considered less burdensome than that of the Persians.

The Afghans of the tribe of Ghildjzyes, dispersed over the province of Kandahar, were, however, the most restless and the most constant enemies of Persia, so that, towards the close of the seventeenth century, they had pretty nearly rendered themselves masters of the principality.

In 1698, a little before his accession to the throne, the Shah, Sultan Hoosein, felt that it was absolutely necessary that they should be put down, and with a view to effect this object he selected as their governor the Walee of Georgia, Gourguin Khan, surnamed Shah Nawaz Khan, a clever and energetic man, and sent with him a well-appointed and numerous army, and instructions to take severe measures with the Afghans.

Shah Nawaz Khan arrived at Kandahar in 1702, and treated the Afghans without pity, as a conquered but rebellious people; nothing could escape his inflexible and harsh proceedings—neither rank, age, nor sex was any protection; his troops, surfeited with murders and pillage, reduced the women and girls to a state of slavery, and made them the unhappy victims of their base violence. The Afghans, bewildered and alarmed at this state of things, sent a deputation to Ispahan, in 1706, to entreat the King to put a stop to the calamities which weighed upon them; but this embassy did not succeed as a similar one had done in the reign of Shah Abbas, for their delegates were received with haughty and harsh indifference; and the individuals who composed the deputation returned to their countrymen to share with them the despair they also fel.

Disappointed in their hopes, the Afghans could not dream of emancipating themselves by force of arms from the heavy yoke of Gourguin Khan, for his vigilance was equal to his severity; flight being impossible and complaint useless, and seeing no other mode by which they could put a stop to the cruelties that were practised upon them, they awaited in silence, and bowed down with grief, the moment when they should be able to take vengeance upon their oppressors for so many outrages; and this was not far distant, for an act on the part of Gourguin Khan soon presented them with an opportunity.

CHAPTER III.

The Kelauter of Kandahar is sent prisoner to Ispahan — His intrigues against Gourguin Khan — He makes a pilgrimage to Mecca — Obtains a *fetvo* from the chief mollah of Islam — Returns to Ispahan, and finally to Kandahar — Indignation of Gourguin Khan — Events consequent upon this — Opinion of Abdullah Khan upon them — Death of Gourguin Khan — Mir Weis enters Kandahar — Statement of Mirza Mehdee — The Ghildjzyes declare their independence, and exterminate the Persian troops — The tribe of the Abdalees establish themselves in Herat — The Persian generals attack the Kelauter and are beaten — Kaee Khosroo Khan besieges Kandahar — He is defeated and killed with 30,000 of his troops — Mohamed Roostem succeeds him, but is also beaten — The Afghans acknowledge Mir Weis as their sovereign chief — Death of the Mir in 1715 — His brother Mir Abdullah succeeds him — His negotiations with Persia — Is put to death by the eldest son of Mir Weis, who succeeds him — Alayar Khan, Governor of Herat — Zeman Khan appointed by the Persian monarch to succeed him — Heyat Sultan — He marches against Kandahar — Attacked by Assad Ullah and defeated — Enters Herat — Persian campaign against the Usbeks — Sefi Kooli Khan — Is defeated by the Afghans — Independence of the Afghans established — Assad Ullah lays siege to Furrah — Is attacked by Mir Mahmood of Kandahar — A Belooch chief, Mir Mohamed, seizes Herat.

AMONGST the Afghan nobles who had signed the petition to the Shah against Nawaz Khan was Mir Weis, the *Kelauter* * of Kandahar, and chief of a branch of the tribe of Ghildjzyes. This Serdar had, by his amiable manners, liberality, persuasive powers, and great intelligence, made himself much beloved by his countrymen. Gourguin Khan feared him, and knew that he was the principal instigator of the hatred which the Afghans bore him; he therefore ordered the Kelauter to be arrested, under the pretext that he was conspiring against the government, and sent him, with several other *rich Sefid* † Afghans, to Ispahan, there to explain his conduct to the Shah.

Mir Weis did not on this occasion belie his reputation for ability. On his arrival at the court of the Seffavyes, he at once perceived the corruption which reigned on all sides; and scattering a little gold about him, he endeavoured to turn his captivity to account. In a

* The duties of *kelauter* in Persia are not exactly defined. In different towns they are more or less important: but in the case of Mir Weis, at Kandahar, the office must have been Governor in chief. And he had probably amongst his other functions to superintend the administration of the police, but with very extensive powers.—*Ferrier.*

† Literally *white beard*, but in this instance *eminent*.—*Ferrier.*

solemn audience granted him by the King he succeeded in obtaining from the sovereign an acknowledgment that he was innocent of the accusations which had been brought against him; and such was his tact, and the ductile character of his mind, that in the course of a few days he became one of the principal favourites of Shah Sultan Hoosein, and the friend of all the great nobles of his court.

Assured of having for the future an influence over the degraded courtiers of the Persian King, the views of Mir Weis took a wider range than they had hitherto done, for he concluded that a country thus delivered up to men so worthless and corrupt might become an easy conquest if attacked by some brave men well led. Strong in the power of his own genius, he deeply reflected upon the mode in which he might carry out so gigantic an enterprise as an invasion of Persia; and, to give himself the best chance of success, he determined to work upon his countrymen by that most powerful of agents, fanaticism. Instead of evincing a desire to return to his country, he solicited and obtained the Shah's permission to undertake a pilgrimage to Mecca, and also his consent that the *rich sefids* who had accompanied him should return to Kandahar; but before they left Ispahan he instructed them secretly to prepare the Afghans for revolt. A few days after their departure Mir Weis was on his way to the Holy City, where, having enlisted the sympathies of the chief mollahs of Islam, who, like the Afghans, were Soonees, he found no difficulty in obtaining from them a *fetvo*, in which they declared that his countrymen were bound by every means in their power to throw off the thraldom of the Shiah heretics.

Mir Weis returned to Ispahan as soon as he had performed his pilgrimage, and occupied himself in carrying out the intrigue which, with no little ingenuity, he had set on foot before his departure.

Like all Persian nobles in high situations, Gourguin Khan had enemies at court anxious for his downfall, as much from jealousy as in the hope of succeeding to the government of Kandahar, or replacing him by one of their own creatures. Amongst these enemies was the vizier of Shah Sultan Hoosein, who could not forgive Gourguin Khan and his nephew, the Sipahee Salar Kaee Khosroo Khan, the estimation in which they were held by the Shah, and the influence which they had always employed against him. Mir Weis, with considerable penetration, saw that this personage intended to compass the ruin of both uncle and nephew by prejudicing the mind of the Shah against them whenever an occasion should present itself; he made, therefore, secret advances to the Vizier with the hope of inducing him to associate himself in his design. The Vizier, well convinced of the bad feeling which the Afghan chief entertained against Shah Nawaz Khan, and believing him to be entirely devoted to the interests of the Shah, entered into his views, and became one of Mir Weis's warmest protectors. In order the more rapidly to bring about the fall of Gourguin, the Vizier made every effort to support the Afghan chief against him, and solicited the Shah's permission for Mir Weis to return to Kandahar. This feeble prince had been persuaded that Gourguin Khan and his nephew, secretly supported by the Tzar of Russia, wished to raise the standard of revolt in Georgia, and declare themselves independent. This was sufficient to induce the Shah to give Mir Weis permission to return to his native city, with orders to resume the important functions of Kelauter, satisfied that his fidelity and vigilance would enable him to penetrate the real sentiments of Gourguin, and at the same time serve as a counterpoise to his power, which had considerably increased, and given rise to some apprehensions. Mir Weis, well assured that every one would be in his favour, returned to Kandahar by Kerman and the Seistan, observing attentively on his journey the state of things in each locality. On his arrival he saw that the power and tyranny of Gourguin Khan had attained their utmost limits, and thought that his adversary might refuse to recognise the firman which conferred on him the functions of Kelauter. But the Governor, though indignant at his return, conformed to the orders of his sovereign, and reinstated the Mir in his post. Nevertheless, to humiliate him in the eyes of the people, and to prove that he himself was absolute in his own government, he ordered him to send one of his daughters, a girl of great personal beauty, to his harem without delay—his intention being not to make her his wife, but his concubine.* The Afghans, informed of the affront which had been put upon their chief, and eager

* The manuscript of Abdullah Khan is here at variance with that of Mirza Ali Mohamed, whose account of the transaction I have followed. Abdullah Khan states that Gourguin Khan was really desirous of an alliance with the Mir, with whose talents and influence he was well acquainted, and that he wished by means of this marriage to put an end to the differences that existed between himself and that chief. —*Ferrier*.

to avenge it, rushed immediately to arms; but Mir Weis, secretly assembling the principal chiefs, arrested their ardour, and they decided upon temporising in order that they might take measures which should better ensure the success of their plans. "The time which must prove our courage," said he to them, "is arrived, but the prudence of the serpent that watches overcomes the strength of the lion who permits himself to slumber; we must conceal our swords in a bed of roses, and those who have sufficient faith in me to place their destiny in my hands may be convinced that the most profound secresy is the first condition of success."

After this conference Mir Weis affected to submit to the governor's wishes; but instead of sending him his own daughter, he substituted one of his slaves, also a very beautiful girl, who, dressed in the richest attire, was conducted in great state to the harem of the Shah Nawaz Khan. Not less animated than Mir Weis against the oppressors of her country, his slave accepted, and with delight, the part she was called upon to perform. Gourguin Khan, not in the least suspecting the plot, believed the Afghan was really desirous of forgetting the past and being on friendly terms with him for the future; he therefore trusted him implicitly.

Mir Weis profited by the favour which he now enjoyed with the governor to bring about his fall with greater certainty; at the same time he secured the co-operation of the officers of the palace, and excited the turbulent Abdalee and Kaukeree tribes to commence a revolt, which soon spread its ramifications over all the southern part of the province of Kandahar. This rising occasioned Gourguin so much anxiety, that he decided on sending his best Georgian troops to put it down, and retained only twelve or fifteen hundred men near him to defend the citadel.

Mir Weis took advantage of the absence of these troops to put the projects he had so long meditated into execution, and sent Shah Nawaz an invitation to a feast which he had prepared at one of his country houses, situated about half an hour's ride from the city. This he accepted, and without suspicion, and such was the security felt by Gourguin after he had arrived there, that he quaffed immoderate quantities of wine during the repast, and with his suite, who had indulged to an equal extent in their libations, eventually fell asleep. Everything, in short, worked well for Mir Weis; the conspirators slaughtered all the inebriated sleepers, after which the Kelauter dressed himself in the robes of Gourguin, and ordered the Afghans in his own service to put on those of the Georgians who had accompanied their Walee. Thus disguised, they returned to Kandahar in the middle of the night, put to death the Persian troops on guard at the gate, and entered the city without being recognised. The insurgents, at first but few in number, were soon reinforced by the Afghans from the environs, who had previously been prepared for the movement, and the Persian garrison was so completely exterminated, that not one soldier was left alive. Mirza Mehdee, a Persian, and author of the 'Life of Nadir Shah,' gives a different account of the death of Nawaz Khan. He states that the governor had quitted Kandahar to chastise some rebels of the Kaukeree tribe, when Mir Weis arrived, who fell upon the Georgian Walee at Dehchir, defeated and took him prisoner, and subsequently put him to death by the hands of Murad Khan, a low Afghan. This statement seems, however, to be inaccurate.

The natives of different countries residing at Kandahar were at that time at variance with each other, and, after this tragedy was over, Mir Weis assembled them together with a view to their reconciliation. In his usual persuasive style of eloquence he showed them the advantages they might obtain from the liberty which had thus been given them, and invited them to form that bond of union which alone could emancipate them, and for ever, from the Persian yoke. He then drew forth the *fetvo* he had obtained from the chief mollahs at Mecca, which had an irresistible effect upon the feelings of this fanatical people, whose warlike instincts, having been powerfully excited, required only to be cleverly directed. They were not long in deciding what course to take, and swore that they would obey the Mir, inviolably attach themselves to his fortunes, and respect his person.

Three days after this unlooked-for event, the Georgians who had been despatched against the rebels in the south, and succeeded in their mission, arrived under the walls of Kandahar. Here they were suddenly attacked by five thousand Afghan horse, commanded by Mir Weis; and though they fought with a heroism worthy of a better cause, they were unable to stand the unexpected shock or make good their retreat: only eighteen escaped and returned with the disastrous intelligence to Persia. Such is the account given by Mirza Ali Mohamed, from whom Abdullah Khan again differs. The latter states "that Gourguin Khan himself marched at the head of his troops against the Abdalees and Kaukerees, who had taken up a position about twenty leagues from Kandahar, and, refusing to pay the taxes, massacred without pity every Persian they came in contact with. Gourguin Khan was scarcely ten miles from the city, when Mir Weis, having quickly assembled the principal chiefs and all the fighting men of the Abdalee, Ghildjzye, and Kaukeree tribes then in Kandahar, followed rapidly in the rear of Gourguin Khan. It was the habit of the governor and his Georgians to get drunk regularly every day after sunset, and no precautions were ever taken to guard a camp in which every one was plunged in debauch. Mir Weis knew this, and fell upon them during the night: it was a massacre rather than a combat, for the Shah Nawaz and his troops were put to death almost without resistance. After this coup-de-main Mir Weis returned immediately with his men to Kandahar, to which he laid siege, and after a few days obtained an easy victory over the remaining half-starved Persians that defended the place. These he put to death, as well as those individuals who were not of Afghan origin, or who held an appointment under the late governor. Discord ensued when the plunder was to be divided, and swords were drawn; but the Abdalees and Kaukerees were beaten by the Ghildjzyes, and finally obliged to submit, nor could they have remained in Kandahar without their permission. The Abdalees up to this time had always inhabited the country to the south of the Urghendab and the Helmund without having ever obtained the consent of the Mogul or Persian kings to pass those rivers; but now, by virtue of a fresh agreement with the Ghildjzyes, they were enabled to do so, and many of them settled amongst the mountains of the Siah-bend, situated between Kandahar and the principality of Gour. The emigration of the Abdalees into the principality of Herat dates from this period, and there in the course of a very few years they greatly increased in numbers and became very rich. Nevertheless the Afghans agree in stating that a branch of the Noorzyes had been established in the plains of Obeh and Chehrak for more than one hundred years before the bulk of that tribe came to reside in the principality."

Mir Weis, having driven out the oppressors of his country, turned his attention to the manner in which he might best consolidate his work: he restored union between the different tribes, established a kind of discipline amongst them, and released them from the heavy imposts which had till then weighed heavily upon their exertions. Finally, in 1713, the principal families acknowledged him as the Sovereign Prince of Kandahar.

The Court of Persia, instead of putting down this rebellion with vigour, adopted a system which exposed all its weakness. It commenced by negotiating; but Mir Weis, having detained the ambassadors who were sent to advise him to return to his duty, the Shah at length determined to march an army upon Kandahar. With this view the chiefs who commanded in Khorassan were ordered to unite their forces and attack the rebels. This they did, and, though outnumbering the Afghan troops in the proportion of eight to one, they were, in consequence of the want of co-operation between the Persian chiefs, completely beaten by Mir Weis in three successive battles. These events took place in 1713.

The Shah, on receiving information of this catastrophe, saw at once the imminence of the danger. The revolt might gain ground in other provinces of his empire, in which alarming indications had manifested themselves; however, two years elapsed before he ordered his army of 30,000 men to take the field. It was composed of Persians, Arabs, and Abdalee Afghans, at enmity with the Ghildjzyes, and commanded by Sipahee Salar Kaee Khosroo Khan, Walee of Georgia, and nephew of the unfortunate Gourguin Khan.

In this campaign Mir Weis was not successful. He lost all the territory he had taken from the chiefs of Khorassan, was completely defeated by Kaee Khosroo between the Helmund and the Urghendab, and, retiring from thence, was obliged to seek refuge within the walls of Kandahar, to which city his adversary soon laid siege. This the Sipahee Salar pushed forward with great activity and perseverance, and ravaged all the environs of the city, which, ere many days had passed, became a complete desert. As a reprisal for the acts which the Abdalees and Kaukerees had committed, he put to death all the Afghans who fell into his power, and did not even spare the women and children.

The besieged were soon reduced to the greatest extremity, and, alarmed at the terrible consequences that might befall them if the city was taken by assault, they insisted that Mir Weis should offer terms of accommodation to the Persian general. But Kaee Khosroo Khan, thinking himself sure of success, and eager to avenge the death of his uncle by that of his murderers, demanded the unconditional surrender of the place. The garrison saw by this reply that they had nothing to hope for, and, gaining courage from despair, continued the defence with renewed energy, the abilities of their chief rising with the difficulties which he had to contend with.

Mir Weis, having succeeded in baffling the vigilance of the besiegers and escaped from Kandahar, assembled several thousand Afghan cavalry, ravaged the localities Khosroo had spared for the purpose of supplying his own camp, and harassed the Persians day and night. The result was obvious. The Sipahee Salar was obliged to raise the siege to obtain provisions, of which he stood greatly in need; but constantly molested on his march, he found it impossible to secure a moment's repose for his troops, who, decimated and discouraged, began to disband. This new danger induced him to offer battle to the Afghans, who accepted it on the 26th of Ramazan 1714 (Hejira 1126), and they so completely annihilated the Persian army, that only one hundred out of thirty thousand men escaped with their lives. Khosroo Khan, borne down with despair, threw himself at the head of a few brave companions into the thickest of the fight, and there sought an honourable death, which defeat had made more welcome to him than life. This narrative is also from the text of Mirza Ali Mohamed. Abdullah Khan assures us that Khosroo did not attack the Afghans, but that they surprised and defeated him in a night attack.

Mohamed Roostem, another Persian general of some repute, was subsequently sent with a third army to subdue Mir Weis, but he was not more fortunate than his predecessor. Defeated by the Afghans in several encounters, he owed his own safety only to a rapid retreat, which left the Mir absolute master of the whole province of Kandahar. After this fresh success all the Afghan tribes gave in their adhesion to him, and acknowledged Mir Weis for their sovereign chief, as the inhabitants of the capital had done after the death of Gourguin Khan. Unfortunately, however, this adroit and courageous man could not continue the great work which he had up to this time so cleverly conducted, for he died towards the close of 1715, in the eighth year of his rule over the Afghans, and in the succeeding one to that in which he obtained his last victory over the Persians. It was also the very moment at which the measures he had taken with a view of insuring the independence of his country and ameliorating the condition of the people afforded every hope that they would be realised; but, though checked for a time, these hopes were not extinguished, for those measures received a fresh impulse under the government of his son Mahmood.

Mir Weis left two sons, Mir Mahmood and Mir Hoosein. The former, who was the elder, had scarcely attained his eighteenth year at the time of his father's death, and in consequence of this the Afghan chiefs declared that he was not competent to succeed him. Their uncle, Mir Abdullah, was therefore placed at the head of affairs, but the expectations which had been raised by the bold and characteristic conduct of his brother were not realised by him: his first act was to open a conference with the Persian government, whose suzerainty he agreed to admit, and also to pay a tribute, if the Shah would give him the government of Kandahar, make it hereditary in his family, and withdraw the Persian garrisons from the principality.

Two years were consumed in these disgraceful negotiations, and, though the projects of Mir Abdullah were but imperfectly known to the Afghans, they were mistrustful of his intentions, and opposed him as best they could; but when these projects came to be revealed to them by the Persians, who in so doing hoped to sow the seeds of dissension amongst them, they were in the highest degree indignant.

The eldest son of Mir Weis, who was already distinguished by many of the qualities the Afghans had admired in his father, and who, though so young, had displayed daring acts of courage bordering on rashness when engaged with the Persians, took advantage of the discontent which the interested conduct of his uncle had given rise to in the minds of his countrymen, and seized the sovereign power of which he thought he had been unjustly deprived. The unpopularity of Mir Abdullah made his success easy; he attacked his house with only fifty men, killed him with his own hand, and made the Afghan chiefs then at Kandahar elect him governor in the room of his murdered relative. The people themselves demanded his election, which, however, was not agreeable to a few ambitious Serdars; but when they saw the young chief had obtained the general support of the nation, they adhered to the new order of things.

Abdullah Khan, the Heratee, gives a different account of the motives which led to this murder of the Mir. Abdullah, observes that historian, was less active, less impetuous, but not less intelligent and prudent than his brother Mir Weis. After the death of the latter several Ghildjzye chiefs talked openly of their intention to dictate to those in power; the seeds of much discord had also been sown amongst the tribes, and Mir Abdullah was perfectly aware that he could not expect to retain the sovereign authority in any degree of tranquillity unless he could prevent new hostilities on the part of Persia. The negotiations therefore which he had entered into with the Shah had only that object in view, and there is no doubt that whenever he had found himself able to do so he would have thrown off a vassalage the light fetters of which he now consented to wear. The fiery Afghans could not understand the wisdom of this system, and the constant opposition of his nephew Mahmood finished by lowering his influence with the Serdars, several of whom hoped and were desirous of occupying his position themselves. The Mir's death was as unjust as it was to be regretted, and the more to be deplored, as his successor displayed warlike qualities only, which led to the decimation of the tribes, and weakened them to such a degree that, under the reign of Nadir Shah, they again fell under the Persian yoke. The power also after Mahmood's time passed into the hands of the Abdalee tribe—to the injury of the Ghildjzyes, who had been the first to proclaim and establish the independence of the Afghan nation.

At about the period when Mir Weis died, the population of Herat tried also to withdraw from their allegiance to the Seffaveans. The Khorassians, of whom it was for the most part composed, had obtained from Nadir Shah the privilege of being governed by their own chiefs. Alayar Khan, who was governor of the province at the time of Roostem Khan's defeat, though not declaring himself independent as Mir Weis had done, acknowledged only from that time a nominal submission to the Persian court; but whether the Persian garrison of Herat, though very small, still inspired him with awe, or whether he hoped by cunning and temporising finally to become completely independent, he continued to keep up appearances, and observe a respectful bearing towards the Shah Hoosein; and as anarchy reigned in several Persian provinces, he thought the monarch might possibly look upon these faint proofs of his obedience as submission.

Alayar Khan, as well as Mir Weis, with whom he had secretly allied himself in a common determination to resist the Shah, died before he could put into execution the plans which he had conceived. The court of Persia appointed Zeman Khan, Koortchee

Bashee, his successor. This officer, who commanded the troops quartered in the province of Herat, was instructed to reinforce his division by enlisting all the volunteers in the locality and march against Mir Abdullah. If this chief had been as prudent as his predecessor, he might have hoped, if not to obtain a positive and complete success against the rebels in the south, at least some advantages which would, without doubt, have prevented Mir Mahmood from undertaking the expedition which he made some time after in Persia; but Zeman was a dull and dissipated man, and had not the tact to foment the elements of discord which existed amongst the Afghans. The Abdalee tribe, almost the whole of which was settled in his government, were the hereditary enemies of the Ghildjzyes, and might have been led against them with success; but he had affronted them, and was obliged to take the field with a weak corps-d'armée composed almost entirely of Persians. Neither the importance of the undertaking he had to carry out, nor the burden of the responsibility which rested upon him, operated as any restraint upon his conduct, and his excesses were such that they effected his ruin even before he was in presence of the enemy.

A short time before this a branch of the Suddozye tribe had established itself in the neighbourhood of Sukkur, and their chief, Heyat Sultan, anxious to obtain certain favours from Zeman Khan, committed a most fearful outrage against his own son. Incredible as it may appear, he sent Assad Ullah, a young and beautiful lad, to this wretch in human shape for an infamous purpose. The crime accomplished, the unfortunate youth took the first opportunity of making his escape from the Persian camp, and, returning to his tribe, which shared with him the feelings of fury that animated their young chief, they determined upon taking a deep revenge. Assad's first step was to seize his vile and unnatural parent and imprison him in a fortress, after which, accompanied by a few thousand horsemen, he started in pursuit of Zeman Khan, and such was the rapidity of his movements, that he surprised the Persian commander at midnight in the district of Zemindavar, before he had received the slightest intimation of his being in arms, attacked with great bravery and impetuosity the weary and sleeping troops, and put them nearly all to the sword. The villain who had so deeply injured him was the first that fell, and by the hand of Assad; after which the victorious youth marched on Herat, and, having obtained an entrance to the city, exterminated the few Persians he found there. After this he again took the field, and made himself, almost without opposition, master of the whole province, which, on the 26th of Ramazan, 1716, he constituted an independent principality.

As to the Persian troops which had succeeded in effecting their escape from the massacre at Zemindavar, finding themselves without a commander, they disbanded, and returned to Ispahan. All that the government could do to induce them to return to Afghanistan under a new general was ineffectual; they refused to march; and the Shah Sultan Hoosein was under the necessity of relinquishing his project for bringing that country again under his dominion. Assad Ullah Khan raised himself to power about a year before the period at which Mir Mahmood became by the murder of his uncle Prince of Kandahar.

Persia, already so much weakened by the loss of two of her finest provinces and three armies, ravaged by the Uzbeks, menaced by Turkey and Russia, and governed by a degraded and superstitious court who ruled the feeble Sultan Hoosein, had no little difficulty in making a stand against so many disasters. Nevertheless, the Persian monarch made a last effort, and in 1719 raised an army of 35,000 men, well provided with artillery, which he placed under the orders of Sefi Kooli Khan, a general of reputed talent, to whom he allotted the task of driving back in the first instance the Uzbeks, and then of reducing Herat and Kandahar.

The Khan obtained an easy victory over the undisciplined hordes of Uzbeks, who, badly armed and badly led, having pillage only in prospect, and not the permanent occupation of Khorassan, took to flight at the first shock of the Persian army. Puffed up with pride at a success thus easily obtained, Sefi Kooli Khan pompously announced his intention to exterminate the rebel Afghans, to whom he sent an imperious order to come to his camp and implore his mercy. On the receipt of this message, Assad Ullah Khan moved forward to meet him at the head of 12,000 Afghans and Hazarahs, and, in spite of the disproportion of the two armies, attacked him directly. The Afghans were armed only with bad swords and worse matchlocks, but they did not hesitate to face the fire of the formidable Persian artillery, and maintained during a whole day a most obstinate combat, in which 3000 of their best troops lost their lives. The victory was still undecided at sunset, when by some accident never accounted for a dreadful explosion took place amongst the Persian artillery. This caused an instantaneous panic in their army, and they took to flight, leaving on the field of battle all their baggage and the greater part of their guns. Sefi Kooli Khan and several members of his family, together with a large number of chiefs as well as 10,000 Persian soldiers, were slain in this battle fought near the village of Kariz.

This victory decided the fortunes of the Afghans. Independence was henceforward theirs, and the power, but half-established, of Assad Ullah Khan was consolidated, not only in Herat, but also through the greatest part of Khorassan, of which he took possession, with the exception of Meshed, its capital, and that resisted all his attacks. Seeing that his efforts to reduce it were ineffectual, he was satisfied with keeping a watch upon it, and marched to the south of his territories, in order to extend them in that direction. He seized, in the first instance, upon Subzawar, and afterwards moved on Furrah, to which place he laid siege, when he was attacked by Mir Mahmood of Kandahar, who thought these proceedings might be detrimental to his own interest, more particularly as Assad Ullah exhibited the courage and capacity of a good general, and belonged to the tribe of the Abdalees, the rival of his own. But Assad Ullah Khan was unfortunately killed at the commencement of the battle, a ball having struck him in the middle of the forehead; his troops, discouraged, retired to Herat, where anarchy reigned during several months, until a Belooch chief of the Seistan, one Mir Mohamed, seized the power and established order in the city.

CHAPTER IV.

Intrigues of Persia in Afghanistan — Preparations of Mir Mahmood — He outwits the Persian court — Is appointed Governor-General of Kandahar — His ambitious projects — Seizes the fortresses on the Helmund — State of the Persian army — Besieges Kerman — It surrenders to his troops — They are beaten by the Persian general Leuft Ali Khan — Mir Mahmood retreats to Kandahar — Leuft Ali is disgraced — Revolt against Mir Mahmood at Kandahar — The Mir marches with his army against the Persians — Provisions the fortress of Bam — Kerman surrenders to him — He is repulsed before Yezd — Moves on Ispahan — State of Mir Mahmood's troops — A singular recipe for courage — Pusillanimity of the Persians — Disunion amongst them — The consequences — Their army is routed by the Afghans — The Ethemad Dooulet and the Walee of Georgia — The chief command of the army is given to the latter — Proposition of Shah Hoosein to Mir Mahmood — The siege is pressed closer — The Persians endeavour to leave the city — Great scarcity prevails — The result — Dreadful sufferings of the inhabitants — Shah Hoosein proceeds to the Afghan camp — He abdicates the throne — Mahmood's conduct after his victory.

THE Persian Government, while sending armies to subdue Kandahar, also employed the arts of negotiation, and tried to deceive successively Mir Weis, his brother, and his son, with intrigues and promises of which Eastern nations are so prodigal. But these chiefs did not fall into the snare prepared for them: nevertheless Mir Mahmood, who put his uncle to death because he had received certain propositions from the Shah, found somewhat later that this plan was a good one, and adopted it himself; less, however, because he was afraid of the Shah of Persia, than because he required a few years of repose to prepare himself for the invasion which he had projected against that kingdom. As the victory over Assad Ullah Khan might awaken the fears of the Persians, and induce them to march one of their everlasting armies upon him, he hastened, immediately he had relieved Furrah, to inform Shah Hoosein that he had attacked the Abdalees only to prevent them from taking the town from him, and that it was now entirely at the disposition of the Shah. The letter which Mir Mahmood sent to the Shah was placed in his hands by the same minister who had been the accomplice of Mir Weis, and on this occasion he did not give the lie to his own base antecedents. Instead of enlightening his master on the manifest ambition of the Afghan prince, he did all that lay in his power to convince him that the Ghildjzyes were excellent vassals, who had rendered him a very great service, and furthermore that they had only exterminated Gourghin Khan, his nephew, and the Georgians, on account of the excesses they had committed, and to deliver themselves from a most odious tyranny. By such representations he sought not only to revenge himself on the Georgians, whose chiefs were his most dangerous antagonists, but also to endeavour to calm the resentment the Shah had always felt against him, in consequence of the efforts he had made to induce him to give Mir Weis permission to return to Kandahar.

The poor feeble-minded sovereign, deceived once more, bestowed upon Mir Mahmood the surname of Hoosein Kooli Khan (the slave of Hoosein), and sent him a firman appointing him Governor-General of Kandahar, and making that high office hereditary in his family. Mir Mahmood accepted these honours with apparent gratitude and respect, and this good understanding between the Mir and the Court of Ispahan enabled him to augment in all security the force which he intended to employ in carrying out his ambitious projects. To clear away, however, all difficulties, he also wrote to the Shah and represented that the Abdalees recently established in Herat had been in revolt for the last two years and paid no taxes, and he solicited the Shah's permission to subdue them. Sultan Hoosein was foolish enough to consent to this expedition, which Mir Mahmood at once undertook, but, instead of directing his steps to the north, he sent there a small flying detachment, while he himself marched with the mass of his army along the banks of the Helmund and seized all the fortresses on that river, for they commanded the principal roads of the Seistan leading into Persia. It is true he took possession in the name of the Shah, but his secret purpose was to fortify himself, and to collect provisions, in order that he might command an easy passage to the southern provinces, and at a future time with little difficulty invade the Persian territory. It will be remembered that his father had travelled through them on his return from Kandahar, and the invaluable information which he then collected was now to be utilized by his son, whose preparations for this invasion were prolonged up to 1720. But even then his army numbered only 12,000 men; however, they were all picked men, inured to war and hardships of every kind, and prepared for any eventuality that might arise. Persia, on the contrary, was at this time in a most deplorable condition; everything was in disorder; and the only emulation that could be said to exist at that court was who should exhibit the greatest weakness and degradation. The right of holding the appointments of the public service, instead of being a privilege belonging to high birth or a recompense for meritorious services, was sold to the highest bidder; the troops, without discipline, received neither instruction nor pay, and, frequently disbanding themselves, pillaged the villages and the caravans. The towns were infested with thieves, who openly followed their villanous profession with the utmost assurance, knowing they could do so with impunity. In short, everything announced the complete decadence of this great monarchy, which, attacked on all its frontiers, by the Afghans, the Tartars, the Russians, and the Arabs, seemed likely to become an easy conquest to the first who should attempt to invade it.

It was the young Mahmood, breathing vengeance for the miseries which his country had suffered under the Persian rule, who was the first that engaged in this difficult enterprise. In 1720, under the pretext of attacking Chedad Khan, a Belooch chief, who with his nomades was ravaging the province of Kerman, Mahmood placed himself at the head of his small army, and traversed amidst unheard of difficulties the arid and desert countries of the south of Persia. On this march his soldiers were soon decimated by privations and fatigue, and of the 12,000 men who set out with him only 7000 arrived under the walls of Kerman, to which he laid siege with a courage and determination utterly disproportioned to the means of aggression at his command. Simultaneously with these operations he again endeavoured to put the Shah Hoosein on the wrong scent and lull the vigilance of his government, to which he wrote stating that he had besieged Kerman merely to force the Governor to furnish his troops with provisions, and thus repay him the expense of moving his army in the interest and for the benefit of the Shah of Persia.

Mahmood was joined by a great number of Persian malcontents, who soon filled up the casualties in his army. The town, hard pressed, held out only for a few days, and then surrendered at discretion; nevertheless the victor thought it necessary to punish the inhabitants for the feeble resistance they had offered, and not only them but those of the whole district. During four months his soldiers, gorged with plunder, committed every imaginable excess, at the expiration of which time they were attacked and put to flight by the Persian General Leuft Ali Khan, who marched to the assistance of the invaded province with a very superior force. The defeat of Mir Mahmood was so complete that he was obliged to make a rapid retreat to Kandahar, taking with him only a miserable remnant of that army which had followed him with so much enthusiasm to the conquest of Persia! Not one man would perhaps have survived if the evil genius which presided over the destinies of that empire had not arrested the progress of her victorious commander. Leuft Ali Khan, the only good general the Shah then had, was, by way of recompense for the brilliant success which he had just obtained, deprived of his command and thrown into prison. A court intrigue, originating in the Vizier, brought about this unjustifiable result, for the letter of Mir Mahmood had been perfidiously misinterpreted by him to the Shah Sultan Hoosein. But if Mir Mahmood had not been defeated, more important interests would have obliged him to abandon the province he had just conquered, for he received intelligence that his rear was seriously menaced. Beiram Sultan Lakzee, governor of Furrah, and Malek Djaffer Khan Sistanee, having formed an alliance, succeeded in exciting a portion of the province of Kandahar to revolt against his authority. Supported by a few thousand men, they had even seized upon the city in the name of Shah Hoosein, but were driven from it by Mir Hoosein, brother of Mir Mahmood. The latter therefore hastened his return, and his presence soon restored order. His resolution had not been shaken for one instant, for he had reflected, and wisely, on all that had passed, and had seen his own faults. These had arisen rather from ignorance than want of courage—they appeared to him therefore easy of correction: and the bravery and intelligence which he had shown in his fatal expedition of 1720 secured for him the obedience and admiration of his soldiers, which enabled him with little trouble to raise another and a larger army, one not less enthusiastic than the first. The Afghans of every tribe, even those living in the provinces of Herat and Kabul as well as the Hazarahs, hastened with alacrity to the standard of a chief who promised to enrich them with the spoils of their ancient oppressors. The Belooches settled to the south of the Helmund also furnished him with a contingent of several thousand men, and he determined to take an ample revenge for the disasters inflicted upon him by Leuft Ali Khan.

After having installed his brother Mir Hoosein as Regent of Kandahar during his absence, he again entered Persia, in January, 1722, at the head of an army of 28,000 men, carrying with him immense stores of provisions in order to guard against the privations his troops had suffered on his first expedition from the scarcity of food and forage.

Mir Mahmood opened this campaign by rapidly crossing the Seistan, and without encountering any obstacle he reached the fortress of Bam, where he remained for a few days. This fortress he repaired and strengthened with great care, and made it an immense depôt of provisions and munitions of war. The garrison was ordered to collect within its walls all the corn which the inhabitants of the surrounding country could supply above what they required for their own use, and also to keep numerous beasts of burden ready to take the road whenever instructions were given to that effect. The command of this important place was confided by Mir Mahmood to his relative Noor Ullah Khan, a brave and energetic man, on whose fidelity he could rely; and having thus completed his preparations, he again advanced and arrived before Kerman, intending to besiege it once more, but the inhabitants opened the gates almost without offering any resistance: the garrison, however, in the citadel, composed of picked men, refused to surrender. The commander wrote to the Afghan chief that, if his object was to amass great riches and become Shah of Persia, he would lose his time and uselessly exhaust his resources in undertaking the siege of a place that was provisioned for ten years, and the defenders of which were determined to bury themselves beneath its ashes rather than capitulate; but he added that if the Mir chose to march on Ispahan he might accomplish his purpose, and he offered to give him 18,000 tomauns towards the expenses of the campaign, if he would raise the siege. Mahmood accepted these conditions, far less because, according to the custom of his country, it saved the honour of his arms, than because he had no heavy artillery to batter the place—the only guns at his disposal, those called in Persia *zimboorek*, being wholly inefficient for this purpose. Of these he had an hundred carrying a ball of from one to two pounds, each zimboorek being carried by a camel with the artilleryman who served it.

Directly Mahmood had received the sum agreed upon he moved upon Ispahan by Yezd, the direct road, and made an attempt to take the latter town by assault as he passed; but several attacks having, in spite of the brilliant courage of his soldiers, been vigorously repulsed, he abandoned this siege also. It was likely to prove a lingering affair and occasion him the loss of much precious time, so he continued his march upon Ispahan without troubling himself about his rear, for the country was too denuded of the enemy's troops to give him any anxiety on that subject. As to his line of operations, that lay wherever provisions could be obtained, and he carried with him a pretty large supply, which was renewed from time to time in the villages on his road. In this manner he arrived at Guluabad, a village situated ten miles from Ispahan, without having met one Persian who attempted to oppose his passage. Here he entrenched his army, which had been somewhat reduced since its departure from Kandahar by privation and fatigue, as well as in the combats before Kerman and Yezd; but these losses he had repaired by a few thousand Gheber recruits, who were not less desirous than the Afghans to revenge themselves on their common oppressors the Persians. Mahmood had still 23,000 combatants under his command when he arrived at Guluabad, but, in spite of their courage and the advantage they derived from the reputation of their arms, they could have been easily exterminated if the Persians had possessed the least sentiment of national feeling, and been animated by the remembrance of the ancient grandeur of their country; but this debased people learnt from their weak monarch only how to lament their misfortunes, instead of warding them off by fighting manfully to prevent them, and it was not till the last moment, when money and arms were distributed amongst them, that they decided upon defending the capital of the empire.

Mir Mahmood's troops arrived at Guluabad in wretched condition: the rags they wore scarcely covered them; they were destitute of warlike stores; with rare exception, their sabres were the only arm of which they could make any use, and their light artillery was unfit for siege purposes. Ispahan, on the contrary, besides its population, which was at this time estimated at more than 600,000 souls, had a garrison of 60,000 soldiers; the city walls were strong, and the besieged in possession of a formidable artillery. Unfortunately, however, the spirit of the army was cowardly and superstitious, and it was in those days more advantageous for a minister to deceive and betray the monarch, or flatter his predilection for theological discussions, than to do his duty. One of his favourite generals, Fath Ali Khan Kadjar, assured Shah Hoosein he had heard from an old woman of Asterabad, who was said to be inspired, that two legs of a he goat, boiled with 325 peapods in water over which a young virgin had repeated 1200 times "Là illah, illah là,"* made a broth which would render invisible the men who drank it: the superstitious monarch therefore ordered that his troops should be daily supplied with goat-soup thus prepared. A thousand absurdities equally efficacious were decreed for a like purpose; and there were only one or two high-minded men who, stimulated by the calamitous state of affairs, endeavoured to raise the drooping spirits of the garrison; but owing to the weakness of the monarch, they and the few followers who adhered to them soon fell victims to his imbecile conduct. Traitors alone were listened to and intrusted with the command of the troops; there was no mutual understanding between them, and they daily accumulated acts of cowardice, treason, and folly, one upon the other.

The Ethemad Dooulet, first minister of the Shah, and the Walee of Arabia, who was General in Chief, were always of opposite opinions. The first asserted that, as they had hitherto done nothing, but had allowed the Afghans to arrive under the walls of Ispahan, it would be better to remain on the defensive, and let them wear themselves out in useless efforts; but the Walee made light of the opinion of that eminent personage, and went out nearly every day skirmishing round the enemy's camp, in a manner, moreover, that appeared to be much more in the interests of Mir Mahmood than in those of his sovereign. His subordinate officers committed similar faults; sorties were made without judgment or discipline, and the Persian troops gave ground at the first onset, while the rivalry existing amongst the commanders produced daily collisions in their army, that frequently ended in bloodshed.

A council of war having been summoned by the King, who presided in person, it was at length decided that a general attack should be made upon the Afghans. Mahmood had only twenty thousand fighting men to withstand the Persians, but, accustomed to conquer, the power of this force was increased three-fold by their own courage: they heeded not the numbers of the enemy, and blindly obeyed a prince who possessed all their sympathies, and who had the command entirely in his own hands; while the Persians, being formed into several divisions, all independent one of

* God is God, and there is no God but him.

the other, and receiving different orders, were essentially deficient in combination and resolution, the chief elements of military success. At daybreak on the 8th of April, 1721, the Persians left the city in great confusion to attack the Afghan camp. The Ethemad Doulet and the Walee of Arabia had not been able to come to an understanding as to the order of battle, and were no better agreed in opinion as to the attack; thus each of them commenced with the corps-d'armée under his command, and in accordance with his own individual ideas, without dreaming of the mutual support they ought to afford to each other when required.

At first the Ethemad Dooulet remained inactive, and, advantageously posted on the defensive, waited for the Afghans to advance, and this plan was approved by the majority of the other generals. But the Walee, a man of little reflection and of an ardent temper, looked upon this inaction as disgraceful, and, without listening to the advice of his colleagues, exclaimed, "We are not here to deliberate, but to fight." With these words he galloped forward to his men, who poured down upon the left flank, which gave way at the first onset. It now required a slight effort only to turn the Afghans and put them to a complete rout; but the Arabs, far more anxious for plunder than for glory, rushed into the camp of Mir Mahmood and began the work of pillage. The Ethemad Dooulet, observing the Walee thus engaged, fell upon the Afghan right, which was moving up to attack the Arabs; but Aman Ullah Khan, the most talented of Mir Mahmood's lieutenants, who commanded this wing, perceiving his intention, faced about, and for some time retired before the Persians; then suddenly halting, he opened his squadrons and unmasked his one hundred zimbooreks, which instantly sent forth a hail of balls into their ranks. The enemy, instead of rushing at once upon the guns, which could not have been reloaded in time for another discharge, suddenly halted, and finally decamped. Aman Ullah, seizing the propitious moment without hesitation, fell upon the fugitives with his cavalry, and made a terrific carnage; their artillery, consisting of twenty-four pieces of large calibre, which they had placed in their rear, were also captured, and turned against the royal army. From that moment the rout of the Persians was complete, and the soldiers, instead of entering Ispahan, regained each his own province, and there waited the issue of events. The Afghans obtained an immense booty in this battle, in which 25,000 Persians remained upon the field: amongst them was Roostem Khan Gooulaye Agassee, chief of the slaves, and Ahmed Khan, General in Chief of the Artillery, two of the most important officers in the army.

This event spread the greatest consternation in Ispahan, and the Shah held another council of war, at which the Ethemad Dooulet proposed that the King should leave the capital without delay, and retire to Kasbeen, from whence he could make an appeal to his faithful subjects, raise a powerful army, and, returning, rescue Ispahan from the Afghan invaders. The Walee of Arabia, whose troops had behaved so ill in the last battle, and had been the cause of the defeat, again held a different opinion, which obtained with the feeble monarch, who, influenced by traitors and cowards, blindly consented to his own ruin. He gave the Walee the supreme command of his army; but in thus concentrating the power into one hand he did not succeed in imparting greater unity to the subsequent operations. The successive reverses which overwhelmed the Persians, instead of opening the eyes of the Shah to the incapacity of his general, served only to increase his absurd caprices, which always ended in partial defeats, and eventually so decimated and discouraged his army, that the troops were afraid to expose themselves beyond the walls of the city.

While the Shah Hoosein confided the destinies of his empire to a man so little worthy of this trust, Mir Mahmood, though a conqueror, was a prey to the most cruel anxiety, for the number of his troops diminished without his having the power to recruit them; a turn of fortune in favour of the Persians might place him in a most critical position; and at one moment such was his indecision that he ceased to give any orders to his generals. Finding that Ispahan did not surrender after the victory he had gained, he was on the point of retiring to Kerman to reorganize his army; but having been informed of the alarm which reigned in the city, and that provisions were running short, his hopes again revived, and another motive arose to dissuade him from fulfilling his intention of retreating. Instead of preserving that firmness of demeanour, which will frequently sustain a drooping cause, instead of energetically battling with his enemy, the Shah Sultan Hoosein was seen to drag the imperial purple through the mire, and, following the example of his governor of Kerman, beseech his enemy to accept immense sums of money to evacuate the Persian territory. It was evident that his proposition originated in fear and discouragement; and

Mir Mahmood was convinced that he should soon be master of the city if he persevered in the investment of the place. He hourly saw the Persian generals committing the grossest faults, and neglecting to take the most simple measures for their preservation. He knew that imprudent and ignorant counsellors gave the Shah advice which must infallibly lead to his destruction; and all these circumstances determined him to abandon his project of retreat and press the Persians with additional vigour.

The errors, or rather the treachery, of the Persian nobles, enabled Mahmood to surround the city by a line of circumvallation, which it would have been impossible to defend with his small army if the Walee had made the least effort to dislodge him; but he sent a succession of feeble detachments against the Afghans, which, badly directed, failed in every attack. Ferahabad and Djulfa, abandoned by the Walee, were now taken by assault, and, regardless of the heroic resistance of their inhabitants, the general in chief made not the least demonstration in their favour; it was supposed that the fanaticism of this barbarian was gratified by the ruin of Djulfa, for it was inhabited by Armenian Christians. In short, the Walee and his troops always moved in the direction where the enemy was not; and if he did meet the Afghans, he was sure to retreat under some frivolous pretext or other; he boasted in loud terms, when in presence of the Shah, but always remained in a state of inaction when he ought to have shown energy and determination.

Feeling that he was victorious on all points, Mahmood drew closer the line of circumvallation in which he held the Persians, who made not the least attempt to check his operations: debased by the tyranny and superstitious bigotry of the court, they became utterly helpless; while the Afghans, elated by their success, and possessing all the *élan* of a people who had recovered their liberty, fought with the greatest enthusiasm. They carefully guarded the roads, intercepted the convoys of provisions that endeavoured to enter the capital, and laid waste the environs with fire and sword, preserving only what was necessary for themselves; until this country, hitherto so fertile, became an arid desert on which nothing could be seen but the bleached skeletons of men and horses, and the charred ruins of forsaken villages.

At the commencement of the war the rural population, harassed and plundered, flocked to the capital, where they were of no use in the defence, and their presence only increased the scarcity, which soon became extreme, and many thousands of the famished citizens of Ispahan let themselves down from the ramparts and fled from the city, hoping to reach some other province where food was in abundance. But the Afghans, who closely watched their movements, slaughtered them without remorse, and but a very few succeeded in effecting their escape; nevertheless the bare possibility of doing so induced crowds of them daily to make the hazardous attempt. Heaps of human bodies were seen here and there wanting the common rights of sepulture, while many more floated on the surface of the Zendehrood, the tainted waters of which were no longer fit for the ordinary purposes of life; and at length even these did not reach the capital, for the Afghans cut off the canals which supplied the city; the tanks were insufficient to meet the general consumption, and thirst was superadded to the pangs of hunger. Provisions of all kinds were soon exhausted; the few camels and other beasts of burden which remained were sold at so high a price that the great men about the court could alone purchase any animal food; and the people were reduced to such extremities that they were compelled to give chase to the most unclean animals, which by their religion they were forbidden not only to eat, but even to touch. At night the inhabitants of one quarter made incursions into other parts of the city to search for provisions supposed to be concealed, and frequent scenes of violence and bloodshed were the result; for here the father was often found armed against his son, and brother against brother; all affection was banished amongst the members of the same family; they looked upon each other as deadly enemies, and fought for the wretched scraps of food they had perchance procured. At length meat of every kind disappeared, and the trees were stripped of their leaves and bark to satisfy the cravings of these miserable beings, who, searching the very dunghills and common sewers, lived upon any soft substance, whatever it might happen to be, which they found there. Old pieces of leather were soaked, boiled, and eaten with avidity; the plaster from the walls, mixed with sawdust, also offered them another species of food which was sometimes the object of angry dispute even to the death. The population of Ispahan, so healthy, light-hearted, and rich a few months before, now presented the spectacle of a mob of attenuated creatures, wan and of a sinister aspect, scarcely able to drag themselves along the streets and public places, that were covered with the corpses of their countrymen, and which, horrible to relate, were sometimes eaten to alleviate the terrible pangs of hunger. Many put an end to their own existence to avoid these sufferings. Amidst all this appalling misery the people evinced to the last their devotion to their King, who assured them of the speedy arrival of his son Thamasp. This prince had succeeded in eluding the vigilance of the Afghans, and gone to the north of the empire, where he expected to raise an army and march to the relief of Ispahan; but five months having elapsed without any tidings of him reaching the capital, its inhabitants despaired of his return, and besought the Shah to bring their calamities to a close. This prince, more weak than ill-intentioned, afflicted with the fearful condition of his subjects, determined to put an end to it; besides, it was utterly impossible that he could prolong the defence. All his armies had been destroyed, the few soldiers that remained in Persia were in distant provinces, and many of them in the interest of ambitious chiefs, who, profiting by the miserable state of their country, united with each other to create an independent power.

Eight months had elapsed from the commencement of the siege, when, on the 14th of Sefer, 1135 of the Hejira, and 23rd October, 1722, the Shah Sultan Hoosein left the city, escorted by the great officers of his court, and arrived at the camp of Mir Mahmood, in whose favour he publicly abdicated the throne, and with all solemnity delivered to him the sword and crown of the Seffaveans, the attributes of his power as monarch of the Persian empire. The same day the invader took military possession of the arsenals and other public establishments, but it was not till five days after that he made his triumphant entry into Ispahan. His first act was to assign a place of residence to the fallen Shah, and a sufficient pension to meet his requirements; his second, to order a general massacre of the troops remaining within the city, not so much with a view of taking revenge upon them for the resistance they had made, as to strike terror into those who, under the command of the Prince Thamasp, might be tempted to renew the contest. This massacre continued during three days, after which Mir Mahmood ordered it should cease, and occupied himself in restoring tranquillity and security in the capital. Having very little confidence in the administrative powers of the Afghans, who, up to this period, had never taken part in public affairs, and not daring to place any faith in the Persians so recently subjected to his rule, the Mir appointed two officers at the head of each department of the administration—an Afghan and a Persian; the former to watch the latter, and at the same time acquire from him all that it was useful for him to know.

The measures taken by Mir Mahmood to protect the vanquished from insult, the severe discipline he observed in his army, and the even-handed justice he dealt out to every one, soon acquired for him the esteem of the Persians. The Persian chiefs, who, traitors to their king, had furnished him with information during the siege, he treated with the greatest severity; he, nevertheless, made an exception in favour of the Walee of Arabia, whose life he spared in conformity with a vow that he had made so to do if he should come victorious out of the contest; and in order not to give any opportunity for a false interpretation to the motives which dictated this, he loaded with favours those who had remained faithful to the fortunes of the Shah Hoosein.

Up to the day on which Mir Mahmood attained a position so elevated, his conduct was that of a man animated by magnanimous sentiments; but, from the time he felt securely seated on the throne of the Seffaveans, he adopted a line of conduct which tarnished the glory of his previous career; the innate ferocity of the Afghan, suppressed for a time, soon reassumed its empire over his mind; he became suspicious and even cruel towards those who had served him with the greatest fidelity. But, in spite of his tyranny, he endeavoured to tranquillise Persia by his judicious administration, and to extend his dominion over those provinces which had not recognised his authority. He would, perhaps, have succeeded, but for the change which had taken place in his character, and which became every day more and more cruel.

CHAPTER V.

The Prince Thamasp — Mahmood sends an army against him — Kasbeen surrenders to the Afghans — Duplicity and cruelty of the victors — The inhabitants take their revenge — Defeat of the Afghans — Mahmood is furious at this — Reconciliation with Aman Ullah Khan — Mahmood massacres the Persian nobles — Sanguinary scenes in Ispahan — State of the provinces — Prince Thamasp is proclaimed Shah — Assembles troops in the Azerbaidjan — The Turks and Russians seize upon Armenia and Georgia — State of the Afghan army — Desertions from Mir Mahmood's ranks — Shiraz besieged — Tyranny of Mahmood — Mir Echreff appointed to the chief command — The Afghan army march upon Yezd — Mahmood becomes deranged — Losses in the Afghan ranks — The troops return to Ispahan — Mahmood in a paroxysm of madness puts to death the sons of Shah Hoosein — Death of Mahmood — Mir Echreff succeeds him — He puts the Serdar Ullah Khan to death — Policy of Russia at this period — Echreff marches against the Turks — Battle of Kiemereh — Defeat of the Turks — Treaty with the Afghans — Events in Afghanistan — The Russians take possession of Guilan — Echreff fortifies the Afghan quarter in Ispahan — Nadir joins the Shah Thamasp — He takes Nishapoor — Echreff seizes Yezd — Battle between Nadir and Echreff — Defeat of the Afghans — Battle of Bagh Mirane — The Afghans retire from Ispahan — Conflict at the Bend-emir — Retreat upon Shiraz — Destruction of the Afghan army — Death of Echreff — Reflections.

AFTER the abdication of his father in 1722, the Prince Thamasp Mirza assumed the title of Shah at Kasbeen; but when Mir Mahmood despatched an army against him, the prince fled at its approach, and retired into the Azerbaidjan. The inhabitants of Kasbeen, seeing themselves thus abandoned, immediately made their submission to the Afghans, to whom they gave a most friendly reception. The invaders reciprocated this feeling, and appeared desirous of being on the best terms with them; but, after they had been some time in the town, renewed the scenes of carnage which took place at Ispahan, and during three days gave the reins to their passion for murder and pillage. The Kasbeenians, finding that submission had not disarmed the vengeance of their conquerors, assembled in arms after the first moment of surprise, massacred in their turn nearly half the Afghans, and drove the remainder from the city. The survivors at once dispersed; some of them regaining Ispahan, while others followed the Serdar Aman Ullah Khan, and Mir Echreff, the cousin of Mahmood. These two Afghan chiefs had, more than any others, contributed to the victories and elevation of the son of Mir Weis; but Mahmood, jealous of their popularity, instead of recompensing them for their services, basely accused them of treachery and threatened them with death, from which they escaped to Kandahar.

Mir Mahmood was highly incensed at the defeat his troops sustained at Kasbeen, and not less so at the defection of the two serdars; he was also apprehensive that the Persian nobles whom he had retained at his court might attempt to overthrow him or take his life, and thought, therefore, that, having merely a small body of troops to make a stand against a general revolt, terror alone could retain the Persians in obedience. Well convinced of this, he determined upon adopting the most barbarous measures, and, having succeeded in reconciling himself with Aman Ullah Khan, turned that circumstance to account by making it the opportunity for holding a great festival. To this he invited all the Persian dignitaries of rank and other persons of note in Ispahan, who, anxious to please their new sovereign, and entertaining no suspicion of his villanous design, accepted his invitation, and arrived at the palace to the number of one hundred and fourteen, but, instead of the banquet which they had expected, they found Afghan troops posted in the royal gardens, who, in conformity with the orders they had received, put them all to death. This horrible butchery accomplished, the soldiers spread themselves over the city, and slaughtered, to the number of several thousands, the near relatives of the victims, as well as a great number of syuds and ulemas of the capital. It was only when this bloody tragedy had been played out that Mahmood's fury was temporarily appeased. Two days after, five hundred youths, of the first families in the kingdom, and who within the walls of their colleges had escaped this massacre, were taken from thence into the country, and hunted down like deer, the Afghans piercing them through with their jereeds as they fled terror-stricken across the plain. Not long after, three thousand Persians, who had taken service in the tyrant's army, experienced a similar fate; they were suddenly attacked at a banquet which he gave them, and, being unarmed, were exterminated to a man. Finally, he put to death every Persian who had held any employment or received any favours from the Shah's government. These horrible proceedings, which lasted during a month, plunged all the first families of the country into the depths of despair, and denuded Ispahan of half its population; the carnage subsequently extended itself to the provinces, and murder, pillage, and desolation reigned on all sides.

At length the cruelties of Mir Mahmood became a species of madness, but the Persians, utterly debased, did not attempt to deliver themselves from his frightful tyranny. In the midst of these sanguinary scenes they lay prostrate at the feet of him who had but yesterday deprived them of a father, a brother, a son, or a friend, and, while waiting till they received the same fate at his hands, were vile and degraded enough to submit to be used as the instruments of his ferocious nature. But the torrents of blood thus shed brought no sense of security to Mir Mahmood, and his position was certainly well calculated to inspire him with uneasiness. Thamasp Mirza had recently been acknowledged Shah by the population of Azerbaidjan, and a party which began to be powerful in that province had pronounced in his favour, and threatened to march, at no distant date, upon Ispahan. On the other hand, the Turks and the Russians, taking advantage of the distracted state of Persia, had seized upon Armenia, Georgia, Guilan, Kurdistan, and a part of Irak, and made further dispositions for advancing towards the south. The army of Mahmood numbered only at this time a few thousand Afghans; it is true, their name alone was in itself sufficient to make the conquered tremble; but the ranks of these hardy and ferocious soldiers were daily thinned, and everything indicated that they would not be able to resist the storm which was gathering against them in the north.

All these considerations, and the retirement of Mir Echreff, a chief beloved by the troops, led to much desertion amongst the Afghans; the most devoted servants and the nearest relatives of Mir Mahmood fled from the effects of his tyranny, and he soon found himself isolated in the midst of his court. In this extremity he recruited his army with Kurds, who, as well as the Afghans, were Soonees, thinking that he could rely more upon them than upon the Persians, who were of the hostile sect of Shiahs. He thus raised a new army, with which, in 1724, he took possession of several districts in Irak and Fars, though Shiraz, the capital of the latter province, did not surrender until it had stood a siege of eight months and suffered all the horrors of famine.

But the Afghan nation were not dazzled by these successes. Mahmood never regained their confidence, and such was the impression his actions had produced that the reinforcements he had haughtily demanded from Kandahar arrived but tardily, and amounted only to the tenth part of what he anticipated, for no one would serve a prince who had delivered them from the Persian yoke only to impose a more cruel and despotic tyranny of his own. The Serdar Mir Echreff was at the head of these troops, and they insisted that he should be confirmed in his command as the absolute condition of their services. Mir Mahmood the more readily complied with this request, because, having been abandoned by his principal officers, the co-operation of his cousin had become an absolute necessity for him, not only to direct the military operations, which, by reason of his bad state of health, he was unable to conduct, but also to retain in Persia, through his influence, many Afghans who would otherwise have left the country. On the arrival of this reinforcement Mir Mahmood marched upon Yezd, which he attempted to seize, but he was not fortunate in this enterprise. He issued orders to his troops which it was impossible to execute, and derangement of his intellectual faculties was clearly manifested upon this occasion; his eccentricities were very nearly causing a revolt in his army, which, indignant at the losses it had sustained without obtaining any corresponding success, obliged him to raise the siege and return to Ispahan. This check soured and excited him, and his irascible nature was still more aggravated by the unreasonable demands of his officers, who were supported by the troops. Alarmed also at the progress of Thamasp Mirza, the Russians, and the Turks, and a prey to remorse, his mind was filled with visions of his victims ready to torment him, so that he abandoned himself to superstitious devotion in the most exaggerated form; he shut himself up in a subterraneous cell, observing the strictest fast, and when, at the end of two months, he left this retreat, he was in such a state that he could scarcely be recognised. Livid, emaciated, and his features contracted, he seemed to dread the light of day, and reappeared more fearful and more cruel than ever; haunted by the darkest suspicions, gloomy and taciturn, he shuddered at the approach of his best friends, dreading to find in every one an assassin. During one of the paroxysms of his disease he was informed that the sons of the Shah Sultan Hoosein had made an attempt to escape, when, trembling with rage at this intelligence, he ordered them all to be brought into his presence, and, drawing his poignard, put thirty-one of them to death with his own hand. Their unfortunate father, hearing their cries, broke through the guards, and, rushing to the scene of carnage, endeavoured to protect them at the risk of his own life; a blow from Mahmood's dagger wounded him in the arm, and the sight of his blood alone recalled the Mir to himself, and induced him to spare two of the princes, still very young, the only ones that escaped from this fearful massacre. His insania was at length complete: to this were added an attack of paralysis, a painful disease of the intestines, and want of sleep, and in this condition he sometimes tore pieces of flesh from his body, and devoured them. His mother, as some say, in despair at his sufferings—or Mir Echreff, as others affirm, to obtain the power to which he was called by the general wish of the Afghans—ordered him to be smothered under the cushions of his own divan; his remains were thrown to the jackals. But whoever gave the order for the death of Mahmood, it is certain that this prince was still alive when the Afghans acknowledged Mir Echreff as their sovereign.

The antecedents of this young soldier and his brilliant qualities, in no way inferior to those of his predecessor during the first years of his reign, raised great hopes of him in the minds of his subjects. Accordingly, he applied himself earnestly to the task of mitigating the misery inflicted by his relative, and expressed publicly the horror he felt at the merciless deeds which had rendered the very name of Afghan odious; he paid the greatest honours to the remains of the sons of the Shah Sultan Hoosein by magnificent funeral rites, at the close of which he declared to the assembled Afghan and Persian nobles that he devoted the memory of Mahmood to the execration of future ages. In short, he did everything in his power to attach the Persians to his interests, and bestowed favours upon them, even to the detriment of the Afghans. The latter were not long in perceiving that they had chosen a master who was quite determined to take every advantage of the power they had just placed in his hands, for his first act was to put the Serdar Aman Ullah Khan to death. This brave but ambitious general of Mir Mahmood, as well as several other chiefs, had done everything to prevent his election, and he was also suspected of holding a secret correspondence with Shah Thamasp. No real crime could be imputed to them, but Mir Echreff thought their deaths necessary to his security. He confiscated to his own profit the wealth which they had accumulated during the conquest of Persia, and this enabled him to meet the immediate necessities consequent upon his succession and the embarrassments that met him on all sides.

Echreff entertained no delusions on the difficulty of his position. It was evident that he must put an end to the divisions amongst his own people, and obtain the confidence of the Persians; he had also to repel the invasion of the Russians, who had seized upon the Guilan; that of the Turks, already masters of Georgia, the Azerbaidjan, Kurdistan, and part of Irak; and finally to subdue the party of Thamasp Mirza, which had been organised in the south of the Azerbaidjan and the Mazanderan. This prince was the only one of the three surviving sons of the Shah Hoosein, who was then in possession of his liberty: by the abdication of his father he considered himself King of Persia, and had, as Shah, treated with the Russian and Turkish governments. To the first he had promised the cession of the provinces bordering on the Caspian; and to the second, the countries they had already seized, on condition that they assisted him in regaining the throne of his fathers. Agreeably to the terms of this treaty, which accorded so well with the views of territorial aggrandizement projected by the remarkable sovereign who then reigned in Russia, the army of Peter the Great disembarked in the Guilan, and there established itself; and as everything denoted that the Russian generals did not intend to leave the positions they had taken up, Echreff turned his first efforts against the Turks. In his endeavours to establish peace he at first tried what he could effect by negotiation, offering to make great sacrifices to obtain that result. But the Sultan, Ahmed Khan, seeing the state of anarchy that reigned in Persia, determined to retain the provinces already mentioned; the negotiations, therefore, were broken off, and he ordered Ahmed Pasha, the Walee of Bagdad, and Hoosein Pasha, the Walee of Mosul, with the troops under their command, to converge first on Kermanshah, and afterwards to concentrate them on Hamadan. These two towns were already occupied by detachments of the Turkish army under the orders of Abdul Rahman Pasha. The Walee of Bagdad, who had the command in chief, was instructed to send a flag of truce to Mir Echreff directly his army had assembled at Hamadan, and imperatively demand that the Shah Hoosein and his sons, at this time imprisoned in the fort of Teberruk, at Ispahan, should be set at liberty. He was also to insist upon the immediate evacuation of the Persian territory by the Afghans, as well as the restitution of all the treasure they had laid their hands on during their occupation. The rejection of any one of these conditions was to be followed by a declaration of war.* And in this manner the matter terminated, for the Turkish envoy was unable to come to any understanding with Mir Echreff. Ahmed Pasha took the field with an army of 60,000 men and 70 pieces of artillery, and marched direct upon Ispahan. Echreff met him about four days' march from the capital, his army not being half as numerous as that of the Turks, and very ill provided with artillery. A battle was fought at Kiemereh, a town situated between Ispahan and Boroodjird, and the victory was for a long time undecided, but at length the Turks were routed, leaving 12,000 men upon the field, and 50 pieces of cannon; the baggage also fell into the hands of the Afghans. Echreff showed himself as great after the victory as he had been reasonable and moderate during the negotiations, and, retaining only the arms, returned all the booty his soldiers had made to the Turks. To Ahmed Pasha he wrote that he could not consider as legitimate spoils of war the plunder he had taken from misguided Mussulmans; that his greatest desire was to live in peace with his brethren; that he trusted the Sultan would not again disturb him in the possession of a throne which he had taken from heretics, and to which he had an incontestable right by every law, human and divine. This generous conduct, and the cession to the Turks of the districts of Tauris, Zinguian, Sultanieh, Tefrich, Ferahane, Kezaz, Kurdistan, Looristan, and Koozistan, as well as admitting the religious supremacy of the Sultan, which Mir Echreff engaged to acknowledge in future, induced the Turks to make peace. This he ardently desired, for he had to contend with immeasurable difficulties; and in these negotiations with the Turks, as well as his conduct in the field, Echreff displayed the talents of a consummate diplomatist and a first-rate general. He obtained from Turkey the formal recognition of his right to the throne of Persia: and the year following, the Sultan Ahmed Khan sent Reshid Pasha to congratulate the Afghan chief on his accession to the throne. Echreff afterwards sent Mohamed Khan, a

* Abdullah Khan, the historian of Herat, remarks in his manuscript, that Echreff was so thoroughly indignant at the insolence of this message, that immediately after the receipt of it he ordered the Shah Hoosein and his sons to be beheaded in the presence of the Turkish envoy; but as Abdullah Khan is the only eastern authority which records the death of the Shah Sultan Hoosein as having taken place at this epoch, I thought it right to mention the circumstance in a note, adopting myself the opinion more generally accredited.—*Ferrier*.

Beloochee, to acknowledge the compliment, and he was received at Constantinople with great honours.

In consequence of the treaty thus concluded between Echreff and the Sultan, the Prince Thamasp was left to his own resources; and when the Turks entered the Azerbaidjan he evacuated that province, followed by a few devoted adherents. Subsequently to this he again took possession of Kasbeen and Teheran, and in these cities he resided alternately; but no sooner had Echreff got rid of the Turks than he marched against and completely defeated the Prince, forcing him to retire into the Mazanderan. Nevertheless the troops of Thamasp refused to surrender Kasbeen and Teheran to the victor, who, called to Ispahan by the urgency of his affairs, left an army to prosecute the sieges under the command of the Serdar Seidel Khan Nassaree, who soon reduced these cities.

While Echreff was courageously fighting in Persia to establish his power, he lost his hold upon Kandahar, which remained definitively in the hands of Mir Hoosein, a brother of Mir Mahmood, whom he had endeavoured to overthrow by an intrigue. In the Seistan, the governor Malek Mahmood, a descendant of the ancient Persian sovereigns, had taken the title of king, and subsequently seized upon the greater part of Khorassan. Herat had acknowledged his authority for many years past, so that the Afghans were driven out in this direction. These changes were the cause of further complications amongst the chiefs, between whom there was already anything but a good understanding.

It was, therefore, evident to Echreff that there was no hope of his being assisted by his own nation, and that for the future he could reckon only upon those who had, up to this time, followed his fortunes. He now saw, without much regret, the Russians masters of the Guilan; and when he was convinced that the possession of that province would satisfy their ambition, and that they had no intention of disturbing him in Irak, he determined to act with the utmost energy in the East, where his affairs were much embarrassed; but before leaving Ispahan he ordered the quarter in which the Afghans resided to be enclosed with high and thick walls, within which they would be secure against all the vicissitudes of war. Shah Thamasp, on the other hand, made every effort to recover the throne of the Seffavyes, and had the good fortune to secure the services of one of those extraordinary men that Nature produces only at long intervals. Nadir, subsequently Nadir Shah, a powerful robber-chieftain, offered his services to the son of the Shah Sultan Hoosein, who accepted them with eagerness. The military reputation of Nadir, to which was now added the authority derived from his position as commander-in-chief of the troops of the legitimate king, attracted numerous partisans to his camp, and he soon saw himself at the head of a large and well-disciplined army inspired by his own peculiar and energetic impulses.

During the years 1726 and 1727 Nadir employed himself in reconquering that part of Khorassan which Malek Mahmood, the Prince of Seistan, had seized, and also in taking Herat; after which he marched towards Mazanderan, that he might, in concert with his sovereign, adopt some plan for driving the Afghans from the kingdom. The capture of the city of Nishapoor, and the slaughter of 3000 Afghans, was the prelude to this enterprise. After this he dislodged successively all the Afghan garrisons in Khorassan, and drove them from post to post, until they had entirely evacuated this province, which soon acknowledged, and to the fullest extent, the authority of the Shah Thamasp.

While Nadir was thus occupied, Mir Echreff seized upon Yezd, which had resisted the arms of Mir Mahmood: but the conquest was dearly bought, for he there lost his tried and veteran soldiers, the élite of his army. This was indeed a great misfortune, and, aggravated by the fact that, Mir Hoosein having declared himself independent in Kandahar, he was unable to fill up the casualties in his army with Afghans, who were no longer anxious to take service under him. Mir Echreff was, therefore, constrained to recruit his army with Persians, and march without further delay against Nadir, whose victorious battalions were daily augmented by men eager to deliver their country, and take a deep revenge for the odious tyranny under which they had groaned for six years. Mir Echreff had never been in such a critical position, and the measures of precaution which he took to protect his rear plainly showed the disquietude he felt; his soldiers participated in this feeling, they had lost all confidence in themselves, and it was under such apprehensions that they moved forward to meet the enemy.

Shah Thamasp, impatient to recover his capital, was desirous that Nadir should march in all haste on Ispahan; but the prudent general respectfully but firmly declined to comply with his wishes, convinced that such a movement would be inopportune. Nadir felt confident that, if he kept his troops fresh, it would be easy for him to beat the Afghans, if they attacked him after a long forced march, exhausted by privations and fatigue. In acting thus he also had the advantage of choosing the ground on which he intended to give battle without removing from Mazanderan. The population of this province was entirely devoted to Shah Thamasp, and he could therefore, in case of a reverse, effect his retreat in all security across the mountains, which offered at every step admirable positions for defence.

The army of Echreff numbered 30,000 men, scarcely the half of which, at the utmost, were Afghans, and on coming up with the forces of the enemy he found them entrenched in a well-chosen position on some small hills selected by Nadir. The Afghans, never having seen the Persians hold their ground, were anxious to attack at once; but Echreff, who had a higher opinion of his adversaries, repressed, perhaps inopportunely, this impulse, which might have given him the victory, and remained several days in a state of inaction. It was only when it became impossible for him to obtain supplies that he decided upon giving his adversary battle, and on the 23rd of Rebý-i-ul akher, 6th of November, 1728, he took up a position in front of his army échelloned from Moomineabad to Boordj-meyoos, or Meimandoos. The latter place is situated about seven miles east of the town of Damghan, having the village of Naimabad on the west, and at the same distance from the village of Deh Mollah. The attack commenced along the whole line; but the Persians received it with great steadiness, and, perfectly cool, waited till the enemy had advanced within half musket-shot before they poured in their fire. The Afghans fought with the courage and savage energy that was natural to them and the confidence of men accustomed to conquer; but they were unable to make any impression upon their adversaries. Echreff, surprised at a resistance to which his troops were not accustomed, attempted to destroy Nadir's order of battle by turning his left flank; but the Persian commander, perceiving his intention, formed his infantry into squares, and routed in detail with his cavalry Echreff's detachments, after which, leading the mass of his forces against the Afghan reserves, he put them to flight.*

* Abdullah Khan states there were ten French officers, for the most part belonging to the artillery, serving in the Persian army, and that his father, who was placed by Nadir under their special orders, had frequently told him that this sovereign held them in great consideration, gave them the absolute authority over his troops, and that he owed the greater portion of his success to the faithful support which they gave him.—*Ferrier*.

The Mir's troops performed, indeed, prodigies of valour; but they were unable to rally, and left 12,000 of their comrades on the field of battle. The Persians, who lost only 3000 men, followed the retreating enemy and came up with them at the defile of Khar, called also by the Persians Tingui-serdaree.* Here the Afghans rallied and renewed the fight; but they were again defeated, and abandoned all their baggage to the victors—Nadir himself was wounded in this second engagement. The distance from the defile of Khar to Teheran is forty-five miles, and the remnants of the Afghan army reached that city in one day; they subsequently pressed on to Ipsahan with all speed, spreading alarm, desolation, and death on their route. On their arrival there they hastened, with their families and their treasure, into the fortress which Echreff had constructed in the centre of the city; but after having confided its defence to a garrison of picked men, the Afghan commander again took the field with his remaining troops, consisting of Afghans, Tartars, Kurds, and Ghebers, in all 20,000 men, marched to the north of Ispahan, and at a spot twenty-four miles from thence took up a position on a table-land in advance, and to the north-east of the village of Moortchekhor. There he waited for the Persians, over whom he still hoped to prove his superiority in arms. The Afghans were posted between the village and a trench which they had thrown up in front of their camp in the form of a demi-lune, their right resting on a watercourse and their left on a caravanserai difficult to take. Seeing them in so good a position, Nadir did not think it advisable to attack immediately: he wished to refresh his troops, and for this purpose pitched his camp about two miles west of the high road and round the village of Bagh-mirane. The reconnaissances which he ordered to be made on the Afghan camp having satisfied him that it could not be carried in front, he determined to turn the position, and taking advantage of a dark night, which occurred three days after his arrival, he found himself at the near approach of day in the rear of the Afghans, separated from them only by the village. Fortune, which favoured him at all points, again declared for him, for a violent wind arose and drove clouds of dust in the faces of

* This spot is cited by several travellers, and with reason, as being the Caspian Pyles.—*Ferrier.*

the Afghans, and, favoured by this circumstance, Nadir fell upon them with the same intrepidity and vigour which he had already displayed. The enemy, in despair, maintained an obstinate resistance; but they had to do with men flushed with recent victories, which gave them the solidity of old soldiers. If the Afghans fought to preserve their conquest and their lives, the Persians were animated by the remembrance of the injuries they had suffered, and were burning to avenge. The village was at length carried, and afterwards the entrenchments, in defending which 4000 Afghans found a soldier's death. The survivors retreated in disorder to Ispahan, where each of them collected in the course of the night his most valuable effects, and at daybreak, accompanied by their wives and children, mounted on mules and camels, fled southward. Mir Echreff, furious at his reverses, put the Shah Sultan Hoosein and his two sons to death, and in a gloomy and savage mood was the last Afghan that left the walls of Ispahan. He carried with him all his treasures and jewels, and, with 12,000 horsemen still under his command, directed his course on Shiraz, from which city he hoped again to reassume the offensive against the Persians; but Nadir did not allow Echreff time to reorganise his army, and after a few days' repose he was once more on foot, intending, if possible, to force him to evacuate the province of Fars. The Afghans advanced to meet the enemy as far as Peulee Khan, a bridge over the Bendemir, ten miles south of Persepolis, and disputed with tenacity and fury the passage of that river; but they were again defeated and retired to Shiraz in the greatest confusion. Nadir doggedly pursued them step by step, invested the city, and informed the beleaguered host that, if Echreff was not delivered up to him within forty-eight hours, he would put every soldier to death, and with torture. The Afghans agreed to his conditions, on ascertaining which the Mir prepared for flight, and, accompanied by two hundred brave men who remained faithful to his fallen fortunes, cut his way sword in hand through the investing army, taking in hot haste the road to Afghanistan—a portion of his army fell under the swords of the Persians, who gave their adversaries no quarter, and the remainder dispersed. As to Echreff, he was so rapidly pursued that he was obliged to abandon his baggage and treasure to avoid being made prisoner: his followers, seeing that they could no longer be of the least service, left him. When he reached the Seistan, he had only two servants with him, and they, as well as the Mir, fell by the hand of Abdullah Khan, a Belooch chief, who sent his head and two large brilliants which were found on him to the Shah Thamasp.*

Thus terminated the dominion of the Afghans in Persia. If any individual was capable of maintaining it for a longer period, it was certainly Mir Echreff, who to extraordinary courage united great talents of every kind; but the elements on which his power rested were too unstable for it to be possible that he could eventually come forth victorious from the conflict which arose between himself and the robber chieftain. This extraordinary invasion of Persia ended in the extermination of all those who had taken part in it—a just retribution for the crimes and atrocities with which they had sullied their cause. During the seven years that the Afghans held Persia, that empire lost more than a third of its population; the soil remained without cultivation, the canals and watercourses for irrigation were dried up, and the greater portion of the public buildings completely destroyed. The invaders had to contend against a people enervated, effeminate, and devoid of every sentiment of honour and national feeling; they triumphed, therefore, by an obstinate determination to succeed, and, in spite of their inferiority in numbers, they did so. Such examples are, it is true, rare in history; but the Afghans were better qualified to fight than to govern. To appropriate, wherever they went, and without any reason or pretext whatsoever, money or money's worth, was their practice; revolts and disturbances naturally ensued, and necessitated the employment of a large army. They were in the end weakened by twenty combats, and found it impossible to recruit in Afghanistan, except in the small and scarcely organised state of Kandahar, which ceased to provide them with further reinforcements; they were, therefore, obliged to admit foreign soldiers within their ranks, whose fidelity was at least doubtful, and who rarely acted with vigour; but they maintained themselves seven years in Persia, much more by the terror which their first victories and their cruelty inspired, than by the material means at their disposal. If Echreff vanquished the Turks, it was because he had the support of the

* Several Eastern authors contradict this account, and assert that Echreff died of disease.—*Ferrier.*

Persians, who detested them much more than they did the Afghans, and served voluntarily against them; but directly Nadir appeared, this unreal and unstable dominion was dissolved and overthrown in four successive battles. Shunned and dreaded everywhere for their turbulence and barbarity, they were repulsed on all sides, and found, with great difficulty, an asylum or even a shelter in those desert wastes; the greater number of them were tracked like wild beasts, and killed like them, or perished from misery and hunger, and it is doubtful whether more than a few hundred Afghans ever returned to their own country.

CHAPTER VI.

Nadir takes Herat and Furrah — Marches upon Kandahar in 1737 — Admirable defence by the Ghildjzyes — Mir Hoosein capitulates — Nadir reduces Afghanistan — His policy in that country — Insurrection of the Afghans after the death of Nadir Shah — Expulsion of the Persians — Ahmed Khan Suddozye elected King — Hadji Djemal Khan — Revolt of the Serdars — Nasser Khan surrenders Kabul and Peshawur — Ahmed Shah marches against Lahore — Hayat Ullah Khan obtains the assistance of the Mogul Emperor — Admirable tactics of Ahmed Shah — Passage of the Tchenab — Ahmed Shah takes Lahore — Makes a treaty with the Mogul Emperor — Revolt at Kandahar — Execution of the conspirators — Ahmed Shah advances into Khorassan — Siege of Herat — Defence of the citadel by Emir Khan — Timoor Mirza marches against Meshed — Defeat of the Khorassian chiefs in that city — Meshed relieved by Shah Rokh — Defeat of Mir Alem — Ahmed Shah retires from Meshed — Besieges Nishapoor — Is obliged to retreat — Disasters of the Afghan army — Passage of the Heri-rood — The remainder of the army arrive at Herat — Ahmed Shah reaches Kandahar.

It not having been our intention to write a history of Persia, we shall not follow Nadir Shah in his wars with the Turks and other nationalities under the Persian rule, but proceed at once to speak of his campaigns in Afghanistan.

After the victory at Shiraz Nadir reconquered in succession all the Persian provinces which had become detached from the empire. In the year 1730 he seized upon Herat, that city having revolted from his authority; he also took Furrah, a strong and very important fortress, situated about one hundred and forty miles south of the first-mentioned place; but he did not extend his conquests on that side, and it was only after having obtained several fresh victories over the Turks, and imprisoned Thamasp, that he placed the crown of the Seffavyes on his brow. In 1737 he marched on Kandahar at the head of 100,000 men without meeting any resistance on his road, for the inhabitants submitted to his authority or fled at his approach. Nevertheless the population of the city, which had been considerably augmented by the influx of persons whom his victorious march had driven into it, prepared to resist the Persian invader.

Mir Hoosein Khan, who was still in command there, reminded the Ghildjzyes of the struggle they had made for their independence, their victories over the Persians, and their conquest of that country; and, being eloquent as well as brave, he easily succeeded in exciting them to make a spirited defence. The position of Kandahar was at this time very strong, the city being situated at the foot of a rocky mountain which flanked it on the north and east: innumerable stone towers, connected by curtains, surrounded it, and followed the sinuosities of the mountain, the summit of which was occupied by a fort, believed to be impregnable, and commanding the citadel, placed half way between it and the city. Nadir Shah, against whom no resistance had as yet been offered, was obliged to halt before these obstacles, to which art had also added all that could render the defence effectual. Despairing of being able to take the city by assault, he established a strict blockade, hoping to reduce the garrison by famine; but it was in vain that he enclosed Kandahar within a double wall, between which his soldiers were sheltered from attacks both from within and without; a year and a half elapsed without his having obtained the least advantage against the city—however, he was more successful towards the country, for his detachments brought the whole of the environs under submission. When, therefore, he was master of the province, he resolved to carry the place, and ordered a general assault. The preparations for this had been most formidable, the bravery and devotion of the troops admirable, but, after a furious and desperate conflict of two days' duration, Kandahar was not only not taken, but not one of the advanced works was carried, though several attacks against them had been made. A feeling of discouragement began to pervade the Persian army, when a newly-raised corps, of the tribe of the Bakhtyarees, which had already distinguished itself on several occasions by its firm and courageous bearing, obtained an advantage which raised the hopes of the rest of the troops, and induced them to redouble their efforts. Though received with a storm of bullets, this gallant band had succeeded, by climbing the almost perpendicular rocks and clinging to their projections, in reaching a little plateau, from whence they were enabled to carry several towers on the north side of the mountain. Into these they managed, simply with ropes and their own strong arms, to raise some pieces of artillery, which opening their fire upon all the other towers, a breach was made, and in six hours the Bakhtyarees were in possession of them; the town and citadel were therefore obliged to surrender at discretion. Mir Hoosein Khan retreated into the fort on the summit of the mountain, where he successfully resisted every attack, and might still have made a protracted defence had it not been for the generosity of Nadir, who promised to spare his life, and give him high rank in his own army. This noble offer led to a capitulation, and Mir Hoosein afterwards became sincerely attached to the Persian invader, and one of his favourite generals.

Once master of Kandahar, the Persian monarch took measures to consolidate his power, and, with a view of preventing the inhabitants from again offering a similar resistance, which their bravery, their means of defence, and the strength of the place might tempt them to do, he dismantled the fortifications, and transferred the population to a new town which he built during the blockade at about a gunshot from the old city. But the new one was scarcely inhabited fifteen years, for immediately Ahmed Shah Suddozye came to the throne he built a third city, about one mile and a half further east, when the city of Nadir was deserted.

To the conquests of Herat and Kandahar Nadir was not long in joining that of Kabul, and thus became master of the whole of Afghanistan. By great political ability, and more especially by the generous manner in which he treated the people and their chiefs, he completely secured their good will, and raised a contingent of 16,000 horse in that country. They were recruited amongst those who could claim descent from the Abdalees and the Ghildjzyes, twelve thousand being taken from the former tribe, and four from the latter: the chiefs of these tribes, to the number of ten, namely, eight Abdalees and two Ghildjzyes, had the command of these troops, the command in chief being given to Noor Mohamed Khan Alizye, one of them. This body of men accompanied Nadir Shah in all his expeditions, and participated powerfully in the successes and glory of that conqueror. They rendered him more especially a signal service, and certainly saved his army from complete destruction, when, on his return from India, he was engaged with the enemy in the mountains beyond Peshawur, and harassed on all sides by the Khyberrees. The Persian conqueror was in a most critical position on that occasion, and extricated himself only by paying a large sum of money by way of toll to the mountaineers who closed the defiles against him. In short, this contingent of the Abdalees and Ghildjzyes showed so much devotion to Nadir, and rendered him such important services, that he at length preferred them to his own troops, which led to great jealousies on the part of the Persians; and when Nadir was assassinated in 1747, they gave vent to their resentment, and attacked this favoured corps with fury. Being very inferior in numbers, the Afghans were obliged to consult their own safety by a prompt retreat, and returned to their country under their own commander Noor Mohamed Khan, but they immediately took measures to deliver themselves from the Persian yoke, by no means a difficult task, for, after Nadir's death, anarchy reigned in every part of the empire.

The serdars who had served in the Persian army were, as we have already remarked, ten in number. Ahmed Khan Suddozye, descended in a direct line from Sudoo, who had been ambassador to Shah Abbas the Great, was the most noble amongst them; and Hadji Djemal Khan Mohamedzye, lineally descended from Mohamed, a companion of Sudoo in that embassy, was the most influential. Experience had clearly demonstrated to all these chiefs that the divisions amongst themselves, much more than the power of their enemies, had, up to that period, brought them under the subjection of the various invaders of their country; and they swore therefore to remain strictly united, and adjourned for one month the completion of the code of laws which they had determined to give to their nation.

After the return of the Afghan contingent to Kandahar, they remained some days in the enjoyment of those social and family ties to which they had been for so long a time strangers, and their turbulent spirits took some repose; but whether from a discontented feeling towards their chief, or intrigues which led them to rebel against him, they withdrew the chief command from Noor Mohamed Khan, giving as a reason that his origin was not sufficiently noble. After the fall of this personage the principal serdars of the Abdalee and Ghildjzye tribes assembled in the tomb of Sheik Seurk, situated in the village of Nadir-abad, now Kichk-nookhood, thirty-five miles from Kandahar, to decide upon the best method of organising a regular government in Afghanistan. At this meeting it was agreed that a fusion of their nation with the Persians was henceforward impossible—that they ought to elect a chief taken from amongst themselves, who should be obeyed in all things, and assisted in giving that unity of purpose to all military operations, and the civil administration, without which there was no chance for them to preserve their independence. This proposition was not agreed to without delay, and more especially without great difficulty; each tribe was anxious to advance the claims of its own candidate for the throne, and the good understanding between the chiefs who represented the tribes was far from being impressed with sentiments of a conciliatory or unselfish character. Ahmed Khan Suddozye, whose family lived at Herat, where he enjoyed great consideration, was present at eight of these tumultuous assemblies, and had listened attentively to all that had been said without offering one word on the important questions which had been discussed. The dervish who had the care of the tomb of Sheik Seurk, and whose opinion was always received with respect, had remarked the reserved manner of Ahmed Khan, and the holy man, wearied with the interminable discussions and repetitions which had taken place during several days at these meetings, advised their breaking up the conference at once. "Why all this verbose talk?" said he to the serdars; "God has created Ahmed Khan a much greater man than any of you; he is of the most noble of all the Afghan families. Maintain, therefore, God's work, for his wrath will weigh heavily upon you if you destroy it." After having pronounced these words in a most energetic manner, he took a handful of barley from an adjoining field, and, having formed it into a wreath, placed it on the head of Ahmed Khan, adding, "and may this serve as your diadem." Hadji Djemal Khan, the most powerful of the serdars present at this meeting, and who appeared to have the greatest number of votes, immediately withdrew his pretensions in favour of Ahmed Khan, and supported his election with all the weight of his persuasive eloquence—conduct that obtained for him the general respect of the Afghans. The serdars, seeing that he who would certainly have been chosen their sovereign was so disinterested, followed the example thus given them; but they separated well convinced that Ahmed Khan, who had been the most silent of them all, had also been the most clever in not allowing his claim to be advanced till the last moment, when the diversity of opinions had wearied the meeting, and, above all, in having these qualifications brought forward by a third person, which made him appear modest and disinterested, when they well knew he was neither the one nor the other.

Ahmed Khan, who took the title of Shah, was crowned in the mosque at Kandahar towards the close of the year 1747, when there were great rejoicings, which were prolonged during several weeks. The ceremony of his coronation was of the most simple kind: the Mollah of the highest rank poured a measure of wheat on the head of the new monarch, announcing to the assembled Afghans that he was the chosen of God and the nation. This emblematical investiture of the regal power is followed at the present day amongst the Afghan tribes each time that they elect a chief; the signification which is attached to this ceremonial is, that abundance and prosperity will result from the acts of him whom they make the depository of power.

The Afghans were still in the midst of their coronation festivals when there arrived at Kandahar Eaghee Khan Chirazee, chief of the customs to Nadir Shah in Scinde and the Punjab, having in his custody two *kooroors*, 1,360,000*l.*, in money, diamonds, and shawls. This Ahmed Shah seized and immediately distributed amongst the officers and men of his army and the employés of the government; and this great liberality on his part did more for his future career than all his private virtues and his noble origin. Several tribes who had not as yet positively recognised his election, but the chiefs of which were on this occasion the recipients of his generosity, now attached themselves to his person, and he profited by this feeling of unanimity to consolidate his power, and during the first years of his reign to raise a large army, with which he subsequently marched on Kabul with a view to its capture. This was not so easy as an offensive operation, for Nadir Shah had settled twelve thousand Persian families in the Bala Hissar, the citadel of that capital; but Ahmed Shah having, through his partizans, entered into a secret understanding with them, they made common cause with the Afghans on their arrival, under a promise that their chiefs should participate in the official appointments and advantages in the gift of the sovereign, and be treated in all things on a footing of equality.*

In spite of this defection, Nasser Khan, the governor of Kabul, obstinately refused to recognise the authority of Ahmed Shah, and did everything in his power to recruit the garrison amongst the

* The Persians inhabiting Kabul are known by the name of Kuzzilbashes, because they form part of one or more of the seven Turkish tribes that embraced the party of the Shah Ismail, the founder of the tribe of the Seffavyes. This sovereign, to distinguish them from the others, gave them a kind of red cap; hence their name of "Red head," Kezzel bash. These seven tribes were Oustadjaloo, Chamloo, Nikaloo, Baharloo, Zoolkadder, Kadjar, and Afchar.—*Ferrier.*

Hazarahs and Usbeks, but all in vain; and despairing at length of being able to make head against the Afghans, he fled, after a feeble conflict, to Peshawur. Ahmed Shah then took possession of Kabul without meeting with the slightest opposition; appointed as governor of the province a clever man devoted to his person and interests; and left the city in pursuit of Nasser Khan, who, abandoned by the greater part of his followers and seeing clearly that a longer resistance could only end fatally for himself, surrendered Peshawur to the Afghans and submitted to their king.

Ahmed Shah was aware that war was a necessity to the people over whom he reigned; their turbulent nature, and the rivalry which existed between the various tribes, would certainly have led to grave disorders against the prosperity of the state and been dangerous to his rising power, if they had remained inactive. Besides, the kingdom of the Afghans was to be constituted, the limits and boundary of which had not up to this time been defined by any one. Ahmed Shah resolved to extend these limits wherever an Afghan tribe was to be found, and, in order to carry his views into effect, he remained no longer at Peshawur than was necessary to subdue and organize the tribes which inhabited the mountainous districts of that province; and when he was convinced that there was nothing more to apprehend from their opposition, he crossed the Indus and marched against Lahore.

Hayat Ullah Khan, son of Zekeria Khan, honoured by Nadir Shah with the surname of Shah Nawaz Khan, who had succeeded his father in the government of this city, hearing the intentions of Ahmed Shah, assembled an army and took up a position at a little distance north of Lahore. He also wrote a letter to the Great Mogul at Delhi, Ahmed Shah Gourkanee,* informing him of the advance of Ahmed Shah Suddozye; the capture he had recently made of Kabul and Peshawur; of his projects on Lahore, and those which he presumed he might have on India; and for these reasons claimed his assistance. The Mogul Emperor conceded all that he desired, and placed himself at the head of the troops destined to co-operate with Hayat Ullah. Immediately the Lahore chieftain felt certain of this he did not wait for their arrival, for, thinking that Ahmed Shah Suddozye, when he saw him so well supported, would

* Gourkanee is the name of the tribe to which Tamerlane belonged, also Mirza Baboor and his descendants.—*Ferrier.*

not dare to tempt fortune against him, he made a bold demonstration in the hope of arresting his march, and moved his camp to the left bank of the Tchenab. The Afghans, however, neither halted nor delayed their onward movement as he had expected, and soon arrived in his front; but as the river was considerably swollen, the two armies were obliged to wait till it had fallen before they could attack. The impatience of the Afghan monarch in particular was great, for he was anxious to engage his adversary before the Moguls, of whose expected arrival he was aware, had joined, but the want of pontoons obliged him to remain passive during several days. Directly his cavalry could attempt the passage of the river with any security he put the whole of that arm in motion at midnight and in profound silence, and crossed at a spot a few parasangs above the enemy's encampment. Ahmed Shah had conceived the idea of marching straight to Lahore, carrying the place by a coup-de-main, and baffling the vigilance of his opponent by leaving his infantry behind him on the right bank and in sight of the enemy. His anticipations were well founded, for the army of Shah Nawaz Khan, thinking they had still before them the whole of the Afghan forces, slept in fancied security. On the following day, however, the Governor of the Punjab learnt that Ahmed Shah was marching on the capital with his cavalry. Leaving therefore his infantry face to face with that of his opponent, he hastened in pursuit of their horse with his own, and came up with them on the following day half-way between the Tchenab and the city; but having reconnoitred and found the enemy much superior in numbers, he did not dare to attack, and filed along his flank, protected by a chain of hills, south of which he expected to fall in with Gourkanee, who was marching to his assistance.

The Afghan King saw clearly the movement of his adversary and divined his object, and, a fresh project having suddenly suggested itself to his mind, he permitted Shah Nawaz to make this retrograde movement without offering any opposition to it; but when he supposed him to be at a good distance Ahmed returned by the road by which he had advanced, and fell upon the Sikh infantry on the left of the Tchenab, routed them completely, captured their artillery and a considerable booty. He then passed his own infantry over to the right bank of the river, and moved rapidly on Lahore, which he seized without difficulty.

Shah Nawaz Khan, ashamed of a flight which must be explained to his ally by some reason or another, attempted to justify it by exalting to the highest degree the numbers, courage, and cleverness of the Afghans; this imprudent speech brought discouragement into the Mogul ranks, and their inclinations, which up to that period had been unanimous in favour of fighting, were transformed into an ardent desire for peace.

After having fortified Lahore and confided it to the care of a picked garrison, Ahmed Shah Suddozye marched to meet Ahmed Shah Gourkanee, but he had scarcely traversed half the distance which separated him from the Mogul Emperor, when he was met by his envoy, who was the bearer of pacific proposals from his master. After long hesitation Ahmed Shah Suddozye decided for peace, for the chances of the war in which he was engaged were great; his power was as yet in the bud; he was also not without uneasiness as to his rear, and even regarding the state of his own country; he thought therefore that it would be imprudent on his part to risk his fortune on the uncertain issues of a battle, and therefore agreed that all the provinces in the Punjab which had been under the rule of Nadir Shah should remain in the hands of the Afghans, and should form the dower of a Mogul princess, who was some little time afterwards married to the prince Timoor Mirza II., son of Ahmed Shah Suddozye. All the countries situated beyond the Sutlej on the left bank of the Indus remained in the hands of the Moguls, and the rivers before mentioned were to form the line of demarcation between the two empires. A treaty based upon this convention was signed by the two parties in 1750; and the Suddozye prince, after having nominated governors in his new conquests, returned to Kandahar, where several Afghan serdars, jealous of the power of their sovereign and of the glory which he had recently acquired, secretly endeavoured to excite the masses against him. No sooner, therefore, had he arrived in his capital than they resolved to assassinate him, but the king, informed of this conspiracy a few moments only before the time at which they had fixed to carry it out, frustrated it entirely by his firmness and presence of mind. The leader in this plot was the same Noor Mohamed Khan, Alizye, who was removed from the command of the army when the Afghans returned from Persia, and upon whom Ahmed Shah had conferred the title of Mir or Prince of the Afghans; his accomplices were Meuheubet Khan, Kedoo Khan, and several other Afghans of less note, who with him perished by the hands of the executioner, as well as ten men from each of the tribes most deeply compromised. These executions were the first which had taken place by order of Ahmed Shah, and many of the chiefs, being apprehensive that he might on some other occasion adopt the same severe measures against themselves, disputed his right to inflict the punishment of death. After the executions were over they agitated the question whether or not the *lex talionis* should be applied to the Shah and his family; they also wished to limit his power, or rather to subject it to their approbation; but Ahmed Shah suppressed with energy this feeling on the part of the chiefs, and his determination and justice soon produced tranquillity in the countries subject to his dominion.

Reassured by this favourable result, he meditated the conquest of Khorassan, a project which he had conceived immediately he ascended the throne. At that period Shah Rokh, grandson of Nadir Shah, reigned in this province, where he had with difficulty established himself after great opposition on the part of the chiefs. His principal antagonist was Moomeen Khan, governor of Tchinaran, who had even succeeded in taking possession of Meshed, and induced the army to proclaim him Shah of Persia; but after having exercised the sovereign power for a few days only, he gave umbrage to the troops, who mutinied and put him to death. This event enabled Shah Rokh to reassume his rights; his satisfaction, however, was not without alloy, for several other chiefs who had the same object in view as Moomeen Khan spread anarchy and confusion in all parts of Khorassan. Ahmed Shah thought, therefore, that this was a most propitious opportunity for his purpose; and in 1750 he marched into that province with an army of 70,000 men. Herat was then governed by the Arab Serdar Emir Khan, an old commander-in-chief of artillery under Nadir Shah, who held the city in the name of Shah Rokh Mirza; this chief, feeling that he was not strong enough to meet the Afghans in the field, placed the citadel in a good state of defence, and with a garrison of picked men retired within its walls. To the townspeople who were ready to defend the city he ordered that money, provisions, and arms should be distributed, and despatched a messenger to Shah Rokh Mirza requesting his prompt assistance.

The inhabitants of Herat now sustained a siege for fourteen months in the most heroic manner, trusting always that this assistance, twenty times demanded, and as often promised by the prince, would at length reach them; finding themselves, however, deceived in their hopes, and being reduced to the greatest distress, they surrendered at discretion and opened the gates.

Emir Khan, who, from the citadel, witnessed the fall of the city, determined to make one last effort in its defence, and descended into the suburbs with his little band; but being assailed in front by the Afghans and in the rear by some Heratees who were of their party, his soldiers were soon exterminated, and the Emir hacked to pieces on the spot. Fifty men whom he left in the citadel were the only troops that surrendered to the Afghans, and their lives were spared.

Shah Rokh Mirza had been prevented from going to the relief of Emir Khan by circumstances which he could not control, for he was hardly able to maintain his own ground in Meshed, the possession of which was disputed by a score of competitors. The general-in-chief, Yoosoof Khan, had at the outset beaten them all, but this chief, as brave as he was faithful, fell in a combat which took place between his troops and those of two princes of Khorassan. One of them, by name Mir Alem, belonged to an Arab tribe of the Seistan; the other, Djaffer Khan, was chief of the Kurdish colonies of Boodjnoord. These Khans, after the death of the brave Yoosoof Khan, seized Meshed and imprisoned Shah Rokh; but when the moment arrived for dividing the authority and the plunder they could not agree, and, assisted by their respective partisans, came to blows. In this conflict Mir Alem proved the victor, and remained sole master of the city. After having obtained this advantage he made every preparation to resist Ahmed Shah Suddozye, repaired the fortifications, provisioned the place, and after having confided its defence to the inhabitants, whom he believed he could trust, he left Meshed, determined if possible to pounce upon Herat. In this attempt he was disappointed, for, on arriving at Toorbut-Sheik-Jam, he was himself surprised by the prince Timoor Mirza, who, with the advanced guard of the Afghan army, was marching on Meshed. Recovering from the first feeling of astonishment at this untoward incident, Mir Alem attacked his adversary with the greatest intrepidity and made him give ground; but a charge of 3000 Belooch cavalry commanded by Nasser Khan, chief of Kelat in Beloochistan, carried disorder into the Emir's ranks, and his army was cut to pieces. Mir Alem immediately gave up all idea of keeping Meshed, and retired in the direction of Ghain to his tribe.

Nasser Ullah Khan, the son of Shah Rokh, who was in the field with a small party of horse when he heard this good news, entered Meshed, delivered his father, and placed him at the head of affairs. Anxious to terminate the object of his expedition, Ahmed Shah now appointed Dervish Ali Khan, Hazarah, to the government of Herat, and, rejoining his advanced-guard with the rest of his troops, a few days afterwards arrived under the walls of Meshed, which he invested on all sides, and vigorously besieged. His attacks were, however, repulsed with energy, and he suffered during several months considerable losses that were not compensated by any corresponding success. In spite of the vigilance and the discipline which Ahmed Shah maintained, a night rarely passed without his being surprised by Nadir Mirza or Nasser Ullah Khan, who, at the head of a few select horsemen, came down upon the Afghan camp when they were least expected, and did not retire until they had placed a good number of their adversaries *hors de combat*. Asiatic armies have no conception how to protect themselves from night attacks by placing main guards, pickets, or videttes; so that Ahmed Shah's forces were always surprised by these onsets, which, being cleverly conducted, annoyed them much. Mamech Khan Zaferanloo, governor of Tchinaran, who had attached himself to the fortunes of the grandson of Nadir, gave him also very useful support; he supplied the town with provisions, his cavalry made daily attacks upon the rear of the Afghans or pillaged and laid waste the environs of the city and their camp. Although the besieging army amounted to an effective force of 60,000 men, they were never able to overpower, or even seriously to check, this handful of cavalry, who dealt such heavy blows and numbered not more than a thousand men. Matters remained in this state during four months, after which Ahmed Shah, who had not expected to meet with so obstinate a resistance, finished by listening to the propositions that were made with a view to an amicable arrangement, and consented to raise the siege of Meshed on condition that his son Sindjar Mirza, who had remained a prisoner with the Persians after the death of Nadir Shah. should be restored to him. Several of Ahmed Shah's relations, whom Emir Khan had carried away from Herat where his family resided, were also to be given up, and on the receipt of a large sum of money the Afghan king agreed to retire from before the place.

These conditions having been duly fulfilled, Ahmed Shah, without troubling himself about his rear, proceeded at once to lay siege to the fortified city of Nishapoor, situated in a plain exceedingly fertile, where his army could easily find subsistence. This town was then governed by two persons of equal authority—one, Abbas Kooli Khan, of the tribe of Beyat, which numbered 10,000 families, residing around Nishapoor, and on which he relied for support; the other, Hadji Seif Eddin, a native of the city; and both determined to offer a stout resistance. Ahmed Shah was satisfied by simply investing the place, deferring the siege to a later period, when, according to a promise made him by the latter, he hoped to be able to obtain possession of the city. For himself, said this personage in his letter to the Afghan monarch, he laid down his arms the very day of Ahmed Shah's arrival; but he added that it would require some time before he could overcome the obstinacy of Abbas Kooli Khan, who had decided upon fighting. In thus acting the cunning Hadji was only desirous of gaining time, and the Afghan sovereign was his dupe, for he negotiated and temporised so long, that the winter set in before he had opened his trenches; the snow fell heavily, the army were soon in want of provisions, and cold and hunger cruelly decimated the troops. At length the severity of the season was such that the beasts of burden perished, and the Afghans were compelled to abandon their tents, baggage, ammunition, and artillery. After having destroyed the former and spiked the guns, they threw them into the *kariz*, or subterranean aqueducts, communicating with the surface by shafts, and then retreated, leaving a long line of corpses and baggage-animals on their track. Another division of their army, which had been detached against Ali Murad Khan, the chief of Tubbus, was also nearly exterminated; those who escaped the sword succumbed in their flight to the severity of the weather; and such was the intensity of the cold that at the halt made at Kiaffer Kaleh 18,000 of Ahmed's soldiers died in one night, and on the following day very nearly the same number perished in attempting the passage of the Heri-rood, near the town of Kussan. The river was frozen, but it gave way under the crowd of fugitives, who were swallowed up in the icy waters; those who had retreated by other roads were scarcely more fortunate. The Serdar Djummeh Khan, who held a command in this expedition, left a short sketch of it, and one of the incidents that he relates is worthy of mention, as it appears to us unique in history. He assures us that, in order to preserve himself from the excessive cold, and therefore from death, which was the certain consequence, only one way suggested itself, which he adopted; this was, to disembowel some of his camels, in the inside of which, enveloped in a blanket, he each night took up his quarters, and in this way he passed from one to another as they got cold, killing seventeen between sunset and sunrise. The disasters of this retreat continued until the wretched remnants of the Afghan force reached Herat, at which time all that remained of Ahmed Shah's brilliant array of troops were a few miserable beings more resembling skeletons than soldiers. A few days after his arrival in the city, Ahmed Shah perceived that the governor, Dervish Ali Khan, profiting by his distressed position, was intriguing to seize his person and raise himself to power upon his master's ruin; but Ahmed, anticipating his intention, ordered him to be arrested and thrown into prison, appointing his son Timoor Mirza governor in his stead; he then left for Kandahar, with a view of recruiting his army.

CHAPTER VII.

Second siege of Nishapoor by the Afghans — Clemency of the victor — He invests Meshed — Battle of Kakhak — Death of Ali Murad — Capture of Toon and Tubbus — An ambuscade — Treaty with Shah Rokh — Ahmed Shah retires to Herat — Campaign against the Usbeks—Beghee Khan seizes Balk, Khulm, &c.— Assad Khan Ghildjzye — His successes in Persia — Defeat of Kerym Khan — Assad Khan is attacked in the mountains — Last attempt of the Afghans to annex Persia — Nasser Khan, Belooch, revolts — The combats of Pringues and Mestook — Siege of Kelat — Favourable terms made by Nasser Khan — Ahmed Shah proceeds to India — Insurrection of the Mahrattas — Ahmed Shah Gourkanee deposed — Assassination of Alemguir — Ghazi Khan seizes the throne of the Moguls — Ahmed Shah, Suddozye, reaches Lahore — Marches on Delhi — Shooja ed Dooulet — Passage of the Bar — Desertion of Delaver Khan and Zal Beg — Shah Alem cedes his rights to the English — Revolt in Kandahar — Abdul Khalek Khan — Abdullah Khan suppresses the insurrection — Ahmed Shah marches on Peshawur — Arrives at Kandahar — Zal Beg is executed — Delaver Khan flies to Herat — Timoor Mirza is made viceroy — Ahmed Shah's reasons for this — Death of Ahmed Shah — Yaghoot Khan — The Serdars declare for Suleiman Mirza — Character of Ahmed Shah.

IN the following year, namely, in 1751, having completely repaired his disasters, Ahmed made a second inroad upon Khorassan. Every cavalry soldier carried with him two battements* of iron for casting shot, which were placed in store directly he arrived with his army under the walls of Nishapoor. The siege of this city was now pressed with great energy; the Afghan monarch cast a gun upon the spot, which threw a projectile weighing 472 lbs. English, and one month was employed in casting, boring, and placing this monster gun on its carriage. When fired it produced a most terrible effect, the walls and houses being pierced through and through, but it burst the very first time it was used. The citizens of Nishapoor, ignorant of that fact, were so terrified by the destruction which this single bullet occasioned, that they despatched several of their chiefs to Ahmed Shah to inform him that they surrendered at discretion. Abbas Kooli Khan, who held the citadel, refused however to acknowledge this surrender, and attacked the Afghans at the moment they were on the point of entering the city; but he was repulsed in an instant, and reduced to the alternative of soliciting in person the clemency

---

* A *battement* of Herat is equal to 6 lbs. English.—*Ferrier.*

of the conqueror. Ahmed Shah detained him as a prisoner in his camp, and he subsequently accompanied him to Kabul: the Afghan conqueror, having perceived in this chief very considerable talents, and a frankness of disposition in which he thought he could confide, gave him his sister in marriage; he also bestowed one of his daughters on Abbas Kooli's son, after which he sent him back to Nishapoor, as governor of that city. Having thus satisfactorily established his power there, Ahmed Shah, thinking he had cause of complaint against Shah Rokh Mirza and his sons, who had been hostile to him in his second campaign in Khorassan, again laid siege to Meshed. Contemporaneously with this movement he detached a corps of cavalry under the orders of the Serdars Jehan Khan and Nasser Khan of Kelat, to subdue the districts of Toon and Tubbus, and take revenge for the defeat which the Afghans had sustained during the preceding year at the hands of Ali Murad Khan. These Serdars commenced operations by devastating the country, after which they marched against the governor of Tubbus, whom they met at Kakhak, a small village situated near Gourmabad, and there fought one of the most obstinate and bloody battles that is to be found in the annals of Persian history; such was the tenacity and fury of the combatants, that, when ammunition failed on both sides, they dismounted from their horses, and, drawing their sabres, did not cease to strike till the death of Ali Murad, who arrived at the close of the conflict; this determined the issue of the battle, and the remainder of his men, for the most part of Arab tribes, took to flight. Much of the credit of this victory was more especially due to the bravery of Nasser Khan and his Beloochees, who behaved like heroes.

After this the Afghans took possession of Toon and Tubbus, and committed every kind of excess upon the inhabitants of those towns: fire and sword did their work, and to these were added violation, murder, pillage, and devastation; in which having indulged sufficiently, they again joined the royal camp, carrying with them a considerable booty. While the serdars of Ahmed Shah were obtaining these successes, that sovereign pressed on the siege of Meshed with vigour, but he had, up to this period, been scarcely more fortunate than in the preceding year. The inhabitants, animated by religious fanaticism, defended themselves with intrepidity, and the Afghans suffered heavy losses in their encounters with the enemy; their resources also diminished daily, and provisions became very scarce, which obliged Ahmed to detach 2000 of his cavalry in the direction of Subzawar and Shah Rood Bostam, to procure supplies. In this enterprise they perfectly succeeded, and were returning to camp with 2500 beasts of burden laden with plunder, which had greatly encumbered and delayed them, when on reaching the halt of Abbasabad the foragers fell into an ambuscade, in which were posted 1500 Kadjar horse from the environs of Asterabad, who fell upon and completely routed them. A great number of Afghans were killed or made prisoners in this affair; the plunder fell into the hands of the Kadjars, and the survivors, numbering scarcely a thousand, regained the Afghan camp.

Ahmed Shah, seeing that his efforts to take Meshed would prove ineffectual, and fearing that the winter, which was now approaching, might cause a repetition of the disasters of the preceding one, accepted the terms offered him by Shah Rokh Mirza. These were, that Ahmed should leave him in quiet possession of Khorassan and support him against the ambitious chiefs of the province, on condition that Shah Rokh should acknowledge his suzerainty, that money should be coined in his name, firmans and other official documents bear his seal, and the districts of Toorbut Sheikh Jam, Bakharz, Toorbut-hai-darieh, and Khaff, be made over to him. A treaty, drawn up on this basis, was signed by the two contracting parties, after which Ahmed Shah, thinking that the power which he had thus consolidated was a sufficient guarantee against the ambitious projects of Assad Khan, an Afghan chief, of whom we shall have occasion to speak hereafter, returned to Herat, where he occupied himself in carrying out numerous reforms in the army and administration. It was from hence that he sent Beghee Khan, one of his viziers, with an army to subdue the countries beyond the Oxus, inhabited by Uzbeks, Hazarahs, and a few Afghan families, who had not yet acknowledged his dominion. After having engaged in several combats, but not very serious ones, Beghee Khan seized upon Meimana, Andekhooye, Akhcheh, Shibbergan, Serpeul, Balkh, Khulm, Badakshan, and Bamian: he organized the various districts he had conquered; and having appointed governors, with whom he left troops to keep the inhabitants in awe, he returned to Kandahar, where Ahmed Shah had previously arrived, and this sovereign, to recompense Beghee Khan for the services he had rendered him, added to his title of vizier that of Sedre-azem.

It has been mentioned that in isolating Khorassan from Persia, and placing the former under the authority of Shah Rokh Mirza, his vassal, Ahmed Shah acted with a view of protecting himself against the projects of Assad Khan, an Afghan Serdar, of the tribe of the Ghildjzyes. After the death of Nadir this Serdar had been fortunate enough to maintain his authority in the Azerbaidjan, of which province he was governor. He was a man of great firmness, brave, and more enlightened than are ordinarily the individuals of his nation; and his justice, his equitable views, and the partiality which he manifested in favour of the sect of Shiahs, drew around him a great number of partisans. Seeing his power and popularity thus increased, he declared openly his pretensions to the possession of Irak, Khorassan, and even proposed to push on to Afghanistan, and dethrone Ahmed Shah, whom he considered as an usurper, for in his opinion the throne belonged by right to a chief of the tribe of Ghildjzyes; but he was arrested in his march eastward, and recalled to Irak, by serious events that occurred in 1753. Kerym Khan, of the tribe of the Zends, after having made his authority acknowledged in Fars and the other southern provinces of Persia, took advantage of the hatred which their populations felt for everything that bore the name of Afghan, to raise a large army, and with this he marched against Assad Khan, with the view of forcing him beyond the Persian border. This chief, who had already advanced as far as Damghan, retraced his steps, met his antagonist at Kasbeen, attacked him immediately, and with such effect, that Kerym Khan was completely beaten, and so hotly pursued, that he was obliged to abandon Ispahan and Shiraz, without being able to offer even the slightest resistance. He subsequently retired to the mountains in the south of Persia, to shelter himself from further pursuit; and discouraged by the reverse he had just experienced, was on the point of seeking refuge in India to enjoy the repose he so ardently desired, when he was dissuaded from taking this step by Roostem Sultan, the chief of the district of Khecht. This chieftain informed Kerym Khan that Assad Khan had committed the imprudence of entangling himself in the defiles which led to his place of retreat; that this ill-judged movement would infallibly lead to his destruction, because the country people, who were on the side of the Zend chief* and

* Of the army of Assad Khan one-third were Afghans, and the other two Georgians, Kurds, and Turks of Azerbaidjan.—*Ferrier.*

detested the Afghans, were acquainted with all the advantages and difficulties of the ground, and, profiting by such knowledge, would make the narrow gorges and defiles through which the latter were marching a last resting-place for his enemies.

Convinced by this reasoning, Kerym Khan decided upon renewing hostilities, and placed his troops under the orders of Roostem Sultan, giving him full power to act as he thought fit; accordingly this chieftain halted for Assad Khan at the defile of Kooma, which extends about a mile and a half along the summit of a high mountain, and through this the Afghans could only advance in single file. The Persians placed themselves behind the fragments of rocks which lay scattered along the pass, and waited till the enemy occupied it from one extremity to the other before they attacked, when, with a perfect unity of action and inconceivable energy, they fell upon the whole line. Every shot from the long matchlocks of these expert marksmen carried death into the Afghan ranks, while their bullets fell harmlessly against the rocks, behind which their adversaries had ensconced themselves. All those who could escape from this hornet's nest endeavoured to make good their retreat and regain the plain, but here they found fresh opponents, who had turned the position and attacked them with fury. It was in vain that Assad Khan tried to rally his troops and renew the fight; his efforts were unavailing, and he was obliged once more to retire. A few days after, while continuing this retrograde movement, he was overtaken by Mohamed Hoosein Khan, Kadjar, another aspirant to the Persian throne, when the remainder of his army was destroyed, and Assad Khan only escaped with his life by seeking refuge in Bagdad. Not meeting here with the support he expected, he passed on to Georgia, where the Prince Heraclius gave him no better reception; and worn out and dispirited by his many disappointments and personal sufferings, and being without a hope of success, he finished by making his submission to Kerym Khan, who gave him high rank at his court and treated him with every consideration. Assad Khan remained to the end faithfully attached to Kerym Khan, and this was the last attempt made by the Afghans to seize the throne of Persia. Ahmed Shah experienced some disquietude in seeing Assad Khan thus submit to the Persian monarch, but Kerym Khan, having plenty to do in maintaining the tranquillity of his own kingdom, never again made the slightest hostile attempt to annex Afghanistan to Persia: it was however believed at Kandahar that he was no stranger to the revolt of Nasser Khan, chief of Kelat and Beloochistan, of which we shall have occasion to speak.

Subsequently to his return from Khorassan Ahmed Shah had been under the necessity of proceeding three times to India, as well to establish his authority in the Punjab, where great agitation, fomented by the Mahrattas, was almost permanent, as to curb the turbulent spirit of that people, who were not less unmanageable than the Afghans. Nasser Khan had taken part in all these expeditions, and distinguished himself in each of them: he had recognised the suzerainty of Ahmed Shah from the time he ascended the throne, and had always been well treated and generously recompensed by that sovereign; but nevertheless the Belooch chief revolted against him and proclaimed his own independence in 1758. Ahmed Shah exhausted every means of conciliation towards Nasser Khan, whom he esteemed, without being able to bring him back to his allegiance, and at length sent a division of his army against him, but the chief, who had been for some time prepared for this crisis, was not intimidated, and directly he was informed of the arrival of Ahmed's troops he marched to meet them. A battle was fought near the village of Pringuez, situated about seventy miles from Kelat, in which the Afghans were completely beaten, and obliged to retire to a distance of thirty miles from thence. The Serdar in command immediately despatched a messenger to the king to demand reinforcements, and Ahmed, fearful lest such a check, though of little consequence in itself, should acquire importance from the exaggerated manner in which the circumstances might be detailed to the tribes recently subdued, put himself at the head of this second division, and hastened to the support of his discomfited troops. Nasser Khan, assailed by him near the camp of Mestook, situated three miles and a half from Pringuez, was defeated, and obliged to retire in all haste to Kelat: this town he had previously placed in a good state of defence, and within its walls he now took refuge. Ahmed Shah followed him close and invested the place; the position of the citadel on an eminence was exceedingly strong, and this circumstance, and the want of unanimity that existed amongst the Afghan serdars, were the causes that led to a protracted siege, and eventually to no advantageous result. It was in vain that assaults were made on five different occasions; they all failed, because the various chiefs would not, and did not, support each other; and at length the Shah, perceiving he could gain nothing by prolonging the conflict, consented to a treaty which replaced Nasser Khan under his suzerainty, and obliged him to furnish a contingent of troops on every occasion that the Afghan monarch made war beyond the boundaries of his kingdom. In this case the chief of Kelat was to receive a sum of money and munitions of war every time he took the field. Nasser Khan also stipulated that he should not be compelled to furnish such contingent for the sake of supporting this or that Suddozye chief, or their successors of that or any other tribe, or be obliged to take part in the internal quarrels that might arise amongst the Afghans themselves. This was the only condition bearing the charactor of vassalage imposed upon the Belooch chief, who was now exempted from the tribute which he had previously paid to Ahmed Shah; and in order to make the treaty more binding the king married a cousin of Nasser Khan's, after which he returned to Kandahar, and he was shortly obliged to leave for India to put down the troubles which had again broken out owing to the intrigues of the Mahrattas. This people incited the population to revolt, and seized the country, which was the appanage of the Mogul Princess, the wife of Timoor Mirza.

"The Mahrattas," remarks Sir John Malcolm, "became formidable in the reign of Shah Jehan, and during thirty years that Arungzebe passed in the southern provinces of his empire his chief occupation was to subdue the Mahrattas; but this he found impossible, for they never awaited his attack. The country was laid waste and his troops continually harassed by men who, from the lightness of their frames, were no burden to their horses, and who, from habits of hardihood and abstemiousness, required little either for shelter or support. It seemed in vain to war with a foe who was intangible, and whose glory lay in the rapidity of his retreat; for the Mahratta soldier, though brave, boasts more of his power to elude than to attack his enemy. When the empire of India fell to pieces at the death of Arungzebe, and Mahomedan princes and nobles were all ranged against each other, the Mahrattas, by continuing united, made a rapid and surprising progress. Besides the great possessions which they actually occupied, they had compelled not only the paramount sovereign of India, but almost every ruler of a province, to pay them a considerable part of their annual collections,* that their habitations and fields might remain in safety. At the period when Nadir threatened invasion, the city of Delhi itself was subject to this *disgraceful* tribute." †

The disgraceful tribute of which Sir John Malcolm here speaks was agreed to by the Indian princes at the period when Ahmed Shah marched against the confederation of the Mahrattas, and the latter used all the influence they possessed in the various principalities of India to force those princes to send their contingent of troops to take part in the war in which they were about to engage against the Afghans.

Ahmed Shah Gourkanee, the sovereign of Delhi, had been deposed in 1753 by his vizier Ghazee Khan, and that functionary placed his nephew Alemguir on the throne in his stead. This prince, utterly destitute of ability, was assassinated by Ghazee in 1760, when the usurper seized upon the sovereign power himself; and Ahmed Shah, Suddozye, heard of this event a few days before he arrived at Mooltan, as well as of the junction of the Mogul troops with those of the Mahrattas.

The various populations of India had been in an unsettled state ever since Nadir Shah seized upon Delhi; but at the death of Shah Mahmood, emperor of the Moguls, anarchy was rampant. The princes of India, tributaries of the Mahrattas, ardently desired to deliver themselves from the yoke imposed upon them by this confederation of plunderers, and Ahmed Shah, Suddozye, sent secret emissaries to their courts in order to work upon and strengthen this feeling. With a view of giving them time to do this he advanced but slowly, and occupied himself in organising the territory which he had recently conquered in Scinde and Mooltan. He then entered the Punjab, which the Mahrattas evacuated at his approach without fighting, so that he arrived at Lahore unopposed, and there he encamped. The Indian princes obeyed the injunctions of the Mahrattas, and, in spite of the intrigues of Ahmed Shah, sent their several contingents, which, when united, formed an army of 200,000 men, of which 70,000 were cavalry, supported by twenty pieces of artillery of large calibre and 200 zimbooreks.

Ahmed did not take the field until the whole of this formidable

* This was levied under the various names of Choute, Desmokee, &c.

† Sier Musakhereen.

army was assembled in the environs of Delhi. He then advanced to meet it, and came up with the enemy on the banks of the river Bar; but in consequence of the depth of that stream and the want of pontoons, he was obliged to wait a few days until the water had subsided. This was all the more disadvantageous to him, inasmuch as he could only obtain provisions for his troops on the side occupied by the enemy; and as the Mahrattas were vigilant in watching the fords which they fortified, the Afghans soon felt the effects of a scarcity in their camp; some of them murmured loudly, and others prepared to desert, when a fortunate occurrence, the result of the clever policy of their sovereign, took place, which, producing abundance at once, revived their hopes. Shooja-ed-Dooulet, the Prince of Lucknow, had submitted to the Mahrattas only because he could not avoid it, and, suddenly leaving them, proceeded to the Afghan camp, followed by several other Indian rajahs and 25,000 men, which made the effective force of Ahmed Shah's army 85,000 men—45,000 being cavalry and the remainder infantry—with seventeen pieces of cannon and eighty zimbooreks. There were about 10,000 non-combatants in the Afghan army, whereas in that of the Mahratta confederacy one-third might be set down as belonging to that class, such, for instance, as servants, sutlers, drivers in charge of oxen, ponies, camels, &c., and thus not more than from 100,000 to 110,000 troops could be brought into position.

Shooja-ed-Dooulet, having provisioned the Afghan army, and overcome the hesitation of the Serdars, who considered the passage of the river as a thing impossible, it was resolved to give battle. On the 7th of January, 1761, therefore, Ahmed Shah, Suddozye, ordered the Serdar Samut Khan, Yoosoofzye, to cross the river with 5000 cavalry and attack the Moguls—which order he promptly obeyed; but the greater portion of his horsemen were carried away by the rapidity of the current, and the fire of the enemy's artillery made such havoc amongst them, that the survivors remained in a state of indecision. Ahmed Shah, perceiving this corps required support, sent two others to its assistance; but the Serdars Delaver Khan, Isakzye, and Zal Beg, Popolzye, who commanded them, and who were at variance with Samut Khan, did not heartily execute the order they had received, and allowed Samut's troops to be cut up. The king saw the state of affairs at a glance, and, alive to the least thing that might compromise him as to the issue of the conflict, mounted his horse and plunged into the river, followed only by his guards. The Serdars commanding the divisions which had remained immovable were now obliged to advance, for the troops were ashamed to see their sovereign braving death while they remained passive spectators of the combat. The Mahrattas redoubled the fire of their artillery to repulse this attack, and this was so terrible that the surface of the river was covered by the corpses of men and the carcases of horses, and its waters became crimsoned with their life-blood. But the Afghans gained at length, though with heavy loss, the opposite shore, and with hearts burning for revenge fell upon the enemy, whom they finally put to the rout; 20,000 of them remained on the field of battle, also their artillery and baggage, and the victors obtained a rich booty. This memorable and bloody battle was fought on the plains of Paniput, a few parasangs north of Delhi.

Shooja-ed-Dooulet had up to this time formed but an incorrect estimate of the bravery of the Afghans; but after having been an eye-witness of it, and remembering that they were not very conspicuous for their notions of gratitude, and might perhaps be wanting in that which they owed to him, he regretted that he had assisted them—nevertheless he remained faithful to his new ally; as to Delaver Khan and Zal Beg, who had not obeyed the order of Ahmed Shah to march to the assistance of Samut Khan, and feared his anger, left the camp by stealth, taking with them their men, even before the issue of the day was known. The king, without making himself very uneasy at this defection, continued rapidly to advance, and seized upon the Mahratta country, after which he passed into the Mogul territory, when the usurper Ghazee Khan, seeing his kingdom invaded, determined to obtain, if possible, the mediation of Shooja-ed-Dooulet, and thus make his peace with Ahmed Shah. The Prince of Lucknow was not averse to undertaking this negotiation; but on condition that Ghazee Khan, as in duty bound, should surrender the crown to the legitimate sovereign, and further pay an enormous contribution to the expenses of the war. These severe terms having been accepted, Ahmed was desirous of placing Shah Alem, the son of Alemguir, on the throne, and, upon his refusal to be reinstated in his rights, his son Jehan-booght, as yet only a child, was raised to the musnud.

Matters at Delhi having been thus settled, Ahmed Shah proceeded in the direction of the Punjab to maintain order there, and was preparing to march to the southern provinces of India when he learnt that the Mahrattas had moved upon Delhi. He returned, therefore, in haste to the support of his new ally, whom he had the good fortune to save from the danger that menaced him, for the Mahrattas retired at his approach. Whether Shooja-ed-Dooulet had really intrigued with them to bring about the fall of Jehanboogbt, or whether the serdars, jealous of his influence with the Shah, deceived Ahmed in order to effect his ruin, the result was that the Afghan monarch, who ought to have shut his eyes, at least for the moment, to the accusations brought against the Prince of Lucknow, demanded from him a large sum of money; but Shooja, indignant at the request, determined not to comply with it, and, clandestinely leaving the camp with his troops, retired to his own country. This desertion, added to that of Delaver Khan and Zal Beg, with their 10,000 horse, seriously reduced the strength of the Afghan army, so that Ahmed Shah was no longer in a position to prolong the campaign, but, satisfied with the immense treasures he had collected during the war, he returned towards his own territory, to which he was, as it happened, recalled by an event of some importance.

Some ambitious, and consequently discontented serdars, had, after their flight from the royal camp, joined Delaver Khan and Zal Beg, who, supporting the revolt of a nephew of Ahmed Shah's, by name Abdul Khalek Khan, proclaimed him king at the fortress of Girishk, and subsequently moved in triumph towards Kandahar. Previously to this Hadji Djemal Khan, of the branch of the Zergueranees, had likewise proclaimed himself king at Kandahar after the departure of Ahmed Shah for India, and had even coined money in his own name; but having heard of Ahmed's victories, he thought it would be more prudent to renounce the royal position he had assumed and stand on one side. Abdul Khalek, less judicious, made incredible efforts to secure his object. When Ahmed Shah became thoroughly aware of what was passing in his capital, he considered the circumstances of so little importance, that he did not think it necessary to return there in person, but sent the Isakzye Serdar, and Abdullah Khan, surnamed Shah Pecend Khan, with a strong division of cavalry, to put down the rebellious proceedings of his nephew and the serdars who had joined him, recommending the Khan, above all things, to use the utmost despatch and endeavour to arrive at Kandahar before they could reach it from Girishk; he was not, however, in spite of his exertions, able to do so until after the revolt had taken root there, and Suleiman Mirza, the eldest son of Ahmed Shah, who governed in the absence of his father, had been expelled from the capital. The greater number of the revolted serdars had only supported the usurper because they believed the report which had been circulated by Delaver Khan and Zal Beg that Ahmed had lost the battle of Paniput, and met with great reverses and disasters in India; but they deeply regretted their folly in this unlucky business when they were made acquainted with his success and saw Abdullah Khan and his cavalry make their appearance. Thinking, therefore, that the only way to obtain the Shah's pardon was to make a prompt submission, they, with few exceptions, went to the camp of the latter, to whom they delivered up the city, and also Abdul Khalek himself. When he left Delhi, Ahmed Shah had gone to the Punjab, and thence to Peshawur, to re-establish his authority, which had been somewhat questioned; and it was during this journey that he received a letter from Abdullah Khan, announcing the manner in which he had terminated his mission—the king, in his reply, desired him to strangle his nephew secretly, a command which he immediately put into execution.

The disorder at Peshawur was great when Ahmed arrived there, as well in the town as in the neighbourhood; and several months elapsed before tranquillity was restored, and matters resumed their ordinary course. At this period snow covered the ground to the depth of three feet, and the Shah was obliged to wait for the spring until he could return to his capital; he wrote, therefore, to his son Suleiman Mirza, desiring him to take every possible means in his power to capture the serdars Delaver Khan and Zal Beg, who had so treacherously deserted him, and to put them to death. The prince wrote therefore to the latter, feigning a friendship and promising perfect oblivion of the past—and this in the name of his father—if he would pay him a visit at Kandahar. Zal Beg accepted the invitation, and, with perjury truly Eastern, Suleiman Mirza put him to death directly he entered the town. Delaver Khan was less inclined to confide in the prince's word than his unfortunate friend, and instead of proceeding to Kandahar, as he had previously promised to do, he fled to Herat, and placed himself under the protection of the prince Timoor Mirza, second son of Ahmed Shah, and governor of that city. From a spirit of opposition to his brother Suleiman, with whom he was on bad terms, Timoor received the fugitive in a somewhat eager manner, and showered honours and benefits upon him, which were increased, even to prodigality, each time that the reiterated orders arrived at Herat to put him to death.

Ahmed Shah left Peshawur at the commencement of spring,* and remained the whole summer at Kabul, arriving at Kandahar about the middle of autumn, at which period he experienced an attack, and with more intensity than ever, of that terrible malady which had forced him long before to substitute an artificial nose of silver for his own, which had sloughed away. This malady, called by Abdullah Khan *Djuzam* (which in Persian signifies leprous, and a small ulcer) arrived towards the close of this year at such a fearful height, that the Shah determined to proclaim his second son, Timoor Mirza, his viceroy and successor to the throne of Afghanistan. The serdars, astonished at this decision, which appeared to them unjust, inasmuch as it was to the prejudice of his eldest son Suleiman Mirza, assembled, and, having come to a resolution, presented a respectful request to the Shah Ahmed in favour of that prince. In this document they allowed a feeling of something like discontent to appear, that they had not been consulted in a matter of so grave a nature. The Shah replied, that in acting thus he had not consulted his own particular bias, and that in making his selection he had been guided entirely for the public good. "Timoor," said he, "it is true, is younger than Suleiman, but he is infinitely more capable of governing you than his brother." The serdars wished for a proof; the Shah simply replied that Suleiman had never been able to conciliate the esteem and affection of the tribes; that he was violent without clemency; that he had never been able to foresee or put down a revolt; and, in short, that he hastily put to death the Serdar Zal Beg. "But," said the serdars, "it was by your order." "Did I not also order Timoor to put Delaver Khan to death?" replied Ahmed; "and what did he do? Political reasons might induce me to order two culprits to be put to death, but other secret reasons, which were known to the

---

* The manuscript of Abdullah is entirely without dates, the author is therefore unable to give any.—*Ferrier.*

prince Suleiman, ought to have led him to disobey me, as his brother did." The serdars appeared satisfied with these replies, which seemed to embody, as it were, his opinions for the future guidance of the princes of the blood.

When Ahmed Shah had induced the serdars to acknowledge his son Timoor Mirza as his successor, he retired to a palace he had built at Tobeh-Maharoof, situated in the midst of the Suleiman mountains, the cradle of his tribe. From hence he watched over the government; but after four or five years had elapsed, his disease having rendered him incapable of any further continuous labour, he entirely abandoned public affairs to the governors of the various provinces of his empire, and expired shortly after, namely, in 1773. Yaghoot Khan, the chief of his eunuchs, and a person in whom he had great confidence, kept his death a profound secret, and wrote immediately to Timoor Mirza, who was still governor of Herat, to come with all speed to Kandahar and take possession of the throne. At the same time that he transmitted this information he set out himself, taking the royal corpse with him; this was placed in a litter, and the curtains being carefully drawn was completely concealed from every one. The adroit eunuch approached the litter from time to time, as if to receive some order from his sovereign, or give him some refreshment, remarking to those of his escort who wished to make any request or an inquiry about his health, that, being extremely unwell, the Shah had ordered that no one should be allowed to disturb him. Yaghoot Khan also took with him the Shah's jewels and treasure, which were carried by mules, and always preceded the royal litter, so that he might be able to have his eye constantly upon them. No one discovered the deception during the greater part of the journey; and it was only about a day's march from Kandahar, when the prince Suleiman Mirza came out to receive his father, that it was necessary to make the Shah's death public. The serdars, who were present on this occasion, were nearly all attached to the party of this prince, from whom they had received brilliant promises, and they immediately returned with him to the city, and proclaimed him Shah of the Afghans.

Ahmed Shah, Suddozye, reigned twenty-five years and a few months: he was free from most of the crimes commonly found in individuals of Eastern nations; such as drunkenness, whether from wine or opium, duplicity, avarice, cruelty, and one which need not be mentioned; he was always a most firm supporter of religion. On his accession to the throne he changed the name of his tribe, which was *Abdalee*, to that of *Dooranee*, which signifies a person of noble and ancient birth; and he took the title of Doorveranee, *i. e. he around whom converges the noble and ancient tribe.*

In order to increase the numbers of the Afghan nation Ahmed connected with it all the tribes of doubtful origin, Eimak or Belooch, speaking the Pushtoo language, who were settled in the various provinces, particularly in the district of Furrah and on the banks of the Helmund. There was a clause in his will forbidding his successors to cut off the nosé or ears of any one, no matter whom; and this was based upon his own sufferings, for the leprous disease having destroyed his nose, and Nadir Shah, to punish him for an act of insubordination, having cut off one of his ears, he had deeply felt the deprivation of these organs. He also desired the Dooranees to ally themselves one with another, and not to give their girls in marriage to strangers; that for the future the succession should go entirely to the son and to the exclusion of the daughters, who up to that time had participated in the property left by their father; that at the death of an Afghan his nearest relative, the father and son excepted, should marry his widow; and if there was no relative, the widow should reside in the house of her deceased husband, and live on the proceeds of his property till her death; that when a married woman died without having a child, her father, brother, or other relative could not demand her dower from the husband; he also abolished divorce, and withdrew from the master his right to kill his slave. He abrogated the custom of bending the body and kissing the earth before the sovereign, whom he commanded henceforth to be saluted by carrying the hand straight to the forehead; he granted permission to sit in the presence of the monarch only to the syuds and priests, to whom he conceded the privilege of dining every Thursday evening with the sovereign, in order that he might be able to converse with them on the sciences and religion. The laws he made during his reign he caused to be rigorously executed, and commanded that his descendants and successors should do the same after him. He accumulated great riches, but they consisted of the plunder which he had taken from his enemies; the revenues of

Afghanistan, properly so termed, never found their way into his private coffers: he gave his troops their pay in person. The name of Ahmed Shah became glorious throughout Asia after the battle of Paniput, which was one of the causes that led to the rapid decay of the Mogul empire. The petty chiefs of Khorassan, who all acknowledged his suzerainty, and offered but a timid opposition, he would have brought into complete subordination, had it not been for the six campaigns which he made in the Punjab, India, and Beloochistan, which absorbed all his time. He saw that repose demoralized his troops, and he kept them always in a high state of discipline. It was by this system that he was enabled to maintain himself securely upon the throne, as much as to the great clemency that he constantly manifested, and which induced him so continually to pardon the rebellious chiefs who could not bring themselves to bow under the yoke of obedience, and between whom he was obliged to be the peacemaker. His reign was remarkable for the good which he spread around him, and his generosity and simple and modest demeanour in the midst of courtly pomp made him loved by all who approached his person; he was of easy access, and administered justice upon the most equitable principles, without a harsh word even to those who deserved it; he was conciliating, persuasive, and no one ever complained of the judgments that he gave. He greatly extended the limits of his empire, which, at the moment of his decease, were as follows: the frontier to the north was defined by the Oxus and the mountains of Kiafferistan; to the south, by the sea of Oman; to the east, by the mountains of Thibet, the Sutlej, and the Indus; and to the west, by Khorassan, Persia, and Kerman.

But Ahmed Shah is much more deserving of eulogy for the talent with which he subjected the various Afghan tribes to his laws, than for having given such a vast extension to his kingdom, or for the victories he won. The princes who prior to him governed the Afghans exercised but a nominal authority over the nomade tribes, for they listened only to the orders of their own chiefs. Ahmed Shah conciliated the majority of these, and reduced to obedience the few who were hostile to him. The nine Serdars who had served with him in the army of Nadir formed a Council which he always consulted in questions of state: he adopted no measure of importance without their approbation, and never failed in any promise that he made them. His government in short resembled much more a federative republic of which he was the head, than an absolute monarchy. After a victory he always gave up a large part of the spoils of the enemy to his soldiers; he never adopted an arrogant tone of superiority with their chiefs which could hurt the feelings of those with whom he had once been on equal terms, and who had elevated him to the sovereign power.

CHAPTER VIII.

Kabul becomes the capital — Sons of Ahmed Shah — Dervish Ali Khan — Afghan principles — Walee Khan and his sons put to death — Flight of Suleiman Mirza — Timoor Mirza enters Kandahar — Resides at Kabul — Kuzzilbash cavalry organised — Timoor marches against Scinde — Conflicts between the Kaloras and Talpooras — Timoor Shah takes Bawalpoor — Establishes the Kaloras in Scinde — Fresh disturbances in Scinde — Medad Khan is beaten at Djioond — Fethi Khan Talpoora succeeds to power — Timoor takes the field against the Emir of Bokhara — Balkh and Akhcheh become independent — Timoor returns to Kabul — Events in Khorassan — Afghan army marches on Meshed — Mamech Khan — Capture of Tchinaran — Death of Medad Khan — Fresh insurrection in Khorassan — Afghan army advances into that province — Conspiracy to take Timoor Shah's life — The plot fails — Arseleh Khan is put to death — Value of an oath in an Afghan sovereign — Death of Timoor Shah — Character of that monarch — Sons of Timoor.

THE Afghans never really enjoyed their independence till the reign of Ahmed Shah, and the national disposition was probably modified at this epoch. The liberty of speech and action in which they were permitted to indulge contributed without doubt powerfully to develop that independent manner and rustic pride which still characterize them in our own day—a conquered nation for generations, they became all at once conquerors. This sudden transition took place it is true under Mir Mahmood, but was only thoroughly developed under Ahmed Shah, Suddozye; it inspired them with confidence in themselves and roused a superiority which had up to that period been dormant; in a word, the national mind had been formed.

The city of Kandahar was considered the capital of Afghanistan during the reign of Ahmed Shah, but he only resided there during the autumn and winter; he went to Kabul in the spring and summer, alternately changing his place of abode from one city to the other, that he might constantly enjoy an agreeable and temperate climate. His son Timoor Shah altered this state of things; for he withdrew the title of capital from Kandahar and transferred it to Kabul, which was subsequently the royal residence during the whole period that the dynasty of the Suddozyes occupied the throne of Afghanistan.

Ahmed Shah left eight sons, namely, Suleiman Mirza, Timoor Mirza, Chahab Mirza, Sindjar Mirza, Yezdan bakhch Mirza, Sikander Mirza, Darab Mirza, and Perviz Mirza. The Prince Timoor, Walee of Herat, named by his father as his successor, did not hear of his death till he received the letter written to him by the eunuch Yaghoot Khan, but he learnt before he left Herat that his brother Suleiman Mirza had been proclaimed king at Kandahar by a few Serdars, at the head of whom was the Shah Walee Khan, first minister of the deceased Shah. The delay which took place before Timoor proceeded to his capital arose from the uneasiness occasioned him by Dervish Ali Khan, Hazarah, a subtle chief, and a dangerous traitor, who had recently escaped from the dungeons of Herat, in which Ahmed Shah had imprisoned him after his return from Meshed. A party hostile to Timoor had rallied round this Khan; nevertheless the prince, under a promise of pardon, was clever enough to induce him to come within the precincts of his palace; where, according to Afghan usage, which consists generally in a perfect disregard of the value of the most solemn oaths, he put him instantly to death, and gave the command of the Hazarahs to the Serdar Mohamed Shah Khan, a member of the same tribe. After this he appointed his own son, Mahmood Mirza, Governor of Herat; but as he was desirous that he should accompany him to Kandahar, he named Islam Khan, Popolzye, his vizier, as the *locum tenens* of his son in that office, after which he assembled his troops and marched against Suleiman Mirza. On his arrival at Furrah he was joined by a great number of partizans who had already abandoned the cause of his brother, but amongst all those who deserted Suleiman the most important accession to his cause was the Shah Walee Khan, who had great influence over the Afghans. This personage brought his two sons and two of the principal Dooranee Serdars to the camp of Timoor, which was then at Siah-ab; but the prince, fearing to be hampered in the government by this old servant of his father, and desirous also of striking terror into the traitors by a severe example, ordered their heads to be struck off directly they appeared before him. The party of Suleiman Mirza, terrified by these executions, was at once dissolved, and the usurper finding himself thus deserted fled to India, accompanied by four followers who alone remained faithful to him.

Timoor, surrounded by all the great and powerful families in the kingdom, and accompanied by a numerous army, now made his public entry into Kandahar with much pomp and circumstance, and was at once acknowledged king by the assembled Serdars; but he made only a short stay in this city, the population of which had become odious to him from having taken his brother's part: as a punishment he deprived it of its title of capital, which as we have already said he transferred to Kabul, to which place he at once proceeded with his army, leaving his son Mahmood provisional Governor of Kandahar. The reign of Timoor continued for twenty years, and during this period he almost always passed the winter at Peshawur, and the remaining seasons of the year at Kabul. On ascending the throne he augmented the pay of the Afghan chiefs, and gave the tribes a great extension of territory; several of the serdars received appointments of great trust and high command and titles much esteemed at the court of an Asiatic sovereign.

The Serdar Payendeh Khan, son of that Hadji Djemal who had renounced his pretensions to the throne in favour of Ahmed Shah, Suddozye, was confirmed in the command of the powerful tribe of the Barukzyes, and honoured with the title of Sera-fraz Khan. Delaver Khan, the Serdar who deserted at the battle of Paniput, received the title of Medad Khan, and the grade of Serdaree Serdarane, "General of Generals." Kazee Feiz Ullah, Pich-nawaz of the king, received the title of Kelane Kelauter, "Greatest of the Great." Timoor Shah had such an implicit confidence in this Serdar that he never did anything without consulting him. Abdul Latif Khan, one of the descendants of Sheik Ahmed Zindeh Pir, was appointed lieutenant of the kingdom and receiver-general of the taxes. Noor Mohamed Khan, Baberee, was made president of the court of accounts; and lastly, Iltifat Khan, chief of the eunuchs, was appointed chief treasurer and custodian of the crown jewels. All these personages had the rank of ministers, and Timoor ordered as a general rule that the principles of justice, equity, and a mild course of conduct should be observed towards every one; but he recommended them to employ the chiefs of tribes as little as possible as public functionaries, for up to this period they had generally held the appointments, and almost always abused their authority. The Shah's guards were selected from the tribe of Isakzye, and to this the Serdaree Serdarane belonged. A division of 12,000

Kuzzilbash horsemen was also organized under the command of the Serdar Mohamed Khan Beyat, the pay of their officers was augmented, and Timoor chose from amongst these the companions of his debauched habits, for he had a great predilection for wine and other pleasures. He paid with great punctuality every half-year the salaries of the officers of his court, and the army every year.

Timoor Shah was only twice at the head of his troops to meet his enemies; all the other wars in which he was engaged were conducted by the Serdaree Serdarane, Medad Khan, Isakzye. The first occasion on which Timoor took the field was in 1779 in the campaign against Scinde, which had revolted. The governor of this province, a vassal of the Afghan sovereigns, and admitting their suzerainty, had endeavoured to throw it off at the time the Mahrattas rose in his father's reign, and Ahmed Shah had subdued him even before the battle of Paniput, making him pay a very large sum of money as arrears of tribute, and as an indemnity for the expenses of the war; after which Ahmed forgave him, and maintained him in his government. This chief belonged to the tribe of the Kalora, and had the title of Emir of Scinde. Mir Fethi Khan, chief of the Talpoora tribe, a rival of his, attacked him in June, 1779, massacred a great number of his people, and dispossessed him of his government. The Kalora chieftain fled to Kandahar, from whence he addressed a petition to Timoor Shah, who at once took the field with his army to reinstate him in his rights. The king began by seizing Bawalpoor, in which place he found immense riches, and upon these he laid his hands. The insurgents after this success did not hold their ground anywhere, and their chiefs fled from the province, which the Shah placed under the control of the Kalora Emir, and then returned to Kabul; but he had scarcely left Scinde when the chief of the Talpooras again entered that territory and once more drove out the Kaloras. The embarrassments under which Timoor laboured at that time prevented him from promptly repressing this fresh outbreak: and it was only in 1786 that the Serdaree Serdarane Medad Khan could march there with a small corps d'armée, with which, on its entering Scinde, the contingent of the Khan of Kelat was to form a junction; this chief, however, was bound to the Talpooras by family ties, and on various pretences did not bring the reinforcement which by treaty he was obliged to furnish. In spite of this contretemps

Medad Khan marched upon the insurgents with his small force, but, being attacked by very superior numbers near the village of Djioond, he was beaten and obliged to retire and fortify himself in that locality.

Mir Fethi Khan then entered into negotiations with the Serdaree Serdarane, demanded to be invested with the same rights that the Shah of Afghanistan had formerly acknowledged, and which had been held by the chief of the Kaloras, promising for the future an exact payment of the tribute as well as the sum then due for arrears. Medad Khan accepted this arrangement, which was confirmed by his sovereign, but Mir Fethi Khan, who only wished to gain time to collect his treasure and his forces, in order that he might defy his suzerain with the greater chance of success, refused to pay the tribute the third year after his installation as Governor of Scinde, and proclaimed his independence. Timoor Shah being unable to send troops and thus oblige him to return to his duty, Scinde remained independent of Afghanistan up to the time of the Shah's death.

The second occasion on which this sovereign took the field in person was in his conquest of Sarmacand and Bokhara, to punish the inhabitants of Balkh and Akhcheh, who had driven out their Afghan governor and revolted against him at the instigation of Sultan Murad Khan, Emir of Bokhara, and of Mavar-ul-nahar. When the Shah approached Balkh, those who had raised the standard of rebellion, and in whose support Sultan Murad Khan had sent a contingent of troops, left the town to oppose the Shah, and encamped at a short distance from him. If Timoor Shah had at once attacked the Uzbeks he would most certainly have crushed them, for his army was much superior to theirs, not only in numbers but in the spirit of the troops; but the rivalry which existed between the serdars, and the vexation felt by those who commanded the tribes at being obliged to leave their lucrative appointments, caused them to temporize and thus compromise the success of the Afghan arms; and his attempts to conciliate these chiefs were so prolonged that the army was at last completely without provisions.

The fall of Timoor Shah was the object of the serdars, and this they hoped to accomplish without its appearing to be their fault, trusting that his successor would grant them the advantages which they had hoped, but in vain, to receive from him. The king penetrated their design, and to avoid an irreparable disaster came to an understanding with the rebels, withdrew from the conquest of Navar-ul-nahar, and retired to Kabul, preserving a feeble appearance of authority on Balkh and Akhcheh, which from this day became pretty nearly independent. They accepted, it is true, a governor named by Timoor Shah, but they took care previously to point out certain persons from amongst whom that officer should be taken. The authority of the governor thus chosen was very limited; the people he governed merely furnished him with the means of subsistence for himself and a very small number of personal servants; but they paid him neither taxes nor salary and subjected him to every kind of annoyance. The consequence of this was that Timoor Shah was at length unable to find any person who would accept the appointment of governor of these turbulent cities, which led to a hundred jokes and witticisms more or less wounding to the feelings of the sovereign, particularly from those who were hostile to him. The Loutis, who wandered from town to town with monkeys and other animals, taught them to cast earth upon their heads (a sign of the deepest grief amongst Asiatics) when they were asked whether they would be governors of Balkh or Akhcheh.

From the period at which Timoor Shah succeeded to the throne Khorassan had been in a permanent state of revolt. Shah Rokh Mirza, who recognised the suzerainty of this sovereign as he had done that of his father, claimed his assistance against his old friend Mamech Khan of Tchinaran, who had five years before seized and continued to hold possession of Meshed, in which city he exercised a most fearful tyranny. Timoor Shah sent 30,000 men, under the orders of the Serdaree Serdarane, to overthrow the usurper. On his arrival at Meshed Mamech Khan left the city and shut himself up in his fortress of Tchinaran, in which place Medad Khan thought it would be as well not to disturb him; he contented himself therefore by ordering his villages to be pillaged, his territory ravaged, and, replacing Shah Rokh at the head of the government of Meshed, he returned to Kabul; but he had scarcely reached the capital when news was brought to him that Mamech Khan had been enabled to collect a few thousand horsemen, and once more devastate the province, and that his position became every day more menacing. Timoor Shah was obliged to send Medad Khan to put down this fresh revolt, and on his arrival Mamech Khan again retired within the walls of his fortress, but this time the Afghans laid siege to the place, and soon forced him to surrender at discretion. The Serdaree Serdarane, however, treated Mamech with generosity, left him in possession of his Khanat, and was satisfied with accepting a light contribution in money towards the expenses of the war and a thousand beasts of burden loaded with provisions: after which he set out on his return to Kabul; but the simoom blew with such intensity when he arrived in the plains of Furrah that he died, and with him a great number of his soldiers.

A few days subsequently to this circumstance the Khorassanees were informed of it and immediately rose against the Afghans and their protégé Shah Rokh Mirza, which obliged Timoor Shah to send a third army the following year to reduce them to obedience. He placed these troops under the command of Ahmed Khan Noorzye, son of Nasser Ullah Khan, who, although with great difficulty, succeeded in putting down the revolt. From this moment up to the end of the reign of Timoor, the Afghans were never engaged in any conflict; nevertheless the year preceding the death of that prince was remarkable for an event in which the Shah was nearly coming to a violent end.

In accordance with his usual custom Timoor went to pass a few months at Peshawur, but this year he remained at that city a longer period than usual, detained there by an insurrectional movement which threatened to develop itself further and extend as far as Lahore. Arseleh Khan, of the Mohmund tribe, and Yaghoot Khan, chief of the eunuchs of the late king, who with several other Afghan chiefs were dissatisfied with Timoor, determined upon his ruin. It was agreed amongst them that Yaghoot Khan, who commanded the guard of the royal harem, should connive at the entrance of Arseleh Khan and his people when the king retired there, and put him to death, after which they were to proclaim his nephew, Iskander Khan, a son of Suleiman Mirza, king in his stead.

On the day agreed upon for the execution of this conspiracy, 2500 hill-riflemen, and as many resolute inhabitants of Peshawur, well armed, suddenly assembled in a large open space covered with ruins, habitually deserted and situated on the side of the grand square opposite to the citadel, on which a few thousand Kuzzilbash horse, forming the king's guard, were always encamped. It was about two hours after noon, the time at which eastern nations take their siesta; the palace guard were therefore all asleep, or very nearly so, and the conspirators made choice of this moment to penetrate into the citadel by a sally-port, of which Yaghoot Khan had given them the key. By a rare chance Timoor Shah had not yet fallen asleep, and, hearing the tumult and a distant hubbub of voices, he perceived at once that he was threatened by some impending danger, and quickly retired to the summit of a tower at one of the angles of the citadel looking into the large square. The assassins, never thinking for a moment that he would hide himself in a place where no one ever put his foot, did not search for him there and went on; but when they returned they were attracted by his shouts, and saw the king waving his Cashmeer turban in the air as a signal of distress to the Goolam Kuzzilbashes, who were snoring below; the conspirators endeavoured to get at him by breaking the doors, but one of them, being iron-bound and padlocked, resisted all their efforts to open it, which gave the guards time to come up and vigorously attack the insurgents, who were quickly reduced to the simple contingent of the mountaineers, for the Peshawur men had dispersed when they saw that the alarm was given. The Goolams, who were soon supported by other troops, cut the conspirators to pieces, and but very few of them were enabled to escape—Arseleh Khan fled to his tribe, who lived in the valleys enclosed between the mountains of the Haicht-naggar, a rough country, full of difficulties, in which the Afghan cavalry would have had but very little chance of success had they ventured to pursue him. Timoor employed cunning in his attempts to seize the culprit; he feigned forgiveness and a wish to pardon Arseleh Khan, declaring daily at his *durbar*, and also in private, that he admitted he had been occasionally unjust towards him, and that he desired nothing more than to be able to repair the injuries he had done him. He made these sentiments well known in public; and when he knew they had reached the ears of Arseleh Khan, he sent one of the great nobles of his court to him, accompanied by a large suite of servants carrying a Koran, on a page of which he had inscribed an oath that he would pardon his fault, and affixed his seal to this document. Arseleh Khan, placing confidence in the sanctity of the book which had received on its pages this solemn promise from the king, invited the envoy and his suite to lodge in his own house, treated him with great splendour and consideration, and after a few days returned with the embassy to Kabul; the Khan's throat was cut the day that he entered the city.

Timoor Shah, a little reassured by the death of this chief, now ordered a massacre of the people of Peshawur who had joined in the revolt, and fixed the extent of it to one in three of its inhabitants; this command was unfortunately but too well obeyed, and Peshawur was very nearly depopulated by these executions, which were preceded and followed by a general emigration.

From this period Timoor Shah became suspicious, morose, and restless, and his clemency, which had till then rendered his reign remarkable, entirely ceased, and it terminated in an act of unparalleled cruelty. His last days passed away in alternate paroxysms of remorse and fear; he could not quiet his conscience and absolve it from the guilt of the wholesale slaughter of which we have just spoken, nor the murder of Arseleh Khan, brought about by perjury, and also having carried off by force the wife of an Afghan of Kandahar, to give her to a certain Mohamed Khan, one of his favourites, who had conceived a passion for her. Timoor Shah survived only ten months after the attack on his life; and his death, in 1793, was occasioned by an inflammation of the intestines, accompanied by violent fits of vomiting. Several of his contemporaries, whom we have had occasion to consult on the subject of his death, assure us that he was poisoned by one of the women of his harem, the sister of a Popolzye chief, who was hostile to him.

In spite of the several acts which have just been mentioned, the reign of Timoor Shah is cited in Afghanistan for the justice, equity, and paternal feeling with which he treated his subjects. He had many difficulties to surmount; for the serdars who had placed his father on the throne, and divided with him the direction of affairs, considered themselves much more like the tutors of his son than his councillors. The king endeavoured for a long period to release himself from this thraldom, but, seeing that his efforts were vain, he gave himself up to that life of ease and effeminacy with which European authors have so sharply reproached him, without reflecting whether it was possible for him to follow a different line of conduct. They would have been less severe if they had given themselves the trouble to inquire what were the causes of this apathy. They heard from the Afghans that which they have themselves repeated; but we must not forget that this people admit amongst the number of their great men those only who gorge themselves with pillage, who carry war and devastation everywhere, and who satisfy them in their eager desire for riches; it was only by employing such means that the great Ahmed Shah, a sovereign, be it observed, highly to be respected as an Afghan, was enabled to make himself popular with the plundering tribes of which his nation was composed. His son, instead of enriching them by continual wars, was obliged to come to the assistance of those he had to protect by taking funds from his own treasury; and this was quite enough to bring upon him the slander and ill feeling of the people. An Afghan loves to live at other people's expense; everything which tends to make him respect the property of his neighbour, to be subject to laws which prevent him from ransacking and destroying, is opposed to his nature; is it, therefore, astonishing that, being animated by such sentiments, the reign of Timoor Shah should appear to him weak and effeminate? I had occasion, during my journey in Afghanistan, to converse with some respectable serdars, who, having held high positions at the court of this sovereign, were able to appreciate his character. These individuals assured me that the intelligence and activity of this prince were equal to his courage and firmness; and it was these qualities which had led his father to give him the preference over his other sons; but it would have been absolute folly for him to have entered into an open struggle with the old serdars, who were venerated by the Afghans, with a view of concentrating all the power within his own hands, for this contest could terminate only to his disadvantage, and would have ended in his complete ruin. He preferred the wise and prudent path of reasonable concessions to that dangerous, and always uncertain, one of civil war; if he was debauched, it may be affirmed that in this he only imitated the majority of Eastern sovereigns—even those who rank highest in the pages of historians. They have always considered, and will always consider, so long as there is no change of habits in Asia, the abuse of the physical powers and pleasures as the first and most imprescriptible of their rights. Timoor, however, without doubt would have been less effeminate if, like his father, he had had the power in his own hands; but, not having serious subjects to attend to, he gave himself up to frivolous ones.

When the serdars who had been the companions of Ahmed Shah were dead, their sons succeeded to the influence which the former had taken in the affairs of government, and Timoor was unable to resist their demands. These chiefs disposed of the tribes; they could alienate them from him in a moment, and he was, therefore, obliged to be on good terms with them. Unfortunately these young serdars were passionate and ambitious; being without the experience of their fathers, they never knew how to preserve amongst themselves that union which had existed amongst the latter; and Timoor, instead of finding in them the characteristics which are necessary to triumph over difficulties, passed his time in endeavouring to heal their misunderstandings, which could not be done without a great deal of tact, so that their feelings should not be wounded and that he should still appear to preserve the authority of a sovereign over them. It was the just medium that Timoor adopted with them all, and the clever concessions which he made to ambitious chiefs eager for change, which assured to him a reign of twenty years, exempt from the scenes of anarchy that stained with blood those of his successors. It was in consequence of his sons not having followed their father's example that they were hurled from the throne of Afghanistan, and ended their days by the sword or in exile.

Timoor Shah left thirty-six children; of these twenty-three were sons, namely—

Humayoon Mirza.—His mother was of the tribe of Suddozye.

Mahmood Mirza, Hadji Firooz Eddin Mirza.—Their mother was of the tribe of Popolzye.

Abbas Mirza, Kohendil Mirza.—Their mother was of the tribe of Isakzye.

Zeman Mirza, Shoodja-ool-Moolk Mirza.—Their mother was of the tribe of Yoosoofzye.

Ahmed Mirza, Mohamed Sultan Mirza, Yezdane Bakhch Mirza.—Their mother was of the tribe of Noorzye.

Kechver Mirza, Sultan Ali Mirza, Nadir Mirza.—Their mother was a great-grandchild of Nadir Shah.

Eyoob Mirza, Hassan Mirza.—Their mother was a Popolzye.

Echreff Mirza, Muzafer Mirza, Djehan Wala Mirza.—Their mother was of the tribe of Etchekzye.

Mohamed Murad Mirza, Mirane Mirza, Hoosein Mirza.—Their mother was of the tribe of Mohamedzye.

Achem Mirza, Chapoor Mirza.—Their mother was a Mogul.

It is essential that the reader should notice with attention the names of those princes who are born of the same mother, because the half-brothers habitually detest them, and in cases of revolt are nearly always united against them. In taking up arms they are nearly always sure to have the support of the tribe to which their mother belonged.

Nearly all these princes were, as may be seen by the above table, born of Afghan mothers, with the exception of Kechver, Sultan Ali, and Nadir, who were descended from a great-grandchild of Nadir Shah, and Achem and Chapoor Mirza, whose mother was a daughter of the Mogul Emperor Ahmed Shah Gourkanee, whom Timoor married in 1750. All these princes had each from ten to fifteen children; those who survived the disasters which have befallen their dynasty have sought refuge in India, where the greater number of them are pensioners of the East India Company.

CHAPTER IX.

Afghanistan at the death of Timoor — Intrigues for the succession — Payendeh Khan supports Zeman Mirza — Afghan tactics — Zeman is proclaimed Shah — He marches against his brother at Kandahar — Flight of Humayoon Mirza — Tyranny of Zeman Shah — His sanguinary acts — Gives up Balkh to Persia — Zeman marches against the Punjab — Humayoon seizes Kandahar — Zeman takes the city by treachery — Humayoon is made prisoner — His brother puts out his eyes — Zeman advances upon Scinde — Mahmood Mirza endeavours to intercept him — Battle of Gourrek — Zeman advances on Herat — Takes the city — Mahmood Mirza retires to Persia — Advances on Furrah — Battle of Emaret — Mahmood invests Herat — Cunning of Zeman Shah — Mahmood quits his camp — His allies are beaten and disperse — Zeman Shah arrives at Herat — Mahmood retires to Bokhara and Khiva — Revolt of the Sikhs — Zeman reduces Lahore — Disasters of his army — He reaches Kabul and Kandahar — Fatal tendencies of Shah Zeman — Discontent of the Afghans — The vizier Vefadar Khan — Conspiracy of the Serdars — Payendeh Khan and his accomplices executed — Flight of Fethi Khan — Revolts — Fethi Khan accompanied by Mahmood takes Furrah and Kandahar — The army deserts Zeman — Battle between the brothers — Zeman is beaten and his eyes put out — Vefadar Khan is executed — Zeman retires to Bokhara — Character of the Shah.

AFGHANISTAN, at the death of Timoor Shah, comprehended the principalities of Cashmeer, Lahore, Peshawur, Kabul, Balkh, Khulm, Kandahar, Mooltan, and Herat; those of Kelat and Beloochistan, as well as Persian Khorassan, acknowledged her as suzerain. Scinde also, though not having paid for five years the tribute agreed upon by Mir Fethi Khan, chief of the Talpooras, was nevertheless classed as amongst the number of her dependencies. Less far-sighted than his father Ahmed Shah, the deceased prince had neither designated the son who was to succeed him to the throne, nor obtained the recognition of any one of them by the serdars. The majority of his sons at the time of Timoor's death were governors of various provinces. The eldest, Humayoon Mirza, his successor to the throne by right, was at Kandahar, Mahmood Mirza at Herat, Abbas Mirza at Peshawur, Zeman Mirza at Kabul, Shoodja-ool-Moolk at Ghuznee, Kohendil at Cashmeer; and the royal corpse had not received the rites of sepulture when his sons were already disputing the succession. The majority of them had hastened to Kabul to be present when their father drew his last breath; the others, amongst whom were Humayoon Mirza and Mahmood Mirza, remained at their governments, where they had made themselves beloved by the people, and might reasonably hope for their assistance and support in retaining their power. Mahmood Mirza had promised his support to Humayoon Mirza to aid him in seizing upon the throne, supposing that his accession to it was disputed; and the latter, in acknowledgment of this service, had promised to confirm him in his government of Herat. The good understanding was not so complete amongst the other brothers assembled at Kabul.

Abbas Mirza, the fourth son of Timoor Shah, renowned for his Herculean strength, had, in the first instance, a chance of obtaining possession of the throne; but the serdars having refused to sanction his election before his father's obsequies were performed, the untoward delay modified the chances which he might have had of success; for each serdar attached himself to one or other of the princes, and endeavoured to influence him in favour of his own particular interests. The consequence of this was a complete dissension amongst the chiefs—each party flew to arms, and blood flowed in the streets of Kabul.

The most powerful and influential of all the serdars was Payendeh Khan, a son of that Hadji Djemal who withdrew his pretensions to the crown in favour of Ahmed Shah. Like his father he was the head of the family of the Mohamedzyes, and commanding-in-chief the tribe of the Barukzyes. This position gave him great influence amongst the people, who, after the descendants of Sudoo had been raised to the throne, had withdrawn from them a portion of their regard, which, replaced by fear, had been bestowed upon the descendants of Mohamed, whom they considered as alone capable of maintaining their privileges against the excessive power which they had given to their kings. Payendeh Khan gave his adhesion to Zeman Mirza, the fifth son of Timoor, and succeeded in attaching to his party the most influential of the Afghan nobility and the chiefs of the Kuzzilbashes at Kabul. Amongst the former were Ahmed Khan, Noorzye; Fath-Ullah Khan, Suddozye; Noor Mohamed Khan; Emin-ool-Moolk; Emir Islam Khan, Djevanchir; Djaffer Khan, Djevanchir; Mohamed Khan, Beyat; Emir Ullah Khan, Logheree; and many others of as high rank and equal power. With their assistance he was enabled in the first instance to calm the general excitement, and subsequently to elevate the Prince Zeman to the sovereign power in the following manner:—

On the proposition of Payendeh Khan, the princes agreed to assemble with the chiefs of tribes in order that the latter might proceed in all liberty to the election of a sovereign taken from amongst the former. Each of the sons of Timoor, accompanied by the serdars, came to this meeting; and in conformity with an understanding which had been already agreed to, no one had any arms, either concealed or otherwise, about his person. The place selected for this gathering belonged to Payendeh Khan; he had previously, and with great secrecy, strengthened all the doors and windows, and arranged the apartments in such a manner that no prison could have been more secure. When the princes were assembled, and some time had been occupied in discussion, Zeman, whose partisans had purposely abstained from appearing there, suddenly, under some slight pretence, left the assembly. Payendeh Khan, who, to prevent any suspicion, had not uttered a word in favour of his candidate, followed him out of the room, after which all those who remained in the house were placed under lock and key, and troops stationed round it.

The various factions, deprived of their chiefs thus retained prisoners and receiving no instructions, allowed themselves to be persuaded by Payendeh Khan, and acknowledged Zeman Mirza as their king. The new sovereign kept his brothers in confinement during five days without giving them anything to eat save two or three ounces of bread daily, the only way in which he could bring them to recognise his election. When they and the chiefs who had shared their captivity were released, they resembled so many skeletons, and left the inhospitable and treacherous roof under which they had passed these five days of suffering, only to be transferred to the citadel of the Bala Hissar, within the walls of which Zeman thought it would be prudent to place them.

The new sovereign commenced his reign by settling a pension upon the old and devoted servants of his father, and by various concessions attached to his person those serdars who had been opposed to him; but some few others, for the sake of example, he put to death; and as, after all, the Afghans were obliged to have a king, they contented themselves with the one that had thus been elected, who met with no further opposition in Kabul.

Humayoon Mirza, informed of the blow thus levelled at his

rights as the eldest son of Timoor, protested against the usurpation of Zeman, and accelerated his preparations for war; his brother, Mahmood Mirza, did the same; and a good many partisans came forward at their appeal to overthrow the usurper. But Zeman Shah, who could dispose of the greater and the richest portions of the kingdom, who was in possession of the royal treasure and the most warlike of the troops, did not remain inactive; in a very short space of time he had assembled a sufficient force to put down his two antagonists, and, directly he was in a position to take the field, he marched on Kandahar. Though Mahmood had not yet come to his assistance, Humayoon Mirza advanced boldly to meet Zeman, and came up with him at the little town of Kelat-i-Ghildjzye; a battle ensued between the rival brothers; Humayoon was completely beaten, and obliged to fly into Beloochistan, where he found an asylum at Kelat with the Emir Nasser Khan.

Mahmood Mirza, retained at Herat by the necessity of calming the excitement that reigned there, was not able to act up to the promise he had made his brother Humayoon to come to his support; and Zeman, after the defeat of the latter, made preparations to subdueMahmood, when several revolts which broke out at Kabul forced him to return there. At this period evil councillors obtained a power over the mind of the Shah; they persuaded him that the weakness and condescension of his father to the serdars had alone checked the increasing impulse given to the prosperity of Afghanistan by his ancestor Ahmed Shah, and they recommended him to alter this system, and concentrate the absolute power in his own hands.

To effect this object Zeman Shah commenced by taking the great appointments of the state from those who had inherited them as sinecures since the reign of that monarch. Even Payendeh Khan himself, to whom he was indebted for his throne, was not made an exception by the instigators of this violent change, for his influence considerably diminished, and these dismissals did not long suffice to appease the fears that his ambitious advisers suggested to Zeman Shah. Individuals of consideration were attracted to court on the faith of solemn oaths, arrested, imprisoned, or put to death, and these sanguinary executions spread consternation in Kabul, the citizens of which were soon brought under a yoke of iron. Such useless cruelties alienated the

Afghans from their new sovereign; and his brothers, who were released from the citadel almost immediately after they had been incarcerated, dispersed over the different provinces, and everywhere excited disobedience to his authority. Obliged to conspire in secret in presence of the troops that were sent to suppress the disorders of which they themselves were the instigators, they nevertheless ceased not by their intrigues to endeavour to accomplish the fall of their relative, and continued very dangerous to his power. Shah Zeman, fearing that a general reaction would be manifested against him, was afraid to put those who were in his power to death, as it was in the first instance his intention to do; but these quarrels between the sons of Timoor Shah were the prelude to scenes of carnage, in the midst of which the dynasty of the Suddozyes was to end.

It was about this time that Agha Mohamed Khan, founder of the dynasty of the Kadjars in Persia, sent Mohamed Hoosein Khan, Karaguzloo, as ambassador to Shah Zeman, requesting the cession of Balkh, which he required in order that he might be able to undertake in all security the expedition which he proposed to make against Beghee Khan, at that period king of Bokhara. Zeman Shah, being then greatly embarrassed, could not refuse this concession to the Kadjar, who was at Meshed with a numerous army; he consented, therefore, not only to his demand, but promised also to assist him with his own troops. Subsequently Agha Mohamed Khan having been called to the west by the menaced invasion of the Russians, this treaty was never carried out.

During the events that we have related above the fire was smouldering which was so soon to burst forth in the midst of the Afghan nation. The Punjab, annexed to the kingdom by Ahmed Shah, attempted to regain its independence, and the Shah Zeman immediately took the field to chastise the rebels; but he had scarcely crossed the Indus when he learnt that, assisted by the Emirs of Beloochistan, his brother Humayoon had seized upon Kandahar. This intelligence obliged him to put off his expedition to Lahore, and he set off by forced marches, and by the direct road across the mountains, to attack the former city. On the approach of his brother, Humayoon was betrayed by his Afghan partisans, who wished to seize and deliver him up to Zeman; but, assisted by the Beloochees, he succeeded in escaping from them, and again fled to Beloochistan. The Shah sent a thousand cavalry in pursuit of him, from whose clutches he escaped for several days; but having, unfortunately for him, returned on his road to gain Herat, they came up with and arrested him in the district of Zemindavar, after which, and in obedience to the orders they had received from Shah Zeman, they put out his eyes. The Shah, delighted with this fresh act of cruelty, which, he fancied, ought to strengthen the power he had usurped, thought of marching against the Emirs of Scinde, as much with the desire of punishing them for the support they had given to Humayoon, as to force them to pay the arrears of tribute which they owed, and which they had ceased to pay several years before the death of Timoor Shah.

Shah Zeman had reached the Bolan Pass when he heard that Mahmood Mirza, after having established his power at Herat, had just taken the field with an excellent army, and intended to advance upon his rear while he was engaged with his enemies in Scinde. Forced therefore by necessity, he came to terms with Fathi Ullah Khan Talpoora, and for the sum of 300,000*l.* gave up the remainder of the arrears, which amounted to three times that sum, and confirmed him in the government of Scinde, after which he moved by forced marches to meet his brother.

Mahmood Mirza, quite as well informed of the movements of Zeman as the Shah was of his, halted when he heard of the king's return to Kandahar, and having taken up a position in the mountains of the Siah-bend, across which he had advanced, only moved forward when he learnt that Zeman was two or three marches from his encampment. The two armies came in sight, and attacked at Gourrek, a large village situated between Girishk and Zemindavar, and fought with fury during fifteen successive hours. At length fortune declared itself against Mahmood Mirza, who, beaten, turned, and cut off from his communications, was obliged to fly and retire within the walls of Furrah, followed only by a hundred of his dependants.

After this Shah Zeman, without giving himself any further trouble about his antagonist, marched straight upon Herat, and encamped under its walls, but several assaults which he made were repulsed with energy, and he was on the point of retreating when the mother of Mahmood Mirza arrived in his camp to make proposals in the name of her son, who she assured Zeman had no desire for the throne, and would be quite satisfied simply with the government of Herat. The Shah, who was anxious to carry his arms to other points that were seriously menaced, was delighted with the proposition, and accepted it immediatetly.

Kamran Mirza, the son of Mahmood, and Hadji Firooz Eddin, his brother, who had been appointed governor of the city in Mahmood's absence, had remained within the citadel, and were afraid to go into the town lest the fortress should be taken from them by some treacherous act on the part of the garrison. Not having received any information respecting the transaction which had just taken place between the two brothers, their joy was not greater than their astonishment when they saw Zeman Shah in full retreat, which they attributed to the arrival of Mahmood Mirza at the head of fresh forces. Desirous, therefore, of making a diversion in his favour, they assembled in haste the troops that were at hand, and pursued the Shah; but they had scarcely reached the royal residence of Roouz-bagh, situated seven miles south of Herat, when the Parsivan, Kalech Khan (a serdar of the Taymoonis, suzerain lord of Khaff, a man of great influence in the principality, and reputation in warlike affairs), who had been intrusted by Kamran and Firooz Eddin with the command of the citadel during their absence, despatched a messenger to Zeman Shah to inform him that he held the fortress at his disposal, and that he ought to come immediately and occupy it with his own troops.

The princes, informed of this unfortunate circumstance, returned instantly to Herat, which still held out for them, and attacked the citadel on all sides; but it was in vain that they cannonaded it. Kalech Khan, whom they summoned, and ordered to return to his duty, answered only by redoubling his fire. The place was strong, well provisioned, and capable of resisting any assault for several months, while it required only two days for Zeman Shah to come and occupy it. Directly he appeared, the princes, seeing themselves abandoned by their partizans, fled in the direction of Khorassan; and Zeman, meeting with no further opposition, took possession of Herat, where he remained four months. He appointed his son Kaissar Mirza governor of the province, and gave the command of the Heratee troops, as well as 1000 Afghan horse, to the Serdar Kalech Khan, who had delivered up the place to him. Zeman Khan, Popolzye, was appointed Vizier to Kaissar Mirza, and received the title *in partibus* of governor of Persian Khorassan, which Zeman Shah had the intention of uniting with

Afghanistan. With this view he left a corps of troops with the Popolzye Serdar, independently of those commanded by Kalech Khan, in order that he might be enabled to invade that province, the conquest of which was resolved upon. After having taken these measures the king returned to Kandahar, where he remained but a short time, and a few days after arrived at Kabul.

But Mahmood Mirza, without either money or an army, could do but little, and came to the determination of going to Teheran and demanding assistance from Feth Ali, the Shah of Persia, who had for some years been seated on the throne of the Kadjars; and this sovereign promised him support and his reinstallation in the government of Herat, on condition that he admitted his suzerainty. This occurrence took place in the year 1798, during which the revolt of Sedik Khan obliged Feth Ali to proceed to the Azerbaidjan; but before his departure he recommended Mahmood Mirza to the care of the Emir Assad Ullah Khan, governor of Kachan, and son of the Ethemad Dooulet, Hadji Ibrahim of Shiraz. Mahmood Mirza followed the Emir Assad Ullah Khan to Kachan, but, observing that Feth Ali Shah prolonged his stay in the north of his kingdom, the prince got weary of waiting for the support that had been promised him, and wrote to the Shah, requesting that he might be permitted to leave the residence which he had assigned him. The King of Persia having consented to this request, Mahmood proceeded to Khorassan, where he hoped to be able to raise some recruits; nor was he deceived in this hope, for Mir Ali Khan, an Arab, the governor of the district of Ghain, espoused his cause, and they took the field with 3000 infantry, marching in the first instance in the direction of Furrah. The inhabitants of this city were favourable to the cause of Mahmood, and directly they heard of his approach they came out several days' march to meet him, when a great number of them enrolled themselves in his army.

The news of the arrival of Mahmood Mirza had spread rapidly in Herat, much exaggerating his success, and he was described as having arrived at Furrah with 50,000 men, subduing everything on his road. These reports carried consternation into the minds of the citizens; all those who had deserted the Prince Mahmood, dreading his anger, made their preparations for departure; and the Prince Kaissar, himself believing in the accuracy of the intelligence, repaired and provisioned the citadel in great haste; but more truthful accounts followed and modified the alarm of the prince and the scared inhabitants.

The report of this triumphant march brought to Mahmood Mirza's standard a reinforcement of several thousand men; amongst these was the Noorzye Serdar, Djabber Khan, who brought with him a contingent of a thousand horsemen; but when he saw what a small army Mahmood's was, he repented of the step he had taken, and under cover of a dark night quitted the camp, and proceeded in great haste to Herat, where he made the real state of things known. Reassured by this information, Kaissar Mirza assembled the troops of Kalech Khan, and, uniting them to those of Zeman Khan, Popolzye (who, on learning the news, had returned promptly from Khorassan, in the direction of which he had moved), marched with these two divisions against his uncle. Mahmood, seeing that Furrah was favourable to his cause, left that town on his right, advanced at once to meet his opponent, came up with and attacked him near the village of Emaret, and routed him completely.

The vanquished army retired in haste to Herat, and closed the gates. Mahmood Mirza followed, but, being unable to invest the place entirely by reason of the smallness of his force, he determined to encamp at a spot on the banks of the Heri-rood about three miles from the walls. The Vizier Zeman Khan, having discovered that the sympathies of the Heratees were in favour of Mahmood, conceived that a temporizing line of conduct could not but be advantageous to the latter: he resolved therefore, as force was not on the side of Kaissar, to obtain the victory by cunning. After having obtained the permission of that prince, he wrote a letter to Mir Ali Khan, the Arab, as if it was the reply to some terms of arrangement which the latter had made to Kaissar Mirza, and which consisted in his obtaining some favour of that prince, in exchange for which Mir Ali promised to deliver Mahmood Mirza into his hands. The adroit Vizier confided this letter to an intelligent man, and advised him to manage in such a way that he should be suspected and arrested by some of the prince's troops, and then pretend great anxiety that the letter in question should not be seen. The scheme was carried out as he wished; the camp guard seized the messenger and conducted their prisoner to Mahmood Mirza, to whom they presented the letter which they had taken. Mahmood, alarmed at the snare thus revealed to him, asked the advice of an Afghan noble, Mohamed Akrem Khan, as to what steps should be taken, and he advised him to avoid by flight the trap that had been laid for them.

Nevertheless, the contents of this letter did not remain so entirely a secret from Mir Ali Khan, but that he received some information respecting it. He hastened, therefore, immediately to Mahmood, and swore and protested in the most energetic terms to the truth of his devotion to his person and his cause. The prince feigned to believe him; but, when night came, he fled from the camp, accompanied by his son Kamran, his brother Hadji Firooz Eddin, the Serdar Akrem Khan, and a few devoted servants; and when he thought himself in safety he sent his son and his brother to Teheran to claim the promised assistance of Feth Ali Shah, proceeding himself to Bokhara to endeavour to interest the Emir in his favour.

Mahmood Mirza had scarcely left the camp and his ally Mir Ali Khan, than Kaissar Mirza was informed of the fact, and he profited by the confusion and astonishment into which this event had thrown the Ghainians, to fall upon and rout them thoroughly—a great many were made prisoners and brought to Herat. As for Mir Ali Khan, he had great difficulty in effecting his escape, and reached Ghain with only a few horse, having met much privation and danger on the road.

Shah Zeman, then at Kabul, was soon informed that his brother Mahmood had returned to Afghanistan, and some false reports induced him to believe that Kaissar Mirza, after having been beaten at Emaret, had also evacuated the city of Herat on the approach of Mahmood, who had taken possession. He therefore assembled his army without loss of time, and took the field with a view to its recapture, for the country and the roads were so thoroughly scoured by the partisans of Mahmood, that no messenger had been able to reach him with true intelligence of the actual state of things; it was only on his arrival at Herat itself that he knew positively what was passing. Delighted to find that the evil was not so great as he had anticipated, he encamped his army on the banks of the Heri-rood, and, followed by his court, subsequently entered the city. When he learnt that his brother had gone to Bokhara he immediately despatched the Kazee, Abdul Irak, to the Emir of that country, to represent that by the terms of the treaty concluded between Timoor Shah and the Emir he was bound to deliver up Mahmood Mirza to him as a disturber of the tranquillity of the Afghan kingdom; but that, nevertheless, if he found himself bound by the duties of hospitality, he should remain satisfied if he would order the prince to be watched at Bokhara in such a manner that he could not escape and again foment discord in his dominions. Sultan Ali Murad detained the Afghan envoy for some time at his court without giving him a categorical answer: he finished, nevertheless, by promising that Mahmood Mirza should be detained in his capital, and that he would answer for it *with his head that he should not leave it.* The Kazee left Bokhara without having comprehended the meaning of these words of the Emir, who had dwelt especially upon the last part of his reply, the real and secret intention of which was to gratify upon the fugitive prince the mortal hatred which he felt for the family of the Suddozyes; his death was indeed only deferred at the earnest request of a great and influential Uzbek nobleman, by name Fezl Ahmed, who interested himself in his behalf. Mahmood, informed by Fezl Ahmed of the plot which was in preparation against his life, managed to deceive the vigilance of his guards and fled to Khiva, when Mohamed Rahim Khan, the sovereign of that Khanat, for some time treated him with great hospitality; but as in the end he was unable to render him the assistance which he required to renew the war, Mahmood Mirza left Khiva and rejoined his son and his brother at Teheran, to which city he had sent them subsequently to his flight from the camp of the Emir of Ghain.

After a residence of four months at Herat, Zeman Shah received letters from the governor of Peshawur informing him that on his departure from Kabul the Sikh mountaineers of Yambou had made a descent upon Lahore, and plundered and sacked the city. The Serdar Ahmed Khan, at the time governor of Lahore, did his best to frustrate their intention; he went out and attacked them, but his soldiers fled at the first onset, and the Khan was killed in endeavouring to cover their retreat. On the receipt of this disastrous intelligence, Shah Zeman appointed Mir Efzel Khan, son of the Serdaree Serdarane, Medad Khan, vizier to his son Kaissar, after which, taking with him Zeman Khan, Popolzye, in whose military talents he had the greatest confidence, he left immediately for Kabul by the difficult and mountainous road which traverses the country of the Hazarahs, Poocht Kooh, accompanied only by one hundred and fifty horse. As to the mass of his army, artillery, and baggage, he sent them by Kandahar, under the conduct of his minister Vefadar Khan and the Serdar Ahmed Khan Noorzye. Zeman Shah, who arrived in the capital in twelve days, took a large sum from his treasury to make formidable preparations for carrying on the war with activity; and directly the troops which arrived by way of Kandahar had joined those he had just raised he left for the Punjab. The Sikh mountaineers abandoned Lahore at his approach and retired into their fastnesses; he therefore took peaceable possession of the city. As the inhabitants had taken no part in the last revolt, in which they had been maltreated by the mountaineers, he thought he could place confidence in them, and consented to the request which they made, namely, that in future the governor of Lahore should be selected by the Shah from amongst the principal Sikh chiefs, to the exclusion of the Afghans. He chose, therefore, for this post one of them, by name Runject Sing, who had even then acquired a great reputation for talent and courage; and after having duly installed him, Zeman Shah departed on his return to Kabul. This march was for him and his army one long series of misfortunes; his artillery and a great part of his baggage were lost at the passage of the Jelum; the rain, which fell in torrents and almost daily, had so broken up the roads that they were impassable; the soldiers, worn out by their sufferings, either dropped to the rear or deserted, and the plundering tribes took advantage of the distressed condition of the army to pillage the baggage and strip the stragglers, who were incapable of defending themselves. In fact, it was the *débris* of an army of attenuated men, which, harassed by a thousand miseries and privations, that Zeman succeeded in bringing into Peshawur. Here he remained a month to rest and refresh his troops, after which, having installed his brother, Shooja-ool-Moolk, as governor of the city, he proceeded to Kabul, where he made but a very short stay, for he was under the necessity of going on to Kandahar in spite of the severity of the winter to suppress the disposition to revolt in that city.

Such revolts originated more especially in the discontent which the powerful tribe of the Barukzyes felt at seeing their chiefs, the Mohamedzyes, set aside and debarred from holding any public appointment, and meeting with no consideration at court. The reader should remember that, from the day on which Sudoo and Mohamed had been raised to a superior rank by Shah Abbas the Great, the descendants of the first had enjoyed under the Seffavean dynasty an almost regal power in Afghanistan. The descendants of the second, without having so great an influence, held nevertheless the highest appointments in the state, and were not less venerated than the Suddozyes. When Ahmed Shah ascended the throne, he, out of gratitude to Hadji Djemal, a chief of the Mohamedzyes, respected the privileges of that family, the chiefs of which constantly held the most important commands in his army and the great offices at his court. Timoor Shah, who followed the example of his father, had the tact always to attach them to his party, and Zeman Shah was the first who dared to alter this state of things, which, sanctioned by time, had all the force of law.

Payendeh Khan, chief of the Mohamedzyes, was, as we have already remarked, stripped of all the appointments that he held, and this was the first grievance of the Barukzyes against royalty. The prime minister of Zeman Shah, Vefadar Khan, although belonging to the royal tribe of Popolzye, was of low extraction. The Shah did nothing without having first taken his advice, and this personage was the instigator of all the harsh measures which the Shah had adopted against the great families of the kingdom ; Vefadar Khan found his own interest in the confiscations which habitually followed, and they also delivered him from dangerous rivals. Zeman remained deaf to the milder counsels which were given him, and a fatality seemed to urge him forward from day to day in this impolitic and unjust path. The prime minister, having sprung from the lower ranks of the nobility, was despised by the higher, and he revenged himself by oppressing them and elevating unknown persons in their place, who became so many tools in his own hands. The system thus adopted by Zeman of governing in the most absolute manner, without the concurrence and support of the serdars, had nevertheless, up to this time, produced only irritation in the public mind, and some partial revolts ; but the discontent was general, particularly amongst the most influential and powerful chiefs, who had all of them been more or less despoiled. Although Vefadar Khan was not ignorant of the extent to which he was detested by these persons, he played nevertheless a double game, and nourished in their minds sentiments of hostility to the king. The Khan endeavoured to compromise his sovereign in their eyes, by making them believe that, in whatever he did, he simply executed the wishes of the Shah, and that his intervention with the king was the means of saving them from much greater disasters. His friendly protestations were always accompanied by hypocritical marks of interest in their behalf, such as the remission of a tax or the concession of some land, and led them to believe that he had great difficulty in procuring these favours from the Shah, regretting that it was not in his power to render them a greater service, thus leading them to hope that they would be in a much better position in future. In this way he by turns flattered and caressed all parties, boasting everywhere the favours he had granted, and seeking every opportunity of laying upon the king all the odium of his tyranny and the bloody executions of which he himself was the sole originator, hoping by such conduct to overthrow his sovereign, and by these intrigues attain himself the regal power. He fancied he should obtain his end by exciting, when the propitious moment arrived, a tumult amongst the people, and expected to receive the support of the new serdars of his own creation, who were devoted to him. His numerous emissaries glided amongst the populace, and, though apparently perfectly disinterested, worked upon them for the vizier's own purposes. The brothers of the king also were under his influence, and he made use of them and led each in his turn to believe that he was endeavouring to raise him to the throne. The intrigues and underhand practices of this ambitious man proved that he had as much craft and subtlety as he had talent for governing; the steps he took were always well considered, and to the point, and his plan was so well conducted that it might have succeeded if he had had the boldness to bring it more rapidly to an issue; but the heads of a few more serdars, who had taken umbrage at him, were wanting: he temporized, therefore, and this delay was fatal.

The Afghan serdars, for the most part discontented, formed a secret league, in order that they might come to some understanding as to the measures that must be taken to free themselves from the iron yoke and sanguinary persecutions which weighed upon them; but to give a greater chance of success to their enterprise, they delegated five of the most powerful amongst them, who alone were to decide upon the means to be employed—the others binding themselves to be ready on the day appointed, and to execute without hesitation whatever should be determined upon. As the police of Vefadar Khan was perfectly organized, and nothing escaped their Argus eyes, the five delegates fixed upon the house of a dervish, in high repute for his sanctity, as their place of meeting, for his residence had been always frequented by the most considerable of the Afghan nobility, who went by the appellation of his *murids*. He never received more than six persons at a time, and his door was shut against every one until these six departed to make way for others. Payendeh Khan had the cleverness to induce this holy man to join the conspirators, and he trusted that, by meeting at his house and taking advantage of the custom so long established there, he and the other delegates would escape the inquiries which might arise. After a lively discussion at one of these meetings, in which each of them stated the grievances of his tribe, it was admitted that their nation had suffered beyond what any men of spirit could tolerate—that Zeman Shah and his minister ought to be overthrown, and the first replaced by the prince Shooja-ool-Moolk, his half-brother, at that time governor of Peshawur.

The chiefs present at this meeting were Payendeh Khan, Mohamed Sherif Khan, Moonshee Bashee (cashier-in-chief), Yoosoof Ali Khan, chief of the eunuchs, Sultan Khan, Noorzye, and Rahim Khan, Alizye. Before separating they fixed upon a day for the execution of their project, and also drew up several articles, forming a kind of constitution, which they were to give to their countrymen. The principal clauses in this document were, that henceforth the crown should be elective; that the Serdars alone had the right to vote at such election, and also to depose those sovereigns who proved themselves unworthy of the trust which had been reposed in them. But unfortunately the conspirators procrastinated, and their plans were betrayed to the prime minister by the Moonshee Bashee. Vefadar Khan, thinking this an admirable opportunity of getting rid of his principal opponents at one fell swoop, immediately informed the Shah of the conspiracy which had been revealed, who recommended that the greatest secrecy should be observed, and at once relieved his guards, of whose fidelity he was doubtful, replacing them by others on whom he thought he could rely. The following day he made considerable presents to his servants and officers, and also to the people, to dispose them in his favour, and on the succeeding one sent for all the chiefs who were concerned in the plot; but separately, and under the pretext that he was desirous of conversing with them upon public affairs, so that they should not have the least suspicion of his motive. However, on their arrival at the palace, they were seized and imprisoned in the citadel. A few hours after the Shah ascended the throne in great state, and, ordering them to be brought into his presence, demanded why they had conspired against him? to which they replied, that they had sworn to dethrone him, but not to put him to death; that they never could have had an idea of attacking his royal person if they had not been firmly convinced that all their representations to induce him to dismiss his vizier would be fruitless; it was his ruin alone they were bent upon, and it was the hope of putting an end to this wretch that had led them to conspire against their king. After having listened to this avowal, Zeman Shah ordered them to be executed in his presence, their bodies to be left on the public square outside the citadel, and remain there for three days exposed to the public gaze.

As he now feared some movement on the part of the Barukzyes, the chief of which tribe he had just put to death, he ordered that all the Mohamedzye serdars should be arrested, but the greater part of them, having been warned in time, were enabled to save themselves by flight, or take refuge in the mosque of Ahmed Shah,—a sanctuary never violated. Fethi Khan, the eldest son of Payendeh Khan, who was more particularly sought after by the express orders of the Shah, with a view of putting him to death, also escaped the vigilance of the soldiers that were sent in pursuit of him. Having received notice of their intentions, he got over the walls, and, having excellent horses awaiting him in a garden adjacent to the city, he reached Girishk, seventy-three miles distant, in eight hours. From thence he took the road over the mountains and across country, in order that no trace should be found of him, and directed his course to Persia, where he rejoined Mahmood Mirza, who, as we have already remarked, had, for the second time, taken up his residence at the court of the Kadjars. On this occasion, as on the former one, he had been very well received by Feth Ali Shah, who had placed himself at the head of an army, with a view of reinstating him in his government of Herat; but on his arrival at Nishapoor he learnt that fresh disturbances had broken out in the Azerbaidjan, which obliged him to return to Irak with his troops, and dismiss Mahmood Mirza, to whom he gave a subsidy and assigned Turchiz as his place of residence, promising that he would send him troops when order was restored in the north of the empire, so that the prince might proceed against Herat. It was at Turchiz that the Serdar Fethi Khan joined Mahmood Mirza, and the greater part of his brothers soon arrived at the same place, who, like him, had also their father's death to avenge.

After the sanguinary executions of the chiefs at Kandahar, the Afghans in all parts of the kingdom rose against Zeman Shah. The Punjab and Peshawur in particular openly raised the standard of revolt. There were also some attempts at insurrection in Kabul, which obliged the King to proceed there in great haste; but fearing also for the tranquillity of Kandahar, he left there a part of his army, and the Serdar Mir Ali Khan, a devoted, energetic, and intelligent man, as governor.

While Zeman Shah was in a state of complete uncertainty as to what step he should take to pacify his kingdom, Fethi Khan, who had, as well as his brothers, devoted himself to the cause of Mahmood Mirza, urged that prince to enter Afghanistan once more, and overthrow his brother. Their pressing solicitations at length prevailed, and he marched on Ghain, but, on his arrival in that district, he saw that the inhabitants did not feel disposed to pardon him for the check they had sustained, owing to his flight when they formed part of his army before Herat, and that in consequence they were very little inclined to assist him. Mahmood almost regretted having left Turchiz, and thought of returning; but Fethi Khan somewhat restored his courage, and induced him to renounce this intention. At the same time he sent two of his brothers to the fortress of Furrah, to endeavour to keep matters quiet and obtain intelligence; this was easy enough, for the inhabitants of that town were entirely devoted to Mahmood Mirza, to whom they opened their gates when he presented himself before them, accompanied only by eighteen horsemen, which formed all his army. This success obtained for him the support of some chiefs of Khorassan, and he soon found himself at the head of a small force. He then made an appeal to the Afghan nation, and in the manifesto which he issued he drew a vivid picture of the cruelties and vices of Zeman Shah and his minister Vefadar Khan, and announced his design of marching on Kabul, to deliver the people from their oppression. The tribe of the Barukzyes, who recognised Fethi Khan as their chief, hastened *en masse* to place themselves under the orders of their young general, and this example was soon followed by the greater number of the Dooranee tribes, when Mahmood marched on Kandahar. The governor, Mir Ali Khan, informed of his approach, went out to meet him at the head of four thousand cavalry, but, completely routed and forced to fly, he had scarcely time to retire within the citadel. Mahmood Mirza followed him step by step, and invested the city, which he besieged without success during forty-two days. At length, on the forty-third the assault was given, and Fethi Khan, who conducted it, was the first man that scaled the walls, and his soldiers followed rapidly. They were treacherously aided by Bakhch Khan and Hassan Khan, two Afghan chiefs, who, ostensibly of the Shah Zeman's party, were secretly doing all they could to make that of Mahmood Mirza triumph, and but for their help the place would not have been taken without great difficulty. When Mir Ali Khan saw that the affair was desperate, he ordered these two traitors to be brought into his presence, and, feeling sure of their perfidy, put them to death on the spot, after which he mounted his horse and escaped by a secret door, accompanied only by a few horsemen.

Directly Mahmood Mirza was in possession of Kandahar he was obliged to levy a large sum upon the inhabitants for the maintenance of his army; but the persuasive manners and talents of Fethi Khan induced them to support this contribution without murmuring, and they remained devoted to the prince. On hearing what was passing at Kandahar, Zeman Shah sent an army of 15,000 horse, under the command of the Serdar Ahmed Khan, against Mahmood, for he was averse to leaving the capital himself for fear he should lose it in his absence. This officer was but little satisfied with the Shah, and still less so with his minister Vefadar Khan, and, in the hope that he would be better treated by Mahmood, he went over to him, with all his army, at Mookpoor. In anticipation of ulterior events, Shah Zeman had, after the departure of Ahmed Khan, assembled fresh troops, but when they heard of the defection of the corps under that serdar they at once disbanded and retired to their homes. An outbreak occurring at the same time in Kabul, Zeman Shah was under the necessity of evacuating the city and retiring in the direction of

Jellalabad. On leaving the gates of the capital he had with him only two hundred cavalry and four hundred artillerymen, with their guns, stores, and ammunition ; his minister, Vefadar Khan, and the Serdar Zeman Khan, Popolzye, were the only chiefs who remained faithful, and they retired with him and his party within the fortified village of Kaleh Acheg, the name of its owner, and immediately set to work to repair the walls and provision it. From hence a fresh appeal was made to the partizans of the Shah, and, as the royal treasure was still in his hands, he was joined by a pretty good number of recruits, but much more in the hope of receiving high pay than from any devotion to his person. However that might be, Zeman again found himself in a position to give battle to his brother.

After the 15,000 cavalry of Ahmed Khan had joined the army of Mahmood Mirza, the prince marched rapidly upon and seized Kabul, without meeting with the slightest resistance. The Emir Islam Khan and Djaffer Khan, two Kuzzilbash chiefs, who only could have defended the city, were allied by marriage to the Mohamedzyes, and went over to their side the moment they appeared.

Mahmood, thus successful, decided upon dislodging Zeman Shah from the fortified position he had taken up. The task was a difficult one, for the latter had saved all his artillery, while the prince had not one single piece to oppose to him. Nevertheless, he hesitated not, and again took the field. The armies of the two brothers met at the halt of Ouchpane, when that of the Shah was completely beaten and dispersed, and he had the greatest difficulty in regaining Kaleh Acheg. Mahmood followed him, and immediately assaulted his adversary's stronghold, but, defended by both nature and art, and garrisoned by brave men determined to die for their king, it resisted for eleven days the continuous efforts of the besiegers. However, the time had arrived when they could hold out no longer, and the Shah, accompanied by the serdars who were with him, escaped during the night, and retired into another small fortress near Jugdulluk, also belonging to Acheg Khan. This chief, alarmed at the probability that disastrous consequences might result to him for the hospitality he had shown to his sovereign, sent a messenger to Mahmood to inform him of the Shah's retreat. The prince immediately sent a serdar, with a strong escort and a surgeon, to the spot which the Khan had designated, when Zeman was taken prisoner, and, in conformity with the orders of Mahmood, his eyes were immediately put out — a punishment he richly merited for the same cruelty which he had practised upon Humayoon Mirza, his elder brother. Vefadar Khan, Zeman Khan, Popolzye, and Mohamed Khan, the brother of the Vizier, also taken prisoners with Shah Zeman, were sent to Kabul, and there publicly executed. Thus terminated the career of this ambitious minister, who could only govern by intrigue and murder, and this in order that he might supplant his master, which he would have done, had not his courage failed him at the moment his plan was on the eve of execution. He perished by a death to which he had condemned hundreds, and which he so thoroughly deserved himself.

Though blind, Shah Zeman, with the assistance of a few devoted friends, subsequently managed to deceive the vigilance of his guards, and fled to Bokhara, where fresh misfortunes awaited him. His daughter, who followed him in his exile, and who was remarkable for her great beauty, was torn with violence from him by the Emir Haidar Turreh, who had inherited from his father a hatred of the Suddozye family. After this abduction he was on the point of putting Zeman to death, which would infallibly have happened, if he had not again succeeded in making his escape.

From Bokhara this king, hitherto so powerful, but now so unfortunate, went to Herat, which was then governed by the Prince Hadji Firooz Eddin, half-brother of the Shah Mahmood, who respected his misfortunes and gave him a generous reception; and after having treated him in the most hospitable manner during several months, he gave him an escort which secured his safe retreat to India. Zeman retired to Loodiana, where he lived on a pension from the East India Company, devoted to the observances of his faith, and did not at any subsequent period mix himself up with the revolutions of which his country was so frequently the theatre after his fall. He was still living in 1846. This prince, like all the Afghans, was cruel; but this arose much more from the fact that he was influenced by a bad minister, in whom he placed too much confidence, and who knew how to inspire him with chimerical fears, than because he was of a naturally cruel disposition, and wished to gratify it. His greatest crime was, that he was absolute, and would reign on that principle. This wounded the pride of the serdars, and was in opposition to the received opinions amongst them as to the extent of the sovereign power. With a different vizier, he might have hoped that his reign would be as long, and possibly more glorious, than that of his father, for he was personally very brave, very active, always on horseback, bringing one war to a conclusion only to commence another; nor was he wanting in intelligence: but he lost all his future chances by making the Mohamedzye chiefs discontented, for their rights to the great offices of the state were quite as sacred in the eyes of the Afghans as those of the Suddozyes to the throne. The moment he endeavoured to abrogate those rights his fall became certain; but, in spite of the sanguinary executions he was guilty of at the instigation of his minister, the Afghans have a greater respect for his memory than that of any of the other sons of Timoor Shah.

CHAPTER X.

Mahmood ascends the throne — First acts of the Shah — Revolt of the Ghildjyes — Kaissar Mirza is driven from Herat — Hadji Firooz Eddin made governor of that city — Kaissar Mirza attacks him, but is obliged to retire — Kamran, a son of Mahmood, and Kaissar alternately take possession of Kandahar — Disorders and conflict with the Kuzzilbashes — Peace is restored at Kabul — Conspiracy against Shah Mahmood — He is dethroned — His brother Shooja succeeds him — Mahmood remains a prisoner — Kamran is expelled from Kandahar by Kaissar Mirza — The latter, defeated by the Heratees, evacuates the city — The Persians besiege Herat — They are beaten and retire — Shah Shooja marches against the Talpooras — Returns to Kabul — English embassy to Kabul — Difficulties of the reign of Shah Shooja — The Serdar Fethi Khan intrigues and flies from Kabul — He is arrested by Kaissar Mirza — Dost Mohamed escapes and pillages Bakooa — Shere dil Khan assists Shah Mahmood to escape — The latter and the Mohamedzyes release Fethi Khan — Mahmood marches on Kabul — Seizes the city — Battle of Neemla — Shooja is put to flight — Endeavours to keep the field — Retires to Loodiana.

AFTER seven years of conflict and misfortunes Mahmood Mirza ascended the throne of his fathers in the year 1800, and when Zeman Shah was overthrown he took the title of Shah, and made his solemn entry into Kabul. He behaved with the utmost generosity to his troops, even to such an extent that he exhausted the greater part of the treasure accumulated in the coffers of the state by his father and grandfather. He also enriched the chiefs who had assisted him, and gave them the highest appointments at his court: the Serdar Fethi Khan received the title of Shah Doort Khan;* Shere Mohamed Khan, son of the Vizier Shah Velee Khan, was named Mooktar-ed-Dooulet, and to him was delegated the government of the kingdom; the Serdar Abdullah Khan, Ali Kioozye, father of Yar Mohamed Khan, who had been confined in the Bala Hissar by Shah Zeman, was released from that fortress, and made Governor of Cashmeer; and, finally, he sent his son Kamran Mirza, with several brothers of the Serdar Fethi Khan, against Shooja-ool-Moolk, who commanded at Peshawur, to take the city and seize that prince. Shooja did not wait for them, but fled at their approach; so Kamran took possession of Peshawur without any fighting.

* Friend of the king.—*Ferrier.*

A few capital punishments, which Mahmood ordered after his installation to power, excited a little irritation amongst the nomade tribes, the chiefs of which had more especially felt the effects of his anger; but as these rigorous measures affected his adversaries only, the Shah's party felt no uneasiness, and considered that he had a right to chastise those who had been opposed to him. Nevertheless the Ghildjzyes, the born enemies of every Abdalee sovereign, revolted at the outset against his authority, and were desirous of placing one of their own tribe upon the throne; Mahmood was obliged to send the Serdars Fethi Khan and Ahmed Khan against the rebels, who beat them in four or five encounters, and terminated the revolt by makng them conform to the existing state of things.

On the other hand, fortune came to the aid of the Shah Mahmood; for Kaissar Mirza, the son of Shah Zeman, lost the government of Herat, and this without any attempt on the part of Mahmood to dispossess him of it. The circumstances were as follows:—

Mir Efzel Khan, the Vizier of Kaissar Mirza, conceived the idea of overthrowing the prince immediately after the fall of his father, and at this intrigue he worked ardently, and formed with great ease a powerful party on which he could entirely rely. When he thought he was sufficiently powerful, he resolved on putting Kaissar to death, but the prince, informed of the plot in time, escaped from Herat, and sought refuge at Kaff-rooge, a town of Khorassan, leaving his wives and children under the protection of the Serdar Kalech Khan, who, though less influential than Mir Efzel Khan, was still sufficiently powerful not to be apprehensive on account of the support and protection he gave to this unfortunate family.

After the flight of Kaissar Mirza, Mir Efzel, well convinced that Shah Mahmood, occupied at this time with the Ghildjzyes, could not by any possibility come and disturb him, endeavoured to establish his authority in Herat. The inhabitants, who were attached to him, would not agree to this except with a certain reservation; but, on the other hand, they rejected and repelled the secret intrigues of Kalech Khan, the antagonist of the usurper, who wished to assassinate him. The Heratees demanded that Efzel Khan, though retaining the appointment of vizier, which they guaranteed him, should receive as governor, in the place of Kaissar Mirza, one of the blood royal, unless he preferred the return of that prince himself; but Mir Efzel, fearing the resentment of the latter, hastened to find a successor agreeably to the wishes of the people.

Hadji Firooz Eddin, who, as we have already remarked, retired to Teheran, had on leaving that capital gone on a pilgrimage to Mecca. On his return Afghanistan was groaning under the sanguinary executions of Shah Zeman, and the war was then going on between him and Mahmood Mirza; the Hadji, who was anxious not to be a witness of these sad scenes, retired therefore to Turchiz in Khorassan, which the Shah of Persia had assigned to him as his residence, and here he occupied himself in the purchase and sale of horses, camels, and other beasts of burden. An envoy from Mir Efzel Khan came to him there, and proposed for his acceptance the government of Herat; but this prince, devoid of ambition, and caring little for the grandeur of such a position, declined the offer, preferring to continue his commercial pursuits. This refusal was not at all to the taste of Mir Efzel, who, pressed by the intrigues of Kalech Khan, was more earnestly solicited from day to day to recall Kaissar Mirza. To allay, therefore, the impatience of the people, he pretended that he had received a letter from Hadji Firooz Eddin accepting the government of the city; this, however, he had himself forged, and, contemporaneously with making the letter public, despatched in haste a few horsemen to Turchiz, who, under the pretext of wishing to purchase some horses, induced the prince to meet them in a retired spot, when they carried him off by main force, and brought him to Herat, *nolens volens*, where he was obliged to accept the title of Governor.

Kaissar Mirza, seeing that his uncle had carried the day against him, would not submit to the decision of the Heratees, and marched against Herat at the head of a small army of Afghans and Khorassanees, which he had succeeded in raising. Hadji Firooz allowed him to advance as far as Shekivar, a village situated twenty-one miles west of Herat, where he attacked his adversary, when Kaissar was completely worsted, and obliged to take to flight. In accordance with a plan agreed upon previously, and of which the troops had been informed, the prince after his defeat directed his course southward into the plain of Bakooa, where the fugitives went to rejoin him; when they all arrived he marched against Kandahar, hoping to surprise Kamran Mirza, who commanded there, and capture that city. In this attempt, as it turned out, he was successful, but a few days after the inhabitants revolted, and drove him out of Kandahar. Kamran Mirza, who had retired to Kelat i Ghildjzye, was recalled by them, so that these two princes succeeded each other three times during the space of two months, according as the party which supported either had the upper hand; nevertheless Kamran Mirza finished by remaining master of the position, and Kaissar fled once more.

Mahmood Mirza had been the sovereign ruler of Afghanistan during two years and six months, when the city of Kabul became the scene of sanguinary disorders, originating in a religious schism between the Afghans, who are Soonees, and the Kuzzilbashes of the sect of Shiahs; these riots seriously compromised the power of Shah Mahmood, nevertheless he surmounted the difficulty, but the support he gave to the heretical Shiahs alienated the Afghans from him, and contributed greatly to his fall, which took place some short time after.

These disorders were occasioned by a circumstance arising out of the horrible inclination the Persians have for a vice which it would sully these pages to mention. Some of the Kuzzilbashes secreted for several days a young Afghan lad of great beauty in their house, during which time he was treated in the most infamous manner, and this not only from their depraved passions, but from their hatred to Soonees. Restored to liberty, the youth informed his parents of what had taken place, when they immediately complained to Shah Mahmood; but the king, not wishing to alienate the Kuzzilbashes, whose adhesion had been, and might be again, of great service to him, refused to legislate upon the matter, and forwarded it to the religious tribunal from which it came. The injured parties, although dissatisfied in that the Shah eluded their complaint, nevertheless conformed to his orders, and proceeded to the mosque to consult the Syud Mir Vaëz, a man highly venerated by the Afghans, and whose hostility to the Shah Mahmood was no secret to any one. When the complainants appeared, the Syud was preaching to an immense crowd of persons, and they interrupted him to make known their business with loud cries and rending their clothes. On learning the nature of it, Mir Vaez at once gave them a *fetvo* authorising the extermination of all the Shiahs in Kabul, whom he held in detestation. When it was known that this *fetvo* had been issued, the Afghans assembled in arms, and in great numbers, around the mosque, and afterwards went, full of excitement, to exterminate the Kuzzilbashes. The first place to which they proceeded was the quarter of the Khaffis, a people originally from Khaff, massacred all those whom they met, and pillaged and burnt their houses. Recovered in some degree from the first movement of surprise which this sudden attack had caused them, the Kuzzilbashes assembled, fully determined to defend their property and their lives to the last extremity. Nevertheless, their situation became every moment more critical, for, after a stout defence of two days, they saw, on the morning of the third, all the heights that commanded their position occupied by the Afghans from the neighbouring villages, who had come to the assistance of the citizens. The Shah Mahmood had sent Mooktar ed Dooulet and Ahmed Khan several times to the assailants, to endeavour to prevail upon them to desist from their sanguinary intentions, but this step, instead of appeasing, only irritated them the more, excited as they were by the mollahs and some serdars, who were jealous of the favour shown to the Kuzzilbash chiefs by the Shah. After four days' fighting, during which four hundred persons at least, and on either side, had lost their lives, the Serdar Fethi Khan, who, by reason of the alliances which existed between his family and the Kuzzilbashes, had, up to this time, refrained from taking any part in the affair, became alarmed, and, apprehensive that things might take a still more serious turn, was anxious to put some bounds to the furious harangues of Mir Vaëz, who spared not even royalty itself. Fethi Khan therefore stepped forward, and, with his brother, declaring in favour of the Kuzzilbashes, rushed at the head of their partisans upon the disturbers of public order, and dispersed them with matchlock and sabre, to the great regret of the serdars opposed to Mahmood, who were also envious of the favour in which he was held by his sovereign. From this moment they conspired against them, and swore to overthrow them both. An occasion for doing this did not present itself for two years, when Fethi Khan was obliged to march with an army to Bamian to put down some disorders amongst the Hazarahs. Immediately after his departure, Mir Vaëz, the Serdar Ahmed Khan, and Mooktar ed Dooulet, the principal chiefs of the conspiracy, sent an express to the prince Shooja-ool-Moolk, the younger brother of Shah Mahmood, requesting him to come immediately to Kabul, and overthrow the latter, promising to give him their support and that of the Afghans in general. This prince, who had received information of this plot long before, was not very far distant from Peshawur, which he had secretly approached, and, on the receipt of the letter written him by the conspirators, advanced rapidly towards Kabul with all the men he could collect. Shah Mahmood was one of the last persons who heard of his arrival, for no one had revealed the fact to him, and he only ascertained it by remarking the excitement which everywhere prevailed. He was not a person who could suggest to himself the energetic measures which the exigencies of the moment required, and the man of action who had placed him on the throne, and through whom he governed, namely, Fethi Khan, was at a distance, and wholly ignorant of what was passing at Kabul—all the warriors who had been despatched to him by Shah Mahmood had also been detained, and could not join him in person, for he was closely watched in his palace.

Feeling the imminence of his danger, Mahmood took refuge in the Bala Hissar, and the inhabitants, satisfied by keeping an eye upon him from the outside of the citadel, went in crowds to meet Shooja-ool-Moolk, whom they brought into the city in triumph, and placed on the throne amidst the loudest acclamations.

I have, up to this point, followed the manuscripts of two Eastern authors, whose works I have frequently quoted in the course of my narrative: that of Mirza Ali Mohamed has led me only to the close of the Afghan dominion in Persia; from that period, up to the arrival of Shah Shooja at Kabul, I have drawn my materials from the writings of Abdullah Khan Heratee, *pich-Khetmet*, gentleman of the chamber, or equerry, to the Shah Kamran of Herat; but I must add that his narrative is very summary and destitute of dates; and I have been obliged to make researches elsewhere to find those I have recorded. I have also joined to the information taken from his manuscript many other particulars which I collected myself during my travels in Afghanistan, from the mouths of contemporaries of Shah Timoor and of his sons, who themselves took part in the events of those times. The reign of Shah Shooja-ool-Moolk is the one upon which I am not so well informed, and, having no European library to refer to, it will be impossible for me to fill up the very important omissions which, without doubt, exist in the history of this reign.

The first act of Shah Shooja, as king, was to seize Shah

Mahmood, delivered up to him by his own guards, and to order the *lex talionis* to be enforced by putting out his eyes, as Mahmood had done those of the Shah Zeman; Mooktar ed Doonlet having interceded for him, Shooja revoked this order out of consideration to his supporter; but he detained the ex-king a prisoner, and confined him in a dungeon of the Bala Hissar.

After having taken this precautionary measure, the king confided a division of his army to his nephew Kaissar Mirza, the son of Shah Zeman, in order that he might turn Kamran Mirza, a son of Mahmood Shah, out of Kandahar, where he commanded; but, meeting half-way Alem Khan, nephew of the Serdar Ahmed Khan, he learnt, greatly to his satisfaction we may presume, that this had already been done. The inhabitants had risen at the instigation of Alem Khan, and driven Kamran from the city; no opposition, therefore, was offered to the prince on entering Kandahar, of which, in virtue of new orders from his uncle, he became governor. On leaving the city, Kamran Mirza took the road towards Herat, where his uncle Hadji Firooz Eddin gave him a kind reception, and confided to him the government of the district of Furrah, adjacent to Kandahar, where he was in a position to observe the events that were passing in that city, and to lay hands upon it by surprise, or otherwise, as occasion might present itself.

Some time after Hadji Firooz Eddin, influenced by his mother, who was also the mother of Shah Mahmood, consented to march an army against Kabul, and make an attempt to release his brother; he gave the command of these troops to his son Malek Kassem Mirza and his nephew Kamran Mirza. The prince Kaissar, tardily informed of their march, came out nevertheless from Kandahar and attacked the Heratees near Kaleh d'Azim Khan, but he was beaten and forced to fly once more, leaving the victors masters of Kandahar. Hadji Firooz Eddin had scarcely obtained this success when he learnt that Mohamed Velee Mirza, Governor-General of Khorassan, had marched an army commanded by the Naïb Mohamed Khan Kadjar to take Herat. He therefore recalled his nephew and his son, who abandoned in their turn Kandahar to Kaissar Mirza. While awaiting their arrival, Hadji Firooz Eddin assembled in haste a few thousand horse of the Eimak tribes, and moved out of Herat to meet the Persians; the encounter took place near Chekivan, but he was beaten and obliged to make a speedy retreat into Herat, which was soon besieged by the victors. The Persians had good artillery, and their troops had received for some time past a certain amount of instruction and organization on the European system; they might therefore hope to make themselves masters of the place in a short space of time. But this hope was not realized, owing to their want of vigilance, for the Afghan princes, returning from Kandahar, fell upon their rear, which they put to the rout, while Hadji Firooz sallied from the city and attacked them in front, so that, taken between two fires, they must have thought themselves fortunate in being able to effect their retreat with the loss of a few hundred men killed and three or four guns taken. They repaid themselves however for this check by ravaging the country through which they retreated, and bringing with them to Meshed more than one hundred thousand cattle.

This was the first time after the death of Nadir Shah that the Persians put forward their claims to Herat; since then they have made very many attempts to take it, without more success than in this instance: nevertheless they have exercised from this period a certain influence upon its governor, who, for the sake of being at peace with them, acknowledged, although evasively, the suzerainty of the Shah of Persia after this attack; and agreed to pay a tribute, the terms of which were left altogether undetermined: neither the amount nor the time it was to be paid was stated; it was much or little according to circumstances and the means which the Persians might have of enforcing payment. Shah Shooja had enough trouble to consolidate his power in Kabul, for a thousand factions were in a state of agitation around him; he punished some and compromised matters with others, and had at length succeeded in establishing some order. The Serdar Fethi Khan, after his return from Bamian, attached himself to his party and became one of his ministers; it was this chief who advised him to give up his life of repose and make war, which alone could conciliate and obtain for him the respect of the Afghans. As the Shah had a predilection for a military life, this advice was adopted, the invasion of Scinde resolved upon, and, after having assembled an army of 30,000 men, the king marched on that country. The chief of the Talpooras endeavoured to avoid the storm, and sent his minister Walee Mohamed Khan to the Shah, offering to pay him 320,000*l.* which he was indebted to him for arrears of tribute; but the Serdar Fethi Khan, who saw the king was inclined to accept this offer, opposed it in every way that he could. His advice would most probably have been listened to if disastrous intelligence had not been received from Kabul: the northern tribes were in a state of agitation, and the capital itself was not tranquil; which reasons induced the Shah to terminate his misunderstanding with the Emirs of Scinde and accept the 320,000*l*., which having done he returned in great haste to Kabul. Having restored tranquillity there, he made an expedition eastward, with a view of retaking possession of Cashmeer, and reducing the Serdar Runjeet Sing, Governor of Lahore, to obedience; but he failed in this enterprise also, and returned to Kabul, having suffered considerable losses.

Though Shah Shooja's reign was so short, it was nevertheless one of those which had the greatest chance of being prosperous. The Afghans seemed tired of the demon of discord, but unfortunately there was nothing of a conciliatory character about the Shah; he alienated those whom he had the greatest interest in attaching to his cause, and an unforeseen occurrence, by which he ought to have obtained strength, served only to excite in him the love of absolute authority, and in the end turned to his prejudice.

The British government, after having subdued in succession all the sovereigns of India one after the other, saw itself menaced in the middle of its triumphs by a danger against which it sought to protect itself by all the means in its power. The Emperors Napoleon and Alexander had just agreed to undertake an hostile expedition against India, passing through Persia. Feth Ali Shah, who then reigned in the latter country, was not so staunch an ally that England could trust him; she thought therefore of establishing her first line of defence beyond the Persian frontier, and sought the friendship of the Afghans to form her advanced guard. With this policy in view, the Governor-General of India sent Mr. Elphinstone as ambassador to Kabul, where he made a treaty of alliance offensive and defensive with Shah Shooja-ool-Moolk; the ambassador was exceedingly well received, and each day the Shah gave him a fresh entertainment in the royal palace. The siege of Herat, which Mohamed Velee Mirza had just undertaken, and the result of which had been so unfortunate, was the counterpart to this embassy. It is well known how the rupture which took place between France and Russia, and the ascendancy obtained by England at the court of Teheran by scattering her gold on all sides, led to the failure of Napoleon's plans, which might otherwise have been completely successful, and overthrown the then political state of India.

Shah Shooja-ool-Moolk had the reputation, and with reason, of being the most talented of the sons of Timoor Shah. With great firmness of character and tried courage, it was plainly to be seen by more than one circumstance that he was not a man to support intrigues, or serve as an instrument to a party. It was, therefore, a little against the grain that the serdars had submitted to the coercion of Mir Vaëz, Ahmed Khan, and Mooktar-ed-Dooulet, the result of which was the elevation of Shah Shooja to the throne; for they clearly saw that under such a sovereign they must take a straight course and obey without making those representations which the Afghans love so much to present to their superiors. Pressed by circumstances, they could not do otherwise than accept the candidate for the throne without conditions, for his usurpation was the only means by which they could withdraw themselves from the vengeance of Shah Mahmood, and that of the Serdar Fethi Khan, in the eyes of whom they had become ostensibly compromised since the unfortunate day when the Soonees and Shiahs had massacred one another in the city of Kabul. Nevertheless, they still hoped that in accepting Shah Shooja as king he would keep his authority within just limits; but they were mistaken, for the Shah, who at once penetrated their intentions, cut short all their demands from the very day he ascended the throne, by an act of sovereign power of the most absolute character. This tyrannical feeling soon became habitual to him, and it increased by degrees with all those who displeased him, however powerful or influential they might be. The Mohamedzyes themselves were deprived of their appointments, and their chief, Fethi Khan, disgraced by the king. The serdars, who vegetated in obscurity and were the least to be feared, were taken from their retreats and placed in positions of importance—in a word, Shooja shook himself free from the yoke, and transformed everything, and he never afterwards gave any proofs of that independent spirit which had led others to have such an high opinion of him when he was only a prince of the blood. But it must be admitted, and to his praise, that he was always grateful to those who had raised him to power: Mir Vaëz, Ahmed Khan, and Mooktar-ed-Dooulet, were much more his friends than his dependents; but this friendship could not preserve them from the sad fate that awaited them; and they fell all three from the elevated rank in which fortune had placed them by the revolutions which the Barukzyes and their numerous adherents stirred up amongst the Afghans. Mooktar-ed-Dooulet, obliged to give up the post of vizier in favour of the Serdar Akrem Khan, was in prison, and it was without doubt from the day that he retired from affairs that the decadence in the reign of Shah Shooja may be dated. The Serdar Ahmed Khan, less unfortunate than Mooktar, died sword in hand, while putting down a revolt in which the most faithful of the Shah's friends lost their lives. The sons of these two chiefs, who exercised so great an influence over the Afghans, took from that time part in the revolt, and from this moment the reign of Shah Shooja-ool-Moolk was nothing more than a succession of dangers, sufferings, and bitter anxiety. If he had been content to remove with some show of reason those who impeded the march of government by their intrigues, or if, while repressing them with more severity, he had acted with justice on the flagrant proofs of their crimes, the restless disposition of the Afghans would not have been alarmed, and he might have aspired to a reign not less glorious than that of his grandfather Ahmed Shah, with whom he had more than one point of resemblance. But he was capricious and singular like his brother Zeman, whose cruelty was necessary to consolidate the power in his own hands.

Discontent soon became general amongst all classes of Shah Shooja's subjects, even amongst his most devoted adherents, who also murmured loudly; but without taking into consideration their irritation and remonstrances, he continued to give vent to his haughty and absolute disposition. The Afghans, who saw in him the most talented of the Suddozyes, resisted for a long time the wishes of their serdars, who, habituated to raise and depose their kings, were anxious to be rid of him; and the want of agreement on the choice of a successor which they must give the nation was the reason why they delayed his fall indefinitely. There is even some probability that this prince would have been able to maintain his hold upon the throne if the Serdar Fethi Khan had not been amongst the number of his adversaries; Shooja imagined he could despise him, and, instead of conciliating him, which would have been the wisest course, he did everything to increase his dissatisfaction. This false policy cost him dear.

After his disgrace Fethi Khan, disliking Kabul as a residence, proceeded to Kandahar, his native city, and in the environs of which the greater part of the tribe of the Barukzyes resided. When he arrived Kaissar Mirza was governor, and he promised that he should be respected and protected by him as long as he did not interfere in the affairs of government. Fethi Khan was not then in a position to make conditions, and was obliged to accept those which were offered him; but he prepared everything in secret for the restoration of Shah Mahmood. Whether Kaissar was informed of this, or whether he thought the step necessary to his uncle's safety, he ordered the serdar to be seized on his leaving an audience which had been accorded him; and the officers who were commissioned to arrest him precipitated themselves upon him with such violence that he fell with his face to the ground, and knocked out several of his teeth. Profiting by this circumstance, they gagged him to stop his cries, bound his feet and his hands, and made him a close prisoner; his young brother, Dost Mohamed Khan, who was near him, assisted by a few servants, attempted his rescue, but, overpowered by numbers, he was obliged to take to flight to escape the same treatment. He succeeded, however, in collecting a few hundred Barukzyes in the city, and with these attacked the citadel, but, received by a volley from the garrison, he was obliged to retire, and, hastily leaving the town, retreated to the fortress of Girishk, the governor of which was devoted to his family. After this he scoured the plain of Bakooa with the Barukzyes who had followed him, plundered the caravans, and soon found himself in possession of 600*l.*, which he spent in obtaining recruits and adherents to his cause.

The Serdar Fethi Khan had previously to his arrest despatched his brother Shere dil Khan to Kabul, with the view of facilitating the escape of Shah Mahmood from prison, and recommended him, above all things, not to permit any Afghan to take part in this enterprise, but to employ Kuzzilbashes exclusively. This Persian tribe, as we have already stated, consisted of 12,000 families when they were brought to Kabul by Nadir Shah, but subsequently to the death of that conqueror their numbers had considerably augmented. Up to the reign of Shah Mahmood the Afghans treated them upon a footing of equality, but after the sanguinary conflict which arose between them on the occasion of the horrible crime committed by these Persian colonists they were oppressed in every kind of way, though Fethi Khan had always remained on good terms with them, which led them very naturally to assist him in delivering Shah Mahmood. The undertaking was a difficult one, for Shah Shooja kept him closely guarded; but whatever might have been the vigilance of his gaolers, the Kuzzilbashes finished by evading it. Tools were secretly conveyed to the prisoner, and such was the energy with which he used them, that in eight hours he had dug down to the conduit by which he was to escape beyond the city walls. It was night when he gained the outside, and the Kuzzilbashes, who were on the watch, conducted him to a tomb in a churchyard situated near the walls of the Bala Hissar, and, having covered the place of his retreat with branches and earth, they retired, recommending him to have patience for a few days until the pursuit which it was certain would take place began to slacken. The next morning a hundred emissaries were despatched on every side, with orders to put him to death directly he fell into their hands, but the majority of them soon returned to inform the Shah that their endeavours to find him had been unavailing. After having passed several days in this subterranean abode, Mahmood learnt that his brother had made useless search for him: he therefore left his retreat in the middle of the night, and, accompanied by Shere dil Khan and a few devoted adherents, galloped southward, when they were soon joined by Dost Mohamed Khan, in whose company they plundered three rich caravans. With the proceeds of these robberies they were enabled to raise a small force, after which they acted upon a larger scale; the villages were in their turn put under contribution, and they then laid siege to Kandahar.

During three months Kaissar Mirza repulsed all the attacks of the besiegers, but after this, being without either provisions or munitions of war, he came to a compromise with them, setting the Serdar Fethi Khan at liberty, on condition that they raised the siege and retired from Kandahar. When the serdar was released, Mahmood Shah was strongly inclined to break his promise, and constrain his nephew to give up the city, but Fethi Khan prevented him; he represented to him that the throne was at Kabul, and not at Kandahar, and this determined Mahmood to march on the capital; they left, nevertheless, two thousand Barukzye horse encamped within a short distance from the former city.

When Shah Shooja heard that Kandahar was besieged by Mahmood, he collected his troops and left Kabul with 25,000 picked men to relieve it, but after a few days' march more than half deserted; the Kuzzilbashes especially all left his court and returned to Kabul, which obliged the Shah to fall back on his capital, but he had scarcely arrived there when a revolt forced him to evacuate it, and he retired and took up a position in a vast plain surrounding the gardens of Neemla, near Gundamuck. Shah Mahmood and Fethi Khan, who followed him close, remained in Kabul only long enough to take possession of it; they then confided it to the care of the Kuzzilbashes, and hastened against Shah Shooja, whose army was advantageously posted and numbered 20,000 combatants. Though mustering only 3000 horse, Fethi Khan charged them with impetuosity at a moment when they least expected it, and before they had even time to form up in order of battle: the result was a complete rout, for it threw the mass into utter confusion; fear took possession of them, and they fled from the field. Akrem Khan, the vizier of Shah Shooja, was killed, and the king escaped to the mountains of the Khyber, abandoning on the field of battle all his baggage and the royal treasure, which, independent of a sum of 2,000,000*l*., contained precious stones of immense value. Shah Mahmood secured an enormous booty, and entered Kabul amidst the acclamations of the inconstant people of that city, mounted on an elephant which Shah Shooja had ordered to be richly caparisoned for his own triumphant entry into the capital.

Shah Shooja remained only a short time in the Khyber, and retired soon after towards the south, where he hoped, by joining his nephew, Kaissar Mirza, to take the offensive and regain his crown. Directing his course towards Kandahar by the mountains bordering the Indus, he obtained some recruits on the road; but in spite of the secrecy with which he endeavoured to conduct his march, it became known, and, to add to his disgrace, his nephew was driven from Kandahar by the Serdar Poor dil Khan, a brother of Fethi Khan. After this Poor dil Khan attacked Shooja with superior forces, who was fortunate in being able to escape by a rapid flight; this was in 1809, four months having elapsed between his first and second defeat. Powerless rather than discouraged, he retired shortly after to Loodiana, where he resided near his brother the Shah Zeman, living from that time, like that prince, on the bounty of the East India Company, but not before he had gone through many severe trials.

CHAPTER XI.

Sir A. Burnes' sketch of Shah Shooja — Fethi Khan is appointed Vizier — Shah Mahmood devoted to pleasure — Influence of the vizier — Kamran, the son of Shah Mahmood — His ferocious disposition — He kills his cousin Kaissar — Fethi Khan reduces the Belooches — Establishes order and security — Afghan alliance with the Sikhs — They unite and seize Cashmeer — Fethi Khan breaks his word to the Sikhs — The latter seize upon Attok — Brilliant exploit of Dost Mohamed — Panic of the Afghans — Runjeet Sing pillages Cashmeer — The pretensions of Persia on Herat — Hoosein Ali Mirza marches against that city — Fethi Khan marches to the relief of Herat — The vizier arrests Hadji Firooz Eddin — The prince's harem is violated and plundered by Dost Mohamed — Flight of Mir Efzel Khan to Meshed — Battle of Kiaffir Kaleh — Retreat of both parties — The Afghans obtain the plunder — Kamran conspires against Fethi Khan — Shah Mahmood commands the vizier's eyes to be put out — Kamran arrives at Herat and executes the order — The brothers of the vizier, Shere dil Khan and Kohendil Khan, escape — Poor dil Khan remains a prisoner.

SIR ALEXANDER BURNES, an enlightened and conscientious traveller in Afghanistan, gives a sketch of the life which Shah Shooja led after the battle of Neemla. This narrative was taken from a little work written by Shah Shooja himself; I made every endeavour when in Afghanistan and Persia to procure this book, but without result—as it is highly interesting, I present it here from the pages of Burnes.

"After Shah Shooja-ool-Moolk had been defeated at Neemla he had wandered as a fugitive in various corners of his dominions; and his adventures, which have been detailed by himself in a small volume, are replete with interest. After his discomfiture at Kandahar he was seized by Ata Mohamed Khan, the son of his former vizier, and subjected to much indignity. He was for some time confined in the fortress of Attok. The lancet was frequently held over his eyes; and his keeper once took him into the middle of the Indus, with his arms bound, threatening him with instant death. The object of such severity was to extract from him the celebrated diamond called Koh-i-Noor, or mountain of light, which he was known to possess. In the mean while Ata Mohamed Khan proceeded to Cashmeer, and carried the captive monarch in his train. On the fall of that valley he was released by Futeh Khan and joined his family at Lahore. His queen, as I may well call the Waffadar Begum, the most influential lady of his harem, had used every persuasion to prevent Shooja's placing himself in the power of Runjeet Sing, but he disregarded her advice, and in the end had ample reason to regret his having neglected it. This lady was a woman of most bold and determined character; and her counsel had often proved valuable to her husband, both in his days of power and disaster.

"At Lahore, while at the mercy of the Sikhs, and absent from her husband, she preserved her own and his honour in a most heroic manner. Runjeet Sing pressed her urgently to surrender the Koh-i-Noor, or valuable diamond which was in her possession; and evinced intentions of forcing it from her. He also sought to transfer the daughters of the unfortunate king to his own harem. The queen seized on the person who conveyed the message, and had him soundly chastised. She also intimated to the Maharadja, that, if he continued his dishonourable demands, she would pound the diamond in a mortar, and first administer it to her daughters, and those under her protection, and then swallow it herself: adding, 'May the blood of all of us be on your head!' This lady succeeded in the end in escaping from Lahore disguised as a Hindoo; and planned the deliverance of her husband, which shortly followed. This was only effected at the expense of the great diamond. A narration of the circumstances relative to its surrender would prove interesting, but it would be out of place in this sketch. It is sufficient to mention that an imprisonment of the closest nature, insult, and even hunger, fell to the lot of this unfortunate monarch.

"The ungenerous part which the king of the Sikhs was enacting towards her husband aroused the energies of the queen, who had settled herself at the British station of Loodiana. She arranged the placing of horses on the road, and Shooja and his people made every exertion in Lahore. They hired all the houses which adjoined those in which they lodged, and opened a passage into the street by cutting through seven walls. A few hours after the household had retired to rest, the king descended by the aperture and issued into the street in the dress of the Punjab. The city wall had yet to be passed, and the gates were shut. Shooja crept through the common sewer of the city, and fled with two or three servants towards the hill country of Kishtwar. Here he once more raised the standard of a monarch, and planned an attack on Cashmeer, in which he was assisted by the Rajah of Kishtwar. The expedition would have been successful, for the Governor of Cashmeer had evacuated his frontier position, but an untimely season blocked the roads with snow, interrupted the supplies, and once more frustrated the hopes of Shah Shooja. Wandering by a cheerless and ungenial country, the Shah at length reached the British station of Sabathoo in the outer Himalaya, from which he repaired to Loodiana, where his family had found an asylum. He here joined them, and has since shared the bounty of the British Government. Few monarchs and few men have been subjected to greater reverses of fortune than Shooja-ool-Moolk; and we find our sympathies enlisted in his cause by a knowledge of his misfortunes."

Shah Mahmood had now for the second time reaped the fruits of the clever combinations of Fethi Khan, whose military talents were completely developed. It was much more in answer to his appeal that the Afghans, particularly the powerful tribe of the Barukzyes, had responded, than from any wish which they had to see Shah Mahmood again upon the throne. This prince, although tried by many vicissitudes, had learnt nothing by adversity; he wished for power with reference only to the sweets of life and the pleasures which it procured, leaving to others the cares of government. It was on the Serdar Fethi Khan that he heaped these, either because he was convinced that it was impossible for him to reign without the co-operation of that chief, or from a feeling of gratitude, or, more likely still, because he was convinced of his great capacity; he made him his prime minister, gave him the most extensive powers, and laid upon him the difficult task of governing the Afghan nation. From this time he gave himself up to, and gratified, his depraved inclinations; effeminate and self-indulgent, he thought of nothing but his pleasures and orgies of every kind and description, living in utter ignorance of all that was passing around him. Fethi Khan did not abuse this unlimited confidence, and soon restored to his country the splendour and glory of the days of the great Shah Ahmed, which had totally disappeared since the pacific reign of his son Timoor.

The name of Fethi Khan soon became celebrated and popular throughout Central Asia; the Afghans more especially held him in the greatest admiration, and had, on the contrary, the greatest contempt for their king. Nevertheless such was at this epoch the veneration they had for the Suddozyes, that they never thought of dethroning him in favour of his fortunate and able general. It is true many persons have given Fethi Khan credit for the most ambitious views, but on a close examination of the facts one remains convinced that this chief was sincere when he protested his devotion to the Shah, and was contented with the high position to which his sovereign had raised him. What indeed could he gain by becoming king? only another title, which would have caused him immense embarrassment, and a host of enemies, without giving him more power. All the affairs of the kingdom were submitted to his discretion; he made his brothers in succession governors of all the provinces; he had the administration of the finances and the army; his orders were not subject to the least control. What could he desire more? Nothing! and Shah Mahmood considered himself extremely fortunate in having as his minister a man who fulfilled his responsible and arduous duties so well. But those who envied the minister did not find him to their liking, and were constantly seeking for an opportunity of inspiring the weak monarch with chimerical fears; amongst these was his son Kamran, but his intrigues had no other result in the first instance than to cause his own removal from office, and under the following circumstances.

Kamran Mirza, after having rejoined his father under the walls of Kandahar, returned with him to Kabul. This prince, although still young, had already become remarkable for his haughty exterior, cruelties without number, and a great inclination for debauch, and he was on the point of proceeding to Kandahar as governor of that province when he made himself conspicuous by circumstances of a most odious character. His cousin Kaisear Mirza, son of Shah Zeman, had not followed the example of Shah Shooja, as after having been removed from his government, of which Kamran was going to take possession, he made his submission to his uncle Shah Mahmood, and remained from that time at Kabul under the special protection of the Serdar Fethi Khan. Kamran Mirza, who still entertained great resentment against the prince for all the disappointments he had made him feel on various occasions at Kandahar, ordered him to be seized one morning, and put to the torture, with a view of forcing him to give up some diamonds which he had forgotten to take with him in one of his hurried flights from that city, and which he pretended had fallen into his cousin's possession. Shah Mahmood, having been informed of this circumstance, immediately interfered, and made him release his nephew, but a few days after, Kamran, meeting Kaissar Mirza in one of the royal gardens, apostrophized the latter in most opprobrious terms. Kaissar had the imprudence to reply, when Kamran felled him to the earth with a wrestler's club which he took from the hands of a person in his suite. Fethi Khan seized this opportunity of representing to Shah Mahmood how his son with such a disposition might compromise himself with a nation so susceptible as the Afghans, and it was determined between the king and his minister that no appointment should be given to Kamran Mirza, and that he should for the future remain at court under the surveillance of his father. From this moment the hatred of the prince was redoubled against the vizier, and he was ever after mixed up in all the intrigues and conspiracies that were formed against him.

The first object of Fethi Khan, after the restoration of Shah Mahmood to power, was to make the Emirs of Scinde and Beloochistan return to their duty; he then reduced to obedience the greater part of the tribe of the Hazarahs, settled in the heart of the mountains of the Paropamisus. He also restored order in all the provinces; made the laws, the observance of which had been very much relaxed, to be respected; regulated the administration, which, up to that period, had been in a most intricate state, giving rise to the most nefarious exactions and embezzlements of the most scandalous kind; and lastly it might be said that security reigned everywhere. This remarkable man united to a superior genius a great aptitude for governing and for war: not one of his predecessors had been able to reduce rebels to obedience with the same promptitude, or keep them afterwards in the path of duty; he struck hard, but he was generous after the victory was gained, and shone by his excessive liberality: always in the midst of combats, he still found time to direct the helm of state, and was ready for everything,—in activity he had no equal. He was the eldest of twenty-one brothers, all men of mark, who powerfully assisted him by their support; he placed them, as we have already said, at the head of the provincial governments, putting much more faith in them than in the princes of the blood or ambitious serdars, who, jealous of his fame, were occupied only in creating embarrassments for him, or in endeavouring to injure him in the opinion of his sovereign. Hadji Firooz Eddin was the only prince whom he allowed to remain undisturbed in his government of Herat; and this, simply because the troops were occupied elsewhere; his fall was therefore delayed. He intrusted the government of Beloochistan to his brother Rahim dil Khan, who resided at Shikapoor. Poor dil Khan was installed at Kandahar; Sultan Mohamed Khan at Peshawur; Shere dil Khan at Ghuznee; Kohendil Khan at Bamian; and the others under their orders in districts of these provinces; he nevertheless retained some of them near his person. Amongst these were Mohamed Azim Khan, Djabber Khan, Nawab Assad Ullah Khan, who were men of capacity, and assisted him in the administration of affairs. His young brother, Dost Mohamed Khan, had the entire charge and management of his household, which did not prevent him from mounting his horse and fighting like his other brothers.

After having completed the preparations for war, in which he had been engaged during two years, Fethi Khan marched in 1811 against Cashmeer, which had thrown off the Afghan dominion, and was then held by the Serdar Attah Mohamed Khan, a son of the vizier Akrem Khan, killed at the battle of Neemla. He would also have willingly marched against Runjeet Sing, governor of Lahore, who, after the fall of Shah Zeman, had proclaimed his independence in the Punjab, but it would have been undertaking too much at a time; moreover the vizier preferred making use of him in his plans for the reconstruction of the empire, and falling upon him afterwards when he had no further necessity for his services. He therefore induced him to sign a treaty, in which he gave him nine lacs of rupees (90,000*l.*), to be taken from the revenues of the province of Cashmeer, on condition that the Sikh army should assist him in reconquering that country: this treaty was concluded on the banks of the Jelum, where the two chiefs met, attended with a sufficient escort. The Afghan minister had with him eighteen of his brothers, who advised him to put an end to the Sikh chieftain at this meeting, offering themselves to be the assassins. Fethi Khan rejected this proposition, but much less because he would not be guilty of a base action, a thing which Asiatics never look upon in the light that we do, than because he required the support of the Sikh army, twelve thousand men of which formed a junction with his immediately after the treaty was signed. On receiving this augmentation of his forces, he proceeded towards Cashmeer, by way of Bember. The little army of the rebels had posted themselves in the defiles of the Pir-pindjal to dispute his passage, but, seeing themselves menaced in front by Fethi Khan, and in the rear by his brother Kohendil Khan, who had turned their position with a corps of cavalry, they retired without fighting. The Afghans had, therefore, no one to disturb them in their advance, and they took possession of the plain of Cashmeer without opposition. The city also had scarcely been invested when it surrendered at discretion, and the citadel alone, to which the Serdar Attah Mohamed Khan had retired, continued to offer any further resistance; nevertheless, after thirteen days of negotiation, that chief, rather than be besieged, capitulated. He was a man of great talent, energetic, brave, influential, and respected by the Afghans. Fethi Khan wished to make a friend of him; he treated him, therefore, with great distinction, and recommended him to the good offices of Shah Mahmood. Runjeet Sing tried, but without success, to induce Fethi Khan to confer upon him the government of Cashmeer; but the vizier, who saw the drift of his proposal, namely, to reimburse himself in the first instance the expenses of the war, and afterwards to ensure to himself the payment of the sum guaranteed by the treaty, eluded his request, and confided the administration of this fair province to his brother, the Serdar Mohamed Azim Khan, who, after him, was the eldest son of Payendeh Khan—Runjeet was therefore minus his expenses, and did not even receive the nine lacs of rupees which had been promised him. Frustrated in his ambitious design, he turned his attention to Attok, a fortress situated on an eminence close to the Indus, commanding the principal passage of that river; and the governor, who was a brother of the Serdar Attah Khan, having surrendered this important place to him, in consideration of a lac of rupees, and certain promises which satisfied his ambition, the Sikhs, on entering Attok, openly abandoned the Afghan party, and hastened to put the place in a good state of defence.

When Fethi Khan was informed of the desertion of his allies, he quitted Cashmeer to march against Runjeet; sending forward his brother Dost Mohamed Khan, at the head of two thousand horse, to clear the way, and followed close with all his forces. On the approach of the advanced guard of the Afghan the Sikhs descended into the plain of Tchatch, which lies to the east of Attok, and took up a position about three miles and a half from the fortress, on some hills where they had not only the advantage in the ground, but also that of securing the only spring of water in the country. Dost Mohamed Khan, who, for a reason so important, felt the necessity of seizing this point, and desirous of distinguishing himself in the first command with which his brother had intrusted him, fell with impetuosity upon the Sikhs without waiting for the arrival of the Afghan army, which followed him a league in the rear. In this charge he captured the enemy's artillery; but his success did not last long; the Sikhs rallied, and, after having received reinforcements, renewed the attack with a force eight times superior to his. Finding that he had committed himself, he sent an express to Fethi Khan to hasten his march, and while awaiting his reply valiantly resisted the enemy, and would neither retire himself, nor could the Sikhs force him to do so. Unfortunately the Dost's message never reached Fethi Khan, the messenger taking a wrong direction and losing his way. The vizier was also led into error by persons ill-informed of what had transpired, who assured him that his brother had been killed and his division nearly destroyed, and he made therefore an échelon movement towards the Indus in order to avoid the Sikhs, ordered the heavy baggage to be burnt, and crossed the river without being disturbed by the enemy. Though tardily made acquainted with the movements of the Afghan army, Dost Mohamed hesitated not to retreat by the road it had taken, the Sikhs retiring to Attok. Fethi Khan, under the pressure of threatening circumstances which arose in the west of Afghanistan, was obliged to give up for the time his belligerent policy against Runjeet Sing; indeed he was compelled to weaken the garrison of Cashmeer to reinforce his army. This encouraged the Sikh chieftain to make several inroads on the territory of that province, the revenues of which he seized, an act the Afghan governor could not prevent.

Before entering upon the details of the new campaign which the Serdar Fethi Khan had to sustain against the Persians, it is necessary, in order that the reader may comprehend the motives which led to the war, that we should look back a little at the events recorded in the preceding pages.

It has been mentioned that the prince Hadji Firooz Eddin,

removed with violence from Turchiz by the orders of Mir Efzel Khan, had in the year 1800 been elected, in spite of himself, sovereign Prince of Herat. The just and mild character of his rule had obtained for him the love and respect of all classes of the population: ambitious individuals, who wished to overthrow him, were unable to find support anywhere, and during the sixteen years that he had governed this province he was never seriously disturbed except by the unfortunate expedition of Kaissar Mirza, and those which were almost annually sent against him by the Shah of Persia, Feth Ali, who laid claim to the principality as having once formed part of that kingdom. But up to this period Hadji Firooz Eddin had paralyzed his efforts, sometimes by repelling the Persians by force of arms, but more frequently by paying a small tribute which was exacted from him; nevertheless, he had always protested against the pretensions of the Persian monarch, and declared that Feth Ali Shah had no more legitimate claim upon Herat than he had upon the other countries which had emancipated themselves from the dominion of Persia during the last century; that the dynasty of the Kadjars had, it is true, established itself on the ruins of a vast empire, but that these remains had been absorbed in the organization of several kingdoms, which in forming themselves had taken less account of territorial limits than of the races which inhabited them; that none of them had the right to impose laws upon the others without their consent; that the independence of these races, particularly that of the Afghans, had been made sacred by the elevation of the Suddozyes to the throne, the king then on the musnud being the third of that tribe; that as the grandson of Shah Ahmed, founder of this dynasty, he reigned as the legitimate sovereign over a province the majority of the inhabitants of which were Afghans; in short, that Feth Ali Shah in his capacity of Shah of Persia was not more justified in making this claim upon Herat, than the Afghan princes would be in laying claim to the possession of Ispahan, Shiraz, or Kerman, for the simple reason that Mir Mahmood and Mir Echreff had reigned over those provinces. In support of these arguments, Hadji Firooz Eddin sent detachments of troops across the frontier to the assistance of some chiefs in Khorassan whom Feth Ali Shah had not yet been able to bring under his rule. Of this vast province he really possessed only Meshed; Nishapoor, Koochan, Boojnoord, Tubbus, Toorbut, Haidarieh, and Ghain were pretty nearly independent, and, under the authority of the khans with whom the Governor of Herat had just entered into alliance, and in exciting whom against Feth Ali Shah he hoped to give the Persian army enough occupation to prevent it from being sent against himself. He was, however, mistaken, for after a vigorous effort Feth Ali Shah finished by triumphing over their insubordination. The anger which this sovereign felt against Hadji Firooz Eddin, who had provoked it, became fatal to the latter; he soon saw Herat menaced by a formidable army, and necessity obliged him to have recourse to the aid of Shah Mahmood, whose assistance was almost as dangerous for him as the enmity of the Shah of Persia.

When the Persian battalions were all assembled at Meshed, Hoosein Ali Mirza, son of Feth Ali Shah, took the command. Kalech Khan, the celebrated Serdar of the Taymoonis, a man dreaded by the Heratees, also joined the Persian prince with a contingent of excellent troops, and, if they had at once entered upon the campaign, there can be no doubt that they would have taken Herat; but Hoosein Ali Mirza delayed the march of the army for a reinforcement of several guns of large calibre which he could have done very well without. This gave the Vizier Fethi Khan time to come to the relief of the place; his troops cleared the two hundred leagues which separated them from Herat with a rapidity unexampled in that country, and arrived there before the Persians had even crossed their own frontier.

It was not without good reason that Hadji Firooz waited till he was in the last extremity before he claimed the assistance of his brother. During the sixteen years that he governed Herat he had always been independent of him, though they were on good terms. It was only when the successes of Fethi Khan in Beloochistan and Scinde made him fear that he should be removed from his government, that he wrote to the latter protesting the truth of his respect for and submission to the king; but directly the vizier had left those provinces to proceed to Cashmeer, he kept only half the promises he had made. It is true he coined money in the name of the Shah Mahmood, but he never paid him a farthing of the tribute which had been agreed upon.

Fethi Khan, who was too much occupied in the East to enforce a more complete submission, appeared for the moment to rest satisfied with this state of things at Herat, but Hadji Firooz Eddin clearly understood that the vizier was only temporizing with him, and that, as soon as he was relieved from the embarrassments which had arisen with Runjeet, he would in his turn be obliged to conform to his brother's views. It was, therefore, with very great regret that he saw himself obliged to call this general to his assistance, whom he had so great an interest in seeing employed anywhere rather than at Herat; but there was no time to hesitate, for the danger that menaced him left him no other alternative.

Fethi Khan arrived at Herat towards the close of 1816. Hadji Firooz received him with great honours, and made him protestations of fidelity and friendship; but his conduct betrayed the fears that assailed him, and contributed more than anything else that had occurred up to that time to deprive him of his government. Well convinced that if Fethi Khan entered the city his own power was at an end, he permitted him to do so with an escort of fifty horsemen only; the army was obliged to encamp under the walls. The vizier dissimulated his displeasure, and even accepted the proposition with an outward appearance of respect; but he rendered this of a very illusory character by the choice he made of the persons who accompanied him. All these were allied to some family or other in Herat, and they soon induced their relatives to make common cause with them; so that on the fourth day after the vizier's arrival they delivered up to him the gates of the city—the citadel surrendered on the following day. He also arrested Hadji Firooz Eddin, and sent him, but under honourable escort, to Kabul, to give the king an account of his long administration. Fethi Khan had not up to this point passed the limits of justice; but whether he was animated with a certain feeling of resentment against the prince, or that his orders were exceeded, he was deprived of all his riches, and, as they were concealed in his harem, this sacred asylum was forced, and the party deputed to seize them, of whom his brother Dost Mohamed was the commander, made an indiscriminate pillage; the princesses were even stripped of their clothes, and the Dost himself tore off a sash ornamented with precious stones which supported the trousers of the daughter of Shah Mahmood, the wife of his own nephew Malek Kassem Mirza, son of Hadji Firooz Eddin.

Mir Efzel Khan, Isakzye, who had much assisted in the elevation of Hadji Firooz Eddin to power, afterwards became his prime minister. He was the most influential person at Herat after the governor, and strongly opposed any appeal to Fethi Khan for assistance, but the advice of Hadji Agaï, one of his officers, had prevailed over his. Foreseeing that which subsequently took place, Mir Efzel Khan resigned the command of the army and retired to Persia before the arrival of the vizier, and it was a happy thought of his, for the latter put out the eyes of Hadji Agaï, and Efzel Khan would have shared a similar fate.

After these measures, which Fethi Khan thought necessary for the security of the kingdom, had been taken, he marched against the enemy, encamped in front of the town of Kussan, about sixty miles from Herat, situated in the plain of Kiaffir Kaleh, on the extreme frontier of Persia and Herat. The battle commenced at dawn of day. The Persian prince, Hoosein Ali Mirza, had a splendid army under his command, which he disposed as follows:—In the first line he placed four regiments of regular infantry, under the orders of the Serdar Zoolfagar Khan;* this general, to give confidence to his newly organised troops, who, appreciating only cavalry, were grievously disconcerted at not being in that arm of the service, killed his magnificent Arab horse in front of his division, and placed himself at their head on foot. In spite, however, of this proof of courage, when his corps was attacked by the cavalry of Shere dil Khan, brother of the vizier, it was completely routed; they rallied, however, after a time behind the caravanserai and ruins on one side of the plain, and furiously recommenced the combat, which lasted till four o'clock in the afternoon, when the Persians, having 10,000 men *hors de combat*, began their retreat. A charge of cavalry made just at the right moment by the Serdar Kohendil Khan, also a brother of the vizier, turned this retreat into a complete rout, and the Persians precipitately abandoned the field. Fethi Khan immediately advanced to ascertain the position of things in his front, but he received a spent ball in his mouth, and, falling from his horse, was obliged to be carried to his tent. This fact having become known amongst the Afghans, they thought their chief was dead, and the Persians victorious; and losing at once all the courage they had so recently displayed, broke as if seized with a sudden panic. The first fugitives who arrived at Herat spread terror through the city; a part of the inhabitants left at once, and the remainder prepared to receive their

* The Sabre of Ali.—*Ferrier.*

new masters, when Fethi Khan arrived very *à propos* to restore confidence, for his wound was not a serious one, and he was always able to direct the affairs of government.

The Persians retreated with scarcely a halt as far as Meshed, and were not a little astonished to learn a few days after their defeat that the Afghans believed that they were the victors, in spite of their having lost their artillery and baggage, which were not, it is true, taken possession of by their adversaries until nine days after the battle.

After this victory, which disgusted the Persians for some time with the idea of attempting to take Herat, Fethi Khan occupied himself in fixing the revenues of the province, and in reconstructing the dilapidated fortifications of the city. His just and enlightened administration obtained for him the esteem and affection of the inhabitants. I have had opportunities of conversing with many Heratees who were acquainted with this remarkable man, and they spoke of him with veneration. His virtues were as great as his courage; he was completely devoted to the glory and interests of his country; his fame was carried to the highest point by his last victory; and he was making his preparations for the conquest of Khorassan, when a fearful catastrophe deprived Afghanistan of this worthy man, and annihilated the generous designs which he had conceived for her, and which would have made that kingdom as prosperous and powerful as it had been under the great Ahmed Shah.

Kamran Mirza, a monster of vice and ferocity, guiltless of ever having felt one noble or generous sentiment, witnessed with the greatest displeasure the successes of Fethi Khan, by whom he had been prevented from taking part in the government on account of the murder of Kaissar Mirza. From that day he had thought only of taking vengeance upon the vizier, and sought every opportunity of rendering him an object of suspicion to his father, to whom he spoke in depreciating terms of all his actions; he tried also in every possible way to excite the jealousy of the other serdars, who were already only too much disposed to side with him, and who always fell in with his views when he brought any complaints to the notice of the Shah; but Mahmood, delighted to find himself powerful with so little trouble, and enabled to gratify his own depraved inclinations without being obliged to take any part in public affairs which were so well conducted, refused for a long time to believe in the disloyal and infamous accusations brought against his minister. Obliged however to listen continually to a repetition of them, and thinking over his extraordinary success, and the influence he had obtained in consequence, he at length finished by entertaining a few misgivings, but he was completely amazed when he saw Hadji Firooz Eddin arrive at Kabul. This prince protested loudly against the manner in which he had been treated by the vizier, the invasion of his harem, the loss of his property, and spared no exaggeration to make his brother believe the accuracy of his statements. Kamran Mirza came to his aid, and used every effort to convince the king that his royal dignity had been insulted in the person of his brother, thus brought before him loaded with chains like a vile criminal, and also in that of his own daughter, the wife of Malek Kassem, from whose person Dost Mohamed Khan had stripped the last vestment which could protect her from his gaze and that of his associates. The serdars, who were jealous of the vizier's power, supported these representations, bringing to the notice of the feeble monarch a host of other disgraceful actions of which they said Fethi Khan had been guilty. They assured the Shah that he had determined upon his ruin; that the king ought to be beforehand with him, and put him to death; that there were at his court twenty chiefs braver and more capable than he was; until at length Mahmood Shah, yielding to the lowest feelings of jealousy, had not the strength of mind to resist their arguments, and he gave an order that the eyes of Fethi Khan should be put out.

Kamran would not rely upon any one but himself to execute this diabolical sentence: he kept the king's instructions as secret as he could, and left for Herat immediately, towards the close of 1817, to be sure of his victim. The prince had broken his parole, for it had been agreed between Mahmood Shah and his vizier that he was not to leave the court, and that fact must have been a warning to the latter, who was also told by his friends of the fate that awaited him; but he would not believe in such base cruelty and ingratitude, and took no precautions to guard himself from the malice of his enemies. He received the son of his sovereign with the most profound respect and the greatest honour, and, instead of evincing any mistrust, seemed as if he wished to induce him to forget the past, intreating him that he would for the future go hand in hand with him in consolidating the power of the Suddozye dynasty and raising the glory of the Afghan nation.

The vizier had been to him every morning to receive his orders since the prince arrived at Herat; the best intelligence seemed to exist between them; and Fethi Khan had already accused his friends of having given themselves up to chimerical fears, when, one day on entering the Bagh-Shah (a royal palace outside the city, and the residence of the prince), he was arrested with his suite, which consisted only of twenty persons, and his eyes were immediately put out.

The same fate was reserved for the three brothers of the vizier, namely, Poor dil Khan, Shere dil Khan, and Kohendil Khan, who, during the time that this abominable cruelty was being committed, were in the royal palace of the Tchahar-bagh in the city, quietly playing at chess. Generally speaking, they accompanied their brother in his visits to the prince, but on this day, Poor dil Khan being indisposed, he dispensed with their attendance. When Kamran saw that the three other victims had not come within reach of his vengeance, he was suffocated with rage, and sent a detachment of soldiers to arrest them immediately. Fortunately, however, one of their servants, hearing by accident of the danger which threatened them, ran to the palace and informed them of what had occurred, but he had scarcely fulfilled this act of devotion when the satellites of Kamran Mirza filled the court of the Tchahar-bagh. Flight was now almost impossible, for every mode of egress was carefully guarded, and the only mode of escape was to put a bold front upon the matter, which the three brothers did. They were accompanied by only two servants, one armed with a sabre, the other with a dagger, and Poor dil Khan, being unwell, retired to a terrace of the house with them; but Shere dil Khan, arming himself with the sabre, and Kohendil Khan with the dagger, rushed upon the soldiers with such impetuosity and resolution, that the fellows, thinking, in all probability, that they were supported by their servants, fled terrified from the house. Taking advantage of this moment of panic, the two heroes promptly rejoined their brother, and from the terrace leaped on to that of a house adjoining the palace without being seen, and escaped to their residence with the utmost haste. After having armed themselves to the teeth, they mounted their horses, and accompanied by a few of their followers took to flight, but on arriving at the city gates they found two hundred soldiers there to dispute their passage, and through these they had to cut their way. Shere dil Khan and Kohendil Khan were fortunate enough to do so without receiving a scratch, but Poor dil Khan, weakened by sickness, had his horse killed under him, when a score of men threw themselves upon him, bound his hands, and carried him to Kamran Mirza. The prince, seeing that two victims had still escaped him, dissimulated the regret he felt, and assured Poor dil Khan, whom he put in prison, that no harm would befall him, hoping that he would be able to make use of him at a future time as a means of securing by craft his principal adversaries.

Kamran Mirza remained some time longer at Herat, endeavouring by promises and presents to secure the army to his own interests; but always preoccupied with the idea of completing his sanguinary work, and putting to death the brothers and adherents of Fethi Khan, he went to Kandahar, where he hoped to succeed in this object.

CHAPTER XII.

Shere dil Khan raises Kandahar — Kamran proceeds there — Poor dil Khan escapes — Cruelties of Kamran upon Fethi Khan — Brothers of the Vizier — Dost Mohamed Khan — Cause of his quarrel with Fethi Khan — He seizes Kabul — Flight of the Royal Family — Mahmood and Kamran meet at Ghuznee — Dost Mohamed puts them to flight — Murder of Fethi Khan — The Shah and his son are pursued and arrive at Herat — Misunderstanding between the princes — They acknowledge the suzerainty of Persia — Quarrels between Mahmood and Kamran — Hadji Firooz and Kalech Khan attack Kamran — The latter is killed and Hadji Firooz made prisoner — Kamran and the Persians at variance — Revolt of Furrah — Kamran proceeds to that place — Moustapha Khan and Mohamed Hoosein revolt at Herat — Cause of this — Djehanguir Mirza is proclaimed chief, and afterwards deposed — Hadji Firooz succeeds him — Death of Meuhvali Khan — Hadji Firooz retires to Meshed — Moustapha Khan closes the gates of Herat against Kamran — He besieges the city, but retires on the approach of Shere dil Khan — The latter also retires — Cruelty of Moustapha Khan — Conspiracy of Syud Mir Sedik — Kamran enters Herat — Miserable end of Moustapha Khan — Vengeance of Kamran — Reflections on the Afghans.

AFTER their flight from Herat Shere dil Khan and his brother sought refuge in the fortified village of Nadalee, situated about twenty-three miles from Girishk, which belonged to Adeh, the mother of Fethi Khan. From thence they despatched emissaries in all directions to rouse the nomade tribes. A great number of the Barukzyes responded to their appeal, which formed the nucleus of a little army, and this was soon increased by numerous deserters from the royal forces, who would not serve under Kamran.

The prince, observing that the detachments which he sent from the city were constantly destroyed or repulsed by the partizans of Fethi Khan, employed the arts of cunning to lead his brothers to fall into his net. He had dragged about with him the unfortunate minister, and endeavoured to persuade Poor dil Khan, whom he took from his prison, that he had put his brother's eyes out only to raise him to the post of vizier: at the same time he gave him a magnificent robe of honour, made him a serdar, promised that the firman of vizier should be sent to him as soon as Shere dil Khan and Kohendil Khan had made their submission, and pressed him to write and tell them to come to Kandahar. Poor dil Khan appreciated this brilliant promise at its exact value, but he appeared as if he believed the prince and entered into his views; he assured him of his entire devotion, and behaved as if he intended to keep his word, but two days afterwards he fled, and to their great joy reached his brothers at Nadalee, for their measures had been almost paralyzed up to that moment by the fear they experienced that he would be treated by Kamran in the same way that he had dealt with their eldest brother. His presence also brought fresh recruits to their ranks, for the Afghans had great confidence in him; they considered him as one of the most talented of the sons of Payendeh Khan, and in the differences which existed between themselves almost always requested him to be the arbitrator.

Kamran Mirza, irritated by the flight of Poor dil Khan, which he might have foreseen, revenged himself on the unfortunate Fethi Khan, upon whom he inflicted a thousand outrages and cruel tortures. Having perceived that a ray of light still remained in the eyes of his victim, he himself introduced a hot iron into the orbits in order to dry up every part. It was in this condition that the butcher dragged him to Ghuznee, where the Shah Mahmood awaited him, but his courageous minister never asked for mercy, and, by his firm and resigned bearing, showed himself as great in adversity as he had been generous in the exercise of his power.

Such cruelties practised upon such a man merited punishment indeed, and seventeen brothers of the victim soon united to take their revenge. Their names were as follows:—

The Vizier Fethi Khan	By the same mother	Dead.
Mohamed Azim Khan		"
Timoor Khan		"
Poor dil Khan	By the same mother	"
Shere dil Khan		"
Kohendil Khan		Living in 1846.
Rahim dil Khan		"
Mir dil Khan		"
Dost Mohamed Khan	By the same mother	"
Emir Mohamed Khan		Dead.
Djemal Khan		"
Sultan Mohamed Khan	By the same mother	Living.
Yar Mohamed Khan		Dead.
Pir Mohamed Khan		Living.
Syud Mohamed Khan		"
Nawab Assad Khan	By the same mother	Dead.
Nawab Samut Khan		"
Nawab Djabbar Khan		Living.
Djumbè Khan	Son of a slave	"

Mohamed Azim Khan, who, after Fethi Khan, was the eldest of the sons of Payendeh Khan, governed Cashmeer. Being ill at the time he heard of the atrocious cruelties inflicted on his blind brother, he could not then join his relatives, but he raised the standard of revolt in this province against the Shah Mahmood, and sent Dost Mohamed Khan before him to Kabul, in order that he might work upon the population to rise in favour of their cause. This young chief was the very man for such an undertaking, for, as it has been shown, he had already made himself remarked on several occasions for courage and military talents, though at the moment his services were required he was in prison, and the following were the reasons that led to his captivity.

A few days prior to his attacking the Persians at Kiaffir Kaleh, Fethi Khan ordered him to give up some magnificent pearls the Dost had purchased, but which the vizier had already selected for himself, and stated thus much to the merchant who had them on sale; he also required him to restore the girdle ornamented with brilliants which he had taken from the daughter of Shah Mahmood when he broke into the harem of Hadji Firooz Eddin. But Dost Mohamed obstinately refusing to comply with his wishes, it produced a rupture between them, when the latter, fearing the consequences of his brother's anger, departed secretly from the royal camp, and went to Cashmeer; Mohamed Azim Khan, who was own brother to the vizier, took his part, and demanded that the brilliants and the unlucky pearls should be surrendered to him for the purpose of being forwarded to Fethi Khan, who had foreseen that the theft would give rise to complaints and fresh intrigues against his family.

The Dost, again refusing to restore these valuables, was detained a prisoner until they came to release him in order that he might assist in avenging the brother by whom and for whom he had been so severely treated. The voice of honour, and revenge for blood, and still more the conviction that he had been in error, spoke more powerfully to his heart than his resentment; he therefore collected a small corps of men, and advanced boldly against the capital. Shah Mahmood, plunged in debauch, was incapable of watching over his own safety, and from the moment the insurrection broke out confided the care of Kabul to his grandson Djehanguir Mirza, son of Kamran, with whom he associated, as his lieutenant and responsible adviser, his new vizier Mohamed Attah Khan, Popolzye: after this Mahmood retired to the fortress of Ghuznee, from whence he wrote to his son to come and rejoin him. Dost Mohamed Khan, having completely beaten the detachments which Djehanguir Mirza sent against him, entered Kabul, and obliged that prince to seek safety in flight; he also took Attah Mohamed Khan prisoner, had his eyes put out on the public square, and subsequently sent him away into the mountains.

After having been rejoined by Djehanguir Mirza, and a few soldiers who were with him, it was not long before Shah Mahmood was surrounded by the troops which his son Kamran brought from Kandahar—much weakened it is true in numbers, and much discouraged, but still able to afford him the hope of reducing the insurgents if he had been a clever man. The army having halted a few days at Ghuznee to give Kamran a little repose, he marched to Kabul to put down the rebels; but Mohamed Azim Khan, who, now re-established in health, had just joined Dost Mohamed, spared him half his journey, and, midway between Ghuznee and Kabul, offered him battle at the head of four thousand men. The prince, who had twelve thousand, was not in the least doubtful of success, but he was wrong in his estimate of the feeling of his troops; for, on the night preceding the conflict, they passed over to his adversary. Mohamed Azim and the Dost pursued Kamran immediately to the walls of Ghuznee, and soon obliged his father and himself, and those who supported their party, to evacuate the town.

Shah Mahmood, made desperate by this last disaster, ordered Fethi Khan, who had now been deprived of his eyesight eight months, to be brought into his presence, and commanded him to write to his brothers, and desire them to return to their duty. But the unfortunate vizier calmly replied that in losing his sight he had lost also all his influence over his fellow-men, and that he no longer occupied himself with the affairs of this world. The king, enraged at this answer, ordered him to be put to death, and his enemies, the nobles of the court, were charged with the execution of the sentence; Kamran Mirza, himself the most cruel of the Suddozyes, struck the first blow, and at this signal the rest drew their daggers, rushed upon him, and strove who should make him feel the greatest torture and suffering. They flayed him alive, disjointed his members, which they drew from his body one by one, and at length decapitated him, which put an end to his agonies. His corpse, thus mutilated, was abandoned to the public executioner, who cut it in pieces, threw them into a sack, and carried them to Ghuznee, where they were interred.

Not a sigh or complaint escaped Fethi Khan amidst these horrible tortures: he was sustained by the courage of a hero, and the calm of a pure conscience.

A general cry of indignation arose from one end of Afghanistan to the other against the murderers of this great man, and those who had remained faithful to the Suddozye party, not from a feeling of sympathy, but from a sentiment of duty, now left it; even the personal friends of the king were moved with compassion at the manner in which his old and faithful servant was put to death; and there were very few serdars whose jealousies were not subdued by his sad end.

Shah Mahmood, a wanderer and a fugitive, had now only a few servants around him, repulsed, harassed, and tracked, and obliged to shun inhabited places, he dared not stop even in the most desert spots, so hot was the pursuit. The dangers he underwent were incessant; he suffered every kind of privation, having nothing to support life but roots and wild fruits. Nearly dead from hunger, and in the last stage of despair, the fugitives endeavoured to reach Kandahar, which Kamran, on leaving Ghuznee, had confided to the care of Gul Mohamed Khan, Popolzye; but he soon learned that the city had fallen into the hands of the Mohamedzyes, and that with the assistance of Mir Efzel Khan, Isakzye, Poor dil Khan had seized it. After Fethi Khan lost his sight, Efzel returned from Persia to live in the midst of his tribe, encamped in the environs of Koohnichine, a fortress situated on the banks of the Helmund, which belonged to him, and Poor dil Khan, without giving himself any concern as to the antagonistic feeling which existed between Mir Efzel Khan and his elder brother, came to him and demanded his assistance and that of his tribe; this was conceded, and the Mir joined the Mohamedzyes. The two chiefs then marched against Kandahar, which surrendered to them after a feeble resistance; but the governor Gul Mohamed Khan escaped, and reached Herat, the garrison of which was devoted to Kamran Mirza, and the former knew how to keep them in obedience.

Shah Mahmood, being informed of this fortunate circumstance, immediately directed his steps towards that city, but, being completely without provisions and menaced on all sides, he was obliged to take the least frequented and accessible roads; the number of his followers diminished day by day, hunger, fatigue, and privation accompanying them everywhere. It was in this condition that they crossed the Paropamisan chain, inhabited by the Hazarahs Poocht-Kooh, who, though enemies of the Afghans, nevertheless inspired them with less terror than the latter. At length Mahmood reached Herat, having with him only his son Kamran, his brother Hadji Firooz Eddin, and eleven servants who were devoted to him.

But discord soon divided this royal trio. Kamran Mirza had only desired the fall of Fethi Khan in order that he might himself direct the government; he commenced therefore by seizing upon all authority; Shah Mahmood, who, not without reason, attributed his misfortunes to his son, resisted these attempts and determined to govern for himself, which daily produced between them the most violent scenes; and Hadji Firooz Eddin, wearied with these interminable discussions, obtained permission from the king to retire to Meshed, which he did immediately.

For some time after their arrival at Herat Mahmood and his son were alarmed by the threats of the Persians, who seemed disposed to set up anew their claims upon the city, but Shah Mahmood and Kamran did not make this matter so much a question of *amour propre* as did Hadji Firooz Eddin, for they admitted without protest the suzerainty of the Shah of Persia, bound themselves to pay him tribute, and thought themselves fortunate in being able to remain on such conditions the peaceable possessors of the last refuge that they were able to find in Afghanistan.

In 1819, a short time after this agreement had been concluded, Kamran Mirza, tired of the tenacity with which his father maintained his rights as sovereign, drove him from Herat, but Shah Mahmood, having collected a small army amongst the Eimaks, laid siege to the city in 1820. He was however beaten and obliged to fly to the Hazarahs Zeidnat: nevertheless he did not consider himself vanquished, and for a time appeared to have recovered the energy of his youth to fight his son. After having reinforced his army he returned in 1821, and besieged Herat a second time; but having invested it for a few days, the serdars interfered between father and son, and effected a reconciliation, upon the understanding that Shah Mahmood was to have the title of king, and enjoy all the honours, and his son the power he so much coveted.

While these two princes were disputing in the west the possession of one corner of Afghanistan, the other portions of the kingdom passed into the hands of the Mohamedzyes and the Sikhs. The former were too much occupied with their war against the latter, and their differences with one another, to carry their arms against Herat, and repaid themselves by agitating that province with rumours and secret conspiracies, so that Kamran had at first great difficulty in making his authority respected, and when it was a little strengthened he had to repulse the attacks which were made by his adversaries from the exterior.

When Hadji Firooz Eddin, by no means satisfied with the conduct either of his brother or his nephew, retired to Meshed, he met there the famous Serdar Kalech Khan, Taymooni, who represented to him how wrong he had been to leave Herat, where neither Mahmood nor Kamran had the least chance of being able to maintain his position, while he, Firooz Eddin, who had governed that country for years to the general satisfaction of the people, would most assuredly have been before long raised by them to the sovereign power. This serdar said, in short, all that he could to awaken his ambition, and offered his support to reinstate him in power. The prince for a long time resisted these arguments, but at length, overcome by his solicitations, decided upon taking Kalech's advice and reign again over a people and a province which he had rendered happy and flourishing for sixteen years of his paternal administration. Kalech Khan made all the preparations which could suggest themselves to the mind of a clever man, and the expedition was undertaken in 1822. It was kept so secret that Kamran Mirza, who had gone to hunt in the country round Kussan, a town situated about fifteen hours from Herat, on the road to Meshed, was surprised by the advanced guard of Hadji Firooz, and very nearly made prisoner; the devotion of four of his servants, who defended his house, and were all killed at the entrance, while he gained the fields by a back door, alone secured him the opportunity of flight. Arrived at Herat, he immediately despatched his minister, Attah Khan, and several other officers, in all directions to assemble the contingents of the nomade tribes, who promptly arrived to his assistance and relieved the city. While these troops, under the orders of Attah Khan, Ali Kioouzye, attacked the army of Hadji Firooz, the prince Kamran left the city at the head of two thousand Afghans, and fell upon the enemy's rear. The conflict lasted thirteen hours; very little powder was expended, for the two armies fought with cold steel foot to foot, and perhaps no more obstinate battle was ever fought under the walls of Herat; when it was over there might be counted more dead bodies than living men. The victory nevertheless remained for a long time uncertain, but the death of Kalech Khan turned the tide of battle in favour of Kamran. This serdar had singled out and pursued the prince with fury, and in a few yards more he would have crossed swords with the miscreant torturer of Fethi Khan; but fortune was not in the ascendant for him, his horse came down in a ravine and injured the khan's neck in the fall. His soldiers, seeing him in this disabled state, turned and fled, and, the enemy having made him prisoner, Kamran sabred his foe himself—on this occasion as on every other he showed himself ferocious in the combat, and cruel when victorious. Hadji Firooz was also captured, and he would not have been spared any more than his general if Shah Mahmood had not interfered energetically in his favour; but he was subsequently confined in the citadel, where he was closely watched.

The prince Kamran was scarcely delivered from this danger when he was called upon to deal with another. The united chiefs of Khorassan attacked Herat in 1823; this expedition was undertaken by order of Feth Ali Shah, King of Persia, to force Kamran to pay the tribute, which under various pretexts he had never done. During three months the Khorassanees made many unsuccessful efforts to take the city, and they did not leave the province until they had completely ravaged it. These inroads of the Persians were frequently renewed, and Kamran repulsed them all by force of arms whenever there was a chance of his coming victorious out of the contest; but he much more frequently met and bent to the storm, as Hadji Firooz had been forced to do before him, by paying a small tribute to the Shah of Persia, and in conforming to some frivolous ceremonies of vassalage.

Kamran Mirza had scarcely shaken off these enemies from without when he had to contend with disagreeable complications within the province of Herat, and in the year 1824 they extended to the districts which up to that time had been pretty quiet. That of Furrah more particularly pushed matters to the last extremity: the inhabitants finished by separating themselves from the capital to form an alliance with Kandahar, and Kamran was obliged to march in person with an army to reduce them to obedience.

Before departing on this expedition the prince took every precaution to preserve the tranquillity of Herat in his absence. At the time Shah Mahmood accommodated matters with his son, he lost all his influence, and was forced by Kamran to retire to the Bagh Shah, a palace situated about a gunshot from the city, where he could at his ease give himself up to his depraved inclinations. The citadel with a good garrison was confided to the charge of Moustapha Khan, Zoori, who had always been devoted to him, and he appointed his maternal uncle Mohamed Hoosein Khan governor of the city, with the title of *vekil*. These two personages were to have equal authority and a voice in the direction of affairs, and Kamran hoped that in opposing one to the other he would be able to secure a greater guarantee for their fidelity. His eldest son, Djehanguir Mirza, was left in Herat to control their actions, but they held this prince in little consideration, who became simply the promulgator of the orders which they gave, and not the representative of the regal authority.

The Vekil Mohamed Hoosein Khan had great influence in the city, and the Serdar Moustapha Khan a still greater in the army. At first they seemed to act perfectly well together, but they were united only in appearance; each sought secretly to overthrow the other, and to put Kamran on one side that he might govern in his place. They also attempted to dissimulate their ambitious purpose from one another, when an occurrence wholly unexpected arose, and made them participate in concert in a revolt which each of them had individually premeditated.

The troops left for Furrah in the hope that, as stated by Kamran, they would receive their pay directly they arrived in that district, but this promise not having been performed they began to murmur, and the prince was forced to send to Herat for money. One of the officers of his household, by name Meuhvalee Khan, was charged with this mission, and to him Kamran gave a note of hand for six thousand tomauns, which he ordered his uncle Mohamed Hoosein Khan to pay with the least possible delay.

Meuhvalee Khan performed this duty in the most haughty and arrogant manner, because the money was not ready; the Vekil begged him to have patience for a few days, but the officer demanded that the sum should be given him on the instant, and apostrophized Hoosein Khan in menacing and opprobrious terms. The Serdar Moustapha Khan, who was present during this altercation, represented to his colleague that Meuhvalee Khan must be cognizant of some evil intention which Kamran entertained towards them: "For," said he, "if a subordinate addresses us in such a manner, what will not the prince do when he returns?" The imagination of these chiefs, already prepared for revolt, soon became heated; they immediately arrested the messenger, and decided upon overthrowing Kamran; but when they came to discuss the basis upon which the government was to be established, and who should be its chief, they found it was not easy to come to an understanding between themselves, and the question was adjourned. Nevertheless, they agreed upon the main point—namely, the overthrow of the prince Kamran; and also that his son Djehanguir must be compromised in the eyes of the people, and rendered odious by being induced to commit some unnecessary act of cruelty. They began, therefore, by making him issue a proclamation that his father's rule was at an end; and it would seem that this prince, then about twenty-two years of age, agreed very willingly to this proposition, thinking without doubt that there was no more harm in taking the place of his father Kamran than there had been in his dethroning Mahmood Shah. Accordingly Djehanguir was proclaimed Sovereign Prince of Herat, and his first act was to pronounce the condemnation of Meuhvalee Khan. The sentence was a terrible one: they first cut off his nose, his ears, and his fingers, and from hour to hour scored him with sabre-wounds. The agonies of this unfortunate man lasted two days, after which one of the officers of Djehanguir Mirza dragged him through the bazaars, and in a loud voice invited all those who were friends of the new sovereign to throw a stone at the wretch, while two hundred men, who had been assembled there previously by the serdar and the Vekil, also stoned the miserable sufferer.

Directly Mohamed Hoosein and Moustapha Khan had attained their object by compromising Djehanguir with his father, and making him detested in the eyes of the Heratees, they improvised a revolt by which the prince was overthrown and imprisoned, and the executive power placed in their own hands. This was the critical moment for these ambitious men, for they had penetrated the intentions of each other. The Vekil, who did not feel himself strong enough to attack the serdar openly, and dislodge him from the citadel, released Hadji Firooz from the prison in which he was confined, and made the citizens acknowledge him as their sovereign. Moustapha Khan, thus forestalled, saw very well that he could not obtain anything from the inhabitants if he stood alone, for Hadji Firooz was their idol; they still remembered how much happiness they had enjoyed during his administration of affairs, and his return to power filled them with joy. As a counterpoise to this, the serdar went to the Mahmood at Bagh Shah, where he lived pretty nearly forgotten, and was ignorant of what was passing in the city, with the intention of setting him up as an opponent to Hadji Firooz. This done, blood soon flowed in Herat, and Moustapha Khan, defeated in the first conflict, was obliged to shut himself up with the old king in the citadel, from whence he cannonaded the city, which, to avoid complete destruction, surrendered at discretion.

This second reign of Hadji Firooz Eddin lasted only eighteen days: the victor Moustapha Khan obliged him to return once more and seek refuge at Meshed, to which city he was followed by the Vekil. The former was still alive in 1845; I saw him in my way through Meshed in that year, and received these details from his own lips.

After the deposition of Djehanguir Mirza, and when he saw the power as he thought escape from him by the election of Firooz Eddin, Moustapha Khan, thinking his chances of success were small, and calculating still less upon Shah Mahmood, sent an express to Kamran Mirza to beg him to hasten his return, promising to stand firm for his party until he made his appearance. The prince hastened to adopt this suggestion, and arrived under the walls of Herat the day after his uncle Hadji Firooz and the Vekil had retired from the city, but he found the gates closed; for the victorious Moustapha, having now no other competitor, replied to the summons to open them that he knew no other sovereign than Shah Mahmood, would obey his orders only, and that those orders were that his son should not be allowed to enter the city.

Kamran invested the place immediately after he received this message, but he had scarcely opened his trenches when he was obliged to retire to Laush-Jowaine, a fortified castle and position to the south of Furrah, to avoid a battle with Shere dil Khan, Mohamedzye, whose forces were much superior to his. This serdar had been sent against him by his brother Poor dil Khan, the sovereign of Kandahar, as much to avenge the death of Fethi Khan as to seize upon Herat, and this conquest, added to the others which he had made to the eastward since the fall of Shah Mahmood, would have made them masters of the whole of Afghanistan, as we shall see hereafter.

Shere dil Khan, not having succeeded in obtaining possession of the place by simple summons as he had expected, commenced the siege, but he was soon forced to raise it, and finally to retreat towards Kandahar, finding himself between two fires; for an army from Khorassan, commanded by Mohamed Khan, Garai, whom Moustapha Khan had called to his support, was in the neighbourhood.

The usurper, now being rid of Hadji Firooz, of Kamran, and of Shere dil Khan, satisfied the expectations of his ally Mohamed Khan, Garai, with a sum of money, and by paying his expenses during the campaign; but not feeling sufficiently secure even after this, he thought that the best method of maintaining his position was to destroy all those who had opposed him. Blood again flowed on all sides, and revolt was the only resource that remained to the miserable Heratees by which they could deliver themselves from this tyrant.

Syud Mir Sedik Khan, chief of the Afghan branch of the Berduranees, a tribe from which the majority of the citizens of Herat had sprung, invited the prince Kamran to approach the town as secretly as he could, declaring that when he arrived they would admit him. Though Kamran had since his last flight been deserted by very nearly the whole of his army, he did not hesitate to accept this dangerous invitation to regain his power, and, reaching Herat about midnight, his march not having been discovered, the Syud admitted him into the place without the prince having been compelled to fire a single shot. The remainder of the night was occupied in making the arrival of Kamran known to the inhabitants, and the citadel in which Moustapha Khan resided was surrounded at sunrise by ten thousand armed men, who aroused him by a well-sustained fire of artillery and volleys of musketry. The serdar, surprised by this sudden attack, lost a few men in the first instance, but after a few hours he completely organised the defence, which during a month was most vigorously conducted, and he only made up his mind to surrender when the towers, shaken to their foundations by the explosion of mines, were on the point of falling, and large breaches opened a wide passage for the besieging army. In this extremity he sent the Serdar Dost Mohamed Khan, Popolzye, one of his party, to Kamran, to offer his submission: at the same time he invoked the clemency of the conqueror, and sent him a Koran, opened at the verse which recommends Mahomedans to bear no hatred, and forgive each other their faults; but the prince, certainly very far from a good Mussulman, and, as I have already remarked, a rare example of ferocity, fell upon the messenger and cudgelled him with a dervish's stick which he happened to have in his hand.

Moustapha Khan, appreciating clearly from this incident the kind of fate that awaited him, defended himself with desperation for ten days more—it was a lion encaged. . . . At last the assault was given; the place fell; Moustapha was taken prisoner, and suffered the most dreadful of deaths. His body was burned with hot irons, his flesh torn with red-hot pincers by shreds; covered with wounds and nearly flayed, he was bound to a large tree at the entrance to the citadel, and on this spot the people congregated to spit in his face, and covered him with every kind of excrement. At last they ripped open his belly, and he expired after enduring seven days of the most fearful agony. The tree to which he was bound was standing in 1845. Kamran Mirza punished his father, Shah Mahmood, for having assisted the serdar in this revolt, by depriving him of his wine during one whole month, which was to him a terrible infliction. As to his son Djehanguir Mirza, he gave him his liberty, but with it, as a small recompense for having assisted in dethroning his father, two thousand cuts with the bastinado on the soles of his feet, forgetting that he had been guilty of the same crime himself. In this family the son, grandson, and grandfather were all equally worthy of each other, and strove to distinguish themselves by the most odious crimes. Such is the Afghan character: the people of Afghanistan honour that which is vile with us.

From the death of Moustapha Khan, not one year went round

without Kamran's seeing some ambitious character putting his sovereignty in question. Alternately victor and vanquished, his reign was nothing more than a long drama of intestine wars, conspiracies, and revolts, followed by the most atrocious executions. He cruelly put to death all who were opposed to him, even those whom he merely suspected: and numbers of these unfortunate beings were thrown under the feet of elephants, or to hungry tigers, which he kept for this purpose. There was in his revenge a barbarous ferocity of which it would be difficult to form a conception; and the most disgusting feature in it was, that he delighted to be himself the executioner of the sentences which he pronounced. In Europe the memory of Kamran would have been execrated for ages, but the Afghans see things in another point of view; courage so called is in their eyes the greatest of all virtues: it stands in place of every other, and to take vengeance upon an enemy, to kill and massacre plenty of human beings, passes with them for courage. Directly a prince, a chief, or a person of lower grade is in the possession of absolute power, he ought to prove that he has it by the massacres he orders. They cannot comprehend why an enemy vanquished or disarmed should be pardoned, and they regard this as an act of weakness and pusillanimity. In their estimation he who makes the most victims is the most powerful, the most honoured; and it is very doubtful whether there is a family in Herat which has not been deprived of some one of its members by Kamran. Now that he is dead, the people flock in crowds in pilgrimage to his tomb. With such sentiments it is not surprising to see the history of this nation broadly traced in characters of blood.

CHAPTER XIII.

Death of Shah Mahmood — Kamran is suspected of murdering his father — He indulges in every kind of excess — Death of Attah Khan — Yar Mohamed Khan is made Vizier of Herat — Hostility of the Persians against this principality — Intrigues of Abbas Mirza — Yar Mohamed arrives at Meshed — He is put to the torture by the Persian prince — Is delivered by the Athar Bashi — Measures of Yar Mohamed — Revolt of the Syud Mohamed Sedik — He is betrayed by Kamran and executed — The Shah is closely watched by Yar Mohamed — His sons are disgraced — Project of Mohamed Shah on Herat — The Barukzyes consent to the restoration of Shah Shooja — He plays the despot, and is overthrown — Eyoob succeeds him — Mohamed Azim Khan marches against the Sikhs — Runjeet Sing successful against the Afghans — The battle of Noochero — The Afghans are beaten — Death of Azim Khan — The character of that serdar — His son Habib Ullah Khan succeeds him.

KAMRAN MIRZA was generally suspected of having abridged the days of his father, the Shah Mahmood, who was found dead in his bath in 1829; some assert that he was poisoned, and some that he was strangled, by the command of his son, who was tired of seeing him raised to power like a puppet every time an ambitious man revolted against himself. From the time of his father's decease Kamran took the title of King; he then seemed to have lost all energy, and retired within the walls of the citadel of Herat, remaining almost a stranger to the affairs of government, the direction of which he gave up to his minister, the Serdar Attah Khan, Ali Kioouzye, who had given him many marks of his attachment, and in whom he had entire confidence; after which, and following the example of his father, he commenced a life of drunkenness, opium-eating, and every Eastern vice.

This alteration in the conduct of the prince awakened the hopes of every party, and each wished to try its strength in several disturbances, but the vigilance of Attah Khan suppressed them with so much energy that they withdrew into the shade, and made no further attempts during his lifetime. This able man, who had distinguished himself as much in war as in the civil administration of his country, died in 1830, leaving three sons, serdars like himself. In conformity with the custom of Afghanistan, where the office of prime minister is hereditary like the crown, it was expected that the eldest of these sons, the Serdar Dine Mohamed Khan, would succeed his father as vizier. Though young, he had shown himself worthy of this distinction by his bravery in the field and his military capacity, of which he had given proof on several occasions; but, surrounded by intrigues, he refused to accept power, and abandoned his rights to his cousin, the Serdar Yar Mohamed Khan, who, having lost his father at a very tender age, had been brought up with him in the house of Attah Khan. The minister had always evinced a great predilection for his nephew, and frequently expressed an opinion anticipatory of his future greatness; and Shah Kamran, influenced by a certain mollah, Mohamed Athar Bashi, the apothecary-in-chief, who flattered his passions, and administered his drugs to excite them, accepted Yar Mohamed Khan as his vizier.

This young serdar, who was distinguished for his courage and cleverness, had made numerous partizans amongst the Heratees. His father Abdullah Khan, Ali Kioouzye, although of noble extraction, was not in the outset a very great personage; but he rose by merit, and became governor of Cashmeer at the period when Shah Mahmood first ascended the throne. That sovereign released him from prison, in which he had been confined by Shah Zeman, and placed him in this high position; thus fortune favoured him, and his son's career was even more successful.

The début of Yar Mohamed in administrative affairs justified the selection which had been made in his person; it is, however, to be presumed that he at once turned his views towards the assumption of supreme power, for all his acts tended constantly towards the accomplishment of his ambitious projects. As firm as he was vigilant, he always held his adversaries in check by depreciating them; he successively removed those most dangerous to his interests in a manner that did not produce too much discontent, and endeavoured to smother the rivalry existing between the various tribes on whose support he could rely; he proceeded, in short, like a clever and intelligent man, and the Shah Kamran, confiding in him, followed his advice in all respects. But Yar Mohamed had been minister scarcely a year when one of those events so frequent in Afghanistan arose to check for a moment his dawning fortunes.

At the commencement of 1832 Feth Ali Shah, always preoccupied with the idea of joining the province of Herat to Persia, assembled 30,000 men at Meshed under the command of Abbas Mirza, the heir apparent to the throne. For some years past Russia had encroached considerably on the north of the Persian territory; England had done the same thing in the south, to the prejudice of the Indian princes. Nevertheless, she had not made a progress that would enable her to secure as much influence in Persia as the Tzar. She commenced, therefore, by fearing that the Shah of Persia, whom she had abandoned to the Muscovites, would undertake the conquest of Herat, and this much more in accordance with the wishes of the Emperor Nicholas than his own. England was alarmed at this demonstration on the side of India of which Herat is the key, and brought forth all the springs of her clever policy to prevent it, or at least to paralyze the effects of it. She was, however, in the first instance, somewhat reassured by the reflection that, the Persian army being directed by English officers, could only obtain such success as they would permit. The East India Company was also clever enough to induce Feth Ali Shah to turn the expedition from its original object for a time, and reduce the petty chiefs of Khorassan, who had given only a nominal obedience to Persia since the reign of Nadir Shah.

On his arrival at Meshed the prince Abbas Mirza despatched one of his officers to the Shah Kamran to request him to send his minister there in order that they might consult together, and endeavour to terminate their differences in an amicable manner. The character of the prince inspiring the vizier with every confidence, he accepted this invitation, and went to Meshed attended by five hundred Afghan horse; but instead of coming to an arrangement as Yar Mohamed hoped, Abbas Mirza originated fresh and serious difficulties, and Yar Mohamed was very soon obliged to confess to himself that he had been led into a snare. With great secrecy, therefore, he immediately sent off his men by small detachments to Kootchan, then governed by Reza Kooli Khan, who had not been subdued by Abbas Mirza, and recommended them as brave fellows who could powerfully assist the ally of his sovereign in the defence of his fort, which Yar Mohamed considered one of the outworks of Herat. He then addressed a communication to the Persian prince containing most energetic protestations on his strange proceedings with regard to himself; but it was all very fine for him to invoke the inviolability of an ambassador's person, or the rights of individuals; no one listened to him, and a few days after, the prince, fearing his energy and talents, gave an order that his movements should be carefully watched. After this Abbas Mirza endeavoured to bring him to consent to an arrangement relative to Herat, but the vizier would not concede anything which he considered prejudicial to the interests of the Shah Kamran. The prince even went so far as to extract two of his teeth to cure his obstinacy, when by the intervention of some great personages this cruelty, unworthy of one of the Persian royal family, was abandoned. The Athar Bashi, however, soon arrived to offer himself as an hostage in the place of Yar Mohamed, who returned to Herat; but the vizier not having sent the prince the ransom which he had consented to pay to save his life, the Athar Bashi was placed in great danger: the death of Abbas Mirza, which took place towards the close of the year 1833, facilitated his release, which he succeeded in obtaining at the cost of 1000*l.* paid to those who had charge of him. He also promised to send them a similar sum when he reached Herat, but this he of course took very good care not to do.

The intrigues of the English at the court of Feth Ali Shah to prevent the expedition against Herat from being carried out, only partially succeeded; the troops were occupied in reducing the small fortresses still unsubdued of Khorassan, and two years elapsed between the period at which they reached Meshed, and the time when Mohamed Mirza, the eldest son of the hereditary prince of Persia, encamped under the walls of Herat with a *corps d'armée* to effect a preliminary investment of the place. This was to be succeeded by a regular siege on the arrival of the rear-guard under the command of his father, but Mohamed Mirza had scarcely pitched his tents under the city walls when he heard of the death of Abbas Mirza, in consequence of which he raised his camp, and retreated on Meshed.

When Yar Mohamed escaped from the Persians he retook, and with a strong hand, the reins of government: nevertheless his vigilance could not prevent the revolt of the nomade population in some of the districts situated in the north and east of the principality; but, an active gĕneral as well as a clever politician, he marched without delay against the rebels, and subdued them with as much promptitude as vigour. He subsequently led his troops southward, and made Kamran's authority respected in all the Seistan. After this he returned to Herat, and continued to take a firm course in furtherance of his secret designs.

Towards the close of the year 1834 an Indian Mussulman, who had been a sergeant in the East India Company's service, came to Herat, and offered his services to the Shah Kamran, which the vizier accepted, and from this time the infantry, till then held in little estimation there, was drilled, though very indifferently, on the European system.

Taking advantage also of a few years' peace which ensued after the retreat of the Persians, Yar Mohamed repaired the fortifications of the city, which in consequence of the numerous assaults they had sustained were partly in ruins. He created villages, invited the populations from a distance to settle in them and cultivate the land lying untilled or unreclaimed, and would have done at that time what he did at a later period, encouraged industry and commerce, and cleared the roads of myriads of robbers who had infested them, but such measures would then have injured his own interests. It is true that he governed, but Shah Kamran reigned, and he had the tact to make the odium of the plundering and discontent on the part of the people, fall upon the king, while he managed to secure to himself all the praise of whatever was good. If from the moment of his elevation to the post of vizier he was remarkable for those qualities which are with difficulty found united in an Afghan, he was nevertheless not exempt from the vices of his countrymen. During the entire reign of the Shah Kamran he was as avaricious, cruel, and implacable as it is possible for an Afghan to be; but unfortunately this is frequently necessary with people of this nation, though in his extortions and sanguinary executions he was not always guided by any regard for the public weal: his ambition on such occasions was concealed under a veil of devotion which he affected to feel for his prince and his country, and the serdars, who were not his dupes, were continually on the alert to overthrow him, but without the least success.

Amongst the numerous revolts which he had to repress, that which broke out at the commencement of 1837 gave him the most serious uneasiness. It was headed by the same Syud Mir Sedik Khan, Berduranee, who had surrendered the town of Herat to the Shah Kamran when he was dethroned by the Serdar Moustapha

Khan; but less fortunate on this occasion, Mir Sedik, having failed in his enterprise, was taken and executed. The unfortunate Syud had entered into this conspiracy with the full knowledge and consent of the king, who, beginning to perceive that his vizier was more powerful than himself, and even restricted his personal liberty, was anxious to throw off the shackles which impeded the freedom of his actions. But he did not dare to strike openly, and it was actually the Shah himself who in a drunken fit revealed the plot to Yar Mohamed, and thus caused the death of Mir Sedik Khan as well as that of many other chiefs who were completely devoted to him.

After this occurrence the vizier removed from the court such of the king's advisers as were attached to him, and by degrees replaced them by his own creatures. He preserved to the Shah all the external appearances of respect and obedience, but he found a thousand ways of eluding his orders and his wishes when they were not in accordance with his own views; and in fact he did as he pleased.

Shah Kamran, warned by his wives, his sons, and other relatives, who detested the vizier, at length perceived clearly where all this would end, but there was not one spark of that feverish ambition remaining in him which caused the death of Fethi Khan. The state of drunkenness in which he continually lived paralyzed all his energy, and he never seriously attempted to deliver himself from the tyranny which his minister imposed upon him. He readily gave his consent, it is true, to a secret league formed by a powerful party to overthrow Yar Mohamed, a conspiracy at the head of which were his own sons; but he withheld his co-operation on two or three occasions at the very moment when his minister was to have been put an end to, and at length finished by discovering the plot to him himself. Yar Mohamed disposed of the chiefs who had formed these intrigues, and punished the sons of his sovereign by reducing to a very small sum the allowance which they received from the state.

Such was the situation of affairs at Herat, when towards the close of the year 1837 Mohamed Shah, King of Persia, again laid siege to that capital, and took up the idea which his grandfather Feth Ali Shah had entertained, of adding this province to his dominions; and this desire was all the more intense, inasmuch as he considered that he was bound in honour to recommence a siege which the death of his father Abbas Mirza had alone induced him to abandon before he had even fired a shot. The execution of this project was highly satisfactory to the Russian government, for it admitted the validity of the Shah's claims upon Herat, and found independently of these many other legitimate and powerful motives for approving of the expedition undertaken by that monarch. Amongst them was the refusal of Shah Kamran to liquidate the arrears of tribute which he had pledged himself to pay, and the sums of money taken by his vizier from several Persian caravans travelling through his territory. The English, who had done everything in their power to prevent the first expedition against Herat from being carried out, opposed the second in a still more decided manner; but as the consequences connected with this event were of so grave a nature that we cannot treat them summarily, we will enter at a later period into the details of the various phases through which it passed. In the mean while we must retrace our steps a little to give some account of what happened in Kandahar, Kabul, and Cashmeer after Shah Mahmood and his son Kamran had been driven from Afghanistan proper.

Once master of Kabul, the Serdar Mohamed Azim Khan, who, on the death of the vizier Fethi Khan, became the oldest surviving son of Payendeh Khan, reunited the scattered remains of the Afghan army, and re-established security and order; but his brother the Nawab Djabbar Khan, by whom he was represented in the government of Cashmeer, had great difficulty in escaping the snares set for him by Runjeet Sing, and in suppressing the revolts which arose from the intrigues of his clever and powerful neighbour. His other brother, Rahim dil Khan, had been obliged to fly from Shikapoor immediately after the death of Fethi Khan to escape from the Beloochees, whom Shah Shooja, who had hurried from India, had induced to revolt against him.

Poor dil Khan had remained master of Kandahar, but not thinking himself sufficiently strong to maintain his power as sovereign, and having no hope of receiving any succour from Mohamed Azim Khan, who had quite enough to do in Kabul, he sent his brother Kohendil Khan to Shikapoor, to propose certain terms to Shah Shooja, which, if accepted, would lead to his restoration to the throne of his ancestors. This prince insisted that the sons of Payendeh Khan assembled at Kandahar should swear on the Koran that they were sincere in their devotion to his person, and after having obtained this pledge he proceeded to that city, from whence he wrote to Mohamed Azim Khan to claim his rights over Kabul and Peshawur. Mohamed Azim having given in writing, a similar declaration to that of his brothers, and sent it to the Shah, Shooja set off immediately to join him at Peshawur where he then was, and Poor dil Khan accompanied him with a strong escort. Mohamed Azim Khan was in perfect good faith when he consented to the restoration of Shooja-ool-Moolk, for his position was not less embarrassing than that of Poor dil Khan, and he had very great difficulty in maintaining his authority over the northern provinces of the kingdom. Foreseeing well that the divisions which had crept in between his brothers would lead, ere long, to the loss of the sovereign power in his family, he thought that the only way of consolidating the influence of the Mohamedzyes was to call in a Suddozye prince, whom they would place like a puppet on the throne, and preserve for themselves all the executive power. The restoration of Shah Shooja was therefore to be effected on this basis and understanding; but such a mode of proceeding was by no means satisfactory to that prince, whose imperious and absolute character had not been softened in exile, and who wished to ascend the throne without making any conditions, or entering into any engagement, either with individuals or the people at large. Mohamed Azim Khan, thinking that he might bring the king to admit as sacred the right of his family to the first offices in the state, re-established him on the throne, and this in spite of the knowledge that he had of his intractable character. But Shooja, without taking any account of the ulterior consequences of his conduct, manifested almost from the outset his arrogance without disguise; he treated Mohamed Azim Khan and Poor dil Khan as rebels, took offence because one of their cousins used a palanquin, and ordered that for the future this honour should be reserved for the princes of the Suddozye family alone.

Mohamed Azim and his brothers exhausted all the powers of argument that could be dictated by consideration and wisdom to induce Shah Shooja to listen to reason, but, finding him immovable in his absolute views, they would not permit him to proceed to Kabul; the prince therefore left the camp, situated thirty-five miles from Peshawur, and retired within the walls of that town, with a small body of Sikhs who had attached themselves to his person, to which were added a thousand Afghans of the discontented tribe of the Mohamedzyes. Mohamed Azim Khan, desperate at having created fresh difficulties for himself by thus recalling Shah Shooja, immediately laid siege to Peshawur with all his army. The prince could not hope to hold the place for any length of time; nevertheless, he defended himself, but was eventually obliged to evacuate the town sooner than he had expected. His magazine took fire and destroyed all his munitions of war; two hundred of his men were killed by the explosion; and an enormous breach was made in the city wall, which opened an easy passage for the troops of Mohamed Azim.

Obliged to make a precipitate retreat, the Shah managed to reach Shikapoor, where the Emirs of Scinde consented to receive him. Sir Alexander Burnes states that they ceded the place to him and adds,—"A series of intrigues set on foot by his enemies expelled him even from this retreat, and he fled by the circuitous route of the desert of Jaysalmere to Loodiana. The conduct of Shah Shooja was ill-calculated to support his falling fortunes: he forgot the dignity of a monarch in low intrigues with his subjects, in which he tarnished their honour as well as his own. The fitness of Shooja-ool-Moolk for the situation of sovereign seems ever to have been doubtful. His manners and address are highly polished, but his judgment does not rise above mediocrity."

In the year 1819 Mohamed Azim Khan gave way to the representations of Eyoob Mirza, another son of Timoor Shah, who came to his camp, and promised him that, if the Khan would place him on the throne, he would appoint him his vizier, and give him all the power, having no other ambition than that of perpetuating the possession of the throne of the Afghans to the descendants of the great Shah Ahmed, and to see money struck in his own name. "In short," remarks the author of the work we have just quoted, "Eyoob said, 'Make me but king and permit money to be coined in my name, and the whole power and resources of the kingdom may rest with yourself; my ambition will be satisfied with bread and the title of king.' These conditions were accepted, nor did this puppet monarch ever violate or attempt to infringe the terms by which he had gained the name and trappings of royalty, but continued a tool in the hands of Azim Khan, who was nominally his vizier. So degraded was now the state of the Royal house of Kabul, that the very robe of honour with which the minister was installed into the viziership of the empire, was a portion of his own property, and had been sent privately to the

Shah, who conferred it on the vizier with all the pomp and display of royalty. Several of the young princes who aspired to the throne were delivered over to Eyoob and put to death."

Eyoob kept therefore the promise which he had made to Azim Khan, even beyond what he had permitted himself to hope. The Afghans will have in their kings activity, courage, and energy of character, but Eyoob was distinguished only by nullity the most complete: he thought of nothing but himself, and yet he could not escape the fatality which seemed to pursue the sons of Timoor Shah. Some letters which he wrote to his brothers Shah Mahmood and Shah Shooja having been intercepted, Mohamed Azim drove him out of Kabul, and put his brother Sultan Ali Mirza to death, as he appeared to have encouraged the king in breaking the pact which united him with the Mohamedzyes.

This would seem to indicate that Eyoob, in giving up so readily the royal authority, obeyed from necessity rather than choice, and without doubt only waited for a favourable opportunity to obtain it; but be that as it may, neither plan succeeded. At the same period at which Sultan Ali Mirza was put to death at Kabul by Azim Khan, another brother of that prince, Mohamed Murad Mirza, fell under the sword of Kohendil Khan at Kandahar, for a reason similar to that which had led to the fall of Eyoob.

For several years past the affairs of government had weighed heavily upon Mohamed Azim Khan; the order he established after having driven Shah Shooja from Peshawur had, after the dismissal of Shah Eyoob, again given place to agitation: the public mind was to be quieted; the serdars were to be satisfied or put down to procure tranquillity for the kingdom, and that was not an easy thing to accomplish. Mohamed Azim Khan in his desire to smooth all these difficulties wished to proceed with some degree of regularity; he commenced therefore by marching against the Sikhs, who, since they had occupied Attok, had taken possession of some of the Afghan territory which surrounded it, and began to be very unpleasant neighbours to the Dooranees.

That remarkable man Runjeet Sing, profiting by the enfeebled state to which so many troubles had reduced the Afghans, had taken from them in succession Attok, Mooltan, Derrehghazee Khan, Leya, and Cashmeer. Nawab Djabbar Khan, the governor of this last province, had been forced to evacuate it, and suffered great loss in effecting his retreat; the Sikh troops had even pursued him to the right bank of the Indus, and at one time menaced Peshawur. Eight thousand of Runjeet's soldiers, under the command of Boodh Sing, had also just made, from weak entrenchments hastily thrown up, an heroic defence against a population of fifty thousand Afghans. The Sikhs, up to this time enslaved, proved by these brave deeds of arms that their nationality had boldly developed itself; they felt the necessity of constituting themselves a separate and compact power; and as this first and sudden impulse of the natural genius of this people might become fatal to their neighbours, there was not a moment to lose in repulsing such formidable adversaries. Azim Khan therefore marched a body of troops towards the quarter that was threatened; but though they obtained marked and somewhat numerous advantages over Runjeet, they were not able to force him to recross the Indus, which on his invasion of the Afghan territory his cavalry had passed by swimming at a spot where there was no ford—a feat unheard of before in the annals of war in that country.

Mohamed Azim Khan had endeavoured to rouse the fanatical feelings of his soldiers by proclaiming a holy war, but, not having been able to arrest the success of this modern Porus by that device, he was obliged to march in person against him. The Sikh and Afghan armies met at Noochero in 1822, the latter being divided into two corps by the Kabul river. The vizier Azim Khan had conceived his plan of operations very badly: for he and the greater part of his brothers were on the southern side of the river with the second division, which it was impossible to move to the support of the first when it was attacked in person by the whole of Runjeet's forces. Nevertheless it sustained the fight valiantly: the infantry, posted on an eminence, and protected by several pieces of cannon, received the onset of the Sikhs without flinching, and repulsed four successive charges which they made with the whole of their cavalry; it was only when a fifth was given that the Afghans were obliged to fall back, and with the loss of their guns—Runjeet conducted this charge in person, and brought up the whole of his reserves. Mohamed Azim Khan and his brothers were spectators of this sad disaster without the power, as it is said, of being able to remedy it; a circumstance which seems incomprehensible, for the runaways found no difficulty in crossing the river and rejoining them, as did likewise a corps of Sikhs who pursued them. How then did it happen that Azim Khan could not do the same?

But supposing the Afghan general had committed this first error, it was easy for him to repair it by attacking the Sikhs in their passage of the river, which he did not do; the fact was, his heart failed him, and he took to flight. His apologists have endeavoured to justify his retreat by saying that it was caused by the shouts that were heard in the Sikh camp on the night preceding the battle, which led Azim Khan to believe they had received large reinforcements. But even if this version of the affair was correct, the error, not to say stupidity, of allowing the Sikhs to cross the river without making any attempt to stop them, is not the less great; besides, it may always be said that the Afghan general did not advance merely to retreat, but to fight, and that he might at least have saved his guns and his baggage which he abandoned. The Sikhs, taking advantage of the panic that seized their adversaries, marched on Peshawur, of which they took possession, and destroyed the citadel.

The right bank of the Indus remained in the power of the Sikhs after the battle of Noochero, and Peshawur was an advanced post over which Runjeet reserved the right of suzerainty. He gave the government to Sultan Mohamed Khan, one of the brothers of Azim Khan, enforcing a small tribute, hoping by this means to increase the disunion amongst the sons of Payendeh Khan, and turn it to greater account.

Mohamed Azim Khan, overwhelmed by all these reverses, and suffering from the effects of a wound which, from his habits of drinking, had become very irritated, left the army, the temporary command of which he gave to his brother Dost Mohamed Khan, and took the road to Kabul, where he hoped to recover; but this hope was never realized, for he had not sufficient strength left to reach the city, and died at the village of Latu-bend about two days' journey from the capital. For some time past he had felt convinced his end was approaching, and hastened to collect all his wealth, which amounted to 2,700,000*l*.* Azim Khan left this enormous sum to his son Habib Ullah Khan, and a few hours before his death he made him swear to employ it and his life in revenging his father's defeat and the misfortunes of his country.

The character of the vizier Mohamed Azim Khan has been estimated very differently by different persons according as they were partizans of the Suddozyes or the Mohamedzyes, but the

* I learnt this from Kohendil Khan, his sons, and his brother.—*Ferrier.*

majority of impartial individuals in Afghanistan are of opinion that he was a man of moderate abilities, and not equal to his mission; that he was wanting in firmness; that his military talents were of a mediocre character; and that his love of wine and ardent spirits was so great that he had the command of his faculties but for a very short time during the twenty-four hours. He was, however, gentle, conciliating, and showed great urbanity of disposition.

CHAPTER XIV.

Proceedings of Habib Ullah Khan — Divisions between the sons of Payendeh Khan — Habib Ullah Khan at war with his uncles — Poor dil Khan interferes in Kabul — Union of Sultan Mohamed and Dost Mohamed Khans — Shere dil Khan and Poor dil Khan establish peace between their brothers — Dost Mohamed again at variance — His rivalry with Sultan Mohamed — That prince at Peshawur — Sir A. Burnes's opinion of him — Kandahar — Poor dil Khan and Shere dil Khan — Character of the latter — Sir A. Burnes's opinion of the Kandahar chiefs — Character of Dost Mohamed — Sir A. Burnes's opinion of him.

HABIB ULLAH KHAN had sworn to his dying father that he would take no rest until he had exterminated the Sikhs, but his courage did not correspond with his promise; it is true he continued the war, but without energy; and it was only by the power of money that he was enabled to maintain for a short time his troops in obedience. Brutalized by his passion for drink, a vice which he inherited from his parent, he felt very little for the misfortunes of his country. His mother endeavoured, but in vain, to stimulate his zeal, and lead him to appreciate more honourable sentiments; but he remained deaf to her solicitations. This apathy in their chief discouraged the inferior officers, who by degrees abandoned him, while the serdars and his uncles neglected the national defence and interests to quarrel for power amongst themselves. From this period the sons of Payendeh Khan were more disunited than even the Suddozyes, and rushed into a number of little wars which continued during several years, until a few of them had succeeded in definitively establishing themselves in the Afghan principalities. Balkh, Khulm, Koondooz, and Badakshane had shaken off the yoke since the fall of Shah Zeman, and governed themselves. As to Scinde, Shah Shooja was the last of the Afghan kings who received tribute from that country, and after his disasters the Talpoora Emirs considered themselves as completely independent.

Habib Ullah had scarcely exercised his power six months when, his money being spent, all consideration for him was at an end; in Kabul he had only a mere shadow of authority remaining, and that was soon disputed by his uncles. As to Sultan Mohamed Khan, who had been made governor of Peshawur by Runjeet, he was not satisfied with the small revenues of that province, which he was obliged to share with his two brothers, Pir Mohamed Khan and

Syud Mohamed Khan. Dost Mohamed Khan had made a party for himself, and resided at Ghuznee.

The army of Hahib Ullah Khan, considerably weakened by desertion, was not in a condition to measure its strength with those of his uncles united. Aware of this, he sent his brother Akrem Khan to Kandahar to represent to their uncle Poor dil Khan the danger there would be to him if he permitted his brothers Sultan and Dost Mohamed Khan, who then had the reputation of being ambitious and restless characters, to acquire an influence in his neighbourhood superior to his own, for it might lead to their creating disturbances in the principality of Kandahar, and possibly end in their taking it from him if he was not upon his guard; Akrem Khan also sent him a few of their letters which had been intercepted, and in which such intentions had been clearly manifested.

Poor dil Khan, alarmed at the danger which menaced him, sent his brother Shere dil Khan to Kabul at the head of a few thousand men, and this serdar met Dost Mohamed Khan on the road, beat, and forced him to retire upon Jellalabad, and then proceeded to Kabul. There, however, instead of giving any assistance to his nephew Habib Ullah Khan, he deposed him, plundered him of his riches under a threat of killing him, and united the remnants of his army with his own. The vanquished chief by way of consolation now plunged into every kind of debauch, and continued to reside at Kabul, where he still lives in a miserable plight, given up to excesses of the most filthy kind. Akrem Khan, his younger brother, died after his return to Kandahar; he was a brave and resolute man, and no friend to ambitious characters: his death was supposed to have taken place from the effects of poison.

When Sultan Mohamed Khan and Dost Mohamed Khan saw the turn affairs had taken at Kabul, they put a stop for a time to the fratricidal war they had carried on since the death of Azim Khan, and united their forces with a view of seizing that province. They then marched against their brother Shere dil Khan, who at their approach retired within the walls of the Bala Hissar, not having sufficient troops to meet them in the field. Here he had great difficulty in maintaining himself during the winter of 1825. The season was very severe; the roads were covered with snow, and impasseable; and it was only in the spring, and after he had been five months besieged, that Poor dil Khan could bring him reinforcements from Kandahar. Directly these arrived they attacked

Sultan Mohamed and Dost Mohamed, and defeated them after a most sanguinary struggle. Nevertheless, these serdars did not consider their cause a hopeless one, and again prepared to try the fortune of war, when Poor dil Khan, by a generous resolution, stopped the further effusion of blood. He went almost alone to the camp of his brothers, and pictured to them all the calamities which the quarrels and divisions of the sons of Payendeh Khan had brought upon their country. "Let us stand close," said he; "and to prove to you to what extent our union is dear to me, I will return to Kandahar, and abandon Kabul to Sultan Mohamed Khan, our eldest brother; but, before I retire, you must swear to me, as well as all our brothers now present in both camps, that nothing shall disunite us for the future." This generous proposition was accepted, and a good understanding reappeared for some time amongst the members of this heroic family.*

But Dost Mohamed Khan took the oath that Poor dil Khan had exacted only because he felt convinced that his brothers would never support *him* in his resistance, but he felt very angry that Sultan Mohamed Khan, who was already in possession of Peshawur, had been preferred to him as sovereign of Kabul, in contempt of the rights that he thought he had acquired by the courage he had everywhere displayed, and by his great popularity with the Afghans; and without doubt this chief was the bravest and the most talented politician amongst the brothers of the vizier Fethi Khan, and had thus contributed more than any of them to overthrow the Suddozye family. With him vexation and spite overruling every other consideration, he foreswore himself and prepared to carry arms against Sultan Mohamed Khan; however, there was, it is true, a deadly enmity between these two brothers, which had its origin in a love affair. One of the widows of the Serdar Azim Khan was a member of the royal family of the Suddozyes, and, according to the established custom in Afghanistan, was obliged to marry one of the surviving brothers of the deceased. Sultan Mohamed Khan, who greatly admired her, had, in the first instance, some chance of becoming her husband, and a few conferences had already taken place on this subject, when Dost Mohamed, who knew how to render his homage acceptable, made his appearance and married the beautiful widow. Sultan Mohamed Khan never forgave him this outrage, and swore to wash it out in his blood whenever an occasion should present itself.

* All the sons of Payendeh Khan were then in one camp or the other.—*Ferrier.*

During the space of two years did Sultan Mohamed and Dost Mohamed carry on a merciless war one against the other, but it terminated in 1826, when Dost Mohamed, victorious on all points, was enabled to establish definitively his authority at Kabul. Mohamed Khan, Beyat, a serdar of the Kuzzilbashes, gave him his support in consequence of the blood relationship which united them. His sister was the mother of Dost Mohamed Khan; and without the support of the Kuzzilbash chief the Dost would have had great difficulty in obtaining this triumph over his opponent, who was assisted by the Sikhs.

Sultan Mohamed Khan, thus thrown back upon Peshawur, had also the annoyance of finding himself more and more brought under the power of Runjeet Sing. The Maharadja had, up to this time, been satisfied with receiving a small annual tribute from the Afghan chief, but, when he saw that Sultan Mohamed was beaten by the Dost, he demanded that one of his sons should be delivered up to him as a hostage, and reside at Lahore. It would have been easy for Sultan Mohamed to escape this difficulty by becoming reconciled to Dost Mohamed Khan, who was quite willing to receive his advances, and had even taken the initiative in this respect; but Sultan Mohamed thought it preferable to persevere in the hatred he felt to his brother, and made his complete submission to the Sikhs—the sworn enemies of his country and of his religion.

I was not able to reach Peshawur myself, and could not therefore judge of the state of this province or collect any information respecting the manner in which it was governed by Sultan Mohamed Khan, but I will supply such information by giving some passages from the work of Sir A. Burnes, who visited that city in 1832.

"The government of Peshawur has been held by a member of the Barukzye family since Futteh Khan placed Shah Mahmood on the throne of Kabul. Peshawur owed allegiance and contributed to the support of the kingdom till the year 1818, when the vizier was put to death. Azim Khan, his successor, exacted tribute for it during his lifetime in the name of Eyoob Shah. Since that time it has formed a separate chiefship like Kabul and Kandahar, now subject, however, to the payment of a yearly tribute to the Sikhs. It is governed by the Serdar Sultan Mohamed Khan, who shares its revenues with two other brothers, Pir and Syud Mohamed Khan. A large portion of the country is alienated to different individuals, and the net revenue falls short of nine lacs of rupees per annum. The younger brothers enjoy three lacs, and the chief defrays from the remainder the entire expenses of the country, the tribute to the Sikhs, and likewise supports the numerous families of two elder brothers, who fell in battle and to whom he succeeded.

"The power of the chief is confined to the plain of Peshawur, and the hills of Kohat, which form its southern boundary. That plain is well known as one of the richest portions of the Kabul dominions. It is of a circular shape, about thirty-five miles broad, highly peopled and cultivated, watered by nature and art. Within this limited space there are numerous villages which pay no taxes. The Khuttuks, a tribe of Afghans in the east, hold the country for twenty miles west of the Indus for the small sum of 1200*l.* annually, which they render to the chief of Peshawur. The villages on the west, and the Khyber hills, do not pay anything; and those north of the Kabul river, with some few exceptions, enjoy a like immunity. The only places of note in the chiefship are Peshawur and Hushtnuggur, which are described by Mr. Elphinstone. Peshawur has fallen into a state of decay with its change of rulers, and it is doubtful if it boasts of a population of one half the hundred thousand souls which occupied it in 1809. Hushtnuggur is the seat of one of the younger brothers; Kohat is held by the other. The military strength of Peshawur is unimportant. Its contingent of troops cannot be rated above 3000, two-thirds of whom may be cavalry. The chief might rally round him a numerous body of irregulars, or, as they are called, 'ooloosee;' but they are badly armed, and not to be relied upon. Six pieces of artillery, and two hundred regular infantry, complete the power of the chief of Peshawur. With money the services of the Khyberees, and other hill tribes, may be purchased on an emergency; but the chief has no treasury. In a religious war with the Sikhs, an infuriated population may be always raised, and has proved itself formidable on a late occasion, when the Syud Ahmed preached his crusade in this country; yet the whole of these combined form a diminutive force, as compared with his neighbours on the east and west—the Sikhs, and his brother of Kabul. The political influence of Peshawur is as limited as its military power. The Sikhs have exacted a tribute from it since the death of the vizier's brother, Azim Khan, and retain a son of the chief as a hostage for its fulfilment. It now amounts to sixty horses, with some rice, which is peculiar to Peshawur; and it is annually enforced by an army which crosses the Indus, and lays waste their territories if not speedily paid. The amount of the tribute depends on the caprice of Runjeet Sing, but the Sikhs will not make a conquest of this country. Without Mahommedan auxiliaries they could not retain it.*

"The chiefs of Peshawur and Kabul, who are brothers, are at enmity. The power of Kabul is far more consolidated than that of Peshawur, but the latter has an ally in his brother of Kandahar, who would resent any attack either on Peshawur or his own country.† The chiefs of Peshawur and Kandahar have been some time past concerting an attack on Kabul; but it is not improbable that the territories of both may ere long be threatened, and perhaps taken, by the Khan of Kabul. In such an event, the chief of Peshawur would call in the aid of the Sikhs. This would probably be given, since Dost Mohamed of Kabul would never consent to the annual tribute now paid to Lahore by his brother of Peshawur. Serdar Sooltan Mohamed Khan entertains hopes of being able to interest the British Government in his cause should it decline. No chief in the kingdom of Kabul entertains a higher respect for the British Government than Sooltan Mohamed Khan. This has always been shown by his attention to Europeans who have entered his country. If misfortunes fell upon him, he might be a useful or a dangerous partisan. He might espouse the cause of the King Shah Shooja-ool-Moolk; though that monarch is no favourite with his family; yet the inconsistency and inconstancy of the Afghan chiefs are proverbial. In any difficulty the chief of Peshawur would be ably assisted by Pir Mohamed, but his other brother is destitute of energy and enterprise. The whole of the Barukzye family‡ entertain a dread of Shah Shooja-ool-Moolk, and the Prince Kamran of Herat. The one, if aided by the British, would drive them from their usurped authority; and the other, if assisted by the Persians, might perhaps fix himself on the throne of his ancestors. Sooltan Mohamed Khan bears a fair reputation, but his government is most oppressive and vexatious. His agents and underlings practise all manner of exactions; goods are taxed far above their value; and the currency is constantly altered and depreciated. An enormous tax is levied on the water-mills which grind the flour,

* Burnes is not quite accurate here, for Peshawur was actually invaded by the Sikhs and governed for a number of years by General Avitabile, who was the terror of the Afghans.—*Ferrier*.

† Poor dil Khan and Shere dil Khan being dead, Kohendil Khan governed Kandahar when I visited that city.—*Ferrier*.

‡ Burnes should have written Mohamedzye, for Barukzye is the designation of the entire tribe.—*Ferrier*.

and it falls heaviest on the lower orders of the people. The chief is a man about thirty-five; he is ambitious, and at one time held the government of Kabul. He is well educated, and with good talents; possesses an engaging manner, he reads and writes and transacts his business in person. He has not the art of settling disputes, and his court presents a scene of confusion which is hardly to be described or believed. The complainants intrude at all times and places, and state their grievances in the most free and republican manner, yet nothing is ever settled, and the population are heartily disaffected. Like Afghans, the chief of Peshawur and his relatives live from hand to mouth; they are liberal of what they possess, and have no wealth. I have been informed that they could not retain their government without this open-handed liberality. The chief of Peshawur has rallied round him some of the most celebrated of the Dooranee nation, who share his bounty. The sons of Akram Khan, and the Mookhtar o Doula, Shah Shooja's two ministers, as also one of the celebrated Mir Weis, are among the number; the latter is an officer of the chief of Peshawur. The only son of the Vizier Futteh Khan likewise resides with Sultan Mohamed Khan." *

It has been stated that Kandahar had fallen into the hands of one of the Mohamedzyes, namely, the Serdar Poor dil Khan, immediately after the death of the Vizier Fethi Khan. This serdar had, like Sultan Mohamed Khan, divided his principality into several districts which he had given to his half-brothers, Shere dil Khan, Kohendil Khan, Rahim dil Khan, and Mir dil Khan. Shere dil Khan, who had the reputation of being the bravest and the most enterprising of the surviving sons of Payendeh Khan, had received from his brother the command-in-chief of the army of Kandahar. Unfortunately this energetic man died while still young, in 1829; a few months after, his brother Poor dil Khan followed him to the tomb, and the power then reverted to their next eldest brother, Kohendil Khan. Such had been the paternal and enlightened administration of Poor dil Khan, that his successor, on whom the Kandaharians had founded the same hopes, was by general acclamation placed at the head of affairs. It would appear, however, by the following extract from Sir A. Burnes's work, that these hopes were not realized; for this is the opinion of that officer respecting the government of Kohendil Khan :—

* This serdar has left him, and has long resided at Kandahar.—*Ferrier.*

"It has been already mentioned that Shere dil Khan * fled from Kabul to Kandahar, and formed the present chiefship with the spoil of his nephew. He was a man of singular habits, in some respects resembling his brother Futteh Khan, but morose as well as cruel. They give an anecdote of his lopping off the finger of one of his boys, telling him at the same time, if he cried, that he could not be his child or a Barukzye. The young fellow bore it with great patience. Shere dil Khan in his flight to Kandahar was accompanied by four brothers. He himself is since dead, as also one of his brothers. Kandahar is now governed by Kohendil Khan, supported by his two surving brothers, Rahim dil and Mehr dil. The revenues amount to about eight lacs of rupees; his force consists of 9000 horse and six pieces of artillery; but as the city is situated in the heart of the Dooranee country, and near the native seat of the Barukzye family, he could perhaps increase his cavalry on an emergency.

"The government is not popular, nor would it appear from the acts of oppression that it deserved to be so. The chief is on bad terms with most of his neighbours. In common with all his family, he is inimical to Kamran of Herat, and has at different times attempted to seize that city. He is also at issue with the chief of Kabul. The connexion between the Peshawur and Kandahar branches of the Barukzyes is very close and secure; but their united efforts will not, in all probability, injure their brother of Kabul. The Kandahar chief also seeks to form a settlement on the Indus; and has for several years past sent his troops to threaten Shikapoor in Scinde. The Ameers of that country have been hitherto able to resist his attacks; but, as there is an open and easy communication between Kandahar and the Indus by the Bolan pass, the chief is not likely to discontinue his endeavours in that quarter. In a disorganized state of Scinde he might easily possess himself of Shikapoor; and such a state of events seems by no means improbable in the country of the Ameers. The chief of Kandahar would gladly interest the ruler of the Punjab in his cause; but it is not probable that he will procure his assistance, as he himself looks upon Shikapoor with an eye of cupidity."

* Burnes appears to have thought that Shere dil Khan was the sovereign of Kandahar; and this is not surprising, for Poor dil Khan gave up to him the entire direction of affairs, and the Afghans considered him as their chief *de facto*; but Poor dil Khan enjoyed by right the prerogatives of a sovereign, which were never contested by his brothers, and Shere dil Khan died without ever having positively reigned. —*Ferrier*.

After having endeavoured to show the manner in which the principalities of Herat, Peshawur, and Kandahar were constituted subsequently to the dismemberment of the kingdom of the Suddozyes, it is desirable that we should throw a glance at Kabul, the most wealthy and important of the Afghan provinces; and let us in the first instance commence with its chief, Dost Mohamed Khan, who came forth victorious in 1826 from his conflict with Sultan Mohamed Khan.

Dost Mohamed was the favourite brother of the Vizier Fethi Khan, and this predilection was not the effect of chance; but in spite of the good qualities which were remarkable in the young and intrepid chieftain, he was certainly not exempt from the ordinary vices of the Afghans, though distinguished from them by superior intelligence and courage, which manifested itself in many heroic deeds when he was still a very young man. His manners were polished and attractive, and one felt irresistibly drawn towards him. The preference evinced for him by Fethi Khan obtained him the hatred of his brothers; nevertheless they affected to be anxious to pay their court to him to please the vizier, but when an opportunity offered never failed secretly to play him some shabby trick. Dost Mohamed was not one to be made their dupe, but not wishing to irritate them he took no trouble to conceal his actions, and repaid them in kind a hundredfold for the evil he received; this increased their hatred, which gave him very little concern, for, though brave soldiers, his brothers were far from possessing his capacity and resolution, and in the quarrels which ensued between them and him he was sure to have the upper hand. The success which crowned all the projects of the Dost, and the tenacity with which he met these misunderstandings with his brothers, had procured him the *sobriquet* of *Gurkek* (the little wolf), a name by which he is distinguished amongst them at the present day. They were very nearly all opposed to him when he wished to seize upon Kabul, and yet he triumphed over all their intrigues, and defeated them every time they came to blows. Directly his power was consolidated in the principality, he occupied himself in healing the wounds which so many intestine wars and revolts had inflicted on the country, and it soon felt the vivifying and paternal influences of his government. It is true that the small portion of the kingdom which had fallen to him did not allow of his raising a large army and subduing all the other provinces which had detached themselves from Kabul, like the Vizier Fethi Khan, but the finest prize in Afghanistan was still within his grasp; he had the good sense to be satisfied with it, and, instead of taking his revenge against his jealous and ambitious brothers, by dispossessing them of what they had, which he might easily have done, he preferred to leave them in quiet enjoyment of their conquests, and occupied himself in making order, security, and abundance in his own territory succeed to the disasters of war and the convulsive throes of revolution. His justice and equity were admitted by all, and he repressed violence without mercy from whatever side it arose. The rock upon which all the Afghan sovereigns had made shipwreck up to this time was the insubordination of the serdars, who, having the power and influence over the warlike portion of the population, and possessing very productive fiefs which considerably lessened the revenues of the state, took advantage of these circumstances to agitate the public mind, and to change the sovereign as it suited their fancy; but the Dost soon made it clear to them, and at their cost, that it was as difficult as it was dangerous for them to endeavour to throw off their allegiance to him. Without evincing any want of generosity, he obliged them to moderate their tyrannical conduct towards their dependants, and lend their support to the development of commerce and agriculture, which he was anxious to improve amongst a people so idle, as well as to engender in their minds sentiments of a humane character. The great families submitted unwillingly in the first instance to this state of things; but they thought that it was better to bend to a monarch who was generous, than to attempt revolts the issue of which must be at the least uncertain, and which might again place them under the insecure and cruel despotism of the Suddozyes. But we have seen how Sir A. Burnes estimated the characters of the two brothers at Peshawur and Kandahar, and it will not be out of place to give here the parallels which he has drawn between those chiefs and the state of their dependencies, and Dost Mohamed and the condition of Kabul.

"In the year 1826 Kabul fell into the hands of Dost Mohamed Khan, the present chief, and a brother of the vizier Futteh Khan. Since then he has greatly extended and consolidated his power. He intrusts the town and dependencies of Ghuznee to a brother, and admits no one else to share his fortunes. The limits of the chiefship extend to Hindoo Koosh and Bamian. On the west it is bounded by the hill country of the Hazarahs; to the south is Ghuznee, and to the east it stretches half way to Peshawur, terminating at the garden of Neemla. Much of the country is mountainous; it contains a large proportion of arable land which is most productive. It lies along the base of hills, and derives a richness from the soil washed from them. The revenues of Kabul amount to eighteen lacs of rupees. Its military force is greater than any among the Afghans, since the chief retains a body of good horse, who are well mounted and accoutred. He has also 2000 infantry, with other auxiliaries, village troops, and a park of fourteen guns which are well served for a native state. This country is by nature strong and mountainous, though it has good roads through it.

"The reputation of Dost Mohamed Khan is made known to a traveller long before he enters his country, and no one better merits the high character which he has obtained. He is unremitting in his attention to business, and attends daily at the Court-house with the Kazee-o-Mollahs to decide every cause according to the law. The Koran and its commentaries may not be the standard of legislative excellence; but this sort of decision is exceedingly popular with the people, since it fixes a line, and relieves them from the *jus vagum aut incognitum* of a despot. Trade has received the greatest encouragement from him, and he has derived his own reward, since the receipts of the Custom-house of the city have increased 50,000 rupees, and now furnish him with a net revenue of two lacs per annum. One in forty, *i.e.* 2½ per cent., is the only duty levied in his territory; and the merchant may travel without guard or protection from one frontier to another, an unheard of circumstance in the time of the kings. The chief of Kabul, in his zeal for orthodox government, has deprived his subjects of the luxury of wine and spirits as being prohibited by his creed. The enactment has driven the Jews and Armenians from his country, since they had no other means to procure a subsistence. A good Mahommedan ought not to regret the loss of such luxuries; but with this single exception I heard of no complaint against the rule of Dost Mohamed Khan. That chief, in common with many of the Afghan nation, was addicted in early life to wine and its concomitant vices. His prohibition of them may be, therefore, capricious; but he as well as his court hold out a bright example to the community. The justice of this chief affords a constant theme of praise to all classes: the peasant rejoices at the absence of tyranny; the citizen at the safety of his home and the strict municipal regulations regarding weights and measures; the merchant at the equity of the decisions and the protection of his property; and the soldiers at the regular manner in which their arrears are discharged. A man in power can have no higher praise. Dost Mohamed Khan has not attained his fortieth year; his mother was a Persian, and he has been trained up with people of that nation, which has sharpened his understanding, and given him advantages over all his brothers. One is struck with the intelligence, knowledge, and curiosity which he displays, as well as his accomplished manners and address. He is doubtless the most powerful chief in Afghanistan, and may yet raise himself by his abilities to a much greater rank in his native country.

"The differences which exist between Dost Mohamed and his brothers lessen the influence of all parties, and would lay open the state to intrigue and faction if invaded. The family of Barukzye * have nothing to fear from any other Afghan tribe, since they surpass all in numbers as much as in power.† The chiefs of Peshawur and Kandahar do not want the wish to injure their brother of Kabul, but they cannot accomplish their purpose. Both of them have had a footing in Kabul, and look with envy on the prosperity of Dost Mohamed Khan. Both have emissaries at his court, who excite disturbance; and both cherish hopes of rooting out one whom they consider a usurper. The task will be found difficult, for the chief of Kabul, besides the moderation and justice which secure him so many friends, enjoys an advantage in his Persian descent which will prove of material service to him in adversity. He holds the warlike clan of Juwanshire in his interests, and takes every occasion to conciliate this tribe, which has so often turned the scale in favour of different pretenders to the throne. He has acquired their language (the Turkish), and promoted their interests and wellbeing.

"The Persians of Kabul amount to 12,000 families; they reside in a separate quarter of the city, which keeps up an *esprit de corps* among them; it also gives them a knowledge of their power which may prove salutary or prejudicial to the factions that divide the country according to circumstances. The state of fear which an enemy on both sides must inspire has had a bad effect on Dost Mohamed Khan's administration. With his own house as an

* Mohamedzye.—*Ferrier.*

† This is an error into which Burnes has fallen; if it is the family or branch to which the sons of Payendeh Khan belongs that he refers to, he should have mentioned them as Mohamedzyes, and that consists of only four or five thousand families. If it is the tribe of Barukzye to which he alludes, it is probable that it contains 45,000 or 55,000 familes.—*Ferrier.*

object of care, he is not likely to pursue conquests abroad, or retrieve the fallen state of Kabul. This alone deters him from taking Herat, the only province of the kingdom of Afghanistan now held by a descendant of the royal family, and the Prince Kamran rules more from tolerance in his enemies than his own power. He receives no aid from his countrymen, since the whole of the chiefs of Afghanistan are his enemies, and desire his destruction, in revenge for the assassination of their brother Futteh Khan. Herat has, therefore, become a dependency of Persia. The town itself has of late been several times entered by the troops of that nation, and only spared by the ready tender of money on the part of its governor.* It was threatened in September, 1832, by the Prince Royal in person, who made a pecuniary demand, and also required that the coinage of the city should be struck in the name of the King of Persia. It is probable that both these requests will be granted,† since Kamran would gladly hold his power on any terms. The Persians do not appear to contemplate any permanent settlement in Herat, since it would incur the expense of retaining a force that would diminish the tribute now gained from it. Kamran is said to be in possession of some of the crown jewels of Kabul, and derives a large revenue from Herat, which is situated in one of the most fertile countries of the world. By this wealth he is yet able to retain about his person some of the Afghan chiefs, and can raise a body of 4000 or 5000 horse. He has no political connexions in any quarter; but still clings to the hope of being able to re-establish the monarchy of his father. He has the character of a cruel and tyrannical man, is destitute of friends, and odious to his countrymen.

"The same causes which prevented Dost Mohamed from marching against Herat prevented him also from making some endeavours to wrest Mooltan and Dera Ghazee Khan from the Sikhs. He last year made a demonstration against Jellalabad, a district between Kabul and Peshawur, worth about seven lacs of rupees a year. He will probably annex it to his power, but until able to coerce or subdue either Peshawur or Kandahar, Dost Mohamed Khan cannot rise above a chief, or be aught than one among many in Afghanistan. In the present state of politics in that country he is nevertheless the most rising man in the Kabul dominions."

* This is an error; the territory has been entered, but the city not.—*Ferrier.*

† I have witnessed the contrary.—*Ferrier.*

CHAPTER XV.

Shah Shooja takes up arms against the Barukzyes — Dost Mohamed Khan marches to the relief of Kandahar — Shah Shooja receives a check — That sovereign is completely defeated — He retires to Kelat — Sultan Mohamed arrives at Kabul — Machinations of that serdar against Dost Mohamed Khan — Resolution of the latter — The Dost, now elected Emir, marches against the Sikhs — Defeats them at Djamrood — Sir A. Burnes at Kabul — The English are hostile to Dost Mohamed — Sumner's account of the Russians and the English in Asia — Mohamed Shah determines to invade Herat — He is supported by the Russians.

SUCH was the state of things when Burnes visited Kabul in 1832. The result of his opinion, as of my own, which is also that of the Afghans in general, is that Kohendil Khan, the sovereign of Kandahar, had not the same superiority of mind as his brother, and was far from following in the same steps. The people were discontented with him, and he might have been reproached, as well as Sultan Mohamed Khan, who did not govern at Peshawur a whit better than he did, with sentiments of jealousy and hostility to Dost Mohamed, whose enlightened and loyal government they sought to impede and ridicule in a manner little honourable to themselves. Ambition is an unfaithful mirror, which reflects things much less in their natural aspect than that in which mankind is pleased to colour characters and personal interests. With these perverted feelings, Kohendil Khan and Sultan Mohamed Khan constantly pursued a hostile line of conduct towards their brother, who was desirous of being on the best terms with them; and they accused him, but without the least reason, of wishing to seize their territories—there was danger for them it is true, but this danger was in another quarter. Sultan Mohamed Khan, already subdued by Runjeet Sing, was on the eve of being totally overthrown by the Maharadja, and, if Kohendil Khan did not succumb to him first, it was because he owed his preservation entirely to the generous support which he received from his brother Dost Mohamed Khan, as we shall now see.

Shah Shooja-ool-Moolk, although often beaten, had not renounced his right to the throne. From the period at which he was, for the first time, overthrown by Fethi Khan, he had made eight attempts to regain it by force of arms; he failed—but his courage remained unshaken, and he had succeeded in interesting the Anglo-Indian government in his fate. They required a sovereign in Afghanistan devoted to their views, but, afraid to assist him openly, the Governor-General supported his cause with some Sikh regiments, with which, through his intervention and promises of concession of territory on the part of Shah Shooja, Runjeet Sing agreed to furnish the Suddozye prince. This fact has been proved by the letters of Sir Claude Wade, at that time political agent at Loodiana, which letters were found amongst the baggage of Shah Shooja-ool-Moolk after his defeat; a good many amongst them were addressed to some of the Afghan serdars. The British agent excited these chiefs to revolt, and assured them that his government would know how to appreciate the support that they might give to their legitimate sovereign.

In January, 1834, Shah Shooja quitted Loodiana; in the month of May he crossed the Indus, and, in the first instance, seized upon Shikapoor, belonging to the Emirs of Scinde, but to which he laid claim. He then marched towards Kandahar at the head of an army of 22,000 Afghans and Hindostanees, the latter drilled and manœuvring on the European system, and observing its discipline, some of them being deserters from the Company's service.

Kohendil Khan, having assembled in haste what troops he could collect, marched to meet the king as far as the valley of Pisheen to close the passage, but he was defeated and obliged to make a rapid retreat on Kandahar, whence he despatched messenger after messenger to inform Dost Mohamed of the storm which had burst upon him. On the reception of this news the chief of Kabul made the following reply: "Whenever you are menaced let me know, and, as I am your enemy now, so I will be your friend then." After which, forgetting the just complaints which he had against this ungrateful brother, he remembered only the ties of kindred and blood which united them, and hurried to his assistance with his army. But, before setting out, he despatched an officer to Sir Claude Wade to ascertain from him if it was true that the Shah was openly supported by his government? that if his reply was in the affirmative, he should think about it; if, on the contrary, it was in the negative, he should fight. The political agent of the Company replied that the Indian government had taken no part in the expedition, but that Shah Shooja had its best wishes for his success.

The "best wishes" of the English government did not stop Dost Mohamed; his march, which he had delayed in order that he might receive the reply of Sir Claude Wade, he now hastened; and it was indeed high time that he should arrive at Kandahar, for Shah Shooja had taken up a position between the old and the new city, and pressed the siege closely. The ground from which he opened his attack was intersected by numerous watercourses and covered with large gardens, enclosed with mud walls, in which the soldiers made many gaps to pass through; and these obstacles were far from favourable to the manœuvres of cavalry, of which arm the greater part of both armies was composed; nevertheless, conflicts took place daily on both sides in these labyrinths. The encounters were the more murderous, inasmuch as the combatants, surrounded by walls, preferred being killed on the spot to yielding one inch of ground, and such close fighting soon weakened both parties. Shah Shooja had great difficulty in repairing his losses, though the advantage on the whole was on his side, and on the 29th of June, 1834, he made a general assault upon the place. His troops displayed great bravery; four times repulsed, four times they returned to the assault, but at last they were obliged to retreat, leaving the ditches of the town filled with their dead and wounded. The Dost's army arrived at this juncture, and from that day Shah Shooja was under a double disadvantage, for he was obliged to divide his forces to repel the sorties of the besieged commanded by Kohendil Khan, and the attack of the Dost in his rear. This war, or rather this butchery, lasted during fifty-four days, and the Afghans affirm that 16,000 men were killed before the place.

After having lost a pitched battle against Dost Mohamed Khan, Shah Shooja fought only to clear a passage for himself and his troops, and make good his retreat to Shikapoor; but hotly pursued by the Mohamedzyes, he was cut off from his communications, and thrown back upon the interior of the kingdom. Soon after he was abandoned by his soldiers, and had only fifty horsemen with him when he arrived at Herat, and demanded a refuge and hospitality of the Shah Kamran; but his nephew, who never loved him, and was afraid that he might intrigue with a view of supplanting him, refused him permission to enter the city. The defeated Shah was therefore obliged to retire upon Furrah, through the arid deserts of Beloochistan. What he suffered in traversing its parched and burning sands, under the scorching rays of the sun, without food or water, wanting in short everything, is incredible, and the Mohamedzyes, who pursued him, were on the point of taking him prisoner at the moment he entered Kelat Nassir and was safe from further molestation. The Emir of this town had freed himself from the Afghan dominion during his reign, but he received him hospitably, and furnished his guest with the means of gaining Loodiana in a manner suitable to his rank. Here he again resided, pensioned by the English, who reserved him for a new invasion in which he subsequently lost his life, and England met with the greatest disaster that she was ever called upon to register in the military annals of her Indian empire.

Mohamed Akbar Khan, the favourite son of Dost Mohamed Khan, distinguished himself, in the campaign that had just terminated, by a courage which might almost be termed foolhardy, and military talents which even then gave indications of what his future career might be.

This victory definitively confirmed the Mohamedzyes in the possession of eastern Afghanistan; but, instead of profiting by it to strengthen their position, it became the signal for fresh dissensions amongst them, the result of which was the recall of Shah Shooja a few years later, supported by an English army. While Dost Mohamed Khan was gone to assist his brother against this expatriated sovereign, Sultan Mohamed Khan had been removed from his government of Peshawur by Runjeet Sing; forced, therefore, to retire to Jellalabad, he, with a view of remedying this reverse, thought he might profit by the absence of Dost Mohamed Khan to seize Kabul. His two brothers, Pir Mohamed Khan and Syud Mohamed Khan, joined him in this enterprise, which they had already commenced when they heard of the victory the Dost had gained at Kandahar and at the same time his return to Kabul. They therefore remained some days undecided as to what line they should adopt; but the success of their plan being, to say the least, doubtful, and they not as yet committed to it, they gave up the project, pretended to feel an ardent desire to be on the most friendly terms with their victorious brother, and went boldly to meet the Dost to congratulate him on a success which, as it annihilated all their hopes, they cursed from the bottom of their hearts. Although informed of their faithless proceedings, Dost Mohamed thought it would be better to leave them to think that he was ignorant of their schemes, imagining that in acting thus he might bring their dissensions to a close. He received his brothers, therefore, with courtesy and all the appearance of sincere friendship, and spared nothing to attach them to his cause. Moreover, directly he returned to Kabul he determined to revenge the affront which had just been put upon them by Runjeet, and proclaimed a holy war against the Sikhs; nevertheless, before undertaking it, he was desirous of exalting himself in the eyes of the Afghans, and received from a council, composed of the serdars of the principality, the title of Sovereign Prince. Mir Vaez, the grand Mollah of Kabul, proclaimed him Emir ool Moamerime,* and on this occasion repeated the same form of ceremonial that had been used at the coronation of Ahmed Shah and his successors. When the festivities of his enthronement were over he sent 9000 horse against the Sikhs commanded by one of his brothers, but, as they obtained only a doubtful success, he left Kabul and placed himself at their head; the Afghans were encouraged by his arrival, but the result was not more fortunate than before. This was owing to the intrigues of Sultan Mohamed Khan and his brothers, who were negotiating secretly with Runjeet Sing; and the Emir Dost Mohamed, having convinced himself of this fact, abandoned the war, which could only be disastrous to him, and returned to Kabul. There he occupied himself in reinforcing his army, intending to enter at some future time upon another campaign, with greater chances of success, which were not to be hoped for so long as Sultan Mohamed Khan was ready to play the traitor.

All the public functionaries of whose fidelity the Dost was not perfectly sure were now dismissed; he made his sons governors of the various provinces and districts, and further intrigues failed in consequence of the wise measures which he adopted. Sultan Mohamed Khan and his two brothers, seeing that they were wholly powerless in Kabul, threw themselves completely into the hands of Runjeet Sing, who appointed the former governor of Rota, a

* Commander of the Faithful.—*Ferrier.*

fortress in the north of the Punjab, the inhabitants of which were for the most part Mohamedans.

The Sikhs, finding that Dost Mohamed hesitated to renew the attack, mistook his discretion for fear, and Haree Sing, governor of the Maharadja at Peshawur, threatened some villages dependant on Kabul, and was guilty of numerous exactions against the Afghans of that country. The Emir, wearied with all these annoyances, declared war against Runjeet, and gave the command of his army to his sons Mohamed Efzel Khan and Mohamed Akbar Khan, with orders to advance immediately against the Sikhs. This time fortune declared in favour of the Afghans. They attacked their enemies at Djamrood, near the entrance of the Khyber-Pass, to which they had advanced, and defeated them completely; their general, Haree Sing, being killed in this battle. The Emir, who evinced great moderation after his victory, respected the territory of his enemy, and claimed the intervention of Lord Auckland, Governor-General of the British possessions in India. He demanded that the Indus should for the future be the line of demarcation between the two states, and consented on this condition to abandon Cashmeer to the Sikhs for ever, though it was an Afghan province, and the majority of the population were his countrymen. Lord Auckland rejected these reasonable propositions; and, in his reply, left Dost Mohamed only a *hope* that Runjeet Sing would be requested by him to restore the government of Peshawur to his brother, *Sultan Mohamed Khan;* adding, that he could not, consistently with the friendly relations existing between the Maharadja and the East India Company, force him to make a restitution, the legitimacy of which was, in his eyes, a questionable point. Burnes was sent to Kabul to make known this decision of his Excellency to Dost Mohamed; and the Emir naturally preferred leaving Peshawur to Runjeet, to seeing it again in the hands of his mortal enemy, Sultan Mohamed Khan. It was about this time that the army of Mohamed Shah, king of Persia, marched against Herat, and the Emir was far from desirous of forming a treaty with that sovereign, for all his sympathies were with the English, and he had done everything in his power to enter into a sincere alliance with the East India Company; but Messieurs the Directors would listen to nothing; they had admitted as a principle, that the consolidation and extension of Runjeet Sing's power, under their immediate protection, was a counterpoise against every evil that could happen to them, and every advantage the Russians could gain arising from the Treaty of Turkomantchai signed between the latter power and Persia in 1827. Hence arose the tenacity with which the East India Company supported the invasions of the Maharadja and rejected the loyal concessions of the Emir Dost Mohamed, who from that moment had no other hope of safety than by allying himself with Russia and Persia.

Let us not, however, anticipate, but come to that famous siege of Herat, which was nearly altering the status of every country in Central Asia. Almost all those persons who have written on the changes which it occasioned during the last few years in Afghanistan have allowed a party spirit more or less strong, with which, God be praised, the author has nothing to do, to influence their opinions. Merely a traveller in the country, my constant aim was to search for truth, and to speak it with impartiality; having no political interest to defend, nor dignity or diplomatic pride to maintain, free from constraint, and having been able to mix with all classes of the population, information came to me from all sides, and many fresh circumstances were revealed to me. In adding them to those already known, I have given a sketch of the whole, and endeavoured to make it as accurate as possible with respect to the events that have recently taken place in Central Asia. To attain this object with the greater certainty, I have selected from amongst the narratives, which have hitherto appeared, those which seemed to me to contain the most exact detail of facts, borrowed from them whatever appeared to be true, and rejected all that seemed open to the suspicion of a single doubt.

The extracts are from the text of these authorities, which could not gain by a transformation of style, and the information that I have collected is added. I shall begin by giving the reader an idea of what were the respective positions of the English and the Russians in Asia at the time the siege of Herat was undertaken, but a reservation is necessary on my part. Though assenting to the mode in which the writers whose works I am about to make use of, and who have examined matters to the core, have appreciated them, I do not intend to be responsible for any remarks that can wound the susceptibility of any nation which is the subject of them. My object is to make known facts without malice or prejudice, to give these facts impartially, with simply their historical interest attached to them, and not to recriminate against any individual whatever. The first quotation is taken from a work by Mr. George Sumner of Boston, who seems to me to have treated what relates to the English in a manner which is tolerably satisfactory. The following is his opinion :—

"It has been generally thought that the war made on the Afghans by the English was to be attributed to a fear of the encroachments of, and invasion by, Russia, but it has since been acknowledged that this fear was only a chimera. Let us examine this question. First, to make the subject more clear, we will speak of the position of England in the East: there we see an immense empire, with more than 100,000,000 of subjects, a large army, large revenues, and towns containing a million of inhabitants, entirely under the control and government of a company of merchants and capitalists, who, tranquilly seated behind their counters, give their instructions and orders to their agents, and in less than eighty years have succeeded in raising a power which seems almost to equal that of Alexander or Tamerlane.

"The condition in which they found the various states of India was no doubt exceedingly favourable to the increase of this empire; but another cause, tending almost equally to that increase, was the vast field that it opened to talent of every description, and the facility that every able officer, however low his rank or position, there found of attaining wealth and distinction, by courageously devoting himself to the interests of those whom he served.

"It ought to be remarked, in speaking of the facility with which India was subjugated, that the plan of conquest adopted at the commencement by Clive, and since constantly followed by the English, did not originate with them. It was conceived by the French General Dupleix, when that talented officer commanded at Madras. His proposition to the French government was immediately rejected, and drew upon its author reproaches that the most recent biographers have not endeavoured to remove—indeed they have continued them. It was to employ only a small number of European troops in the conquest of India, and to take advantage of the dissensions amongst the princes and rajahs of the country, to foment discord in their different states, and, finally, to assist any one of them who, after his success, showed a disposition to become a docile instrument in the hands of the nation that had supported him. *Divide et impera.* By adopting this plan the East India Company has worked by degrees to the north and north-west, invading, one after the other, princes, rajahs, and emirs, and even the Great Mogul himself had to accept their alliance and submit to their rule. The Company has occupied Delhi, the capital of the empire of Aurungzebe, crossed the Sutlej, rendered tributary the sovereign of Lahore, and has travelled thus far without knowing when or where it ought to stop, until it found itself face to face with another power, of which the mind was as active and the resources as great, of which the interest and capability of advancing southwards were just as unlimited as those of England acting in the opposite direction—that power is Russia.

"When the expedition of the Shah of Persia against Herat, in 1835 and 1836, was determined upon, the northern limit of the states belonging to the English, and paying taxes to them, was the river Sutlej, which flows south-west, and joins the Indus at a distance about 200 miles north of Delhi.

"Beyond, and in the delta formed by the Sutlej and the Indus, is the Punjab, the kingdom of the Sikhs, with their remarkable sovereign, Runjeet Sing of Lahore. He had hastened to treat with the British government in 1832; Burnes said of him that he might be regarded as one of the most faithful allies of the English, and the Maharadjah proved this by joining with them against the Afghans.

"Crossing the kingdom of Runjeet, we come to the unhappy country of Afghanistan, which witnessed the recent disasters of the British army. To the north of Kabul, the capital of that province, extends a portion of the Himalaya range of mountains, across which, in summer, there are at least two passes open to caravans, leading direct to the Khanats of Badakshane, Balkh, and Bokhara. With these Russia has formed great commercial interests, but the government of that country pretends that she has not yet any well-established political relations there.

"From Kandahar, another city in Afghanistan, the road is open towards Herat, on the Persian frontiers, and, passing through Persia, we reach the Caspian Sea and the southern boundary of Russia. Between Afghanistan and Russia then there is on one side, besides the three Khanats that we have mentioned, a vast extent of deserts, and on the other side is Persia, which, like Turkey, seems scarcely to have forgotten its past splendour and ancient renown. This nation, enfeebled within and powerless without, has become more and more tottering, and seems ready to fall before the first enemy who shall attack her with vigour.

"Thus it is evident that the country of Afghanistan, of which Europe thought very little fifty years ago, is without doubt destined to be the theatre of important events, on which the powers of Central Asia will be tested, and their destiny decided.

"It was in Afghanistan, that Alexander the Great, on his march towards the Indus, stopped to rest his soldiers, who ate with delight the refreshing fruits of the villages in which we now find Kabul. Through it also passed Ghengiz Khan and Tamerlane, when they undertook their expeditions to India. On this distant point is now fixed the attention of the two great countries, who look upon it as the pivot on which, in some degree, must turn their respective interests in India. Count Nesselrode, in a despatch of October 20th, 1838, recommended England to respect Afghanistan. 'Great Britain and Russia,' said he, 'can have but one desire, that of maintaining peace in Central Asia, and supporting the independence of the peoples who are the legitimate possessors and the ancient inhabitants.'

"The friend of England, Runjeet Sing, was not arrested in his progress by this manifestation on the part of one of the greatest powers of Asia. He had already committed depredations in Afghanistan, reduced Peshawur to a state of vassalage, and prepared other more hostile movements towards the south-east. When the Shah of Persia, remembering that his dominions had in former times extended to Delhi, determined to recover or reduce Herat (which had been part of his legitimate possessions, and which is the capital of that province of Afghanistan situated farthest to the north-west), he was probably instigated to attempt this reassumption of his ancient rights by Count Simonich, then Russian minister at Teheran; at least it was supposed so."

The position of the English in India, and the tendency of their future policy, are clearly set forth in this extract; but it would not be of much interest if it were not followed by a sketch of the Russian policy in Central Asia. This question was considered in 1843, in a monthly review, by "A. Chodsko," who has proved himself as well informed as the philologist of Boston. After having rapidly traced the efforts which had been made by the cabinet of St. Petersburgh to render its policy dominant in Europe, and, above all, in Turkey, the writer turns his attention to Asia, and unfolds, with startling truth, the successive invasions of the Colossus of the North on that continent. The reviewer commences by citing the opinion of a contemporary historian: "Vainly," say Lesur, "were the dangers pointed out of permitting this intrusion of an enslaved and barbarous people into the system of European politics; Rüssia has been elevated as much by the errors of others as by her own genius. The last treaties with Turkey, Persia, and the powers assembled at Vienna, have established her dominion on the right bank of the Danube, at the extremity of the Gulf of Bothnia, and from the Vistula to Kamtchatka. She commands the Black Sea, she suffers none but her own armed flag to float over the Caspian, and the shrine of the Kadjars is placed under her protection." After this quotation the reviewer continues: "Subsequently to the year 1819 Russian agents left Tiflis, envoys to the Khans of Khiva and Bokhara. Their instructions were to obtain the abrogation of the trade in slaves, and to announce their mission as the accomplishment of a great duty on the part of the head of the Russian empire. Russia, who had generally imposed slavery upon civilized nations, pretended to restore liberty to slaves, and she knew not how to proceed otherwise than by the sword: she threatened to conquer. The Autocrat expected the refusal that his envoys returned with, but he wished to give a colour to the war for which he was preparing, and his battalions were already marching from Tiflis upon Orenburg. Their reports also informed the Emperor Alexander that his projects against Turkestan were premature; he could not ensure his object until he had deprived Persia of the states she possessed on the borders of the Caspian Sea, and that conquest could not be attempted without further success against Turkey. But the patient constancy with which Russia carries on her schemes is well known; aggression against Turkey would dissipate any suspicions that might arise, while an invasion of Persia would only confirm them. The disposition of the Greeks to revolt was therefore encouraged, and Alexander showed himself again in the character of defender of an oppressed people. But he contented himself with pleading their cause with the Sultan; and several influential personages of his court having endeavoured to turn to their advantage the discussions that arose in 1823 with the Porte, to provoke a rupture, the Emperor sent them into exile.

"The long looked for epoch for the achievement of the project to the accomplishment of which all his intrigues had been directed, arrived in 1824. In the spring of that year he saw the ambassadors of the Khirghizes arrive at his court to render him homage as the supreme chief of the Tartars. In virtue of this title he granted them a code of civil laws, drawn up in the Russian language and in the language of their country; this he bestowed upon them in consequence of their having acknowledged themselves vassals of his empire; the Emperor also promised to visit them, and did in fact very soon after set out for Orenburg.

"Such was the rash and inconsiderate contempt of the nations of the west for the people whom they called the barbarians of Asia, that this step on the part of Alexander occasioned no suspicion. The country of the Khirghizes attracted no attention, though it was the very same kingdom of Kharism, formerly so powerful, and which once entirely ruled Central Asia.

"A brilliant reception awaited the Tzar at Orenburg. The khans of the most distant tribes came there to acknowledge their prince, and proclaim aloud his sovereignty. The Russian journals were filled with accounts of the homage which the numberless hordes scattered over Asia came to offer to their new chief. They had bestowed upon him, as formerly on their celebrated Temondjine, the Tartar surname which signifies *The Greatest*—Djenghis.

"The Emperor soon quitted Orenburg to visit some of the Khirghiz hordes, and was satisfied that he should find in them all the submission that he could expect from their nomadic habits.

"Alexander went again to Orenburg in 1825, and took the empress, then an invalid, with him, intending to leave her at Tangarsk, the climate of which place, the mildest in Russia, would, it was hoped, re-establish her health: but as, on the contrary, she grew worse, he would not quit her. It was then that he was attacked by the mysterious malady which had already carried to the grave his father, the Emperor Paul, and which also terminated his own life, for he had drawn upon himself the same enemies.

"Everything was in readiness for the Persian war, and the commencement of it was in the following year the first act of his successor; it might therefore from that moment be concluded that Nicholas was worthy to continue the policy of Alexander. The rupture of the treaty of Gulistan appeared to be the work of

Persia, and the conjecture might be read in the papers that she was emboldened to that step by the secret intervention and promises of England.

"The treaty of Turkomantchai, of which the preliminaries were signed November 3rd, 1827, was the result of this clever comedy. Russia acquired two khanats which in a military point of view commanded the Persian provinces, occupied the countries south-west of the Caspian Sea, and succeeded to the rights which Persia had preserved over that Turkomania which had been the ancient kingdom of Samarcand. These rights were of the same nature as those recognised by the Khirghizes, and became much stronger, being thenceforth exercised by the acknowledged chief of the Tartar nation.

"Nevertheless, whatever dangers were revealed, the blindness of England continued and manifested itself by the impolitic battle of Navarino, in which the Turkish navy was almost entirely destroyed. The result of it was the treaty of Adrianople, and afterwards that of Unkiar Skelessi, which confirmed to the Emperor Nicholas his preponderating influence in Turkey.

"The successor of Alexander then appeared sure of the expected triumph of the policy so long followed in Asia. His numerous army was concentrated upon Orenburg, and orders were given for the opening of the campaign in the first fine weather of 1831, when the insurrection in Poland suddenly obliged him to march his troops to the Vistula.

"The British ministry was the first that opened its eyes, as is proved by its intrigues to cause, though prematurely, the breaking out of the rebellion; and it sacrificed that unfortunate people to its own safety, by hurrying them into action to avoid being taken at a disadvantage itself.

"Taking immediate measures for the protection of the Indian Empire, of which the chiefs, absorbed in commercial calculations, had too much neglected the political interests, the ministry addressed to the Governor-General, Lord Auckland, fresh instructions; and it was at this time that Captain Conolly and Lieutenant Burnes were sent on their respective journeys. The first started from St. Petersburg to pass through the countries of the Khirghizes, Turkestan, and Persia, while the second left Delhi to explore Afghanistan, Bokhara, and Persia. Burnes had already shown great capability in other expeditions, but the object of his travels was not dissembled. It was evident that his purpose was to investigate the intrigues of the Russians, and the extent to which their efforts to lay the foundations of political power in Turkestan, under the appearance of commercial intercourse, had succeeded. Burnes allowed it to be seen that he was convinced the project of marching an army across so much arid and uncultivated steppe was impracticable; but the passage of his narrative in which he insists with the greatest force upon this assertion suffices to prove that he had presented Lord Auckland with notes and information to the contrary. Here follows the passage: 'When one has met with and felt such a horrible scarcity of water, and found pasture for the horses so difficult to obtain, ophthalmia so prevalent, and so many other impediments, it will be understood that this desert can with difficulty be crossed even by a few squadrons of light cavalry. But who would think of crossing it? If the descendants of the Scythians and the Parthians have the pretension to enter upon this conflict, they can do so without exciting much attention from Englishmen.' If the traveller thus deluded himself, one may be allowed to think that his British pride had strangely blinded him. What difficulty could there be in procuring water in a country from which the river had only been turned aside? What obstacles could hinder the raising of forage in a country lately so fertile and of which the sterility* was so recent?"†

This sketch gives a very accurate idea of the object the Tzar had in extending his dominion towards the south; it is astonishing therefore that the English Government should have been alarmed at the project formed by the Shah of Persia, under the advice of Russia, to sieze Herat. We will admit, like many other persons, and as several newspapers have done, that the possibility of a Russian expedition to India is a chimera if we had based our opinion, as there is everything to lead us to suppose these writers did, on the authority of Burnes; but as the Government at Calcutta knew very well that the obstacles were not so serious as this

* The district of Merv here spoken of was ravaged by the Tartars and Usbeks in 1786.

† The critic is perfectly correct in his remarks upon Burnes, and, had he possessed more information, he might have added, that in the winter and in the spring grass and water are to be found everywhere in the deserts of Khiva and Bokhara. The facility with which a Russian expedition could thus reach India has been shown in 'Caravan Journeys.'—*Ferrier.*

officer wished them to believe, the Governor-General in Council was right to take precautions against any invasion which could be made from the north of Europe into Central Asia. He ought indeed to have done this with more energy at the outset, and with less delay, by which means he would have avoided many diplomatic embarrassments, and many important disasters, the wounds from which will not be healed for a long space of time, though, without doubt, England gained her object. Herat has remained independent, and Russia has retired within the limits stipulated in the treaty of Turkomantchai, while England has brought her frontier up to the west bank of the Indus, and passed that river at two points; Peshawur in the north, and Shikapoor in the south, are two *têtes-de-pont* which cover the principal approaches to the river, and menace the Afghans. But let us not anticipate.

CHAPTER XVI.

First diplomatic discussions relative to the siege of Herat — Mr. Ellis is succeeded by Mr. M'Neil — The Persians invade the principality of Herat — The minister of the Shah plays a double game — Captain Eldred Pottinger at Herat — Russian officers in the Persian camp — Samsoun Khan — Colonel Blaremberg — General Boroffski — Colonel Semineau — Siege of Gorian — Recrimination against the latter officer — Russian and English agents in the Persian camp — Their hostility against Colonel Semineau — Operations at the siege of Gorian — Fall of the place — Shere Mohamed Khan — Yar Mohamed's reply to his brother — Duration of the siege.

IT has been already remarked that the idea of laying siege to Herat for the purpose of effectually putting a stop to the incursions of the Heratees on the Persian territory, and forcing Kamran to pay tribute, originated with Mohamed Shah, but it should be said that immediately the subject was made known to the Russian Government it met with its eager support and encouragement; not because the views of Russia extended at that period so far as to undertake an invasion of British India, for she was not then in the least prepared for so great an enterprise, but because she ever obeys that spirit of forecast, evoked by Peter the Great, which always leads her, whenever an opportunity presents itself, to extend her influence in the direction of the Indus, as she did not long ago to the banks of the Bosphorus at Constantinople. At that time the Russians were contented with the possessions which they held in Asia, but they could not, as clever politicians, see without jealousy the successive invasions of England; they therefore forced her to extend her frontiers out of all reason, exciting her fears by demonstrations of an ambitious character, hoping by that means to make her consume with greater rapidity the immense resources at her command, and to irritate the numerous peoples she has subjected, who serve her much more from a sentiment of fear than because they are habituated to, or love, her rule.

The projects of Mohamed Shah on Herat began to see the light about the commencement of 1835. Mr. Ellis, then British minister at the court of Teheran, at once informed his government of the fact by pointing out the active part which the Russian minister in Persia, General Simonitch, had taken in connexion with the resolution which had been formed by the Persian monarch. The British Ambassador danced atttendance in the diplomatic antechamber eighteen months to persuade Lord Palmerston, the Foreign Minister of Her Majesty, of the complicity manifested by Russia in this war, which was evidently undertaken with views hostile to England. It was in vain Mr. Ellis informed his Lordship that, after having offered his mediation to smooth the misunderstanding existing between the Shah of Persia and the sovereign Prince of Herat, the Persian Government had refused to allow Major Todd, the officer attached to his mission, to be the bearer of his letter to Shah Kamran; and that he was obliged to place it in the hands of the Persian authorities in order that it might reach its destination; in other words, to be submitted to the supervision and control of Russian agents. The British minister further stated that Count Simonitch openly encouraged the war against Herat, that each day he hastened forward the preparations as well as the concentration of troops at Teheran, promising, in the name of his government, subsidies of all kinds and even the support of some Russian regiments. It was equally useless that, under the profound impression that he foresaw a very serious misfortune impending over his country, Mr. Ellis wrote to his superior thus:—"I have the complete conviction that the English Government cannot permit the extension of the Persian Empire, in the direction of Afghanistan, without placing the interior tranquillity of British India in danger. This extension will bring Russian influence to the very threshold of our Indian Empire; and as Persia will not, or dare not, enter into a sincere alliance with England, our policy for the future should be to consider her not as a barrier which covers India, but as the first parallel from whence the assault will be given."

Lord Palmerston* was not much moved or affected by this information: his policy at that time was not anti-Russian, and he persisted in seeing in the reports of his subordinate at Teheran, only, and perhaps unreasonably, timid anticipations which nothing could justify. Left without instructions, obliged very frequently to have recourse to his recollection as to what the English policy had

* An article from the pen of Mons. A. Thomas, in the 'Revue des Deux Mondes,' has furnished me with valuable information on facts relating to these negotiations.—*Ferrier.*

been during his service in India, to enable himself to make a few feeble remonstrances to Mohamed Shah, and almost always censured by his chief for the fears which he expressed, the unfortunate Mr. Ellis did not know what part he was to play at Teheran.

The minister of Russia, on the contrary, always advanced boldly in the warlike policy which he counselled, and had driven the Shah to carry on: supported by his government he dared everything, and his most trifling wishes were accepted as orders by the Court of Teheran. If Lord Palmerston, pressed by Mr. Ellis, was hardy enough to make a few weak remonstrances to the cabinet of St. Petersburg, Monsieur de Nesselrode denied facts as clear as the sun, and it was almost by menaces that he replied to the constant demands of the English minister that a good understanding should exist between the two governments upon the affairs of Persia. The noble Lord, deceived by Russian duplicity, considered it a crime in his minister at Teheran to have seen too well and appreciated too clearly the state of things there. The Prime Minister had been disturbed at a moment when the Russian alliance was without doubt necessary to him, as a balance, and he could not make up his mind to open his eyes to an event and give his attention to a subject which took him by surprise and deranged his plans.

The correspondence of the Foreign Office relative to this affair is nothing more than a series of reproaches upon what Lord Palmerston then denominated chimerical ideas, which his subordinate had conceived respecting General Simonitch; his Lordship requests Mr. Ellis to act in concert with that diplomatist, respecting whose intentions, so far as he is concerned, he is quite satisfied, and to make confidential representations to the Shah's Government on the embarrassment which his inconsiderate aggression against Shah Kamran must expose him to. In short, he has nothing to transmit to Mr. Ellis but timid counsel to assist him in meeting an evil, the cause of which his Lordship obstinately refuses to comprehend; he will see nothing because he is determined to avoid a conflict with Russia, and he keeps on such good terms with that power as to embolden her to redouble her exertions in encouraging the Shah to seize upon Herat. However, this cautious policy could not save Lord Palmerston from the consequences of the entanglements which it created for him, and he finished by being completely the dupe of his own acts. He believes the word of the Cabinet of St. Petersburg, and yet he doubts more and more the accuracy of the reports of his own minister at Teheran. The far-sighted Mr. Ellis then has to endure all the ill-humour of Lord Palmerston, and he is recalled without mercy for not having been able to stop events the development of which was owing to the too great confidence of his chief in the assertions of the Russian Government.

The noble Lord still endeavoured to disguise to himself the check which his policy had inflicted upon English influence in Persia; nevertheless he subsequently made choice of an energetic man, well known for his hostility to Russia, to fill the post of British minister at the court of Teheran. Mr. M'Neil belonged to that school of diplomatists who are perfectly happy in the midst of agitation, and for whom European principles disappear before the necessities of the tortuous diplomacy of Asia. After having passed twenty-five years in India or Persia, he had returned to England towards the end of the year 1834, and, not approving of the policy that had been followed by his government in Persia since the accession of Mohamed Shah to the throne, he had, through the press, fought the question with all the obstinacy inherent in the English character, stating that there was no necessity for drawing the sword from the scabbard to baffle the Russian intrigues at Teheran, that it was only requisite for England to declare distinctly to the Shah her opposition to the war with Herat for that monarch to abstain from carrying on any further the preparations for the expedition. This view of the subject, one so simple, which Lord Palmerston ought to have adopted from the first, at length broke in upon his Lordship's mind, but nevertheless he preserved it as a last resource in case he should find the Shah intractable in every other way; and as he was aware that Mr. M'Neil was active even to restlessness, resolute even to temerity, his instructions were similar to those which had been given to Mr. Ellis. The new Envoy was desired to discourage the ambitious projects of the Shah, and to offer his mediation in arranging the misunderstanding which had arisen between Persia and Herat; in short, he was to continue a spectator of Russian intrigues without being able to offer one energetic word in opposition to them. Mr. M'Neil was not more successful than his predecessor, and complained to his government with as much force as perspicuity, demanding that his instructions should be extended in order that he might have the power of acting with some hope of success. But Lord Palmerston appeared to send him duplicates of all the replies that he had formerly given to Mr. Ellis. His Lordship could not yet make up his mind to take the initiative in a vigorous opposition to Russia, and he endeavoured to maintain a peace which that power seemed little anxious to preserve. Lord Palmerston was not very fortunate in his appreciation of diplomatic affairs, for, when he certified in his letters to the sincerity of the part played at Teheran by Count Simonitch, that nobleman admitted his bad faith in his own correspondence. The noble Lord waited with imperturbable tranquillity till reparation should be made by the Persian Government for conduct with which he was offended, and this at the very moment when Mr. M'Neil received the assurance that the Shah declined to make any; and as Lord Palmerston had purposely deferred sending his instructions, his envoy found himself opposed, with his hands tied, to the ever active manœuvres of Russia, and the determination of the Shah to seize Herat.

That which Messrs. Ellis and M'Neil had foreseen at length occurred; the Persians took the field in 1837, and in the month of October entered the province of Herat; but it is necessary to add that the energetic representations which Mr. M'Neil made to the Shah *on his own responsibility* had led to indecision and a slight sensation of fear in the council of his ministers, which the non-realization of the promises made eighteen months before by General Simonitch also powerfully contributed to develop. The Persians had waited, but in vain, up to this time for the material intervention promised by Russia, and the Russian diplomatist, who had been urged to give a guarantee in writing to the effect that it would be forthcoming, had just refused to do so. Mohamed Shah had conceived some just apprehensions upon this subject, which led him for a moment to think of renouncing his project, for he was afraid that his quondam ally would abandon him in the height of the conflict which the war with Herat might cause between himself and England. But the cleverness of Count Simonitch surmounted this difficulty also, and the Shah took the field without an afterthought, determined to seize upon the fortress which he was going to attack; but his prime minister, Hadji Mirza Agassee, an old and obstinate man, directing as he pleased the opinions of the King, was far from sharing these sentiments. He readily consented that the Persian army should invest Herat, but he had secretly decided in his own mind to allow the siege operations to languish until the Russians had fulfilled the verbal stipulations which their diplomatist had made with him, and, as these engagements were never carried out, the city was not taken. This resolution of the Vizier is the solution of the enigma which so many persons have attempted, but in vain, to discover. Twenty-five days at the utmost ought to have been sufficient to take Herat; nevertheless it sustained a siege of more than nine months, to the great displeasure of Mohamed Shah, who, deceived by his ministers and generals, was ignorant that there were some amongst them who had been gained over to the English party and intended to retreat without having accomplished the projected conquest. But the folly and incapacity of the Persian officers in directing the operations of the siege, as well as the eccentric measures adopted by the prime minister, were more than sufficient to cause the failure of the enterprise without the addition of bad faith.

The newspapers assured us at the time, and many persons still think so, that the Persian army was accompanied by many Russians, officers and men, when it marched against Herat, and that the place was defended by several English officers; there is exaggeration in these two assertions which I will clear away.

In the treaty of 1813 between England and Persia it was stipulated that, if war broke out between the Persians and the Afghans, the English Government should remain neutral, but it might nevertheless become a mediator if requested to do so by both parties. We have seen that England up to this time had not failed on her part with respect to that clause; but the eagerness with which the Russians had advised the Persians to undertake a siege that threatened the dearest interests of England, without doubt induced the Governor-General to pay very little attention to it, and he sent Captain Eldred Pottinger to defend Herat. The Indian newspapers pretended that "this officer, travelling in the neighbourhood of that city, entered it by chance at the moment the siege commenced, and that it was with his assistance and advice *as well as the encouragement given by the English Government*, that the inhabitants were enabled to hold out for nine months." The first part of this assertion is not accurate. Captain Pottinger, *sent by his Government with a secret mission*, arrived at Herat disguised as a Hindoo physician, and was known there only to three merchants of Herat, who were devoted to English interests—Shah Kamran and his vizier did not hear of his arrival until the army invested the place. This was the moment chosen by the English officer to offer the support of his professional services, as well as subsidies of all kinds on the part of his Government, to assist the Shah Kamran in making a stand against the Persians. This offer was accepted with joy, but such was still the discretion of the chiefs of Herat that the inhabitants were actually not aware that the pretended Hindoo physician was an English officer, until Mr. M'Neil arrived in their city in March, 1838. From that moment Captain Pottinger resumed his European uniform, and did not attempt to conceal himself any longer. He was the only Englishman who remained in the place during the whole period of the siege; but it should be added that Major Todd and some few other officers, who were like himself attached to the Persian embassy, entered the city on several occasions with a flag of truce, and it is reasonable to suppose that the advice of these officers was calculated to strengthen the resolution of Yar Mohamed Khan in continuing the defence.

As to the Russian officers, there was not one in the Persian army, for the Sertip* Samsoun Khan, of Russian origin, could not be considered such; he had resided in Persia for many years, and, having refused to take advantage of the amnesties granted by the Emperor of Russia to his subjects who were deserters, Samsoun Khan was much more of a Persian than a Russian, as all those who knew him could aver. Besides, his military knowledge was too mediocre to influence the operations of the Persians, for his rank in the Russian army had never been higher than that of a quartermaster sergeant of dragoons. At the time of the siege he commanded the Persian battalion of the Chaldean, Armenian, and Nestorian Christians, to which were attached seven or eight hundred Russian deserters, nearly all of whom were common soldiers; a very small number of these had been sergeants and corporals, and they had for the most part arrived in Persia long before there was any question of the siege of Herat. [These deserters were, in 1839, in consequence of the representations of the British Government, reclaimed and given up to the Emperor of Russia, and that event led to a new conflict between Russia and Persia. The Shah, on the ground of the duties of hospitality, refused to give up these Russian deserters, but the Emperor Nicholas just at that moment visited his Trans-Caucasian provinces, travelling

* General of Brigade.

indeed as far as Erivan ; and to this place Mohamed Shah sent his eldest son, Nasser Eddin Mirza, to compliment his Russian Majesty. Count Simonitch then declared to the Shah that, if he did not give up the Russian deserters, the heir to the Persian throne should remain an hostage in Russia until he did so ; there was therefore nothing to be done but to yield, and to this alternative the Shah consented.]

Nor can it be said that Lieutenant-Colonel Blaremberg, of the Russian Engineers, was attached to the Persian army, for he formed part of the mission of Count Simonitch. It is true that these two superior officers were actively mixed up in the affairs of Herat, but in a diplomatic sense ;—they never ostensibly directed the operations of the siege, and their position was simply that of advisers.

Two other European officers were in the service of the Shah : one of them, General Boroffski, a Pole and a Russian subject, had, through the protection given him by the English, advanced to this rank in the Persian army, but he had never served in any part of Europe, and had no military experience whatever ; he was reported brave, but courage alone is not sufficient to direct the operations of a siege.

The other was General Semineau, at that time Colonel of Engineers, a Sardinian subject, and an old officer of the Empire, serving in the Shah's army as a Frenchman—his mother was French and born at St. Tropez, his father at Nice. The English accused General Semineau of serving the interests of Russia, because he performed his duty ; they were, however, in an excellent position to know that, when the campaign against Herat commenced, this officer was on the very worst terms with Count Simonitch. In Persia, however, duty is a thing which always comes after personal interest, and there is nothing astonishing in the fact that the English had great doubts of the Colonel's conduct being disinterested.

The Count Simonitch and Mr. M'Neil had remained at Teheran, but each of them detached an officer of his legation to the royal camp. The Russian dragoman Goutt, and the English Colonel Stoddart, taking example from their chiefs, carried on an active paper war. To the first was attached an officer of cavalry of the same nation, by name Vikovitch, who had made himself a reputation for talent in Tartary, and been employed in several missions with success. He spoke with fluency several languages and oriental dialects, and his government destined him, as we shall see further on, to prepare the way for Russian influence in Afghanistan.

Amongst the Persian nobles, too numerous to mention, to whom the Shah had confided the various commands of his troops, there was not one who was capable of taking up the encamping ground for an army, or directing scientifically the operations of the siege. His Majesty was obliged to make Colonel Semineau take upon himself the duties of chief of the staff, and director of the artillery and engineers, which brought upon him from the first the jealousy and opposition of the Persian officers, who were besides urged to annoy him by the Russian and English agents, according as his acts happened to be adverse to the policy or proceedings of either. The Russian was the first who endeavoured to injure him, in the opinion of the Shah and his minister, stating that the Colonel paid and received visits to and from Colonel Stoddart, which was a great impropriety in the eyes of Count Simonitch, but subsequently, when facts proved that Colonel Semineau was a loyal and honest man, though on terms of good social feeling with men of all parties, and performed his duty before every other consideration, the attacks came from the opposite side. Unfortunately the Persian Government lent but too willing an ear to this gossip, and such weakness annihilated all the good that could result from the active co-operation of this officer in carrying on the siege.

The Persian army advanced very slowly upon Herat, and turned aside to wage an irregular warfare against the Turcomans, Yamoods, and Goklans, before repairing to its ulterior destination; nevertheless, when it arrived under the walls of Gorian, a fortress garrisoned by the troops of Shah Kamran, and situated thirty-five miles west of Herat, in the middle of a large plain ten miles in width, it then numbered from 34,000 to 35,000 men, well provided with artillery and munitions of war. Colonel Semineau ordered the army to encamp a gunshot from the fortress on ground sheltered by a ridge of hills which covered it at this short distance. After having marked out the encampment for each corps, he proceeded to make a still closer reconnoissance of the town, and was received by a sharp fire of musketry, but he continued his examination of the place, and, this duty having been accomplished, he retired to a short distance from the noise of the camp, and traced a sketch of the plan of attack which he thought it desirable to make. While thus employed, other divisions of the army arrived in succession, and with them the Russian agent Goutt, who, seeking every opportunity of annoying the Colonel, was loud in his exclamations against the spot he had chosen for the camp. "It is treasonable," exclaimed the Russian, "placing us so close to the poignard of the Afghans; he wishes our throats cut; he is sold to the English," &c. &c. Great confusion and tumult followed, and maledictions without number were hurled at the Colonel. The mules remained still laden, and every one was on the point of carrying his baggage elsewhere, when the arrival of the Shah put a stop to these irregular proceedings. The Persian chiefs made their complaints in bitter terms, but the King well knew their ignorance, for his military studies, which had been directed by French and English officers, enabled him to form a correct judgment of the circumstances; he went himself to the summit of the hills adjoining the camp to ascertain the eligibility of the position, and saw at a glance that the spot chosen by Semineau was a most favourable one, as the enemy's shot flew over the camp. The Shah therefore maintained the dispositions made by Semineau, who, ignorant of what had taken place, went to communicate with the sovereign about half an hour after, and was received by him in his usually kind manner. The Colonel's plan of attack presented three points, on either of which it could be made with a fair hope of prompt success: but the one selected was on the reverse side of the ridge of hills against which the troops were encamped, for from thence the ground sloped towards the place. "Well, then," said the Shah to Semineau, "it is you who shall direct the attack," and gave him written orders to the colonels of four battalions to place themselves immediately under the Colonel's command, and obey him in everything. These four regiments were the Bahader-hane or grenadiers, the Khasseh or guards, the Demavend, so called from the district of that name, and Karaguzloo, of the tribe of that name. These troops were employed in making the gabions and fascines that were necessary, and on the following night Semineau broke ground and commenced his trenches, but he had then to avoid a danger which he did not in the least suspect. The Persian chiefs, who were ordered to conduct the other attacks, did not advance methodically and in silence like the Colonel, but discovered their position to the besieged by a brisk cannonade, under cover of which their troops advanced on the open plain, but the besieged Gorians replied with a musketry fire so well kept up that many of the Persians were soon *hors de combat.* The Persian guns being badly laid, the shot passed over the town at a considerable height, and, after having described their curve, fell into the middle of Semineau's division, who was not a little astonished; nevertheless, after taking some precautions, he proceeded with his trenches. His plan consisted in dividing his corps into two brigades, to attack an angle of the bastion that it was intended to destroy; and when the trenches had arrived at the point at which the two brigades were to separate, they were to construct their respective batteries, at a good distance from one another. But the semi-Russian Sertip, Samsoun Khan, of the grenadier regiment, to whom the Colonel had given the command of the second brigade, obstinately determined to remain where he was and batter the angle in front, being at a distance equal to the point blank fire of one of his own pieces.

His adviser on this occasion was a gunner, like himself a deserter from the Russian service, who had convinced him that a cannon-shot striking a mark at a short distance would not make a hole, but fall to the ground after having struck the wall, and that, to obtain the most completely destructive effect, it was necessary that it should acquire greater power in a longer trajet. I mention these trifling circumstances, to a certain extent foreign to the subject-matter of this work, only with a view of showing how ignorant the Persian officers were in general, and Samsoun Khan in particular. Colonel Semineau, after having made reiterated representations to this officer, and threatened to retire if he persisted in this obstinacy, at length acceded to his wishes, leaving to him all the responsibility of his conduct. As to his own operations, he continued his trenches in order that he might be able to place his guns on the spot he had determined upon at the outset.

Samsoun Khan had constructed the embrasures of his battery with old wooden boxes filled with earth, which were of course knocked all to pieces by the first fire, and ten of his men were killed at day-break; his casualties soon amounted to forty-five or fifty, and his battery was laid completely open This decided him in coming round to Semineau's opinion, and to construct a fresh battery in the proper place.

If I have been diffuse upon these accessory details of the siege of Herat, it is not that they are of any real importance, but that I wish to give an idea of the obstacles raised by Persians, English, and Russians, at every step, to impede Colonel Semineau, who alone was sincere in the prosecution of the war which had been so rashly undertaken. Samsoun Khan, as a Russian deserter, exercised some influence over the troops, and he was also considered one of the most experienced generals of Mohamed Shah. What has been stated above will give a correct idea of his capacity, and enable the reader to imagine that of his Persian colleagues, which was inferior to his, both on scientific grounds as well as courage.

Colonel Semineau had not advanced so rapidly with his trenches, or rather towards a result, as the commanders of the other attacks, who had from the first established their batteries at too great a distance from the place; but with a view to more satisfactory proceedings, he arrived after several days' hard work within five-and-forty yards of the fortress, and this without losing a single man. His batteries, constructed upon the ordinary rules of engineering, being ready, he gave notice to the king of the hour at which he intended to open his fire, and Mohamed Shah, anxious to see the effect, took up a position on the neighbouring heights to have a good view. Semineau obtained the success which from his able dispositions he had reason to expect: the great tower at the angle gave way, and the ricochet fire would soon have destroyed the smaller towers, which were on the prolongation of this face and the upper part of the wall which connected them one with another. Mohamed Shah, who had served in the wars against Russia and been present at different sieges, had never witnessed anything like this, and exclaimed, when he saw the result of the fire, "It is only to-day that I understand what may be done with artillery." The Afghans, not less surprised than the Shah, and alarmed at the disastrous consequences which would follow if the town were taken by assault, hung out a flag of truce near the angle of the bastion, and, Semineau having given orders to cease firing, they advanced to the top of the breach and declared that they surrendered at discretion. Two hours after, the Serdar Shere Mohamed Khan, the brother of Yar Mohamed Khan, who commanded in the town, came to the Shah and made his submission;

the Persian troops occupied Gorian the same day, and their army, which was now at liberty to advance to the siege of Herat, arrived under the walls of that city in the beginning of November. The Serdar Shere Mohamed Khan wrote to his brother from the camp to inform him of the reason which had induced him to surrender Gorian, and advised him not to continue a conflict which the insufficiency of his means of defence would not permit him to prolong against the Persian army, for, said he, "there is an European officer with it who can in forty-eight hours raze Herat to the ground." He also stated that in persisting in his resistance he would only lead to the ruin of his country and great misfortunes for himself; that it would therefore be much better for him to throw himself upon the generosity of Mohamed Shah and open to him the gates of the city. Yar Mohamed, indignant at this message, replied, "It may be very well for you, who knew not how to die at your post in defence of the fortress which I confided to your care, to give such advice, but for myself, as long as there remains one cartridge to fire, a sabre in my hand, and one breath of life in my body, I will never bow my head before the Kadjars: I will not surrender Herat until the teeth which Abbas Mirza ordered to be pulled out of my head at Meshed are replaced. If till then the fortune of war goes against me, I shall know how to escape dishonour by dying in the breach." He kept his word, and his heroic defence during nine months is one of the finest military exploits which modern history furnishes in Asia.

CHAPTER XVII.

Herat — Appearance and position of the city — Its fortifications and environs — Attack of the Persians on the suburbs — Colonel Semineau's plan of attack — Absurdities of the Persians — Underhand intrigues and eccentricities of Hadji Mirza Agassee — Means adopted by him to prevent success — Conspiracy in Herat in favour of the Persians — The plot is discovered — Monster cannon — Treachery and death of Mirza Naghi — Distinguished conduct of Colonel Semineau — Cowardice of Meuhbalee Khan — Colonel Semineau declines to take part in the operations — The Afghans surprise Hadji Khan — Scarcity of provisions in the Afghan camp — Privations of the enemy in Herat — Difficulties of their position — Djellal Eddin Mirza and Chems Eddin desert to the Persians — Mr. M'Neil arrives at the Persian camp — Proceedings of that minister — Diplomatic notes between the Russians and the English — Mr. M'Neil breaks with the Persian government — His messengers are arrested — Mr. N'Neil's conduct in the Persian camp — He leaves for Tauris.

THE fortified town of Herat, supposed to have been founded by Alexander the Great, is a quadrangle of 3½ miles long on the north and south sides, and rather more on the east and west. Its extent would be immense if all the suburbs were included, particularly those stretching to the west of the town beyond the Dervazeh Irak, or Gate of Irak; all these suburbs are partially covered with ruins, and numerous walled gardens about half a gunshot from the town. A thick rampart, constructed of earth brought from the interior of the city, surrounds it and forms its defence. The height of this rampart is not everywhere equal, but the average may be about 90 feet, and it is supported on the inside by counterforts of masonry. Earth has also been taken for a distance of 108 yards beyond the ditch, and used in the construction of this work, and being a pure clay it has become exceedingly solid. The rampart has the appearance of a long hill surrounding the city, and on the crest of it a thick wall has been built about 32 feet high, flanked with round towers, which, as well as the curtains that connect them with each other, are loopholed for musketry; it is only in the enormous and massive towers at the angles that cannon can be mounted.

Generally speaking, the ground from the edge of the ditch towards the country, in a radius of 250 yards, is of a marshy nature; water is found at a depth of from 8 to 10 feet, especially on the southern side of the city, for the general inclination of the ground is from north to south. Streams, which all run east and west, water the environs and supply the ditch; and it flows out on the south side opposite the large tower which forms the angle of the place, called Koordj Khakhister, or Tower of Cinders. When the Persians first arrived before Herat the immediate neighbourhood was well wooded—an immense number of vines and vast plantations of poplar, willow, cypress, and above all fir, filled the Bagh Shah, or King's Garden, and bordered the avenue which extended about a mile thence up to the gate of the city.

At half a cannon-shot south of the town is a canal with steep banks, supplied with water by the Heri-rood, which is four miles distant from the city, and on this canal are a great number of mills; it is fordable only at a few points, on which account at different distances little bridges have been built, each of a single arch.

There are five gates to the city of Herat. To the north of it, near the Dervazeh Melek, or Meshed, are two citadels—Ark Noon or the New Citadel, and Ark Keuheuneh or the Old Citadel—which nearly join each other. The first commands the second, in which there is an enormous round tower, that then served as the palace of the Shah Kamran.

Also on the north, parallel to the walls, and about 1250 yards from them, rises the long hill of Talleh-bingui, which forms a ridge on that side. Beyond this hill stands one of the most beautiful mosques ever built in Asia: it is surmounted by nine minarets, from the summits of which the interior of the town can be seen, and its distance from it is about the longest range of a twelve-pounder. Herat is not commanded by any of the hills in the environs; Talleh-bingui, which is used for a cemetery, is the highest.

Mohamed Shah pitched his camp about a mile and a half south-west of the city, on the right bank of the great canal already mentioned, and as soon as his troops arrived he commanded them to invest the place on all sides. To do this was not difficult, for the Persians were ten times as numerous as the Afghans, who had only 4000 men to defend it. They had confined themselves to this small nnmber in order to economise the provisions they had stored up a long time previously, having foreseen the attack they were now called upon to repel.

The first day that the Persians attacked the city the Afghans opposed the occupation of the suburbs with as much courage as obstinacy; it was necessary to dislodge them from each house in succession; the smallest tuft of trees, the smallest piece of wall, were cover of which they availed themselves with great readiness, and from thence directed a most murderous fire on their aggressors. Artillery did no further service for the Serbaz or Persian infantry than batter the towers and covered ways, from which a treble fire of musketry proceeded. The Afghans had a few pieces of heavy calibre which they had placed on the large towers, and the fire from these guns took the assailants in flank and occasioned them immense loss. However, their ardour was not abated, and such was the progress they made, that, in the evening, the Afghans, fearing their position would be turned and their communications cut off, at last retreated and abandoned the suburbs to the Persians, who immediately surrounded the city and took up a position wherever an inequality in the ground presented itself to shelter them from the uninterrupted fire which proceeded from the ramparts.

Colonel Semineau then made a careful reconnoissance of the fortifications, and traced a plan of attack, which he submitted on the following morning to the Shah. In this he indicated, as the best point on which to make a regular approach, the great tower at the angle of the city, called Koordj Khodja* Abdul Hamid, of which he had the opportunity of examining with a glass, from the minarets of Talleh-bingui, the front within the town. The King thought the plan was an excellent one; but such was his wretched vacillation, and so strong were the intrigues of the English party, that it was never acted upon, and the attack was indefinitely delayed.

The Shah was afraid of offending the different Persian commanders, for, moved by presumptuous vanity, they refused to be directed by an European, and promised, if allowed to act for themselves, to take the city in eight days. This emulation amongst his lieutenants, which evinced itself by false oaths and hollow protestations of devotion, the Shah thought he ought not to discourage; and as each asserted he was braver and wiser than all the rest, he made each independent in his command, and ordered them to take up positions according to their own good pleasure on whatever points they considered most eligible: they were also to attack as they

* Master-tower.

pleased, without any regard to acting in concert, as each would then derive from his own deeds the honour that would attach to them.

Sad indeed were the consequences of these incredible arrangements: everything in the trenches was done at random, excepting that it might be said they agreed on one point only, namely, to make the greatest possible noise without arriving at any result. The artillery played without judgment on the whole circumference of the place, and wasted their shot in a point-blank fire against the rampart, which all the cannon-balls in the world could not destroy. The first operation in each trench was an endeavour to bring down the tower and curtains on the crest of the rampart, before they thought of how they were to pass the ditch: to effect the latter purpose the Persian generals could devise no brighter scheme than letting off the water; therefore they broke the dam and laid it dry, greatly to the convenience of the Afghans, who till then could not get in or out of the city excepting at the gates, which were masked. From that time they constantly harassed the Persians by surprises on all points, the great advantage of exit and entrance having been given them by their enemies.

Although the operations were thus disjointed and subject to the caprice of a score and a half of commanders in the trenches, Hadji Mirza Agassee, an old Mollah, entirely ignorant of military science, reserved to himself the chief direction of the siege; his object, as before stated, was to prolong it till the diplomatic struggle in which he had, with Russia, engaged against England, should be decided. But as the Shah had not at that time been convinced by his arguments, and pressed his generals to take the town as quickly as possible, the prime minister gave them secret counter-orders to do nothing; they fought therefore without a purpose; men were lost without necessity, and treason was the order of the day.

Colonel Semineau alone was ignorant of these disloyal intrigues, and conducted his operations on the side assigned to him, the Gate of Kandahar, with his habitual resolution, but the prime minister found means to paralyze his best measures by giving him as coadjutors Persian officers who did not execute his orders. On the other hand, Hadji Mirza Agassee committed a thousand extravagances, more like the lucubrations of a diseased brain than the rational conceptions of the commander of an army. The following facts will only give a slight idea of his eccentricities; were they all to be chronicled, they would fill volumes—a few only shall be mentioned.

Two or three of the commanders in the trenches, being sufficiently powerful to have nothing to fear from the minister, and being even hostile to him, had not been favoured with his views, and having pushed their works with ardour were more prepared to attempt an assault; but it was necessary that a diversion in their favour should be made by the troops in the other trenches. This diversion was ostensibly promised to them by Hadji Mirza Agassee, but he secretly forbade those who were to carry it out from doing so; the gallant fellows therefore who made the assault found themselves betrayed, and, crushed by the Afghans, lost heart for any future attempt.

At another time ammunition was wanting at the moment of attack; or the cartridges for the guns and musketry were blank. This happened several times in the trenches commanded by Prince Seifet Dooulet; nevertheless he was not discouraged, and, after having made the necessary arrangements, applied to the prime minister for permission to make an attack that should reach the very heart of the city. His request was granted, but a condition was attached to it, namely, that he must trust nothing to chance, but make a trial first. "If you succeed," said he to the prince, "do not advance too far, retire after a slight engagement; be satisfied with knowing that you have the advantage, that should be sufficient for you; we shall see later what can be attempted definitively." In vain the gallant prince represented that the Afghans were quite ignorant of the works in his trenches, that to make a simple trial would only serve to expose them, and enable them to construct other works that might completely neutralize the effect of his. The minister remained immoveable in his determination, and this spirited officer was obliged to give up his cherished hopes of serving his sovereign and distinguishing himself. From that time the intriguers tempered his zeal by withholding the ammunition and projectiles that were requisite for the operations he had to conduct; and Hadji Mirza Agassee, saying that he had scarcely enough himself to defend the king's camp if it should be attacked, coldly added, "You must do the best you can, it is your affair." Upon receiving this reply, Seifet Dooulet, and those chiefs who were similarly circumstanced, cut some thousands of balls out of the ruins of the marble tombs on the Talleh-bingui, but after they had put their troops to all that labour the powder requisite to discharge them at the enemy was denied these energetic officers. The king had masked all the gates of the town as soon as he arrived before it, but a few days after the Hadji said that they ought to give the Afghans the power to move out; and the reason he assigned for this strange conduct was that the rebels should have an opportunity of escaping. "If I were to be master of the town in ten days," he said, "there would be too many of them to punish." At the same time he by degrees formed a Persian party in the city, who conferred with him, proposing to admit during the night some of the king's troops, and deliver to him all the artillery of the Shah Kamran; everything was agreed upon, and the sound of the trumpet was to be the signal for the Persians to enter the city. The trumpet did sound, but the Persians never appeared; and, in their stead, the accomplices in this treason saw approaching the troops of Yar Mohamed Khan, who came down upon them and cut them to pieces. Hadji Mirza Agassee had himself revealed the whole plot to the Vizier of Shah Kamran!

Again: Mohamed Shah had ordered that a 96-pounder should be cast upon the spot, which with some difficulty was done, but when it was mounted the prime minister discovered that it required too much ammunition, and he was very indignant with the commander of the artillery. "What a fool you are!" he said to him; "cannot you see that this piece was cast far more for the purpose of terrifying than of destroying the Afghans? tell your men to fire over the town; that will frighten the Shah Kamran, and every morning you can send a waggon and a few artillerymen round to the other side to pick up the balls that will have fallen beyond it."

Thus it will be seen that the prime minister was in no hurry to take Herat, but neither was he disposed to abandon the siege, for as soon as the troops were installed he made each battalion clear a piece of ground and sow it, which plainly showed that he intended to remain till the next harvest. As long as Mohamed Shah was not prevailed upon by the Hadji to waive his original ideas of the siege of Herat, he showed himself far less benevolently inclined to the Afghans and their adherents than his minister was, and ordered that all who were taken prisoners should be put to death: he often commanded that these executions should take place under his own eyes, and, when beholding the vast space of bloodstained ground, was once heard to say "In Gulistan est," "This is a garden of roses."

In another instance, when the treason of Mirza Naghee was detected, the same savage feeling was manifested. That officer was in a high position at court, and his guilt was proved by an intercepted letter of his to the Shah Kamran, in which he informed the Afghan prince of what was doing in the Persian camp, and recommended him also to warn Mr. M'Neil to hasten his arrival, if he wished to prevent the fall of the town. The Shah sent immediately for the criminal, and, perfectly regardless of the entreaties of the Hadji, ordered that he should lose his life under the bastinado, and that his body should be exposed on a gibbet before the ramparts of the city.

The prime minister was well aware that his sovereign would have more than enough to do to annihilate all the traitors in his camp, and for this simple reason—they were most of them his own friends; from that moment he determined to induce the Shah to participate in his views, and finally succeeded in his object. But both the one and the other stood so much in awe of General Simonitch that they concealed from him the little inclination they had to continue this war with the Afghans, and they prolonged it only to avoid incurring the indignation of that diplomatist.

Colonel Semineau was no longer an obstacle to the proceedings of the prime minister, for, shortly after the arrival of the army, he had by a series of intrigues forced him to abstain from taking further part in the active operations. The day after that on which the place was invested the Colonel advanced, with 200 recruits who had arrived in camp the evening before, to an Imaum Zadeh,* situated at a short distance from the Gate of Kandahar, and there took up his position; the ground about it was undulating and very much broken, and for a considerable space covered with burial-grounds, gardens, and the ruins of houses and out-buildings. Once in possession of the Imaum Zadeh, he entrenched it, and connected it by some small earthworks with an ab-ambar,† situated about 11 yards in front of his position. This brought him so near the gate of the town as to give rise to a hope that some lucky chance or clever *coup de main* might one day or other put the place in his hands,

---

* Saint's tomb. † Reservoir of water.

and, had he been at all supported in his plans, that would have happened.

The first night he held this post was exceedingly dark, and favoured an attack that 2000 Afghans moving silently out of the town attempted against it. The Imaum Zadeh was at the time but imperfectly protected by a slight earthwork scarcely finished, and the enemy crept up to it unperceived, until noticed by Colonel Semineau himself, who was returning from an inspection of his works. He had scarcely regained the tomb when a Herculean soldier who had followed him crawled up the breastwork with his sword raised to cleave him to the ground, but before he could do so he fell by a ball from the Colonel's pistol. The Afghans, seeing they were discovered by this rash action of their comrade, at once rushed towards the work, and, as they gained the top, would certainly have remained masters of it if Semineau had lost his coolness for a moment. His recruits, under fire for the first time, stood astounded at being thus assailed by at least twice their number, and but for the energetic conduct of their commander, which restored their courage, would have been massacred without dealing a blow even in self-defence. When they had repulsed their enemies with the bayonet, the Colonel placed them round the breastwork, conjuring them to stand, which they had every inclination not to do, annoyed as they were by a well-sustained fire from the walls, though the stupidity and clumsiness of the Afghans assisted them in no slight degree. The besieged threw fire-balls from the town to guide their party, but these never reached the Imaum Zadeh; they fell short amongst the Afghans, and consequently rendered them visible to the Persians, by whose bullets they were cruelly decimated. They could not return the fire because they had only their sabres with them, and therefore fell by hundreds on the work; and after four hours' hard fighting, seeing that it was impossible to overcome the resistance maintained by the little garrison, they retired into the city.

A Persian Sertip, Meuhbalee Khan, and a relation of the prime minister, who was posted 200 yards in rear of the Imaum Zadeh with 300 men, with orders to support the Colonel, instead of executing the duty assigned to him, as soon as he heard the firing made all his preparations to escape in case the enemy should reach his position; but the next morning, when he heard that the men whom he had abandoned had been victorious in the struggle, and still held the post intrusted to them, he could not believe it, and gave as an excuse for his inaction that he did not consider himself in sufficient strength to advance to their assistance, that he believed they were all killed, and consequently that it was useless to try to help them. The truth was that this inaction fell in with the views of the prime minister as well as of this coward.

A Persian proverb says, "It is not always those who sow the corn who reap the crop," and Meuhbalee Khan remembered it: hastily wrapping a handkerchief round one hand, he hurried with his feigned wound into the presence of Mohamed Shah, and gave his sovereign a most flowery description of the courage he had displayed in the defence of the Imaum Zadeh, without even naming the brave Semineau, but the monarch, enlightened by more truthful informers, presented the Colonel with a watch set in jewels, an acknowledgment of the royal appreciation of his services, which is in Persia considered as equivalent to receiving a decoration. Notwithstanding the flagrant falsehood in which this craven Meuhbalee Khan was thus detected, the Hadji insisted upon his remaining the colleague of Colonel Semineau in the intrenchments in front of the Kandahar Gate, to the great annoyance of that officer, who well knew the cowardice, ignorance, and treachery of the Sertip: in an evil moment, however, he yielded to the desire of the Hadji, and very unfortunately, for a few days after, in his absence, the Khan allowed the Afghans to take the works constructed with so much trouble and defended at such a cost of life, decamping with the men under his orders.

From that moment Semineau, who till then had constantly struggled against the cowardice and treachery of others, ceased to take any part in the siege, and retired to his tent in disgust, a result which perfectly fell in with the schemes of Hadji Agassee. Nevertheless, when he waited upon the Shah, this brave soldier hesitated not to tell him his opinion, and point out to him that he was betrayed. The weak-minded monarch bent his head and reflected; but never profited by the information and advice given to him. His minister directed his conduct as he pleased, and knew how to remove from his mind the most unfavourable impressions regarding himself.

The Afghans distinguished themselves daily by the most daring attacks upon the besiegers: sometimes a handful of horsemen would issue from the town, charge a whole corps of Persian infantry, and never retire without making many prisoners or committing great slaughter; sometimes a detachment would fight till the death of the last man amongst them: theirs was always hand-to-hand work with the sabre, and was perfectly murderous. One day they surprised two battalions of Chaghaghis posted on the Talleh-bingui, killed 400 of their men, and carried off two guns. Their commander, the Sertip Hadji Khan, had very imprudently at nightfall of the previous day admitted within his lines 100 Afghans, who besought him to grant them hospitality, assuring him that they had always been on the side of Mohamed Shah, but that it had never been possible for them to escape from the city till then. The too confiding Sertip allowed them to remain with his own men, and at midnight they sprung upon the piled arms of the soldiers sleeping beside them, and with the aid of 200 of their countrymen, who had followed them and crept up the hills to the works, made a frightful carnage, after which they retired with one prisoner, a captain of artillery, and the two guns that he commanded.

The Persian army, harassed without intermission by sorties of this description, never had a moment's repose: it maintained itself with difficulty, for the provisions were brought from a great distance, and often intercepted by parties of Afghans who scoured the surrounding country. The neighbourhood of Herat had supplied the bazaars of the camp very well for three or four months, and these resources would have lasted three times as long if they had been properly managed; but they were wasted and misused, and it was not long before the half-famished soldiers of Mohamed Shah were reduced to browse upon clover, and seek for wild roots to satisfy their hunger. By marauding, in which they were great adepts, they sometimes managed to procure a little corn or barley, of which they made coarse bread, and ate it ravenously half baked.

The beleaguered city was in no better condition; the Afghans felt the miseries of famine even in a worse degree than their enemies. They were in want of the first necessaries of life—salt was sold at 20*s.* an ounce; the horses, camels, mules, asses, and even animals reckoned unclean by Mussulmans, had been consumed, and the population was dreadfully reduced by hunger. The water in the canals which supplied the city having been turned off by the Persians, it was necessary to have recourse to that in the tanks, which was very brackish, and also insufficient, for most of them being supplied from the outside of the town were soon dried up, and this added one more to the terrible sufferings of the inhabitants. Yar Mohamed placed sentries on all the cisterns that were supplied by springs, and the water that rose in them was parsimoniously dealt out to the people every twenty-four hours. The bazaars, public squares, and mosques were crowded with sufferers imploring the pity of the serdars as they went by, and begging for food; to prove their misery they laid out before them the corpses of their townsmen who had died of hunger, but the chiefs, reduced to extremity themselves, could only encourage them by words and their own stern resignation. To all these horrors was at length superadded the failure of ammunition. Yar Mohamed Khan, it was true, ordered some to be made, but either the materials were bad or the workmen ignorant, for the powder burned in the cannon and left the ball as it was put in.

The original defenders of the city, who amounted at the beginning of the siege to 4000, were reduced to half that number in the first month of the operations, owing as much to the defections produced by the intrigues of the Russians and Persians, as from their losses in action; but, as the Afghans are nearly all soldiers by birth, Yar Mohamed filled up his ranks with tradesmen and workmen. Those who were for defending the place to the last extremity, at the head of whom were the Vizier, his cousin the Serdar Dine Mohamed Khan, and Captain Pottinger, were immoveable in their resolution; but those who were for submitting, and who affected to act in the name of the Shah Kamran, were daily intriguing, and tried frequently to give the city up to the besiegers; so that but a handful of brave Afghans were frequently obliged to repel the attacks from the enemy outside the walls, and those from their countrymen within as well; but this contest was of short duration, for the traitors, seeing the fruitlessness of their disloyalty, took refuge in the camp of Mohamed Shah, with the exception of their nominal chief Shah Kamran, who was imprisoned and closely watched in the citadel, where he could get drunk at his ease; he ceased not to urge the surrender of the place, but, though Yar Mohamed treated him with external respect, it was long since he had paid the least regard to his commands.

Amongst the Afghans who had joined the Persian army were Djelat Eddin Mirza, a son, and the Serdar Chems Eddin Khan, a brother-in-law, of the Shah Kamran; the former was governor of

Subzawar, the latter of Furrah, fortified places south of Herat. They had brought with them 1000 Popolzyes and Noorzyes, who were a valuable reinforcement to the Persians; also 2000 Hazarahs of Kalehnoon, who, by the clever policy of Assaf Dooulet, the maternal unole of Mohamed Shah, were attached to the Persian party. This welcome addition to his forces saved the king from the necessity of raising the siege so soon as from the utterly destitute state of his army he must otherwise have done, and he afterwards proved his gratitude to these chiefs by bestowing lucrative grants upon all, and continuing their rank in the Persian army when they followed him in his retreat.

It has been stated that General Simonitch and Mr. M'Neil had remained at Teheran after the departure of the Shah for Herat, the latter greatly distressed at an event which he had long before announced by anticipation to his own government, but which he had constantly assured the Persians would never happen. "In the present state of his finances," he said, "the Shah will never get 10,000 men together to take into the field." The facts had not justified his predictions, and he persisted against them so far as to doubt that Herat was attacked, even after the arrival of the army under its walls; but at last he was obliged to believe it. Learning that the siege had commenced, and that the place was on the point of being taken in spite of his intrigues amongst the Persian chiefs, and the useless efforts of his agent Colonel Stoddart to induce the Shah to retire, he became so alarmed that he determined to visit the royal camp himself. He had, it is true, no order from his government to authorize his taking this journey, but he provided himself with a very indirect one from the Governor-General of India, and arrived on the 8th of March, 1838, under the walls of Herat. The coldness of his reception, and the displeasure evident in the king's countenance, would have daunted any less hardened diplomatist than himself; but in spite of the insufficiency of his instructions, he attacked the question of the retreat afresh with his usual tenacity, and used all the arguments that diplomacy or even threats could furnish to induce the Shah to retire, but without success.

The following extracts are from the work of M. Alexandre Thomas, 'Simple à propos de l'Histoire Diplomatique,' which has been my guide in all that concerns the negociations that took place between Russia, Persia, and Great Britain. This excellent work is exceedingly dry, but that has not prevented me from consulting it; its length has obliged me to make a close abridgment of a portion; and to the extracts, which I shall give nearly verbatim, I have only added circumstances that had been forgotten—for the asperity of his opinions I leave Mons. Thomas responsible. "Mr. M'Neil," says this author, "pressed and menaced, but the Shah excused himself as he did to Mr. Ellis—'he is not a free agent, he is afraid of giving umbrage to the Russian Government by abandoning the place; if he had known he was running the risk of losing the friendship of the British Government, he would not have gone so far; if Mr. M'Neil was in a position to inform him that if he did not at once desist he would be attacked by the British, he would desist at once: he must absolutely be so spoken to, so treated by Great Britain, to support him against Russia.'

"Mr. M'Neil did his best and gained time: he went from the besiegers to the besieged, from the city to the camp, carrying, dictating, changing the concessions of both parties; but when he went into Herat he was always careful to take with him Major D'Arcy Todd of the artillery, in order that he might assist Captain Pottinger with his advice. However, by dint of perseverance and parley, the British Envoy had succeeded in settling the preliminaries of peace, when the Russian Ambassador reached the Persian camp; a despatch also arrived from Lord Palmerston dated February 12, 1838, enclosing an extract from one from Lord Durham, the British Ambassador at St. Petersburg, in which it was stated that 'Count Nesselrode said that he was convinced that our minister had been misinformed, and that Count Simonitch had never given any such advice to the Shah as that which had been attributed to him, namely, to seize Herat.' Lord Palmerston proceeded, therefore, to address fresh reproofs to his agent, though it appeared that his lordship was not entirely convinced by Lord Durham's assertion, for he demanded, timidly it is true, but still he demanded, from M. de Nesselrode the recall of Count Simonitch from Teheran, and also that of the Russian deserters employed in the army of the Persian sovereign; however, this did not prevent him from writing to Mr. M'Neil that the general was offended at his bad opinion of him, recommended him to be less suspicious for the future, and to live on good terms with his colleague; information which, instead of extinguishing, only added fuel to the fire. Its first effect was to break off the preliminaries of peace to which the British envoy had brought both parties to consent; and the second was immediately to restore to Count Simonitch his influence in the councils of the Shah, while Mr. M'Neil lost all his. This letter from Lord Palmerston deprived him of all power of action, for it contained not a word about Herat—no notice whatever of Russia; it seemed to reduce the pacific conclusion of the whole affair to the secondary question of a good understanding between the two diplomatists.

"Mr. M'Neil had then nothing more to say; his credit fell rapidly when it was seen that he was not supported; annoyances and affronts of all kinds were put upon the English; Russia, who recalled her deserters, exacted the withdrawal of all the English officers in the service of the Shah; and by one of those unhappy coincidences to which Lord Palmerston always exposes himself by his consideration for doubtful friends, and which only produce vexatious results, the British officers were requested to withdraw from the camp before Herat, just when Mr. M'Neil had received the order to leave them at the disposition of the Shah as long as he was not obliged to quit the Persian territory himself.* He was almost driven to the last extremity—he ought to break all diplomatic relations with the Shah, and retire without having even officially opened any discussion touching upon Russian intrigues. He did break them, and retired for a doubtful and almost insignificant affront from the Persian court. Notwithstanding the strict orders of Mohamed Shah that no one should have any communication with Herat, Mr. M'Neil continued to have secret correspondence with the besieged, and a courier with some despatches addressed to him was arrested by the Persian videttes; the Persian monarch had perhaps a right to be more indignant at this than he was, but he only sent the letters to the British envoy, and begged him not to expose himself to have others intercepted. Probably few sovereigns would have shown more moderation on such an occasion, but Mr. M'Neil considered himself affronted by this act, which he looked upon as an infringement of his rights, and insisted upon an apology from the prime minister; this was refused, and he adopted the refusal as the basis of his rupture with the Persian Government. Without taking into account the continued hostility of Russia, which for

* Despatch, March 10, 1838.

three years had menaced the barriers of British India, Mr. M'Neil announces to his own Government his rupture with that of the Shah in the following terms :—

"'*Meshed, June* 25, 1838.

"'After having exhausted all the means I could devise to induce the Persian Government to grant me reparation and satisfaction for the violence offered to the messenger, and finding that I could obtain nothing, I felt compelled, not only in consequence of the evident determination of the Persian Government not to grant what I had demanded, but also because of its perseverance in a course of proceeding towards me in camp which I felt was lowering the character of the mission in the estimation both of Persians and Afghans, to quit the court, and I am now on my way to the Turkish frontier, where I shall hope to receive further instructions from your Lordship. What course the Persian Government will now pursue I know not: some public act of reparation, which will prove to the people of Persia and of Central Asia that we are not with impunity to be insulted, is in my opinion indispensably necessary—I will not say to restore us to our former position, but to enable us to retain one of any credit or respectability. Both the Persians and the Afghans in the Shah's camp saw with amazement the Persian Government treating a British mission as a proscribed body, and punishing persons who ventured to hold even a casual communication with it; while some of the members of the Russian mission took to task, and threatened to get punished for that offence, persons who occasionally visited at my tent, taking some precautions to prevent their being discovered.'

"In the month of May, 1838, before he quitted the camp, the British envoy despatched Major Todd to Lord Auckland, Governor-General of India, with despatches that informed him of the rupture which had taken place. After rapidly crossing Afghanistan the Major arrived in July at Simla, where he found his Lordship, who was greatly impressed with the importance of the letters placed in his hands; it has even been affirmed that they were the cause of his determination to make war on Kabul the following year.

"On the eve of his departure from the camp Mr. M'Neil obtained permission to go into the city once more to make a last attempt at a reconciliation between the Persians and the Afghans; he passed the night in Herat, but, instead of fulfilling his promise, it was found that he had only been there to make presents to Shah

Kamran and his adherents to induce them to renounce their project of surrendering the place. The next day he went to the Shah, and told him that the Heratees would not hear of peace, and that he must raise the siege. On the refusal of the Shah, the British ambassador struck his tents, and left for Tauriz, where he decided to wait for further instructions from his Government, to which, on the 11th April, 1838, he wrote as follows: 'The question of Herat seems therefore to be the question of all Afghanistan, for it is no secret to any one that the British Government has been desirous to prevent its fall, and that Russia, on the contrary, has been solicitous to see it in the hands of Persia.'"

CHAPTER XVIII.

Mr. M'Neil's letter to the Muchteid of Ispahan — Lord Palmerston no longer continues his half-measures — The English occupy the island of Karrack — Captain Vikovitch at Kandahar and Kabul — He returns to the Persian camp with the envoys of these two principalities — Treaty between Persia and Kandahar — Violent declaration of Lord Palmerston to the Persian government — General Simonitch arrives in the Persian camp — The Persians take courage — Hadji Mirza's opposition to Count Simonitch — Colonel Semineau's plan of attack adopted — Siege operations renewed — The assault — Treachery of the Persian chiefs — General Boroffski is killed and the Persians are repulsed — Colonel Semineau is wounded — He sends in his resignation, which is not accepted — Is promoted to the rank of General, and receives a Persian order — The English ultimatum arrives at the Persian camp — Conduct of the Heratees during the assault.

MR. M'NEIL had scarcely reached Meshed when he allowed free scope to his resentment against the Persians; and he carried matters to such extremes, that one is in truth tempted to ask if his actions ought not to place him under the ban of civilised nations.

On his accession to the throne Mohamed Shah had met with opposition from three of his uncles, and one, Seifet Dooulet, Governor of Ispahan, had been supported in a semi-revolt against him by Syud Mohamed Bagher, the great Muchteid of that city, whose power over the masses was great; indeed he could raise them with a word. The British envoy knew that after the fall of Seifet the chief of Islam had retained a feeling of resentment against Mohamed Shah, which he did not even take the pains to conceal; Mr. M'Neil wrote, therefore, a furious letter to the Suyd, in which he insinuated that he ought to preach a crusade against his sovereign, and left him to believe that he would in so doing be supported by the British, who were, he said, attached to the Persian people, and were angry only with their unworthy monarch. Happily the enlightened mind of Syud Mohamed Bagher saw this attempt in its proper light; he sent Mr. M'Neil's letter to the Shah, and replied thus to the Envoy himself: "The Persians have always been remarkable for their attachment to their kings, and to you, an European Envoy, less than to any one else does it appertain to raise a storm in a country where the English have always been received according to the dictates of the laws of hospitality." Thus was arrested the progress of an evil which might have proved immense. "Mr. M'Neil," says Monsieur Thomas, "had not reached Tauriz when he received from Lord Palmerston a reply to one of his despatches, anterior to that in which he had announced his rupture with the Persian Government. It was after having stretched his patience to the very utmost, and when there was not the least hope of gaining his point by wisdom and firmness, that the British Agent received from his Lordship the permission to act energetically in the name of Great Britain.

"'The Shah should have been told from the beginning,' said Lord Palmerston, 'that the British Government perceived in this expedition a hostility entirely incompatible with the spirit of the alliance entered into between Persia and Great Britain.'

"At the same time an English fleet sent by the Indian Government disembarked on the coast of Persia, and took possession of the Island of Karrack. As soon as Mr. M'Neil received this intelligence he sent Colonel Stoddart, as the bearer of an ultimatum, to the camp of Mohamed Shah, informing that sovereign that Great Britain had determined to arrest his projects of conquest in Afghanistan, and that, if he did not immediately raise the siege of Herat, the taking of Karrack by the English would be followed by further and more significant acts of hostility on their part."

England was not ignorant whence this injury proceeded, but she could hardly attack the source without creating a fresh complication of interests, and English pride is not so hasty as to be unable to resign itself, when desirable, to a cold-blooded policy. Not daring to go direct to the Russian Court, whose incognito, though but loosely kept, she respected, she dealt a side blow, as if to warn and disconcert those who would be tempted to try to profit by their manœuvres. However that might be, Mr. M'Neil, armed with the last despatch that he had received, was perfectly at liberty to act or threaten as he pleased, but the power came too late, as the opportunity was lost; the rupture with Mohamed Shah was complete, and in his reply the British Envoy could only inform Lord Palmerston of the extent of the mischief.

It has been stated that when the Persian army marched fron Teheran it was accompanied by a Russian officer named Vikovitch, who quitted it at Nishapoor, having had numerous audiences of the Shah and his prime minister: very soon after he reached Kandahar, where in twelve days he concluded a treaty offensive and defensive with Kohendil Khan, Sovereign Serdar of that principality. After this he went to Kabul, where he remained several months. Burnes, who had been some time in that city when the Russian officer arrived, was charged by his government with the fulfilment of a mission very similar to that of the Russian; namely, to smooth the existing differences between the Emir of Kabul and the Maharadjah of the Punjab.

Vikovitch was at first not well received by Dost Mohamed, whose tendencies were entirely English; but the Emir, having found only hesitation and injustice in the mediation he had requested of Lord Auckland for the settlement of the difficulties existing between himself and Runjeet Sing, he was in despair, and turned to the side of the Russians and the Persians.

When the Russian diplomatist quitted Kabul he was accompanied by an Afghan Syud named Yaya, whom the Emir sent to Mohamed Shah to follow up the negotiations commenced by Vikovitch; they remained several days at Kandahar, and left with Mohamed Omar Khan, the second son of Kohendil Khan, who was charged by his father with a mission to the Persian monarch analogous to that of the Syud of Kabul. These three personages arrived at the royal camp at Herat some time after Mr. M'Neil had quitted it, and the following is his appreciation of the results of the Russian officer's embassy.

He writes to his government, "Before my messenger (Colonel Stoddart, bearer of the ultimatum) could reach the Shah of Persia, a treaty had been concluded between the Prince of Kandahar and his Persian Majesty, and the Russian minister had formally guaranteed the fulfilment of the engagements contracted by the two parties. A treaty of the same nature was in course of completion with Kabul also, and Captain Vikovitch, after having been received by the Shah in his camp, had set out a second time for that city and Kandahar, furnished with immense sums of money for the purpose of terminating arrangements so auspiciously commenced to establish Persian domination and Russian supremacy in all the Afghan states. The entire country from the Russian frontier on the Araxes to the banks of the Indus had been secretly tampered with and raised by Muscovite agents, some openly accredited, others without any ostensible public duty, all engaged in forming a line of influence which not only counteracted the views and interests of Great Britain, but disturbed and threatened her empire in the East."

"Lord Palmerston," observes Mons. Thomas, "replied to Mr. M'Neil on the 27th July, 1838, and wishing to ward off fresh perils, as well as the embarrassments pointed out by his agent, he at last gave up the reserve and temporising with which up to that period he had acted towards Persia; he discovered in the treaty of 1814, not a reason for political inaction, as he had affirmed at the commencement, but a perfect right of intervention, which is what the terms of the treaty most positively deny: nothing can be more clear. 'If war,' it is said therein, 'should be declared between the Afghans and the Persians, the English Government would not interfere on either side, unless its pacific mediation should be solicited by both the contending parties.' His Lordship went further even than he had ever done before, and, not content with pointing out Russian influence as a permanent stumblingblock in the way of Persia, as a fatal snare which Persia should mistrust for her own sake and in her own interest, he loudly proclaimed that 'the suggestions of Russia were antagonistic to the peace and prosperity of Great Britain.'

"This was a great effort," says Mons. Thomas, "an useless effort after the extremities to which he had been reduced with Persia, aimless and without result, if it did not bear upon a point other than that on which it seemed to be directed." The following is an extract from Lord Palmerston's despatch to Mr. M'Neil, dated Foreign Office, July 27th, 1838:—"I have to instruct you to state to the Shah of Persia, that, whereas the spirit and purport of the treaty between Persia and Great Britain is that Persia should be a defensive barrier for the British possessions in India, and that the Persian Government should co-operate with that of Great Britain in defending British India, it appears, on the contrary, that the Shah is occupied in subverting those intervening states between Persia and India which might prove additional barriers of defence for the British possessions, and that in these operations he has openly connected himself with an European power for purposes avowedly unfriendly, if not absolutely hostile, to British interests; that, under these circumstances, and as he has thought fit to enter upon a course of proceeding wholly at variance with the spirit and intent of the above-mentioned treaty, Great Britain will feel herself at liberty to adopt, without reference to that treaty, such measures as a due regard for her own interests and the security of her dominions may suggest." *

"Lord Palmerston," remarks Mons. Thomas, "had failed to preserve the Persian alliance at a time when it might have been done by moderation and firmness only, and now that it was lost he adopted violence and menaces to regain it. It was the British Government, throwing aside the indecision caused by the fear of Russia, taking at last an extreme line, not against Russia, which it always treated with deference,—not against Persia, which remained its sturdy enemy under the protection of the Tzar,—but against the whole of the East, which it then wished to terrify with the power of Great Britain, and this after having displayed her weakness for four years. It now became necessary to raise Persia from the depths into which she had fallen by accepting the Russian alliance, and some great exploit was to be performed in the name of England alone; the weakness with which the Tzar's proceedings in Persia had been combated was bitterly repented of, and they must now be stopped in Afghanistan as by a thunderbolt: so great was the fear of being outstripped by the indefatigable activity of Muscovite diplomacy, that it was thought preferable to destroy it at the outset." We shall see to what this new system led, and will judge of it by its fruits.

General Simonitch made up his mind to leave Teheran when he saw that Mr. M'Neil had gone to the royal camp, and, in proportion as the reception of the British minister had been cold and reserved, was his Majesty's manner to the Russian gracious and expressive of his anxiety to please; for as Mr. M'Neil had, in consequence of not being supported by his government, lost the influence that he had at one time succeeded in obtaining, and had even come to a rupture with the Persian Court, General Simonitch had become more powerful than ever, and the Shah, against the advice of his first minister, was devoted to him body and soul. This diplomatist was a Dalmatian, who, being in the French army in 1812 or 1813, was taken prisoner by the Russians, and after the fall of Napoleon entered their service. It is true he

* Mohamed Shah had renounced this convention long before the British Government; and when pressed by Mr. Ellis and Mr. M'Neil to conform to it, he said that in his eyes it had been annihilated ever since the day on which the Cabinet of London had refused to pay to that of Teheran the subsidies that Great Britain had by the same treaty engaged to furnish.—*Ferrier.*

treated the Persian King with rough respect, which had a certain effect upon the weak but goodnatured monarch, who entertained a species of veneration for all those who had served under that Emperor; and after having been sharply rebuked by the Russian ambassador for all the deception that had been practised from the commencement of the siege, the Shah ordered the chiefs of his army to act henceforth in conformity with the instructions of the Russian minister.

Hadji Mirza Agassee, thus thwarted in his scheme of retreating, exerted himself as much as possible to get these orders revoked, but in vain. He then tried to paralyse their effect by manifest ill-will in furnishing the materials, ammunition, and stores requisite for the works necessitated by the new arrangements that were adopted. He did not conceal the vexation he felt even to General Simonitch, and explained his opinion to him very categorically. "Why should I take Herat?" he said to the dragoman; "why should I expose a crowd of innocent people to perish for the fault of one individual only?—of Yar Mohamed Khan, who takes all the revenues of the province for his own profit, instead of paying me the tribute; and who authorized all the pillage that has been committed by the Afghans upon the Persian merchants. And then, it would be impossible for me to keep Herat with Persian soldiers, idle gluttons, who the moment they are masters of the place will think only of eating pillau, and amusing themselves with the women. The Afghans, whose baggage is light enough, for they have never anything to lose, will come back some day and cut their throats. Besides, you have not given me the material support that you promised; on the contrary, you have taken away the Russian deserters: all this ought to induce the Shah to raise this unhappy siege, which ruins the country and creates difficulties with England."

But General Simonitch was not to be impeded by this obstinate old man. He immediately sent for Colonel Semineau, whose straightforward conduct had won his esteem, and in some degree reproached him for the tardy manner in which the operations were conducted. The Colonel exculpated himself by showing it was not his fault, as treachery and the general ill-feeling had obliged him to hold himself aloof after the first few days of the siege; at the same time he submitted to him the plan of attack which he had presented to the Shah seven months before, but never received authority to put into execution. The General then desired Lieutenant-

Colonel Blaremberg, the Russian officer of Engineers attached to the embassy, to inspect the works in the trenches, and as speedily as possible report his opinion of them. M. Blaremberg was soon convinced that they were conducted in a manner entirely contrary to the rules of common sense, and that the wisest course to take would be even then to adopt the plan of Colonel Semineau, and this was the one subsequently carried out by General Simonitch. Fascines and gabions were immediately made in great numbers; and as the soldiers would do nothing without being well paid, the Russian minister drew from his own treasury the funds necessary to satisfy them, and they worked accordingly, but he alienated the chiefs from his cause because he never gratified their avarice. They had taken English gold as a soothing antidote to the excess of their zeal, and would not have been less happy to pocket that of the Russians as a stimulus to it; but the General, thinking perhaps that he should not want their help, never bestowed an obolus upon them, which led to a thousand intrigues on their part to baffle the new plan of attack. The following, taken from Colonel Semineau's notes, will give a rough idea of the disconnected character of the operations.

"For eight months," it is therein stated, "have we fought without result, and 4000 soldiers have been disabled, which in Persia very nearly means killed, for the slightest wound cannot be successfully treated, excepting by astrologers, who take the title of doctor without having the slightest idea of the knowledge that belongs to it; besides, they are particularly careful to keep out of the way when the army is in the field.

"After the expiration of these eight months, during which we had only experienced heavy losses, and without any corresponding result, his Persian Majesty, by the advice of General Simonitch, sought to enlighten himself by a council of war, at which he presided in person. After many propositions more or less extravagant had been made, my turn came, and I reverted to the plan that I had given in at the commencement of the siege. But this raised a terrible storm against me; not a chief would confine himself to a uniform and well-considered line of operations. Each persisted in wanting to act separately with his own force, and claiming for himself the honour of taking Herat or any other success he might obtain: they therefore with one voice rejected my project. However, addressing myself to his Majesty, who seemed on the point of yielding to his officers, I represented to him that it would be folly to sacrifice the public interest for the sake of individuals; that each corps would take its turn in the trenches that I intended to open, according to the rules of war; and that in point of fact the city could only be taken in the name of Mohamed Shah, who ought to have the honour of the victory, without that circumstance in the least detracting from the glory that would belong to the generals. This advice pleased the King; and as nothing more was wanting to induce the council to hold the same opinion, the order was immediately given to commence the attack upon the angle of Khodja Abdul Hamid under my direction in chief. But I had yet to encounter many a spiteful impediment in the construction of my trenches, and it was entirely owing to the determination of General Simonitch that I could partly surmount them. For example, one day, in the middle of a most difficult work, the Shah sent for me and commanded me to throw a bridge over a ravine twenty miles from the camp, which would have occupied several days, and during my absence my trenches must neccessarily have been at a standstill. Happily Lieutenant-Colonel Blaremberg prevailed upon the King to revoke this order.

"I opened my first trench at the farthest ruins of the Meuhelle Arabha,* and, having arrived within 437 yards of the edge of the town ditch, I constructed large and spacious cavaliers, using only gabions, palisades, and fascines, which I raised to the height of 326½ feet; this height was not sufficient to enfilade the second covered way, but one of our batteries had a plunging fire into the first and the ditch. From the cavaliers I had a good view of the prolongation of the curtains in the enceinte, as well as along those of the second covered way. I placed in battery eight 12-pounders on each cavalier, and made the embrasures *à portière*, and it was not till everything was complete that I worked from this point to reach the edge of the ditch of the angle attacked. The Afghans had made galleries with *fougasses* to defend the approaches, from which they hoped to obtain great results; but as these underground works had been executed some time, it was not difficult to discover, by the colour of the grass withered above them, the direction they had given to their mines. A *caponière*, which they had made in the ditch, and in sight of my battery, enabled the enemy to communicate

* Arab quarter.

with his mines. These I turned by counter-mines, at which we secretly worked. When our chambers were charged and matches ready I sent two balls at the *caponière*, which swept it away, and the people who were in it took refuge in their mines. At that moment I ordered ours to be sprung; the explosion destroyed the Afghan works, and the miners were suffocated; from that day they abandoned all their works beyond the counterscarp, and of this circumstance I took advantage to push my trenches without delay up to the ditch. But the Afghans, perceiving the object of the cavaliers, altered their determination, and early in the night established traverses to defend the covered ways on both sides of the angle of attack; I was not uneasy at that, because the space that I required opposite the batteries was free, and they in no way impeded me in forwarding my works, foot by foot, up to the crest of the rampart of the town. I would not breach it till I had sufficiently filled up the ditch at the point at which we were to pass it; this I managed to do by three chambers outside the counterscarp, and, springing them all at once, the earth was thrown into the ditch and filled it. We then opened from the two batteries in the cavaliers, each of which was armed with eight pieces of heavy artillery, consisting of twelve, eighteen, and twenty-four pounders. The fire from these guns at forty-three yards from the edge of the ditch, and sixty-five yards from the large tower, took it obliquely, and after a cannonade of four hours, not only was that vast and massive work razed to the ground, but also the adjacent one on either side of the angle; I wished to use some field-howitzers, but, being short, they blew out the cheeks of the embrasures. On the night of this day, the results of which had as much astonished the Persians as the Afghans, we filled the ditch with the fragments of the wall and bags of hay, and at daybreak we might have made the assault, but, knowing the daring of the enemy, and the inexperience of our own troops, I conceived it my duty to save bloodshed as much as possible, by conducting the approach in zigzags up to the crest of the breach, where I had intended to establish a *nid de pie*, to protect the infantry, who were to descend into the city. I asked for the requisite quantity of timber, fascines, and gabions to construct this, which could have been done in three days, but a cabal at court had vowed to baffle me as much as possible; on this occasion they put the very stars in requisition against me, declaring that it was absolutély necessary the assault should be made on the following day, the 24th of July, because a happy conjunction of them promised infallible success. In consequence four battalions were told off for the assault, and noon was the hour appointed for storming the place. It was well chosen, for the Afghans, overcome by the heat, habitually gave up a few hours to repose in the middle of the day, and, till then, the Persians had done the same; the former therefore were far from supposing that this would be the moment selected for the attack,—it was indeed a complete surprise. But unfortunately, of the four battalions that ought to have marched, one only, the Karaguzloo, and that reduced by its losses to 400 men, appeared at the breach. Pressing had been the demands, the entreaties of these devoted men for ammunition, and yet seven rounds per man was all the prime minister would grant them; and as he knew full well that the other battalions, being his countrymen, Makooees, would not stir a foot, he gave but four to each serbaz. The messengers I sent into the camp, one after another, to procure what I required, always returned with a vague answer, and, in short, it was impossible for me to obtain anything. On the other hand, the Sertip Hadji Khan, who had behaved so ill some months before near the Imaum Zadeh, and who had received orders to hold his brigade in reserve to support, if necessary, the storming party, went in quite a different direction, and attacked another part of the city, in the hope of having the credit of taking it. But this absurd diversion injured far more than it contributed to the success of the enterprise. The 400 serbaz who threw themselves into the breach quickly disposed of the guard in the covered ways; they were half asleep, and a crowd of their comrades, who rushed to their assistance, were swept away by our batteries, which then crossed their fire behind the point of attack. This brave band of Karaguzloos carried the Persian colours to the very crest of the breach, and had the courage and constancy there to maintain themselves for hours, waiting for ammunition, in the mean time using their bayonets, bricks, and stones, to keep off the Afghans, who in very superior numbers fired on them in front and flank. The science of the engineer, and the devotion of the soldier, could avail nothing in such a position. The Afghan serdar Dine Mohamed Khan, who commanded the defence, fought like a hero. With his pistol he laid at his feet the brave Nabee Khan, chief of the Karaguzloos, whose courage and loyalty merited a better fate, and cut down the trumpeter who sounded the advance, and had just planted the flag on the breach, but he could not force that handful of Persians to retreat; the death of their chief had only doubly excited them, and the majority of them preferred death on the field of honour to retreating one single step. In vain they called upon the other three battalions to help them; a secret order retained them where they stood. The gold of England and the orders of the Hadji Mirza Agassee had tied them hand and foot. The soldiers looked on like the *habitués* of the pit of certain theatres: each gave his opinion, and with more or less noise or sympathy. 'They'll mount, they'll mount;' or, 'They will never do it.' Such were the cries that accompanied these noble Karaguzloos to the top of the breach. I had also demanded the aid of 400 riflemen of the Garai tribe, well known for the correctness of their aim, in order to maintain a sharp and continuous fire from the foot of the entrenched cavaliers upon the faces of the angles of attack, but what were my astonishment and indignation to see them remain passive spectators of the fight! These sharpshooters were under the command of a great Persian nobleman, a relative of the Shah's, who ought to have been more interested than I was in the taking of Herat; and when I approached him to express my feelings at the conduct of his men, he replied, in the most ironical manner, 'Give them powder and ball, of which they are perfectly destitute, and they will do anything you require.'

"I then saw clearly that treachery on all sides would cause the failure of the assault, and there remained but one man in whom I had yet a hope left,—this was General Boroffski. He had in the first instance been protected by the English, but his proud nature could not adapt itself to their demands, and General Simonitch had endeavoured, and with tolerable success, to attach him to the Russian cause, promising to interest the Emperor in his position, and to endeavour to procure his recognition of the General as the son of Prince R., of whom he was the natural child. Boroffski had no military acquirements, but he was brave, and the serbaz always followed him with the utmost confidence; about two sections rallied round him, and hurried to the breach to support those who were already engaged, but he had scarcely reached the ditch when a ball struck him in the lower part of the body, and gave him the wound which sent him to his grave. My eyes followed Boroffski on his way to the assault, and I saw him fall mortally wounded; I have always thought, from the direction the ball took, that it came from a Persian musket; and I can state as much with regard to myself, for I was hit in the shoulder by a ball from behind me as I faced the rampart.

"The unhappy serbaz, who were as much disappointed at this fresh misfortune, and as heartily enraged with their chiefs, as I was, addressed them in the most insulting terms, but they were at last obliged, to their bitter regret, to abandon the breach they had so valiantly stormed and held for five mortal hours; they slowly obeyed the bugle that sounded the retreat, and, mutilated as they were, the shattered survivors of this heroic battalion retired with mournful steps to their encampment. After having visited the minister to report to him the result of the operations, and reproach him with his disloyal conduct, I, like those brave men, shut myself up in my tent, and I determined to renounce the Persian service for ever, and even my arrears of pay. I told Hadji Mirza that I should resign, but the Shah, always kind and considerate to me, pressed me so much not to do so that I yielded to his persuasions; and as soon as he had obtained my promise to that effect, he sent me the brevet of General and the red ribbon of the order of the Lion and the Sun."

General Semineau, having been in entire ignorance of everything that passed, had acted with his accustomed loyalty of character, and especially regretted that he had been refused the three days to carry his works to the crest of the breach, for then treason itself could not have prevented him from taking this important place. Under cover of the *nid de pie* crowning the culminating point of the attack, he could have established one or two pieces of cannon in battery, the fire of which would have protected the troops in their descent into the town; this would not have been easy, because the interior side of the épaulement was raised to the height of nineteen to twenty-two feet *à pic*, and supported by brickwork which served as a counterfort. At the top of the épaulement was a banquette on which two men would have difficulty in walking abreast, and the Persian soldiers in following this must have been under the murderous fire of the besieged from the surrounding houses, before they could get to the rampe which led into the city: all therefore was not done when the breach was gained. General Semineau, who devoted himself solely to his profession of engineer, and interfered not in politics, was absolutely ignorant of the reason for which he was so pitilessly refused the three days he so much required; but on the 24th of July, 1838, Colonel Stoddart was expected to arrive at the royal camp, with the ultimatum of Mr. M'Neil, by which the Shah was threatened with war with England if he did not raise the siege. On the 22nd General Simonitch had received a despatch from M. de Nesselrode, which informed him that he had been disavowed by him, that he was recalled from Teheran, and that he was besides charged to inform the Shah that his Majesty must no longer expect to be supported in his undertaking by the Russian Government. Count Simonitch thought less of the blow thus dealt to himself than of the failure of an enterprise that he had conducted with such ability, and, partly by persuasion, partly by threats, obtained the order for the assault on the day named. Colonel Stoddart could not arrive till night, the place might be taken by the Persians before the ultimatum arrived, and, its fall being a *fait accompli*, negotiations might be continued on a different footing; Russia could then more positively resist the demands of England: but the treachery of the prime minister annihilated all the operations of General Semineau, to whom fortune was adverse in every way. The city itself, in consequence of the intended flight of Yar Mohamed, was on the point of yielding. That chief could not imagine that the Persians would loose their hold after having advanced their works so near, and, when the fight was at the sharpest, he retired from the assault in all haste to make preparations for departure. In the act of mounting his horse he sent to the troops to say they might surrender, but he was detained by Captain Pottinger, who entreated him to grant an hour's delay, at the expiration of which time he could leave the city if success attended not the efforts of his gallant soldiers on the breach, when the vizier acceded to his request.

The British officer, well acquainted with the details of Mr. M'Neil's policy and negotiation, was not ignorant of the reasons which led General Simonitch to hurry the assault; and his practised eye soon perceived that, though made with vigour, it was not supported: he saw the irresolute battalions quite undecided as to what they ought to do, and could not mistake such characteristic signs. British policy had once more the upper hand, and Captain Pottinger had not prejudged the circumstances when he hoped for the retreat of the assailants. In this terrific struggle the Afghan women and all the children over ten years of age hastened to the breach to exert their feeble power in aid of their defenders, and showered down bricks and stones upon the Persians. The Afghans had determined to slay all their women and children, and afterwards each other, if the Persians succeeded in getting into the place.

Mohamed Shah remained two months inactive under the walls of Herat after this assault, and in September, 1838, he raised the siege and retired to his capital. Scarcely had he arrived there when the Russian Government, not very grateful for his docility, obliged him to pay a fourth part of the expenses of the war stipulated in the treaty of Turkomantchai.

When the Persians retired, Syud Yaya, the envoy of Kabul, and Mohamed Omar Khan, the envoy of Kandahar, accompanied the Shah to Teheran, while Captain Vikovitch, who had presented them at the royal camp, followed them as far as Kussan, a frontier town of Herat; here he turned to the south, and, after having examined in a strategical point of view the road which passes by Khaff, Birdjan, Duroo, and Furrah, he went to Kandahar. There he had several audiences of Kohendil Khan, to whom he paid 5600*l.* in consideration of an engagement entered into by that prince to recommence the siege of Herat, which the threats of Great Britain had forced Mohamed Shah to abandon. In consequence the Serdar Mohamed Sedik Khan, the eldest son of Kohendil Khan, at the head of three or four thousand men, entered the territory of Herat and commenced hostilities. Captain Vikovitch remained forty days at Kandahar, and when he left that city to return to Teheran great was his astonishment, on arriving at Furrah, to find the army of Mohamed Sedik Khan encamped there and perfectly unoccupied, except in the appropriation of the booty it had levied in the district by carrying fire and sword into every house. He had detached a small advanced guard, but that had not proceeded beyond the small town of Subzawar. This fatal delay, of which Vikovitch felt the full importance, brought on an angry contest between that officer and the Afghan serdar. Vikovitch demanded the prompt execution of the convention between himself and Kohendil Khan, or, in case of further delay, the immediate restitution of the 12,000 ducats; but Mohamed Sedik Khan was highly indignant. "The money you gave me," said he, "would not provide my army with horseshoes. If you wish me to advance, give me as much again." Vikovitch, who knew well that to pay more was simply throwing the money away, decisively rejected this proposition, which at one time the serdar seemed inclined to enforce, and not by words only. He even thought of plundering the Russian officer, and would perhaps have proceeded to personal violence, had he not been restrained by the fear that the Shah might make some retaliation upon Mohamed Omar Khan, then at his court on a mission to that sovereign. These facts were told me by the ruffian himself.

Mohamed Sedik hesitated not to abandon the project of seizing Herat, and returned to his father to confer upon the plan for opposing the English invasion, then vaguely rumoured in Afghanistan. As to Captain Vikovitch, he was obliged to continue his journey without recovering the 12,000 ducats that were extorted from him by the Serdars of Kandahar. After having visited the fortress of Laush Jowaine and the north of Lake Roostem, he took the road by Toon and Tubbus towards Teheran, and very soon after returned to Russia, where, as the reward of all his exertions, he found hinself in fatal-disgrace. This crying injustice wounded him so deeply, that he put a period to his life with his own pistol in a hotel at St. Petersburg: it is stated that before he committed that deplorable act he destroyed the documents that he had collected on his various journeys in Asia.

CHAPTER XIX.

The Persians abandon the siege of Herat — The Serdars of Kandahar and Captain Vikovitch — Desolation of Herat — Yar Mohamed implores the assistance of the neighbouring principalities — Yar Mohamed sells the Heratees to the Turcomans — The English prepare to invade Afghanistan — Misunderstanding between Dost Mohamed and Runjeet Sing — Intervention of the English — Their want of good faith towards Dost Mohamed — Their partiality for Runjeet — Negotiations between the English and the Dost — Battle of Djamrood — Burnes at Kabul — He meets with Vikovitch, who is coldly received by the Emir — The Dost makes frank explanations to the English — He is supported by Burnes at Calcutta — Burnes is triumphant over Vikovitch — Note of Lord Palmerston to M. de Nesselrode — Reply of the Russian cabinet — The last attempt of the Dost to secure the alliance of the English — Efforts to the contrary on the part of Sir W. M'Naghten and Sir Claude Wade — Lord Auckland declares for Shah Shooja — Consternation of the Dost at this intelligence — Reflections on the English policy.

It is impossible to conceive the reckless devastation committed by the Persian soldiers in the principality of Herat during the ten months of the siege of its capital: they made a perfect desert of that once rich and fertile country. The city, torn up by shot and shell, was nothing but a mass of shapeless ruins, and the houses, caravanserais, and bazaars, were all pulled down to repair the breaches in the ramparts; it was in fact a heap of cinders, ruin, and desolation.

To crown their misfortunes, the wretched citizens, who had been nearly starved during the siege, were for a long time short of provisions after it was raised, and the famine was almost as bad as it had been previously, for the ground had not been tilled, and every one had consumed the provisions he had laid by before the arrival of the Persians. All the villages, from seventy to ninety miles round, had been completely pillaged to supply the besieging army, and the population of the country stripped of everything, as were the citizens who left the city before the siege, and now returned in crowds to Herat, where there was not a grain of corn to support them. The famine soon made frightful ravages, and produced every day horrible scenes worthy of cannibals—in fact, its condition was fearful to contemplate.

To put an end to this misery, Yar Mohamed Khan appealed to

the chiefs of the small principalities round Herat, and, in the name of Mahomet, implored their generosity, and entreated them to send corn to the desolated city; at the same time he remitted the duty on every description of grain.

The merchants of Turkestan, Kandahar, and the Eimak Khanats quickly responded to this appeal, but much more with the view of realizing enormous profits than of relieving such bitter distress. The majority of the Heratees, not having a groat in their pockets to purchase bread for their families, in many instances sold themselves to the Turkomans for ten battemens of corn: fathers sold their children for as small a sum, and the children thankfully sanctioned the bargain which saved them from the terrible pangs of hunger.

Yar Mohamed entered largely into this traffic, not, as his unhappy people did, to save their lives, but to replenish his coffers, the contents of which had been considerably exhausted by the war. He sold to the Uzbeks all the Heratees who were guilty of the most trifling misdemeanours; and when they saw this, and ceased to commit them, thereby destroying his source of gain, he sent agents into the bazaars to excite disorder, and by that means secured a supply of slaves for his market. The slightest altercation or a loud word amongst a harmless group of citizens, and his satellites were always at hand to pounce upon these unfortunate beings; even those who were attracted to the spot by curiosity only were taken, and a couple of hours afterwards sold or exchanged by their relentless vizier for a camel, or a mule, or anything else that might better suit him. Twenty young men was the price that he usually gave for a Turkoman horse, a hundred tomauns in value. This trade continued for some considerable time, but the English at last succeeded in putting a stop to it, the inducement being a subsidy which they paid to the court of Herat.

Western Afghanistan had scarcely escaped the Persian yoke, at the cost of all these fearful calamities against which it had still to struggle, when the English, to repay Russia and the Shah for all their provocations, prepared a formidable expedition to invade Kandahar and Kabul. This important act was preceded by negotiations sufficiently singular, of which I will endeavour to give a rough sketch.

We have stated that Runjeet Sing, the ambitious Maharadjah of the Punjab, after having wrested from the Afghans their finest

S 2

provinces, prepared to push his conquests still further into their territory, when his intention was seen through by Dost Mohamed, who, as the English said (but the fact has not been proved), sought the alliance of the King of Persia, and proposed to assist him in his expedition against Herat, provided that the Shah would on the other hand protect him against the Sikhs, who were supported by the East India Company. The English also reproached the Dost with having written to the Emperor of Russia requesting his alliance. This letter was, it is said, sent to St. Petersburg by an Afghan envoy, properly accredited; but the assertion is denied by M. de Nesselrode, who declared in one of his despatches, bearing date October 20th, 1838, that this envoy was simply a commercial agent, having no instructions or authority to meddle with politics. The adversaries of the Emir went so far as to give a copy of his letter, but Dost Mohamed declared that it was a lying invention of the enemy; and to those who are acquainted with the extent to which false documents are made use of in Asia, and the advantages which the English have themselves derived from them in subduing the princes and rajahs of India, one doubts the propriety of giving an opinion on the validity of the one which the Emir is reproached with having written. This doubt is all the more admissible, inasmuch as at the epoch at which this document was said to have been prepared he was the warmest partisan of the English in Afghanistan, and remained so after they had driven him from that country. The following is the letter referred to, written in the early part of the year 1836:—

"There have been great differences and quarrels between myself and the royal house of the Suddozyes. The English Government is inclined to support Shoojah-ool-Moolk. The whole of India is governed by them, and they are on friendly terms with Runjeet Sing, the lord of the Punjab, which lies in their neighbourhood. The British Government exhibit no favourable opinions towards me. I (literally the creature of God), with all my power, have been always fighting with the Sikhs; your Imperial Government has made friendship with the Persians; and if your Majesty will graciously be pleased to arrange matters in the Afghan country, and assist this nation (which amounts to twenty lacs of families), you will place me under obligations.

"I hope your Imperial Majesty will do me the favour by allowing me to be received, like the Persians, under the protection of the government of Russia. Under your royal favour I can perform, along with my Afghans, various praiseworthy services. It would be highly proper, whatever your Imperial Majesty may be pleased to do."

Supposing that Dost Mohamed did write this letter, where was the crime in his doing so? Had he not a right to look for alliances against his enemies? Was there more justice therefore in the English supporting Runjeet Sing in his spoliation of the Afghans? But who was this Runjeet—who were the Sikhs? A nation of yesterday; always in subjection, without ancestors or traditions, and governed for the first time by a chief of their own nation: and this chief, this Runjeet, who it cannot be denied possesses some very great qualities, how was he brought up? From whom did he hold his power? Was it not from an Afghan sovereign, the Shah Zeman, who made him governor of the Punjab? Has he not thrown off his allegiance to that monarch's successors, and proclaimed himself sovereign of that country? Is then the origin of his power more legitimate than that of Dost Mohamed, who at least has in his favour the old traditions of his family to prove that his ancestors always had in his country a power almost equal to that of the Afghan sovereigns?

The English had, probably, thought of this more than once; but reason is a poor argument in the eyes of those who for twenty years had been wishing to have in Kabul a sovereign who would be a docile and submissive instrument of theirs. They also sanctioned the spoliations committed upon the finest Afghan provinces by Runjeet. He had seized Mooltan in 1810, Cashmeer in 1819, Peshawur in 1823, and that Runjeet affirmed, with the entire consent of Shah Shooja-ool-Moolk, the dethroned king, who had placed himself under his protection, and was considered by him and the English as the legitimate sovereign of Afghanistan, qualified by that title to make whatever concessions of territory he pleased. But why should Shooja be the legitimate sovereign of Afghanistan more than any other of his twenty brothers?—than Zeman or Mahmood, for instance, who had been kings before him, and had done nothing to disinherit their children or deprive them of their rights to the throne? Shah Kamran and Shah Eyoob had always protested against the pretensions of Shooja to the throne. Why, then, should the English be so regardless of their remonstrances and opposition, and the opinions of the generality of the Afghans? This policy concealed an ambitious project; the Anglo-Indian Government was possessed with a passion for territorial extension, and in no way sensitive as to the justice of the cause of Dost Mohamed from the moment they found that he would not bend to their wishes; and not being in a condition to depose him themselves, they weakened his power as much as possible by means of their ally Runjeet, who annually sent an army to ravage some part of the Afghan kingdom.

Although the Government of Calcutta showed a marked predilection for that ruler, it did not fail still to maintain its relations with and show some consideration for Dost Mohamed, who had on his part been guilty of very great duplicity, if he had really written to the Emperor Nicholas the letter which they accused him of sending, for very nearly at the same time, viz. on the 31st May, 1836, following, he addressed Lord Auckland, who had recently arrived in India, in the most humble terms, as follows:—

"It may be known to your Lordship that, relying on the principles of benevolence and philanthropy which distinguish the British Government, I look upon myself and country as bound to it; and the letters I have received from that quarter have all been replete with friendly sentiments and attention, and to the effect that, in the time of need, the obligations of friendship should be fulfilled. The late transactions in this quarter, the conduct of reckless and misguided Sikhs and their breach of treaty, are well known to your Lordship. Communicate to me whatever may now suggest itself to your wisdom for the settlement of the affairs of this country, that it may serve as a rule for my guidance.

"I hope your Lordship will consider me and my country as your own, and favour me often by the receipt of your friendly letters. Whatever directions your Lordship may be pleased to issue for the administration of this country, I will act accordingly."

Lord Auckland replied to this communication on the 22nd of August, 1836, with the greatest kindness, very highly praised his discreet policy, and promised his impartial intervention to effect a reconciliation between the Afghan prince and the Sikhs.

During the time that this correspondence was passing, the Persian expedition against Herat was prepared and openly encouraged by General Simonitch; but it was November, 1837, before the army of Mohamed Shah arrived under the walls of that city. Early in the same year, however, Dost Mohamed, grown weary of the provocations of the Sikhs, and finding that he derived no benefit, but rather the contrary, from the intervention of Lord Auckland, determined upon avenging his own cause, and seized upon the opportunity offered him in the month of May by the indiscretion of the Maharadjah (who recalled his troops from the Afghan frontier in order to celebrate, with the greater pomp, the marriage of his grandson Nahal Sing), to march 15,000 men into the province of Peshawur. They were commanded by the Dost's two sons, Mohamed Efzel Khan and Mohamed Akbar Khan, who attacked the Sikhs at Djamrood on the 1st of May, 1837. The combat was obstinate and the carnage dreadful, but victory crowned the banner of the brothers at the heavy cost of 7000 men.

The Government of Calcutta, already sufficiently alarmed by the Persian expedition against Herat, became still more so on hearing of the defeat of their faithful ally Runjeet, and despatched with all speed Sir A. Burnes to Kabul, to endeavour to arrest the progress of the victorious Afghans.

The British Envoy arrived in that city in September, and was received with great honours by Dost Mohamed, who greatly esteemed him. The instructions of Lord Auckland were, that he was simply to enter into commercial relations and pacific intervention between the Emir and the Maharadjah; he added also that he was authorized to do this in the interest of the Afghan chief and to avert his ruin. It was sufficiently surprising that his Lordship should use such language respecting a prince who had hitherto so well known how to defend himself, who had set forth no demands but what were perfectly reasonable, and in accordance with which he would, if admitted, have laid down his arms. The task of Burnes was difficult; but he was fortunate enough to obtain from the Emir a temporary suspension of hostilities, and it was while he was occupied in this negotiation that Captain Vikovitch arrived at Kabul, namely, in December, 1837. The English have asserted that he brought the reply of the Emperor Nicholas to the letter the Emir had written his Imperial Majesty in the commencement of 1836.

Whatever might have been the real object of his presence there, Vikovitch met with a cold reception, and Dost Mohamed made his arrival the pretext for paying a visit to Sir A. Burnes, and requesting his advice as to what he ought to do under the circumstances. The Emir declared from the first that he had determined not to adopt an alliance or political relations with any other foreign power than England, that he would receive no foreign agent so long as he had the hope of conciliating the sympathy of the Anglo-Indian Government, and that for all he cared he was willing to dismiss the Russian officer, or arrest him on his journey; indeed, to treat him as Burnes might wish. It must be admitted that this was very extraordinary language for a man to use who had been recently accused of having written to the Emperor of Russia in the most respectful and submissive terms. Nevertheless Vikovitch was allowed to enter Kabul, but only at the request of Burnes, who took copies of all the letters brought by the latter to the Emir, and the conduct of Dost Mohamed was in every way calculated to inspire the English Government with confidence. The following letter from the Envoy to Lord Auckland proves this to have been the case:—

"*January* 15, 1838.—Since I have been here I have learnt that a Persian agent, bearing presents for Dost Mohamed, has penetrated the country as far as Kandahar,* and he has announced himself as the bearer of most seductive promises; but he was nevertheless obliged to leave Afghanistan almost immediately, because no one invited him to come on to Kabul. After him a Russian agent came, by name Vikovitch; he brought flattering compliments and offers of lasting engagements, but he was received with only the respect due to any stranger and the regular forms of hospitality. The Emir has said that his interest was in the English alliance, and that he would not abandon that while he had a hope of obtaining it."

The reasons which Burnes gave to his Government seemed to him so conclusive, that he did not for a moment think that the authorities at Calcutta would reject the alliance of a chief so devoted to the English as Dost Mohamed; and to smooth every species of difficulty, he exerted himself to establish a friendly understanding between the Dost and the Sikhs. The Emir, a witness of his efforts, testified his gratitude for them; but his confidence in the equity of the Directors of the East India Company towards him was not so great as that of the English officer.

Knowing how strong was their predilection for Runjeet Sing, and

* This agent arrived with Vikovitch in October, 1837, and remained there when the latter went on to Kabul.—*Ferrier*.

having a vague suspicion that the Court would come to a partial determination, the Dost neglected no means of persuading them of his entire devotion. "In return," said the Emir to Burnes, "I ask but little, but that little is just and reasonable. I ask the English to protect me from the spoliations of the Sikhs and the resentment of the Persians, who will never forgive me for having made common cause with your countrymen; they must also force the former to give me back Peshawur, which is the only point that protects my frontier on this side of the Indus, and oppose any attempt of the latter to reduce Herat and Kandahar to a state of vassalage: then I am theirs, body and soul. I shall never have recourse to others till I have lost all hope in you, and even in acting thus it would be with regret to save only Afghanistan and my own honour, not from ill-will towards England. On the contrary, I should be happy to be advised and protected by her, and in return should make every effort to second her views, political and commercial."

This frank and explicit declaration of the Dost's could not leave Lord Auckland in any doubt of his loyalty or sincerity. It was quite sufficient to induce him to fall back upon the natural course of British policy in India, and to maintain the Afghan independence against every other state, instead of joining with the Sikhs to attack it on the one hand, while the Russians, in alliance with the Persians and the Serdars of Kandahar, ruined it on the other.

The arrival of Vikovitch at Kabul, and the copies of the letters presented by him to the Emir, produced a lively sensation at Calcutta, and formed the subject of a note sent by Lord Clanricarde to the cabinet of St. Petersburg, which plainly allowed the determination of the British Government to act vigorously to be perceived. The following is an extract from that document:—

"The undersigned is further instructed to state that the British Government possess a copy of a Treaty which has been concluded between Persia and the Afghan ruler of Kandahar, the execution of which has been guaranteed by Count Simonich, and has given to this Treaty, which tends to afford Russia, if she adopts the guarantee, a pretence to compel the Shah of Persia not only to make himself master of Herat, but to deliver over that city afterwards to the rulers of Kandahar, to be held by them, together with their other possessions, in the capacity, which those rulers engage by the Treaty to acknowledge, of tributaries to Persia.

"The guarantee, moreover, contains a promise to compel Persia to defend the rulers of Kandahar against attack from any quarter whatever. It is true that in this stipulation no specific allusion is made to England; but the intention of the parties may be inferred from the original draft of this treaty, of which also Her Majesty's Government have a copy, and which was less cautiously worded, and in which specific allusion was made to England as one of the powers against whom assistance was to be given by Russia to the rulers of Kandahar.

"The undersigned is further instructed to state that a Russian agent of the name of Vicovitch, but sometimes calling himself Omar Beg, and said to be attached to the staff of the general commanding at Orenburg, was the bearer of letters from the Emperor and Count Simonich to the ruler of Kabul, copies of which are in the possession of the British Government, and that Count Simonich observed the most perfect silence towards the British minister at Teheran with respect to the mission of this agent; a reserve which might seem unnecessary if this agent was merely to deliver the letters of which he was the bearer, and if his mission was to have no tendency prejudicial to the British interests.

"But the British Government have learned that Count Simonich announced to the Shah of Persia that this Russian agent would counsel the ruler of Kabul to seek assistance of the Persian Government to support him in his hostilities with the ruler of the Punjab; and the further reports which the British Government have received of the language held by this Russian agent at Kandahar and at Kabul can lead to no other conclusion than that he strenuously exerted himself to detach the rulers of those Afghan states from all connexion with England, and to induce them to place their reliance upon Persia in the first instance, and ultimately upon Russia.

"If the British Government could entertain a doubt of the correctness of the foregoing information, that doubt would, in a great measure, be removed by the unfriendly language with respect to the British Government which Count Simonich held some time ago to the agent of Kabul at the court of Persia, and of which the British Government possess proof in the report made by that agent to the ruler of Kabul."

Lord Clanricarde concludes by declaring "that Russia is free to pursue with respect to the matters in question whatever course may appear to the Cabinet of St. Petersburg most conducive to the interests of Russia. But the British Government considers itself entitled to ask of the Cabinet of St. Petersburg whether the intentions and the policy of Russia towards Persia and Great Britain are to be deduced from the declarations of Count Nesselrode and Mr. Rodofinikin to the Earl of Durham, or from the acts of Count Simonich and M. Vikovitch in Asia."

The Russian Government was not much disturbed by this note, nevertheless it did vouchsafe to give a few explanations, but in a most ironical manner. It denied facts as clear as the sun, with an audacity so sustained and so calm that any minister less experienced than Lord Palmerston would have allowed himself to be deceived by the language of Count Nesselrode. The following are some extracts from the despatch which that diplomatist addressed to Count Pozzo di Borgo, to be communicated to the Foreign Office, October 20th, 1838:—

"You state that on this occasion Her Britannic Majesty's Principal Secretary-of-State for Foreign Affairs did not conceal from you, Monsieur le Comte, that public opinion in England ascribes to Russian influence a decisive part in the events now passing in Persia, and attributes to our Cabinet intentions dangerous to the security of the British possessions in Asia.

"This consideration is so serious, it is calculated to have so pernicious an influence on all our relations with Great Britain, that we do not hesitate a single instant to meet the English Cabinet with a frank and spontaneous explanation. The policy, M. l'Ambassadeur, which the Emperor pursues in that quarter is guided by the same principles which direct it in Europe. Far from any idea of encroachment, that policy has only for its object the maintenance of the rights of Russia, and respect for those legitimately acquired by all other powers.

"The idea of assailing the security and tranquillity of the possessions of Great Britain in India has consequently never presented itself, and will never present itself, to the mind of our august master. He desires only what is just and what is possible.

"If the British Government places in those principles the confidence which they are calculated to inspire, it will be easy for you, M. l'Ambassadeur, to clear up the doubts which it has conceived as to the conduct which we have adopted in the midst of the recent events in Persia, and specifically with regard to the expedition of Mohamed Shah against Herat.

"If we adduce these facts, if we point out the restless activity of certain unaccredited and unrecognised individuals, it is certainly not our wish to impute to the Government to which they belong the blame of which they are deserving. On the contrary, we consider the British Cabinet to be altogether a stranger to the tendency which we have just alluded to. But in like manner as we place a just reliance on the rectitude of the intentions of the English Government, so also are we entitled to expect that it will not raise a doubt as to our own.

"These remarks, M. le Comte, which the Emperor commands you to communicate with the most perfect frankness to the English Ministry, will serve, I hope, to satisfy it, above all, as to the intentions of our Cabinet, and to place in its true light the conservative and disinterested policy of our august master. Our attitude, M. le Comte, will necessarily be regulated according to the definitive determination which the British Government shall think fit to adopt."

After this display of principle M. de Nesselrode gives his explanations. He declares that the siege of Herat appears to him a thing just in itself, but defends himself from the charge of having instigated the Shah to undertake it. Nevertheless, he adds, that if Herat were joined to Kandahar all contests would cease, and that country would then become accessible to every nation interested in the commerce of Central Asia.

The Emperor could not have any reason to injure England, and the natural obstacles which separate the two empires render a collision between them impossible. M. Thomas continues his narrative, and states that "According to Count Nesselrode it was England who had made the first attack, and he finished by no longer concealing that Russia well knew, when necessary, how to manœuvre up to the Indus. It was therefore for England to refrain and be careful; as to the Russians, they had nothing to reproach themselves with; they denied the existence of any grievances that could be brought against them; they had wished to prevent the attack upon Herat; Simonitch and Vikovitch were pacificators; the latter had been charged simply to fix the extent of security that Afghanistan would grant to Russian merchants, and not to establish a treaty, or any other political combination, Russia having no other object than to secure a market for her manufactures in Central Asia. If by accident the agents had slightly deviated from their instructions, England could not complain. Where is the government that is always served as it wishes to be? Had England herself the power to control those turbulent travellers who continually excited disturbances in Asia?

"Further, Count Nesselrode announced the recall of General Simonitch, and that Colonel Duhamel, who was appointed to succeed him, was on his way to Teheran—terminating his despatch as follows:—

"'If we recall these facts—if we notice the activity of certain individuals who put themselves forward without having been accredited, or even recognised, by their government—it is not because we wish to impute to the British Government itself the blame which belongs to them; on the contrary, we consider the British Cabinet as being entirely above such actions as we point out; but as we place confidence in the rectitude of her intentions, we consider that we have a right to expect she should not throw any doubt over ours.

"'These remarks, which the Emperor commands your Excellency to communicate in full to the British Cabinet, will, I hope, serve to satisfy it, and place in its proper light the conservative and disinterested policy of our august master. Our attitude must necessarily be regulated by the definitive determination that the British Government will think fit to adopt.'"

But Lord Palmerston, who, to the last, strove to preserve the illusion that the Cabinet of St. Petersburg was sincere, wrote to Count Pozzo di Borgo in the following terms on December 20, 1838:—

"I can assure your Excellency that her Majesty's Government have given to this important communication all the attention which it so justly demands; and I have great pleasure in being able to state to your Excellency that this communication has in its general result been highly satisfactory to her Majesty's Government. The leading principle which invariably directs the British Government in the management of its relations with foreign powers is an anxious desire to preserve for the British nation the blessings of peace. But as regards Russia this wish is peculiarly strong; because an alliance of long standing between Great Britain an

Russia, commercial intercourse valuable to both countries, and common interests of the highest order, must necessarily lead her Majesty's Government to deprecate as a great misfortune any event which might tend to interrupt the good understanding which so happily subsists between the Cabinets of Petersburg and London."

Count Nesselrode, delighted to have succeeded in calming Lord Palmerston's fears, wished probably to make him feel that from the explanations he had given it did not follow that the Russian Cabinet was determined henceforth to concede to him on all points, for after having received his reply he addressed the following dry answer to his Lordship on January 29, 1839, a reply which reads far more like a threat than an approach towards the good understanding upon which the Noble Lord seemed so self-satisfied:—

"Those explanations," remarks Count Nesselrode, "have afforded to the two Cabinets the opportunity of receiving and of offering on either side assurances which bear the character of just reciprocity, and which are inseparable from one another. Our Cabinet, in taking note of that assurance, expects to receive the proof of its entire fulfilment."

Is it possible to show more ability, more subtlety, more acuteness, than Russia did in these negotiations, or rather deceptions, of four years' duration? Nothing in her conduct can seriously give offence to the English. They reproach her with treaties made by her agents; she disavows them. They are offended at the siege of Herat, which they attribute to her; she immediately abandons the Shah to his own resources and withdraws from him the Russian deserters. She has extended her influence to the frontier of the British empire in India, without its costing her the smallest sacrifice; she fails, it is true, but she retires without shame and without loss, and in her retreat she shot a Parthian arrow at her rival, who only triumphed for the moment, subsequently to meet with the most dreadful catastrophe.

Though Russia and Persia had appeared to give way on all points, and Lord Palmerston had shown himself satisfied with the explanations of M. de Nesselrode, the British nevertheless continued their preparations in India for the purpose of driving the Emir Dost Mohamed and Kohendil Khan from the principalities of Kabul and Kandahar. Five of the Company's ships of war also entered the Persian Gulf in the spring of 1838, and the troops they had on board took possession of the island of Karrack, where they waited for flat-bottomed steamers to convey them into the heart of Persia by the river Karoon. When the siege of Herat was raised, this expedition was given up; but the one to Afghanistan was carried on with vigour to depose a prince who had wished, at all risks, to become the ally of England, and whose proposals and concessions she, in her blind policy, constantly rejected.

Dost Mohamed was thought to possess considerable administrative ability, and a courage not common even amongst the Afghans. These qualities did not constitute any recommendation in the eyes of the Directors of the East India Company; but the Emir, who by inclination and conviction felt that the power of retaining his position could only be derived from them, and that nothing but their concurrence could enable him to found and maintain a monarchy, allowed himself to be persuaded by Alexander Burnes to make one last attempt to secure the friendship of England, by intrusting him with a letter to Lord Auckland:—

"Let his Lordship," said he, "give me but two words of encouragement; let him recognise me as Emir of Kabul, and I will forget the mortal feud between me and the Shah Kamran, my enemy by blood, and I will rush to his support with my best troops to defend him from the Shah of Persia, on the simple condition of receiving a subsidy for the troops that I shall employ in the service of the Company." He even added, "that for the present he would not say another word about the restitution of Peshawur."

There was so much disinterestedness and so much good intention in these propositions, that Sir A. Burnes conceived himself justified in promising the Dost that he could induce his Government to accept them; but what did that avail against a prior decision? It was in vain that he wrote to Calcutta, "There is but one way of making Afghanistan a barrier against the Russians, and that is to form a strict alliance with Dost Mohamed, to strengthen his authority, which has been compromised by family quarrels, and let every one be thoroughly convinced that the government of India will never allow any attempts to be made to injure or subvert it."

But the Court of Directors was far from entertaining the same opinion, and in its insatiable avidity had long meditated the re-establishment of Shah Shooja in the government of Afghanistan, in order to have the finances of that country entirely at its own disposal. Lord Auckland laid the conflicting opinions of Burnes and of the Court of Directors before the English Cabinet, who decided in favour of that of the British officer, as being the only rational and practicable one; but the contrary opinion, supported by Sir W. M'Naghten, Sir Claude Wade, and Sir John M'Neil, which favoured the secret views of the Directors, prevailed. Sir Claude Wade, the resident at Loodiana, who was the warmest partisan of Shah Shooja, encouraged the warlike propensities of the East India Company by leading them into the error in which he had himself been held many years by his protégé, namely, that the Barukzye tribe did not contain 60,000 families, as Burnes had stated, and that their numbers did not amount to more than 6000; also that their chiefs were generally hated by the serdars of the other Afghan tribes. Opinions so different held by two officers, both of whom enjoyed in a high degree the confidence of their Government, arose from one common source, ignorance: like the greater part of those authors who have hitherto written on Afghanistan, they confused the tribes with their *subdivisions* or branches. Thus:—Ahmed Shah and his descendants (Shah Shooja, &c.) were of the tribe of Popolzye, and the branch or family of the Suddozyes. Hadji Djemal Khan and his posterity (Dost Mohamed, &c.) were of the tribe of Barukzye, and the branch or family of the Mohamedzyes; and it is probably of this latter branch, which does consist of four or five thousand families, that Sir C. Wade intended to speak; for in Afghanistan, when a descendant of Hadji Djemal is spoken of, he is not called a "Barukzye chief," but a "Mohamedzye chief." In the same manner Ahmed Shah is not called Ahmed Shah Popolzye, but Ahmed Shah Suddozye.

The advice of Burnes was rejected and his acts completely disavowed. Lord Auckland also took upon himself to offer to the Emir of Kabul the most merciless ultimatum, first demanding, but in the most polite manner possible, that he should immediately dismiss Captain Vikovitch; and next, that he should renounce all his rights to the Afghan provinces conquered by the Sikhs, because the noble Lord had determined not to interfere in his favour, from a fear of displeasing his faithful ally, the Maharadjah of the Punjab. Burnes exerted all his powers of persuasion and argument, which marked the intense interest he took in the cause of the Emir, to induce him to accept these hard conditions. The Dost, though indignant at this unworthy treatment, had not actually given his definitive reply, affirmative or negative, when he received information from his agents in India, which left him no doubt of the fact of the concentration of a British army at Ferozepore with the well-determined purpose of replacing Shah Shooja on the throne of Kabul. Simultaneously with this information the Dost received letters from Captain Vikovitch, written from Kandahar, in which the fairest promises were made to him. These letters decided him in his course of action, and he broke off his negotiations with Burnes, who, having failed in his mission, retired, leaving Dost Mohamed in a state of great consternation.

Mons. Thomas then proceeds with his remarks:—"The Dost could not, he said, hold out a month against England, and the thoughts of displeasing her filled him with terror. He was not ignorant that Runjeet was the friend of the English, and that it would not be wise to attack him. They could at any moment support Peshawur, if not with troops at least with simple remonstrances, which would have restrained the Maharadjah of Lahore; but, on the contrary, they were now more than ever Runjeet's declared friends, and preferred him to the Afghans, who were ready to place themselves at their disposal. Certainly that was not the provocation of a very determined enemy. Burnes himself, when he left, did not think that the Afghans would ever throw themselves into the arms of the Russians, and unite with the Persians. The fatal policy of England, however, constrained the Dost to do so, and left him no alternative but ruin or war.

"After having been four years at peace—after having forced the Shah of Persia to retire from Herat—after having ascertained with certainty the devotion of Dost Mohamed—what could excite the Government of India to such a violent determination? Why make war on the Afghans? Had all Asia risen in arms? Had the Persians taken Herat and Kandahar, the Russians Bokhara and Khiva? No; but, as Burnes said, it was only because a Cossack captain, without state or suite, had galloped up to Kabul. Lord Palmerston, who had hesitated so long before he interfered officially in Persia, adopted in less than six months a vigorous intervention in Afghanistan. He required a war with Kabul, because he had not known how to ask in proper time for explanations at St. Petersburg, which would certainly have been given him if he had procrastinated, temporised, and tergiversated less. Afraid of losing the alliance of Russia in Europe, because he had the misfortune to place faith in it, and the still greater one of preserving it as a balance of power—necessitated to defer to her, though the Foreign Office had been obliged during four years to pass over in silence the Muscovite intrigues, he had not warned the princes of the East that England considered herself affronted, but endeavoured to detach them from these intrigues out of regard for their interests. He never spoke in the name of his Government, and they had therefore never listened to him; however, seeing India seriously threatened, he at length took a side, but which? Lord Palmerston let loose the demon of war all over the East; he created perils without end for the British empire; he raised up against it resentment and vengeance; he mixed England up more and more with the internal quarrels of a country in which her dominion could only be maintained by neutrality; he hurried her purposely into the path of conquest, and struck wherever the Russian had set a foot or intended to set one, hoping these grand strokes of his genius would astonish and lead to reflection, without remembering that such flagrant injustice is never pardoned."

CHAPTER XX.

Lord Auckland sends Sir W. M'Naghten to Lahore — Treaty with the Sikhs — Manifesto of the Governor-General from Simla in justification of his policy — Reflections on this document — The possession of Scinde adjourned — The Emirs are opposed to the advance of the British army through their territory — Mir Roustem of Khyrpoor — Averse to *lending* the fortress of Bukkur to the English, but at length accedes to their request — The result of this to himself and his family — Conduct of the British authorities in Scinde — Strength of the army when concentrated at Shikapoor — Extract from Mr. Sumner's work — Seizure of Kurrachee — English appliances to success in the invasion of Afghanistan — Proceedings of Shah Shooja.

As soon as war had been determined upon, Lord Auckland sent the Secretary of the Government of India, Sir William M'Naghten, to negotiate a treaty with Runjeet Sing and Shah Shooja-ool-Moolk, which he concluded without difficulty; the Shah agreeing to cede to the Maharadjah all the Afghan provinces he had conquered, including even Peshawur, which Dost Mohamed had refused to give up. This point settled, Lord Auckland published the following manifesto, in which he set forth his reasons for making war upon the Afghans:—

"Simla, October 1st, 1838.

"The Right Honourable the Governor-General of India having, with the concurrence of the Supreme Gouncil, directed the assemblage of a British force for service across the Indus, his Lordship deems it proper to publish the following exposition of the reasons which have led to this important measure.

"It is a matter of notoriety that the treaties entered into by the British Government in the year 1832, with the Ameers of Sinde, the Nawab of Bahawulpore, and the Maharajah Runjeet Sing, had for their object, by opening the navigation of the Indus, to facilitate the extension of commerce, and to gain for the British nation in Central Asia that legitimate influence which an interchange of benefits would naturally produce. With a view to invite the aid of the *de facto* rulers of Afghanistan to the measures necessary for giving full effect to those treaties, Captain Burnes was deputed, towards the close of the year 1836, on a mission to Dost Mohamed Khan, the chief of Kabul. The original objects of that officer's mission were purely of a commercial nature. Whilst Captain Burnes, however, was on his journey to Kabul, information was received by the Governor-General that the troops of Dost Mohamed Khan had made a sudden and unprovoked attack on those of our ancient ally, the Maharajah Runjeet Sing.* It was naturally to be apprehended that his Highness the Maharajah would not be slow to avenge this aggression, and it was to be feared that, the flames of war being once kindled in the very regions into which we were endeavouring to extend our commerce, the peaceful and beneficial purposes of the British Government would be altogether frustrated. In order to avert a result so calamitous, the Governor-General resolved on authorizing Captain Burnes to intimate to Dost Mohamed Khan that, if he should evince a disposition to come to just and reasonable terms with the Maharajah, his Lordship would exert his good offices with his Highness, for the Maharajah, with the characteristic confidence which he has uniformly placed in the faith and friendship of the British nation, at once assented to the proposition of the Governor-General, to the effect that in the mean time hostilities on his part should be suspended.†

"It subsequently came to the knowledge of the Governor-General that a Persian army was besieging Herat; that intrigues were actively prosecuted throughout Afghanistan for the purpose of extending Persian influence and authority to the banks of, and even beyond, the Indus; and that the Court of Persia had not only commenced a course of injury and insult to the officers of her Majesty's mission in the Persian territory, but had afforded evidence of being engaged in designs wholly at variance with the principles and objects of its alliance with Great Britain.‡

"After much time spent by Captain Burnes in fruitless negotiation at Kabul, it appeared that Dost Mohamed Khan, chiefly in consequence of his reliance upon Persian encouragement and assistance, persisted, as respected his misunderstanding with the Sikhs, in urging the most unreasonable pretensions,§ such as the Governor-General could not, consistently with justice and his regard for the

* What then of the spoliation of the Afghan provinces by Runjeet.—*Ferrier*.

† I have no doubt that the English, foreseeing that the Punjab would ere long be theirs, supported Runjeet in his spoliations.—*Ferrier*.

‡ An alliance which was obligatory on both parties, and which England had been the first to break by refusing to pay the subsidy she had promised to Persia.—*Ferrier*.

§ The restitution of Peshawur, the bulwark of his country, extorted by Runjeet.—*Ferrier*.

friendship of the Maharajah Runjeet Sing, be the channel of submitting to the consideration of his Highness; that he avowed schemes of aggrandizement and ambition injurious to the security and peace of the frontiers of India; and that he openly threatened, in furtherance of those schemes, to call in every foreign aid which he could command. Ultimately he gave his undisguised support to the Persian designs in Afghanistan, of the unfriendly and injurious character of which, as concerned the British power in India, he was well apprized, and, by his utter disregard of the views and interests of the British Government, compelled Captain Burnes to leave Kabul without having effected any of the objects of his mission. It was now evident that no further interference could be exercised by the British Government to bring about a good understanding between the Sihk ruler and Dost Mohamed Khan; and the hostile policy of the latter chief showed too plainly that, so long as Kabul remained under his government, we could never hope that the tranquillity of our neighbourhood would be secured, or that the interests of our Indian empire would be preserved inviolate.

"The Governor-General deems it in this place necessary to revert to the siege of Herat, and the conduct of the Persian nation. The siege of that city has now been carried on by the Persian army for many months.* The attack upon it was a most unjustifiable and cruel aggression, perpetrated and continued, notwithstanding the solemn and repeated remonstrances of the British envoy at the court of Persia, and after every just and becoming offer of accommodation had been made and rejected. The besieged have behaved with a gallantry and fortitude worthy of the justice of their cause; and the Governor-General would yet indulge the hope that their heroism may enable them to maintain a successful defence until succours shall reach them from British India. In the mean time the ulterior designs of Persia, affecting the interests of the British Government, have been, by a succession of events, more and more openly manifested. The Governor-General has recently ascertained, by an official despatch from Mr. M'Neil, her Majesty's envoy, that his Excellency has been compelled, by a refusal of his just demands, and by a systematic course of disrespect adopted towards him by the Persian Government, to quit the court of the

* At the date of this manifesto the Shah had abandoned the siege and retired.—*Ferrier.*

Shah, and to make a public declaration of a cessation of all intercourse between the two governments. The necessity under which Great Britain is placed of regarding the present advance of the Persian arms into Afghanistan as an act of hostility towards herself, has also been officially communicated to the Shah under the express order of her Majesty's Government.

"The chiefs of Kandahar (brothers of Dost Mohamed Khan of Kabul) have avowed their adherence to the Persian policy, with the same full knowledge of its opposition to the rights and interests of the British nation in India, and have been openly assisting in the operations against Herat. In the crisis of the affairs consequent upon the retirement of our envoy from Kabul, the Governor-General felt the importance of taking immediate measures for arresting the rapid progress of foreign intrigue and aggression towards our own territories. His attention was naturally drawn at this conjuncture to the position and claims of Shah Shooja-ool-Moolk, a monarch who, when in power, had cordially acceded to the measures of united resistance to external enmity which were at that time judged necessary by the British Government, and who, on his empire being usurped by its present rulers, had found an honourable asylum in the British dominions.

"It had been clearly ascertained, from the information furnished by the various officers who have visited Afghanistan, that the Barukzye chiefs, from their disunion and unpopularity, were ill fitted, under any circumstances, to be useful allies to the British Government, and to aid us in our just and necessary measures of national defence. Yet so long as they refrained from proceedings injurious to our interests and security, the British Government acknowledged and respected their authority ; but a different policy appeared to be now more than justified by the conduct of those chiefs, and to be indispensable to our own safety. The welfare of our possessions in the East requires that we should have on our western frontier an ally who is interested in resisting aggressions and establishing tranquillity, in the place of chiefs ranging themselves in subservience to a hostile power, and seeking to promote schemes of conquest and aggrandizement. After serious and mature deliberation the Governor-General was satisfied that a pressing necessity, as well as every consideration of policy and justice, warranted us in espousing the cause of Shah Shooja-ool-Moolk, whose popularity throughout Afghanistan had been proved to his Lordship by the strong and unanimous testimony of the best authorities. Having arrived at this determination, the Governor-General was further of opinion that it was just and proper, no less from the position of Maharajah Runjeet Sing, than from his undeviating friendship towards the British Government, that his Highness should have the offer of becoming a party to the contemplated operations.

"Mr. M'Naghten was accordingly deputed in June last to the court of his Highness, and the result of his mission has been the conclusion of a tripartite treaty by the British Government, the Maharajah, and Shah Shooja-ool-Moolk, whereby his Highness is guaranteed in his present possessions, and has bound himself to co-operate for the restoration of the Shah to the throne of his ancestors. The friends and enemies of any one of the contracting parties have been declared to be the friends and enemies of all.

"Various points have been adjusted which had been the subjects of discussion between the British Government and his Highness the Maharaja, the identity of whose interests with those of the Honourable Company has now been made apparent to all the surrounding states. A guaranteed independence will, upon favourable conditions, be tendered to the Emirs of Scinde; and the integrity of Herat, in the possession of its present ruler, will be fully respected; while by the measures completed, or in progress, it may reasonably be hoped that the general freedom and security of commerce will be promoted, the name and just influence of the British Government will gain their proper footing among the nations of Central Asia, that tranquillity will be established upon the most important frontier of India, and that a lasting barrier will be raised against hostile intrigue and encroachment.

"His Majesty Shah Shooja-ool-Moolk will enter Afghanistan surrounded by his own troops, and will be supported against foreign interference and factious opposition by a British army. The Governor-General confidently hopes that the Shah will be replaced on his throne by his own subjects and adherents; and when once he shall be secured in power, and the independence and integrity of Afghanistan established, the British army will be withdrawn. The Governor-General has been led to these measures by the duty which is imposed upon him of providing for the security of the possessions of the British crown; but he rejoices that, in the discharge of his duty, he will be enabled to assist in restoring the union and prosperity of the Afghan people. Throughout the approaching operations British influence will be sedulously employed to further every measure of general benefit, to reconcile differences, to secure oblivion for injuries, and to put an end to the distractions by which, for so many years, the welfare and happiness of the Afghans have been impaired. Even to the chiefs whose hostile proceedings have given just cause of offence to the British Government, it will seek to secure liberal and honourable treatment on their tendering early submission, and ceasing from opposition to that course of measures which may be judged the most suitable to the general advantage of their country."

The explanations that have preceded this manifesto do justice to its inaccuracies, its reserve and want of frankness. I shall not therefore comment upon it, but have reproduced it here to give an idea of the manner in which the Anglo-Indian government proceeds in Asia.

The invasion of Afghanistan was only a prelude to that of Scinde, but there existed friendly treaties with the Talpoora Emirs, sovereigns of that country, and the Indian Government could not then attempt to seize their territory without creating for themselves too much embarrassment at once; the taking definitive possession of it was therefore postponed, but forcing the Emirs to consent to the passage of the British troops through their country was a prelude thereto. At one moment war was on the point of breaking out between the East India Company and the Emirs of that part of Scinde which is watered by the Lower Indus, for they energetically opposed the passage of an English army; but Mir Roustem of Khyrpoor, their aged chief, prevented them from going to that extremity, and succeeded in conciliating all parties.

When the British forces entered Scinde this venerable chieftain acceded to all the sacrifices imposed upon him. When asked by the English to *lend them during their operations in Afghanistan* the fortress of Bukkar, situated on an island at the mouth of the Indus, the demand appeared to him too humiliating. "It is," he said, "at once the bulwark and the heart of my country, and my honour forbids that I should trust that in the hands of strangers." Nevertheless he allowed himself to be persuaded. His whole family threw themselves on their knees before him to induce him not to grant this extraordinary request, but he preferred exposing himself to their lively and incessant reproaches, to displeasing his friends the English, in whose word he believed. He *lent* them the fortress of Bukkar—it has never been out of their hands since, and to recompense his generous conduct towards them they despoiled him five years afterwards of the rest of his territory, and possessed themselves also of that of his brothers and nephews. The officers of General Napier invaded even the harems of these unfortunate princes, and carried off the treasures, jewels, and even the clothes of their women.

The Government of India had ordered that the Expeditionary Army of Afghanistan should consist of 27,000 men, who were to be ready to take the field in the month of November, 1838. But when it was known at Calcutta that the Persians had raised the siege of Herat it was reduced to an effective force of 21,500, and this force was assembled on the eastern bank of the Indus, January 16, 1839, under the command of Lieut.-General Sir John Keane. Here Shah Shooja hastened to join him, and a week afterwards the Emir Roustem placed the troops in possession of the island fortress of Bukkar; they subsequently crossed the river on a pontoon bridge, and were concentrated at Shikapoor in the earliest days of March.

" This concentration," says Sumner, " was preceded by one of those acts of violence too often found in the pages of British history, and which tarnish the glory of the brilliant actions recorded in it.

" Near the town of Kurrachee, which is situated about fifty miles north-east of the second mouth of the Indus, on the Scindian side, is a small fortress belonging to a state with which England was at peace, and which was attached to her by treaties of friendship and commerce. It was thought that it would be useful to hold this place; and a British vessel of war and steamboats having arrived before the fort, February 2, 1839, with two sepoy regiments and a detachment of European artillery, a messenger was sent on shore to inform the officer in command that its position rendered the possession of it indispensable to insure the safety of the vessels of the Company intrusted with the transport of the munitions of war and *matériel* of their army. The message required the officer to deliver up the place in a quarter of an hour, if he did not wish rigorous measures to be taken against him.

" The Scindian officer having refused to yield to the summons, the troops disembarked, and under cover of the fire of the ships, moored broadside to the shore, took possession of the fort and town of Kurrachee, and it now forms part of the British dominions in the East Indies."

The English had neglected nothing that could tend to secure a successful issue to this undertaking; they had exerted all their arts of seduction and corruption to induce the serdars of Afghanistan to attach themselves to their party, and a few of the most influential had responded to their appeal. Amongst these were Iskander Khan, Popolzye; Mohamed Attah Khan, Popolzye; and Walee Mohamed Khan, Isakzye; who left their tribes on the first rumour of the war, and joined Shah Shooja at Loodiana, where, with their concurrence, he formed the nucleus of a government. As soon as that was constituted, they sent numerous emissaries to their own country, with a view of parading to the Afghans the power and generosity of the English, and to persuade them that not only would all resistance be useless, but that it would be more beneficial to themselves to receive them, as they would effect the restoration of their own royal family. A crowd of serdars, who were jealous of those of the Barukzye tribe, whom the Mohamedzye chiefs greatly favoured, allowed themselves to be easily persuaded by these emissaries, and joined without delay the British camp. A small number only, having no greater sympathy with the Mohamedzyes, nevertheless feared the consequences of a return of fortune in favour of that branch, and retired to their homes to wait till the course of events should be more decided before they took an open part.

CHAPTER XXI.

Introductory note to chapter — Character of the Afghans — Their physical development — Mental qualities — Indifferent Mussulmans — Their turbulent nature — Spirit of independence — Love of marauding — Their cupidity extreme — Insensible to good faith — The law a dead letter in their eyes — The citizen and the nomade — Hospitality — Prandial habits of Yar Mohamed — The character of their food — Kooroot — Mode of eating — Ignorance of the Afghans — Their superstitions — Education — Costume — Dirty habits — Religious feeling — Administration of the laws — The *lex talionis* — Punishments — Diseases — Remedies — Public buildings — Roads — Private houses — The zoology of Afghanistan — Domestic animals — Nature of the soil — Productions of it — Aridity of the country — Minerals — Geographical position — Climate — Difficulties of rapid communication — Population.

AT the conclusion of General Ferrier's manuscript are some pages devoted to a description of the Afghan nation, their habits, customs, education, laws, and religion, and much other general information respecting Afghanistan, its productions, climate, &c. The author left it to the translator to decide in which of the two volumes this information could be placed to the best advantage, namely, 'Caravan Journeys,' or the present work. The translator has, therefore, though it certainly does interrupt the continuous character of the history, introduced a portion of that Addendum here; for the reader will thus have an insight into the character of the Afghan people before he enters upon that period of their history which is so closely interwoven with our own, and be, therefore, better able to form an opinion of it and that sad military catastrophe which is still and must ever remain so deeply interesting to every Englishman.

The Afghans are tall, robust, active, and well formed; their olive and sometimes sallow complexions and strongly-marked hard features give their countenances a savage expression; the lids of their black eyes, which are full of fire, are tinged with antimony, for this, in their opinion, gives force and adds beauty and a dazzling brilliancy to them; their black beard is worn short, and their hair, of the same colour, is shaved off from the front to the top of the head, the remainder at the sides being allowed to fall in large curls over the shoulders. Their step is full of resolution, their bearing proud, but rough.

They are brave even to rashness, excited by the smallest trifle, enterprising without the least regard to prudence, energetic and born for war. They possess all the qualities essential to carry it on successfully, but are utterly ignorant how to take advantage of and turn them to account; their courage is impulsive, and displays itself most readily in the attack; if that fails they are easily disheartened, and show no perseverance, for, as they are soon elated, so are they as easily discouraged. They are sober, abstemious, and apparently of an open disposition—great gossips, and curious to excess. Their anger is not betrayed by any sudden burst of passion; on the contrary, all that is brutal and savage in their nature is manifested with the most perfect calmness, but it is the volcano slumbering beneath the ashes.

Courage is with them the first of virtues, and usurps the place of all the others; they are cruel, perfidious, coarse, without pity, badly brought up, exceedingly inclined to theft and pillage. In the latter they differ from their neighbours the Persians, who are, however, as great scoundrels as themselves, for they endeavour by every means in their power to conceal their knavery under the appearance of law or rhetoric, while the Afghans do the very reverse—they at once place the knife on your throat, and say, "Give, or I take." Force is their only argument, and it justifies everything; an individual who is merely plundered considers himself extremely fortunate, as, generally speaking, they act inversely to the cut-throats of Europe, who demand "your purse or your life;" the Afghans take life first and then the purse. In religion they are more tolerant and well disposed towards those who profess a different faith than any other sect of Mussulmans. Like the people of most Eastern nations, they are also addicted to a crime which it is not necessary to name; but this remark applies rather to the rich than to the people in general. An injury is never forgotten, and vengeance is a passion which they love; even at the cost of their lives they will satisfy it should an opportunity present itself, and this in the most cruel manner.

There is no nation in the world more turbulent and less under subjection; the difficulties in rendering them submissive to a code of just laws would be almost insurmountable. To make them observe the rules of good breeding, or even common civility, would perhaps be still more difficult; the people are as gross and coarse as savages. The chiefs and upper classes are more civilized; but their politeness is always tinctured by a rudeness of manner very offensive to Europeans. No matter what the condition or rank of an Afghan may be, he considers that he has a right to seat himself in the presence of his superiors; to this privilege he attaches the greatest importance, and enters into conversation with them perfectly at his ease and without the least hesitation, giving his opinion on every subject; in short, forcing himself and his views upon them as he thinks fit, eating with them uninvited, and all this as if they were upon a footing of the most perfect equality. These habits do not wound the pride of the rich and powerful Afghans; on the contrary, they encourage this independent spirit, and admit their right to make their requests and volunteer their opinions in this way. These are prerogatives which in their eyes constitute liberty.

The Afghans do not attach the same importance to some words as Europeans do; "country" and "honour" are to them as empty sounds, and they sell them to the highest bidder without scruple. This is so true, that they will almost always submit to and obey a conqueror; and if they have been pretty nearly independent since the time of Ahmed Shah, Suddozye, it has been owing quite as much to the weakness of the neighbouring states as because there was no one who thought it worth his while to purchase them. It cannot be denied that the conquest of Persia, under Mir Mahmood in 1721, is a very remarkable page in their history; but if we take into consideration the feeble state in which that unfortunate country was at the time, we shall be the less astonished; a similar invasion, and composed of the same elements, would now have every chance of success, though the means of defence on the part of Persia are much more considerable than they were then. After all, the Afghans were not long in losing their conquest and their liberty, and being in their turn subdued by those whom they had vanquished and humiliated.

In mentioning this circumstance, Heaven forbid it should be supposed that I desire to undervalue the courage of a people who have given so many proofs of it; but I wish to establish the fact that the Afghans are as incapable of a continuous course of action as of ideas; they do everything on the spur of the moment, from a love of disorder, or for no reason at all: it matters little to them who gives them laws; they obey the first comer directly they find it is to their advantage to do so, and allow him to play the tyrant and govern them if he pays them well and does not interfere with their passion for rapine and devastation. Pillage, fighting, and disturbances are at times necessary to their very existence, and are followed by long days of repose and idleness, during which they live on the fruits of their depredations.

Their cupidity and avarice are extreme; there is no tie they would not break, no duty they would not desert, to gratify their avidity for wealth. This surpasses all that can be imagined; it is insatiable, and to satisfy it they are capable of committing the greatest crimes. For it they will sacrifice all—their native and independent pride; even prostitute the honour of their wives and daughters, whom they frequently put to death after they have received the price of their dishonour. Gold in Afghanistan is, more than anywhere else, the god of the human race; it stifles the still small cry of every man's conscience, if, indeed, it can be admitted that an Afghan has a conscience at all: it is impossible to rely on their promises, their friendship, or their fidelity.

They enter into engagements, and bind themselves by the most solemn oaths to respect them, and, in order to give them a sacred character, transcribe them on a Koran, to which they affix their seal, but nevertheless perjure themselves with an impudence perfectly inconceivable. Towns and villages by hundreds have surrendered on the faith of such obligations, stipulating that the lives of the inhabitants should be spared, and yet the examples are rare, that, once in the victors' power, they have not been exterminated. It is extraordinary that, knowing their own bad faith, they allow themselves to fall into these snares. The majority of the wars which they wage against one another generally terminate by one or more of these massacres. Murder is a game, and they evince a feeling of vanity when they commit one, and glory in the perfidy and cruelty which they show in their acts of devastation; when they can cite an example of a town which they have depopulated and razed to the ground, they imagine they have given the grandest idea of their power and valour: they are, in short, real Huns, and Attilas are never wanting amongst them.

They submit to the laws only after they have tried every means to evade them; they consider it perfectly lawful in those who are stronger or more powerful than themselves to plunder them, and consequently they have no scruple in despoiling those who are weaker. Accustomed from their childhood to see human blood spilt, to hear murder not only excused but gloried in, they are soon familiar with the idea of death, which they confront with the greatest coolness. It is rare to see them make war for the simple purpose of defending their nationality, for this sentiment does not exist, and can be considered applicable only to the tribe, its district, or encampment. Their ideas are of a totally different character; the hope of enriching himself by booty, of bathing himself in blood—these are what from his earliest youth an Afghan proposes to indulge in, and these are the principles in which he is brought up. They hate all governments which introduce law and order into a country, or enter into treaties of peace with their neighbours; to do so is in their eyes an attack upon their rights, which deprives them of pillage, and consequently the best part of their revenues.

If an Afghan is put to death by his sovereign for marauding, his countrymen look upon him as a victim; but they establish between him who exposes his life in combat and the obscure domestic thief who does not an immense difference; the first is in their estimation a brave man, whereas the other is treated with contempt, banished from the tribe, and sometimes put to death. At first sight an Afghan pleases, and this in spite of his rough and savage physiognomy and exterior: the fact is, that, when he has an object in view, and he has something to gain, he knows how to play, and with great suppleness, the part which policy dictates; but if he loses the hope of obtaining anything out of you, it is easy to see into the details of his character, and he will stand without scruple unmasked, and in all the aridity of his evil nature.

Excitement, the clash of arms, and the tumult of the combat are to him life; repose is for an Afghan only a transitory state of being, during which he leads a monotonous existence; the sweets of domestic life, mental quietude, the endearments of his family, have no charms for him, and a life without commotion and agitation loses all its poetry. He is only really a man when he is fighting and plundering; then his eye is full of fire, his hand grasps convulsively the hilt of his sabre, and he presses his sinewy legs against his horse's sides until the animal can scarcely draw his breath: man and horse are one, each understands the ardour of the other, and it is difficult to distinguish which of the two is then the most vicious. As there is nothing in the world of which an Afghan makes so light as life, he hastens to live, but in his own way, a slave to his passions, for who knows whether he will not fall to-morrow by his neighbour's sword, as others have fallen to-day by his?

There is no shade of difference between the character of the citizen or the nomade; a town life does not soften their habits; they live there as they live in a tent, always armed to the teeth, and ready for the onslaught, devoid of a right-minded feeling, and always animated by the most ferocious instincts. Though they are full of duplicity, one is nevertheless frequently liable to be taken in by their apparent frankness; but a traveller is not long the victim of their clumsy cheating, which can succeed only amongst themselves, for their minds are rather heavy than acute. Strangers, and particularly Europeans, easily see through them; their kind attentions, or an appearance of politeness to an individual, are rarely the result of a natural and sincere feeling on their part, for they are sure to have an interested object in view; and if they are so liberal as to present you with an egg, it is because they expect to have an ox in return: if they are of any service to you, and they ask for nothing in exchange, you will find that the gift, or whatever the service may be, has cost them nothing, whether trouble or money. They are hospitable to travellers, but only because this is an ancient custom, which has the force of law, and is not a virtue which springs from the heart; those who are not in good circumstances consider it a burden which they would willingly cast aside, were it not that they fear public opinion; in all cases they take every means in their power to evade it; the rich practise it only from ostentation, and always parsimoniously.

Idleness being the dominant vice of this people, they rarely ever work; and when the amount of plunder is insufficient for their requirements, they are always thinking of some expedient by which they can procure money; their greatest anxiety, however, is to ascertain how they can get their daily bread without having to pay for it. This is their one only thought all their lives; after having provided for their wives and children the barest pittance, they will go from door to door in the hope of getting a dinner: hangers-on are indeed so numerous that the chiefs, and even the sovereign himself, are obliged to enter into the most minute details of their housekeeping, and give instructions to their servants as to the character and quantity of the food they are to place before their voracious visitors. If with some bread they give a little soup, they have the reputation of being exceedingly hospitable; but if to these they add a ration of rice or meat, no praise, however expressed, would be sufficiently strong to mark the estimation in which their generosity is held. The common people are not alone in this love of putting their hands into other people's plates, the highest personages do not object to refresh themselves at their neighbour's expense; and I have more than once seen the Vizier Yar Mohamed Khan, and other chiefs, after having finished their own repast, present the remains to some of their guests, many of them generals, governors of towns, &c., who pounced upon and cleared them off in the twinkling of an eye, seizing the bones with as much alacrity as would have done the most famished poodle. It is rare indeed that an Afghan's appetite fails him, at any rate it is a fact that never came within my knowledge; and when they have the good fortune to meet with a table well furnished, and an easy host, they put all reserve aside, and, as they themselves express it (kharabi singuin), make an enormous feed.

This habit of living at the expense of other people forces the Afghans to practise sobriety and frugality. They live on fruit nearly half the year, rice forming the best and most appetising part of their food; but notwithstanding the low price at which it is sold, it is only persons in easy circumstances who can afford to eat it every day. They season it in their pilaus, like the Turks and Persians; like them also they take their meals sitting on the ground, with their heels tucked under them, and convey their food to their mouths with their fingers. Meat is not much liked unless it is swimming in grease; then it is delicious. They throw away the lean, as they say it produces diarrhœa. The principal food of the villagers and nomades is *kooroot*, a kind of pudding made of boiled Indian corn, bruised between two stones, or simply bread, on which they pour rancid grease, mixed with a substance which in the East is known under the name of *kechk*.* The flesh of the sheep or goat is what the Afghans prefer; but, as with the rice, the rich only can afford to purchase it: the ox, the camel, and the horse, that age or infirmities have rendered unfit for further service, is the animal food of the people.

They will not eat meat unless it is *halal* (lawful), that is, the

* The settlement in whey.—*Ferrier.*

animal must have its face turned towards Mecca, and its throat cut in a particular part of the neck, the following sacrificial words being pronounced during the operation, in accordance with their law and rule of faith—*Bismillah rahman rahim* (In the name of the most merciful God). In eating, they mix one dish with another, knead them together with their fingers, and then stuff it into their mouths.

The highest personages not only permit the lowest to eat with them out of the same plate, but the dirtiest and the most disgusting: it is sufficient that they are Mussulmans for them not to feel the least annoyance, and yet they will be scrupulously careful not to eat with a person who is not of their religion, no matter how clean he may be. They make two meals, one at noon, the other at nine o'clock at night; they frequently smoke the *tchilim*, a kind of water-pipe, but very inferior to the *narghile* of the Turks, or the *kalioon* of the Persians.

It would be difficult to conceive the ignorance of the Afghans, which does not, however, prevent them from being excessively presumptuous; they are brutes, not, however, unintelligent, but they like to be within a circle of ideas of the narrowest kind. They have neither the genius of creation nor the faculty of imitation, and are satisfied with the bigoted and confined views which have been handed down to them by their ancestors. They refuse to take the least trouble to learn anything which would open their minds and add to their well-being, convinced that science is a useless burden, which only fatigues and enervates those who pursue it, without making them at all happier. "Are not these Europeans fools," say they, "to give themselves so much concern in acquiring all these things here below, while they are preparing for themselves the most dreadful punishments which they must suffer for ever in another world, for refusing to believe the unity of God * and the power of our revered prophet Mahomet, on whom be praise?"

Their wise men are the mollahs and astronomers; the last, especially, are in great reputation amongst them, for they cannot, will not, undertake anything without consulting the stars and the auguries. They believe also in magic, and hang a number of amulets about themselves and their horses.

The Persian language is met with all over Afghanistan; the great families speak it, and their correspondence is carried on in

* They cannot in the least imagine in what way we comprehend the Trinity.—*Ferrier.*

that tongue: the people are acquainted with it, but they prefer speaking the *Pushtoo*, the language of their nation, which is a mixture of ancient Persian, Arabic, and Hindostanee. They have a few works in this language, but they read Persian authors by preference, and have through them formed imperfect ideas of geography, astronomy, medicine, and history; but these works, full of fictions and deficiencies, have not materially assisted in developing their faculties.

The Afghans wear their clothes long. They consist of two large robes, very ample, and are either of cotton or a cloth made of camel's hair, called *barek:* this is the dress of the people. The only difference in the garments of the rich is in the material, which is silk, cloth, or cachemire. In summer they are made without any lining, but in the winter they are wadded with cotton or lined with fur. The under garment is confined by a piece of muslin, or long cloth, which is wound round the body; the outside one and sometimes a third robe is used as a cloak, and a person would be considered wanting in politeness if in visiting a superior he did not put it on. The shirt is very full, and the sleeves, which reach below the hands, particularly so. The former is open at the side from the neck to the waist, and falls over the trowsers: these, which are excessively large, open at the foot, and are drawn in at the waist with a string. The head is covered by an enormous blue or white turban, and the feet with slippers without quarters. The upper classes are, for the most part, simply dressed, and consider luxury in this respect as enervating; but some young chiefs have their robes ornamented with gold lace or embroidered with gold thread. This is done in the harems by the women, who excel in this kind of work, particularly in Kandahar. The Afghans are not careful of their clothes, and soil them the very first day they are put on, for they squat on the ground without taking the least thought whether the spot on which they sit is clean or dirty. They never change their garments, not even the shirt, until they are completely worn out; and as they very rarely wash themselves, they are constantly covered with vermin, great and small.

The Afghans are Mussulmans of the sect of Soonee, with the exception of the tribe of Beritchees, who belong to that of Shiah. The Parsivans and Eimaks, who are subject to the Afghans, equally profess the faith of Islam, but besides the two sects just mentioned some of them are of a third, called Ali-illahee, who worship Ali as

God. The Afghans did not embrace Islamism till very late, and after their conquerors the Moguls: this assertion is in contradiction to their own, but is nevertheless true. They are religious more from habit than conviction, though they are not on that account guilty of hypocrisy. While the English occupied their country they relaxed considerably the practice of their worship, and the influence of the mollahs was much reduced; but when the Anglo-Indians withdrew from Afghanistan, they recovered it with a powerful hand, and from that moment have endeavoured to excite a spirit of fanaticism in the people, and inspire them with a hatred of Europeans.

It is probable that the Afghans are not more persuaded than formerly of the infallibility of Islam, but, as the mollahs are supported by their chiefs, they have resumed their previous habits. They make the five prayers every day, observe the fast of Ramazan, and everything is comprised in the most rigorous observance of external forms. Let the English return, and they would again relapse into indifference on this subject.

Justice is administered amongst the Afghans according to the commands of the Koran, though in some cases they use their traditional laws, which have, they say, descended to them from the remotest antiquity. The Kazi is the head of the religious tribunal; the sovereign, and, under him, the Kalehbeghi and the Daroga, administer the ordinary law. The Afghans of Herat and Kabul may congratulate themselves on the equity and justice with which they are governed, but it is not the same in Kandahar, where the laws are construed to the benefit of the judges in an unjust and violent manner: they are always anxious to find the accused guilty, and, as the sovereign inflicts heavy fines, this system much augments his revenues.

The *lex talionis* is rigorously observed amongst the Afghans, and the murderer is put to death by the nearest relation of his victim. It sometimes happens that the person on whom this duty devolves is a child, when the punishment remains in abeyance till he is strong enough to hold the dagger which is placed in his hands, and with which he performs the office of executioner. He possesses the right to grant the murderer his life, but there is no instance of this ever having been exercised, excepting for a compensation, which the criminal is obliged to make in a sum of money or in land; sometimes he gives one of his daughters in marriage to the son or the brother of the murdered man, without the father being obliged to give her any dower.

Thieves are treated with great leniency: for the first theft the offender is obliged to restore the stolen property to its owner, and receives from him a paternal admonition; the second is treated in a similar manner, but with the addition of a fine; the third is followed by the bastinado; and a further repetition of the offence by torture or death. In a country where the population is so fond of laying hands upon other people's property, it is not surprising to find the judges exercise so much forbearance, for the generality of them might with more propriety be placed at the bar than on the seat of justice. It must be added that torture, or any other punishment, may be remitted, with the consent of the injured party; and as he has ever before him the probability that he will one day need pardon himself, it is seldom that he is too severe.

The punishments inflicted for political crimes, and others which in France would be brought before our courts of assize, are fine, bastinado, cutting off the nose, ears, or hand; opening the body of the criminal, and then hanging him up till death releases him from his sufferings; cutting the throat, stabbing, impaling, strangling, skinning alive, scalping, quartering, hanging (generally with the head downwards), crucifying, stoning, boiling in a caldron, and a thousand other barbarities of the kind. No extenuating circumstances are admitted; no difference is made between a crime which is the result of passion and premeditated guilt, between manslaughter and murder: from a sentence there is no appeal, and the punishment is pitiless.

The Afghans are afflicted with dreadful diseases, which, from their ignorance of medicine, they cannot mitigate; these maladies are owing to their bilious habit, the badness of their food, their extreme dirt, and the little care they take to prevent their development. The nomades are generally of a sickly complexion; this is to be attributed to the pernicious quality of the water, which is almost all alkaline. The diseases to which they are most subject are fevers, cutaneous and nervous disorders, and especially blindness. The last they attribute to the waters of the rice-fields, which they drink; but if this has any effect upon the eye, it is no doubt less injurious to that organ than the incredible treatment it often receives at the hands of their empirics: in fact, there is no country in the world in which diseases of the eye and loss of sight are more frequent than in Afghanistan. When the Afghans are bled they generally avoid drinking for twenty-four hours after; but if they do not do so, they keep the arm elevated as much as possible during absorption, in order that, as they say, the water may not fill up and mix with the remainder of the blood in the vein. They pretend also that, according to the quarter in which the wind sets, or this or that conjunction of the stars, they ought not to be bled in the same vein. They are very careful not to eat sweet food after sour, dressed after raw, or *vice versâ*. Rancid grease three or four years old is in their eyes more easy of digestion and more beneficial than fresh; the latter, which they obtain from the enormous tails of their sheep, they use only as aperient medicine, and, when melted, swallow four or six pounds of it at a time.

For the cure of wounds and abscesses they have but one receipt, but that they say is infallible—it is, to apply a piece of an old waterskin, resoftened by soaking, which they place on the part affected, either to heal or to draw it. There is, however, a schism amongst their doctors as to the treatment of wounds, some of them affirming that it is dangerous to wash them, and that the blood, or the matter, ought to be left to coagulate on the surface to reform the flesh.

The dressing of a broken bone they remove every three or four days; it consists of flour beaten up with the yolks of eggs, which they consider a specific for setting a dislocated or fractured limb. For fever they recommend cold baths, and, if possible, of iced water; they administer mercury internally, but in such quantities as generally to bring the most serious consequences upon the patient.

Every European is a doctor in the eyes of the Afghans, and they have a blind confidence in them: even when in perfect health they will ask for a medicine of some kind, and, be it what it may, will swallow it on the spot. "I am not ill," an Afghan will say, "but I may become so." They have no idea that there is any difference between one medicine and another; in their opinion they all ought to produce the same results.

To carry a Koran in procession, or to place it under their heads when they go to sleep; to repeat one thousand times the name of God or the Prophet Mahomet, are infallible means of curing any malady whatever. As they have a great dread of the Evil Eye, they cover themselves and their domestic animals with amulets. Some of the charlatans whom they look upon as doctors procure different European medicines from India, of the properties of which they are utterly ignorant, and give them without discrimination as to their nature or dose, whatever may be the disease they are prescribing for; in this manner they will kill fifty patients before they cure one. They win the confidence of these unfortunates by assuring them they have seen their disease in a dream, and that they are thoroughly acquainted with it and the remedy that will cure them. The wretched patients trust these liars implicitly; and instead of depending on the efforts of nature, which in many cases would triumph over the malady, they allow themselves to be killed with a resignation worthy of a better fate.

The munificence of the Persian, Tartar, and Indian monarchs has enriched Afghanistan with many fine buildings and works of public utility—mosques, caravanserais, reservoirs of water, &c., but they have long since been in ruins. The Afghans know not how to build, and destroy everything; one may travel whole months in their country without finding any other shelter than the tent of the nomade. At every step may be seen traces of edifices that must have been magnificent, but none have ever been repaired. Here or there the ground is strewed with rubbish; farther in the distance an aqueduct has fallen down, or a river, owing to the dilapidation of the dykes, has overflowed, and the waters, which, well-directed, would have been of immense advantage to the agriculturist, remain perfectly useless; but the people whose interests are most concerned are quite indifferent to the subject.

The roads, if the name can be given to paths made only by the continual passage of caravans, are traced at random over the country, and frequently turn miles out of the way to avoid some slight obstacle that might have been removed at very little cost of money or time; and often, simply owing to the want of a bridge, or even a ferry-boat, all traffic is interrupted for weeks.

The first families who establish themselves in a fertile spot for the purpose of cultivating it find their way to it by taking as direct a course as they can, but entirely by conjecture; their footsteps guide the next traveller, and the next, and there is soon a path. When the snow begins to melt, thirty or forty camels tied one after the other are led over it to trample it well, and the traces of their large feet never disappear. Such is the organisation of the *ponts et chaussées*, or roadmaking, in central Asia.

The same system seems to have been followed for ages in the construction of their houses; sun-dried bricks are the material ordinarily used, the rich have them burnt; up to the present period but little use has been made of hewn stone. The great scarcity of wood in this country has obliged the Afghans to build vaulted roofs, and, like the Persians, they excel in this art; nothing can be bolder or more graceful than the form of some of their cupolas.

They roughcast the wall with mud and chopped straw mixed; as there is little rain, this suffices to consolidate them, and, being neatly smoothed with a trowel, the effect is not unpleasant to the eye. The rich use plaster; and the Kandaharians especially decorate their rooms with great taste and talent. Their houses are generally low, rarely consisting of more than one floor, but they occupy a great space of ground; the inside is concealed from the gaze of the passer by, by a high wall which encircles the whole, and in which there is very rarely more than one entrance. An Afghan house is usually divided into several parts, each having its own rooms, kitchen, court, reservoir, garden, &c. They perfectly understand the distribution of the apartments, with regard to preserving them from the intense heat of the sun; but they are quite ignorant of any precautions against the cold, which is, however, never severe at Herat or Kandahar. Even a royal residence in these countries looks mean externally compared with an European house, and one is surprised to find in the interior every Asiatic comfort combined with much that is luxurious.

All over the East they make an exceedingly hard cement, which they use as mortar, and to form the lining of baths and reservoirs: it is made by some persons with equal parts of wood-ashes, thoroughly sifted, and powdered lime; and by some with two parts of lime to one of ashes; but in either case these materials are well mixed. Water is then poured upon them and they are well kneaded, after which the mass is beaten for six days by two men with large sticks, and uninterruptedly, except at night: when it becomes a little solid on one side, it is turned over and beaten on the other, care being taken to moisten it occasionally lest it should become too dry. When thus well mixed, it is folded and turned and beaten again and again till the sixth day, when it is ready for use. In building, this cement is laid between the bricks, which are tightly pressed upon each other; for lining it is laid upon the surface that is to be covered, and spread with a flat and polished flint, for it must not be touched with the hand, as it would burn. Three layers are put on successively, and the third is washed over with oil, but of what kind is immaterial; when it is dry nothing can equal the beauty and solidity of this cement, which is called *saroodj*. There is another description called *saroodj maghrebi*, but it is not so much used: this is composed of one third of hot lime, one of sifted sand, and one of pounded brick.

The domestic animals of Afghanistan are the camel, the ox-with-a-hump, the horse, the ass, and a few fine mules, goats and sheep, pigeons and fowls. The camels are of two sorts; those from Turkestan and the country of the Hazarahs are exceedingly large and strong, but not very active. Those from the Seistan are slenderly formed and wiry, but, though small, are as hardy an animal as can be found, and incredibly swift; they will travel five-and-twenty leagues in a day without feeling fatigue, and are never affected by the great heat of the sun; these are generally used for riding, and those of Turkestan as beasts of burden.

The ox is used in the plough, in the transport of goods, and, as a last resource, for food. The horses of Kandahar and Kabul are not particularly good, but at Herat, and amongst the Hazarahs, there are splendid animals, probably the finest and most capable of enduring fatigue in Central Asia. The Afghans take many of them to Shikapoor, where they are bought by the English for remounts for their cavalry, and particularly for the artillery.

Amongst the wild animals of Afghanistan are the royal tiger, the panther, bear, hyæna, wolf, wild boar, jackal, fox, polecat, and various kinds of rats; myriads of scorpions and reptiles swarm in the plains and mountains. Deer, the wild goat, and wild ass are seen in numbers of which it is difficult to form an idea; the gazelle is found only on the south bank of the Helmund. Hares, partridges, pheasants, bustards, indeed every variety of game and waterfowl are in abundance.

The soil of Afghanistan resembles that of the rest of the great table-land of Central Asia. Within the principality of Kabul and the northern part of that of Herat are high mountains covered with forests, having between them vast argillaceous plains well supplied with water, covered with fields, and susceptible of every species of cultivation; the portion south of Herat and Kandahar also consists of immense plains, but generally arid, running from East to West, and bordered by a chain of sterile mountains. The soil of these plains is sandy, and absorbs so much water as to create a great scarcity of that necessary of life within their limits, and the inhabitants are obliged to obtain by long and toilsome labour that which nature has denied them at the surface. They dig a deep hole at the foot of a mountain where they expect to find water, and, having succeeded, lead it to their villages by a subterranean canal connecting a series of wells. Experience is generally their only guide in performing these works, for very few of them understand anything of the art of taking levels; nevertheless, they rarely make a mistake.

Before a population resolve to undertake such a work, they must have found it impossible to select a spot near a natural stream which they could turn to purposes of cultivation. It requires much time and trouble to make these wells, or kariz, as they are called; and if the country unhappily becomes the theatre of war, the first operation of the invading army is to destroy them, and deprive the people they come to attack of their supply of water. It is to this unhappy mania of destructiveness, especially in this particular form, that the depopulation of Afghanistan is principally to be ascribed: immense tracts of country have in consequence been abandoned and become arid; they belong to no one—the land is valueless and cannot be sold; water only has a value, whether in a well or from a river led by conduits to the spot that it is required to fertilize. It is always part of a bargain that, whenever land can be irrigated by this water, the water shall belong to the purchaser.

Notwithstanding the bad quality of the soil in Kandahar, vegetable productions are extremely good and cheap. The Afghan plough is simply a piece of wood sharpened and hardened in the fire. The Afghans cultivate wheat, barley, maize, tobacco, cotton, and rice, sesamum, and palma-christi. The rice from Jellalabad is esteemed the best; and from the sesamum and palma-christi oil is expressed. Asafœtida is exported, but of the other crops they raise only enough for their consumption. They rear also a few silkworms.

All the fruits of Europe, excepting the gooseberry and strawberry, are found in Afghanistan, but the absence of these is amply compensated by the water-melon and the pomegranate. In Kandahar the latter are superior to those grown in any other part of Asia.

In the mountains of Afghanistan are found vast quantities of iron, lead, and sulphur; quicksilver abounds; also asbestos, which is called *singui pembe*. Gold and silver are washed down in many of the little streams; the mountains, therefore, contain much of the precious metals—but all this mineral wealth is useless, for the Afghans will not take the trouble to turn it to account.

Afghanistan lies between 32° and 36° of north latitude, and 60° and 68° of east longitude, and within this confined space the climate varies amazingly according to the locality—the heat or the cold is felt in different spots in the same latitude with very different degrees of intensity, according to the configuration of the country. By the side of plains, on which the sun darts his burning rays, are table-lands at a very high elevation, and gigantic mountains where summer and winter seem to stand side by side. At Herat, in the July of 1845, the Centigrade thermometer never stood higher than 37° in the shade, and that rarely; it more frequently ranged between 32° and 34°. From the commencement of May to the middle of September the wind blows constantly from the N.W. over this province, and often with such violence as to prostrate houses, uproot trees, and cause much devastation. The winter is tolerably mild; on the plain the snow melts as it falls, and does not lie long even on the summits of the mountains. Three years out of four it does not freeze hard enough for the inhabitants to store up any ice for the summer; in general the temperature is moderate, and the climate one of the most agreeable in Asia.

The province of Kandahar is everywhere subject to intense heat. In the fortress of Girishk, on the banks of the Helmund, in the month of August, the Centigrade thermometer stood at 48° or 49° in the shade. This principality is bounded on the S. by the deserts of moving sand of the Seistan, and is on this side open to violent winds, surcharged with exceedingly fine sand, which is very injurious to animal life.

For nine months the sun shines with the greatest possible splendour on Afghanistan, and the nights are even more beautiful than the days; travellers can journey in perfect safety by the brilliant starlight only. The atmosphere is, during the night, much charged with electricity, and the least friction will draw sparks from almost any object whatever, with a slight noise like the breaking of an osier twig.

The N.W. wind of the spring and summer is as violent in Kandahar as in Herat, but the winter is still milder; the mountains which bound it on the north attract much rain, but snow is rarely seen there, and then only in small quantities.

In Kabul the climate is very temperate in the summer, and it is delightful to reside there in that season; but during half the autumn, the winter, and half the spring, the ground is covered with snow three feet deep. The frost is constant and intense, and the roads are impassable for five months in the year.

That which has contributed more than the turbulence of the serdars and the rivalry of the tribes to break up the Afghan kingdom, and keep the three principalities separate, is the difficulty that has been always experienced by the Suddozye monarchs of marching from Kabul with sufficient promptitude upon any part that might be in a state of revolt. The extent of the Paropamisus, which is occupied by independent tribes, and is at any time difficult to pass through, always obliged them to make a long circuit with their armies to reach Herat. This occasioned a loss of time which the insurgents turned to their advantage by strengthening their position. It is difficult to determine the boundaries of the three Afghan principalities from each other in those parts where there is neither river nor mountain to fix them definitely: in such case the frontier of each is defined by an imaginary line which shall just include the ground on which a tribe subject to its power has planted its tents.

The population of Afghanistan is not in proportion to the extent of its territory, and the conditions which govern this question contribute powerfully to arrest its development, and even cause a sensible diminution of its numbers. The inhabitants withdraw more and more from the agitation and instability that reign there; a fourth part of its fighting men have either been killed or taken service in Persia or in India in consequence of the intestine or foreign wars with which Afghanistan has been afflicted.

There are two causes which make it very difficult to estimate the population of Afghanistan: first, the itinerant character of the nomadic portion of it, for the passion for change of place is pushed to the greatest extreme—a remark which sometimes applies even to the inhabitants of towns; secondly, the mountanious country of the Paropamisus is very imperfectly known, and this is specially inhabited by nomade tribes, of which it is impossible, even approximately, to ascertain the number.

The population of Afghanistan is divided into two very distinct parts: first, the Afghans, properly so called; secondly, the Tajiks, the descendants of the ancient conquerors of the country, and who may be subdivided into two classes—the Parsivans,* or inhabitants of the towns, and the Eimaks or nomades. The Afghans are at the present time the dominant race, and the Tajiks are subject to them both in Herat and Kandahar; nevertheless Yar Mohamed Khan has in the former city shown them great consideration, and permitted them to obtain an influence which may at some future time become fatal to the Afghans. At Kabul their superior numbers, their warlike instincts, and the fortified position which they occupy in that city, have obtained for them the same privileges as the Afghans; they share with them the appointments of the public service, and in the political troubles which often arise the party to which they give their support is very frequently triumphant.

The Kuzzilbashes or Persians established in Kabul by Nadir Shah, and numbering 12,000 families, hold to the Tajiks, to whom they assimilate in religion, both races being of the same sect, that is to say, Shiahs.

The following may be considered, but approximately only, as the amount of the population in Afghanistan.

In the province of Herat	300,000	Afghans, and	600,000	Parsivans or	Eimaks.
,, Kandahar	600,000	,,	300,000	,,	Belooches.
,, Kabul	1,600,000	,,	800,000	,,	and Kuzzilbashes.
Total	2,500,000		1,700,000		

General Total, 4,200,000 inhabitants.

* The meaning of which is, "speaking Persian."—*Ferrier.*

CHAPTER XXII.

Government of the Afghan provinces — Power of the Emirs — Influence of the priests — Turbulence of the serdars — Ideas of government — Conduct of public affairs — Stability of power unlikely to last — Mode of obtaining it — Character of the serdars — The producing classes — They cannot leave Kandahar — Clannish feelings — Mercenary qualities of the serdars — Fidelity of the troops never certain — The result of their numerous wars — The sovereign and the serdars — Superiority of the Mohamedzyes — The power of the Barukzyes — Probabilities of their retaining it — English marriages in Afghanistan — The Afghan army — Manner in which it is composed — The contingents easily assembled — Ignorant of military discipline, and insensible to its advantages — War a necessity — Cavalry numerous — Mode of fighting — Rights of individuals unknown — Construction of their towns — Tribes of the south — Strength of the Afghan army in each principality — Yar Mohamed's troops — Money — Prices of provisions — Wine—Weights and measures — The Parsivans — Mechanical arts — European manufactures — Taxation.

THE government of the Afghan provinces has somewhat of a monarchical character about it, nevertheless it is rather a military, aristocratic, and despotic republic, the dictator of which is established for life. The sovereign is absolute, and makes any and every change which may appear to him necessary or proper in the government or the administration; he can dispose of the lives and property of his subjects, and is kept within certain limits in these respects only by the calculations which prudence dictates. Religion is the counterpoise to his authority; this gives the clergy great influence, one that he might try in vain to subject to his will and pleasure; and vainer still would be the attempt to infringe and invade the rights and privileges of the serdars or chiefs of tribes, who would never consent to resign a certain influence in the affairs of government. It may be said that in Afghanistan there are as many sovereigns as serdars, for each of them governs after his own fashion; they are jealous, turbulent, and ambitious, and the sovereign can restrain and keep them in some order only by taking advantage of their rivalry and feuds and opposing one to the other. There is no unity, nothing is permanent, everything depends on the pleasure or caprice of a number of despots, always at variance with each other, making their tribes espouse their personal quarrels; a constant feeling of irascibility is the result, which finally leads to sanguinary civil wars, and throws the country into a state of anarchy and perpetual confusion.

In Europe civilization has regulated everything; the majority of her citizens are devoted to science, the arts, industry, and commerce, which enrich and conduce to the well-being of the nations, and ameliorate the habits and condition of the people: when war bursts forth only a very small portion of the population arm for the defence of the country, and this supplies all the wants of the army, which is an element of order and security—the government, in short, is the guardian and watches over the interests of the nation for the general good. But in Afghanistan the ideas and object of the government and the governed are wholly different; there each man thinks only of destruction and disorganization; it is who shall labour least, or who shall enrich himself the most, and by the most culpable means. The depositaries of power, instead of leading those under them in the right path, instead of giving them, by their own conduct, a good example, and ameliorating the condition of the people, load them with exactions and enrich themselves at their cost.

This system of spoliation and embezzlement is practised by functionaries of every class, and has a sad effect upon the minds of the masses, who follow the example of their superiors: seeing that the great, instead of occupying themselves with their welfare, only think of enjoying themselves at their expense, they become egotistical and avaricious in their turn, and prefer idleness to an industry, which serves only to benefit their oppressors, and draws upon themselves additional persecution. To seize without ceremony upon the property of other people is an example which the Afghans receive daily from their chiefs, and it appears to them a practice both convenient and just; the effect of this is a permanent state of disquietude and trouble. They are, as I have already remarked, the most turbulent nation in Asia, and the most difficult to govern: they always welcome, and with enthusiasm, the arrival of a new sovereign, but a reign too long, or a peace too prolonged with their neighbours, is to them insupportable; and when no opportunity presents itself of getting rid of their over-excitement on their foes without, they make war upon one another.

If courage is to them the first of virtues, it may be said also that agitation is for them a first necessity; thus scenes of violence arise which produce a change of government, and with it a change of sovereigns, with inconceivable rapidity. He who possesses a little money and can scatter it amongst the crowd will soon have a sufficient number of partizans to assist in raising him to power; and though this power is hereditary in Afghanistan, the regular succession to the throne is by no means liked and is the most uncertain thing possible. The legitimate heir is always obliged to submit the question of sovereignty to an election and the chances of war; the result is rarely doubtful, and has always favoured the candidate who paid the soldiers best that adhered to his fortunes; hence it is that one sees so many obscure adventurers, enriched by *razzias*, suddenly elevated to the supreme authority. These have, for the most part, been little better than avaricious and sanguinary tyrants, who are overthrown almost as soon as they are set up. In Afghanistan everything that succeeds is legitimate, and in this way success favours the greatest rascal; his crimes or his virtues are of little importance to the people; if he pays well he is their idol; but let his purse get empty, let a reverse of fortune overtake him, he at once becomes an object of contempt and aversion, and is obliged either to expatriate himself or retire into a greater obscurity than that from which he sprung.

Afghanistan is of all countries in the world that in which a man's position is the most uncertain; a serdar to-day wealthy and powerful will to-morrow be despoiled of everything he is possessed of, and be reduced to serve, and in a subordinate rank, those who, till then, had obeyed his smallest wish. The members of his family will be dispersed and reduced to the greatest privations, and hence it is that in this country are seen so many nobles in rags. There are hundreds of khans who take service as private soldiers, and even servants of the lowest grade; but no matter what may be the misery, degradation, or adversity to which they are reduced, they are always wonderfully vain of their birth, and their aristocratic pride is sure to pierce through their plebeian garb.

The sovereigns of Afghanistan bestow every kind of title with a prodigal hand, and that of khan so much so, and upon such perfect nobodies, that it has completely lost the consideration properly due to it. The chance which every energetic man has of rising to power, even the highest, and the facility with which he attains it, has established between the people, the serdars, and the sovereign, a species of familiarity which is seen in no other country. Individuals of the lowest birth and class, clad in rags and covered with vermin, take whatever complaints they may have in person to the king; they approach and seat themselves before him without ceremony, enter at once and without preamble into their story, and with that easy nonchalant air which is so characteristic of Afghan human nature. The sovereign sees, receives, and discusses every petition even on the most insignificant subjects, and his minister, when he has one, generally speaking, merely gives effect to the decisions of his master.

As the Afghan chiefs are never sure of holding for a lengthened period any great appointment in the state, their first thought is always how they can fill their own coffers and ruin the country; however great and politic, and of future advantage, any measure may appear, they will always sacrifice it to the most trifling present benefit, no matter how small. Another mode of enriching themselves is putting up the public offices for sale to the highest bidder, and the purchasers then consider that they are justified in committing every kind of fraud to reimburse themselves the sums they have paid. Individual liberty exists nowhere in the East so perfect as in Afghanistan; every Afghan can go where he thinks fit; he can leave the kingdom with his family if he wishes, neither authority nor passport is required to enable him to do so, no one has a right to interfere with or restrain him; the sovereign certainly would not, for an Afghan is a very unproductive article, which consumes much and produces nothing: but this is not the case either with the Parsivans or the Hindoos, settled in the country, who form the industrial and producing class. They, especially those in Kandahar, are retained in the principality against their wishes, and are severely punished when they attempt to leave it. It cannot be said that there is, as we understand it in Europe, any national spirit amongst the Afghans; they fight much more for their own interests than for their independence; there is, nevertheless, something which resembles it, though not commonly felt: this is a sentiment of affection for, or a jealous pride in, his own tribe, which makes a man detest the neighbouring one, though of the same race: it may be affirmed, therefore, that every tribe of Afghans has its own clannish feeling, and it is that which protects the nation; interest alone effects a passing unity of purpose, and when that is satisfied the rivalries of different castes and clans re-assume their sway.

The serdars are at one and the same time the strength and the curse of the monarch; prompt to take arms and defend him when a good understanding exists between them, they are as ready to revolt against him when they find, or think, they have the smallest interest in doing so; in anything, however, to which they are disinclined, they would not obey even the sovereign of their choice but with reluctance; moreover, they are always impatient to see him replaced by another, from whom they hope to obtain greater advantages. Each subdivision of a tribe is, according to its numerical force and extent of territory, commanded by one or more serdars. These chiefs, though of a different country and religion, may be compared to the dukes and barons of the middle ages in France—the more powerful to the knights bannerets, and those having authority over only a few families to the esquires—who in time of war enrol themselves and their men under the orders of the chief that inspires them with the greatest confidence, and can pay them the best. They have also the characteristic which was common to the old Italian condottieri, namely, that they will sell their services to the highest bidder. In war, as in peace, they are ready to pass from the ranks of the Emir of Kabul into the service of the Vizier of Herat, the chief of Kandahar, the English, the Persians, Sikhs, Tartars, or Belooches, and vice versâ, without the slightest scruple; it is indifferent to them whether their friend of to-day is their enemy to-morrow, or whether they have even to take arms against their relations or not; the love of money enables them to overlook all these considerations. The soldiers imitate on a small scale that which their chiefs do on a large one, that is to say, they will desert one party and attach themselves to another, without feeling any compunction or incurring the least disgrace; the question is simply one of speculation, an admitted custom, and there is no shame in conforming to it.

The consequence of this is that a sovereign is never sure of his troops, and, if any one else will give them higher pay or treat them better than he can, they will pass over to his camp. The authority of the chiefs of tribes is much more effectual over their subordinates, whom they sometimes rule with a rod of iron; these consider the chief as their father, and are accustomed to obey and respect him from their infancy; he is of the same clan as themselves, he has received his power and authority through a long line of ancestors; but these reasons nevertheless cannot always save him from ruin; it requires very little to excite discontent; then he is attacked, followed, and driven forth, and his right to govern, such as it is, passes to a brother, an uncle, or some collateral branch, to any one, in short, so that the feudal rights remain in the family.

The wars that have reddened the soil of Afghanistan for the last seventy years have so completely decimated the old families that many of them have become extinct, and several tribes have remained without a head. On some occasions, when the sovereign has tried to give them a chief of his choice, instead of one of their own, some dreadful and bloody conflict has ensued, which has always ended in the triumph of the chief elected by the tribe. This resistance is natural enough. To accept a leader who was imposed upon them would be to abdicate their rights, to deliver themselves up to the tender mercies of the prince; whereas, he who holds the command by right of election defends his position and privileges with greater tenacity, no matter who may be the individual who attacks him.

The visits of the serdars at the court of the sovereign are rare, for they are generally apprehensive of falling into some trap which is often laid for them, and they dislike the prolonged stay they are obliged to make when once they are there. They prefer residing amongst their tribe, in their fortified villages, generally occupying some eminence, where in case of attack they can the more readily and continuously resist the efforts of their enemies. The most powerful amongst them are caressed by the sovereign, who attaches them to his interests much more by the concessions he makes than by the fear which he inspires; ordinarily, and with a view to preserve a nominal authority over them, he remits the whole of the taxes, and imposes in their stead the obligation to furnish a contingent of troops in the event of war being declared against him by his neighbours. This wretched system gives too much power to the serdars; the sovereign is at their mercy, and it is the ambition of these men that gives birth to the numerous civil wars in Afghanistan, for they are constantly in revolt.

It has been shown in the course of their history to what an extent they carried their excesses under the dynasty of the Suddozyes; if they have not as often deposed and recalled the

Mohamedzyes, it is because that family is as it were an exception to the Afghans in general, and those who compose it are men of superior intelligence and energy of character. They have also an ascendancy over the other chiefs, and know how to control them by the divisions which they so adroitly excite and maintain amongst them, and by settling or encamping the tribe of the Barukzyes, to which the Mohamedzyes belong, in the plains and valleys that, lying south of Kandahar, reach as far as Ghuznee. This central position enables them to move their forces rapidly to any particular spot, and suppress all revolts with alacrity and vigour, and being numerically stronger they control the other tribes. Many of these they have broken up into sections or dispersed, in order to make it almost impossible that they should render mutual assistance to each other, and they thus hold them in check with greater facility. The clan of which the sovereign is a member always enjoys the greatest privileges and advantages over the rest, and this is one of the reasons why each tribe is continually agitating and endeavouring to raise its chief to power.

The princes actually reigning in Afghanistan have up to this time repressed with as much good fortune as severity the revolts that have taken place in their states; but though this has enabled them to hold the reins of government for many years, we must not imagine that the Mohamedzyes have stifled the spirit of rebellion, which is as much a necessity in the Afghan character as the effect of a vicious social organization; the Barukzyes may be overthrown to-morrow, they live on from day to day in a precarious position, and their fate is dependent on the caprices of fortune and the good pleasure of their enemies. Burnes has affirmed that Dost Mohamed is held in veneration by the Afghans, and that he is the first sovereign who made them understand the sweets of peace, and introduced abundance and security amongst them; but how did they treat him when the hour arrived for them to show their gratitude? this chief was abandoned for Shah Shooja, for whom they had still less consideration. The English took possession of Kabul without meeting with any serious resistance on their march; and in spite of what has been said, and what might still be said, I affirm and assert that they were then received with acclamations and protestations of friendship and devotion without the least solicitation on their part, and this from chiefs who subsequently declared them to be their enemies. Then, as now, the serdars were men of bad faith: they expected and hoped for gold; as long as they were given any they accepted it and said nothing; their consciences were dead within them, even the bigoted feeling of fanaticism was hushed in their breasts; the husband sold the honour of his wife, the father that of his daughter, the brother that of his sister, and one saw a circumstance till then unheard of, a number of Englishmen, Christians, become the legitimate husbands of Afghan women who professed the faith of Islam. Money had made these savage Afghans as tame and submissive as sheep, but directly the order was given by the East India Company to reduce the subsidies which had been paid to them, turbulence and fanaticism returned at once; the salaries and donations which they received after this reduction were even then much higher than those they obtained from their own sovereigns, but in this, as in all other circumstances, their avarice, their unstable, restless, and fickle character, brought about the insurrection which re-established the power of the Emir Dost Mohamed in Kabul and that of Kohendil Khan in Kandahar. Their return was celebrated with every circumstance of pomp by their subjects, and yet how often since that period have they not revolted against these chiefs! They will, as they have already done before, turn their backs on them on the first occasion; and if these princes have the good fortune to terminate their troubled lives in power, it is all that in common reason they can expect. It will be impossible either for them, or Yar Mohamed Khan of Herat to establish a dynasty, the foundations of which shall be sufficiently solid to enable them to transmit it with any degree of certainty to their legitimate heirs; the sovereignty in this country exists only on considerations purely individual,—it is frequently brought to a close with the life of the possessor, and becomes afterwards the appanage of some bold adventurer or soldier of fortune.

The Afghan army might in case of necessity consist of the whole male population, for every man is born a soldier, and attaches himself to some chief as soon as he can hold a musket. As the troops have no regular pay, and during their period of service generally speaking live on plunder, it is difficult to say which is the most disastrous to the people, its own army or that of a foreign enemy, for both one and the other abandon themselves to all kinds of excesses, devastate the country, and leave behind the most fearful traces of their passage; ordinarily speaking, the strength of the army of each principality is dependent on the probabilities that exist of maintaining it in the district to which it is going.

At the first news of war the serdars hasten with their several contingents to the camp of the sovereign, each bringing with him the number of men in proportion to the nature and importance of his command. These contingents united form the army, properly so called; but in addition to it is another class of combatants, which, though not the best, are often the most numerous; such, for instance, as the inhabitants of towns, who are not attached to any chief, individuals who make war on their own account and at their own expense, solely for the pleasure of making it, and in the hope of obtaining large booty. It sometimes happens that these irregulars unite in parties, or all together, and elect a chief, or chiefs, under whose command they place themselves; but more often they are broken up into small detachments of friends or acquaintances coming from the same locality, associated together, and intending to share in the profits of the enterprise; they march after their own fashion, and without order, regulating their proceedings according to the movements of the army, or leaving it when it suits their views and convenience. These elements united, or sometimes disunited, form an Afghan army, if one can give such a name to a collection of men, animals, and followers marching pell-mell, and in the greatest confusion. It requires only a few days for the serdars to assemble their contingents, for every man of the tribe is always ready to mount his horse, and each of them carries his provisions with him in a kind of *havresac*, which is slung behind the saddle. The Afghans, such parasites and sponges when at home, are exceedingly frugal and temperate when they are on a journey; their powers of abstinence and endurance are great, and they can live almost upon anything and for a long time; the chiefs, and those whose means enable them to do so, are accompanied by so many servants for their personal requirements, or to look after the baggage, that during the whole of the operations they generally exceed in number those of the fighting men. All these form a mixed and noisy rabble, undisciplined and impracticable, badly equipped, and taking no precautions necessary to their own security, whether on the march or in camp, even when in presence of the enemy. Nevertheless, though in this miserable and confused state, the army moves with great rapidity and over immense distances: the inhabitants of the villages fly at their approach, for they destroy and pillage everything that lies on their road. Sometimes a dearth of provisions is felt in the camp, when the majority of the volunteers quit the army and return to their homes; the serdars, who carry with them only food enough for their personal wants, are also obliged to disband successive portions of their contingents to obtain supplies, so that it often happens that only a fourth, and even a less number, are all that remain with their colours. When war takes place between the Afghans themselves, it generally ends in a combat in which a very small force is engaged on either side.

In the field, the Afghans never think of ascertaining what is going on in their front on the line of march; they form neither advanced nor rear guards, but move straight on without the least uneasiness or apprehension until they meet the enemy; it matters little to them whether or not their communications are left open; the spot on which they find their subsistence is for them the line of operations; they pitch their camp by hap-hazard, without system or order, at the first place they come to, but by preference near villages, which they can plunder, and where they are also sure to find water. As this is in some parts very scarce, and to be found only at certain points well known to all, it often occurs that the various contingents marching in several columns, finding the springs or wells near which they intended to encamp exhausted, retire upon the adjoining ones, but the ground is often occupied, and a bloody conflict is the result, when the strongest party remains in possession of the springs, and the other has to continue its search elsewhere. In the camp each contingent forms an irregular circle, the baggage and the chief's tent being in the centre. The mass of the Afghan army is composed of cavalry, and the national character, and the nature of the climate and soil, are the principal reasons that lead them to prefer this arm to infantry, which, excepting in the mountains north of Kabul, is held in little estimation amongst them: there the country is difficult and the climate temperate, but in the other parts of Afghanistan the people do not fancy traversing on foot miles and miles of desert plains, under a burning sun, and where water is scarce. With a little forethought and arrangement these obstacles would readily and promptly be overcome, but this is not the country in which people care to overcome difficulties: anything that is easy of execution and can be effected in a brief space of time is much more to their taste.

The love of war is felt much more amongst Afghans than all other Eastern nations; nevertheless, in no one instance has so little desire been shown to augment the means of resistance and aggression. War to them is a trade, for it would be impossible to give the name of science to the thousand absurd proceedings which they employ, and which prove that their chiefs are completely ignorant of the first elements of the art. The reason of their success against the other Asiatic hordes up to this day has been their *élan* in the attack, their courage, but not any clever dispositions or a knowledge of military operations; their neighbours the Sikhs, previously subject to them, defeated the Afghans and seized some of the most valuable provinces in their territory, directly they had obtained even a partial knowledge of European tactics. It cannot be denied that the Afghans are excellent skirmishers and experienced foragers, for they possess the necessary qualifications in a much greater degree than Europeans. They are perfectly independent in their manœuvres, each detachment fighting after its own devices, unrestrained by any subordination and discipline, those who command them not being any wiser than themselves. Their instinct tells them what movement will ensure their safety under defeat, or will tend to their advantage in victory. European soldiers would certainly effect as much as they could under the same circumstances; but then they are subject to regular discipline, directed by one impulse, the majority of them confiding in the talents of their chiefs, so that their courage is limited within proper bounds, out of which they cannot step without compromising their discipline, or sometimes endangering the lives of their comrades.

For the theatre of combat between their armies the Afghans always select large plains, in order that their numerous cavalry, on which they place a blind reliance, may be able to deploy freely; if they could charge regularly and in line it would be perhaps the finest cavalry in the world. The sword is their favourite arm, and when they say of any one "chemchiri adam est" (that man is a swordsman) they have paid him the most flattering compliment. They have no idea of the advantages of position, or estimating in a military sense the features of the ground; in their eyes the shortest road is the best; they never seek to turn a position or to make a diversion; they always attack in line parallel to that of the enemy and on all points at once, taking, in the words of the proverb, "the bull by the horns." Before they encounter their adversary, however, they endeavour to weaken him by ruining the country in his front, so that he cannot maintain himself; they burn the villages, expel the inhabitants, destroy the aqueducts; and after he has wandered for days in the desert they have made, panting with thirst and extenuated by hunger, they pounce upon their enemy like a tiger and make a horrible massacre. Strategy and tactics are unknown to them, and not even by compulsion could they be initiated in these powerful agents in obtaining victory. They will have independence of action, opportunities of displaying their address and their physical strength; they place the triumph of individual courage far above that of science, and reject every idea of combination and unity in their movements. But this impulsive ardour, this daring bravery, of which they were so proud, slackened when they had to meet the British, whose artillery cleverly served, and infantry squares solid as walls, made fearful havoc in their squadrons. The artillery especially, that terrible arm in the hands of Europeans, inspires them with no less aversion than it did formerly Montluc or the Chevalier Bayard, the first of whom looked upon it as an invention of the devil, and the second said it was a shame that a brave man should be exposed to die by such a miserable device.

Against cannon the Afghans feel that they cannot trust to the prowess which they value so highly. Their valour is incontestable, but their presumption is greater; they never cease to boast, and are constantly repeating that, if other nations were, like themselves, armed only with the sword, they could give laws to the world. When they attack they utter loud cries, and the most courageous place themselves in front; the rest form a second or third line, more or less distant from the first, according to the degree of ardour they may possess. These are ready to rush forward and plunder if their comrades in advance are victorious, or to run away if they are beaten. The chiefs are far more intent upon signalizing their personal courage than upon directing their troops, who are not under any control when they have been a short time in action. The Afghans never disband until they have failed in three charges successively, but after that it becomes impossible to rally them, because they believe that *talleh*, fate, is against them, and that they would offend God by longer opposing his decrees.

But if they gain the day, woe indeed to the conquered! for an Afghan ceases not from slaughter till his arm is wearied with striking; till then there is no quarter from him, and a hundred times better is it to die on the field than survive to be his slave, certain of the hardest possible toil and the most inhuman treatment: a large ransom is the only chance of liberty. In time of war the Afghans carry on their communications by signal fires on the mountains, the information they are to afford being intimated by their numbers and position, and the length of time they burn.

They have no idea of the rights of individuals, nor any regard for public opinion, or fear of reprisals. To express any humane or generous sentiments after a victory is in their eyes the greatest weakness; and if they have lost the ideas they first formed of the power of the British, it is not because they evacuated the country, but because they did not, before they left it, convert it into a vast desert, deluged with the blood of the inhabitants.

In the Afghans enthusiasm and impulse are not the result of noble sentiments, and but rarely of fanaticism; they are excited by the hope of pillage, or even, like the tiger, for the plain and simple purpose of satisfying their ferocious instincts. Nothing is more natural, in their eyes, than to seize upon a neighbouring state, even upon that of an ally, without having received the slightest provocation; force, the last argument of a nation who respects itself, is with them the first and only one, and justifies all their actions.

Though they are entirely ignorant of the art of attack and defence of towns and fortresses, the Afghans are remarkable for the obstinacy of their resistance and the correctness of their aim when they are behind walls. When they are the assailants they always attack, suddenly, by escalade, surprise, or stratagem, but very seldom succeed. It is by long blockade or treachery, or more often by lying and false oaths, that they possess themselves of a fortified place.

The majority of their towns are square, but more or less perfect in their form, enclosed by one very thick and high wall of earth, embattled and loopholed, and having a banquette within, on which two men, at most, can walk side by side: at intervals are placed small hollow towers; those at the angles being larger, solid, and constructed for artillery. The ditch which surrounds the enceinte is flooded in time of war whenever water can be obtained. The gates are strengthened with large nails and bands of iron, and to give them greater security there is a portcullis with loopholes above it to defend the approach. A great proportion of the villages in Kandahar and Herat are, like the towns, enclosed with mud walls of about 12 or 15 feet in height, and 4 in thickness at the base, but narrower at the top; they are seldom protected by a ditch, and in some instances there are no turrets except at the angles. These defences would be inefficient against artillery well served, but they are all that is required to sustain the mode of attack customary in the country; however, the climate being so very hot and rain so very infrequent, the walls are of considerable solidity, and are difficult to destroy with artillery only,—the mine is indispensable for effecting a practicable breach.

These remarks apply to the towns and villages situated in the plains of Kabul, but not to those in the mountains, which are constructed in positions defended by nature.

The inaptitude of this nation for discipline and military organisation arises from their spirit of impatience under the slightest idea of restraint; and to this feeling their religion contributes, for they are taught to believe that, having proclaimed Djehad, Holy War, the numerous battalions of the Infidels are powerless against a handful of the Ghazees, or soldiers of the Faith. The climate and nature of the soil have also a great influence on the warlike habits of the Afghans. The tribes of the south are less quarrelsome and less able to support the fatigues of warfare than those of the north; and those who inhabit the southern banks of the Helmund are considered by all the others as an effeminate race. There is more than one instance of this pernicious influence of climate upon the human character, and not the least remarkable one is, that the Roman legions gradually lost their manly courage as they carried their conquests eastward.

The arms of the Afghans are the firelock, the carbine, the swivel-gun, or a pair of bad pistols; sometimes a bow, or a lance with a bamboo handle. The fire-arms are coarse and heavy, the hammers of the locks being very defective; most of the barrels are Turkish, and rifled. They also carry a shield, a foot and a half in diameter, covered with copper, or the hide of either the elephant or the horse, which is very hard.

The whole Afghan army consists of the three divisions of

Kabul, Kandahar, and Herat; of these, the troops called Defteris,* present the following effective force:—

KABUL	15,000	Afghan Horse.
	6,000	Parsivan or Kuzzilbash Horse.
	6,000	Afghan Mountaineers, Infantry.
	4,000	Parsivans, Hazarahs, or Usbeks, Infantry.
Total	31,000	

Mohamed Akbar Khan, son of the Emir, Dost Mohamed, perceived the great advantages which order and discipline gave to the British army, and, as soon as he had in some degree established his power, he attempted to train the Afghan cavalry to move in squadrons—but all his efforts failed against the power of habit. He was more successful with two battalions of Parsivans, who were not so intractable as the Afghans under the discipline that he introduced. These battalions, as it is said, manœuvred badly enough; they were drilled by an Englishman of the name of Kervel, who, having been wounded and made prisoner at the time of the disasters in Kabul in 1841, became a Mussulman, and entered the service of Dost Mohamed.

In KANDAHAR there are	12,000	Afghan Horse.
	3,000	Afghan Infantry.
	3,000	Belooch Infantry.
Total	18,000	

In 1833 Kohendil Khan, sovereign of this principality, obtained the assistance of a few Europeans to instruct and organize his army, and after five years of continued exertion they succeeded in bringing into some slight degree of discipline, such as it was, about 2000 Afghan infantry. In 1838, when Mohamed Sedik Khan advanced to Subzawar with the intention of taking Herat, these battalions met the enemy for the first time, but after one volley was given their natural instinct of self-dependence was at once in the ascendant; every man left the ranks, forgetting all he had learnt, and fought independently, the orders of the officers being drowned in tumult and confusion.

Kabul and Kandahar have also a few pieces of artillery, served by Afghans, who learned, to a certain extent, how to serve them during the occupation of Afghanistan by the British.

* Which receive pay.—*Ferrier.*

In HERAT the army consists of	8,000	Afghan Horse.
	4,000	Hazarah Horse.
	10,000	Parsivan Infantry.
Total	22,000	

Of the three Afghan princes the Vizier Yar Mohamed Khan is the one who has placed the most confidence in his infantry, and he persists in keeping up this arm; notwithstanding the little favour with which it is viewed by the people, he has succeeded in forming eight battalions of 1000 men each. He accomplished this with the assistance of a Hindoo Mussulman, who had been a sergeant in the East India Company's service; this man arrived at Herat in 1829, and was killed in the last campaign which the Vizier undertook against the Hazarahs in 1847. In the organization and drill of these battalions there was much room for improvement, but they have done pretty good service. The Vizier, finding the Afghans ill adapted for making disciplined soldiers, recruited these corps from the Parsivans exclusively, and this released him from the exactions of the serdars of his principality, whom he managed with so much tact that he made it impossible for them to injure or even to disobey him. But if this plan had its advantages it had also its evils, for by it Yar Mohamed committed the same fault that Marius did when he received slaves and freedmen into the Roman army, and he prepared the way for much future embarrassment in Herat. The Parsivans are the conquered race, and their number is double that of the Afghans; by putting arms in their hands, which they know how to use, Yar Mohamed Khan has restored to them their prestige and power. Any other chief but him would have already paid dearly for this imprudence, but his policy has been so clever that he attached to himself by the ties of gratitude a race that till then had never borne, but with impatience, the yoke of their cruel oppressors. It is probable that so long as he lives these battalions of Parsivan infantry will always be faithful to him, and give him their staunch support; but his vigilance is unequalled, and he always foresees, and with rare talent provides against, eventualities that might be fatal to him.

The ordnance of the Vizier is composed of sixteen pieces of artillery, 6, 8, and 12-pounders, which are served by the infantry, who make but poor artillerymen.

In the three Afghan principalities the chiefs are too numerous in proportion to the number of the troops they command, and that is particularly the case in Herat. The Vizier is aware of this, but could not avoid recompensing the brave soldiers who so valiantly fought the army of Mohamed Shah, and afterwards supported him against Shah Kamran. Hence the superabundance of officers, even then but poorly rewarded, and having no permanent command.

The pay of the contingents is given to the serdars by the sovereign and is never fixed: it varies according to the influence these chiefs possess, and the number of men they can bring into the field. The tax due to the state is deducted from the pay when the serdar receives it, but it is rarely they distribute the whole to their soldiers—more than half remains in their own hands, and they indemnify the men by small grants of land, right of pasturage, permission to work at a trade, *et cetera*, and no notice is taken. Each Afghan is obliged to furnish his arms and horse at his own expense, for which reason they always take great care of them.

The princes of Afghanistan have not coined gold pieces; those which are current in that country are the ducat of Russia and the tellah of Bokhara. The gold tomaun and the silver *kran* of Persia are also in circulation, but at a depreciation of a tenth of their value, whereas that of the ducat and tellah is augmented in the same proportion. Small silver coins called *djindek* are struck at Herat, in value about fourpence; and at Kandahar rupees, also of silver, and of the value of a shilling. At Kabul the rupee is worth two shillings.

There are two fictitious light coins current in the three principal cities, called *chahee* and *abbasee*; two chahees make one abbasee, and two abbasees a djindek or fourpence; there are three Herat djindeks in the Kandahar rupee, and two rupees of Kandahar to one of Kabul. Fractions of the chahee and abbasee are represented by a copper coin called *poul* or *päiseh*: its value is never fixed, and varies according to the abundance or scarcity that exists in the market at the time. This value is determined every three months by the sovereign on the report made to him by the chief agent of police and the five principal merchants, who previous to the audience consult their fellow merchants of the locality on the subject. There are from three to five pouls in a chahee according to circumstances, but this copper coin has no currency except in the towns, where it is compulsory to receive it. The country-people will not take it, or sell their provisions to the caravans and travellers, unless they obtain in exchange a piece of coarse cotton cloth manufactured in the country, called *kerbas*, with which they make their clothes. They will not even receive silver money; and if the purchaser has no cloth he must present them with some article that will be useful to them; in the way of food there are only two things which they inquire for, viz. tea and sugar.

In a country where the inhabitants are so idle and poor, every article naturally sells at a very low price; a man may live for two pence a day. The following is the current value of the under-mentioned articles of first necessity in Afghanistan in the year 1845.

		s.	d.			s.	d.
Bread ..	the *men* of Herat *	0	1½	Salt	the men	0	0¼
Mutton	,,	0	4½	Tobacco	,,	1	0
Butter and fat	,,	1	1	Wheat	200 lbs.	2	1
Milk of various kinds	,,	0	1	Barley	,,	1	8
Fruit	,,	0	1	Indian corn	,,	1	0
Rice	,,	0	2½	Wine	a battemen	0	5

It is strictly forbidden to make or drink wine at Kabul and Kandahar; at Herat the contrary is the case, where Yar Mohamed has monopolized the right to make it, and this has brought him in a considerable profit by farming that right at a very high price to others. As to the consumption of it, he is one of the greatest wine-bibbers in that city or the principality.

Everything, whether solid or liquid, is sold by weight in Afghanistan; the one which is generally used is the *men* or battemen of Herat, which, as I have just stated, is of the weight of seven pounds. This is divided into 40 *sirs*, the sir into 20 *miscales*, and the miscale into 24 *nookoods*.

Cloth and manufactured articles are measured by the *guez*, which is 3 ft. 3⅜ in. It is divided into 16 *guireh* or knots, and one of these is subdivided into 4 *nokteh* or points. Though this is the only measure sanctioned by the government, it is rare that an Afghan will purchase cloth in the bazaar unless it is measured from the hand to the elbow, and more especially by his own, that is to say, from the elbow to the very extremity of the middle finger.

The Afghans who take any part in commercial affairs are very few in number; they are principally the *Babees*, who live to the south of Kandahar; the rest never occupy themselves in this way

* The *men* of Herat is seven pounds English—that of Persia is only six, and divided in the same manner as the *men* of Afghanistan; but the *sir* is less, and weighs only sixteen *nookoods*.—*Ferrier*.

or in any branch of industry; they have in fact the greatest repugnance to every kind of occupation, and are only qualified either to make war or to plunder.

Those who inhabit the towns are habitually in the employ of their wealthy countrymen, and the nomades or country people who have pasture or arable land never farm this themselves. Directly an Afghan receives a concession of land from his chief, he places it and a few oxen in the charge of a Parsivan, who tills, sows, and reaps it for him, and when the crops are housed he has a third of the produce for his trouble; if they have flocks, the Parsivan is in like manner the shepherd; and if the Afghan is overtaken by poverty, he procures as best he can a horse and arms, and sets out to plunder his neighbours. The Parsivans in the towns as well as in the villages are, as we have already stated, the industrial class; all commercial affairs are in their hands, all manufactures; in a word, it is their activity and intelligence that support the country and those who govern it. The Afghans are incapable of imitating them; they know only how to fight, and live from hand to mouth, rarely making a competency when they have no public appointment; but once invested with the least power, they enrich themselves by every species of exaction.

To the Parsivans must be added some few Hindoos, as forming part of the commercial and industrious class, who are attracted to the Afghan towns by the hope of gain; they are here what the Jews are elsewhere, always ready to enter into commercial transactions, and evincing like the Israelites the same intelligence and activity in all their operations, displaying the same poverty-stricken appearance, and affecting great simplicity in their dress. Everything about them denotes the greatest humility, which does not however protect them from the contempt of the Afghans. Nevertheless, that does not give them much concern, and they console themselves if it does by filling their strong box with Russian ducats or Bokhara tellahs, and some of them are immensely rich. They are considered extremely honest in all business transactions, exact in fulfilling their engagements, and devoted to those to whom they have once attached themselves. The very few Afghan merchants that are met with are, generally speaking, Syuds or descendants of the Prophet, who will not profane their holy origin by serving any master. These are especially employed in the somewhat unsaintly occupation of horse-dealing with the Hazarahs and

Turkomans. They take these horses to Shikapoor, and return from that town with English goods to Afghanistan. Their title of Syud smooths all the difficulties of their journeys, for they are venerated by the tribes, even those most addicted to pillage. It would be hazardous for Parsivans and Hindoos to undertake similar expedtiions and embark in an import and export trade, for they would be stripped before they had traversed half the road between Kandahar and the Indus, they employ therefore these Syuds as their agents.

The mechanical arts of indispensable utility are but imperfectly known in Afghanistan: they manufacture inferior sabres, glass, delf, coarse cloths of goats' hair, called *kourk*, and others of camels' hair, called *barek*, of which they make their robes and cloaks, and export a pretty large quantity to Turkestan and Persia. The kerbas, or coarse cotton cloth, is their principal article of manufacture, and with it they make their shirts and trousers. At Herat, and there only, they raise and weave a little silk of a light texture, and dye it of a red colour: the women's chemises are made of this. A thick cloth, manufactured from the long coarse hair of the camel and goat, is used by the nomades for their tents. Masonry, and carpenters' or joiners' work are pretty generally understood in this country; they also work tolerably well in leather; and sheep-skins, with the wool on, are beautifully dressed at Kabul. This is done with considerable art, and the cloaks made with these skins, which are very handsome, have a great reputation all over Central Asia. It appears that their superior quality is to be attributed to the fact of their being prepared with the rind of the pomegranate, a fruit which grows with peculiar luxuriance near that city: workmen, who have established themselves at Kandahar, and at Herat, have not been able to obtain the same results with the pomegranates grown in those provinces as they did with the fruit of their native city.

The Afghans purchase in Persia, Turkestan, and more especially in India, a number of articles of European manufacture, which they cannot do without, and which are not produced even in small quantities in their own country. Amongst these the following may be mentioned—metals, silk goods, cloth, muslins, woollen and cotton goods, particularly the latter, which they purchase in very large quantities, the lower and middle classes wearing scarcely anything else. Fowling-pieces and watches would find a ready sale in Afghanistan; those that I saw there were generally speaking of French manufacture, and more in demand than the same articles of English make. Delf, cutlery, spectacles, rich and heavy silk goods, woollen or cotton, for turbans and sashes for the waist, paper, and sugar might be imported with advantage.

Afghanistan, Turkestan, and Persia are excellent markets for England and Russia, who have nearly monopolized the trade of those countries; if France had a commercial treaty with Persia, she might hope to introduce several millions of francs of merchandize into Central Asia annually. The Emir Dost Mohamed and Yar Mohamed have endeavoured by every means in their power to encourage their subjects in manufacturing some of the articles which they require from European countries, and thus avoid the high prices at which they are obliged to purchase them, but on such subjects to speak to an Afghan or a deaf man is absolutely the same thing; the Parsivans responded more readily to this appeal, but they were very soon disgusted with the knowledge they acquired, for it was only a source of misery to them: under one pretence or another the wealthy and powerful classes made them work for their benefit and without sufficient remuneration. The best gunmaker in Kandahar was incarcerated in the fortress of Girishk by the Serdar Mohamed Sedik Khan, on the absurd pretext that he was born at a village within his jurisdiction; the khan gave this unfortunate artizan scarcely bread enough to eat, and the man eventually expired under the harsh treatment he received for having attempted to make a visit to his wife and children, who were living only ten hours' journey from Girishk.

Foreign merchandize arrives in Afghanistan by five different routes: the first is that from the west, which traverses Persia by Teheran, and Meshed to Herat; the second is from Turkestan on the north, by Bokhara, Merv, Moorghab to Herat; the third, also from Turkestan, by Bokhara, Karchy, Balkh, and Khulm, to Kabul; the fourth is the eastern one, from the Punjab by Lahore and Peshawur to Kabul; and the fifth is that of the south from India by the Indus, Shikapoor, and Bolan, to Kandahar.

(The revenue in Afghanistan varies according to the abundance of water which irrigates a locality, or the race of persons by whom it is inhabited.) An Afghan, who thinks that any debt he owes his country is repaid by the fact of his arm being at her service, always finds some way of avoiding the payment of a portion of the tax he owes his sovereign: but the Eimaks and Parsivans, who are regarded as a conquered people, think themselves fortunate if the collector takes only double of what they should legally pay; although Mussulmans (the greater part it is true are of the sect of Shiahs) they are obliged to pay the *kharadj*, or capitation tax, called also *ser khanèh*, or house tax, from which the Afghans are exempt.

The following is a statement of the tax, not as it is collected, but as it is fixed in the principalities of Herat and Kandahar.

Though the Afghans are exempt from the humiliating tribute of the ser khanèh, they pay under another name a contribution of two shillings for each tent or house.

The Eimaks, or the nomade Beloochees, pay the contribution of the ser khanèh, which amounts to forty-four djindeks, or fourteen shillings and eightpence for each family: orphans and widows are free of this impost.

The ser khanèh is not paid under this name by the Parsivans and Hindoos living in towns, who are exempt by placing themselves under the protection of some Afghan chief; but the sovereign repays himself by the tax levied on their shops.

At Herat Afghans and Parsivans, &c., pay an annual tax for the horses or other animals which they keep. For a camel and a mare, sixteen djindeks (five shillings and fourpence); for a cow, three djindeks and a half (one shilling); for an ewe or a she-goat, twenty abassees (or two pence); a he-goat or a sheep is free of tax. For all animals without distinction, whether male or female, a tenth of their value is paid when they are sold in the public market.

In Kandahar the tax upon animals is only paid upon sheep at sixpence a head; the tax of *meidane** is levied on all the other animals at the rate of five per cent.

In Kandahar and in Herat it is only on cultivated land that taxes are levied; the sovereign takes as much of the crop as there was seed sown, and also eight djindeks (two shillings and eight pence) on the produce of ten battemens of seed sown.

Fruit gardens are taxed by the *tenef*, or cord, at ten shillings each; this measure comprises a space sixty paces long on every side. Kitchen gardens pay twelve shillings and sixpence per cord. When an Afghan proprietor or farmer lets his land to

* The duty upon sales.—*Ferrier.*

a Parsivan, and furnishes seed, and oxen to work it, the former claims four-fifths of the produce, and leaves one-fifth for his tenant. But when the Parsivan takes the land only, he takes three-fifths, and gives two-fifths to the landlord.

Having merely passed through the principality of Kabul, it was impossible for me to know positively how the taxes are levied there, but the information I obtained by careful inquiry justifies me in supposing that it is nearly in the same manner as in Kandahar.

In the eyes of an European these taxes appear trifling, but it must be remembered that the smallest payment seems onerous to an Afghan; they work so little, and are therefore so poor, that they feel the want of the least thing that is taken from them, and every time they pay a tax they exclaim against what they call violence and tyranny. They might perhaps become reconciled to the impost if, after they had paid it, they were left in peace and idleness to enjoy the fruits of their speculations or their misdeeds, but they are subject to the exactions of subordinate agents, and that provokes them, though they pay less than the Parsivans and others. The inhabitants of the country pay also another indirect tax, which, in proportion to their resources, is rather heavy, but it does not seem oppressive to them, because it is engrafted on the manners of the nation: it is the hospitality they are bound to exercise towards travellers, of whom a great number are servants of the government.

When the travellers are men of rank they have a long train of attendants, all of whom the villages are obliged to feed, and also their horses; it is true they sometimes avoid extortion by concealing themselves if they have timely notice, but they cannot often elude the vigilance of the head of the village, who almost always extracts something from them; this is violence and not hospitality as they like to practise it.

A sa general rule, if an Afghan is obliged to work one month in twelve he considers himself most unfortunate. The repression of crime and levying a tax he designates as *zalm*, tyranny. To live in perfect licence and never to be asked for anything is what he would call the proofs of a paternal government. Nevertheless, the heaviest demands are not made upon him; the Parsivans, who are attached to the soil, obtain for their labour in cultivating it, only just so much as is necessary for the maintenance of themselves and their families. There is no security for them unless they put themselves under the protection of an Afghan, and this protection costs them dear. Those who live in the towns are less oppressed than those in the country, but as they are the working part of the population, they are subject to a host of taxes direct and indirect which they have much difficulty in meeting the payment of, even when they are always in work. Tradesmen pay five pounds twelve shillings per annum, for permission to open their shops. Those who expose their goods in front of their houses, such as *attar, bakal, halva-furouch,** pay upon each shelf a sum fixed by the tax-gatherer, which varies according to the presumed profits of the merchant. Artificers like *kiefch-dooz, zine-dooz, zerguer,* or *khayat,*† are obliged when they sell an article, and before they deliver it to the purchaser, to submit it to one of the inspectors, who perambulate the bazars, to receive the mark of the *dagh,*‡ for which they pay a duty equal to one third of the value of the article sold. Workmen, that is, *benna, nahal-bend,* or *nadjar*§ are obliged to give to the government gratis, two days' work out of seven. In fact, every profession, every species of trade or commerce, is subject to taxation. At Herat in particular, the meat-markets, soap-manufactories, copper-ware, and ironmongery trade, carpentry, the repairing of old furniture and even shoes, and the carriage of water, are all monopolies.

At Kabul, previously to 1839, the Parsivans were much better treated; they did not pay more than two per cent. on their flocks, and four per cent. on the harvest, like the Afghans; but since the power of the Emir, Dost Mohamed Khan, has been hampered by the conduct of his sons, avaricious demands have greatly increased in that principality.

In Kandahar extortion is yet more rampant than in Kabul or Herat. The people live in utter misery, and within the last ten years more than 100,000 of Kohendil Khan's subjects have emigrated. All merchandise entering Afghanistan pays duty as under:—

At Herat	5 per cent.,	but with other exactions it may be calculated at	9 per cent
At Kandahar	2½ „	„ „ „	10 „
At Kabul	2½ „	„ „ „	4 „

Goods are exported from the three principalities free of customs duties, but they are subject to the *badj,*‖ viz.:—

* Druggist. Grocer. Spice shop.

† Shoemaker. Saddler. Goldsmith. Tailor.

‡ Stamp.

§ A mason. Blacksmith. Carpenter.

‖ Tax on transport.—*Ferrier.*

		s.	d.
A camel load, whether entering or leaving the country, pays..	..	12	2
A horse or mule load	..	8	10
An ass load	..	2	0

Every horse sent to India for sale pays 1*l.* 4*s.* 4*d.* to the chief of Kandahar when he leaves his territory.

The revenues of Afghanistan are:—

In Herat	£56,000	and	£24,000	in corn.
In Kandahar	48,000	,,	32,000	,,
In Kabul	140,000	,,	60,000	,,

Whoever looks only at the amount of this revenue will never be able to form a correct opinion of its importance; he must also understand the price of labour, of materials, of cereal and other products, of the requirements of the people, *et cetera*, he will then have an idea of the real value of sums which appear so small. Under the system followed by the Afghan chiefs, these revenues covered all their expenses, and left them a very pretty profit. The English, instead of following the same system, paying the officials regularly and on the same footing, and thus have satisfied every one, thought it necessary to increase the expenses which such a revenue was not able to meet; this was one of the principal reasons that led to their disasters in that country, because every one had enjoyed the augmentation, and revolted when the time came for retrenchment.

We have said that the minerals in the mountainous parts of Kabul and Kandahar are not worked. Yar Mohamed, of Herat, saw better than either of his neighbours, the advantages which he possessed in this source of wealth, and has for some years past worked an iron and a lead mine near his capital. The results, however, have been but moderate as to profit, owing to the ignorance of the workmen, who are unacquainted with metallurgical operations; the silver is not properly extracted from the lead; the iron can be broken, and is as brittle as glass even when hot. The Vizier is most anxious to increase his revenue by these mines; he would like to establish cotton and woollen factories, also spinning machinery for cotton, silk, and wool; to erect cannon foundries and small-arm manufactories, but in the Afghan style. Yar Mohamed would like to have all this without spending any money, and with the assistance of one man, who must be acquainted with every department, and who would find by enchantment, in a country devoid of everything, all the machinery and tools requisite to carry out such projects.

CHAPTER XXIII.

English army leaves Shikapoor — March through the Bolan pass — Kohendil Khan advances to meet it — Defection of the Afghan chiefs — Kohendil retires into Persia — Kandahar capitulates — Assault and fall of Ghuznee — Dost Mohamed endeavours to negotiate, but without success — The Emir leaves Kabul — The English enter the city — Restoration of Shah Shooja — First disagreement between him and the British — The latter interfere in the administration of the kingdom — Results of this — The priests are hostile to the invaders — Avaricious views of the English disappointed — Revenues of Afghanistan moderate in amount — Means employed to raise them — Shah Shooja demands the fulfilment of the treaty — Refusal of the English — Hatred against them augmented — Religious proselytism — English connexions with Afghan women — Revolts in the kingdom — The Dost at Bokhara — Persecutions to which he is subject — Combat at Karchy — Mohamed Shah threatens the Usbek Emir — The Dost is released — His perilous position near the Oxus — He flies to Cher Sebz and Khulm — Returns to the province of Kabul — Conflicts between the Dost and the English — Deserted by his countrymen — Surrenders to the English — He is sent to India.

WE must now return to the History which was interrupted at the close of the 20th chapter, the last incident mentioned being the concentration of a British force at Shikapoor. This army left that place early in March, and after passing Dadur, entered the mountains through which the road winds as far as Bolan, a distance of fifty-two miles, and thence leads to the great table-land of Central Asia, more than 5000 feet above the level of the sea. Notwithstanding the advantages which this defile afforded the Afghans scarcely defended it. The English advanced without serious opposition, though two hundred men well posted might have annihilated them, distressed as they were by a painful march amidst the natural obstacles with which the pass is thickly beset at every step. At Dadur, on this side the mountains, the thermometer stood at 102° of Fahrenheit, while violent snowstorms fell heavily on the way-worn soldiers as they advanced along the Bolan Pass. On the 24th of March, after eight days of a most harassing march from Shikapoor, the army having cleared the mountains, moved on towards Kandahar. Kohendil Khan had ceased to intrigue against Dost Mohamed, and became on friendly terms with him, as he always did when threatened by serious danger. He had determined upon shutting himself up in his capital till his brother of

Kabul should arrive with reinforcements to his assistance, but the Dost having been detained by a movement which the Sikhs had made in favour of the English on this side of Peshawur, Kohendil Khan decided upon assembling all his contingents and marching to meet the enemy. However, he had scarcely reached the valley of Pisheen when the ranks of his army were thinned by numerous desertions. The Serdar Hadji Khan, Kaukeree, was the first to pass over to Shah Shooja with five hundred picked horsemen; this was the signal for the disorganisation of the Kandaharian army, and Kohendil Khan, and his brothers, despairing of then defending themselves and their families with success, determined upon flight. They gained the Helmund, followed its course to lake Roustem, and entered Persia, where the Shah received them most kindly; he bestowed upon them as a fief the little town of Sher-babek, situated between the provinces of Fars and Kerman, and gave them the revenues of the whole of that district, amounting to 12,000 tomauns annually. The flight of the Prince of Kandahar was followed by the immediate submission of the Serdars Hadji Dost Mohamed Khan, Isakzye, Habib Ullah Khan, Surkanee, Peïstalab Khan, Noorzye, Ramazan Khan, Ghildjzye, Akhter Khan Alizye, Ser Firaz Khan Isakzye, &c. &c., who brought with them a detachment of horse to Shah Shooja, and his cause might from that hour be looked upon as triumphant in Afghanistan.

The British Army thus took possession of Kandahar without opposition, and the King and General Sir John Keane made their public entry into that city on the 20th of April. Shah Shooja, as if conscious that his claim to the throne was not very legitimate, was crowned in the mosque of Ahmed Shah on the 8th of May, 1839, hoping by that ceremony to render his claim more important in the eyes of the Afghans. After naming his son Timoor Mirza governor of the city, the King and the Army marched on the 27th of June, in the direction of Ghuznee.

"This town," says Mr. Sumner, "is about one hundred and sixty miles from Kandahar, and sixty-eight from Kabul: although ten days ought to have been sufficient to reach Ghuznee it was not till the 21st of July that Sir John Keane arrived before that fortress. The march of the troops had been much impeded by the difficulties of the road, the great number of camels, and the crowd of camp followers, more numerous even than the soldiers, but no resistance worthy of remark opposed the progress of the army.

"It had been supposed that the town of Ghuznee was not fortified, it is, however, surrounded by a wall and a ditch. To attack it with the few light field-guns that the Anglo-Indian army had with it was impossible, but one of the gates was destroyed with gunpowder in the course of the second night, and on the 23rd of July a fierce combat took place in the streets of the town, in which the English lost two hundred men. The Afghan garrison, numbering 2500, fought with unexpected energy,—it is stated that almost all the dead were pierced by the bayonet, and very few received gun-shot wounds. Nevertheless, the Afghans were vanquished, and Gholam Haidar Khan, one of the sons of Dost Mohamed, who commanded, was taken prisoner; Shah Shooja wished to put him to death, and the English had the greatest difficulty in making him renounce his intention."

Notwithstanding the defection which had so seriously weakened the army of Kabul, Dost Mohamed would not abandon his kingdom without trying the fortune of war, and he marched at the head of the few followers who remained faithful to him, about 6000 men, with his artillery, to meet the British Army; but having at the second halt heard of the fall of Ghuznee, he sent his brother the Nawab Djabbar Khan, as ambassador to Sir William M'Naghten, the British Commissioner, to negotiate with Shah Shooja. The Afghans reproached the Nawab with being too warm a partizan of the English, with whom he had for some time kept up a continuous intercourse; but as he was of a conciliatory disposition and generally appealed to as peace-maker in the quarrels between his brothers, as well as those between the serdars of the different tribes, this partiality was overlooked. The Dost could not have made a better choice of a negotiator with his adversaries, to whom he proposed that he should accept a post under Shah Shooja, analogous to that which his brother Fethi Khan had held under the Shah Mahmood, that is to say Prime Minister. He also demanded the restoration of his third son Haidar Khan and his wives, who had been made prisoners at Ghuznee, and consented to submit on these two conditions; but they were rejected. The Nawab met with an icy reception in the English camp, almost insulting, and returned full of hatred for those who, but a few days before, held the first place in his esteem. The Emir retraced his steps when he heard the result of his last conciliatory offer, and gave up the idea of making head against the invading army with so small a force as his own, the greater part of which were demoralized,—moreover, he could only expect fresh defections. He made, therefore, but a short stay in Kabul, and abandoning that city retired beyond the Hindoo Koosh into the dominions of the Emir of Bokhara, accompanied by his family and three hundred and fifty devoted adherents. As soon as he was gone, Abdullah Khan, Etchekzye, Aziz Khan, Ghildjzye, Emin Ullah Khan, Logheree, and Khan Shireeu Khan, Kuzzilbash, who might still have created fresh difficulties for the English, and caused them considerable loss in their attack upon Kabul, now openly espoused the party of the invaders and made their submission.

The Anglo-Indian army entered that city without opposition on the 7th of August, 1839, and proclaimed the definitive re-establishment in power of Shah Shooja-ool-Moolk. The General-in-Chief had hoped to take Dost Mohamed prisoner, but finding that he had escaped he sent Colonel Outram with one hundred and fifty British cavalry, and seven hundred Afghan horse, commanded by Hadji Khan, Kaukeree, in pursuit. On the 21st of August they had nearly attained their object, for they were but fourteen miles from the fugitive Emir, but having received secret intelligence of this by a messenger from Hadji Khan, he made a forced march, and escaped the danger that threatened him. Before he could reach Khulm he had to repulse several attacks of the Hazarah Deh Zinguis, who had already felt the power of English influence, and his little escort was reduced to half its number by the time he arrived at Balkh. His first intention had been to gain Persia, but the Emir Nasser Ullah Khan Bahadoor having despatched a messenger to offer him shelter in his dominions, he delayed his journey to Teheran, and went direct to the court of the Usbek Emir.

Shah Shooja, replaced on the throne of his fathers, was soon surrounded by the greater part of the Afghan serdars, and with the exception of some partial outbreaks of little importance, had reason to consider himself firmly seated on the musnud. This result was due to the conciliatory conduct that he at first manifested, and his good understanding with the English; but he only acted thus from an apprehension that Dost Mohamed might be near at hand, for as soon as he knew that that chief had arrived at Bokhara, he wished to exercise the sovereign authority to the exclusion of his protectors. They, on the contrary, had determined to leave him nothing but the semblance of it—and Sir W. M'Naghten directed everything. He gave all his orders through the Shah, who every morning repeated, at his durbar, the lesson he had received on the previous evening from the British Commissioner. The serdars were too clear-sighted not to perceive this, and they expressed their disgust in strong terms at all times, and in all places. The English, though affronted at this freedom of speech, dared not openly repress it, lest their own interference in the Government should become too manifest, but they revenged themselves by noting the chiefs that were rebellious in their eyes, and in this way created a great deal of discontent.

Notwithstanding the smothered displeasure that prevailed, the English fancied themselves firmly established in the country, and sent back part of their army to India. They determined also at once, and without the least consideration for the Afghans, to introduce those administrative reforms which they had established in their Indian possessions, where all had been done progressively and without wounding the prejudices of a population, far more timid and more easy to manage than the Afghans. It is true that in Afghanistan they put native officers at the head of the different departments, but they were there like puppets, having no liberty of action and only following blindly the directions of a British officer, who was associated with them. In doing this, Sir W. M'Naghten appeared to be guided by the remembrance of what Mir Mahmood the Ghildjzye had done when he established his government in Persia; but Sir William forgot, or overlooked, the point that the Mir in placing with his officials others more enlightened than themselves, selected the former from among the Persians, a servile people always accustomed to bend to a conqueror, while the English officers on the contrary thrust their own will upon the Afghan functionaries, which was a very different condition of affairs. The plan failed and brought into general contempt with their countrymen those natives who accepted office under such circumstances.

This system gradually disturbed the good understanding existing between Shah Shooja and the English; they wished to be masters, but wanted the courage to act openly, and yet they would not leave the King to his own ideas of Government: they were apparently neutral, and still had the presumption to mix themselves up in everything. This bastard system alienated from them both the people and the court; the Shah testified his great displeasure at it, and at last counteracted every measure that originated with the English. For example, Sir Alexander Burnes, who had been appointed Lieutenant-Governor of the city of Kabul, had established a new and reduced tariff for the merchandize imported into Afghanistan, but Shah Shooja seeing that this was done simply with a view of encouraging the interests of British commerce, secretly authorised his agents to levy higher duties than those which had been determined on. The injured merchants complained to the English, by whom they were referred to the Minister of the Shah, and this officer gave them the bastinado for appealing for justice to strangers before they had applied to the Royal Government. At length an almost open rupture took place between Mollah Chekkar, the Shah's Prime Minister, and Sir W. M'Naghten. A party had been formed by the Vizier with the hope of withdrawing the Shah from the influence of the British, and this party cared not in the least to conceal or dissimulate its intentions. Sir W. M'Naghten and Sir A. Burnes were made aware of its existence, but they despised the information they received on all sides, and when their partisans endeavoured to make them see the extremities to which impunity would encourage the Afghans, they answered in the famous words of the Duc de Guise, "they dare not." The result proved that these gentlemen were no nearer right than was the Duc de Guise.

The Afghans, little initiated in the intricacies of politics, and not as yet completely experienced in the duplicity of the government of Calcutta, remembered the article in the treaty that Lord Auckland had concluded with their king, which stipulated that as soon as Shah Shooja was *firmly* established on his throne, the Anglo-Indian army should repass the Indus. This word "*firmly*" gave him, it is true, a great latitude, but it was not thus that the Afghans had interpreted it; and they were impatient for the hour that should rid them of their protectors.

The uneasiness at length became general, and confidence existed amongst the English only. The Afghans anticipated a catastrophe, and the agitation, at first confined to the towns, soon spread into the country. The Mollahs would no longer recite the "Khoutbe" (or prayer for the King) in the Mosques, alleging that they could only do so for an independent sovereign, and that Shah Shooja was not independent. On the other hand, the maintenance of the British army had nearly exhausted the provinces, all the necessaries of life had quadrupled in price, and a cry of distress was raised everywhere. In vain did the Vizier publish an order placing the sale of provisions on the old footing and forbid monopoly; no one paid any attention to his injunctions. The Shah therefore found himself obliged to arrest the monopolists, whose corn was re-sold at the tariff price, and by public auction. The English were ill-judged enough to interfere in their favor, which increased the irritation amongst the people, and they were accused of wishing to create a famine. It was in vain that they distributed food gratis to the necessitous, the populace valued not this concession as proceeding from charity; that virtue is practised in a different manner by the Afghans, and the English lost more than they gained by granting benefits to one class only, and with an appearance of such method and calculation so totally foreign to Afghan habits. The deplorable mania which the English have for scattering gold by handfuls in Asiatic countries, without any reason for doing so other than to gratify an useless pride, and for valuing things only because they are expensive, created for them in this instance one of the most formidable difficulties they have ever had to encounter. The officers were prodigal in their personal expenditure, and that depreciated the value of money; the British Commissioner had obliged the King to give his officers, civil and military, as much pay for a month as they had hitherto received for a year; and that without having previously ascertained that the revenues of the country would admit of his so doing. It is true the English had calculated on an excess of receipts consequent upon the regularity of their administration, and an amount of revenue founded upon the information given by Shah Shooja when he was at Loodiana. But in that as on many other occasions they were wrong in not remembering the maxim of Machiavelli, "that it is dangerous and imprudent to undertake an expedition upon the representations and hopes of exiles." The English also paid for every species of labour, tenfold what the Afghans had ever received before, so that all the workmen were glad to be employed on the fortifications, or otherwise occupied by the English, and hands were therefore soon wanting to till the ground. Shah Shooja, even, could not obtain the men that he required, because he could not pay them on this footing, and he was therefore obliged to overwork the labourers who were engaged in the repairs of his own palace, and to pay them the ordinary wages of the country. But here the English meddled again, and signified to the Vizier, that if those who complained were not satisfied, and paid according to the English tariff, they should pay them themselves, and place the sum to the Shah's account. This new and insulting injunction irritated the Shah to the last degree, and from that moment he seemed to be indifferent whether or not he was on good terms with his protectors; he even earnestly required of them the promised evacuation of his dominions. But Sir W. M'Naghten refused to comply with this demand, objecting, that he could not be "firmly" seated on his throne while Dost Mohamed remained at liberty, and that the English could not leave him without support as long as there was a chance of the return of that chief. Shah Shooja, forced rather than convinced, resigned himself to their tutelage; but his reiterated complaints created in his subjects the most hostile feelings against the English, and their exasperation broke through all bounds when the people saw that the invaders considered the Afghans incapable of serving them, and found themselves superseded by Hazarahs and Parsivans who up to that time had been looked upon as a conquered people. Perhaps the English were not wrong in having a better opinion of these descendants of the Persian colonists, but such a step should only have been taken with the greatest prudence, gradually, and after they had become perfectly established in the country. Another error was their constant habit of threatening to send some of the restless chiefs to India, and not carrying out the menace. This might possibly have prevented the development of the revolt in which they were overwhelmed at a later period. The Afghans have little or none of that feeling which we understand by the word patriotism, for they are quite indifferent as to which or how many of their tribes may be subdued, provided their own is in the enjoyment of personal freedom; but this indifference as to who governs them, is accompanied in each individual by a deep attachment to his own tribe. The repeated threats, therefore, of separation from them created serious alarm, and these fears being worked upon by the partisans of Dost Mohamed, inspired a still greater distrust and hatred of the English: who never looked with the least anxiety at these various indications of approaching trouble, but slept on in perfect tranquillity.

While they were reforming the administration, their missionaries attempted to meddle in religion also, and distributed everywhere the Bible translated into Persian—a proselytism that was more injurious than profitable to them. Previously to the time at which the English entered Afghanistan, the inhabitants might have been considered as the least fanatical of any people professing Islamism

—but as a set-off, they are the most covetous upon earth, and the result was that the women soon gave themselves up to the English for money, even with the knowledge of their husbands; fathers and brothers sold their daughters and sisters, and it was a novel spectacle to see Christians become the legitimate husbands of Mahomedan wives, for many officers were legally married to Afghan women. The Mollahs did not omit to rouse the anger of the faithful, against this tendency to encroach upon their religion, and they excited on all sides a fanaticism which manifested itself in the provinces by assassination and partial revolt. Colonel Herring was murdered at Ghuznee, and it was only with great difficulty that Colonel Orchard and Major Mac Gregor quelled a seditious movement excited by a certain Syud Kassem. The fortress of Kelat-i-Ghildjzye also rose against the authority of Shah Shooja, or rather the English, and the circumstance that led to this was one of the unnecessary acts of rigour, of which they are so often guilty in Asia.

Lieutenant Lynch, one of the political agents in Afghanistan, made a military reconnaissance on the side of Kelat-i-Ghildjzye and summoned the inhabitants to open the gates of their fort to him. The commandant was one of those men who were tired of the ascendancy so arrogantly maintained over their sovereign by his foreign ally, and replied that he should do as Lieutenant Lynch demanded as soon as he showed him an order from Shah Shooja, or his son Timoor Mirza, and that in the mean time he would visit him the next morning as a friend. Lieutenant Lynch was not satisfied with this answer, and without further negotiation demolished his fortress with his artillery, and the chief and many of the garrison lost their lives. The survivors, who were of the Ghildjzye tribe, bent for a time to the storm, but as soon as the opportunity presented itself, they took their revenge by massacring all the English that fell into their hands. A detachment under Major Clibborne was cut up in the south, and that officer lost his life. The Serdar Akter Khan, Alizye, who had raised a small body of troops of his tribe in the district of Zemindavar, held the English in check in that quarter, and Yar Mohamed Khan secretly sent him reinforcements, for though the English paid him large sums of money the discontented Afghans always found help and shelter in his dominions.

In the midst of these serious difficulties the British were surprised by fresh troubles, the Emir Dost Mohamed re-appeared in arms on the northern frontier, and there was not a moment to be lost in preparing to meet the storm.

The Emir of Bokhara had received the fugitive Prince and his family in a suitable manner when he arrived in his capital, and allotted a daily sum for their maintenance, but from that conduct five or six days after, it became evident that his offer of an asylum was intended to draw them into a snare, for their allowance was stopped and the Dost was left to his own resources. This indifference to misfortune, so foreign to the Mussulman ideas of hospitality, was followed by aggravated insults.

The greater number of Dost Mohamed's sons accompanied him to Bokhara, and the youngest, Sultan Djan, who was remarkable for his personal beauty and graceful and distinguished manners, attracted the attention of the Emir Nasser Ullah. This monster was addicted to the most horrible of Eastern propensities, and one day sent an officer to the Dost's house to bring Sultan Djan to the palace. His father, however, well acquainted with the Uzbek Emir's character, refused to let him go, and immediately ordered the lad, accompanied by his second son Akbar Khan and one hundred Afghan horse, to leave Bokhara. They did so, but were soon pursued, and after a desperate encounter near Larchy, in which the Afghans lost two-thirds of their party, the remainder were obliged to lay down their arms. The two brothers were then brought back prisoners to Bokhara, and it is unnecessary to say what was the fate of the youngest at the hands of Nasser Ullah.

The position of the Emir Dost Mohamed had now become most distressing; he had every day to repulse some new demand from his tyrant; his life even was in danger, for Nasser Ullah Khan, besides his hereditary hatred to the Afghans, wished to make himself popular in the eyes of the English by showing hostility to the Emir of Kabul, as they might some day enter his own dominions. His messengers were frequently crossing those of Shah Shooja, and the two monarchs had concerted together one of those vile plots by means of which Asiatics so frequently endeavour to effect their objects, when the Shah of Persia wrote to Nasser Ullah Khan and informed him that he should hold him responsible for any evil that might befall the Dost, whom he declared he had taken under his own special protection. The Shah also enjoined him to set that chief and his family at liberty, in order that he might make a pilgrimage to Mecca, as he had expressed his intention of doing, and concluded by signifying to the Emir of Bokhara his royal determination of making war upon him if he did not comply with his injunctions.

Nasser Ullah, afraid openly to manifest his indignation against the Shah of Persia, allowed the Dost to leave Bokhara; but he was even then actually planning the death of this unfortunate chief, and taking measures to make it appear the result of accident. Before the departure of the Dost he sent a man to the banks of the Oxus who, in concert with the ferryman, was ordered to upset the boat, and take care that the Emir should never reach the shore alive.

Happily, an indiscreet remark of the wretch intrusted with this detestable commission made the Dost, when he reached the banks of the river, suspicious of some lurking danger; and a caravan from the south travelling to Samarcand coming up at the time, he succeeded in escaping with it, disguised and in a litter, and thus eluded the vigilance of the authorities of Bokhara. His wives had left that city after him, and, having sent a messenger to desire them to alter their route, they rejoined him seven miles from Samarcand, which place he did not think it prudent to enter. Here, however, he took off the female attire in which he had escaped, mounted a horse, and proceeded to ask hospitality of the Khan of Cher Sebz, who generously granted it, but for a brief space only, for, though this Khan detested the Emir of Bokhara, he dreaded his power. Alarmed therefore at his threats, and command to put Dost Mohamed and his sons to death, on pain of being deprived of his Khanat, he secretly sent away his guest, furnishing him with the means of reaching Khulm. Mir Walee, the chief of this province, was by no means easy at the approach of the English, who had already reached Bamian, and he had made warlike preparations to receive them. The moment of the Dost's arrival could not have been more propitious, for the partisans of the Emir had succeeded in agitating Kohistan, of which the population refused to obey the orders, emanating in appearance from Shah Shooja, but really from the English. Discontent was general in the other Afghan provinces, and if the orders of the latter were still acted upon it was feebly and with repugnance on the part of the officials, though they were active enough when they saw a chance of committing some extortion that might prove a benefit to themselves. Sir W. M'Naghten knew not what to do, nor whom to trust—for those Afghans who did not betray him were indifferent to the disaffection that existed and the progress of revolt: he gave orders, and revoked them almost as soon as given; and at last determined on rigorous measures, hoping thereby to eradicate the evil. In doing this he made several arrests of very doubtful legality, and missed the real culprits, who were most of them about the person of Shah Shooja.

Hadji Khan, Kaukeree, the first of the Afghan chiefs who joined the English, was arrested and sent to India, for showing too much independence, and being suspected of having pursued the Dost too leisurely in order to give him time to escape. Two other Ghildjzye serdars, Abd el Rahman Khan and Mahme, who had taken refuge with the Sikhs, were, contrary to all the laws of hospitality, given up to the English, and also sent to India. In Kandahar severity was pushed to its utmost limits; Akrem Khan, Noorzye, convicted of having taken up arms against the invaders of his country, was arrested, and blown from a gun. Hadji Dost Mohamed Khan, Izakzye, died almost at the same time in the prison of Kandahar, and the people, ever suspicious, believed, though it was never proved, that he had been poisoned. Such was the position of affairs when the Walee of Khulm and Dost Mohamed took the field. On the 30th of August, Mir Efzel Khan, eldest son of the Emir and commander of the advanced guard of Usbek Afghans, attacked the British post at Badjguiah, but did not succeed, and he fell back upon the main body of the army. Dost Mohamed waited a few days longer, and on the 18th of September accepted the offer of battle given him by Colonel Denny, and he likewise was unsuccessful; after which the Usbeks retired altogether. This check, however, did not daunt the Emir, who withdrew into Kohistan, where the majority of the chiefs declared for him, and their men, added to those who joined him at Khulm, still presented an effective force of 6000 troops; other reinforcements from various districts also came and ranged themselves under his standard, but Sir W. M'Naghten cooled their ardour for the cause of their ancient chief by lavishly distributing gold amongst the hostile tribes. The Dost and his companions, who well knew the power of this touchstone of honesty over the mind of an Afghan, were alarmed at the probable result of such prodigality, and it was almost with hesitation that on November 2nd, 1839, he engaged General Sale and Prince Fethi Djing, second son of Shah Shooja, at Pervaneh Derreh,

The Dost's soldiers performed prodigies of valour, and the 2nd Regiment of Bengal Regular Cavalry wavered and fled before a charge of eighty Afghans, led by the Emir himself, who broke them at the onset, and then engaged the infantry, upon whom he inflicted considerable loss, especially in officers. The advantage of the day remained with the Dost, and the Anglo-Indian army would have been completely beaten had they renewed the combat on the morrow, but success being doubtful they determined to conquer with gold; their agents entered the camp of the Emir, and manœuvred so well and so quickly, that he only escaped death at the hands of his own mutinous troops by a rapid flight, in which he was accompanied by a few brave men who remained faithful to him. Dost Mohamed now retired to the mountains, and wandered amongst them for some time; his partisans, who were gradually detached from his falling fortunes by English bribes, and being also little inclined to face the hard winter in the hills, returned to their homes. Their noble chief was at length utterly abandoned, and had much to suffer from privation and the rigour of the season; but this was not all,—he found himself hunted by parties of Afghans, who hoped to receive a large recompence for betraying him to his enemies, and this led to the resolution which he finally took of placing himself in their hands.

On the 4th of November, 1840, he went almost alone under the walls of Kabul, and, taking advantage of an accidental meeting with Sir W. M'Naghten to make his submission, he gave up his sword to the envoy, declaring at the same time who he was. The English diplomatist immediately returned it, which mark of respect gratified the Emir exceedingly, and they rode into Kabul together. Dost Mohamed was honourably treated while he remained in his own capital, and was afterwards sent to India with his wives, where he was pensioned, and carefully guarded by the political agents of the East India Company; his sons, whom he had left in Afghanistan, soon joined him in his exile, with the exception of Akbar Khan.

We have seen that this chief was taken prisoner by the Bokharians after having sustained a bloody combat with them at Karchy. On his return to Bokhara he was imprisoned by order of Nasser Ullah Khan, and was consequently prevented from leaving it with his father. But a short time after the flight of the latter the surveillance to which he was subjected was relaxed, and having succeeded in making his escape he reached Cher Sebz: but the Khan of that place, afraid to grant him an asylum for the same reasons that prevented him from sheltering his father, gave him an escort of two horsemen as far as Khulm, where the Walee received the fugitive, and several of his dependents who joined him there.

Notwithstanding the strict watch that was kept over him, Dost Mohamed was treated with great consideration and respect by Lord Auckland, who, wishing to give him a clear idea of the British power in India, took him over all the arsenals, magazines, dockyards, &c., at Calcutta. The Emir was completely amazed at all he saw, and expressed the conviction that afterwards he often repeated to his sons when they wished him to make war with the English, that they were "invincible, and would some day be the masters of the world." After several months' residence at Calcutta the Dost fell ill from the effects of the climate of Bengal, when he sought and obtained permission to join his family at Loodiana.—Subsequently he was allowed to settle in the mountains, the air of which was more favourable to his health.

CHAPTER XXIV.

Shah Shooja demands the evacuation of his country by the English — Their refusal — Forgery of letters — The invaders impose a vizier on Shah Shooja — Unjustifiable acts of this functionary — Complaints of the Afghan chiefs to Shah Shooja — The King conspires with them against the English — Abdullah Khan at the head of the conspirators — Carelessness of the English — Subsidies to chiefs reduced — Revolt of the Ghildjzyes — General Sale marches against them — Is obliged to retire into Jellalabad — Feeling of security in the English — Insurrection in the provinces — Revolt at Kabul — Attack on Sir A. Burnes's house — Assassination of that officer — The English are driven from the city — Bad defensive position taken by them — Commissariat stores pillaged — Death of Abdullah Khan — Zeman Khan proclaimed King — Continual fighting — Weakness of General Elphinstone — Conduct of the 44th Regiment — Suspension of arms — Akbar Khan returns to Kabul — Indecision of the English — Events in the provinces — Plan of retreat abandoned — Embarassment of Sir W. M'Naghten — Suspicions of the Afghans — Meeting between the resident and Akbar Khan — Assassination of the former — Major Pottinger — Treaty with Akbar Khan — The English retreat — Akbar Khan unmasked — The English deliver up hostages to him — English army annihilated — Akbar Khan besieges Jellalabad — Transactions between Shah Shooja and Zeman Khan — The King is assassinated — Character of that sovereign.

AFTER the submission of the Emir, Shah Shooja, thinking the English had no further plausible motive for refusing to evacuate Afghanistan, inasmuch as the tranquillity of the country could not be disturbed by any pretender to the throne, demanded for the second time the fulfilment of the treaty; but, on various pretences, they again rejected this demand, and continued to carry out those injudicious reforms which had already alienated so many from their party. It might have been supposed that they were striving to destroy their own influence by adopting measures so false and ill adapted to the objects they had in view; every day they in some manner wounded the self-love and disappointed the avarice of the Afghans, and expected them to change abruptly the habits, customs, and ideas that had existed amongst them for ages past—indeed, they endeavoured to make them do so.

In a country so recently conquered, and on which a new sovereign had been forced, the opposition must, of necessity, be obstinate; the wisest policy would, therefore, have been to attach the people to them by kindness, to throw, if possible, a veil over the past, and, above all, to be indulgent to minor offences. The British did just the reverse in Afghanistan.

After his flight to Bokhara, Dost Mohamed continued to correspond with the Afghan serdars that surrounded Shah Shooja, and he kept all their letters; these were found in a little bag on the field after the battle of Pervaneh and given to the English, who talked of this discovery, and threatened to make use of them against the chiefs whom they compromised and who were far from docile under their rule. But this indiscreet conduct brought about a result very different from what they intended, for the serdars who were hostile to them, and who were afraid of being sent to join Hadji Khan, Kaukeree, in India, held aloof, and, to prevent any surprise on the part of their conquerors, surrounded themselves with their followers, always appearing in public attended by an escort ready to fight; this warlike attitude was almost a challenge to their adversaries, who scarcely dared to accept it. The English, moreover, drew upon themselves the resentment of those who up to that time had been devoted to their cause, by recompensing the individuals that delivered this packet of pretended letters, the contents of which were, in truth, the fabrications of some artful and avaricious intriguers—a fact that was proved in the sequel.

Shah Shooja profited by the errors of the English to alienate the minds of the Afghans from them, and to strengthen his own party; his vizier, Mollah Chekker, was the soul of all his intrigues, and cared so little to spare the protectors of his sovereign, that in several instances they were able to prove his hostile intentions, and eventually demanded his dismissal.

The king resisted to the utmost of his power, but was at last obliged to accept a vizier of their choice; and the Nizam ed Dooulet, the new minister, who consulted his master simply as a matter of form, entirely followed the instructions he received from the English. This miserable wretch, finding himself supported by them, committed spoliations and exactions of every kind, and was guilty of many acts of tyranny; those whom he plundered sometimes found the means of bringing their complaints before the king; but Shah Shooja informed them that he could do nothing, being himself a slave. Sir W. M'Naghten was far from approving of the vizier's conduct; but having himself made him minister, he could not immediately degrade him. To these causes of discontent and anxiety was soon added a still greater one.

The Directors of the East India Company, who have a habit of judging of the value of a conquest only by the revenue it produces, were more disappointed than can be described at the deficit which the expedition of Afghanistan had occasioned in their treasury. They, therefore, ordered a rigid economy to be practised in the Shah's army, and these instructions were carried out by the British officers with more or less intelligence. Chiefs, whom it would have been wise in the government to conciliate, found themselves deprived of their subsidies; those of others were considerably reduced, and, at the same time that the pecuniary interests of the Afghans were attacked, several Hazarah and Kuzzilbash chiefs received fresh proofs of favour, which irritated the Afghans to the highest degree.

Towards the end of September the serdars met in Kabul and laid their grievances before Shah Shooja, who could only reply that his power as a king was a fiction, that it was impossible for him to do them justice, and added—"It is your own fault that I have fallen thus low; you have abandoned me to the good pleasure of the English; had there been one man of spirit amongst you, he would soon have delivered me from this shameful state of dependence." These words were not uttered in vain. Amongst the serdars present at the durbar was Abdullah Khan, Etchekzye (branch of the Barukzyes), a chief of energy and resolution, who stood forward and offered to be that man. In the afternoon of the same day he met the Shah in secret conference in the garden of his palace, and there a revolt, which was to be postponed till a favourable opportunity should render success certain, was planned. However, it was resolved that the death of Sir A. Burnes should take place immediately; for the king, who well knew the infinite trouble that officer had taken to support Dost Mohamed, detested him, and was very anxious to prevent his being made the Resident at his court, if Sir W. M'Naghten, whose departure had been talked of for some time, should be removed.

On leaving the Shah, Abdullah Khan called together at his own house the serdars Mohamed Attah Khan, Sikander Khan, Mir Efzel Khan, Abdul Samut Khan, and Abdul Selam Khan, all of the royal tribe of Popolzye; also Seidal Khan, Alikioozye, Emin

Ullah Khan, Logheree, and Mohamed Hoosein Khan, Erz Beghi,* and communicated to them the intentions of Shah Shooja: to which they agreed to conform in every particular, and swore to overthrow the British power in Afghanistan. This oath was written on the leaves of a Koran, and the seal of each of the serdars present was affixed to it. The secret was ill kept, and soon came to the knowledge of Sir W. M'Naghten, who was not in the least alarmed by it, being fully impressed with the idea that it was impossible the chiefs should undertake any serious measures. He would not even allow the Koran to be seized for the purpose of learning the names of the conspirators, lest that act should be construed into evidence of timidity on his part: an appearance of perfect indifference was, in his opinion, the best mode of proving to the discontented that the British were not afraid of them; but Burnes took quite an opposite view of the case. Thus the two officers, invested with special power, were never agreed upon the most judicious plan to be adopted for the general interests, and this want of good understanding between the Resident and the political Envoy was, perhaps, of all the causes that contributed to the British fall in Afghanistan, the one that hastened it the most. It is impossible to doubt that, if three or four of the conspirators had been arrested and sent to India, it would have been sufficient to put a stop to these intrigues; but instead of adopting this vigorous course, Sir W. M'Naghten gave them ample time to bring them to maturity, and exasperated the serdars by the most ill-timed measures of economy. Though he did not see that the storm was so close at hand, he was fully aware of the difficulties that were to be surmounted, and modified in a degree the reduction in the pay of the Afghan soldiers ordered by Lord Auckland; but from the moment he received notice of his nomination to the post of Governor of Bombay, he made no further objection to the instructions that the Directors had given, and unhesitatingly reduced all the subsidies which had been pointed out as superfluous.

The Ghildjzye serdars, who occupied the defiles of the Khyber

* This serdar was the brother of that wife of Dost Mohamed who had been previously married to Mohamed Azim Khan. By this marriage she had a son called Sultan Djan Khan, who to this day has influence in Afghanistan. The chiefs of Kabul and Kandahar are both equally anxious to attach him to their cause.—*Ferrier.*

mountains between Kabul and Jellalabad, and held them open or shut at their pleasure, were informed at the commencement of October, 1841, that they must submit to a reduction of 40,000 rupees = 4000*l.*, when they at once hastened to Kabul to ascertain the motive for this alteration. They made their representations in the first instance to Sir W. M'Naghten, and he referred them to Shah Shooja, by whom they were haughtily dismissed, which greatly wounded their self-love and disappointed their cupidity; but a few amongst them he secretly received, initiated them into the conspiracy against his protectors, and assured them that for the future their interests would be cared for.

Sir Alexander Burnes, without actually foreseeing the consequences that would result from these retrenchments, nevertheless opposed them with all his power, though he did not succeed in preventing them; the consequence was, that when the Ghildjzye serdars returned to their homes, they raised their countrymen and cut off the communications in the mountains.

On the other hand, the conspirators at Kabul had sent emissaries to all the Afghan provinces to prepare the tribes for revolt; already discontented, they alarmed them still more by persuading them that their chiefs were to be banished to India, that Shah Shooja was a mere puppet who would soon be upset, and that the British yoke, so heavy only in a protective character, would be far more so when it became absolute. The nomades responded immediately to this appeal, rushed to arms, and the communications between Kabul and Kandahar were closed without delay, as those had already been between Kabul and Jellalabad. General Sale was sent with a brigade to reopen the latter and force the passage of the Hindoo Koosh; this small force quitted Kabul on the 11th of October, entered the mountains the same day, and was very far from expecting to meet with the terrible resistance it found there. Once in this infernal region, however, the Indo-British troops could not retrace their steps, and during eighteen days they were, if the expression may be used, choked in these defiles, where every step of their way was disputed foot by foot. On the first day General Sale was wounded and obliged to abandon his command, and a fourth part of his brigade was exterminated. From the 12th of October the troops could advance only three miles and a half a-day, and arrived exhausted on the 2nd November at Gundamuck, on the other side of the gorge of the Khoord Kabul; here they rested a few days, and then left for Jellalabad, still harassed by the tribes in revolt, and after having reached that town took refuge within its walls with only three days' provisions. Never were troops in such a precarious position; but a most happy incident came to their assistance, for caravans brought them supplies for three months from Peshawur, which enabled them resolutely to oppose an energetic resistance to the insurrection in which the rest of the army perished.

The news of these conflicts of the mountaineers with General Sale's brigade arrived at Kabul on the 1st of November, and was the signal for a serious disturbance which broke out in that city.

The unconquered tribes of Afghanistan waited only for the signal to be given them by the Khyberees to rise simultaneously and commence a war for their faith—a religious war, the most bloody of all wars. They watched attentively the Indo-British troops, who were imprudently dispersed in the several garrisons of Kabul, Ghuznee, Kelat-i-Ghildjzye, Charikar, Kandahar, Jellalabad, and other places; they knew that these detachments could easily be cut off, and also that it was impossible that reinforcements should reach them from India until the month of April, the mountain passes being obstructed by the snow. Of the thirty-two political agents scattered over the country, not one perceived the least symptom of the excited state of the public mind; the unfortunate Burnes himself, blinded by his excessive confidence in the natives, was the first to report to the Indian Government that the Afghan chiefs were sincerely attached to Shah Shooja, and that the British army might be withdrawn from their garrisons. Sir W. M'Naghten wrote more confidently in the same strain: all had fallen into a fatal slumber, from which they were aroused only by surrounding massacre. The British Commissioner had, in the first instance, attempted to parley with the Ghildjzyes and induce them to return to their duty, offering as one of the most persuasive arguments 100,000 rupees = 10,000*l.*; but they rejected every species of temptation, and continued to make war upon the invaders, their attacks being generally made at night.

As soon as the signal of revolt had been given in the country, Abdullah Khan, the head of the conspiracy in Kabul, took no further trouble to conceal his intentions, and said openly that he would kill Burnes before eight days were over. This officer, though warned, paid no attention to these threats, considering them as simple boasting, but, seeing that the serdar's insolence increased daily, he at last became very uneasy, and obtained information which left no doubt as to the serious position they were in; moreover, he saw that the conduct of Abdullah Khan was connected with the revolt in the hills. This enlightened him as to the snare which had been woven round them, and he exclaimed, "There is nothing for it now but to quit this country." The next day, November 2, 1841, early in the morning, he sent one of his servants to the house of Abdullah Khan to request that chief to come to him, but the serdar, suspecting that Burnes intended to seize him and send him to India, conceived that the moment had arrived to execute the project of open revolt, for which he was so well prepared; his first act was therefore to kill Burnes's messenger, and, without loss of time, he proceeded to his residence, accompanied by Seidal Khan, Sikander Khan, Mohamed Attah Khan, Abdul Selam Khan, Emin Ullah Khan, &c. &c., and their followers and servants, in all nearly one hundred and thirty persons, the nucleus of the insurrection.

On the way there they killed the British officers and soldiers whom they met in the streets; the delay this occasioned enabled Burnes, who had been informed of these massacres, to barricade the large outer gate of his house, and the insurgents were therefore a long time before they could force a passage. He had thought of retiring to the cantonments situated three miles from the city, but while putting on an Afghan dress to effect his retreat undiscovered, he changed his mind, and said, "No, I cannot play the coward, and, for the life of one man, compromise the honour of the British name. Were I to escape thus, the Afghans would believe that I was frightened; no, a hundred times worse than death, the prestige of my authority would be lost." With these words he put on his uniform again and remained at his post, but sent messenger after messenger to Sir W. M'Naghten, requesting that a battalion of infantry and two pieces of artillery might be sent to him without delay, for with these he considered he should be able to put down the insurgents. And he was right, for had the British troops appeared in the streets of Kabul 10,000 Kuzzilbashes, Hazarahs, and Parsivans, would have rallied round Burnes and supported him; but seeing that the English did not take the initiative, they feared to commit themselves in the eyes of the Afghans, who might have made them pay dearly for their interference, and thus remained passive spectators of the struggle. To crown his misfortune, the artillery sent for by the beleaguered officer never arrived, and the mob, emboldened by the simply defensive attitude assumed by his countrymen, hesitated no longer; the inhabitants rose in all parts of the city, and to them were soon joined the suburban population. From that moment the impulse given to the revolt was implacable and irresistible, and the nation rose as one man against their foreign invaders. But to continue my narrative; the shopkeepers and workmen, as well as the dregs of the people, now surrounded the residence of Burnes, to take it by assault, and showed themselves exceedingly vindictive in this conflict, a circumstance which might have arisen from his having been governor of the city, and frequently obliged to punish them with severity. The mob showed great perseverance in their endeavours to break their way into the house, but the besieged, twenty-three in number, consisting of a few officers and servants, and ten sepoys, by applying their ears to the ground, learnt from the hollow sound of the blows that were struck against the walls, on which side to expect the attack, and when a hole was made, they shot the first man who presented himself at the opening; this damped the courage of the others, who retired to recommence operations at some other spot. The defence was thus prolonged from eight in the morning till two in the afternoon, and the Afghans having lost many men in their attempts to force an entrance, at last had recourse to other means; combustibles were piled against the great gate, and when it was entirely consumed they rushed in a mass through the passage and gained the interior of the house. The inmates had by this time exhausted all their ammunition, and Burnes received a point blank shot from a pistol; the ball struck him in the right eye, and he died instantly: his body was then hacked to pieces with repeated sabre cuts, and, horribly mutilated, thrown into the garden of his own house.

Three-and-twenty persons perished with Burnes, amongst whom were his brother Lieut. Charles Burnes and Lieut. Broadfoot; Captain Johnson, in charge of the Treasury, escaped by a miracle. Captain Trevor, with his family, and a few other officers, were also fortunate enough to reach the cantonments. His house and that of Burnes were burned to the ground, and the military chest, magazines, and commissariat stores of provisions pillaged.*

* These details of the death of Burnes were given me by Mohamed Hoosein Khan, Kachee, who was the sole survivor of the massacre in Burnes's house. He received six-and-twenty wounds.—*Ferrier.*

On hearing of the outbreak Sir W. M'Naghten detached two regiments under Brigadier Shelton, and some irregulars under Captain Nicholl, to occupy the citadel of the Bala Hissar, in which was the residence of Shah Shooja. This movement was the only measure the envoy adopted, totally regardless of the state of the city and the earnest demands of Burnes, whose repeated messages announced his critical position. It was the greater error, because provisions were short in barracks, and the principal magazine was in Kabul; the Resident considered the small party in charge of it as sufficient for its defence, but the indecision of the officer in command led to its evacuation. Another depôt, gallantly defended, was carried by assault, and it was with great difficulty and loss of life that they subsequently retook two small redoubts tolerably well provisioned, which enabled them to subsist some time longer.

These disasters, the result of want of foresight, were the cause of all the calamities which overtook the British army. Greater success would, without doubt, have followed if bolder measures had been adopted, but General Elphinstone, borne down by age and infirmity, had long lost the qualifications necessary for so responsible a command; he appeared to have fallen into a state of lethargy, and remained complacently satisfied with his defensive attitude, while it was absolutely necessary to proceed by the most opposite means. The staff of the General-in-Chief did not prove itself more competent than their commander, and Sir W. M'Naghten, taking himself to task rather late for the numerous faults he had committed, and which had placed some thousands of his countrymen in peril, strove to repair his error by the energy and vigour with which he conducted the defence. But his efforts were vain, all seemed paralysed around him; his orders, like his requests, were eluded, or timidly and inefficiently executed, and this occasioned fresh disasters, instead of procuring the slightest amelioration of their position.

On the 4th of November Zeman Khan, Mohamedzye,* who possessed immense wealth and had attached the people to his party by his largesses, succeeded, with the help of his uncle Nawab Djabbar Khan, and his cousin Chems Eddin Khan,† both influential personages, in inducing the Afghans to proclaim him king,

* Son of Nawab Assad Ullah Khan, one of the deceased brothers of Dost Mohamed.—*Ferrier.*

† Son of Emin Khan, half-brother of Dost Mohamed Khan.—*Ferrier.*

and he surrounded himself with all the pomp of royalty. This chief, at the head of his partizans, daily exchanged a few shots with the English, who were shut up in their cantonments; but though he captured and murdered a few officers and soldiers who imprudently risked their lives outside the camp, the Mohamedzye chief experienced only reverses in his repeated attacks. In one of these Abdullah Khan, Etchekzye, the originator and promoter of the conspiracy, received a ball in the forehead and died within two days.

After each defeat Zeman Khan retired into the city without being disturbed, for the English never followed him, which they could have done without difficulty; and as they had committed the serious fault of establishing their magazines of provisions at a considerable distance from the cantonments, they should at the outset have displayed a little more energy in endeavouring to dislodge the Afghans from the houses in which they were regaling themselves upon them. At the sight of one battalion and two or three pieces of cannon, they would have fled: they admit it now, and it was the step they most dreaded the enemy would take. Many times did the officers suggest it, but General Elphinstone would not give his consent, and the army saw itself reduced to procure provisions with gold and presents from the insurgents —the conduct of the general was indeed incomprehensible. After Shah Shooja had concerted with Abdullah Khan the revolt against the English, he fell into a far more dependent condition than that from which the latter had intended to withdraw him. The Etchekzye serdar and other conspirators had shown themselves exceedingly overbearing towards him, sharp discussions took place, and there was very nearly a rupture; nevertheless Shah Shooja was not sufficiently clearsighted to discover that they only looked upon him as a tool to be set aside as soon as the annihilation of his protectors was accomplished, and the rising of the Khyberees induced the king to throw himself into the arms of the national party, and conspire actively himself. He first permitted the unhappy Burnes to be murdered, though he could have saved him with the greatest ease, for he occupied the citadel with a devoted garrison of a thousand men; but it seems that he lost confidence in his accomplices while that act was being perpetrated, the cause of which was probably secret information that he received from the Serdar Mohamed Attah Khan. He then thought it prudent to close the gates of the Bala Hissar before the mob could reach it, and, in his blindness, believed that when order was restored the Afghans would hail him again as their king without the concurrence of the British being necessary; he therefore abstained from helping them, hoping by this means to secure the support of his own subjects. He even thought it very wrong when some of the English troops, shut up in the fortress with him, fired upon the townspeople, and turned their artillery upon the city; but it was quite a different matter when the insurgents cut down the trees in his garden under the guns of the place, or when the partizans of Zeman Khan came within range: then the Shah entreated that the sharpest and best sustained fire possible might be kept up. Several British officers, to whom the treachery of Shah Shooja was now evident, proposed that the army should occupy the citadel in which he still resided, as they would then have the town in their power, and could, by threatening its destruction, obtain supplies and provisions. This plan was warmly supported by Sir W. M'Naghten, but rejected by General Elphinstone, who gave as his reason that the discouragement amongst the troops rendered the execution of it impossible; indeed he acted in direct opposition to this sound advice by ordering a regiment, that had been sent to the Bala Hissar when the rebellion broke out, to return to camp. After this, though thus reinforced, the General lost all confidence in himself for any useful purpose; he had despaired of success from the commencement, and waited to the last with the inertness and cold apathy that are the result of a fixed opinion, the annihilation of the doomed army under his command: the troops themselves, cast down by the example of their chief, lost all energy. The British soldier has proved in all times that in bravery he is second to none in Europe; but this is under certain conditions: he must have full rations, his arrack, his beer, and a thousand other stimulants, the privation of which induces discouragement and indecision.

There is no doubt such was the condition of the force at Kabul, and to this must be attributed the feeble and pusillanimous conduct of H.M.'s 44th and the 37th N.I. when attacked by the insurgents in a small entrenched camp on an eminence which protected the citadel; they scarcely made any resistance, the efforts of Brigadier Shelton to animate them were useless, and cavalry and infantry gave way and fled in great disorder to the cantonments, hotly pursued by the Afghans, who would perhaps have forced their enemy's position that day, but for the intervention of the insurgent Serdar Osman Khan, Isakzye, who made a special treaty with Sir W. M'Naghten, in virtue of which a few days of comparative tranquillity were secured to the Anglo-Indian troops. After this check the 54th regiment of N. I., which occupied the Bala Hissar, was withdrawn, and Shah Shooja abandoned to his own resources.

It has been mentioned that Mohamed Akbar Khan, a son of Dost Mohamed, had retired to Khulm after his flight from Bokhara. Not having been able to procure from Mir Walee the assistance he required to maintain the old soldiers of his father who had joined him in his exile, he resolved to go to Persia, where his uncles, the serdars of Kandahar, had been well received by Mohamed Shah, hoping that that monarch would not do less for him than for them; indeed he was on his road there, and near Balkh, when, hearing of the insurrection in Kabul, he changed his course, and arrived on the 25th of November in that city,* where he found everything in the greatest confusion, and his cousin Zeman Khan declared king. Though smarting under this vexation, Akbar was obliged to recognise the election, but only with the secret determination to reverse it on the first opportunity, and such was the diversity of opinions and interests at this time amongst the Afghans, that he had little difficulty in creating for himself, and in a few days, a powerful party, which soon overcame that of all the other chiefs.

Many British officers, alive to the mournful turn that the military operations had taken, and foreseeing the result which the weakness and incapacity of General Elphinstone must produce, were of opinion that negotiations, based upon the evacuation of the country, ought to be opened with all the influential chiefs in Kabul, without regard to the superiority that some chose to arrogate to themselves over the rest. For several days Sir W. M'Naghten repelled this advice, which he received from all sides; but the disastrous intelligence that was brought in from outlying garrisons inclined him to enter-

* The newspapers and some other publications that have touched upon this revolt have stated, on what authority I know not, that Akbar Khan returned to Kabul accompanied by one thousand Tartar horsemen who had been sent to him by the Russian Government, but the assertion is utterly incorrect. He arrived with twelve badly equipped Afghan cavalry, and never received assistance from the Russians, who carefully abstained from any material intervention in favour of the conquered.—*Ferrier*.

tain pacific measures more favourably, for the English had losses to deplore in every direction. The troops at Ghuznee, commanded by Colonel Palmer, had been ordered to Kabul, but could not leave, and, subsequently, being obliged to abandon the town, they retired into the citadel: however, they were pretty well provisioned. The brigade of Lieutenant-Colonel M'Laren, which Sir W. M'Naghten recalled from Kandahar to the assistance of the division in Kabul, had been arrested in its march by the great depth of snow which had fallen and the insurrection that developed itself everywhere with a ferocity and excitement difficult to imagine. This column had pushed forward as far as Ghuznee; but there it was forced to return, and after having thrown a garrison into Kelat-i-Ghildjzye, with a year's provisions, it made its way back to Kandahar. On the other hand Captain Woodburn, who left Ghuznee with one hundred and thirty men, was harassed on the road by the insurgents, and took refuge in some ruins, surrounded by a broken wall. Here, besieged by four or five thousand Afghans, he made a sortie in two divisions, one led by himself the other by a native officer, and, throwing himself into the mêlée, he fell gallantly with all his men; the second division endeavoured to return, but only five Sepoys escaped to tell the tale. Another English officer, Captain Ferris, was besieged with two hundred and fifty men in a miserable fort, which he defended many days against three or four thousand Afghans, and having only twenty-five cartridges a man left, also resolved to try and cut his way through the enemy. This was no easy matter, for he had with him his wife and her sister, but the ladies were tied behind two native horsemen and placed in the centre of the square, and after a frightful conflict the little party reached another fort, whence, with the help of guides, they made their way to Peshawur.

The first idea of Sir W. M'Naghten, on hearing of these disasters, was to force his way through the Khyber Pass and join General Sale in Jellalabad, which he had fortified; but wiser counsels prevailed, and this impracticable project was given up. It was impracticable quite as much from the nature of the ground as from the ill feeling of the tribes, who were in arms all along the pass, and the deep snow presented aggravated difficulties of every kind, which Sale's brigade, if it had been ordered to meet them, must have encountered also. The plans for the retreat therefore were for the moment abandoned by Sir Wm. M'Naghten, and not without regret. Subsequently, and in conformity with the almost universal opinion, he sent Captains Lawrence and Trevor, and a few other officers, to make overtures of peace to the Afghans, by whom the propositions were favourably received; this induced Sir W. M'Naghten to place himself in direct communication with the chiefs, particularly with Mohamed Akbar Khan, with whom the English Commissioner proposed to conclude a treaty, consisting of twenty articles. These were all accepted by him and them, and in several conferences that followed, many of the serdars, who were desirous that tranquillity should be re-established in the country, insisted that the terms of the evacuation should be definitively and promptly decreed. Sir W. M'Naghten, seeing that Mohamed Akbar Khan appeared the most powerful amongst them, and the most inclined to negotiate, preferred treating with him, although he well knew that this chief every day joined the insurgents who fired on the soldiers in the cantonment. But Akbar, having assured him that he acted thus only to pacify the other serdars his rivals, who sought to degrade him in the eyes of his countrymen by representing him as a traitor to the national cause, he succeeded in gaining the confidence of the Commissioner, and an almost friendly understanding was established between them.

Was Mohamed Akbar in good faith when he promised entire devotion to the English, and when he promised even to deliver up the murderers of Burnes? This is doubtful, for it is very improbable he should have forgotten that the ruin of his house had been brought about by those to whom he had offered to devote himself. And then his father, the head of his family, the Emir Dost Mohamed, was he not still a prisoner in India? It is impossible to deny that the position of Akbar Khan was most embarrassing, for, obliged to conciliate the invaders of his country to preserve a hope of delivering his father, he could only do so at the risk of exciting the suspicions of his countrymen, who were but too well inclined to mistrust him. Zeman Khan, his cousin, knew that the return of Dost Mohamed would bring down the crazy scaffolding on which his own dawning royalty depended, and therefore he neglected no means of alienating the Afghans from Mohamed Akbar Khan; he would, perhaps, have completely succeeded if the latter had not, to save his life, adopted an energetic line of conduct, the loyalty of which has been diversely appreciated by those who have considered the subject. Many chiefs had openly quarrelled with the son of the Emir, and on the 22nd of December they reproached him with having treated with the English unknown to them, and sacrificed them to his own ambition. He defended himself with energy from these accusations, but he could not convince his antagonists, and they would certainly have cut him to pieces on the spot if he had not sworn upon the Koran that on the morrow he would bring the British Commissioner into Kabul either as a hostage or a corpse.

The Afghans who took part in the melancholy episodes which concluded the British occupation of Kabul, are generally convinced that in one of his interviews with Mohamed Akbar Khan, Sir W. M'Naghten had solemnly promised to restore his father to him within the space of a month; but the period had nearly expired, and the Emir was still a prisoner in India. This fact greatly exasperated Akbar Khan, and made him more exacting in the terms of the evacuation; several conferences had ended without a successful result, and the negotiations had already become embittered, when on the night of the 23rd to 24th of December, Captain Skinner who was in the Afghan camp, arrived in that of the English, the bearer of fresh conditions from Akbar Khan, who demanded another interview with Sir W. M'Naghten, for the purpose of concluding a definitive treaty. This was acceded to, and the envoy arrived at the appointed rendezvous on Christmas-Day, 1841, accompanied by Captains Lawrence, Trevor, and M'Kenzie; the meeting took place near a bridge, in the neighbourhood of which sixteen Afghan horsemen had been previously posted in ambush. Akbar Khan received the Commissioner with violent reproaches at his having so long delayed setting his father at liberty and evacuating Kabul; he also declared that the arms, ammunition, and hostages had never been given up to him, while on his side he held in readiness and at Sir W. M'Naghten's disposal the cattle necessary to transport the baggage of the army. "In exchange for my promptitude," he said, "I find only delay and duplicity; General Sale, instead of evacuating Jellalabad as agreed between us, has provisioned and fortified himself with more energy than ever." The British Commissioner in vain protested his good and loyal intentions; Mohamed Akbar would listen to nothing: Sir W. M'Naghten had, he said, delayed up to that day to fulfil his promises, and he should therefore consider him and his suite as prisoners, till all the conditions previously determined upon were executed. He then seized Sir William by the arm to take him into Kabul, but the envoy resisted and exclaimed, "Better die than follow you." Akbar Khan instantly put his pistol to his breast and fired,—it flashed in the pan; the second laid the Resident dead at his feet. The pistols which the chief used had been presented to him only a few days before by Sir W. M'Naghten himself. Captain Trevor, who was at a little distance, having seen the first hostile movement of the assassin, instantly dismounted to go to the assistance of his chief, but was killed on the spot by an Afghan bullet. As to Captains Lawrence and M'Kenzie they were seized, stripped, and tied on horseback behind two chiefs, who had infinite difficulty in saving them from their infuriated followers; they were subsequently imprisoned in a fort, but after some days recovered their liberty. The head of Sir W. M'Naghten was carried through the bazaars on the point of a spear, with the green spectacles on that he was in the habit of wearing; it was subsequently fixed on the roof of the Round Point of the bazaar, called the Tchar-sook, as well as his corpse, and that of Captain Trevor: the bodies were left there three days, and afterwards thrown into a dry well.

After the death of Sir W. M'Naghten, the direction of affairs was placed in the hands of Major Pottinger, who had defended Herat the preceding year. On leaving that city he came to Kabul and was appointed governor of Charikar and Istalif, two small towns situated in the mountains, one-and-twenty miles north of Kabul, and about three from each other. The garrisons which held them were after a gallant defence overpowered about the same time that the revolt broke out in the capital, but Major Pottinger, though wounded by a ball in the thigh, was enabled, almost by a miracle, to escape and reach the house of Burnes, which had been sacked and pillaged shortly before. Of this event he was ignorant, but on his arrival there the traces of the disaster were still fresh; he found himself alone in the smoking ruins and in the midst of the insurgents, from whom his lucky star and excellent horse saved him once more, and he arrived, completely exhausted, in the British cantonment. Major Pottinger had but very imperfectly recovered from his wound, when the heavy task of directing the political affairs of Kabul fell upon his shoulders. Sad as had been the result of the confidence which Sir William M'Naghten placed in Mohamed Akbar, such was the desperate position of things, that Major Pottinger could see no better course than to renew the negotiations with that serdar; but the other Afghan chiefs who wished to prevent the concentration of authority in the hands of the son of the Emir, insisted on taking part in the treaty, that was to drive the English out of their country. They all ratified it, and the articles were nearly a repetition of those which had been imposed on Sir W. M'Naghten, namely, the evacuation of Jellalabad by Sale's brigade, and the liberation of Dost Mohamed; but this time it was agreed that the English should keep their arms, and be accompanied across the Khyber by an Afghan escort, commanded by Akbar Khan himself, who was to protect them as far as Peshawur. Wounded, however, as had been his self-love, and foiled in his ambitious views in not having been permitted to treat singly with the invaders, he did not care to assemble the escort immediately. The Indo-British had lost up to this period twenty-eight officers killed in action or assassinated; 10,000 bodies of men and animals infected the air and aggravated the sufferings of the 5000 unhappy survivors, that now formed the army, and who were worn out by the resistance they had maintained for two months against 40,000 insurgents. The cold had become intensely severe; fuel, provisions, and ammunition failed, and the troops being completely discouraged Major Pottinger did not think it advisable to wait any longer for the promised escort, and decided upon making a desperate rush through the midst of the enemy; accordingly, on the 5th of January, 1842, he gave the order for departure.

On Thursday the 6th, after having sustained a siege of sixty-seven days, and endured the most cruel privations, General Elphinstone and the army he commanded quitted, under a humiliating capitulation, the intrenched camp of Kabul, and moved off on a road a foot deep in snow. The force had, however, scarcely cleared the cantonment, when the rear guard was attacked by the Afghans; an officer of the 5th regiment of native cavalry named Hardyman, and some of his men, were killed in this affair, and the army marched only five miles that day. The sky was clear, but the cold intense, and when they arrived on the encamping ground the soldiers had to clear away the snow, before they could rest their weary limbs on the frozen earth; to this was added the want of provisions, and before morning dawned several hundred men and women had died from cold and hunger.

On the 7th the division marched upon Barikhar, and the

Afghan escort which Akbar Khan had promised should protect the retreat appeared in larger numbers and hostile; the rear guard was harassed that day by several bloody engagements, and the enemy carried off three mountain guns. From this moment the English, who had indeed placed but little confidence in the promises of the Afghans, felt convinced they should never reach Jellalabad but by fighting every inch of the way, and, encamping at the entrance of the defile, they there passed a more terrible night than the first. Those who survived till day-break, found the ground covered with corpses; the bewildered Sepoys burnt their clothes to warm themselves, and the British soldiers sinking under cold and hunger had scarcely strength to carry their arms: the most frightful disorder reigned throughout the frozen and famished multitude, and those who had saved anything valuable were here obliged to abandon it.

On the morning of the 8th, the division could not advance one single step. The heights around swarmed with their enemies, who having suspended their fire during the night, recommenced their deadly work at sunrise. In this extremity the English were obliged to enter into a parley with Mohamed Akbar Khan, who was seen encamped on an eminence near, and who, while affecting a great sympathy for them, was not so ignorant of the misfortunes that befell them as he wished to make them believe. He blamed Major Pottinger for his precipitation in quitting Kabul, without waiting for the escort which was to protect the army, adding that he alone amongst the Afghan chiefs had the power to prevent the attacks made upon it, and he offered to control the insurgents, provided the English consented to give hostages that they would not go beyond Tezeen, until Sale's brigade had evacuated Jellalabad. It is evident that the serdar feared the junction of the two divisions in a place that was fortified and provisioned, and in which they could pass the winter in safety, and wait for the spring to resume the offensive. To assure himself therefore that the engagement would be faithfully kept, he demanded at first six hostages, but was subsequently satisfied with Major Pottinger, and Captains Lawrence and M'Kenzie. As soon as they were placed in his hands, the troops moved forward towards the famous defile of Khoord Kabul, but attacked on all sides, notwithstanding the treaty just concluded, this day brought with it the climax of their misfortunes; scenes of carnage and pitiless cruelty were renewed at every step, and the column, crushed by the rolling fire of its invisible foes, at length abandoned the guns to the Afghans. Reduced to twenty cartridges per man, they were obliged to charge with the bayonet enemies sheltered by rocks and well provided with ammunition, while women and children pierced with cold were seen wandering distracted and at random through the fire, amongst the disorganised troops. Mohamed Akbar Khan had no command over his men, for they had proclaimed the Djehad or Holy War, had become Ghazees or soldiers of the Faith, and their fanaticism knew no bounds; the feeling of revenge, that of doing a good work in the eyes of God, and above all the hope of booty, rendered them utterly deaf to entreaty or command; destitute of pity, and reckless of order or discipline, they gorged themselves with blood and plunder.

On the 9th Akbar Khan acknowledged that he was perfectly powerless to restrain these Ghazees, who renewed the scenes of the previous day with increased fury, and the storm which had raged over the wretched troops for three consecutive days ended in one of the most terrible military catastrophes on record. The remnant of the Indo-British army, exhausted by forced marches, by cold, by want of food and fuel, and agonizing sufferings of every description, had no longer the strength to defend itself, and was massacred—annihilated, by overwhelming numbers of merciless enemies. Three natives only and one single European, Dr. Brydon, reached Jellalabad out of a body of five thousand men and a much greater number of camp-followers, who lost their lives in this butchery. Akbar Khan seemed to deplore the conduct of his soldiers and his own want of command over them, and in the height of this bloody tragedy offered shelter to the English ladies, promising to protect them at the peril of his own life; the offer was accepted by several, amongst whom were Lady Sale, Lady M'Naghten, Mrs. Anderson, Mrs. Reid, and Mrs. Mainwaring, and they were perfectly well treated by him.

Akbar Khan having in his camp the hostages that were delivered to him, also General Elphinstone, Brigadier Shelton, Captain Johnson, and a few other officers, remained two days on this fatal ground, waiting for the evacuation of Jellalabad by General Sale, to whom he had sent a copy of the treaty concluded between himself and Major Eldred Pottinger. But that General formally refused to abandon the place without an order from the Governor-General of India in Council; and fortunate was it for him that he came to this determination, for the Afghans had laid a plan for exterminating his corps to the very last man.

After the disaster in the Khoord Kabul, Mohamed Akbar Khan marched his prisoners to Tezeen and Jugdulluk, and then to Thigri, a fortified town situated in the rich valley of Lugman, where, after much hesitation, he determined not to forward them to Jellalabad, but sent them to Buddiabad, a large fortress recently built at the upper end of the valley. On the 11th they were moved to Zindeh and placed in charge of the chief, Mohamed Shah Khan. The death of General Elphinstone from natural causes occurred on the 23rd of April following, and Akbar Khan sent the corpse under escort to Jellalabad; but the Ghazees met it on the road, attacked and dispersed the guard, tore the body from the coffin, and stripped and stoned it.

The massacres in the Khoord Kabul greatly increased the power and influence of Mohamed Akbar and his party became daily more numerous; the Ghazees on all sides responded to his appeal, and the irregular cavalry of the country in the service of the English deserted to join his standard. His army then amounted to seven or eight thousand men, and with these he laid siege to Jellalabad, being fully convinced that General Sale would never evacuate it in virtue of the treaty. This brave officer had entrenched himself in the place with the two battalions under his command, and for more than two months had been living on half rations, determined to hold out to the last man. Jellalabad (Glory inhabited) is situated west of Peshawur, at the opening of the Khyber Pass. In the summer it contains but 2000 inhabitants, but in the winter nearly 20,000, for the severity of that season in these mountains obliges the inhabitants to take refuge in the towns; General Sale arrived at the period of this augmentation, and was necessitated, for the security of his brigade, to take steps to prevent this increase in the population. All Akbar Khan's efforts to dislodge the gallant General proved ineffectual, and instead of succeeding, as he hoped, he was very nearly losing his life here either by mischance or treachery. The rifle of the Isakzye chief, Mohamed Osman Khan, the first of the insurgent serdars who made a treaty with Sir Wm. M'Naghten, went off accidentally—such, at least, was the statement of that chief—and the ball lodged in Akbar Khan's arm, who pretended that the injury was premeditated, and that Osman Khan had been bribed by the English to assassinate him: he, therefore, put him to death.

While Akbar Khan was thus harassing General Sale at Jellalabad, Zeman Khan, the newly elected king of the Afghans, occupied the town of Kabul and besieged Shah Shooja, who from the citadel kept up a cannonade upon the city; several thousand lives were sacrificed in this struggle, for each day brought with it its own combat. The cause of Zeman Khan, however, prospered not; he became anxious and disappointed at this useless waste of his fortune, on which he depended for success, and by which alone he had secured partisans; he, therefore, deemed it prudent to accept the propositions made to him by the Shah, laid down the royalty with which the nation had invested him, and consented to become the prime minister of the Suddozye prince. In acting thus he thought he should be able to prevent the re-establishment of Dost Mohamed if he should return, and also to reduce Akbar Khan to obedience, being well determined, however, to take the first favourable opportunity of overthrowing Shah Shooja and seizing the crown once more; but the events which followed completely neutralized his deep-laid schemes. The Shah, on the other hand, was not more sincere than his vizier, and promised him what he never intended to perform; he made these concessions to his adversaries for no other purpose than to extricate himself from his present embarrassing position, intending to get rid of them all if ever he should find himself firmly established in power. To complete this apparent reconciliation, he named Akbar Khan, *Serdar Serdarùne*,* and sent his appointment to him at Jellalabad; but that chief would not accept it or sanction the treaty concluded with his cousin, unless Shah Shooja agreed to support him in besieging that town. It was hardly possible that any proposal should have better coincided with the Shah's own views, for he ardently longed for some opportunity of leaving Kabul till he could return in force, supported by the English, whose assistance he saw, when too late, was indispensable to him. The conditions offered by Akbar Khan were by no means favourable to the intrigues of Zeman Khan, and the vizier, therefore, advised the king not to accept them, or at any rate if he did to leave him, during his absence, in com-

* General of the Generals.—*Ferrier.*

mand at Kabul; but the king, who perceived the drift of his advice, simply sent him orders to accompany him to Jellalabad, and to prove that he was in earnest in this decision, he appointed the son of the Serdar Emin Ullah Khan governor of Kabul while he was away. Zeman Khan, uneasy at the Shah's persisting in his determination, resolved to ascertain the cause, and found that he had been deceived by his sovereign, whom he had himself intended to betray: he, therefore, to nip the evil in the bud, determined upon his destruction.

Shah Shooja, in pursuance of his intentions, left the citadel to join his small army, encamped about a mile and a half from the Bala Hissar, with the declared object of leading it against the English, but in reality to use it as an escort on his way to place himself under their protection; he had, however, scarcely started when the Serdar Shooja ed Dooulet, a son of Zeman Khan, accompanied by four servants, overtook him, and fired point blank into his palanquin. The unfortunate monarch was wounded by several balls, and still breathed when the assassins took him out of the litter and threw his body into a stream that was near the road, finishing their atrocious crime with their swords. This event took place in February, 1842.

The character of Shah Shooja has generally been too severely criticized. Even his adversaries, the Mohamedzyes, who now govern Afghanistan, admit that he was a very remarkable man, and the only one of Shah Timoor's sons who was capable of reigning. He had both ability and courage, and redeemed more than one vice by the qualities which the Afghans delight to see in their princes. He was after the manner of that country a good administrator, and understood how to conduct a war as well as an Afghan can; he only wanted a little better luck; such is the opinion of all Afghans. Several times beaten and driven out of the country, he never considered himself vanquished, and took the field twelve times in his endeavours to regain the crown. It is impossible to look upon this perseverance as mere obstinacy; it denotes great energy of character, and if he always failed it was because he never would permit the smallest entrenchment upon his absolute rights. When we Europeans form an opinion of the acts of the barbarous nations of Asia we always do so according to our own standard of morals, and political passions, without making the least allowance for the difference that exists between our habits and feelings, and theirs.

There is no question that Shah Shooja, like every other Afghan, was cruel and also despotic, but let us review the position in which he was placed, and it will appear that having to govern a race for whom force is the only law, it would have been difficult for him to act otherwise than as he did. The Mohamedzyes, whose influence in the government was so great, were always conspiring against him during his first reign. After the death of Ahmed Shah, the descendants of that great prince had always been subject to the caprices engendered by the ambition of the serdars who left them only the shadow of regal power. Shah Shooja resisted their intrigues with greater tenacity than his predecessors had done, and was therefore more especially the object of their machinations; he would have been foolish indeed to allow himself to be beaten without making an effort to foil them, and coercion was the only means by which he could succeed in concentrating the power in his own hands: he believed he should secure this object if he did so, and therein was his error. Had he reflected that the tribes, attached to their chiefs by so many ties, would give him but a feeble and uncertain support, he would certainly have abstained from using force for the purpose of attaining it; but weakness on his part would have been worse, for then he must have succumbed at once. His conduct during his second reign is a proof of that independence of character which was ever his misfortune: indignant under the yoke imposed upon him by the English, all the vices of his Afghan nature broke forth; he betrayed his benefactors, resisted his liberators, and died by the hands of assassins—for an Afghan he could have no more glorious close to such a career.

CHAPTER XXV.

Fethi Djing Mirza succeeds Shah Shooja — Combat between that prince and Zeman Khan — The former is beaten — Akbar Khan returns to Kabul and forces Fethi Djing to retire to the citadel — The former becomes his Vizier and recognizes him as King — Akbar plunders Fethi Djing — Flight of the Prince — Akbar remains master of Kabul — The English in spite of the insurrection maintain themselves at Kandahar — Foresight of Major Rawlinson — Occurrences in the neighbourhood of that city — Persian account of them — Akter Khan, Alizye, beaten by the English — Plan of the Afghans to seize Kandahar— They are defeated — Second expedition of the English to Kabul — Akbar Khan is repulsed at Butkhak — Opinions of the press on this second expedition — What is true and what is false — Mistakes of the journalist in military matters — The English evacuate Afghanistan — They place Shapoor Mirza on the throne of Kabul — The English give Dost Mohamed his liberty — Akbar Khan returns to Kabul and seizes the sovereign power — Restoration of Dost Mohamed at Kabul — Seif der Djing is driven from Kandahar by Kohendil Khan.

SHAH SHOOJA left several sons, of whom four took part in the political events that occurred in Afghanistan during the English occupation; these were Timoor Mirza, Fethi Djing Mirza, Seif der Djing Mirza, and Shapoor Mirza.

Although the Shah had appointed a Governor of Kabul previously to his violent death, he had also for further security placed his second son Fethi Djing in the Bala Hissar. When this prince heard of his father's assassination he shut himself up in the citadel with one thousand men of Arab origin who were devoted to him, and sent money to his partizan Emin Ullah Khan, Logheree, who occupied the suburbs with three thousand men, to distribute among the people in his name, and induce them to rise against Zeman Khan: this he did, and a bloody combat was maintained for two days and two nights, after which Emin Ullah Khan was obliged to retire to the Bala Hissar.

Mohamed Akbar had scarcely recovered from his wound when he heard of these events, which determined him immediately to retire from the siege of Jellalabad (an undertaking that had hitherto proved to him only a source of disappointment), and return in haste to Kabul, which he reached twenty days after the death of Shah Shooja. Whether it was because he did not consider himself in sufficient force, or that he thought the moment unpropitious, the serdar did not assume the sovereign power, but resolved in the first instance to beguile his enemies into destroying each other, and for that purpose allied himself with Zeman Khan, and prevailed on him to assist in seizing the person of the Prince Fethi Djing. With their united forces they made four unsuccessful attacks upon the Bala Hissar, but at last succeeded in blowing up one of the towers of the *enceinte*, when they rushed in and either killed or made prisoners all who were within its walls.

Zeman Khan wished to put Fethi Djing to death, but to this proposal Mohamed Akbar refused to consent, and not only took that prince under his special protection, but made the liveliest protestations of devotion to his cause, declaring that he would never recognize any other Afghan as his sovereign. The object of this apparent generosity was simply to crush more decidedly the power of Zeman Khan, who, divining his intention, fortified himself in the suburbs of the town, but in vain, for Mohamed Akbar attacked and drove him back at every point, and he owed his safety to his formal renunciation of his claims to royalty and the post of vizier. After this success Akbar Khan married the daughter of the Serdar Emin Ullah Khan, an alliance which greatly strengthened his party; he was also appointed vizier by Fethi Djing, and maintained in the general command of the army. But these concessions did not affect his original project, and he prepared to bring about the downfall of this prince, who, warned of his danger, once more retired to the citadel, from which, however, he was forced to retire after a siege of forty-eight hours. Akbar immediately seized the treasure that Shah Shooja had left his son, but suspecting that Fethi Djing had secreted a part of it, he ordered his guards not to lose sight of him for a moment, nor to allow him to sleep until he had given up all the diamonds which he acknowledged were in his possession. For three days and nights had the unhappy Fethi Djing Mirza been thus tormented, when Khan Shireen Khan, a Kuzzilbash serdar, who was secretly of his party, and supported the English, found an opportunity of conveying to him two hundred ducats with which he bribed his janitors to facilitate his escape. His prison was one of the large towers in an angle of the citadel, and happily for him a window in it overlooked the town; from this he was lowered by a rope at night, and took refuge in the quarter inhabited by the Kuzzilbashes of Djevanchir, a gun-shot from the place, where Khan Shireen Khan secreted him in his own house.

When his escape became known, Akbar Khan sent in pursuit of him in all directions; the strictest search was instituted for about twelve days, but without success, and when all hope of discovering him was lost, and the search given up, Fethi Djing left his retreat, and under the escort of one hundred Kuzzilbash horsemen, reached Jellalabad. It was not known till some time after that Khan Shireen Khan had assisted the prince in his escape, and though Mohamed Akbar's resentment was great, he concealed it, as it was necessary for him to keep on terms with this serdar. Are not all these intrigues and counter-intrigues the best evidence of the instability of the Afghan character, and of the turbulence, constant craving for change, and uncontrollable love of bloodshed innate in it?

The flight of Fethi Djing Mirza was the last episode connected with the occupation of Kabul by the British. More fortunate or better prepared at Kandahar, they succeeded in holding that city; a result which was due to the firmness of General Nott, and, above all, to the indefatigable activity of Major Rawlinson, who administered the affairs of that Residency with great ability.*

The war in this province was the more difficult to conduct because the principality had never been entirely subdued. The Serdar Akter Khan, Alizye, who had retired to the district of Zemindavar, kept up an unceasing conflict against the English, and though constantly beaten, he, in the most undaunted manner, as constantly

* Major Rawlinson is one of those rare characters who are equally capable of everything — honourable, firm, enlightened, and conciliatory—he is universally beloved. The remembrance of his government, which even in 1845 the author found fresh in the memory of the Kandaharians, and could well appreciate, tells far more in favour of the learned and celebrated decipherer of the Cuneiform inscriptions than anything that can be said in commendation of that officer's talents. The manner in which he defended Kandahar against the insurgents will give the reader only a poor idea of the merit and courage of this brilliant officer. He may justly be classed amongst the great men that have been distinguished in the service of the East India Company, and it is impossible not to feel astonishment, that after such a splendid defence of the post entrusted to his care, his talents and fidelity should remain so ill-remunerated by his government. But, however that may be, such men are always elevated above their fellow men, and whether they are or are not the objects of Government patronage, the esteem and admiration of the world are theirs. — *Ferrier.*

returned to the charge. When the insurrection broke out in Kabul the number of his adherents was considerably augmented, and the serdars Seidal Khan, Mohamed Attah Khan, Saloo Khan, Mir Efzel Khan, and others, with large contingents, then joined him.

Seif der Djing, the third son of Shah Shooja, who lived at Kandahar, fled from the city to join the insurgents; both father and son thus repaying their benefactors the English, to whom they owed everything, with the blackest ingratitude.

Immediately the news of the rising at Kabul reached Major Rawlinson, he secretly despatched messengers in every direction to call in the scattered troops under the guns of the place. He likewise ordered the removal of all the provisions from the different magazines to the citadel, in which he resided, and these wise dispositions were completed before the report of the revolt was known in the city. There were at this time in Kandahar and the suburbs, 4000 Afghan horse, in the pay of the state; these troops were the cause of the greatest uneasiness to Major Rawlinson, and, in consequence, he sent for Mirza Mohamed Khan, Popolzye, the Vizier of Timoor Mirza,* and desired him to say whether he was or was not true to the British cause? To this question he replied in the affirmative, when Major Rawlinson desired him to give instant proof of his devotion by leaving Kandahar with his cavalry, and attacking the Serdar Mohamed Attah Khan, who was advancing on the city from Kabul at the head of the greater part of the insurgent horse. Mirza Mohamed, having first received a large sum of money, at once set out with his division, but, instead of fighting, joined his force to that of the rebel chief. On hearing of this piece of treachery, the Resident adopted a measure most imperatively necessary to preserve the corps under General Nott from certain destruction, and ordered the greater part of the inhabitants who were of Afghan origin to leave the city in the shortest possible space of time, permitting only a few to remain besides the Parsees and Hindoos.

At Kandahar the English had nine incomplete battalions, two batteries of artillery, and a few hundred Indian cavalry, but the atter were outside the town and held the country under the com-

* The eldest son of Shah Shooja and Governor of Kandahar; but only nominally so, for the English had more power here than at Kabul.—*Ferrier.*

mand of Mr. Pattinson. During my residence at Kandahar, I read a Persian account of the mournful event which led to the death of that officer and one of his comrades named Golding. The simplicity of the document tempted me to translate it in the most literal manner, and I give the Persian text in order that those readers who are able may judge of the correctness of my translation.

Dou fooudj Djanbaz ez merdum Afghan-farsi-Kabouli der Kandahar boudend. Douta saheb meuseb inglich serkerdè emin dou fooudj djanbaz boud. Yeki ismech, Golding boud yeki Wilson. Pattinson saheb serkerdi Kull, der tchader Golding saheb boud. Biroun dervaze Herat tchader zedè boudend. Emon cheb ké mi khastend subguiah beurevend der Guirichk, fooudj Golding saheb rikhtend bala tchader. Er dou saheb Khabidè. Boudend der tchader. Dest bè chemchir bala inha rikhtend, Golding saheb kuchtend, Pattinson saheb ez tchader biroun amed. Yozdeh zakhm chemchir dacht. Yek noouker ouchiar dacht; asp hazer mi kouned, vé khodech poucht saheb savar micheved. Emon cheb oura avourd der Kandahar. Bé on saheb diguer, ké Wilson saheb bached, khaberdar micheved; Khodechra bé tchader saheb misresoned—mi bined khoun busior rikhtest vé saheban em nistend—mustereb biroun mi ayed; mi bined yek fooudj djanbaz èmmè reftend. Mi ayed miyan fooudj khodech, migouyet: her guiah chouma em nemek beharam estid, mera beu kuched, vè khod-tu beurevid ouha der djavab mi gouyend: Khouda nè kouned! ma nemek bè haram nistim — migouyed herguiah nemek bé haram nistid ba men bi ayid, ké beurevim khoun béraderan mara biguirim. In savar ez emin fooudj aspha khodra zin mikouned, bé kadr sed savar emera ou mi revend, dou sed pindja savar ez rassalèh. Hindi, alidja mejor Rawlinson, be Komak ou mi furusted, ve gafeul mi rizend bala emon fooudj gurikhté. Fursed tuffeng indaktè nè boud, dest bè chemchir gati mi cheved, alidja Wil-

Two squadrons of Afghan horse, *Djanbaz*, composed of Parsivans of Kabul, were at Kandahar with two English officers, Messrs. Golding and Wilson. Mr. Pattinson, who had the chief command, was in the tent of Mr. Golding, and the squadrons were encamped outside the Herat gate. On the night preceding the day on which they were to march to Girishk the troopers of Mr. Golding's squadron rushed into the tent in which these officers were asleep, fell upon them sword in hand and killed Mr. Golding. Mr. Pattinson, who was wounded in eleven places, having subsequently left the tent, found his servant an intelligent, and faithful man, with his horse ready; this man assisted him to mount, and getting up behind him, he brought him in to Kandahar the same night. The news reaching Mr. Wilson he immediately rode to the tent of these gentlemen, but found only the proof of the murderous onslaught in their blood on the ground. He withdrew from the tent deeply moved, and finding that their squadron of djanbaz had deserted, he at once returned to his own men and said, "If you are traitors kill me and be off;" but the troopers replied, "God preserve us from being any such thing." "Well then," said their officer, "if you are not traitors follow me and let us take revenge for the blood of our comrades which has been shed." The men, about one hundred in number, immediately saddled their horses, and before leaving the ground two hundred and fifty Indian cavalry, which had been sent to his assistance by Major Rawlinson, joined Mr. Wilson, when they at once set off in pursuit of the

son saheb chir del ewel savar boud, mi ressed. Seta ez serkerdèh—buzurk-ra ba chemchir mi zened, kuchtè chudè ez asp mi indazed eukm mi déed, ser yeki-ra mi bourend:—Kalender Khan ismech boud emin fessad-ra ou Kerdèboud Bagui savar, chikest khourdè, rouh bè guriz mi guzarend, aigaib ichan mi revend ta busior ez ichan Kaltl Kerdè vè euldjè busior mi averend, bermiguerdend ser bouridè Kalender Khan-ra avourdend der Kandahar; eukm Kerdend kè sè où rouz der bazar avizou Kerdend. Djartchi Djar kéchid der bazarha ké sezaye kési ké nemek be harami mi kounend.

deserters. It was no affair for fire-arms, they came upon the rebels sword in hand; the very exalted Mr. Wilson, the lion-hearted, was the first to close with them, and killed three of the principal chiefs with his own hand, striking them off their horses. He then ordered the head of one of them, Kalender Khan, who had excited the men to mutiny, to be cut off, and followed the rebel squadron, which had fled in disorder. He pursued them until a great number were killed, and they returned to Kandahar laden with their spoils, bringing back with them the head of Kalender Khan; this was by order placed on a hook in the bazaar to remain there three days, and a crier stood near, who continually announced to the passers by, "This is the punishment of traitors."

Treachery was indeed the order of the day with the Afghans; and fanaticism, till then almost unknown to that people, was added to it. Aroused by the mollahs, it excited every mind, for these sanguinary ministers of Allah unceasingly repeated to the people in their sermons and on all other occasions, the verse of the Koran which says that to kill an infidel is an act pleasing to God, and that every Ghazee will, after his death, go to the Garden of Paradise, and live in the midst of houris always young and beautiful. Is it astonishing that such teaching should instigate this barbarous people to indulge in the most deplorable excesses?

One example, from amongst a thousand, will give an idea of the state of public feeling at this time. An officer of the English commissariat was making some purchases in the bazaar, when one of these fanatics came up to him, and stabbed him in the abdomen with his knife. He was immediately arrested, bound, and brought before Major Rawlinson, who asked him why he had committed so vile an act? "He is mad," exclaimed a certain Mirza Jan, a servant of the English, who wished to save his life. "No, no," replied the Afghan, eagerly, "I have all my senses about me;" and, having heaped upon the Resident every opprobrious epithet he could think of, added, "far from repenting of what I have done, if I had my knife now, and my hands were free, I would do as much for you." The villain was subsequently blown from a gun.

But to return to my narrative. The Prince Seif der Djing, Akter Khan, Mohamed Attah Khan, and other insurgent chiefs, after having united their forces, advanced to within a short distance of Kandahar on the 9th of January, 1842, just in time to give a small body of six hundred men, commanded by General Nott, the opportunity of beating them. They, however, were not demoralized by this check, and persevered in trying to carry out their design of taking the city; but wisely judging that their numbers were quite unequal to accomplish this object by force, they had recourse to an artifice in which they very nearly succeeded. A body of from eighteen to twenty thousand Ghazees attempted to ravage the environs of Kandahar, when General Nott immediately took the field to drive them back. He had only eight incomplete battalions with him, and a few horsemen; amongst these were a hundred Beloochees, commanded by the same Aga Khan whom the English sent into the south of Persia in 1841, and who, having failed in his enterprise, undertaken for the purpose of raising an insurrection there, joined them again. The Ghazees retired slowly on the approach of General Nott, skirmishing all the way, to the mountainous district of Zemindavar, three days' journey from Kandahar, whither the British troops had the imprudence to follow them. When the insurgent commanders saw that they had succeeded in drawing the enemy thus far from the city, they left a few cavalry in his front to occupy their attention, and rapidly returned with the bulk of their troops to Kandahar, the garrison of which then consisted of only seven hundred sepoys and one hundred English soldiers, with a single officer. On this occasion Major Rawlinson showed as much intelligence as coolness and decision. He placed his men most judiciously, the Hindoos on the walls, the few British at the gates; and with these dispositions once made waited the arrival of the enemy in stern tranquillity.

Towards evening some Afghans appeared at the Herat gate with mules laden with firewood, brought, they asserted, for the use of the town, and declaring themselves friends of the English. The sepoy sentry on the rampart, foolishly believing their story, gave them permission to lie down within cannon-shot of the place, which most imprudent conduct, as will be seen, nearly led to the capture of the city. At two o'clock in the dark winter morning, the faggots, which they had secretly piled against the gates, were fired, and a detachment of the insurgent army rushed forward at a concerted signal and threw themselves into the opening made by the flames. They were received with a sharp volley, which did not, however, prevent a few from penetrating to the centre of the city, where they were soon disposed of.

The combat, nevertheless, still raged with fury round the gate; the British artillery, ably served, mowed down whole ranks of Ghazees: and so many Afghans fell there that, entirely obstructing the entrance, the bodies formed a rampart for the besieged. Several attacks which they made at other points were perfectly unsuccessful; and after six hours' hard fighting they retired, leaving more than twelve hundred dead under the ramparts. Intelligence of what was taking place was immediately sent to General Nott, the rapidity of whose movements soon brought him back to Kandahar, near which the Afghans dared no longer remain, and therefore turned their efforts against the little fortress of Girishk. This had been confided to the charge of Mohamed Kooli Khan, a son of the famous Vizier Fethi Khan, Mohamedzye, who had attached himself to the British cause; the young serdar was not to be intimidated either by the threats or by the greatly superior force which held him in a state of siege for many months, during which he made a heroic resistance, and at the close remained master of the place.

That the English maintained themselves in Kandahar through the whole period of the troubles in Kabul was due, as I have already remarked, to the talent and courage of Major Rawlinson, whose measures enabled him to surmount the most serious difficulties, and wait till the relieving army from India arrived to re-establish the prestige of the Indo-British arms in that principality. This expedition obtained permission to pass through the dominions of the Maharadjah of the Punjab, and crossed the Indus about the middle of the summer of 1842. As soon as information of this fact arrived at Kandahar, four battalions of the garrison and the Belooch cavalry, commanded by the brother of Aga Khan, escorted the heavy baggage and guns to Shikapoor, whence they proceeded to India. The five remaining battalions of General Nott's division also quitted the city on the 8th of August, 1842, but marched towards Kabul, where they effected their junction with the corps d'armée which had advanced from Peshawur at the end of the same month.

The Afghans, commanded by Mohamed Akbar Khan, left the

capital to meet the English, and fell in with them at the village of Bootkak, a distance of fourteen miles from Kabul. Khan Shireen Khan, the Kuzzilbash Serdar, had joined him, but after the exchange of a few shots he passed over to the English with the five thousand horsemen who were under his orders.*

The battle of Bootkak, the brunt of which fell entirely upon the light troops, lasted nearly five hours, when Mohamed Akbar Khan, completely beaten, retired to the mountains and thence to Khulm. He had with him at this time a British officer, whom he had taken prisoner in the beginning of the year, and he at first thought of putting him to death, but the fear of reprisals which might be taken on his family, still in India and in the power of the English, suggested to him a nobler line of conduct, and after his flight to Khulm he sent this officer to the British camp, escorted by two Afghan horsemen; those who had been made prisoners on the same occasion, both men, women, and children, having already arrived there. Mohamed Akbar had removed them from Zindeh on the 28th of May, in order that they might be the more closely watched, for two chiefs had, it was said, offered the English to raise two thousand men and deliver the prisoners. They were, therefore, dispersed in various fortresses at about an hour's distance from Kabul, near the river Logur, and at this time they were better lodged and better fed. But when the British force approached, Akbar Khan, dreading that they might be carried off, and that he should then lose the best ground for any stipulation he could hope to make for his exiled family, sent them away on the 29th of August towards Bamian, where they arrived on the 3rd of September, and met with far worse treatment than they had ever experienced.

After the battle of Bootkak, however, Khan Shireen Khan caused search to be made for them by the Kuzzilbashes, who brought them safely into camp at Kabul on the 21st September. He had procured their liberty by his interposition with Mohamed Shah Khan, to whom 20,000 rupees in cash and an annual pension of 2000 more were promised, but never paid.

---

* Khan Shireen Khan, the Serdar Serdarane of the Kuzzilbashes, has four thousand families under his command, and is much looked up to and feared by the Afghans. Six thousand more families of this tribe are distributed amongst different serdars, of whom Gholam Hoosein Khan, Atchar, renowned for his courage, is one, and has authority over one thousand families.—*Ferrier*.

The Indo-British army remained some days under the walls of Kabul before they entered the city, and it was not till the 9th October that Sir R. Shakespear received orders to take in a company of sappers, five companies of Her Majesty's 26th and 33rd, and five companies of the 31st, the Bengal light cavalry and the 3rd Irregular cavalry. As the inhabitants had fled at the approach of the British troops, there was no one to fight: but this officer's instructions were to destroy several parts of this fine city. On the 11th the destruction of the magnificent and glorious edifice of Ali Murdane Khan, the great emporium of this part of Central Asia, was effected, and soon after that of a mosque near the bazaars; the bazaars themselves and every quarter of the city, with the exception of the Bala Hissar and the houses of the Kuzzilbashes, were treated in the same manner, and nothing was left but a mass of ruins. After having destroyed the city, the army retired upon Gundamuck, where they arrived almost without resistance on the 18th, having desolated the country, burnt the residences of the native chiefs and the villages on their line of march. On the 21st the 1st division, under General Pollock, arrived at Jellalabad, and was followed by that of General Nott, which reached it on the 24th. On the 25th October the engineers blew up the bastions of Jellalabad, and all the houses were reduced to ashes—this was the concluding operation of the retributary expedition, and the force commenced its return to India immediately after.

I shall close this episode of the war in Kabul by a quotation from the work of Lady Sale, who was herself one of the prisoners, and who thus speaks of their captivity while sojourning in the mountain fastnesses of the Khyber :—" A woman's vengeance is said to be fearful; but nothing can satisfy mine against Akbar, Sultan Jan, and Mohamed Shah Khan. Still I say that Akbar, having for his own political purposes done as he said he would do —that is, destroyed our army—letting only one man escape to tell the tale, as Dr. Brydon did, and having got the families into his possession—I say, having done this, he has ever since we have been in his hands treated us well—that is, honour has been respected. It is true that we have not common comforts; but what we denominate such are unknown to Afghan females—they always sleep on the floor, sit on the floor, &c. The wuzeer gives us rations of meat, rice, ottah, ghee, and oil, and lately fruit. At first our food was dressed for us, but it was so greasy and disgusting, that we asked leave to cook for ourselves. It is true we have been taken about the country, exposed to heat, cold, rain, &c.; but so were their own women. He has given us common coarse chintz and coarse long cloth, too, wherewith to clothe ourselves; but I do not hesitate to repeat that we have always been as well treated as captives could have been in such a country. But while rendering to Akbar Khan the justice that is due to him, I shall never forget the injury he has done to England. Had our army been cut to pieces by an avowed enemy, whether in the field or the passes, let them have used what stratagems they pleased, all had been fair. Akbar had shone as another William Tell: he had been the deliverer of his country from a hateful yoke imposed upon them by Kaffirs; but here he stands by his own avowal, freely made, the assassin of the envoy, not by proxy, but by his own hand. He treated with his enemies and betrayed them; he massacred under his own eyes thousands of men and women dying of cold and hunger, whom he had promised to feed and to defend; therefore his name will be devoted to eternal opprobrium."

I have examined most of the journals and reviews of the time, in which the British occupation of Afghanistan was discussed, and found that all loudly declaimed against the second expedition to Kabul—those of London as well as Paris, and especially the English opposition press. But why so much heat? so much party spirit? why distort facts or exaggerate them? It is certain that faults were committed, and that bloody catastrophes, even excesses according to our ideas, were the consequences of that expedition; but such invectives will not repair them. Let us state them with the calmness and dignity of civilized people, instead of becoming barbarous ourselves in defending barbarians. In the course of this narrative blame has been awarded wherever it was justly due, and impartiality renders it equally a duty to correct the overcharged statements of the events and circumstances that are said to have occurred in the second invasion of Kabul. The article in the *Journal des Débats* of January 8, 1843, though written with a certain degree of asperity, is on the whole the most moderate that up to that time had appeared on the subject in France, and this induces me to insert it here, adding a few remarks of my own:—

"The principal fact that we find in the Monthly Mail from India, which brings us intelligence from Bombay up to the 1st December, 1842, is the final evacuation of Afghanistan.

"Early in November the Indo-British army of the Indus was concentrated at Peshawur, in the kingdom of Lahore, prepared to return within the boundaries of British India, where it was expected the last brigade would arrive between the 20th and 25th December.

"The events by which this evacuation will ever be remembered are deplorable. In truth, if we wished to take our revenge for the declamations of Lord Palmerston—if we wished to fling back upon England all the accusations unceasingly made by her press against our generals and the system of warfare which they have been forced to adopt in Algiers—the task would be easy, indeed more than easy. The retreat of General Pollock's force was marked by barbarities as odious as useless: every man who fell into the hands of the troops was put to death; and it was not the Afghans who set the example of this cruelty, for they had returned safe and sound the prisoners of 1841.*

"Three towns, one of which contains, or did contain, 60,000 inhabitants, have been reduced to ashes, and why? for what end? For the fruitless pleasure of satisfying the least honourable passion of our nature, the passion of revenge.

"It was not thus that our soldiers and generals behaved in Africa. If the barbarism of our enemies, who knew not, like the Afghans, what it is to make prisoners—if the hard necessities of war forced our generals to adopt measures of extreme severity—they are, at least, in pursuit of a definitive object—positive, honourable, glorious. In those severities the ministers of France may, at least, find consolation in the hopes of a brighter future; they have the right to believe that they will some day rescue that colony from its barbarous condition. The ever increasing sacrifices made by France stand as proofs to the world that it is a real and serious undertaking, in which the country looks for better things than the gratification of brutal passions; but in ordering these burnings and massacres, what object could that general possibly have who was immediately to evacuate Afghanistan for ever?

"'Istalif,' says the letter of an English officer, 'is a pretty little

* But were they not the same Afghans who, in defiance of a capitulation, agreed to by themselves and their chiefs, to allow the British army to make good its retreat, massacred that army to the very last man? The English prisoners were returned, it is true; but would that have been the case if Dost Mohamed had not been the prisoner of the East India Company?—*Ferrier*.

town of 15,000 * inhabitants, against whom we had nothing to say unless that their town stood half way between Kabul and Charikar, where one of our Goorkha regiments (irregular cavalry) † was destroyed the year before by the Afghans.' As, then, they were pressed for time and could not push on to Charikar, Istalif was punished. A brigade, under the orders of General M'Caskill, entered it early in September, after a trifling engagement, and proceeded to put to the sword every one who had not succeeded in making his escape. It appears that even the dead and wounded were not respected. The sepoy soldiers, in the excess of their unmitigable cruelty, set fire to the cotton clothing of their victims, and thus burned the dead and dying, which would, according to their superstitious notions, call down a curse on the descendants of those whose remains were thus disposed of without the honours of sepulture. After the slaughter six hundred women remained in the hands of the victors, who set them at liberty. Were they respected, as had been the European ladies who fell into the power of the Afghans after the disasters at Kabul the winter before? It does not seem that the soldiers saw their prisoners taken from them with much satisfaction.

"Two soldiers of the 9th infantry of the Royal army had at the same moment seized a pretty girl of fourteen years of age, and, not wishing to fight for the possession of the prize, they agreed to decide it with the dice,—with this condition, that the winner should make her an honest woman and marry her the first time he should meet with a priest to bless their union. The dice thrown, the successful player was walking off with the bride elect on his arm, when he received an order to set her at liberty. In vain he entreated and asserted his good intentions; he was obliged to give her up, and it was not without regret.

"A captain of the 26th, having selected one from amongst a group of distracted beauties, purchased for his sultana a magnificent trousseau of the embroidered vests and trousers worn by Afghan women of rank, which after the sack of the town were sold for next to nothing; but scarcely had he time to present them to the lady, when the order arrived to set her free: she did not require to be told twice, but fled as fast as her legs would carry her.

* At the outside 4000.—*Ferrier*.

† Infantry — admirable troops, recruited in the hill country at the base of the Himalaya.—*Translator*.

'Ah,' said the captain, as she disappeared; 'if I had known all the ingratitude of the female heart, they would never have caught me buying these garments.'

"After being regularly pillaged, Istalif was given up to the flames, and the brigade of General M'Caskill returned to Kabul, where another tragedy was to be performed.

"The work of destruction there was accomplished with a refinement of systematic barbarity and cunning which it is difficult to believe. Arriving under the walls of the capital on the 15th of September, the English found it deserted; for the examples they had already made put the whole population to flight. Occupied entirely with the recovery of the English prisoners, General Pollock had never manifested any evil intention against the city; the army was encamped outside, guards were placed at the gates, and the soldiers forbidden to pass them: it might have been supposed that it was a friendly army, an army of pious devotees, for the Rev. Mr. Allen took advantage of the inactivity of the troops during these few days of rest to preach several sermons upon the mercy of God, who had permitted the return of their captive comrades. The event was celebrated by a solemn service, at which all the troops attended, and men selected from the 13th light infantry sang the Psalms. The strict discipline of the army, and these religious exercises, restored in some degree the confidence of the wretched inhabitants, and a great many ventured to return to their houses. It was then, that is to say on the 9th of October, that General Pollock ordered Colonel Richmond Shakespear to enter Kabul with his brigade, and, with the exception of the Bala Hissar, and the quarter inhabited by the Kuzzilbashes,* who had always been friendly to the English, to destroy the city and give it up to the flames.

"At Jellalabad the same scenes were enacted, and it is perhaps still more difficult to understand why that place was treated with such severity. When, in the November of 1841, General Sale, harassed by the Ghildjzyes, and almost overcome by numbers, presented himself at the gates, the inhabitants opened them to him without resistance. He had brought with him only two days' provisions, but they supplied him as well as they were able—moreover,

* These Kuzzilbashes are the same people that Lord Auckland accused of being hostile to the British, and in favouring whom he considered Dost Mohamed guilty of a crime. See his Lordship's Simla manifesto.—*Ferrier*.

on credit. When he afterwards saw that he could not be relieved before the spring and must therefore pass the winter in the town, and found that, to avoid being destroyed with his small garrison by famine, he was compelled to drive out the inhabitants, they left their homes without a murmur, and their provisions in them. Why then was this town so completely destroyed and burnt?*

"Here then are 100,000 people whose houses have been burnt just at the commencement of winter, and in a country too where that season is almost as severe as in Russia. Frightful as all this is, the most odious feature in these cruel transactions is that, in conducting the war as they have done upon the inhabitants of the towns only, the English have punished the inoffensive part of the population, and not the tribes who in 1841 destroyed the army of General Elphinstone. In Afghanistan, as in Algeria, the warlike tribes wander about with their flocks; the towns are inhabited only by Jews, Armenians, Hindoos, Cashmeerians, Tajiks, slaves, merchants, workpeople, handicraftsmen, that is to say, by strangers, who by nature and interest are peaceable, and who have never been known to have a musket in their hands.†

"In all the wars of which this unhappy country has been so long the theatre, these are the people who have to bear the brunt of British vengeance: it is unworthy of the nation. As they had determined that revenge they would have, those who should have been pursued were the Ghildjzyes, the Afreedees, the Chinnarees, the Mohmunds, the Othman-Kails—all those, in fact, whom General Pollock took care not to seek in their mountain fastnesses, and instead wreaked his vengeance upon the citizens. In a word, General Pollock has done that which a French General would do, who, having to punish a revolt of the Flittas or Beni-amers, in Algeria, should burn Mostaganem or Mascara; he has committed barbarities without excuse.‡

"Nevertheless it should be said that public opinion in India has

* The necessities of war are inexorable; and with his knowledge of the Afghan character, General Sale only did what the dictates of prudence commanded for the safety of the troops under his orders. After all, it was only what Davoust did in defending Hamburg, and what any other general in the same position would have done.—*Ferrier*.

† Utterly erroneous: the inhabitants of Kabul were as warlike as the nomades, and in the whole principality there are not six Jews or Armenians.—*Ferrier*.

‡ The case is quite otherwise, for the townspeople in Afghanistan are, as we have already said, quite as warlike as those of the country, and are more dangerous and ferocious in a revolt.—*Ferrier*.

already raised its voice against these ignoble and atrocious excesses, neither do we doubt that in England indignation will be felt by every generous heart. However, the Governor-General, Lord Ellenborough, is preparing a magnificent reception at Ferozepore for the victorious army of Afghanistan. Invitations have been sent to all the native princes to attend the military fêtes, which will, it is said, eclipse the splendour of the courts of the ancient Mogul Emperors; a magnificent triumphal arch is now in course of construction, through which the army of the Indus is to defile, followed by, as trophies of its victories, the gates of the tomb of Mahmood the Ghaznevide, that were captured at Ghuznee, and the twenty-four pieces of cannon taken in 1839 from Dost Mohamed. This last detail is not the least curious part of the ceremony, for it is well known that the English army returned from Afghanistan having lost its own artillery there; the guns were either taken by the Afghans or destroyed by order of the British Generals, who had no means of transport for them.*

"Dost Mohamed and his family, and all the Afghans now prisoners in India, will be present at these fêtes, after which the Governor-General will allow them to return as they may think fit to their own country.

"The government of British India will then believe itself free of all obligation to Afghanistan: it introduced disorder and made war there for three years, and left anarchy which may last for ages."†

The Afghans, from whom I sought to procure evidence by which to test the truth of all the facts that have been related respecting the English occupation of Afghanistan, unfortunately confirmed them, but with various modifications, which considerably lessen the gravity of some of them. They affirm that, in spite of the cruelties and excesses of which, in 1841, they were guilty to the English, the latter showed themselves more humane than could have been expected, and that it was just, because they knew they deserved the utmost punishment that could be inflicted upon them;

* All this display was indeed misplaced; it was sufficiently painful to be reduced to the hard necessity of so severely punishing the Afghans, without adding the mockery of a triumph which could not exist, as there had been little or no fighting. But the procession was intended to make an impression on the Sikhs, the natives of India, and doubtful allies, and that must have been quite as much Lord Ellenborough's object as the gratification of a puerile vanity.—*Ferrier.*

† This is true, perfectly true.—*Ferrier.*

that they abandoned the capital, where the houses were not burnt any more than at Istalif, for the simple reason that, being built of earth, they are not combustible. But it is true that the bazaars at Kabul, which were considered the finest in Afghanistan, were mined and destroyed, as well as some of the adjacent houses. It is therefore untrue, as stated by the *Journal des Débats*, that 100,000 persons were left without shelter.

It is also untrue that the Afghan towns are inhabited by inoffensive people; at Kabul the Jews are not tolerated, and at the outside there are not more than two or three Armenian families there. The mass of the population is of Afghan origin; and whatever be the occupation of an individual of that nation, he is above all things warlike, turbulent, a lover of pillage, murder, and devastation. Proof of this might be found in a thousand instances, but I name but one, the death of the unfortunate Burnes, who was attacked in his house by these same shopkeepers who are depicted as such peaceable people. As I have said before, it was these shopkeeper or merchant soldiers* and other Ghazees, who especially outraged the English, and who therefore, on their second arrival, deserted their homes to take shelter in Istalif, a small fortress which they thought was impregnable, but from which they were driven after only six hours' fighting. The population of that town is 3000 or 3500 souls; and if it held 15,000 when the English attacked it, it is to the emigration from Kabul that the augmentation must be ascribed. The fugitives proceeded to this little town with their families and baggage, believing they would be safe from any hostile attempt; the English soon undeceived them, and many suffered the fortune of war; but the Afghans do not estimate their loss, both at Istalif and Kabul, higher than four hundred and fifty men.

As to the sack of Jellalabad, the history of that episode has also been exaggerated. The fortifications that General Sale threw up for his own defence were demolished in order that the Afghans might not benefit by them, and the adjacent houses fell with them. But the greatest misconception that exists on the subject is to attribute generosity of feeling to Akbar Khan, because he took the English ladies under his protection and preserved them from outrage.

* In Afghanistan the soldiers are not formed into regiments, they are an undisciplined militia; each man lives in his family, and there are sometimes several thousands of them in a town.—*Ferrier*.

It has been ascertained by the author, in a manner which admits of no doubt, that, although they were respected, that fact in no way redounds to the credit of Dost Mohamed's son, for he had more than once in his own mind divided them amongst the harems of some young serdars, his debauched companions. For himself he had reserved the daughter of General Sale, and his confidential conversations with others were frequently enlivened by the prospect of this distribution. One night in particular, after a series of orgies, these ladies were in the most imminent danger, and it was averted only by a riot in Kabul which suddenly called Mohamed Akbar to the scene of action. When, however, this chief was not excited by wine, he allowed but little to be said on the subject, because he remembered that his father was in the power of the British, and he dreaded how far the Dost and the females of his family would be made to suffer if he carried out his brutal intentions. The English might have been reassured as to the fate of the captives in Afghanistan, for the same reasons that caused Akbar to respect them; and when they undertook the second expedition to that country, it was not because it was impossible to deliver them otherwise, for they could have exchanged the Dost and his wives and children for them, but they were determined to prove to the Afghans that the disasters they had suffered in 1841 were not of a nature to damage their power, and that they were perfectly able to take and occupy their country whenever it might please them to do so. So convinced of that fact were the Afghans themselves, that they laid down their arms immediately after the battle of Bootkak, and the British might again have held Kabul by adopting wiser and more politic measures than they did after the first invasion.

But they did not hold it, and were certainly right; for if this possession had not proved a dead weight upon their treasury, it certainly would not have enriched it. It could be of no use to them, excepting as an advanced post against the ambitious schemes of Russia; but until the Caucasus is completely subjugated, it is unlikely that power should undertake any enterprise in earnest in Central Asia, and from this time till then Kabul may be left to itself.* After having sought, and with great care, every species of information connected with the second expedition to Kabul, I am

* Since the English conquered the upper part of the Indus they have commanded all the countries on the right bank of that river east of Kabul, and could take Afghanistan in less than a month.—*Ferrier.*

convinced that I have obtained proof that the actions attributed to the English, and which are to be regretted, took place, but have been grossly exaggerated in their consequences. For the rest, having stated the pro and con, each reader must form his own judgment. It will be most difficult to bring those who know the character and policy of the Afghans to believe that an Indo-British army could follow the one that had been exterminated in that country, and be indifferent or forgetful of the cruelties that the victims who preceded them had suffered. One would have a relation, another a friend, to avenge; and then the Indian soldiers, with their religious ideas, view these things so differently from Europeans, that I believe it would be impossible for their commanders to stop the fearful deeds suggested by their love of revenge, or rather that feeling which they believe to be their duty.

I am far from constituting myself the apologist of these severities; but I have seen war in Asia and in Africa, and know, unhappily by experience, that it is impossible to conduct it as in Europe, where, in the majority of states, the rights of individuals are respected. In vain may we declaim against bloodshed; we shall never be able to convert the battle-field into a drawing-room, where all parties are bent upon the interchange of civilities. When I hear it said, "how many thousands of Circassians the Russian soldiers have slain," or "the French have bathed in the blood of the Arabs!" or "the English have sacrificed myriads of Hindoos to their cupidity;" when I hear it said that the troops of these nations "are the scum of the earth—wretches who have outraged all laws, human and divine," I cannot refrain from cursing the people who say so—men, or rather not men, who possess the miserable courage to speak in favour of barbarians, while they can find only an accusing voice when they speak of the soldiers of their country. Unhappy madmen that ye are! do ye not know that such enemies take your clemency for weakness, your forbearance for fear?—that they have no gratitude but to the God of Islam, who withholds the infidel arm that would have killed them—that their religion enjoins them to massacre without pity or remorse?

The remedy lies precisely in that in which you see the evil. War has its severities, and they are great, therefore it ought not to be undertaken but for sound and legitimate reasons; that is saying enough, and I have not failed to admit that I never approved the one undertaken by the English against the Afghans. But the acts of a government are not to be confounded with those of its soldiers:

to the former all reprobation—to the latter, for their many sufferings and hardships, a few encouraging words is no more than their due. It is easy to forget them in the lazy tranquillity of the closet—it is easy to judge of facts, and in a very humane point of view, when sitting by the fire in a well-stuffed easy chair; but those who endure the misery—who, as the reward of mercy shown in the heat of battle, receive a sword-thrust or a bullet in the breast—who have submitted to tortures worse a hundred times than death, and who then see themselves calumniated and slandered by those who ought, on the contrary, to have exalted their deeds—ask them what they think of your system? Ask the many English, French, and Russian generals, wearied to death with warring against Mussulmans, or consult the writings of others, and they will tell you what is the fruit of your imprudent comments. You destroy the energy of national spirit, and set bounds to nothing but the prosperity of your country; had I any authority over you, you wretched scribblers, I would order you no other punishment than to practise the generosity that you preach with so much volubility. Go, bear the musket for a couple of years only in Algeria, at Tiflis, or Calcutta, and when you return let us resume the conversation.

In assigning to the English expedition of 1842 the probable object of re-establishing the reputation of the Indo-British arms in Afghanistan, I have not pretended to justify it; but if the government of Calcutta had other and more positive reasons for launching into such an increase of expenditure, the public had on its side a right to be surprised at the precipitate return of that army without having effected more than the death of a few hundred men, and the destruction of a bazaar and a few houses. This leaves ground for the supposition that they never knew too well why they went to Kabul, or why they came back, and induced one writer to say that "the English retired from Kabul with a precipitation resembling the retreat of a beaten army as much as the march of a victorious one." Neither can it be believed that they went simply with the intention of re-establishing the legitimate dynasty; but, if such was their intention, then it can only be said that they were not more fortunate in the second expedition than in the first.

Before the English left Kabul they pressed Fethi Djing Mirza to re-assume the regal authority, hoping that, with his own troops and their moral support, he might maintain himself in power after their return to India. But that prince was not dazzled by the splendid illusion; he knew full well that, as soon as his nominal protectors had departed, he should have Akbar Khan upon his hands, and, being determined not to expose himself to the danger of a repetition of the treatment that he had received from that Serdar, he declined the offer. It was, however, accepted by his young brother, Shapoor Mirza, who was very soon destined to see the entire destruction of the ambitious hopes in which his inexperienced miud had indulged. His elder brother's anticipations were realised; for scarcely was the last detachment of the British army out of sight and across the Indus, when Mohamed Akbar reappeared at Kabul, attacked and beat the Mirza, carried off his riches, and obliged him to take to flight. To the English it was now indifferent whether he held his ground or not; they had found out though late that Burnes was right in rejecting the idea of restoring the Suddozyes to the prejudice of the Mohamedzyes; and the proof of this assertion is that Dost Mohamed arrived on the 19th December at Shikapoor, accompanied by Captain Nicholson, who was attached to his escort, and was some days after formally set at liberty. Free to go where he liked or to do what he pleased, the Emir hesitated not a moment, but instantly took the road to Afghanistan. On his arrival at Lahore he was received with great state by Shere Sing, then Maharadjah of the Punjab, and the English conjectured that these princes made a secret treaty; but this was only one of the grievances of which they always assume the existence when they wish to obtain possession of a country. The fact was, the Directors were so astounded at the deficit in their treasury caused by the Afghan war, that they did not know what to be about, and were highly indignant at the brilliant reception given to the Emir of Kabul by the sovereign of the Sikhs.

During the time that the Dost was whiling away precious hours in the enjoyment of the pleasures of the court of Lahore, his son Mohamed Akbar Khan had infinite trouble in managing the various parties that had been formed in Kabul, which, though at first subdued, were now becoming rampant.

Shooja ed Dooulet (the murderer of Shah Shooja), son of Zeman Khan, and Chems Eddin his cousin, both nephews of Dost Mohamed, succeeded in reconstituting the party of Zeman Khan, and forced Akbar Khan to retire into the citadel, where they besieged him for seventy-three days. Intelligence of this fact and his critical position reached the Dost at Lahore, who, being unable himself to go with sufficient rapidity to Kabul, sent his four sons, Mohamed Efzel Khan, Mohamed Akrem Khan, Mohamed Azim Khan, and Goulam. Haidar Khan, to the assistance of their beleaguered brother. Furnished with a firman from the Maharadjah, and with one attendant only, the serdars set out immediately, changed their horses at every village, and, pursuing their anxious journey night and day, scarce drew bridle till they reached Kabul, accomplishing the distance in ten days from Lahore. The great exertions of the princes were indeed all important to the cause, for when they arrived Mohamed Akbar was at bay in the citadel with only two days' provisions. These four young men had been brought up in Kabul, and were beloved by the inhabitants, who had had many opportunities of witnessing their youthful courage, and their appearance at once caused a diversion in favour of their brother, who eventually triumphed over his enemies. The return of the Emir himself, which took place very shortly after, put an end to all further contest; and on remounting the throne, from which he had been three years banished, he at once applied himself to the task of effacing the sad traces of the anarchy brought into his dominions by the English invasion.

At Kandahar, which was also abandoned, General Nott and Major Rawlinson tried to induce Timoor Mirza, the eldest son of Shah Shooja, to remain at the head of affairs in that principality. But the prince coveted not the cares of a throne. Satisfied that the royal honours of Afghanistan were lost for ever to the Suddozyes, he thought that dynasty ought to give way to the Mohamedzyes, and refused the offer, preferring to return to India, where he hoped to live a life of tranquillity, much more in accordance with his own tastes. Upon his declining, the English proposed to his brother Seif der Djing that he should assume the government. The reader will remember that this prince had formerly betrayed them, and made common cause with the insurgents, but his union with the latter was not of long duration; the death of his father completely destroyed it, and he made his submission to and rejoined those whom he had previously abandoned. The Serdar Mohamed Kooli Khan, son of the vizier Fethi Khan, was given him for a minister, and by thus dividing the power between a Mohamedzye who had always been faithful to them, and a Suddozye who had deserted them, though he became more firmly attached to them afterwards—balancing one against the other—the English hoped to retain their influence in this important city. But the plan proved only one more illusion to be added to those by which they had been so often misled, for, about four months after they left Seif der Djing to his own resources, Kohendil Khan returned from Persia and manifested his intention of regaining if possible his principality of Kandahar. For some little time he remained on the banks of the Helmund, where he was joined by the Serdars Akter Khan, Ser Firaz Khan, Shah Pecend Khan, and others; and, when he saw himself in sufficient force, he marched upon his old capital to dispossess Seif der Djing. As to Mohamed Kooli Khan, he at once abandoned the prince, and passed over to the camp of his uncle. Nevertheless, Seif der Djing did not allow himself to be discouraged by the defection of his minister, and gave battle to Kohendil Khan at Haooz Singsar, twenty-eight miles west of the city; but at the very first charge he saw one-half of his army run away, and the other fraternise with his enemy. Kohendil Khan took immediate possession of the capital, amid the acclamations of the inhabitants, who had not, however, the happiest reminiscences of his previous administration, and the serdar possibly mistook the cause of these congratulations; they were not for *him*, but for the success of the principle represented in his person—the choice of the masses, to the exclusion of divine right—the one representing Afghan liberty, the other English domination.

Seif der Djing after his discomfiture was unable to reach and defend Kandahar, and obliged to turn off the road: it was not without difficulty and danger that he gained Shikapoor. Thence he went on to India, whither his brothers had preceded him.

The battle of Haooz Singsar was the last episode connected with the British occupation of Afghanistan, whither the East India Company had sent its army to die and its treasure to vanish! "Such was the conclusion," says an intelligent and clever author, "of this war, and of the policy of Lord Palmerston, vacillating at first, violent at the close. Rather than keep the grand and straightforward path in which states of the highest order should proudly and gracefully tread, in which they can honourably meet and encounter each other—rather than meet the Russians face to face—he preferred disputing with them on distant ground and by paltry counter-manœuvres, a policy which could only engulf his political fortunes, for that was really the finale of the negotiations of which we have given an epitome, and which terminated the sad series of reserve, duplicity, shuffling, and circumspection towards Russia. In this it all ended. The first consequence of his Lordship's policy in Asia was the expedition of Lord Auckland, the second the massacre of the British army by the Afghans, the third reprisals upon the Afghans, and, lastly, the absurd triumph of Lord Ellenborough at Ferozepore. God preserve England from any more such; God preserve her! But it is not the less true that, having exasperated the political animosities and roused the religious fanaticism of Central Asia under the pretence of adding to the terror of her name, she has reduced it everywhere—she has extinguished the hatred of the Russian name that formerly existed—she has destroyed the respect for her own strength, and spread the fear of that power which she dared not to attack but in an indirect manner—she has herself been the pioneer of a Muscovite invasion."

Without adopting the deductions of the writer I have just quoted, it may be stated, and without fear of contradiction, that previously to their ill-starred expedition to Kabul the English never met with anything but sympathy in Afghanistan; opinion is now much divided about them, and the majority of the chiefs are hostile to them. The feeling in favour of them is rather to be found amongst the people, who, with due allowance for their fanaticism, have not forgotten the equitable administration of the invaders, and still regret that it was not continued by their own Afghan rulers. In any case England must now be convinced of the soundness of the advice given by Sir Alexander Burnes. His antagonists were Sir C. Wade, Sir W. M'Naghten, and Sir J. M'Neil, and their policy was accepted by Lord Auckland. Upon these four individuals may England charge the responsibility of her disasters; and upon Burnes did their evil counsel bring the penalty of death: unhappily the survivors cannot replace to their country the loss it sustained in his death and in that of so many other officers—men possessing scientific acquirement, indomitable courage, and a hopeful future.

CHAPTER XXVI.

State of Kabul after the return of Dost Mohamed — Antagonistic feeling between the Emir and his son Akbar Khan — Ambitious projects of the latter — War between the Dost and the Walee of Khulm — Reasons for this rupture — Akbar Khan wishes to dispossess Kohendil Khan of Kandahar — Also to join the Sikhs against the English — His rupture with the Dost — Marriage of Akbar with the daughter of Yar Mohamed Khan — Intrigues of Kohendil Khan to prevent this union — Demonstration of Akbar Khan against Kandahar — He requests the assistance of the Shah of Persia — Favourable reply of that sovereign — Akbar obliges his father to withdraw from the direction of affairs — Death of Akbar Khan — Revolt of Mohamed Shah Khan — Dost Mohamed forces him to return to his duty — Alliance between Persia and Kabul — The English are alarmed — Embarrassment of the Emir — Sultan Mohamed Khan returns to Kabul — Reception by the Dost — The Emir appoints his son Haidar Khan vizier — The Dost joins the Sikhs against the English — Antipathy of the Afghans to the Sikhs, and *vice versâ*—Dost Mohamed takes Attock — His cavalry is defeated by the English — Owes his escape to the fleetness of his horse.

IF absolute calm was not the immediate consequence of the return of Dost Mohamed to his dominions, it at least produced a suspension of hostilities amongst the various parties in the state. The majority of his countrymen rallied round him, but still it was found impossible to re-establish the same governmental unity that had existed before the English invasion; the serdars, especially those belonging to the Ghildjzye tribe, rendered an obedience far less implicit than before, and, though always commanding the respect of his people, the Dost found that he had lost much of that veneration of which he had formerly been the object. This was a consequence of his residence in India: in the eyes of the Afghans he had contracted a kind of pollution from which he could never purify himself; they could not forgive him for having appreciated British civilization, and looked upon his efforts for their improvement almost in the light of a crime.

Akbar Khan, the heir-presumptive of his power, was far from approving of the new policy. Strongly imbued with the same prejudices as the mass of the Afghans, he detested the English, though he was fully sensible of their superiority in the arts of war and government. After he had entrapped and murdered Sir W. M'Naghten he felt persuaded that the blood he had shed must be redeemed by his own, and that his enemies could not without dishonour abstain from taking revenge upon him for that detestable crime; thus circumstances quite as much as his own desire threw him into a line of conduct different from that of his father, and he persevered in his opposition the more tenaciously inasmuch as it was in unison with the opinions of the greater number of his countrymen, who lavished upon him much of the affection that had hitherto been bestowed upon the Emir.

Mohamed Akbar vowed therefore an implacable hatred against the English, and the tenacity of his opposition to them, in despite of all his father's remonstrances, denoted his firm determination not to rest until he had given them a check sufficiently important to disgust them for ever with the idea of attempting further conquests in the north of Asia. He commenced his preparations by inflaming the minds of his soldiers with the wildest and most seductive promises, while his father spared no pains in endeavouring to calm his imprudent ardour and that of his adherents, to extinguish the feuds of the various parties in the principality, and to re-establish security in the hope of giving a salutary impulse to the interests of commerce and agriculture. But Mohamed Akbar, who saw everything through the prism of his own fanatical feelings, and was dazzled with the enthusiasm that his success and constant opposition to the English had excited in the minds of the Afghans, ruined, by the support that he gave to his own turbulent followers, the wise and beneficial measures concerted by his father for the improvement, independence, and prosperity of his dominions. The post of vizier which had been conferred upon Mohamed Akbar by Fethi Djing, and in which his father so imprudently retained him, gave him great influence in the affairs of government, and he used this in a manner very detrimental to their future prospects. He indulged in dreams of re-establishing the Afghan kingdom in the plenitude of its ancient glory and power, and obtaining possession of the other Afghan principalities, the Usbek Khanats, the Punjab, and Beloochistan; even these would not satisfy his ambition, and British India was in his eyes a prize on which he imagined that he should be able some day to lay his hands. Little could be urged against those day dreams if he had intended to carry them out in the spirit of ameliorating the condition of the nations whom he intended to subjugate; but as he would only have renewed the bloody episodes that have rendered mournfully celebrated the reigns of Ghengis Khan and Tamerlane, much cause is there for rejoicing that the Emir opposed, with unshaken firmness and a sincere desire for peace, these warlike and unreflecting manifestations of Akbar Khan.

The disorganization of the Sikhs and the inroads of the British on their territory were the occasions of the first serious outbreak between the father and son; for the latter, seeing that Dost Mohamed opposed his marching to the assistance of his neighbours, and was unalterably determined not to take the initiative in any act of aggression which could again bring the English upon him, was at one moment on the point of breaking with his father completely. He was at this time about to marry the daughter of Yar Mohamed Khan, and endeavoured to interest the vizier in his schemes, informing him that he had decided on withdrawing for a time from Kabul, and requesting he would assign him a district in his dominions where he could establish himself with those Afghans who were attached to him and intended to follow his fortunes. But Yar Mohamed saw many objections to complying with this demand; he interfered only so far as to induce the Dost to endeavour to calm the excitability of his son, and the difficulty was overcome by a concession on the part of the Dost, who promised to send five hundred Afghan horse to his brother and former enemy, Sultan Mohamed Khan. This serdar was serving with the Sikhs, for he had been invested with the government of Rotas, after Runjeet Sing seized Peshawur; and as Nawab Djabbar Khan, also a brother of the Emir, was suspected of having preserved some sympathy for the English, Mohamed Akbar sought to compromise him in their eyes by intrusting to his son, Abdul Ghyas Khan, the command of these five hundred cavalry. But this demonstration against the Anglo-Indian government was not sufficient to satisfy Akbar Khan; he wanted his uncle Kohendil Khan to join him, and on his refusal threatened to invade his territory. He would probably have carried this threat into execution, but for an unforeseen event of which it is supposed the Dost was not altogether ignorant; his son desired war at all risks, and in this wish he contrived to indulge him in the following manner:—

Dost Mohamed had not forgotten the ill-treatment he and his family had received from the Emir of Bokhara, and manifested a desire of taking revenge by proclaiming war against him. He also wished to occupy Balkh, then governed by Ichane Suddoor, under the suzerainty of Nasser Ullah, but to reach that town it was necessary to traverse the territory of Khulm, and the Walee of that principality positively refused to allow the Afghans to pass through it, well knowing what would be the result if he consented. "If you have any complaint against the Emir of Bokhara," he wrote to the Dost, "I will espouse your quarrel and fight him myself, but if you violate my territory I will join him against you."

The negotiations stood thus, and Dost Mohamed, who remembered the Walee's kindness to him, was on the eve of withdrawing his proposition, when Akbar Khan, who also ought to have been grateful for the generous conduct of the Walee to himself, complicated the whole affair by committing an abduction, which, in the opinion of many Afghans, did him more honour than all his triumphs over the English. On leaving Khulm, Mohamed Akbar brought with him from thence a youth belonging to the Khan of that district for a purpose which shall be nameless. This fact was of sufficient importance to induce the Walee to declare war, and Akbar sent his brother, Akrem Khan, at the head of ten thousand horse against the Usbeks. Three battles were fought in 1845 and 1846, but without deciding the quarrel, nevertheless the Khan of Khulm became uneasy, for his rear was threatened by the Emir of Bokhara; he returned therefore to his capital and Akrem Khan to Kabul, where his brother continued to spend large sums of money upon the creature who had been the cause of the war.

When Akbar Khan found that he had nothing to fear from the exasperated Walee of Khulm, he clung with more obstinacy than ever to his project of joining the Sikhs and once more fighting the English. The five hundred cavalry he had sent towards the end of 1845 to assist the former under his cousin Abdul Ghyaz Khan had not arrived in time to be present at the battle of Sobraon, which in 1846 determined the fate of the Punjab, and enabled the British to enter Lahore as conquerors; but Akbar Khan believed that he had only to present himself and his troops before that city to turn them out, and the cession of Peshawur was promised him as the price of his armed intervention. Dost Mohamed was not indifferent to this arrangement, which afforded him the opportunity of including in his dominions that frontier town, which he had always been so unwilling to give up; nevertheless he felt that it would compromise him with the English if he received it from the Sikhs in return for his co-operation, so he preferred seizing it himself at a moment when they were unable to defend it; but Akbar persisted in his wish to cross the Indus. In this purpose he was foiled by the Dost, who secretly retarded the recruiting of the army, and his son was obliged to delay the execution of his projects. To make up for this disappointment, he determined upon marching against Kandahar, alleging that his uncle had sought the alliance of the British and fomented discontent in Kabul, which had brought about changes most disadvantageous to the interests of Dost Mohamed. Several serdars deserted the cause of the Emir on this occasion and passed over to the service of his brother; but none of these defections was so grievous to him as that of his step-son, the Sultan Djan Khan. This young serdar had proceeded to Kandahar with five hundred horse, and been well received by Kohendil Khan—in Akbar's eyes a sufficient cause for declaring war against his uncle, and the Emir had infinite difficulty in preventing him from taking this step. These different views on such serious subjects kept up the irritation between the father and son, and ended in doing more good to their enemies than to themselves. Akbar, who had not the experience of the Emir and was of a restless domineering spirit, never hesitated for considerations of any kind, and, being supported in his violent opinions by chiefs as turbulent as himself, decided on advancing upon Kandahar, in utter disregard of his father's disapprobation; not, however, to drive matters quite to extremity, he thought he would strengthen his policy by the alliance of which the Dost had himself laid the foundations in the preceding year.

Yar Mohamed, after having dethroned and strangled Shah Kamran, had become all powerful at Herat, and it was important that the Emir should secure him in his interest; negotiations were, therefore, commenced between the two families; Akbar married in 1846 Bobodjane, the eldest daughter of Yar Mohamed, and the Vizier's son, the Serdar Syud Mohamed Khan, espoused Goher, only daughter of Mohamed Khan, deceased, a half-brother of the Emir Dost Mohamed.

Akbar Khan's mother went to Herat to bring her daughter-in-law to Kabul; but on her return she was detained a long time at Kandahar, in consequence of an insurrection that had broken out in the district of Kelat-i-Ghildjzye, which prevented her from continuing her journey. This insurrection was attributed to the intrigues of Kohendil Khan, who dreaded the result of the alliances recently concluded, for, as his dominions lay between Kabul and Herat, he was henceforth placed between two fires. He complained loudly to Yar Mohamed of his having given his daughter to Akbar Khan, and before the marriage took place demanded her for one of his own sons, urging his position as a neighbour of the vizier's, which he considered a just ground of preference. But his representations produced no alteration in the arrangement, and the inhabitants of Kelat-i-Ghildjzye having heard that the Emir had ordered two thousand horsemen from Ghuznee to march against them, the matter ended by their opening the road for the affianced bride of Mohamed Akbar Khan. At this the indignation of the serdars of Kandahar was great, and they revenged themselves by sending several thousand cavalry to ravage the plain of Bakooa, belonging to Herat (adding that they intended to seize the town itself), when they were arrested in their project by a diversion made in favour of Mohamed Akbar by his brother Haidar Khan, at the head of eight thousand horse, who advanced by forced marches on Kandahar. The moment Dost Mohamed was informed that the Kandaharians had retreated, he, to Akbar's infinite regret, imperatively recalled him to Kabul. Seizing on this pretext to free himself completely from the authority of his father, Akbar signified to him in the haughtiest and most insolent manner that henceforth he intended to do as he pleased in the principality, and requested him for the future not to interfere in its affairs. Unfortunately Mohamed Akbar Khan was sufficiently powerful to hold this language to his sovereign, and the Emir resigned himself to the passive position in which his son's conduct placed him.

To relate all the rash and foolish undertakings projected by Akbar Khan from this period would be impossible; though he at the same time originated several able measures for the consolidation of his power. It was with this object in view that at the close of 1846 he sent Akhood Zadeh Azim as ambassador to the Shah of Persia to conclude an alliance offensive and defensive with that monarch; his father-in-law, Yar Mohamed Khan, followed his example, and also sent an agent to Teheran for the same purpose. These two chiefs wrote a joint letter to Mohamed Shah in the most pressing terms, showing him how the English were carrying their conquests along the whole course of the Indus, and were ready to enter Afghanistan; the missive concluded in these words: "If your majesty hesitates to take part in the war with us against the English, Allah will require you to account for the neglect with which you allow the faithful to be swept away by the infidels."

The Shah of Persia, without granting the assistance demanded of him, was nevertheless quite inclined to join the projected alliance. The envoys of Herat and Kabul were well received, and richly jewelled swords and decorations were sent to Dost Mohamed, Akbar Khan, and such of their brothers, uncles, and other serdars in the principality as were favourable to the cause.

As to Kohendil Khan, he became daily more discontented with Yar Mohamed and Akbar Khan, and made fresh incursions upon the territory of Herat, in the district of Gulistan, the result of which was that the vizier advanced upon Wachir and Girishk, and made fearful reprisals. Akbar Khan now became anxious to support his father-in-law and march against Kohendil Khan, but Dost Mohamed opposed this, and a sharp altercation took place between the father and son, during which the latter bitterly reproached the Emir with cowardice, and even threatened to imprison him. This quarrel at length opened the eyes of Dost Mohamed, and proved to him what he had up to that time earnestly wished to doubt, namely, the evil disposition of his son; he withdrew therefore from the citadel and took refuge in the kaleh of Djevanchir, where Khan Shireen Khan, the Kuzzilbash chief, received him with all the warmth and respect due to his rank and great misfortunes. Mohamed Akbar threatened, but in vain; he could not induce the Kuzzilbash to give up his guest; and to what extremities he might have proceeded is unknown, for he was carried off by a sudden and wholly unexpected death, caused, as it is said, by taking two aphrodisiac pills, which were given him by a Hindoo doctor. This man had them in a box with some others, of which he took two himself in the presence of his victim, who therefore swallowed those offered to him without suspicion, and died three hours afterwards in horrible convulsions. The conduct of Akbar Khan had scarcely left him the chance of dying a natural death; he thought that in forming a powerful party which would obey his warlike instincts he could oppose his father and the English also, and disdained the prudent warnings often given him to be careful for his personal safety.

Opinions are divided amongst the Afghans as to who was the instigator of this deed. Some lay it to the charge of the English, without being able to produce any proof thereof; others suppose it to have been committed at the instigation of Dost Mohamed and his sons, whom Akbar delivered from the tyranny of the English only to make them feel his own more heavily. However this may be, the Dost obtained some liberty of action after his decease, though not so much as he expected to enjoy. Akbar Khan was dead, but his party was not; some serdars, finding their plans defeated, retired in disgust to their domains, and slighted the old Emir; others revolted against his authority, amongst whom was Mohamed Shah Khan, Ghildjzye, a chief enjoying great influence with the mountain tribes. He had followed the fortunes of Dost Mohamed and his family when the English seized Kabul, and when they returned to Khulm his assistance was most valuable in organizing an attempt against Shah Shooja, as well as during the insurrection of 1841. To this serdar Mohamed Akbar had bound himself by an oath of friendship and brotherhood sworn upon the Koran and legally attested by a mollah; the Mussulman law sanctions ties of this description, so that the two chiefs justly considered each other as brothers. During the lifetime of Akbar, Mohamed Shah Khan received an important command in the hill country to the north of Kabul, and such was the trust reposed in him by his friend, and the difficulty of access to his mountain-home, that he placed all his wealth in his hands as he acquired it, intending thus to secure it from any covetous attack on the part of his own brothers, or even from the English, should they ever return to Kabul; the good understanding between these two chiefs continued uninterrupted till the death of Mohamed Akbar Khan. After that event Dost Mohamed claimed the property that his son had confided to Mohamed Shah Khan, but the latter obstinately refused to give it up, alleging that the oath which bound him to Akbar constituted him the legitimate heir to the deceased serdar, and that the Emir could not without injustice refuse him the title of vizier which he had bestowed upon Akbar; likewise that it gave him the right to marry all his widows in preference to the Dost's sons—Mohamed Shah Khan set up, in fact, an infinity of the most unreasonable pretensions, and supported them by hostile demonstrations. The Ghildjzyes responded to his appeal in crowds, and the Emir was obliged to send an army against them, but it was numerically insufficient to repress the revolt, for it had to operate in a country full of difficulties, with an enemy always fighting under great advantages of ground, and the troops were therefore obliged to return and wait for reinforcements. Dost Mohamed, who was quite alive to the serious character of the circumstances, redoubled his efforts to collect a sufficient force with the utmost rapidity, and in the month of April, 1847, had under his standard 25,000 men—veteran warriors brought up in hatred of the Ghildjzye tribe. With this large army he moved against a comparatively feeble enemy, who had hitherto only been able to maintain themselves against their foes by the mountainous character of their country, and the Emir now determined to strike a decisive blow; concentrating his troops, therefore, he moved towards the point at which Mohamed Shah Khan had encamped with the greater number of the insurgents, and pressed him so vigorously and closely, that the latter was obliged to surrender at discretion and give up the disputed treasure to the lawful heirs of Mohamed Akbar. The Dost also obliged the Khan to enter into and accept other conditions sufficiently humiliating; he seized his sons as hostages, and left him only the government of a small mountain district—measures which rendered another revolt on his part almost impossible. The reduction to obedience of this rebellious tribe gave peace to the principality of Kabul, and the compromised serdars, dreading the loss of their property, liberty, or lives, hastened to join the camp of the Emir, who, after having installed his son Goulam Haidar Khan at Jellalabad in the chief command of the Ghildjzye territory, returned immediately to his capital; there he applied himself earnestly to repair the injuries that years of civil war had inflicted upon some of the finest provinces of Afghanistan, and which originated in the just, though dangerous, antipathy to the British alliance that always existed in the mind of his son Mohamed Akbar.

It was at this juncture that Akhood Zadeh Azim, who had been on his embassy to Persia, returned to Kabul; the Emir could not possibly do otherwise than approve of the conduct of his late son's envoy, and he accordingly ratified all the steps that Akhood Zadeh Azim had taken to perfect a strict alliance between the Afghans and the Persians.

The Anglo-Indian Government watched with some uneasiness the increasing good feeling between these two nations. But although the hostility of Akbar Khan had been anything but encouraging to them, their anxiety was not extreme, for they thought his eccentric schemes would probably commit him sooner or later in some manner very detrimental to his power and introduce perpetual discord and confusion into the Afghan states. Such a man at the head of affairs in Kabul was almost a piece of good fortune for the Company, and it is doubtful whether his violent death was in any way satisfactory to them—at the utmost it might seem to avenge the murder of Sir W. M'Naghten, of which he had been guilty. They might also hope that Dost Mohamed, now emancipated from the thraldom of his overbearing son, would preserve his neutrality towards them, at least for a time. In this, however, there lurked perhaps a greater danger, for, under the able administration of the Emir, the power of the principality would be increased tenfold in a short time; influenced by him the chiefs would more easily become united, while under Akbar they had always been quarrelling: nevertheless, Dost Mohamed might possibly be forced by them to accede to their demands, which, as facts subsequently proved, was the case.

The English thoroughly understood that the tranquillity of Afghanistan was no advantage to their cause, and in place of Akbar Khan provided another brand of discord.

It has been shown in this history that before Dost Mohamed attained the sovereignty he struggled through years of trouble and wars, and fought many a battle, and, if he triumphed over every difficulty, he was not beholden to his family for helping him to obtain that result; nearly all his brothers were hostile to him, and the one whose hatred was the most unremitting and implacable was Sultan Mohamed Khan, who contended with him to the last for the sovereignty of Kabul. It has been stated that this serdar was obliged to be satisfied with Peshawur, and subsequently constrained to cede that province to Runjeet Sing, who made him governor of the fortress of Rotas in the Punjab. After the death of the Maharadjah, and Shere Sing the last of his sons, Sultan Mohamed Khan drew upon himself the enmity of the Sikh vizier Djovaker Sing, and was in consequence taken to Lahore and detained a prisoner there. But the English watched over him; for no one could better carry out their designs than Sultan Mohamed Khan, whose constant enmity and opposition to the Emir was well known to them, and this led them to hope that they might be able to make use of him to counteract his plans. At their solicitation, therefore, the Afghan serdar was set at liberty, and it was believed that he received from them the promise of a pension; after this he returned to Afghanistan, and having lived several months at Peshawur retired to Kohat, a small town situated to the south of the former city.

Dost Mohamed was not blind to all this, but testified no resentment—far from it. After Sultan Mohamed was deprived of the government of Peshawur the Emir's heart was softened by his misfortunes, and he endeavoured on various occasions to effect a reconciliation with him; but the intractable pride of his brother was inaccessible to every attempt of the kind. When he saw him return from Lahore he was not too proud to take the initiative once more with the same object in view, and he sent his eldest son Mohamed Efzel Khan to Kohat to give his uncle every possible guarantee for his security, and endeavour to induce him to return to Kabul. This last step entirely succeeded: the old serdar at last promised to forget his ancient hatred, and go to the Dost. He kept this promise, and a short time after the same roof sheltered these two chiefs of the family of the Mohamedzyes. In this reconciliation the Emir was sincere. Can the same be said of his eldest brother? That is a problem which can be decided by time only.

The return of Sultan Mohamed Khan to Kabul took place at the period at which a fresh revolt of the Ghildjzyes occurred, and Mohamed Shah Khan placed himself once more at their head. Dost Mohamed now declared his military career was over, that he should delegate his authority as a general to his third son Goulam Haidar Khan, the defender of Ghuznee against the English, and should reserve to himself the administration of civil affairs only. The serdars received this semi-abdication with favour; Haidar was dear to them for the same reasons as Akbar, and was besides the son of the same mother: their bravery was equal, and their hatred of the English had been deep and constant.

On assuming the rank of vizier, Goulam Haidar Khan espoused some of the wives of his deceased brother, and amongst them Bobodjane. The first act of his administration was to assemble the chiefs of all the tribes, and make them swear fidelity to his family and war to the unsubdued Ghildjzyes; he won the affections of the army by increasing the pay of the troops, and took advantage of the popular feeling expressed in his favour by at once pursuing Mohamed Shah Khan, whom he speedily reduced to a condition that rendered it hopeless for him ever again to raise the standard of rebellion.

The enthusiasm excited by this success, and the warlike tastes of their new chief, led the Afghans to desire a fresh field for the employment of their arms: they loudly called upon Goulam Haidar Khan to lead them against the English; and, such was the unanimity of feeling, that it was impossible for the Emir to elude or delay the execution of their demands. The Sikhs had for many years offered to restore Peshawur to him in return for the assistance he had formerly given them, and he now decided to accept the proposition which he had till then steadily rejected; for, had he done otherwise, he would perhaps have alienated the affections of his countrymen and lost the throne of Afghanistan for his family for ever.

When the British generals who commanded in the Punjab learnt that Dost Mohamed had descended into the plain of the Indus with 15,000 men, they were anxious as to the course he might take. Having at this time to keep in check Tchatter Sing and his son Shere Sing, who had raised the Sikhs against them on all sides, they were in no position to oppose the invasion of the Afghans, who, having taken possession of the fertile plain of Peshawur, subsequently marched against Attock, then commanded by Colonel Herbert. This officer, being absolutely without the means of defending the fortress, was obliged to surrender, and the Afghans occupied it immediately. However, instead of showing the slightest disposition in favour of the Sikhs, who were their allies, and inhabited the town, they pillaged them, forced their way into their harems, and violated their wives and daughters, in revenge, as they said, for the unheard-of insult of which they accused the army of Shere Sing, namely, of having killed pigs in all the mosques on their route.

Dost Mohamed and his son were utterly unable to restrain their soldiers, and were obliged to excuse these excesses as well as they could to the allies whose cause they had been brought to defend. But the serious nature of the position in which they found themselves led the Sikh chiefs to shut their eyes to these enormities, and the English were thenceforth convinced that, in consequence of their religious antipathies, no alliance could possibly exist between the Sikhs and the Afghans; they were therefore far less concerned than they had been at the advance of Dost Mohamed.

Notwithstanding the prospect which now presented itself to the Emir of seizing Cashmeer, anciently a province of the Afghan kingdom, he appeared by no means anxious to proceed beyond the limits of his re-conquered territory, and displayed no desire to support the insurrectionary movement of the Sikhs. The possession of Attock, where he could concentrate a force sufficient to protect him from a *coup-de-main*, satisfied his ambition, but this was not the case with his soldiers; they had not followed him simply to encamp on the banks of the Indus, and to pacify them he sent a contingent of cavalry to Shere Sing, who had just beaten the English at Chillianwallah. The latter, however, soon took their revenge, and crushed the Afghans and Sikhs together at Goojerat, February 21, 1849. The vanquished were hotly pursued, but the Sikh commanders, Tchatter Sing and Shere Sing, kept the field for another month; they then found they had lost all their positions and the greater part of their artillery, and surrendered to Sir Walter Gilbert, who disarmed the remainder of the Sikh army. This event having set his division at liberty, he received orders from the General-in-Chief, Lord Gough, to march against Attock and Peshawur, and drive the Afghans beyond the passes of Afghanistan.

If Dost Mohamed had cherished a hope that the English would leave him in peaceable possession of the towns which he had just taken, the idea was soon dispelled, for to attack and defeat him was with them an operation equally prompt and easy. He was even driven to seek safety by a precipitous flight, and for two hours the Indian cavalry sent in pursuit of him kept within gunshot of the fugitive Emir; but his gallant horse eventually distanced them, and saved his liberty, perhaps his life.

CHAPTER XXVII.

The English conquer the Punjab — Dost Mohamed loses Peshawur and Attock — He retires to Kabul — Policy of Kohendil Khan at Kandahar after his return from Persia — Retrospective view of affairs at Herat — Yar Mohamed Khan and the English — Major Pottinger and Colonel Stoddart — The latter leaves for Bokhara — Interview between Major Pottinger and Shere Dil Khan — Serious consequences resulting from this — Conduct of Yar Mohamed — Major Todd at Herat — Treaty concluded with Shah Kamran — Yar Mohamed all-powerful in the principality — A scene at Yar Mohamed's dinner-table — Intrigues of that chief — His treatment of Shah Kamran — Misunderstanding between Major Todd and the vizier — Dine Mohamed Khan — Approbation of Major Todd's conduct by the Directors of the East India Company — Official instructions to that officer — Bad faith of Yar Mohamed — Difficulties of Major Todd's position — Treachery of Yar Mohamed — Subsidy to Shah Kamran and his court stopped — The vizier makes fresh demands upon Major Todd — Counter propositions by the latter — He leaves Herat and is escorted out of the city.

ONCE more in possession of Peshawur and Attock, the English installed themselves in a manner to prevent all chance of their being easily removed therefrom; and Dost Mohamed reached Kabul, where he is now less secure than ever, and less satisfied as to the ultimate views of his neighbours. If he has to regret that he could not preserve his conquests, he has at least the satisfaction of having proved to his subjects that he was right in his judgment, and that it was imprudent in them to attack the English, who it was now evident were more dangerous than ever. His defeat was the justification of his past policy; and, having changed that, he is in the worst possible position. The English detest him for having borne arms against them in 1848: to the Afghans he is an object of suspicion, and they will ever suspect that he is ready and willing to treat with the East India Company. Indeed his prospects on all sides are indifferent, and appear as if they were not likely to brighten nor his troubles arrive at any satisfactory conclusion; the fate of the Emir and his kingdom is a problem which time only can solve.

The position of Kohendil Khan at Kandahar is far from being so embarrassing as that of his elder brother. It has been shown how, after having beaten the Prince Seif der Djing, he resumed possession of his principality. After this he found that, besides his quarrels with Akbar Khan and Yar Mohamed, he had revolts to put down amongst the Hazarahs Poocht Kooh and the Beloochees who were under his jurisdiction. But the serdars of his province are not the same turbulent characters as those of Kabul, and therefore he has a far less difficult task in carrying on his government than Dost Mohamed; his political talents are not nearly so good as those of the Emir, but they are sufficient for his position. The Serdar Akter Khan was the only one who could give him the least annoyance, but, notwithstanding the services that he had rendered to his prince when he assisted him in re-consolidating his power, and the family ties that existed between them, Kohendil Khan determined to expel him from the district of Zemindavar; here he was established in the heart of his tribe, the Alizyes, and towards the close of 1847 was attacked by him with a very superior force, when he was obliged to fly, and escaped to Herat. This was a most fortunate event for Yar Mohamed Khan, who was not ignorant of the influence which this serdar exercised over the Afghan tribes established in the south, and the extent to which he might turn it to his own account against his adversaries, the chiefs of Kandahar. The vizier completely neutralised the precautionary measures taken by Kohendil Khan by settling Akter Khan in the district of Gour, situated on the frontier of Kandahar and near that of Zemindavar, which the tribe of Alizye had quitted almost entirely to join its chief in his new abode. This fact was not calculated to re-establish the good feeling that had so long been interrupted between Kohendil Khan and Yar Mohamed; and from this time their intercourse was characterised by constantly increasing asperity: but it is very difficult to foresee the results of this rivalry, Afghanistan being pre-eminently the country in which nothing can be foreseen.

A wish to avoid the necessity of returning to the history of Kabul and Kandahar has induced the author to carry it on without interruption; but, as there is nothing further to add to it, he now proposes to return to Herat, and describe the events that took place in that city after the siege was raised by Mohamed Shah, the period at which the English proclaimed the restoration of Shah Shooja to the throne of the Suddozyes in Kabul, and the independence of Herat under Shah Kamran.

Although the retreat of the Persians and the relief of Herat ought to have satisfied British susceptibilities, Lord Auckland did not the less persist in a most unjust invasion of territory.

It has been related that Shah Shooja, escorted by an Anglo-Indian army, first possessed himself of Kandahar; he had at that time, and in concert with Sir W. M'Naghten, the British resident at his court, agreed that a few battalions, sufficient to seize Herat, should be detached from the expeditionary army to occupy that city. Several reasons apparently combined to induce him to give up this project, the importance of which was thought secondary after the departure of the Persian army; besides Shah Shooja had publicly expressed a hope that his nephew, Shah Kamran, would feel grateful for the assistance that he had received from the English. But these reasons were given only to dissimulate the real state of things, and to anticipate the annoying and disadvantageous moral effect that the truth would produce upon the Afghan allies, whose fidelity was very doubtful. The correspondence of Major Pottinger, who remained at Herat after the siege was raised, and that of Colonel Stoddart, who joined him there after he had carried to the Persian monarch the ultimatum with which he had been intrusted, contained assurances which alone caused the delay of this measure. They informed Sir W. M'Naghten that Yar Mohamed might be considered the real sovereign of Herat, and, after having described him as a man equally energetic and opposed to their ambitious views, finished by stating him to be the *most accomplished villain in Central Asia.* However they admitted the power of upsetting him simply with the aid of Kamran and the Heratees, and *that* was the real motive which led Sir W. M'Naghten to delay and amend the plan first conceived of a military occupation of Herat. They therefore trusted to diplomacy to upset the vizier; but the council at Calcutta had reckoned too much upon the co-operation of fortune, which up to that time had smiled on the execution of their projects in Afghanistan, and the vigilance of the distrustful Yar Mohamed Khan baffled all their calculations.

After the retreat of the Shah of Persia, in 1838, Major Pottinger continued to pay the troops at Herat with money supplied by the East India Company. His efforts, and those of Colonel Stoddart, were mainly directed to saving the wretched Heratees from famine, and preventing Yar Mohamed from selling them to the Usbeks; but as the revenues of the state were exhausted, and the vizier had no means left of raising any funds except by a continuation of this inhuman traffic, the English were under the necessity of granting a pension to Shah Kamran and the principal chiefs of Herat, in order to put a stop to it. This measure, however, did not attain the desired object, and the British officers soon complained of the ill treatment they had to submit to from Yar Mohamed; the motive for which, in their opinion, was the protection they gave the townspeople against their tyrant. After having well investigated the matter and obtained information from the best sources, I have come to the conclusion that they were in error; these gentlemen hoped that gratitude for the support the government of Herat had received from that of Calcutta, and also the fear of the British army in the neighbourhood of Kabul, must bring Yar Mohamed Khan to submit to their wishes. Colonel Stoddart especially would assume to himself the position of a Mentor who expected to be obeyed; of a violent disposition he frequently gave way to passion before the vizier, which impeded rather than served his cause, and only rendered him liable to insult. The consequence was, that an imperative order to leave Herat was given him by the king; moreover, his imprudent conduct placed his comrade Pottinger in a false position. Stoddart, thus dismissed, went to Bokhara, where he had a mission to fulfil, and it was only by great good management that Pottinger could obtain leave to remain at Herat, where he soon had serious difficulties to contend with; these had reference to some concessions that he demanded from the vizier in consideration of the pecuniary aid that he received from the East India Company. The concessions in question were, the reform of the government at Herat, and confiding the administration of it to British agents; the occupation of the citadel with two regular battalions of Heratees, well organized, and officered by Englishmen; and finally, the recapture of the fortress of Gorian, which the Persians had held ever since the close of 1837.

The vizier rejected each and all of these propositions, and the good understanding with him, already compromised by Stoddart, thenceforth ceased entirely with Major Pottinger. The latter, finding that he had failed to obtain any one of his demands, ceased to pay the subsidy hitherto furnished to the Afghan chiefs; but Yar Mohamed, conceiving that the payments which had been made gave him an acquired right to their continuance in future, looked upon this suppression as illegal and unjust. On the 30th of January, 1839, therefore, he sent his brother Shere Mohamed

Khan to Major Pottinger to demand specific explanations of his ulterior intentions. The Afghans are not conspicuous amongst either European or Eastern nations for their politeness, and it is said that the chief executed his mission with such brutal rudeness that Major Pottinger ordered one of his servants, a Heratee, to show him the door; a scuffle ensued, and the servants of Shere Mohamed Khan, hearing his shouts, rushed to the assistance of their master and rescued him from his undignified position: the serdar returned furious into the presence of his brother, his attendants dragging after them the luckless servant of the Major, whose hand was immediately cut off by order of the vizier for having dared to place it upon an Afghan chief. He then ordered Sertip Lal Mohamed Khan, Kaleh Beghi, to surround the British officer's house with a guard of two hundred men, and never to lose sight of him, which order was acted upon forthwith.

Yar Mohamed Khan was most perfectly informed of all the intrigues set on foot by the British envoy to deprive him of his power, and he therefore was not sorry to have an opportunity of making him feel that as yet it had not suffered the slightest diminution from his proceedings; avarice being, however, a dominant feature in his character, he contrived, while asserting his independence and resisting the demands of the English, to bend sufficiently to allow of a reconciliation after this rupture. In adopting this line of conduct he had no other end in view than to enrich himself at their expense, well resolved that he would have nothing more to do with them from the day that they should cease to supply his treasury. "They wanted to despoil me, to ruin me, perhaps worse," said Yar Mohamed to the author; "I must have been a great fool not to be beforehand with them."

Major Pottinger had a perfect knowledge of the character of the Asiatic Mussulmans and the versatility and pliancy of the intellect requisite in treating with them; he was therefore soon relieved from the supervision of his guards, and renewed his negotiations at the court of Shah Kamran, but it was only by continuing the payment of the subsidies, temporarily interrupted, that he obtained his liberty. Although that prince, his court, and his ministers, were absolutely maintained by the English, no one appeared to appreciate that fact, or to esteem them for it, for they well knew that their generosity was exercised much more in their own interest than in that of the Heratees. For his part, Yar

Mohamed was never their dupe, and from the month of March, 1839, he had been in correspondence with the court of Persia endeavouring to obtain support against them. It was at this time that he offered Mohamed Shah to unite his army with that of the Prince of Kandahar and oppose the invasion of Shah Shooja; but the rapid march of the British on that town, and the tardiness displayed by the Shah of Persia in producing the subsidy required to carry on the war, induced the vizier again to attach himself to the English alliance, which he found the most profitable of the two. Having formed his plans upon the events of the moment, he was one of the first to send his congratulations to Shah Shooja upon his success. Major Pottinger knew not which way to turn in the midst of all these fluctuations in the policy of the vizier, and it was with a feeling of inexpressible pleasure that he heard the East India Company were about to release him from his fetters by sending him a successor.

Major d'Arcy Todd, of the artillery, assistant and military secretary to Sir W. M'Naghten, was the officer charged by the Governor-General to accompany Shah Shooja from Loodiana to Shikapoor, and he afterwards went with the army to Kandahar, where the embassy of congratulation sent to the Shah by Yar Mohamed had already arrived. This officer possessed an intimate knowledge of the Persian language, and the affairs of Central Asia, which he had acquired when in the service of the Shah of Persia, and he was therefore selected as envoy to the court of Herat, May 15, 1839. The following were the instructions he received:—

1st. To ascertain the intentions and sentiments of Shah Kamran and his court towards the English Government, and, if he found that in spite of the benefits they had received from it they favoured the Persian Government, to ascertain the cause of discontent, and to do everything in his power to remove it.

2nd. To negotiate a treaty of alliance with Shah Kamran.

3rd. To give Yar Mohamed a written indemnity for his past conduct, in order to obtain his confidence for the future, *but without securing to him and his family the perpetual government of the country.*

4th. To pay attention to the financial relations of the East India Company with the court of Herat.

5th. To take with him engineer and artillery officers to restore and repair the fortifications of the town.

6th. To fix, if possible, the frontier which separates Persia from the principality of Herat.

7th. To make known the objects of the British policy to the chiefs of Bokhara and Khiva; and after having carried out these instructions, to return to Kabul, leaving Major Pottinger as the representative of England at Herat.

Such were the instructions that were transmitted to the British Envoy; but it seems probable that there were secret ones also: at any rate, the last paragraph of the third article leaves room for the supposition—however that might be, Major Todd reached Herat in July, 1839. He exerted himself to the utmost to carry out the mission confided to him, and to establish a cordial understanding between the Shah Kamran, his vizier, and himself; and his efforts were at first crowned with success, for in August, 1839, he concluded a treaty of alliance and friendship with the Suddozye prince. The independence of the principality of Herat was guaranteed by England, and the most substantial advantages stipulated in favour of its chiefs, on condition that the traffic in slaves should be abolished and that all correspondence with other courts should cease unless carried on with the consent of the British Envoy. A monthly sum, equal to the revenues of the principality before the siege, was granted for the maintenance of the government, for the soil had remained without cultivation for eighteen months, and labour of every kind had been interrupted from the commencement of hostilities.

The East India Company also made considerable advances to the agriculturists, merchants, and shopkeepers to enable them to recommence business, and every description of tax was remitted till after the harvest of 1840; large sums of money were likewise expended in repairing the fortifications. The Anglo-Indian Government could hardly have done more had Herat been a British possession, and there can be little doubt they hoped that it would soon become one as they behaved with so much liberality. However, the measures they adopted produced the happiest results for the Afghans; the town was quickly re-peopled, the land covered with crops, commerce resumed its activity, caravans poured in rapidly, and security and confidence were completely re-established. But the sacrifices made by the Company were never compensated by any of the advantages they had expected. Yar Mohamed made not a single concession, and remained absolute master of the principality; he tolerated the English in it only because they satisfied his thirst for gold.

It is true they constantly endeavoured to induce Shah Kamran to displace his despotic minister; but that sovereign could see no other way of disposing of his vizier than by putting him to death—a measure which Major Todd, of course, would not sanction, and the Shah would not commit himself to it unless the English co-operated with him, so that it was very difficult to come to an understanding when the views of both were so conflicting. The Serdar Shere Mohamed Khan, brother of the vizier, and the Ichik Agassi Feiz Mohamed, Alikioozye, both of them warm partisans of the Persian alliance, were constantly originating reports hostile to the English, rendering all hope of coming to a cordial feeling utterly abortive. Herat, indeed, abounded in intrigues, and, if blood was not shed, it was due only to the loyalty of Major Todd, who, constantly pressed by his partisans to consent to the assassination of the vizier, as constantly rejected the idea with indignation; could it have been possible for that officer to wish to terminate the question in this manner, nothing would have been more easy, for, at one of the dinners that he gave to Yar Mohamed Khan, the vizier, being but a bad Mussulman, was so intoxicated as to fall senseless under the table. Here was an opportunity: many of the guests, and amongst them Prince Mohamed Yoosoof (grandson of Hadji Firooz Eddin), the Serdar Dine Mohamed Khan, and the Kazi of Herat, were his declared enemies; Hassan Mohamed, another guest, suggested that the head of the unconscious minister ought to be cut off at once, and the Major had the greatest possible trouble to prevent the company from adopting his proposition, being obliged to sit up with him the whole night to save his life. It was in vain that he represented to these chiefs that such actions were reprobated by Europeans, and contrary to their religion and the rights of men; they looked upon his conduct as simply pusillanimous, and for this reason only several serdars were subsequently much less favourably disposed towards the English,—that the death of the vizier in a chancemedley or an apoplectic fit would not in any way have distressed Major Todd is highly probable. The king was exceedingly ill-disposed towards Yar Mohamed before the arrival of the English envoy, and took no pains to conceal his opinion; he thought no more about the Persians after they had retreated, and when he found the Feringhees paid him his pension with such perfect punctuality and supplied him so lavishly with wine and spirits, which constituted the charm of his existence, he became their warmest partisan and granted them whatever they desired. But the English required also the ratification of his minister, and the minister would never ratify anything. The government of India considered it a crime in Major Todd that he did not give up the old king and try his powers of persuasion and argument upon the vizier; but there is no proof that the British envoy had any chance of success with him, for Yar Mohamed had already come to a determination respecting the power that the English wanted to exert over him, and the substitution of the vizier for his sovereign would have alienated from Major Todd the party that supported Shah Kamran. Furthermore, it was to the Shah that he was accredited by his Government; it was, therefore, his duty to carry on his negotiations in the regular course, and if Shah Kamran had retained any of the vigour of his youth he would at the very commencement have settled his differences with his minister. Every morning the vizier had an audience, at which he made a report to his sovereign on the position of affairs in general; his servants always remained at the gate of the citadel, which was also the residence of the king, and it would have been easy for the Shah to have had Yar Mohamed arrested and strangled before the least assistance could reach him: but instead of taking that step he threatened him in the most violent and absurd manner, and towards the close of 1839 proceeded to such lengths that the loss of his own liberty, and afterwards of his life, were the consequence. It happened thus:—

Shah Kamran, having been informed that the vizier had received 100,000 rupees, demanded that they should be delivered to him; but the minister replied that they were in his charge not only to keep, but to use for the expenses of his administration. In accordance with Eastern custom, Yar Mohamed was at the time seated on his knees and heels before his sovereign, who, being considerably intoxicated, seized his minister by the beard, dragged him forcibly towards him with one hand, drew his dagger with the other, and prepared to strike. However, before proceeding to extremity, he endeavoured to make him restore the sum that he thought the vizier had extorted; but neither menaces nor promises had any effect upon the prime minister, who maintained the most perfect coolness. "Strike," he said, "my fate is in your hands. I have spent the money for the good of the state, and I have none of it to return to you." Kamran, shaken by that extraordinary firmness of demeanour which had maintained so great an influence over him for ten years, replaced the dagger in his belt, and allowed Yar Mohamed to depart. After this the vizier kept a strict watch over his sovereign, and never entered the presence alone to converse upon matters of state policy.

This incident created a further estrangement between Major Todd and Yar Mohamed, and was quickly followed by another event, of which the English were accused of being the instigators.

After the death of Attar Khan in 1830 his father, the Serdar Dine Mohamed, soon repented that he had given up the powerful position of vizier to his cousin; his ambition had increased with age, and he ranged himself amongst the adversaries of Yar Mohamed. Notwithstanding this rivalry the two relatives had not ceased to meet and maintain the appearance of friendly intercourse, and the wily vizier neglected nothing that might attach Dine Mohamed to his cause, for none could promote his ambitious views better than he. This serdar was the true type of an Asiatic warrior —one of those intrepid and fiery chiefs whose sword leaps from the scabbard ere the hand of its master reaches the hilt; his audacity had no equal among the Afghans, and none knew better how to infuse his own courage and enthusiasm into the breasts of others. Yar Mohamed might perhaps have succeeded in securing his assistance if the English had not attached him to their party, but Dine Mohamed submitted to the influence of their persuasions and their gold, and soon fell into their projects. Towards the commencement of 1840 this serdar sent a messenger to the vizier with an invitation to a feast at his house, which was accepted, and arrangements were made by him to seize his cousin on his arrival; of this the minister received warning only at the moment he was passing the threshold of the door, when suddenly retracing his steps he returned home, and despatched a body of five hundred infantry to surround Dine Mohamed's residence, and take him prisoner. Scenes of this description were constantly occurring, and added greatly to the difficulties that the British envoy had to contend with.

Much that I have stated relating to Major Todd was taken from an article in the Bombay Times of November 14, 1847. By incorporating that narrative with my own notes I have hoped to make a simple and explicit statement in defence of that brave officer, so unworthily treated by the ungrateful Government of Calcutta.

The Secret Committee of the Council there had approved of the treaty concluded between their Envoy at Herat and Shah Kamran; they wrote to Major Todd to compliment him on the ability that he had displayed in these negotiations; they also sanctioned all the expenses incurred and promised for fortifying the town, for the maintenance of the Heratee troops, and other purposes, and added, "We continue to attach the greatest importance to the security of Herat, but the sacrifices that we make for Shah Kamran will give you the right to a powerful influence over his councils and conduct, and we hope that he will show himself grateful for all the British Government has done for him." The Council deceived themselves wonderfully in expecting "powerful influence at Herat;" that of Major Todd was barely tolerated; it was far from commanding. The treaty approved by the Council was concluded in August 1839, and in the October following the sacrifices to which they alluded in their letter to their envoy amounted to six lacs of rupees, 60,000*l*.

But Yar Mohamed appeared indifferent to the liberality of the English Government, and at the very moment they supposed they had his *bonâ fide* support he made fresh propositions to the Persian court; the letters which he wrote to Assaf Dooulet, Governor-General of Khorassan, bore in every word the stamp of implacable hatred to the British, and he offered to place himself and his country under the protection of Mohamed Shah. When Major Todd informed the English Resident at Kabul of this fresh treachery, he stated his opinion that to maintain friendly relations with the court of Shah Kamran was no longer possible, and that it was indispensable to the security of the dominion of Shah Shooja *to annex the principality of Herat.* He showed also the precarious and useless position of himself and his mission in that town in comparison with and in despite of the enormous outlay that it entailed, and specially insisted that the Company had no chance of reaping the fruits of its expenditure nor of establishing a permanent and solid influence without the presence of an Anglo-Indian army to awe the vizier. He concluded by saying that if, contrary to his advice, they persisted in maintaining the independence of Herat, the Company would *prepare difficulties for themselves which would attain a fearful height.*

Sir W. M'Naghten supported the opinion of Major Todd with the Court of Directors, and added that he considered the annexation necessary to the complete consolidation of the British dominion in Afghanistan. But on so serious a subject the Directors thought fit to take time for reflection, and after having lost some months in deliberation determined upon placing the conduct of Yar Mohamed before Lord Auckland, that his Lordship might determine what was proper to be done under the circumstances.

While Major Todd awaited his reply the difficulties became daily greater at Herat. The vizier, knowing that his treachery had been discovered, rendered Major Todd's residence there more and more disagreeable by making fresh demands in a most imperious tone; large sums alone would satisfy him, and Major Todd was content to pay them to maintain his position.

In January, 1840, the payments made to the Shah Kamran, his avaricious minister, and his starving people, amounted to 100,000*l*., and yet before that month had expired Yar Mohamed addressed another letter to the Shah of Persia, in which he called himself his faithful servant, and declared that he permitted the British envoy to remain at Herat from mere motives of courtesy. At the same time he wrote a letter to the Russian minister at Teheran asking him to send an agent of his nation to Herat; and so great was his hatred of the English that he offered to give up the city to the Persian garrison of Gorian. Major Todd, exasperated on learning this fact, went instantly to the vizier to expostulate with him, but he could not induce him to forego his intention until he placed his pistol at his breast; this attempt was undoubtedly imprudent, but the British envoy staked everything upon that last throw. Yar Mohamed, awed by his courage and inflexibility, dared no longer resist, and he would probably have behaved with a little more humility afterwards if Lord Auckland had better appreciated the reports of Major Todd; but his Lordship's incredible weakness in his treatment of this barbarian encouraged him to re-assume all his former arrogance. In his reply to the British envoy the Governor-General said that he could only attribute the treachery of Yar Mohamed to a vague idea of danger, and recommended him by every means in his power to endeavour to bring the minister to a cordial and friendly state of feeling with the government of India, and make him clearly comprehend the benefits of the British alliance, instead of proceeding with the duplicity and suspicion which had hitherto marked his conduct towards the Company. Lord Auckland added, that, in consideration of the vizier's former good services, and his resistance to the Persians of several months' duration, he should extend his pardon to every offence of which he might have been guilty before that letter was received. But as this despatch only reached Herat in February, 1840, and Yar Mohamed's last treacherous proceeding took place in January, 1840, it was considered as included in this act of oblivion, and Major Todd was obliged to fulfil the painful duty imposed upon him. He gave the vizier the most positive and solemn assurances that every past infraction of the treaty was forgotten, and Yar Mohamed seemed apparently sensible of Lord Auckland's kindness; but unhappily he was secretly convinced in his own mind that, whatever might be his future conduct to the English, he had acquired impunity for his evil deeds, and therefore proceeded on his old plan of profiting by their folly to fill his pockets with their rupees.

After his rupture with the court of Persia Sir John M'Neil had returned to England, leaving his Secretary, Lieut.-Colonel Sheil, as chargé d'affaires at Erzeroum, who thence kept up an active correspondence with the Persian minister, the good understanding between England and Persia remaining dependent upon the evacuation of Gorian by the Persians and its restoration to the Prince of Herat. Demands the most urgent on this subject were sent to Teheran by Colonel Sheil, at the same time that Yar Mohamed's offer to give the place up to the Shah of Persia arrived there, and with it his request to that sovereign to occupy Herat. This coincidence had caused much altercation between Major Todd and the vizier; but when the latter received full pardon for his delinquencies from Lord Auckland he professed unbounded gratitude for such generosity, and swore to prove it by some brilliant act of devotion; he therefore requested Major Todd to advance him some money, promising that he would employ it in an expedition against the fortress of Gorian. The Major, in his anxious position, trusted to his sincerity, and advanced two lacs of rupees to equip the force, but the cash once safe in the vizier's treasury the preparations, which necessitated only a trifling expense, proceeded slowly, and in a short time he announced on the most frivolous grounds that the undertaking was abandoned. It was afterwards proved in the clearest manner that Yar Mohamed had written to the Persian Governor of Gorian to inform him that he need not be alarmed at any news of a warlike character, for, though the English had obliged him to promise that he would besiege the place, he might dismiss from his mind all fear and uneasiness on the subject, for he did not intend to keep his word. Major Todd, almost in despair at such utter faithlessness, wrote to his Government that the expedition had been given up under circumstances of the most perfidious nature. This took place in July, 1840, by which time the sums spent in efforts to consolidate this most unproductive alliance amounted to 190,000*l*.

The British envoy, seeing the perfect inutility of this vast expenditure, took upon himself to reduce the monthly payment to the court of Herat to 2500*l*.; and Yar Mohamed, wrathful at the reduction, renewed in the following September his intrigues with the Persian monarch. At his request Mirza Massood, the foreign minister of Mohamed Shah, who was at Meshed at the time, came as far as Gorian to meet in person an agent from the vizier; but Yar Mohamed had the address to turn even this perfidious action to his own account, by relating it to Major Todd, and pretending that it had been done unknown to him by his brother, the Serdar Shere Mohamed: he obtained fresh advances for this apparent frankness, but it must be added that he plucked them from the major's hand rather than received them from him. Never was the position of a British agent in the East so exasperating as that of this officer at Herat. Exposed to the craft and cupidity of a man who saw through the ambitious views of the Anglo-Indian Government upon his country, the envoy was entirely at his mercy, and the vizier purposely embittered every hour of every day that he remained at Herat, and rendered endurance scarcely possible. The larger and more liberal were the concessions of that Government, the less did Yar Mohamed dissemble his hatred and hostility to his improvident protectors; and both these increased, while every check or reverse experienced by the British troops in Afghanistan was exaggerated by the vizier, and represented as a triumph of Islamism over the Infidels: he went so far as to say publicly that he should seize the opportunity of the first great disaster of the British arms to join their enemies. At this period clouds hung over the political horizon of Afghanistan; Dost Mohamed had unsheathed his sword in the north, and threatened Kabul: in the south the detachment of Major Clibborne had been cut to pieces, and Kelat-i-Ghildjzye taken from the invaders. The quarrel between the vizier and his cousin caused the former, it is true, some uneasiness, and prevented him from at once taking part against the English; but he indemnified himself by attaching to his party all the discontented spirits of Kabul and Kandahar, with whose assistance he could easily disturb the tranquillity of those provinces and impede the establishment of the dominion of Shah Shooja. It was only by satisfying the rapacious and exorbitant demands which Yar Mohamed daily, nay, almost hourly, advanced on every possible pretence, that Major Todd could retain his footing in Herat at this critical moment.

While thus continuing to draw upon the Company's exchequer, Yar Mohamed actually discussed in council a project for attacking Kandahar, a scheme that he would assuredly have carried out if Dost Mohamed had not been at hand. During all this period scarcely a week passed that he did not speak of his alliance with Persia and his intention of arresting the English officers; in the month of August their imprisonment was so generally expected, that no one would go to their houses, not even persons under great obligations to them. Shah Kamran himself spoke of it, and publicly, but added, the legation had nothing to fear, that he was their friend, and that not one of them would have been alive then but for his interference in their favour. This deplorable condition of affairs had reached such a point that a crisis became inevitable. The money spent upon the chiefs and fortifications of Herat now amounted to 300,000*l.*, which, however, in no way prevented Yar Mohamed from continuing his intercourse with the Persian court; and in January, 1841, he despatched a confidential agent with a numerous suite to Assaf Dooulet, to ask for pecuniary assistance and six guns from the Shah of Persia, to enable him to march against Girishk, a small fortress in advance of Kandahar, as Gorian is of Herat. When Major Todd was certain of the object of this expedition, he represented to the vizier the danger to which he exposed himself by this new infraction of the eighth article of the treaty, and that so flagrant a violation of that solemn engagement would be more than the long-suffering and patience of his Government could submit to; he also declared that he should not consider himself bound to continue the allowances he had paid up to that time—that all the treasure of the Company could not suffice to satisfy his requirements—and that the vizier must provide for the expenses of his own government until such time as he should see fit to act strictly up to the conditions and stipulations of friendship existing between the two nations.

Following up this declaration, Major Todd withheld the payment of 2500*l.* due on the 1st of February, 1841, to the court of Shah Kamran. The vizier, case-hardened by impunity, looked upon this suppression as merely temporary, expected he should be pardoned his last breach of faith as he had been all former ones, and on the 8th of the same month addressed to Major Todd the following fresh demands:—

1st. That the British envoy should pardon all his past conduct, and leave him under no apprehension for the future.

2. That he should receive immediately 30,000*l.* from the East India Company for the payment of his personal debts.

3. That his monthly pension should be augmented and paid a year in advance.

4. That the British envoy should hand over a written agreement not to compromise Herat in any foreign war till after the harvest in July.

5. That the fortifications of the town should be enlarged and finished at the expense of the East India Company, and that it should provide the Government of Herat with the necessary funds to enable it to reconquer several places which had thrown off their obedience to it.

6. That the Company should pay and maintain the Heratee troops while in the field.

After his recent infraction of the existing treaty these terms appeared so exorbitant, that Major Todd replied it was impossible to suppose his Government would consent to make fresh sacrifices, even in a modified form, unless it was for some corresponding advantages, but he offered to grant several of Yar Mohamed's demands if he made the following concessions:—

1. That Yar Mohamed should never again deviate from the spirit of the treaty between the two Governments.

2. That the Serdar Syud Mohamed Khan, his eldest son, should take a contingent of troops to Kabul to serve in the British army.

3. That as soon as this serdar had arrived at his destination the envoy would pay half the vizier's debts and augment his monthly allowance.

4. That the citadel of Herat should receive a British garrison, and that the royal residence of Rooz-bagh, seven miles south of the city, with the land belonging to it, should be made over to the English to build barracks upon for their own troops.

5. That the Vizier should never again expect to receive, and distribute himself, the funds appropriated to the maintenance of the chiefs of the Court of Shah Kamran, and that the sums allotted for that purpose should be paid to the individuals themselves by the agents of the Company.

These propositions of Major Todd's were approved by Sir William M'Naghten, while the Governor-General of India looked upon it as a matter of regret that they had been made. Yar Mohamed appeared quite satisfied, provided the sums he had demanded were paid in advance; but Major Todd knew only too well the character of the man he had to deal with to grant his request, and the result was a most animated discussion. The Vizier pretended, certainly falsely, that Major Todd had in his accounts charged the East India Company with much larger sums than he had paid to him, and that he had used the difference in largesses to the people in order to excite them to overturn the Government of Herat, and substitute that of the Company. Finally—and this seems to be true—that the envoy constantly plotted with Shah Kamran the fall of the Vizier from power, —and the angry minister declared to Major Todd that his presence and that of his subordinates could no longer be tolerated in Herat, and that he must depart with the least possible delay.

Thus ended the anxious and onerous intervention of the Indo-British Government at Herat, and its conclusion was, as might be expected, marked by several acts of rapacity on the part of Yar Mohamed, who immediately made known his intention of marching against Kandahar; and in order to leave no doubt on this occasion of his sincerity, he sent his own brother, the Serdar Shere Mohamed Khan, as ambassador to the court of Persia, with presents for the Shah, and a request that a subsidy might be given him to undertake the expedition he had projected. But it seems evident that in making this demand the Vizier was really not more sincere than he had been with the English; his only object was to obtain from both as much money as he possibly could for the purpose of strengthening his position in his own country.

The British envoy being driven to the alternative of making fresh sacrifices or taking his departure, decided upon the latter, and the Vizier having provided him with the transport necessary for his journey, sent with him the Serdar Fethi Khan, one of his cousins, as his escort to the frontier. Major Todd had, with an object that is easy to understand, collected a considerable quantity of corn at Herat; but the granaries were pillaged by the people even before he had left the town, and a report having been spread that he had carried away four boxes of treasure, the Heratees determined to plunder him of it, and they would certainly have proceeded to do so if the Vizier had not lined the streets and bazaars with troops. His son, the Serdar Syud Mohamed Khan, also accompanied Major Todd and his party to such a distance on their road as secured them against any act of violence.

CHAPTER XXVIII.

Reaction against the English at Herat — Ingratitude of the East India Company to Major Todd — Death of that officer — Russian expedition against Khiva — General Peroffski leaves Orenburg — Disasters and retreat of the Russian army — Aga Khan raises a revolt in Kerman — The Kazi of Herat at Khiva — Conversation with the Khan — Disgrace of Yacooba Mehter — Allah Kooli Khan accepts the English alliance — Snare laid for the Kazi — Captain Abbott at Khiva — His mission there — Intrigues of Yacooba Mehter — Captain Abbott leaves for Russia — The Usbeks take him prisoner — Akhood Zadeh leaves Khiva in search of him — Meeting of Akhood and the captive — The Yuss Bashi and Hassan Bahadoor — Fresh complication — Captain Abbott reaches Russia — Lieutenant Shakespear arrives at Khiva — Obtains the liberation of the Russian slaves and brings them to Astrakan — Lieut. Shakespear's reception at St. Petersburg — Captain Abbott not recompensed — Russia creates difficulties for Khiva — The Shah demands the Persian slaves — Captain Conolly arrives at Khiva — He fails in the object of his mission — Requirements of the Khan.

AFTER the departure of the British Envoy a grievous reaction took place against all those who had participated in the liberality of the English, or who, having served them, received pensions: they were arrested, imprisoned, robbed of every thing, and reduced to the deepest distress. There were but few merchants in Herat who had not transacted business with Major Todd, some of whom had made large fortunes; these the vizier confiscated or grossly overtaxed to his own profit, and insults and oppression continued during several months.

Amongst the families who were the greatest sufferers was that of the Kazi of Herat, Hassan Mohamed, and his son Akhood Zadeh Saleh Mohamed; they were stripped of a fortune amounting to 20,000*l.*, and their wives, daughters, and slaves tortured to make them disclose where the chief judge had secreted his wealth. This venerable old man was actually condemned to death, and his life was saved only by the arrival of a ransom of 1400*l.* sent by Major Todd to procure his release. The villanous nature of Yar Mohamed resumed on this occasion all its original cruelty; and it was in the midst of a sea of blood that he seized the property of so many unhappy people—spoils that he considered legitimately to belong to him only because they had arisen out of, or were reputed to have done so, the corrupt generosity of the English.

It is worthy of remark that nine months before the departure of the mission from Herat, Lord Auckland proposed to the Court of Directors that Major Todd should be recalled, if the measures which the British Government wished to adopt in the principality should be received with suspicion by Yar Mohamed Khan; and his Lordship observed that by such recall the vizier would be made to feel his false position and to defend the independence of his country. But on the arrival at Calcutta of the news that the differences between Persia and England had been terminated by the restitution of Gorian to Shah Kamran, this proposition was abandoned. Dr. Riach, *attaché* to the British embassy in Persia, who had retired to Erzeroom, was despatched to Teheran in the month of January, 1841, and travelled post to Khorassan, to be there at the surrender of the place; this had been stipulated for in a treaty concluded between Great Britain and Persia, the latter being compensated by the restitution of the island of Karrack to Mohamed Shah.

The Court of Directors hoped that this arrangement, and the freedom in which the new treaty with Persia would oblige the Persian monarch to leave Yar Mohamed Khan, would put a stop to the intrigues of the latter. But that was an erroneous anticipation; and the departure of Major Todd from Herat a year afterwards, and just at the moment when Lord Auckland had succeeded in obtaining an amelioration of his position, occasioned the East India Company bitter disappointment—even resentment, and the Secretary of Government received orders to write to Sir William M'Naghten, British Resident at Kabul, to whom Major Todd was attached, that the late envoy at Herat was considered as *incapable of filling a political appointment, and ought to rejoin his regiment with dishonour.*

Here, then, was the recompense which this officer received for so much labour and anxiety, so much devotion to his country, so many dangers braved. Such are the Court of Directors, men who demand of a worthy man full of intelligence and capacity an impossible result—more than impossible; and because he does not obtain it—because he did not rid them of Yar Mohamed, they cast upon him the imputation of dishonourable conduct, which in fact they themselves deserve for the notorious folly and imbecility they displayed, not in the affairs of Herat only, but in all the other provinces of Afghanistan in which they had a policy to carry out. Was Major Todd, then, so guilty? Had he not well estimated the circumstances when he advised they should take everything out of the power of Yar Mohamed and occupy Herat with a British force? Are not those Directors incapable whose avarice was in no degree less than that of Yar Mohamed, who knew not how to value their envoy's advice, and allowed the vizier to believe that he might do as he pleased with perfect impunity? It is disgraceful, scandalous, that writers should have been found in the British press sufficiently stupid and base to sanction the blame with which they sought to tarnish the name of an intelligent and honourable man — blame which could never conceal the black ingratitude of the Court of Directors.

Strong in the consciousness that his conduct at Herat had been strictly irreproachable, the unfortunate Major D'Arcy Todd rejoined in India the corps of artillery to which he belonged; but, constantly oppressed by thoughts of the infamy with which they had so unjustly sought to blast his good name, his laborious life rolled on filled with bitterness, and it was with real pleasure that he received orders to take part in the war that broke out in 1845 between the English and the Sikhs. He went into the field of Feroseshah with the impression that he should there lay down his life, and was conducting himself in the most gallant manner when the iron messenger from one of the enemy's guns realised in a moment his mournful presentiment. Before, however, he met a soldier's death, Major Todd had long been reinstated in the esteem of his countrymen, whose faith in him had for a moment been shaken, and they now respect his memory and take a deep interest in the events of his distinguished career—an interest which will be eternal.

It will be remembered that when Major Todd went to Herat his instructions were also to make known the objects of the British policy in Central Asia to the Khans of Bokhara and Khiva. The English suddenly passed from a state of the most confiding peacefulness to that of the most exaggerated fear, and were no longer satisfied that the possession of Afghanistan efficiently secured their Indian dominions. Turkestan was the barrier they now wished to raise against Russia, by completely establishing their influence in the Usbek Khanats. Moments even appeared precious, for, just at the time when the Shah retired from before Herat, Count

Simonitch boldly announced that a Russian *corps d'armée* was leaving Orenburg and marching upon Khiva, to reduce the Khan of that country, and the cabinet of St. Petersburg gave a very reasonable motive for this new invasion of Tartary. A great number of Russian subjects had been carried off by the Usbeks and sold as slaves in the markets of Khiva, and all negotiations for their deliverance had hitherto proved unsuccessful, for Allah Kooli Khan had obstinately refused to give his consent to their release. The Russian Government at first sought a remedy by making reprisals, and had detained at Astrakan ever since the year 1833 a Khivan caravan, consisting of 200 men and 800 camels, laden with large quantities of merchandise of great value; but this, instead of rendering the Khan more reasonable, only irritated him, and the Emperor therefore determined to employ force to obtain his just demands.

It was at the commencement of the winter of 1840 that General Peroffsky left Orenburg at the head of 6000 infantry, accompanied by 10,000 camels and their army of drivers, to conquer the obstinate resistance of the Usbek sovereign. This season was chosen for the expedition as being the one in which the troops would be less distressed than at any other by the want of water in the arid steppes across which they had to march; but, by one of those strange chances which occur from time to time, this winter was remarkable for its inclemency, and the difficulties that under ordinary circumstances would have been by no means serious became terrible, even insurmountable, in consequence. The cold was intense, and the mercury at 40° below zero: snow covered the earth to a considerable depth, and the wind swept with incredible violence over the naked steppes. Several thousand soldiers were frost-bitten and lost their legs and arms, and the greater number, both of men and animals, perished even before they reached Ak Boolak (a station on the extreme frontier of Russia and Khiva), when General Peroffsky wisely retreated, thus avoiding worse disasters.

Nothing could have served the purposes of the English better, and their satisfaction was proportionably great when the discomfiture of the Russian army became known; but, remembering that another expedition could be sent which might meet with fewer obstacles, and achieve what this had just failed in doing, they hastened to prevent, if possible, a fresh advance of the Russians, by endeavouring to induce Allah Kooli Khan to give them the satisfaction they demanded; and, in order to prevent the Shah of Persia from making a diversion in favour of the Tzar south of Khiva, the British Government created much embarrassment for him in his own kingdom.

In speaking of the affairs of Kandahar, mention has been made of an Ismaelian Syud * greatly renowned for his bravery, and much venerated by the Beloochees, called Aga Khan. This chief, after having escorted part of General Nott's baggage to Shikapoor in 1839, marched at the head of a body of cavalry into Kerman, where he found no difficulty in establishing himself, for he had a great many partisans in that province. His success was so rapid and decided, that the Shah of Persia found himself compelled to send a body of troops against him, and a year elapsed before he could repress the insurrection and drive him from the country.

While Aga Khan was engaged in this irruption into the south of Persia, Major Todd arrived at Herat, and, in conformity with the instructions he had received, sent Mohamed Hassan on an embassy to the Khan of Khiva. The Major could not possibly have selected an envoy better qualified than the Kazi, for, in addition to the influence with Mussulmans which he possessed in virtue of his office of kazi or chief judge, he had also that which arose from his belonging to the Djagatais of Turkestan origin,† a tribe greatly venerated in its own country. The kazi took with him letters from Major Todd, Shah Kamran, and his vizier Yar Mohamed, to the Khan of the Usbeks, and the Afghan prince requested him to conclude an alliance with the English; but, notwithstanding these recommendations, the mission was a dangerous and delicate one, and it required real courage to accept it, for it was generally known at the time that Yacooba Mehter, the vizier of Allah Kooli Khan, had hitherto brought about the death of every one who had supported the British policy. The brave and intelligent Kazi reached Khiva in safety, but met with an exceedingly rude reception from Yacooba Mehter, which occasioned him a momentary regret at håving involved himself in this enterprise; he did not lose, however, either his coolness or his prudence. Having been presented to the Khan on the day after his arrival,

* This chief is thus called on account of his descent from Ismael, the old Man of the Mountain.—*Ferrier*.

† The descendants of Djagatai, a son of Ghengis Khan.—*Ferrier*.

Mohamed Hassan left him to imagine in the first instance that he was simply the bearer of a letter from Shah Kamran, which letter he gave him. After the customary compliments, the Usbek prince assumed an air of severity, and questioned him closely as to the object of his journey; and the following dialogue, which then took place, I now relate as the Kazi himself related it to me:—

The Khan. Strengthen my belief in you, Oh Kazi, by assuring me that you are still a Mussulman. Yet, if you were so, you would never have brought these Kiaffir Frenguis * into the country of Islam.

The Kazi. It is not I who brought them, it is Allah who has sent them to us.

The Khan. How darest thou thus profane the name of Allah, by connecting it with such a bad action?

The Kazi. I only tell the truth, and I can prove it to thee.

The Khan. Prove it, then.

The Kazi. When the rafezis † Kadjars ‡ laid siege to Herat, our illustrious sovereign, who has no equal (*bi nazer*), sent letters to entreat you to come to our assistance—to us—Soonees like yourself, veritable pillars of Islam: Did you come?

The Khan. Never did Mussulman ask my help in vain! My victorious army marched immediately on my reception of the first letter of Shah Kamran; but, when I arrived at Pindjdeh, Mohamed Zeman Khan, Serdar of the Djemcheedis, assured me that my troops were not required to save the place—that the Afghans were all-sufficient, and I then returned to my own dominions.

The Kazi. And who, most mighty Khan, had need of your help, Zeman Khan or Shah Kamran? Why attend to the words of the former, when the fearful extremity to which the latter was reduced was known to all Asia? Not only did you abandon our cause, but you forbade your subjects to bring us provisions. This unhappy example was followed by the Bokharians and the Mohamedzyes, who, instead of coming to our aid, joined the rafezi Kadjars. What did the Frenguis then, whom you call Kiaffirs? They came to aid the true children of Allah, they procured us the

---

* Infidel Europeans.

† Heretics.

‡ The Afghans, in speaking of a nation, frequently designate it by the proper name of the tribe to which the sovereign belongs: thus they call the Persians, Kadjars; the Kandaharians, Mohamedzyes; the Sindians, Talpooras; the Sikhs, Rundjeets, &c.—*Ferrier.*

corn that you refused; they brought us their gold, their blood, and their intellect, to defend our ramparts that were crumbling under the balls of Mohamed Shah, and are now rising again under their beneficent care. It was they who lent the helping hand to the unfortunate, who brought back to us abundance and tranquillity, who distinguished themselves by their justice and equity, and protected the true Mussulman against the heretics. Which, then, are the infidels,—the Persians, who inflicted upon us every kind of misery, and whose part you take; or those whom, deserted as we were by our brethren, God sent to protect us, and whose help you may want ere long to arrest the progress of the Russians?

The Khan. Is it really true, Oh Kazi, that these Frenguis are such as you describe them? Has Islam found support in them?

At this point the Kazi, seeing that the warmth of his discourse had made an impression upon Allah Kooli Khan, drew from his pocket the letter of Major Todd, and handed it to him, saying, "Doubt it not for a moment, great prince; receive this letter that the most exalted elchee (ambassador) accredited to our powerful sovereign addresses to thee; its words are so many precious pearls that he has woven into the wreath of friendship, and in connexion with which he offers his prayers with thine to the Almighty to grant thee a long and glorious reign."

The letter was enclosed in a silken bag embroidered with gold. The Khan took it, broke the large seal of the British arms with animation, and, after having perused the missive, which contained proposals of friendship and alliance, and also of active mediation between him and the Russians, his contracted brow gradually expanded, and from that time he treated the Kazi with great respect. Mohamed Hassan seized this favourable opportunity for complaining of the insolence of the vizier, which brought upon that functionary a severe reprimand. The audience terminated in the delivery of the presents sent by Major Todd to the Usbek prince —optical instruments and splendid arms, at the sight of which the whole court went into ecstasies; and the English cause was further benefited by the disgrace of Yacooba Mehter, their most dangerous enemy, who was kept at a distance from the scene of negotiations.

After having arranged the preliminaries of a treaty, the Kazi promptly set out on his return to Herat, to render to the British envoy an account of the results of his embassy: but when he reached Merv he fell into an ambush, which nearly proved fatal to him. This had been prepared for him by the governor of the town, Niaz Mohamed Khan, uncle of Yacooba Mehter, the exasperated minister. Fortunately some persons who were near, hearing the Kazi's shouts, hastened to his assistance, and delivered him out of the hands of his assassins, though with some severe contusions. Niaz Mohamed, as if to testify his regret at his misfortune, had the hypocrisy to pay a visit to his victim, but no one was deceived by that act of apparent courtesy; the injuries received by the Kazi were intended to impress upon his mind the disgrace he had brought upon Yacooba Mehter, and for some time they certainly answered their purpose.

As soon as Major Todd was informed that the Kazi had succeeded in the object of his mission, he dispatched Captain Abbott to Khiva.* His instructions were, if possible, to induce Allah Kooli Khan to release the Russian prisoners; and, as soon as he had attained that object, to go to Astrakan and procure the liberation of the caravan, which had been detained there seven years by the Russians. Captain Abbott commenced his journey very early in 1840—and at a most auspicious moment, for the army of General Peroffsky had just been decimated and obliged to retire, and therefore a fair field lay open to him in which to bring his negotiations to a favourable conclusion.

If the English were prodigal of their gold in facilitating the conquest of Afghanistan, they certainly were not less so in their endeavours to effect their object in Kurdistan; and Captain Abbott freely employed this means of persuasion. So lavish was he, that at Merv he was obliged to dispatch Akhood Zadeh Saleh Mohamed to Herat, to request Major Todd to send him a further supply of money with the utmost dispatch: he did not, however, wait for this, but continuing his journey to Khiva, was received there with distinction by the Khan, and this in spite of the intrigues of Yacooba Mehter, who had been reinstated in the favour of his sovereign, and who, justly or not, was considered a warm partisan of Russia. One fact, however, appeared to indicate the contrary; he exerted him-

* Captain Abbott published a narrative of his journey, but, being unacquainted with the English language, the author could not avail himself of the advantage of reading that interesting work. His information relating to the British negotiations in Khiva is given as he received it from the Kazi Hassan Mohamed, and his son Akhood Zadeh Saleh Mohamed.—*Ferrier.*

self in every way to prevent the liberation of the Russian slaves, which the English affirm he did only to give the Russians an excuse for marching an army to Khiva. In defiance, however, of the minister's opposition, the Khan made the concessions required of him by Captain Abbott with a view of settling the differences with Russia. Nevertheless, and although the definitive convention was drawn up, the vizier did not consider himself vanquished; the Kazi of Herat had, it is true, escaped his toils, but such he trusted would not be the case with Captain Abbott from those he intended to spread for him.

After having obtained a positive promise that the Russian slaves should be restored, the British officer, anxious to terminate his important mission as quickly as possible, would not wait for the return of Akhood Zadeh with the money from Herat; but, procuring what he required on the spot, he set out for Astrakan, accompanied by seven servants, a *mehmendar*,* and a few horsemen furnished by the Khan of Khiva,—the mehmendar being an officer of high rank, named Hassan Bahadoor. This official conducted Captain Abbott in the first instance to the port of Guedik, and near it was encamped his own tribe, of which he was the chief. Captain Abbott, not finding any vessel here, determined to proceed to Dach Kaleh, four days' journey farther south, occupied by the Russians. But Hassan Bahadoor refused to accompany him, alleging as a reason that his orders from his sovereign were not to go beyond Guedik; and Captain Abbott was therefore obliged to continue his journey without any escort: as to his servants they were like himself, strangers in the country, and consequently ignorant of the road.

The mehmendar was acting upon secret orders from the treacherous vizier, who, foreseeing the difficulty in which Captain Abbott would be placed if he could not find a ship, sent forward a messenger with an order that every vessel that might be there should leave the port. The unsuspecting officer of course saw no danger in going on, though it was on that part of his road that those who had sworn his destruction were lying in wait for him; and he was not more than ten hours' march from Dach Kaleh when he and his servants were assailed by a party of Usbeks, against whom

* An officer whose duty it is to procure food and lodging for ambassadors travelling in some parts of the East.—*Ferrier.*

they at first made a vigorous resistance; but, being in the end overpowered by numbers, they were seized and stripped. Captain Abbott lost two fingers in the *melée* and received a gash on the head, and in this miserable condition he was carried to a camp of nomades ten miles to the north, almost on the borders of the Caspian Sea. His new hosts behaved to him with great cruelty; his servants being all taken from him and dispersed in different camps, were made the slaves of those whose hospitality they had claimed.

While Captain Abbott was thus treated at the instigation of the villain Yacooba Mehter, Akhood Zadeh arrived at Khiva, bringing with him a thousand ducats from Major Todd, but his utmost diligence had not enabled him to reach that town before Captain Abbott's departure; and when he proposed to follow him, he was informed by Yacooba Mehter of the report of the unfortunate officer's death: the vizier at the same time ordered all the letters from Major Todd to Captain Abbott to be taken from Akhood Zadeh, though being written in English he could not understand their contents. After Akhood Zadeh had been ten days at Khiva some information he received led him to suppose that Captain Abbott was still alive, and under the influence of this hope he formed the generous determination of going immediately in search of him. Allah Kooli Khan at first attempted to prevent him from risking his life in so perilous an enterprise; but, finding him resolute, he sanctioned his departure, and ordered him a guard of eight horsemen for his personal security. It was a rough task that the son of the Kazi of Herat undertook; ignorant of the country and the Tartar language, he was obliged to wander from tent to tent over the arid steppes by tracks scarcely to be distinguished, often led astray by false information, and having frequently to contend with the ill-will of his escort. But he did not the less perseveringly continue to scour the country in search of the British officer. On the seventeenth day after he left Khiva, at the encampment of Maukeglag, he first came upon traces by which he trusted he should at last discover Captain Abbott, and he determined to press on without delay to the spot indicated as the place of his detention, when the escort, acting upon secret orders from Yacooba Mehter, refused to accompany him, asserting that this part of the country was in such a state, that to go there was to expose themselves to certain death. However, the noble Akhood Zadeh was not daunted by any of the dangers that were pointed out to him;

he abandoned his camels and provisions to the nomades of Maukeglag, and departed alone on his uncertain way across the steppe. His sufferings in consequence were terrible. Hourly in dread of being robbed and murdered, destitute of water to quench the burning thirst of either himself or his horse, or food to alleviate his hunger, he felt himself, at the close of the fourth day, perishing from inanition, when a traveller on foot happily crossed his path, who gave him a draught of water and a handful of maize. Thus slightly supported, he continued his weary search; for, such was his devotion, that he would have died rather than have failed in it. At length, and on the fifth day, he reached the encampment in which Captain Abbott was detained by the rascals who had plundered him. The unfortunate officer was lying on a wretched carpet, suffering much from his wounds, and expecting his death every moment, when a Kossack entered the tent, and said, "They come to deliver you;" and he had scarcely uttered these words when Akhood Zadeh stood before him. "Barik Allah," * exclaimed his friend, "my eyes are gladdened, for I have found you, and my arrival is the end of your misery." The effect of this most unhoped-for deliverance upon Captain Abbott's feelings may be imagined. Akhood Zadeh then placed in his hands the thousand ducats which he had concealed in his belt during the two-and-twenty days that had elapsed after he left Khiva, and which he all the time dreaded would be taken from him. This act is the more striking, in the eyes of those who know the Asiatic character, than his devotion to the British cause and Captain Abbott, for he could so easily have said that he had been robbed, and no one would for a moment have doubted his word. Few, indeed, are the Afghans who would have acted as he did.† When the first outpourings of the heart between Captain Abbott and his gallant and self-denying deliverer had passed, the latter presented to the chief of the horde the firman of which he was the bearer;

* Glory to God.

† His conduct benefited him but little: others, whose services were not to be compared with his, were rewarded liberally, while he obtained scarcely so much as he had a right to expect. This ingratitude on the part of those he served so well changed his character, and in 1847 he was guilty of an act of bad faith that was punished by the bastinado, under the orders of the governor of Khorassan, Assaf Dooulet, to make him restore some thousands of francs which had been given him by the English for the purpose of proceeding to Khulm to seek for some English prisoners who were said to be there. Akhood Zadeh received the money, but remained at home, quietly sending reports from time to time to the British Legation, as if he had really been occupied in the transaction he had engaged to carry out.—*Ferrier*.

in this Allah Kooli Khan enjoined his subjects to aid him in discovering Captain Abbott, who, as well as his servants, were to be delivered up to him if ever they were found within his dominions. The nomades thus perceived, though rather late, that in obeying their chief and attacking the British officer, they had exposed themselves to the anger of their sovereign, for it was clear he had been quite ignorant of this miserable business, and the responsibility therefore was likely to fall upon themselves. Beseeching Captain Abbott to pardon them, they overwhelmed him with attentions, and conducted him two days' journey on the road to Maukeglag to another encampment; this was composed of two portions of different tribes, one of which was commanded by a chief named Yuss Bashi, the other by a son of the villain Hassan Bahadoor, and it was in the tent of the former that the travellers took up their temporary abode.

Yuss Bashi gave his guest the warmest reception, and the son of Hassan Bahadoor soon paid him a visit; but when he found the British officer intended to make his father responsible for the treatment he had received, he hastened to inform him of the fact, and also that their enemy Yuss Bashi was collecting evidence against them to aggravate his crime. The messenger who carried this letter made such dispatch, that in the short interval of four days Hassan Bahadoor arrived at his son's camp, at the head of 150 horsemen, for the purpose of preventing Captain Abbott from returning to Khiva escorted by Yuss Bashi, who could do them the greatest possible injury in the estimation of their sovereign. When he had pitched his tent he pressed Captain Abbott to be his guest, on the ground that he was his mehmendar, and that it was his duty to watch over the safety of his person. This officer, however, decidedly refused to avail himself of his offer, and rejected the invitation, Yuss Bashi supporting his refusal and sharply reproaching Hassan Bahadoor with his previous conduct. The discussion grew warm, swords were drawn, and blood would have been shed, but for the intervention of Akhood Zadeh, who at last prevailed upon his friend to inhabit the tent of Hassan at night, remaining in the daytime with Yuss Bashi. Captain Abbott now wished to return to Khiva, but Akhood Zadeh dissuaded him. "Allah Kooli," said he, "is not ignorant that the letters I brought for you were taken from me by force; and he will not fail to be influenced by the reports of Hassan Bahadoor, who is so interested in exculpating himself from his criminal proceedings against you. Yacooba Mehter will help him, and possibly you may lose by their fresh intrigues the fruits of your previous negotiations. Hold, then, to what you settled with Allah Kooli Khan; go on to Dach Kaleh and Astrakan, while I return to Khiva to watch over your interests, and be prepared for whatever may occur."

This advice the English officer adopted, and by so doing eventually lost all benefit from his clever and courageous conduct on this anxious and dangerous embassy. He reached the Russian fortress, where his finger was amputated, and as soon as his wounds were healed proceeded to Astrakan to confer with the Russian authorities, while Akhood Zadeh returned to Khiva, with an escort provided by Hassan Bahadoor.

The report to which Yacooba Mehter gave currency, that Captain Abbott had been killed, soon reached Herat; and Major Todd, greatly distressed at the misfortune which deprived him of the co-operation of so good an assistant and compromised the negotiations entered into with the Khan of Khiva, immediately dispatched to his court Lieutenant Richmond Shakespear to complete them, and to ascertain what had really been the fate of their lamented brother-officer. Lieutenant Shakespear, accompanied by the Kazi Hassan Mohamed, arrived at Khiva at the commencement of June, 1840, on the same day that Akhood Zadeh (who the reader will remember was the son of the kazi) reached it from Maukeglag, and from him they heard of the dangers that had befallen Captain Abbott, and of his unlooked-for deliverance.

When Lieutenant Shakespear was thoroughly satisfied of his countryman's safety, he proceeded with the business that Captain Abbott had so well commenced. Allah Kooli Khan, who was at heart favourably inclined towards the English, soon gave up the prejudices that his vizier had instilled into his mind against them, and he even took pleasure in conversing with Lieutenant Shakespear on matters connected with their policy. "How is it," he said to him one day, "that your nation, which is so distant from mine, should wish so much for an alliance with me?" "We possess India," replied that officer; "a vast garden, and, for fear of a surprise, we wish to surround it by walls,—those walls are Khiva, Bokhara, Herat, and Kabul." The Khan, satisfied by this answer, which showed him there was a possibility of obtaining support against the Russians, remained from that moment perfectly willing to treat, whatever his minister might do to induce him to adopt a contrary part. Yacooba Mehter seeing all his plans defeated, sought in every way to multiply difficulties and embarrass Lieutenant Shakespear, and, at the moment when the treaty was about to be concluded, he had the impertinence to say to him, "Thou who wishest to ally thyself to a Mussulman nation, why dost thou not become a Mussulman? Why dost thou remain an infidel?" "Which of us is the infidel?" said the British officer,—"you who, driven by insatiable avarice, daily put slaves to the torture, tear the daughter from her father, the wife from her husband, and sell them to the highest bidder in your bazaars; or those who, like myself, seek the deliverance of so many unhappy beings, and wish to send them back to their country and their families?" Allah Kooli, ashamed of the humiliating reproof that his vizier had drawn upon himself, with some apparent ill-humour, dismissed him with these words: "When will you cease to expose our vices to strangers? this is one who will make them known to the whole world." Yacooba Mehter, after the close of this conference, remained in disgrace for eight days.

Up to this time the Khivan prince had always insisted that the Tzar should return the caravan that had been detained at Astrakan before he set the slaves at liberty; but Lieutenant Shakespear triumphed even over that resolution, by giving him, as a guarantee, a bill of exchange for 4400*l.*, endorsed by the Kazi of Herat, which was to be paid in case the caravan should not be restored after the Russians were given up. This arrangement being satisfactorily concluded, the British envoy collected all the subjects of the Tzar, amounting to four hundred and twenty-four, and having hired camels and men, left Khiva, but on arriving at old Urghendj, he learned that a Russian woman had been detained in the harem of the Usbek prince. Regardless of the consequences that might result from the demand, he immediately sent an express to Allah Kooli Khan, and such was his influence with him, that the woman was set at liberty, in spite of the remonstrances of Yacooba Mehter, and she had the happiness of rejoining her countrymen. The restitution of the caravan took place immediately on Lieutenant Shakespear's arrival at Astrakan with the rescued slaves; thence he went to Orenburg, and from there to St. Petersburg. At the capital he was received in the most courteous manner by the Emperor, and decorated with a Russian order; by his own Government he was knighted. Certainly, the important results obtained by this officer justified the favour in which he was held by the Tzar and his own Sovereign; but his good fortune is one proof more to be added to the many existing in the world that seven-eighths of our success in this life are the result of accident—Sir Richmond Shakespear did but gather the fruits of the labours of the Kazi of Herat and Captain Abbott. The recompense of the former was complete ruin, brought upon him by Yar Mohamed, to punish him for being so useful to the English, and he now vegetates in poverty and misery at Meshed; the reward of the latter is the loss of two fingers, with other wounds—such is the gratitude of governments. Sir Richmond Shakespear, on the contrary, makes a journey to Khiva, the difficulties of which have been removed; above all, he has the Kazi with him, which is a guarantee for his success; and then, because he succeeds, without a thought being bestowed on the exertions of his predecessors, he becomes the centre of rewards, praises, and compliments, while the energetic and courageous pioneers, those who prepared the way for him, fall into the most complete oblivion. What a sad comedy is the world!

Was it persuasion only that induced the Khan of Khiva to give up his captives? This is a point that we have not been able to verify; but even if gold did assist the negociations for the release of the Russian prisoners, can we do otherwise than admire the nation that obtained that result, and made such a judicious selection of its agents to carry out so loyal and noble an enterprise? England, by liberating so many unhappy beings, and restoring them to Russia, destroyed her principal reason for undertaking a second expedition to Khiva. In re-establishing the good understanding between the Tzar Nicholas and Allah Kooli Khan, the English expected to preserve a powerful influence over the latter; but that expectation was completely opposed to the one entertained by the court of St. Petersburgh, which had a direct interest in subjugating, sooner or later, the people of Turkestan, and, therefore, in habituating them never to acknowledge any supremacy but that of Russia. By underhand means, therefore, Allah Kooli was made to comprehend that, if there was danger for him in offending Russia, there was equal risk in seeking support at other hands than hers; and the Usbek sovereign had scarcely settled his troubles with Russia, when he saw his relations with Persia assume a most unfavourable aspect, for the Shah, in the most imperious manner, demanded of him the restoration of 40,000 of his subjects held in slavery in the Khivan dominions. It is easy to see who instigated this demand. Allah Kooli Khan replied that, however desirous he might be to preserve a friendly intercourse with the Shah in Shah,* it was impossible for him to comply with his demand. "The greater part of the Persian slaves," he said, "have been legally bought of the Turkomans settled on my frontier, who are not subject to my laws, and from whom it would be impossible to obtain the sums they have received for them. Many of these slaves have redeemed themselves, married, and become established in my dominions; have raised up families and interests; and to authorize their return to Persia would create a disturbance amongst my subjects that would end in a rebellion, in which I should be the first victim. It is not, therefore, in my power to grant the demand of Mohamed Shah."

The English once more offered their intervention, in the hope of accommodating this difference, and it formed the object of another embassy, which Sir W. M'Naghten, the Resident at the court of Shah Shooja, confided to Captain Conolly, an officer of great ability, and who had already distinguished himself on several occasions.† Moreover, to give him greater consideration and authority, Sir William sent with him an Afghan ambassador, Allah Dad Khan, Popolzye, who was the bearer of letters from his sovereign, Shah Shooja, to the Khan of Khiva.

Escorted by the Hazarahs deh Zingui, Conolly skirted the mountains inhabited by them, travelling direct from Kabul to Meimana, and from that town he wrote to Major Todd, who was then at Herat, to forward him some money, of which he was in need. The major at once despatched Akhood Zadeh with two hundred ducats; and as the latter was now so well known at Khiva, and could be of use to him there, Captain Conolly took him on to the capital. Here the British officer was received with great honour by the Khan, who gave him many proofs of his esteem for himself and his Government, but resisted all his arguments in favour of the manumission of the Persian slaves, and positively refused to liberate them.

---

* King of Kings, the title of the Persian monarch.—*Ferrier.*

† He travelled in Persia, Turkestan, and Afghanistan in 1832. His volume of travels was published in London.—*Ferrier.*

Captain Conolly had been four months at Khiva when a letter arrived from Yar Mohamed, informing the Khan that he had expelled Major Todd from Herat, and recommended him to imitate his example and turn Captain Conolly out of his capital. But instead of adopting this advice, the Usbek sent him a robe of honour, and with it the vizier's letter, assuring him that he spurned such a proposal, and begged him to consider Khiva as his country, and the royal palace as his own house. Captain Conolly failed not to endeavour to turn this evidence of good feeling towards himself to account by urging again the cause of the poor slaves; but his exertions were utterly thrown away. He then took up the idea of purchasing these unfortunate persons on account of the Indian Government.

One of the principal causes of the dissatisfaction of Mohamed Shah with the English was their refusal to pay a subsidy promised to Persia by Mr. MacDonald Kinnear, then British ambassador at the court of Feth Ali Shah, to assist that sovereign in making war against Russia. Captain Conolly thought that, if a sum of money were applied in the interest of Persia as a ransom for the slaves in question, both the Shah of Persia and the Khan of Khiva would be equally well satisfied; and he therefore sent Akhood Zadeh to Kabul to induce Sir W. M'Naghten to sanction the plan, and forward it to Calcutta as the best suggestion he could offer for adjusting the difference that had been created by the demands of the court of Teheran. The departure of this intelligent and faithful friend from Khiva was the signal for a thousand intrigues, which put an end to the influence of England at the court of the Usbek. Sincerely devoted to those whom they served, and united to the Turkomans by the ties of religion, none could better forward British interests in that part of Turkestan than the Kazi of Herat and his son; when they left, Yacooba Mehter regained the ascendant, and Russian interests again prevailed. The Khan, though he conceded nothing to Captain Conolly, became daily more exacting and difficult to please, and finally insisted that he should apply to the Government at Calcutta for a subsidy for him, inasmuch as they paid one to the sovereign of Herat: with this difference, however, that, instead of declining the assistance of English officers, he wished for some to organise his army and cast guns for him. The British agent endeavoured to make him understand that at that moment his request could not be granted, as it would endanger the life of Colonel Stoddart, then a captive at Bokhara, because the Emir would not fail to be offended if support were given to one of his neighbours whose power he most dreaded. The Khan, however, could not or would not be convinced by Conolly's reasoning, and became less and less favourably disposed towards him: finally he made the English officer comprehend that he was in his way, and that he should not be sorry to see him leave his dominions.

CHAPTER XXIX.

Captain Conolly leaves for Kokan — Liberality of that officer — War between Bokhara and Kokan — Colonel Stoddart requests Conolly to come to Bokhara — The Khan of Kokan is averse to his going — Nasser Ullah sends a firman to Captain Conolly insuring his safety — Conolly leaves Kokan for the Emir's camp — Colonel Stoddart — Bad auspices under which he arrives at Bokhara — First meeting between Colonel Stoddart and the Emir — Strange proceedings of that officer when presented to Nasser Ullah — He treats him with insolence — Stoddart is arrested — Barbarous treatment — The Mir Cheb — Stoddart is confined in the Siah-tchah — He turns Mussulman — Russian intervention in his favour — Stoical courage of Stoddart — The Emir changes his conduct towards him — Vicissitudes to which he is subjected — The Sultan interferes in his favour — Also the Russian minister at Bokhara and the Khan of Khiva — Replies of the Emir to those who intercede for him.

AKHOOD ZADEH had left Khiva fourteen days when Captain Conolly determined to quit it also and go to Kokan. He had instructions to explore the road to that town, leaving Bokhara on the right, and passing through Altoon Kaleh, Ak-Mesdjid, and Achkiane; a perfect knowledge of that route was of infinite importance to England, as the Russians were daily drawing closer to it, and it was evidently their object to occupy the points which command it in order to be able to act more powerfully upon the small Tartar states. The Cabinet of St. Petersburg had long since signified to them its intention of constructing a fortress at Ak Mesdjid, for at this spot the three roads diverge which lead from the north to Khiva, Bokhara, and Kokan. A careful examination convinced Captain Conolly of the danger that would ensue to the independence of Turkestan if this encroachment on the part of Russia was permitted, and he advised the Usbek princes to resist it to the utmost. The Emperor Nicholas, however, entirely disregarded their remonstrances, and imperatively informed the Khans that he allowed them three years to make up their minds to leave Ak-Mesdjid and its neighbourhood. This delay expired in 1844; and the following year, when I passed through Meshed, the Usbeks from the north assured me that the Russian fortress was rising fast.

Captain Conolly was six weeks in going from Khiva to Kokan, the Emir of which, Mohamed Ali Khan, gave him a brilliant reception, and he had no great difficulty in winning him over to the interests of his Government; but it should be stated that his presents, amongst which were expensive fire-arms, inlaid and ornamented, and Cashmeer shawls, which he distributed profusely as auxiliaries in his negotiations, contributed not a little to produce this result. He travelled with a train of eighty servants and an immense quantity of baggage, and the principal inhabitants of the towns he passed through shared in his liberality, as well as the Government officials, however low or high might be their rank. This mode of proceeding in a country in which the people are characterised by extreme covetousness could not do less than create an immense number of partisans; and during the three months that Captain Conolly remained at Kokan the inhabitants of that town were almost as much under his influence as that of Mohamed Ali Khan.

The Emir of Bokhara presumes to impose his suzerainty over all the Usbek Khanats which join his own; but it often happens that those which do not recognise his right to that supposititious claim oblige him to place himself on the defensive. The Khan of Kokan, now nearly fifteen years ago, showed the greatest determination not to submit to his rule; but after having been defeated in many engagements, he was obliged to bend to the yoke of Nasser Ullah in 1839. It would appear that the presence of the English officer made Mohamed Ali rather audacious and restive, for he suddenly refused to comply with the conditions of the treaty which he had made with the Emir; and the latter, seeing that negotiation was useless, marched against him at the head of 12,000 men.

When this expedition was undertaken Captain Conolly was still at Kokan, and received about this time a letter from Colonel Charles Stoddart, then a prisoner at Bokhara, in which he pressed him to go to the camp of Nasser Ullah, who had manifested the greatest desire to treat with him for a definitive alliance with England. In this way the Emir hoped he should be able to get Captain Conolly into his power, for, believing as he did that that officer was the instigator of the war which he was now obliged to undertake against the Khan of Kokan, he had a hostile feeling towards him.

Captain Conolly was by no means blind to the danger that lurked under this request of Nasser Ullah's, and he hesitated at first what course he should take; but the hope of attaching the Emir to the British policy, the advantages to be derived therefrom by his Government, and the honour it would reflect upon himself, made him think lightly of his personal safety, and he determined to proceed to the Emir's camp, thoroughly persuaded that it would be easy to induce him to enter into the league which the other Usbek princes had formed against Russia. Nevertheless, before he set out he despatched a messenger to request him to send a firman insuring his safety on his journey. Nasser Ullah, delighted at the facility with which he was drawing the British officer into the snare prepared for him, immediately sent the document, and so much importance did he attach to the fact of his receiving it quickly, that he promised his liberty to the slave who was the bearer of it, across a country covered with the enemy's troops and beset with dangers, if he delivered it within a specified time.

The Khan of Kokan and all the nobles of his court besought Captain Conolly to give up this expedition, and entreated him not to place any confidence in the word of Nasser Ullah: they even detained him a few days by force; but seeing that he was obstinate in his determination, they allowed him to depart, though not without regret, and made him promise to send them an account of his journey, and also the Emir of Bokhara's plan of his intended campaign. It is also worthy of remark, that the Khan of Khiva had advised the English officer on several occasions not to risk his life and liberty on the territory of Bokhara, let the proposal to go there come from whatever quarter it might, for that he would there find nothing but danger and bad faith. It was then something more than imprudence that induced Captain Conolly to throw himself into the lion's mouth; and it is impossible not to respect sincerely such exalted ideas of duty. Which, in truth, is the most deserving of admiration, the men who push the abnegation of the principle of self-preservation to such an extreme solely in the interests of their country, or the country which gave them birth and produces such glorious instances of patriotism?—a country prodigal of its wealth and the blood of its most intelligent and bravest officers, for the merest shadow of an advantage that may disappear in the chances and changes of the future. This is not the optimism of the greater number of European states; and those amongst them who boast of their power and civilization, who shine by their imagination and the wordy eloquence of their Governments, who fence for ever in empty space, would do well to take example from Great Britain.

Ten days after he left Kokan Captain Conolly reached the camp of the Emir of Bokhara. The reception which he met with from this prince at Djizak, though cold and haughty, inspired him with some confidence, and this led him to attempt a reconciliation between the Emir and his vassal. Having succeeded, he left the two sovereigns to discuss the conditions of their treaty, and, under an escort furnished by the Emir, went on to Bokhara, where he took up his residence in the house of a Persian, Abdul Samut Khan,* Naib Top Khane,† whose abode was outside the walls.

Here for a time we must leave Captain Conolly to return to Colonel Charles Stoddart. The reader will not have forgotten that he was attached to the British embassy at the court of Teheran; and was the bearer of the ultimatum sent to the Shah by Sir John M'Neil in July, 1838, in which the British Minister declared war, in the event of the Shah refusing to raise the siege of Herat. After the Persians retired, Colonel Stoddart rejoined Major Pottinger at Herat, whence he was soon obliged to depart on account of the differences that arose between him and Yar Mohamed. He then went to Bokhara, charged by Sir John M'Neil with the difficult task of inducing the Emir to become the chief of a league of the Tartar states against Russia.

This officer had, and with great justice, the reputation of being an excellent soldier—loyal, firm, full of zeal, and of the highest courage; but with these fine qualities there was an impetuosity of disposition and an imperious tone about him, based upon the conviction that he belonged to the first nation in the world, and that

* This wretch, who was of Persian origin, commenced his military career in the army of Abbas Mirza (when that prince was viceroy of Azerbaidjan), and obtained the rank of lieutenant, which he subsequently lost in consequence of some disgraceful conduct that a French officer thought it his duty to report. As this was not the first time he had thus offended, Abbas Mirza ordered that one of his ears should be cut off, and dismissed him from the army. After this punishment he offered his services to the serdars of Afghanistan, and by them he was well received, but was in the end obliged to leave that country for various misdeeds. He afterwards retired to Peshawur, which then belonged to the Maharadjah of the Punjab, but there, as everywhere else, he indulged his intriguing disposition, and joined a conspiracy that had been set on foot against the governor of the town, General Avitabile, a Neapolitan in the service of Runjeet Sing. Abdul Samut and his accomplices were taken: some were hanged, and some put to death in other ways, but the greater number were hamstrung. The rascally Khan escaped with a severe application of the bastinado, and orders to leave Peshawur without loss of time.

It was then that he went to Bokhara, where to a certain extent he organized an army for the Emir, of which he received the command.—*Ferrier*.

† Commander-in-chief of the artillery.

all the others ought to bend before him. Other points in his character also rendered him but little suited to conduct an embassy to the Emir of Bokhara. It was an error of Sir John M'Neil's (who, to say the truth, resembled him in many respects) to select such a man to manage negotiations which required the greatest address and pliancy of disposition.

The following details concerning the captivity of Colonel Stoddart were related to me by the Kazi of Herat, Akhood Zadeh, and several Bokharian chiefs; and I have seen similar information in the account given by Dr. Wolf of the Bokhara victims, translated by Philarête Charles, which I also make use of here, adding to it whatever seems to me to have been overlooked. This courageous traveller describes the Colonel as severe and proud, attached to the habits and religion of his childhood and his country, and inflexible to everything but military discipline. Stoddart, he says, found himself in contact with beasts of prey, destitute alike of pity and good faith, shamelessly perfidious, wedded to the minutiæ of forms, believing themselves justified in doing anything after they have said their prayers and performed their ablutions, and deceiving and killing with perfect tranquillity of conscience. It has been already shown that, in wounding the pride of Yar Mohamed, Stoddart had made him his enemy, and the vizier subsequently wrote a letter to Nasser Ullah, in which he described the British officer as a very dangerous spy, full of intrigue and pride, and an obstinate man; adding that he must be defeated in his views or exterminated. This epistle he sent by one of the colonel's suite to the Emir.

Stoddart, who had no suspicion of the excellent letter of recommendation of which one of his servants was the bearer, nor the habits and customs that he had to encounter, entered the territory of Bokhara full of confidence, and arrived in the capital of Nasser Ullah two days previously to the fast of Ramazan, during which the fanaticism of Mahomedans is always much greater than at any other time. A numerous escort of cavalry, preceded by a mehmendar, received and accompanied him to the residence which had been appointed him in the house of the vizier, Mahzoom Berdi-Reiss, who affected great indignation that the letters with which Stoddart was furnished were addressed to his predecessor instead of to him. But this was only a pretext; for when the colonel left Persia the appointment of the new vizier at Bokhara was not known there; however, it was in this way that the system of intimidation commenced, and after the letter of Yar Mohamed was placed in the hands of the Emir, the latter sought every opportunity of humiliating the stranger who came, as he believed, to meddle in his affairs. Stoddart received these affronts haughtily; the minister did not return his visit, and sent him word that he must come to him; the British agent, however, refused to go; and matters were in this state when Mahzoom Berdi-Reiss entered the colonel's apartment one morning with the vehement apostrophe, "Do you know I have destroyed all the Emir's enemies?" "I rejoice to hear," replied Stoddart, with misplaced irony, "that the Emir has no more enemies." After this unsatisfactory commencement they went on in the same style on both sides.

On the first day of Ramazan the colonel received orders to go on foot to the Registan, the great square in Bokhara, as the Emir wanted to speak to him; but Stoddart refused to walk there, and replied that he should go on horseback, that force only should make him dismount, and that he should do at Bokhara just the same as he would do in London.

To Nasser Ullah, who was already so ill-disposed against him, this answer appeared most insulting; neither a Christian nor a Jew could show himself on horseback in Bokhara, nor any one but the Emir himself on the Registan. However, word was sent to the Englishman that he might do as he pleased; and Stoddart, in full European uniform, caracolled his horse on the forbidden ground, to the great scandal and surprise of the populace. But they were astounded when the sound of the trumpets announced the approach of the Emir; and the stranger, instead of dismounting, settled himself in his stirrups, and received him simply with a military salute.

The Emir, seeing himself thus publicly defied, fixed one long look upon him, and passed on in perfect silence. Some minutes afterwards a maharam * was sent to Stoddart by Nasser Ullah to ask why he had not dismounted in the presence of the sovereign? "It is not the custom of my country," said the colonel. "But it is of ours," replied the officer. "I cannot act otherwise," continued Stoddart. "It is well; the Emir is satisfied, and desires you to go to his palace:" and the chamberlain withdrew.

---

* Chamberlain.

It was not thus that the intelligent Alexander Burnes prepared for his reception by the Emir of Bokhara. He sent a letter, in which he requested "protection and shelter for the traveller from that 'Magnificent Sovereign, the Citadel of true Believers, the Tower of Islam, the Pearl of the Faith, the Star of Religion, the Dispenser of Equity, and Pillar of the Faithful.'" How did Burnes, without any official position, manage to make friends at Bokhara, and to escape every danger? By respecting their bigotry, by conforming to their extravagant etiquette, their Chinese love of forms, and amazing hypocrisy. All obstacles gave way before him. But Stoddart, on the contrary, appears to have taken it into his head to trample under foot every Usbek custom, and to exhibit at the court of Bokhara that unbending pride which is so dear to the English traveller, and at which even Europeans so often take offence.

Before receiving the British envoy, the Emir ordered some Jews, who had traded in Europe, and knew, or were supposed to know, what ceremonies were observed at the courts of Christian sovereigns when they gave audience to an ambassador, to be brought into his presence; and as they affirmed that the salute which Stoddart had made was in conformity with the usages of his country, the Emir was satisfied on the point, and gave an order that he should be admitted at the palace. On his arrival there the colonel was led into a passage that terminated at the interior court of the building in which Nasser Ullah held his durbar and received petitions. Here a chamberlain approached him, and said that he was about to request on his (Stoddart's) part the Emir's permission to introduce him and present his *érz bendèyuiani*—"the supplication of his slave." The colonel was offended at this; he might as well have been offended at the words "Your Majesty," which scarcely belong to any but to God, or have objected to the ordinary phrase "your very humble servant," which signifies nothing. But the stiff and precise ideas of Stoddart thought that such a form of expression was humiliating, and he replied with vehemence, "I address my prayers to God only; I am not the slave of any one: tell your master that I will communicate what I have to say when he has received me, and not before." The same inflexibility was manifested by several other traits of a like nature. The presence of a sovereign in these countries is presumed to have the effect of overwhelming a stranger who comes within reach of the effulgence of his rays; and in consequence of this he is supported under the arms when he enters the hall of audience in which the monarch is seated. Stoddart, who was compelled to submit to this ceremony, shook off with violence the two assistants who introduced him; and this conduct excited the anger of the Bokharians. The master of the ceremonies then approached the colonel to touch his clothes, in order to see that he had no arms secreted upon his person with which he might attempt the Emir's life, and a vigorous blow from Stoddart's fist that laid him at his feet was the result of this unfortunate investigation. Nasser Ullah Khan heard from the inner apartment all that passed in the antechamber, and the proceedings of the English envoy irritated him to the highest degree. At the door of the audience-chamber is placed an officer, who, at the moment a stranger is admitted, repeats the words, "Pray ye all for the sovereign," as if, amidst such a ferocious people, death and danger were always present. Stoddart, who had never made himself acquainted with any of these details, instead of offering up a silent invocation, began reciting in a loud voice a prayer to God in Persian, upon which Nasser Ullah, seated on the royal dais, stroked his beard, full of hatred for this arrogant stranger, and disgusted by his coarse and domineering behaviour.

The Emir, having repeated the accustomed Allah ô Akbar (God is great), received from the colonel's hands the letter which he had brought from Sir John M'Neil, read it, and informed Colonel Stoddart that he could not take into consideration its contents, because it would be derogatory in him to treat with a simple delegate of the British minister. Also, that, in order to continue the negotiations, it would be necessary the colonel should deliver to him credentials signed by the Queen of England herself. Stoddart replied in a dry tone that Sir John M'Neil was likewise the agent and acted for the East India Company, and that this Company had made treaties with all the sovereigns of Asia; that their power was great, and that he did not understand the Emir's objections on this head, inasmuch as there was both honour and profit for him in becoming the ally of that powerful body. Nasser Ullah was far from being satisfied with this reply: he stated that the Emperor Nicholas, his neighbour, a monarch whose power at least equalled that of Queen Victoria, was not too proud to write to him with his own hand, and that he knew of no reason which could prevent the sovereign of Colonel Stoddart from doing as much. "I can," said the Emir to the colonel, "treat only on the grounds of equality; nevertheless, while waiting for the instructions which I recommend you to obtain from London, give me the letters which the *Ferman-Fermar* * has confided to your care for me." The colonel was then obliged to admit that he had no letter to give him but the one that he had presented from Sir John M'Neil, that he was acquainted with the views of the East India Company, and had been instructed to state vivâ voce to his Highness that the Directors would pay a subsidy in money in consideration of a promise to be made on the part of the Emir to resist the encroachments of Russia. Nasser Ullah fixed for a few instants an ironical smile on Stoddart, and said, "Very good; I see that it is your intention to make me your slave: *khetmet kha hem kerd*—it is well, I will serve you. In the mean time withdraw."

This *début* did not augur a successful termination to the negotiations. Stoddart, who had done nothing to conciliate the esteem and confidence of the Emir, arrived at Bokhara without presents, without escort, armed only by his intrepidity; he presented himself as a conqueror rather than as an ally or a friend, and his character as a political personage was equivocal—he neither represented England nor the East India Company. The Emir and his vizier took advantage of these circumstances, and two days after this interview Stoddart received an intimation to proceed immediately to the house of the latter. He hastened, singularly enough —for the hour was inappropriate—to obey the summons: moreover, the colonel had previously refused to attend to a similar request.

It was evening, and Stoddart on entering the house of Mahzoom Berdi confronted twelve armed men stationed in the antechamber of the Reiss, who at once seized and threw him down, and, as he lay on the ground, tied hand and foot, the vizier with a drawn sword in his hand, rushed towards him. "May God pardon your sins!" exclaimed the English officer, who thought that his last hour was come, when Mahzoom Berdi, with sparkling eyes and foaming at the mouth, placed the point of his sword at Stoddart's breast, and loaded him with every kind of invective. "Miserable spy!" he said, "infidel dog! you come here, do

* Governor-General of India.

you, from your English employers to buy Bokhara as you have bought Kabul? You will not succeed—I will kill you!" and he pressed his sabre on the prostrate body of Stoddart; but the Englishman's eye remained firmly fixed on that of the furious minister. This scene lasted a few minutes, and whether the unmoved countenance of his victim arrested the arm of his executioner, or, what is more probable, that this display of force was a concerted plan between the Emir and the vizier, the latter suddenly turned to his servants, and said, "Take him away!" The rain fell in torrents, but the men, some bearing torches, carried him off like a corpse, still bound, and amidst profound silence, along the deserted streets of the city. Sometimes they let him fall on the ground, or drew tighter the cords that confined his bruised limbs; and sometimes they stopped and insulted him with savage gestures and laughter. "Put an end to me at once!" cried the unhappy prisoner; "in pity, prolong not my sufferings!" On hearing this, one of them stooped down, and, bringing his torch nearer to him as he lay upon the ground, said, "Of a truth, you are either a devil or a sorcerer; you know beforehand that you are not going to be killed; if you were only a man, you would certainly have been afraid." In this way they continued to drag him along the streets, and at length threw him, bound as he was, into a dark room, and barred the entrance. After the unfortunate Stoddart had been two hours in this place, alone and stretched on the damp floor, the door opened, lights appeared, and some servants entered, preceded by a man enveloped from head to foot in woollen drapery, which allowed only his eyes to be seen. This personage seated himself on a divan at the extremity of the apartment, the lights being placed in front of him; and Stoddart followed with his eyes every movement of the new comer, who seemed to be some great personage, for every one treated him with profound respect. Raising himself from the floor as well as his bonds would permit, and collecting all his strength, he said, in a firm voice, "I pray that the all-powerful God will pardon you! You have done ill to throw into prison an innocent man, who is charged with a mission from his Government to your sovereign. If you were not disposed to receive me, you ought not to have allowed me to enter your city; it was for the vizier to acquaint me with the wishes of his master; if you desire that I should leave Bokhara, I am ready to attend to those wishes." After having listened with great attention, the disguised person rose and said, "I will communicate what you have said to the Emir."

But this individual, who was the Mir Cheb,* or chief of the police, left the prison to execute the Emir's orders; seized and burned the envoy's papers, sold all his effects and horses by auction, and subsequently transferred him to the Siah-tchah, or Black Well, —a horrible abode. This dungeon, which is in the centre of the town, is twenty-one feet in depth; and here the greatest malefactors are generally confined. The descent into it is made by means of a rope; and when Stoddart was let down he found there two thieves and a murderer, the latter having been incarcerated here for several years. With these criminals for his companions the colonel remained two months in this loathsome and filthy hole, covered with vermin and surrounded by reptiles, in killing which they were constantly occupied. Their food, such as it was, was lowered to them by the rope with which they had themselves descended, and much of their time was passed in smoking.

When the ferocious caprice of Nasser Ullah had been satisfied, and he thought he had humbled the pride of the Englishman and impressed him with the terror of his power, he gave an order to the chief of the police to remove him from the Siah-tchah in which he had been immured, and keep him a prisoner in his own house; but two days after this the public executioner came to Stoddart with an order to put him to death unless he consented to become a Mussulman. To this alternative, borne down by the dreadful sufferings he had endured, and the exhaustion of his mental and bodily powers, he gave a reluctant consent, repeating the Mohamedan confession of faith, after which he was taken to the public square and circumcised in the presence of an immense crowd who had been attracted there by the novelty of the event. Austere and sensitive in his religious feelings, Colonel Stoddart never forgave himself this act of weakness, of which he bitterly repented during the remainder of his wretched existence.

The news of the cruelties that had been perpetrated on the person of the envoy were noised abroad, and General Peroffsky, Governor of Orenburg, instructed the Russian agent at Bokhara to request Nasser Ullah to liberate his prisoner. On receiving this communication the Emir sent for Stoddart, and said, "The Russians claim

* Prince of the night.

you: what will they do with you? Will they treat you well, and shall I place you in their hands?" "I am sure," said his captive, "that the Russians will treat me well; but if my Government demands of your Highness what you have done with me, what reply shall you make?" Such was the answer of this heroic man, after the unexampled tortures he had endured during his two months' confinement in the Siah-tchah with death so near. The Emir, struck by his dignified and bold reply, removed from his own person the rich fur cloak that he wore, placed it on Stoddart, and ordered that he should be led in triumph on horseback through the streets of Bokhara. Restored to health, the first act of the British officer was to proclaim everywhere that he was a Christian, and had become a Mussulman only from the violence offered to him. This conduct was so imprudent, and evinced a strength of mind so rare, that Nasser Ullah, Mahzoom Berdi, the Mir Cheb, and the inhabitants of Bokhara felt as if vanquished; he had been considered as a spy and dealt with as such, but he was again permitted to present himself at the Emir's palace when he gave audience, and received from that barbarian marks of consideration.

Several motives must have led to this singular change in the Emir's conduct to Stoddart. In the first place, the success of the British arms in Afghanistan seemed threatening to Nasser Ullah; he was now desirous of making it appear that the envoy was the object of his munificence, though he had previously made him suffer the weight of his tyranny. He had conceived a hope that he should be able to attach him to his interests, as Runjeet Sing had other Europeans. "Those Feringhees," said the Emir, "so powerful and clever in the arts and diplomacy, so talented in organizing an army, bring everywhere success in their train."

But though lodged in the palace and feasted and overwhelmed with attentions at Bokhara, Stoddart was a captive within its walls, and subjected by turns to the surveillance of Samut Khan, a wretch of avaricious disposition, and Abd ul Haleik, the steward of the royal residence. At this period the envoy was seized with typhus fever, and the Emir ordered his own physician to attend him, who saved his life; and subsequently, when on the eve of sending an embassy to the Tzar, Nasser Ullah offered the colonel the opportunity of accompanying it to St. Petersburg, and undertaking a special mission for him at that court. Once at Orenburg, or rather at the Russian frontier, he would have been out of the clutches of the Emir, but Stoddart declined the proposition; his government had not, he said, as yet intimated to him their wish that he should quit Bokhara. Never was the feeling of devotion to military or diplomatic duty carried to such a height; and scruples like these under such circumstances were perfectly astonishing. Stoddart ought to have known that the great distance from Calcutta, the war then going on, and the state of politics in Central Asia, rendered communication with him almost impossible; the expected despatch might never arrive and this obstinacy renewed the suspicions which had been current as to his motive for coming to Bokhara. One day, when dark shadows came over the mind of Nasser Ullah, Samut Khan received an order to poison the Englishman, who succeeded in preserving his life only by satisfying the cupidity of the Naib with the hope of obtaining a large sum for his ransom; and this the villain increased as much as he could by exciting the suspicions of the Emir. At other times Nasser Ullah felt better disposed towards his prisoner, and sent him tobacco and other presents, requesting him in return to replace the quicksilver on his mirrors, to make him a thermometer, and candles which would burn without smoke; Stoddart might have turned all these matters to account if he had had as much tact as he had courage and piety.

Nevertheless external events advanced towards their climax in the disasters of the British army in 1841—the defiles of Afghanistan were covered with the dead bodies of the troops; and these untoward circumstances made the position of the English agent at Bokhara more and more alarming: moreover war was declared between Nasser Ullah and his neighbour Mohamed Ali, the Khan of Kokan, and at the instigation of the Anglo-Indian government, at least it was thought so. The Sultan, acknowledged by the Soonees as the spiritual head of all Islam, wrote to the Emir of Bokhara to order him to release his prisoner; the Tzar also, through the envoy that was about to arrive at Bokhara, demanded in accordance with the chivalrous customs of diplomatic opponents, the restoration of Stoddart to his country, and when M. de Boutenieff saw him there, he offered him his protection; the Khan of Khiva likewise interceded for him; so that worried by these various applications, and knowing scarcely what to do, the despot became furious. To the Sultan, Nasser Ullah replied that he would obey him provided the Queen of England would remain his friend, and would do him no injury; to the Cabinet of St. Petersburg, that his prisoner was only a traveller, without any official status; and to his neighbour of Khiva in these whimsical words: "You have an Englishman and so have I, why do you wish to take mine?" After which the Emir left Bokhara to make war against the Kokanees.

During this period several letters that Stoddart wrote to his friends, which were entrusted to Khorassanee Kurds, Persians or Jews, who sewed them in the hem of their robes, reached their destination; some of them have been printed, and one is surprised to find in them the style of the Puritans of Cromwell's days. In these letters diplomatic interests, and the feelings of the soldier, take their place far below the religious sentiment which governed the mind and destiny of Stoddart, whose character they invest with real grandeur.

CHAPTER XXX.

Character of Conolly — He is full of hope as to the result of his negotiations — Nasser Ullah returns to Bokhara — His interviews with the English officers — They are both imprisoned — Allah Dad Khan, the Afghan envoy, returns to Kabul — He is brought back to Bokhara — His infamous intrigues — M. de Boutenieff leaves the city — Akhood Zadeh, the son of the Kazi of Herat, and his brother Mohamed Davood — Dangers to which the latter is exposed — Akhood Zadeh is arrested at the frontier of Bokhara — He is imprisoned by the Emir — Obstinate conduct of Stoddart — The servants of the English officers are released from prison — Akhood Zadeh and Allah Dad Khan are confined in the Siah-tchah — They are subsequently released — Joseph, a Greek, is executed — Paper and pens are found on Stoddart — He receives the bastinado — Execution of that officer and Conolly — A register of that event, and other circumstances connected with those officers.

WE must now return to Captain Conolly, who had, as we have already said, fulfilled at Kokan a mission analogous to that of Stoddart, and subsequently, on the invitation of the latter, joined him at Bokhara to share his dangers. This officer united considerable learning to a splendid character—the qualifications of a distinguished soldier and a clever diplomatist. Notwithstanding the grievances that Nasser Ullah Khan fancied he had against him, he was pleased with him at their first interview; and the successful manner in which Captain Conolly had terminated his disagreement with his neighbour of Kokan, disposed him favourably towards that officer. When, therefore, he joined Stoddart at Bokhara he was full of hope that he should be able to induce the Emir to enter into the views of England; but it appears that after he left the camp, Abdul Samut Khan succeeded in working a change in the capricious mind of Nasser Ullah, who wrote to Bokhara and ordered that Captain Conolly should not be permitted to hold any communication with Colonel Stoddart. The latter was at this time living in the house of the Russian Ambassador, and the Emir had a suspicion that he might persist in remaining there, and that M. de Boutenieff would protect him. His order, therefore, to prevent Captain Conolly from seeing his countryman, was given with no other object than that of inducing Colonel Stoddart to remove to the house of Abdul Samut Khan: this fatal step was taken; and Colonel Stoddart, naturally anxious to live with his friend, left the residence of the Russian Ambassador on the 11th of November, 1840, to take up his abode in that of the Commander-in-Chief of the Artillery.

On the return of Nasser Ullah from Kokan, which took place very soon after the arrival of Conolly in his capital, he found himself master of *two* Englishmen; and this was what he wished; for the war in Kabul continued, and the people of Central Asia were animated with the deepest hatred of the power and influence that were brought to bear against them. The conduct of the Emir towards Conolly became haughty and threatening, and Abdul Samut feared, or rather pretended to fear, that the prince's anger would fall upon himself; a house was therefore prepared for the officers in the interior of the city—that is to say, they were treated as prisoners, but an allowance was made them of three tellahs * per day. Conolly had, a month previously, asked for a private audience of the Emir, but never obtained it; however, on the 31st of December, the officers were taken to the palace. "Where are the letters from your government to me?" said Nasser Ullah to Conolly. "You are a spy; but remember that Bokhara is not so easy to conquer as Afghanistan; I shall send you to prison, and your countrymen may come with an army if they like and take you out." Conolly replied with as much firmness as Stoddart, but with more prudence, and both were dismissed. These interviews with the Emir were repeated for three days in succession: the last time they were taken to the citadel, as well as seven of their servants (called in Persian *pich khetmet*, upper servants), and there passed a miserable night of suffering and anxiety. Their house was ransacked and their servants, to the number of forty-four, arrested and thrown into the Siah-tchah (which did not exceed thirteen feet in diameter), for every detail of the successful insurrection against the English in Kabul was then known at Bokhara, and the Emir had ceased to fear them; the wretched captives were to expiate by the most cruel treatment, and finally a barbarous death, the uneasiness that the invasion of Afghanistan had created in the mind of the Usbek tyrant.

It has been said that when Captain Conolly left Kabul on his mission to the Tartar princes, he was accompanied by Allah

* Forty shillings.

Dad Khan, the ambassador of Shah Shooja. This personage followed that officer to the Courts of Khiva, Kokan, and Bokhara; but when he arrived in the latter city he quickly perceived the evil intentions of the Emir towards his master, and endeavoured to obtain permission to retire as soon as possible.

Nasser Ullah had indeed the most profound hatred for the Afghans, and more particularly the Suddozyes, and he would not have been sorry to chastise the ambassador of Shah Shooja; but the fact of his being a Mahomedan, as well as the interest taken in him by the Mollahs of Bokhara who interfered in his favour, induced him to allow Allah Dad Khan to return to Kabul, and he had been gone only a week when the two unfortunate English officers were cast into prison in the citadel. On his road the Afghan was treated with every consideration due to his character of Envoy, and had safely reached the frontier town of Karchy, when he found that the Emir had given an order to the Governor to arrest and send him back a prisoner to Bokhara — which order was carried into effect; and when he returned to the capital he was taken to a place called the Ab-Khaneh,* where the cold was so severe that no person could be left in it two nights in succession and live. Happily for Allah Dad Khan he was, at the expiration of twenty hours, taken out only half dead, and placed in a dungeon adjacent to that to which the British officers had been transferred on their removal from the citadel. This prison was in the house of Mir Syud Sheriff, Kaleh-Beghi,† and from him I received these details. The removal of the Afghan ambassador saved his life, which he so little deserved; for whether he acted by the secret instructions of Shah Shooja as he afterwards pretended, or upon the suggestions of his own mind, it is averred that this wretch instead of assisting Captain Conolly never ceased to embarrass his negotiations at Khiva and at Kokan, by his intrigues and underhand practices.

Monsieur de Boutenieff had not been indifferent to the misfortunes of the British officers, and had energetically protested against the treatment to which they were subjected; but after the disasters of the English army in Kabul the Emir, who now believed himself perfectly secure in his Khanat, considered the intervention of the Russian diplomatist extremely uncalled for, and behaved to him in

* The water-house.

† The commandant.

so violent a manner as to make Monsieur de Boutenieff think he might be treated as the Englishmen had been: he therefore determined to quit Bokhara towards the end of March, 1842.

In the mean time Akhood Zadeh, who was sent to Kabul by Captain Conolly before he left Khiva, had returned to the latter town, accompanied by his brother Mohamed Davood, and brought instructions which it was hoped would induce Allah Kooli Khan to liberate the Persian prisoners. Instead, however, of finding Captain Conolly as he had expected, he received a letter, that the former had written to him from Bokhara, requesting him to join him there. Akhood Zadeh immediately prepared to follow him, but considered it expedient before he set out to send his brother back to Kabul to inform Sir W. M'Naghten of what was passing at Khiva. Fate now pressed heavily and cruelly on the family of the Kazi of Herat, despoiled and exiled by Yar Mahomed, the venerable chief owed his life only to the generosity of Major Todd, who redeemed it from the sordid Vizier at the price of 1400*l.*, and from that moment every member of the family devoted himself body and soul to their deliverers. Mohamed Davood travelled safely as far as Khulm; but at Bamian, four days' journey south of it, he found the whole country in insurrection and, suspected of being a partisan of the English, was stopped and stripped by the Afghans; with a sword-cut on his head and a wound from a ball in his thigh, it was the merest chance that he escaped death and succeeded in gaining Kabul. Arrived there he directed his steps to the entrenched camp, a mile from the city, in which the British army was then blockaded by the insurgents, and delivered his despatch to Sir W. M'Naghten, who, anxious to take advantage of such rare devotion in a native, allowed him only two days' rest, and with wounds yet unhealed, sent him on with letters to General Nott, at Kandahar. At Ghuznee he was seized by the Ghazees, thrown into prison, and searched with great care; but he had concealed Sir W. M'Naghten's despatch in the tuft of hair which Mahomedans allow to grow at the back of the head, and although it escaped their vigilant search, and nothing was found upon him which could establish his guilt, he was tied to the mouth of a gun with the certainty of being blown from it, when he cried out "Allah forgive the murderers of the son of the Kazi Hassan Mohamed." At the sound of that name, so venerated by all Afghans, the Mollahs commanded that he should be set at liberty; and after passing through so many dangers he arrived at Kandahar in safety with his despatches.

Less fortunate than his brother, Akhood Zadeh took the road to Bokhara: he reached Eljik-otoo, a village situated on the right bank of the Oxus, without having heard of the detention of Captain Conolly; and supposing him to be receiving honourable treatment at the Court of the Emir, he did not hesitate in stating openly, when interrogated by the guard at the frontier, that he was in the service of the English and on his way to join one of the officers then at the capital. This was quite a sufficient reason for arresting and sending him there under an escort, and when he arrived the Emir imprisoned him in the citadel, in the house of Syud Mir Sheriff, where Allah Dad Khan was already incarcerated — this occurred ten days after the imprisonment of Stoddart and Conolly. In the various and distressing circumstances which succeeded one another in connexion with the fate of these officers at Bokhara, as much blame was due to the Anglo-Indian government for want of foresight as to Colonel Stoddart, who, though an honest and loyal soldier, was of an unbending disposition, and his national pride led him beyond all reasonable limits; he was perfectly unsuited to the task committed to him, and wanting in the tact and versatility of mind to carry out such a difficult undertaking. The line of conduct he adopted could not fail to end in his ruin, and his blind confidence in the success of the British arms in Central Asia, grieved him to the utmost in his last moments, inasmuch as it caused the death of one of the noblest of his countrymen. Instead of sending word to Captain Conolly to join him, why did not Stoddart follow the instructions of his superiors? In vain the authorities of Calcutta wrote to him that he was free to leave Bokhara, and advised him to seize the first opportunity of flight that presented itself; retained by an exaggerated sense of duty, and disregarding these instructions, he prolonged the critical circumstances in which he was involved till the dangerous period arrived at which the army of his countrymen perished in Afghanistan, and the massacre at Kabul encouraged the Emir to destroy his prisoners: they had not brought him anything that he hoped for, and being demanded from him on all sides, were the cause of extreme embarrassment. Their fate had indeed excited the greatest interest everywhere— neither England nor even Russia had forsaken them: intercessions in their behalf arrived from Persia, Khiva, Constantinople, Kabul, and Herat. The Grand Mollah of the latter town, requested by Major Todd to ask for the release of Colonel Stoddart, drew upon himself a violent attack from Nasser Ullah Khan, who dismissed him rudely, and said, "It is a disgrace to Islam that there should exist amongst the Ulemas one so degraded as to come here to intercede for this infidel." The perseverance with which the liberation of the British agent had been demanded led the Emir to suppose that his life was of great value, and that he might obtain a considerable ransom for him; he even hoped to turn his captivity to good account, and asked the Queen of England to add to his dominions a certain territory on his frontiers, but received only a dilatory reply. Nasser Ullah speculated, in fact, upon his captives, and when he saw that he was deceived in all his calculations, his irascible nature was exasperated in proportion, and he revenged himself in a terrible manner upon the unhappy officers who had placed themselves in his power.

The forty-four servants of Stoddart and Conolly, who were arrested at their lodgings on the day their masters were imprisoned in the citadel, remained forty-four days in the Siah-tchah bound hand and foot to each other, and having for their subsistence only a small ration of bad bread. On the forty-fifth they were taken from this dreadful hole chained by the neck, eleven to a chain, forming four parties, and marched at daybreak to the public square, where they remained all the next night exposed to the deep snow and piercing cold. Two of them had died in the Siah-tchah, a third sunk about noon on the following day from the effects of the temperature of that night, and his corpse was left attached to the chain till sun-down; the feet and hands of the greater number of his surviving comrades were frost-bitten, and they were waiting with great anxiety the execution of the sentence of death which had been passed upon them, when, to their infinite amazement, they were all set at liberty. This was owing to the intercession of the Grand Mollahs of Bokhara who, moved with pity, when they heard of the atrocious order issued by the Emir, went in a body to his palace to protest against it. "They are Musulmans like us, and our brethren," said they to Nasser Ullah Khan, "and may the wrath of Allah descend upon thy head if thou sheddest their blood. They have suffered sufficiently for serving the Infidels. Give them their freedom if thou wouldest avoid the vengeance of heaven and perhaps of men!" The Emir somewhat intimidated by the opposition of the Mollahs whose support was necessary to the maintenance of his power, restored these unhappy beings to liberty, but it was a ten hours struggle to get them out of his hands.

Some Hindoo and Jewish Shroffs,* who had found the means of keeping up a communication with Colonel Stoddart and Captain Conolly, intrusted the servants of these officers with letters which they were anxious to send to their superiors in India; they also gave them some clothes and money, after which many of them departed for Kabul. They arrived there in the midst of the strife of the 22nd of March, 1842, when Mohamed Akbar Khan, master of the capital, was besieging Fethi Djing Mirza in the citadel, and remained here several months in the greatest anxiety, for they dreaded being recognized as individuals who had served the English; but this danger they happily escaped, and when the Anglo-Indian army arrived at Kabul in the August following, they received their arrears of pay, were generously recompensed for their sufferings, and some again took service with British officers. Three of them were for several years my servants; Mohamed, a Heratee, had been with Captain Conolly; another, Ali Bakhtiari, with Captain Vikovitch; the third, Hadji Semnanee, had been cook to Dr. Wolf, and from them I gathered many details respecting their old masters.

Fear alone had induced the Emir to pardon these unoffending men, and he indemnified himself for the blood he could not shed then by treating with still more severity the captives remaining in his power. Four days after the servants were set at liberty he ordered that Allah Dad Khan and Akhood Zadeh should be removed from the prison of the Kaleh-Beghi, and lowered into the Siah-tchah. In this there still remained a Greek from Constantinople, the head servant of Captain Conolly, named Joseph (whom the other servants used to call Yoossoof Khan), and the seven pich-khetmets who had been imprisoned in the citadel, whither they had been taken in company with the English officers the day they were prevented from returning to their own house. Twenty-seven days later the Mollahs obtained the release of these seven pich-khetmets. From that period ninety-two days elapsed, when, and again at the earnest intercession of the Mollahs, Nasser Ullah

* Bankers.

exercised once more his reluctant clemency by releasing the Afghan Envoy, Allah Dad Khan, and also Akhood Zadeh; the former hastened to return to Kabul, and the son of the Kazi of Herat, after having for a few days found shelter with a merchant in Bokhara, reached Persia on foot and joined his father at Meshed, where both sought an asylum from the rapacity and cruelty of Yar Mohamed Khan who had banished them from their country.

Joseph was taken from the Siah-tchah at the same time as Allah Dad Khan and Akhood Zadeh, but the close of his captivity was to be that of his life also. The first time he was brought before Nasser Ullah he said that he was a subject of the Sultan's, which was true; but as he had not been circumcised the Emir thought that he told a falsehood, being persuaded, or pretending to be so, that *all* the subjects of the Sultan must be Mussulmans, and under the impression that he was an Englishman, he ordered him into the Siah-tchah. Suffering horribly from the misery he endured in this dreadful place, he thought that it might be mitigated if he turned Mussulman; he sent therefore a message to that effect to the Emir, who instantly assented to his proposition, but never took him out of the Siah-tchah, where the operation and cure were performed. It was not until the 17th of June, that he saw the light again, when he and the three malefactors, with whom Colonel Stoddart had passed the two first months of his captivity, were brought up to be slaughtered — the execution took place on a Friday, at the hour of evening prayer. The news of the massacre of the English in the Khyber Pass had been sent to Nasser Ullah by the Afghan serdars, who recommended him to get rid of his other prisoners or hand them over to them; and it was their letter which prepared the way for the death of the ill-fated British officers, which was hastened, however, by another cause.

Three days after the execution of Joseph, the Emir commanded that they should be taken from the citadel to a building near the Siah-tchah, but they were not lowered into the well. The guard then forced them to strip off all their clothes, and on inspecting them very closely, found in a small pocket sewn under the top of the sleeve of Colonel Stoddart's *tchoka*,* a pencil, some steel pens, a small phial filled with ink, and some sheets of paper, which were taken to the Emir. Some days previously the police at the fron-

* Bokharian robe.

tier had seized a letter which the Colonel had sent to Mr. Thompson, under-secretary to the British legation at Teheran, who was going to Khiva to continue the negotiations commenced by Captain Conolly; and when this letter was taken to Nasser Ullah he wanted Stoddart to translate it, and also to tell him the use of the articles that had been found upon him. Nothing excites more distrust in Oriental nations than the habit that Europeans have of writing down or sketching, what they see or hear, and in the questionable position in which these officers stood, the double discovery that had been made, could not but exasperate the Emir more and more against them; moreover, Colonel Stoddart at once refused to give the required translation, and he was cruelly beaten with rods on the soles of his feet for three days in succession without overcoming his resolution—he simply declared that the intercepted letter contained nothing hostile to the Emir. But Nasser Ullah would not believe him, and it being his conviction that the purport of the letter was to induce the Khan of Khiva to make war upon him, he condemned the two prisoners to death. No word of weakness escaped Colonel Stoddart when he was informed of the fate that awaited him, but he completely gave way to the violence of his disposition, exhausting the whole vocabulary of personal abuse in Persian against the Emir and his executioner, and ceased not thus to apostrophise them but in yielding his latest breath. He was put to death like a sheep, in some ruins at the back of his prison, and in the presence of a few passers-by who had been attracted to the spot by his cries and his invectives. The officer who was charged with the execution of the sentence then declared to Conolly, who had witnessed his countryman's death, that Nasser Ullah would grant him his life if he would become a Mussulman, but the Englishman replied without fear, as without boasting, "Stoddart and Yoossoof turned Mahomedans and you put them both to death; your proposal is a snare, for you will not spare me any more than you did them. I have no confidence in your promises; I will be no renegade. I die firm in my faith. Finish your work!" They did so, and the bodies of these two heroic men were placed in a common grave that had been dug before their eyes. It was on a Friday evening, the 24th of June.

These sad details were communicated to me by Akhood Zadeh, the Syud Mir Sheriff, whom I saw at Meshed in 1845, my Heratee servant, who had also been Conolly's, and was imprisoned forty-four days in the Siah-tchah, and by many other Bokharians, to whom the particulars of the captivity and death of the British officers were perfectly well known. Dr. Wolf thinks that they were executed on the 17th of June; but, after much investigation, I consider that the event took place seven days later, which is proved by the following dates furnished by the persons above mentioned:—

Stoddart and Conolly were imprisoned in the citadel	Jan. 2, 1842.
Forty-four days after, their servants were released, namely, on	Feb. 15, ,,
Four days later Akhood Zadeh and Allah Dad Khan were imprisoned in the Siah-tchah .	Feb. 19, ,,
Twenty-seven days after, the seven pich-khetmets were released	Mar. 17, ,,
Ninety-two days elapsed up to the death of Yoossoof and the deliverance of Akhood Zadeh .	June 17, ,,
Seven days later, Colonel Stoddart and Captain Conolly were executed	June 24, ,,

This statement is strictly correct; and was copied from the police register at Bokhara by the Syud Mir Sheriff.

Akhood Zadeh, without being so precise himself, acknowledges the accuracy of these dates; he believed the death of the British officers to have taken place on the 2nd of Djemadee el Ewal, or Djemadee el Sanee, *some days after the appearance of the first apricots*—such is the Asiatic mode of marking events.

CHAPTER XXXI.

Mohamed Shah of Persia threatens Khiva — Mr. Thompson, the British minister, arrives at that city — He fails in his negotiations — Nasseli Flores, a Neapolitan, comes to Teheran — Travels to Bokhara, and is thrown into prison there—The Naib, Abdul Samut Khan—Nasseli is condemned to death—Abdul Samut experiences the same fate — Reasons that led to his execution — The watchmaker, Orlando Giovanni — The Emir orders him to be put to death — Character of Nasser Ullah Khan — Measures taken in England to ascertain the fate of Stoddart and Conolly — Dr. Wolf — Policy of Yar Mohamed after the English left Herat — The Shah Kamran in arms against the Vizier — Yar Mohamed besieges him in the citadel —The Serdar Dine Mohamed Khan — Kamran is made prisoner, and plundered by Yar Mohamed — The Shah Zadeh Mohamed Yoossoof — The diamond vest — Negotiations regarding it—Mohamed Yoossoof Mirza the dupe of Yar Mohamed — He flies to Meshed — Revolt to set Kamran at liberty — Yar Mohamed assassinates his sovereign.

SOME months before the terrible tragedy related in the last chapter occurred, namely in the winter of 1841, the British Minister at Teheran made a last effort to induce the Khan of Khiva to give up the Persian slaves; the case was urgent, for Mohamed Shah was marshalling his battalions on the borders of the Atrak and the Gourghan, and threatened to penetrate the heart of Khiva if Allah Kooli Khan persisted in detaining his subjects any longer. The Shah had been driven to this demonstration by the fresh inroads made upon his territory by the Turcomans, who at the instigation of the Khivans, plundered several Persian villages and carried off their inhabitants; in one of these raids they surprised Mohamed Walee Khan, a cousin of the Shah's, and brought him to Khiva, where he was kept a close prisoner. At the time that Mr. Thompson went to that city, accompanied by the Persian envoy Mohamed Ali Khan Kiaffoor, a Russian agent left Orenburg for the same destination, to combine his efforts with theirs in the hope of bringing about a pacific solution of the affair; and notwithstanding the threatened invasion Allah Kooli Khan received them all haughtily. To Mr. Thompson he said, "London is too far off for me to have any intercourse with it, or expect any help from there. Twenty times I have asked the English for instructors of artillery, and they have tantalized me with promises which I have never seen realized; I cannot understand why they interfere in my affairs." He was not so arrogant with the Russian, in whose favour Yacooba Mehter had been endeavouring to prepossess him; but he addressed that ambassador thus: "Petersburg is nearer to Khiva than London, but the bones of the soldiers that the Tzar sent from Orenburg last year to subjugate this country still cover the steppes upon your frontiers, and remain, whitening in the sun, a proof that that undertaking is not easy to carry out." Then, turning to the Persian, he said, "As to Mohamed Shah he may be the cat's-paw of England or Russia, whichever he pleases; Allah Kooli Khan will never imitate his example. You have all taken the trouble to come here to ask me to release the Persian slaves, which I am resolved never to do." And the three ambassadors left Khiva without having in the least advanced their cause.

At Merv Mr. Thompson happily escaped the malevolence of the Emir of Bokhara and Yacooba Mehter, who had sent assassins to the neighbourhood of that town to murder him, but chance and bad information prevented them.* While he was here, Mr. Thompson delivered from captivity a Neapolitan named Nasseli Flores, who had been incarcerated by the Governor Niaz Mohamed Beg. When this young man passed through Teheran he was told by a great many persons, that, in taking the road to Bokhara, he was rushing upon certain death; but he would not listen to their advice, and fate drove him on to his destruction. For many months Flores had enjoyed the hospitality of M. Anitchkoff, the Russian Consul-General at Tauris, and when he put into execution his project of going to Lahore through the Usbek states, Sir John M'Neil, who had a few months previously returned to Teheran, conceived some suspicions against him; he even opened a correspondence with Count de Medem, the Russian Minister, and complained of the direction Nasseli intended taking, protected by a passport which had received the *visa* of the Russian authorities. He said that he considered the journey of Flores across Tartary concealed intentions hostile to England, and offered to send him safely to Lahore free of expense if he would consent to go there by the Persian Gulf and India, but nothing could overcome the obstinacy of the traveller; and the Count de Medem to

* After this was written, Mr. Thompson informed me that that this story was not true. An Usbek woman, in order to get a good reward for saving his life, invented the tale.—*Ferrier.*

set at rest the suspicions of the British envoy, was obliged to erase the Russian *visas* on his passport, and state thereon in Persian that the Neapolitan travelled unprotected by Russia. Flores had not been long enough in Asia to understand the character of Asiatics; he expected to find on his arrival at Bokhara a people resembling the Turks or Persians, and notwithstanding the impediments thrown in the way of his journey, he persisted in his determination and left Teheran with only one servant. He remained some time at Meshed, and I received a letter from him, from this city, probably the last that he ever wrote. The perusal of this may be interesting to the reader. It is dated Meshed, May 22, 1842:—

"MY DEAR M. FERRIER,

"When I left Teheran I promised to let you hear from me when I reached this city. I have been here now a fortnight, and arrived after a fortunate journey of twenty-nine days. Nature has been very niggardly to Persia; but in the Khorassan there is more vegetation than in the provinces of Azerbaidjan and Irak. Should circumstances ever bring you to Meshed I advise you, when you get to Nishapoor, to take the mountain road. You will find villages in the rich valleys; through these water flows in abundance, and a double row of trees following the course of the stream form a pleasing shade for the traveller. Between Nishapoor and this are two small lakes, which I assure you are very picturesque.

"General Semineau, to whom I previously wrote, will have presented my sincere regards to you and have given you a description of this country. I am forced to remain here until the caravan for Bokhara is ready. The days seem an everlasting length; the time passes so slowly when one is obliged to wait and has an object in view.

"Meantime I am in very good company; your countryman M. Jacquet, surgeon of the regiment of Hamadan in garrison here, a person of great merit, is very hospitable to me, and we pass whole days in conversation. He was not aware that there were any French officers in the Persian army; and he will be enchanted, after the report I have given him of your amiable disposition, to make your acquaintance. You can, and with reciprocal advantage, exchange the news of Europe with that of Central Asia, which never fails to reach this frontier city. I am desired by him to say a thousand obliging things on his part, so it now remains for you to write to him, and I assure you that you will be very pleased to know him.

"The Turcomans often visit the villages near the city—they are a perfect nightmare to the Persians; last year they surprised the Vizier of the Governor in a garden out of the town and sold him to the Khan of Khiva. Five months after Assaf Doowlat, the Governor, desirous of making reprisals on a Turcoman tribe in the mountains to the right of Nishapoor, went there with 3000 men of all arms and seven guns to surprise them, but though he made a rapid march the greater part of the enemy were gone, leaving behind them only a few old clothes, swords, and still older camels, and several hundred men within the entrenchment. The powder was not spared; several Turcomans were killed and wounded, also some Persians, but the Governor on the second day fearing an attack from a body of the enemy's cavalry, ordered an assault without making a breach; judge from that how war is conducted in this country.

"The other day the Governor blew a Turcoman from the mouth of a gun and cut off the hands of seven others in the service of Persia who had plundered travellers in the mountains.

"My departure will, Inshallah! be after to-morrow with a numerous caravan. Pray tell General Semineau that as soon as I got here I sent him a letter by a messenger whom Ferez Ullah Khan sent to Teheran. I would write to him again did time permit, but I should only weary him; I beg you to offer him my sincere gratitude and respect. Remember me to your comrades. I do not forget our prince Malek Kassem Mirza; present to him my compliments and tell him that I have given his letters to the Governor, who received me very politely. Adieu, my dear M. Ferrier. May God grant that we meet again in another country rich and happy.

"Ever yours,

"NASSELI FLORES.

"*To the General Ferrier.*"

Flores left, as he intended, with the caravan for Merv, where he had the good fortune to be found by Mr. Thompson, who, as we have said, procured his release, and he then continued his journey towards

Bokhara. His servant—the only one he had—declined to follow him beyond Merv; but this incident, instead of opening his eyes, appeared only to confirm him in his resolution to meet the difficulties and dangers of his undertaking, and he marched on to certain death, with the self confidence of a conqueror. It was twelve days after the death of Colonel Stoddart and Captain Conolly that Akhood Zadeh had the happiness of leaving the city of Bokhara: on his journey from that scene of horrors he met at Tchardjooee, on the left bank of the Oxus, Nasseli Flores, and used every argument he could think of to turn him from his purpose of going on to that capital, relating to him succinctly all that he had so lately witnessed and suffered; but Nasseli understood not a word of any eastern language, and his efforts therefore were utterly vain—he sought to supply the place of words by signs, but he addressed one both deaf and blind. The thought crossed the mind of the energetic Afghan that he would bind him and carry him back to Meshed by force; but he was alone and on foot, devoid of resources of every description, how then could he hope to succeed? moreover such an act on his part might expose him to the danger of being taken himself and sent back to Bokhara. He could therefore do nothing but pray to Allah for the safety of the young traveller, who so confident and light-hearted, was surely going to take his place in the Black Well, and with a heavy heart Akhood Zadeh wended his weary way towards Khorassan. His fears were just; the infatuated Italian continued his journey, and he had scarcely been an hour in the city of Bokhara when he was seized, stripped, and lowered into the Siah-tchah; here he was kept eight days, and fed upon a meagre pittance purchased with the money that had been found on him. He was afterwards brought before the Emir to be present at the investigation of his papers, and as Flores did not understand either Turkish or Persian, an Italian renegade named Giovanni Orlando was ordered to interpret the conversation; the chief of the Artillery, Abdul Samut Khan,* the mortal enemy of all Europeans who had the temerity to go to Bokhara, was also in attendance.

* "I think it well," remarks Dr. Wolf, "to give you a sketch of the life of this Abdul Samut Khan. He was born at Tabrees in the year 1784, and, having acquired some smattering of military science at Kermanshah from M. le Général Court, he was employed there for a while by Mohamed Ali Mirza, the celebrated son of Feth Ali Shah. On account of some misconduct of Abdul Samut Khan, Mohamed Ali Mirza ordered his ears to

We have seen how grievously the intrigues of this villain influenced the fate of Colonel Stoddart and Captain Conolly and aggravated the sufferings of their imprisonment and death; but in his conduct to them he acted quite as much from a sordid love of gain by setting a daily price upon their lives, as from his hatred to all Feringhees: besides, these two unhappy travellers constantly revived in his mind the memory of the most unfortunate events of his existence—the loss of his ears at Tauris and the infliction of the bastinado at Peshawur—both of which occurred in connexion with Europeans, and he had sworn to revenge his injuries on every one of them that might fall into his power. It was enough that Nasseli was an European for him to incur the deadly hate of the Naib; he had also the fault, in his eyes, of being a soldier, for as Abdul Samut was exceedingly ignorant of the military art, he dreaded lest the Emir should keep Flores in his service, and that in comparing the knowledge of both, the result would be very much to his own disadvantage. He had determined to compass the death of Nasseli from the moment that he entered the palace of the Registan: and the fatality which seemed to follow the unfortunate Neapolitan pursued him even here, for the letter of introduction to his countryman Avitabile at Lahore was found amongst his papers; that rendered Abdul Samut perfectly furious, and sentence of death was pronounced

---

be cut off. The khan then deserted, and went over to Ali Mohamed Mirza's antagonist, Abbas Mirza, at Tabreez, but was soon obliged to escape from there. When I arrived at Cabul, in 1832, I met Sir Alexander Burnes, and in conversation he told me: 'When you come to Peshawur be on your guard against a person there who calls himself the vizier of Sultan Mohamed Khan; his name is Abdul Samut Khan, a great rascal, who, if he can do any harm to an Englishman, he will do so; for he knows that we look upon him with contempt.' Therefore, on my arrival at Peshawur I never came near him, but saw him only for one moment, when he called upon me in the company of Sultan Mohamed Khan. A short time after this he intrigued against this prince, fled from Peshawur, and took service with Dost Mohamed Khan; he endeavoured to excite a revolt against that personage, but he was discovered, and fled to Bokhara, where the wise and good Haken Beyk, the Goosh-Beghee of Bokhara (when I was there in 1832) procured him service with the Ameer, to teach the soldiers the military discipline. He lives in great pomp outside the town, and has acquired during the nine years he has been there a fortune of 60,000 tellahs, that is, ducats. He is commander-in-chief of the artillery, and has the title of Nayeb. The Ameer retains by force at Bokhara a certain Giovanni Orlando, of Parma. I had obtained the Ameer's permission to take him with me when I left that city; but having heard that Abdul Samut intended to assassinate me on my road, he requested me to inform the Austrian minister at Constantinople of his position at Bokhara. Abdul Samut had paid ten assassins to kill me on my way to Meshed; and the fact is so certain that I am acquainted with the names of the ten individuals."

against the unhappy traveller. The Emir was only too well inclined to order his execution, and on leaving this audience Flores met with the same fate as the lamented Stoddart and his friend.

Providence often takes upon itself to supply the deficiencies of human justice; of that fact the death of Abdul Samut Khan in 1847 is a proof, and this in spite of the services that he had rendered the Emir of Bokhara. He too well knew the character of Nasser Ullah to believe in his gratitude, and like every high personage in an Asiatic Court, he had no lack of enemies who daily excited his master's suspicions against him. Aware of this, and being a cunning fellow, he sent to his brother, a merchant at Meshed, all the money that he had amassed, whether honestly or dishonestly, at Bokhara, and in 1847 this amounted to nearly 40,000*l.* For many years he had wished to return to Persia, and enjoy at his ease the fruits of his rapacity; but though he had been on the look out for an opportunity of leaving, it never presented itself, and hampered as he was with heavy baggage and several women and children, flight was difficult. To send them away before him would be to reveal his project to the Emir, who indeed had long suspected it, and had given an order that he should be closely watched. Nasser Ullah felt that he was more in the power of the Naib than he liked to be, and had often thought of putting him to death; but then he was so useful—it was only by his assistance that he had been able to impose his suzerainty on the Khans of Cher Sebz, of Kokan, and Balkh, and to deprive himself of his services when he had no other general capable of commanding his army, might prove exceedingly injurious to his interests; he waited therefore, but he was full of suppressed fury against the Persian heretic who had the audacity to be necessary to him. Abdul Samut, however, finding that temporizing did not advance his project of flight, determined to take other means of securing it. In 1847 the Emir marched against the Khan of Cher Sebz, who was in arms to throw off the suzerainty that Nasser Ullah had imposed upon him, and Abdul Samut, thinking that a good opportunity had presented itself for attempting his escape, placed himself in communication with the refractory Khan, and told him that when the armies met he might charge the Bokharians without any anxiety about the artillery, for he would have the guns loaded with powder only, "and then," he added, "as soon as you have forced your way through our lines, I will turn the guns upon the Emir and his troops and we shall crush them at once." This letter was entrusted for delivery to a Persian artilleryman, but he carried it to Nasser Ullah Khan, when the Naib was instantly sent for, and put to death in his presence; his wives and children were given up by the Emir to the merciless soldiery, under whose cruelties many of them lost their lives.

One European still remained at Bokhara—Giovanni Orlando, the Italian renegade already mentioned. This poor fellow, who was by trade a watchmaker, was living at Teheran in 1839, when an ambassador arrived there from the Khan of Kokan, by whom he was persuaded to follow him to the court of his master. Giovanni was well treated by Mohamed Âli; but scarcely had he felt the advantages of his new position when the Emir of Bokhara attacked Kokan, and carried him off to his capital, where he obliged him to mend all the broken watches of his court for nothing. This treatment was widely different from the kindness he had received from the Khan of Kokan; but, as it was impossible for him to escape, he submitted to his sad fate. When Dr. Wolff was at Bokhara in 1844, the Emir consented to allow the watchmaker to return to Persia with him; but on the day appointed for his departure Giovanni was seized with a sudden panic: an idea that assassins had been placed on the road to murder him had taken such firm possession of his mind that he would not leave, and he thus lost his only chance of returning to Europe. Three years rolled on after this misfortune, and he continued to repair the Emir's old watches: however, in the course of time his tools wore out, and it was utterly impossible to replace them; his work, therefore, of course, became inferior, but Nasser Ullah would accept no excuses, insisting upon its being as well done as when he first arrived at Bokhara, and for various failures inflicted the bastinado. One day the Emir's watch stopped in the middle of his prayers, on remarking which he dashed it against the wall, and, furious, ordered the unfortunate Italian to be brought before him. He was obeyed. "Kill him," he thundered to the guard; and the third stroke of a club ended Giovanni's troubles and his life.

The Emir of Bokhara, Nasser Ullah Khan Bahadoor, Melik el Moumenine, is a monster of ferocity. The titles he bears are thus translated:—Nasser Ullah, Khan, The Victory of God; Bahadoor,

The Victorious; Melik el Moumenine, Prince of Believers. He raised himself to the throne by a series of frightful murders amongst his kindred, and other crimes from which even Bokharians recoiled with horror; his bad faith became proverbial amongst them, and his name was pronounced with terror by the people. The Bokharians, however, are now apparently indifferent to the atrocities committed by the Emir, or the disgusting character of his vices, the extent of which is beyond all that can be imagined, and they consider that he is justified by his position in gratifying every passion in any way that he pleases. An increase in the taxation is the only thing upon which they are in the least sensitive; but as on that point Nasser Ullah keeps strictly within the commands of the Koran, and generally speaking the duties are rarely above 2½ per cent., which is fixed by the Zekiat, the Bokharians are satisfied, and do not think the virtue of their wives or daughters of any importance so far as the sovereign is concerned. Besides, the mollahs were the first to set the example of base submission, and the Kazi of Bokhara issued a *fetvo* proclaiming that Nasser Ullah was by the will of God the absolute master of all the women in his territory, that he had a right to do what he liked with them, and that it would be a crime to oppose his wishes; singularly enough, the Kazi was the first person to feel the effects of the doctrine he preached, for his daughter fell a victim to the Emir's brutal passions. One must, therefore, conclude from all this that the inhabitants, though so perfidious and cruel, are in regard to their prince the most easy-going people in existence; of this he seems so perfectly convinced, that when he leaves his palace he never has any escort to attend him, and two or three times a-week the Emir may be seen walking through the bazaars in the dress of a dervish, accompanied only by one servant. The shopkeepers are aware of the order he has given that no one shall pay him the least respect, or treat him otherwise than as one of the public, and for this reason nobody moves away at his approach: he walks from one shop to another inquiring the price of grain or other merchandise for sale; makes here and there a purchase; and, if he finds a tradesman playing tricks, he never offers a remark at the time, but on the following day sends for the delinquent at his public audience, and inflicts the punishment that he thinks he merits. In the year 1845 he appeared to be about thirty-four years of age. This is the man whom the English hoped to make the docile instrument of their wishes; but their agent, as we have already said, was ill-chosen to effect this object, and the sacrifice of his life was the result. The presence of Europeans, Russian or English, alarmed, and not without reason, Nasser Ullah Khan, but though a monster, his jealous terror was the result of reflection, and learning that an English envoy was coming to Bokhara, he resolved to give him the most terrible idea of his power: by this means he hoped to neutralise for the future any desire the English might have to meddle in his affairs, and he determined to keep their agent a prisoner, to be made use of as an hostage in case his countrymen should feel disposed to annoy him—this was not bad reasoning for a barbarian.

The communications with Bokhara being cut off, the Indian Government was for a long time ignorant of what had befallen Stoddart and Conolly, and it had also been absorbed in preparing the second expedition to revenge the disasters of 1841 in Afghanistan; when, therefore, some months after, the Governor-General, in announcing his successes and the punishment of the Afghans, demanded the diplomatic agents of England from the Emir of Bokhara, he found they were no longer in this world!

After the murder of these two officers was ascertained, the Indian Government was utterly at a loss how to avenge it. A large army would be required to attack and successfully punish Nasser Ullah Khan; it must leave in its rear the Sikhs, the Afghans, and all the banditti on the left banks of the Indus and the Oxus. Once at Bokhara, this army would find in its front the advanced posts of Russia, the Cossacks of the Steppes; and Persia and Kokan, obliged to make common cause with the sovereign of Bokhara, a country half as large as Europe with its nomade and warlike mountaineers, would have risen as one man. Certainly there was room for reflection, and the English press and the opposition were not asleep; they pointed out with force the dangers of such an expedition, and this time the Directors dared not oppose the opinion entertained against it on all sides. Nevertheless, the uncertainty which existed as to the fate of Stoddart and Conolly awakened the sympathies of their friends, and steps were taken to ascertain the truth; a Protestant missionary, Dr. Wolff, volunteered to go to Bokhara, and with admirable courage risked his own life upon the bare hope of saving the lives of others. After having exposed himself to great dangers, he has returned to Europe firmly convinced of the death of these two officers, though many persons are still doubtful of the fact; as to myself, who followed closely the steps of Dr. Wolff in Tartary and Afghanistan, I can only confirm his statement as one that cannot be controverted.

The narrative of the British negotiations in Bokhara is so intimately connected with the history of Afghanistan as to have made it requisite for me to give some details of it; but I must now resume that of Herat, which will put the reader in possession of the remaining information that I have been enabled to collect respecting Afghanistan.

The British mission had scarcely left Herat when Yar Mohamed, who had been warmly solicited to expel Major Todd by Assaf Dooulet, Governor of Khorassan, claimed the fulfilment of his promise to pay him a subsidy in money, and gave him six guns and some thousands of firelocks to enable him to march on Kandahar. Assaf Dooulet knew him too well to comply with his wishes; the gifts would, he was aware, be received with the liveliest demonstrations of gratitude, but all would end there, and, under a host of pretences, more or less admissible, he would not take a single step beyond the walls of Herat. The Governor of Khorassan, therefore, evaded his request, but in terms by no means hostile; Yar Mohamed, however, would not consider himself beaten, and renewed his demands more than once without success. The vizier never forgave this refusal, or the just estimate that Assaf Dooulet had formed of his character; he swore eternal hatred to him and his family, and the consequence of this fracas to the Governor of Khorassan will be related hereafter.

Unsuccessful with the Persian, Yar Mohamed was obliged to content himself with the money that he had extorted from the English, and thought no more of invading Kandahar, but he determined to pursue to its completion a scheme that the presence of Major Todd had hitherto absolutely obliged him to delay—there was nothing now to prevent him from compassing the death of the Shah Kamran, and establishing himself on the throne of Herat. This prince at once saw that he could not withstand the sinister projects of his minister without the help of the English; he therefore energetically declared that they should remain at his court and carry out their own views; but as such an arrangement did not suit the vizier, he paid not the slightest regard to his sovereign's wishes.

Shah Kamran had a presentiment that his end was approaching, though after Major Todd's departure he roused himself to avert his sad destiny, and at length determined openly to confront his tyrant minister. His supporters and advisers in this bold attempt were his four sons—Iskander Mirza, Nadir Mirza, Zeman Mirza, and Saadat Mulook Mirza, also his cousin Yoossoof Mirza, a grandson of Hadji Firooz Eddin. These princes secretly assembled at night all those in whom they could place confidence, and, having with their aid overcome the vizier's guard, took possession of the citadel for the king, retiring with him within its walls. It was defended by five hundred devoted soldiers, and as the garrison had provisions for a year, and munitions of war more than necessary to hold it for a longer period, the princes hoped that this stroke of policy would have brought about a reaction against the minister, and that the population of the country would have besieged him in the town, thus rendering them masters of his person. But events entirely falsified their calculations, for the vizier hearing just before midnight that the Suddozyes had taken up arms, without loss of time despatched all the cavalry that he was able to collect at the moment to hold the surrounding country in check, and invested the citadel with six battalions, upon whose fidelity he could depend. From that moment the cause of the Suddozye dynasty became desperate at Herat: its fatal hour had come. Nevertheless, Shah Kamran, or rather his sons, would not succumb; they repulsed the attacks of Yar Mohamed with a perseverance and bravery worthy of a better result, and the vizier finding his attempts were fruitless against the energy of their defence, was obliged to commence a regular siege.

Before he retired to the citadel Shah Kamran despatched a messenger to the English at Kandahar to apprise them of this crisis in his affairs, and to beg them to send him troops, promising to hold the fortress till their arrival, and to place it in their hands. Unfortunately at this period, the spring of 1841, symptoms of agitation had already shown themselves at Kandahar, and the Resident could not without imprudence detach any of the force then stationed in that principality; however, the Anglo-Indian Government were not indifferent to the appeal of their ally, and spared neither money nor promises in their endeavours to induce the Afghans of Herat to exert themselves in his favour.

It has been related that Dine Mohamed Khan, the cousin of the vizier, had been arrested by his order towards the close of 1840, but at the expiration of five months this serdar succeeded in escaping to the mountains of Gour, where he married the daughter of Moustapha Khan, an independent chief of the tribe of Eimak Taymoonis, which gave him great influence in the surrounding country; this made the enmity of Dine Mohamed of some importance to Yar Mohamed, and, as that serdar had always been a partisan of Shah Kamran, Major Rawlinson, the British Resident at Kandahar, thought he could not do better than request him to assemble such of the Afghans as were disposed to help their sovereign, and march on Herat. He also sent Dine Mohamed 1000 Russian ducats; but whether, as the serdar pretended, the money arrived too late, or, as others have said with more probability he remained irresolute too long, when he declared himself ready to march the opportunity of saving Shah Kamran was lost. The Suddozyes, however, though abandoned to their own resources, behaved with the greatest intrepidity; they held the citadel for fifty days, and gave in only when the artillery and mines had partly destroyed the walls, and the *débris* having filled the ditch, the besiegers had obtained an easy access into the body of the place.

In the first moments of success Yar Mohamed acted with some moderation, and sent the four sons of the Shah out of the territory of Herat without doing them any personal injury. As to his sovereign, who entirely lost the little liberty that he had enjoyed, the vizier thenceforth treated him as a state prisoner, and, as soon as he felt that the king was completely in his power, he proceeded to despoil him of his treasures, and seized some splendid diamonds, of the value of more than 240,000*l.*, which were known to have been taken by Shah Mahmood from the crown of Kabul when he reigned in that country. But the deposed prince resisted his demands with more determination than he expected, and refused to tell him where he had concealed his riches.

Yar Mohamed knew his old master so well as to be perfectly sure that neither torture nor death would make him reveal the place; he therefore employed stratagem, trusting that it would succeed better than threats. The vizier acted with less generosity to Mohamed Yoossoof, the Shah's cousin, than to the other princes, for he retained him a prisoner at Herat, but he now determined to make use of him in his endeavours to conquer the obstinacy of

Shah Kamran. He therefore sent for Mohamed Yoossoof, and, after having given him his liberty, informed him that it had never been his wish to usurp the royal power; that he always intended to substitute a prince of the blood-royal in place of the Shah, that his thoughts had always turned upon him, Mohamed Yoossoof; and finally, that his determination was to give him his eldest daughter in marriage, and declare him sovereign of the principality. The only condition, he said, that he should attach to these dazzling promises was that the Prince should endeavour to prevail upon Shah Kamran to divulge where he had hidden his gold and jewels. The old Shah always had a great affection for his cousin, who possessed his entire confidence, and he, therefore, not unwillingly entrusted him with part of the desired information. Mohamed Yoossoof, like a wary man, took one-half of the money which had thus been placed in his way by his confiding sovereign, and carried the other to the vizier, who did not conceal his gratification at this first success. What he most coveted, however, was not yet forthcoming: this was a woman's vest, decorated with precious stones, the value of which was 160,000*l*. Before Kamran retired to the citadel he thought this lady's waistcoat would be no longer safe with him, and gave it into the care of one of his wives, who, uneasy at the responsibility thus thrown upon her, handed it over to her steward, named Nasser Ullah Beg. This trustworthy man had, in the first instance, removed to the country; but, three days after the princes retired to the citadel he went to Meshed, carrying the precious waistcoat with him. Mohamed Yoossoof Mirza was ignorant of the latter circumstance, though he knew that the garment had been given to the Shah's wife, and he told the vizier of this, who put the poor creature to the torture, to force her to give it up; but she bore the agonising trial rather than reveal the secret. He then tried the effect of domestic influences, and signified to her that her only daughter by Shah Kamran should the next day be married to his son, the Serdar Syud Mohamed Khan; but when the unhappy girl heard who was to be her husband, she poisoned herself to escape the detested nuptials. At last Yar Mohamed discovered that the object of his search was at Meshed, and made every effort to get it back, but without success; he then revenged himself on the miserable wife of his sovereign, whom he imprisoned in the citadel, and subjected to daily torture, and it was not till 1846 that she was released, on the reiterated demands of the Shah of Persia. She then fled to Teheran, and joined her brother, the Serdar Chems Eddin Khan, who had long since been driven to take service in the Persian army by the tyranny of the vizier. As for the valuable vest, it never fell into the possession of those who had a right to it. In December, 1845, when I was at Meshed, the faithful depositary of the treasure, Nasser Ullah Beg, died of cholera; he had been ill some time previously, and Assaf Dooulet, seeing his end approaching, appointed him his steward, giving him at the same time one thousand tomauns with which to purchase camels. Nasser Ullah, laid up by sickness, was unable to execute the commission; and when he died, the governor of Khorassan, under the pretence that the deceased had funds of his in his hands, seized everything in his house, and the royal vest thus became his property. It is true that the claims of the Serdar Chems Eddin were supported by the Shah of Persia, and that he ordered his uncle to restore it to him; but Assaf Dooulet settled the question of its restoration by the payment of several thousand tomauns. Since that period he has been deprived of his command in Khorassan, and with the wealth that he accumulated during the thirteen years that he governed that province, his son the Sipahi Salar, created a powerful party, with whose support he raised the standard of revolt against the Shah of Persia, and kept his army in check from 1847 to 1850.

At the same time that Yar Mohamed tortured the faithful wife of Kamran, he disposed of the other wives of that sovereign—and in the Shah's lifetime—to his own friends and partisans; and as they were, for the most part, young and rich, their new husbands were well satisfied with this arrangement, though it is reprobated by the laws of Islam. I was informed of one action of the vizier's of which I should scarcely have believed him guilty, had it not been mentioned to me by his most intimate friends, namely, that he sold three or four of the daughters of Shah Kamran, as well as the eldest of his wives, to the Turcomans, who disposed of them again in the markets of Khiva and Bokhara.

But to return to the Prince Mohamed Yoossoof: after having executed, so far as he had the power, the behests of the vizier, he claimed the performance of the promises which he had made him. Yar Mohamed declared himself ready to fulfil them, but objected that Mohamed Yoossoof had only partly carried out his engagement, and that much of the treasure had yet to be recovered; he did not, he said, intend to alter his determination on account of that disappointment, if the prince would give him a decisive proof of his devotion by having his cousin, the Shah Kamran, put to death. Mohamed Yoossoof now saw clearly the snare into which the vizier wished to draw him, and subsequently throw upon him all the odium of the murder of his relative, for it was in this manner that Yar Mohamed intended to clear for himself, and at the prince's expense, the road to the sovereign power, and thus avoid the disgrace of the crime of regicide. Mohamed Yoossoof at once perceived the danger of rejecting the proposals of a man like Yar Mohamed, hardened in every crime, and, to lull his vigilance, consented to all that he demanded; in the evening, however, under the pretence of enjoying the fresh air, he went out for a ride, escorted by a few servants, and escaped to Meshed, where the Persians received him in the kindest and most generous manner. Before leaving Herat he took the precaution to write letters to several of his friends, in which he warned them of the vile deed meditated by the vizier; but the Heratees had long been accustomed to submit to his tyranny, and were indifferent to, or, at any rate, took no interest in any schemes that he might have against the Shah Kamran, whose conduct had made them callous to his fate. Some few chiefs, who were in favour of a legitimate monarch, endeavoured to revive in the people the prestige which attached to their ancient line of kings; but they could only excite a partial movement, which Yar Mohamed speedily suppressed. This manifestation, however, baffled him in his treasonable plans, and he waited till he should so perfect his combinations that a failure in them would be impossible. His first preparatory measure was to remove Shah Kamran to the citadel of Kussan, thirty-six miles west of Herat, confiding his safe keeping to his cousin, the Serdar Dad Khan, and for some months after this the miserable existence of the dethroned monarch was passed in this fortress in the midst of continual orgies; the vizier commanded that he should be freely supplied with wine and spirits and exciting drugs, in the hope that they would conduct him more quickly to the grave, and also that, in his fits of intoxication he would say or write something that would lead to the discovery of the famous jewelled vest. But his hopes were disappointed, for, however intoxicated the Shah might be, he always recovered the most perfect self-possession whenever his hidden wealth was alluded to. At last Yar Mohamed commanded that torture should be resorted to to vanquish his obstinacy; but this also was fruitless. "Let me go on a pilgrimage to Mecca," said the old man, "and I will send you a rich ransom when I reach Meshed." The vizier was too well versed in the value of Afghan promises to trust to this one, and finding that his prisoner was utterly useless for his principal purpose, and might even create trouble for him, he at length resolved to put the Shah out of his way. The moment was favourable to his project; the defiles of Kabul had witnessed the destruction of one British force, the division in Kandahar could think only of its own safety, Shah Shooja had lost his life, and his death was the forerunner of that of his nephew, the Shah Kamran. After an unsuccessful attempt made by the inhabitants of Kussan to deliver him in the spring of 1842, this unhappy prince was again tortured and cruelly beaten, and at the close of March, Yar Mohamed commanded that he should be suffocated. The Serdar Dad Khan was the executioner, and when he placed the cushion on the poor old man's face, he made no resistance; on the contrary, he testified a certain degree of satisfaction that the moment which was to terminate his sufferings had arrived.

CHAPTER XXXII.

Sons of Shah Kamran — Hadji Firoos Eddin — His sad end, and that of his son Malek Kassem Mirza — Afghan princes in Persia — Conduct of Russia and England with regard to Herat — Yar Mohamed, now sovereign Prince of Herat, attends to the welfare of the Heratees — Strengthens his power, and prepares to attack Gour — Dine Mohamed Khan plunders some caravans — Yar Mohamed takes possession of the province of Gour — Differences with Kandahar — Subjugates the Hazarah Zeidnats — Marches against the Usbek Khanats — He is recalled to the south — Privations suffered by his army — Equilibrium between the states of Central Asia — Mohamed Shah of Persia supports Kohendil Khan in his quarrel with Yar Mohamed — The latter assists the Shah of Persia in his war with Khorassan — Death of the Persian monarch — Alliance of Yar Mohamed with the Shah of Persia.

THE assassination of the Shah Kamran is the vilest of the many atrocious crimes that stain the character of Yar Mohamed Khan. Had he waited but a short time longer, the death of his aged sovereign, whose constitution was broken up by excesses and tortures, must have taken place naturally. To Europeans the cowardly deed appears in the most odious colours: not so to the Afghans. In their eyes it was simply the exercise of a right—the right of the strongest; it was perfectly reasonable that the vizier should kill his enemy, if he could; and the tone in which they would say to each other, "the vizier has killed the Shah Kamran," seemed to express an opinion that he deserved commendation for his conduct, and had by this act added to the glory of his career rather than that he had done anything worthy of reproach.

At his death the Shah left ten sons: their names were as follows:—

Djehanguir Mirza.	Djellal Eddin Mirza.
Seïf ool Moolk Mirza.	Iskander Mirza.
Saadet Mulook Mirza.	Chahab Mirza.
Alemguir Mirza.	Zeman Mirza.
Ahmed Ali Mirza.	Nadir Mirza.

Iskander and Zeman died of cholera at Teheran in 1846.

The eldest son, Djehanguir Mirza, who ought to have succeeded Shah Kamran, will be remembered by his revolt against his father at the time that the latter went to quell disturbances in the province of Furrah, and by the cruel sentence that he pronounced against his envoy, Meuvalee Khan. He showed, however, that the blood of the Suddozyes flowed in his veins, for, like all that family, he was brave, though restless and debauched. Some time after the siege of Herat by the Persians, he declared himself independent in the district of Furrah, of which he was governor, and Yar Mohamed was obliged to send troops to subdue him; which having been accomplished, he was brought to Herat, where he had only half his liberty. When, however, Shah Kamran was removed to Kussan, the Mirza succeeded in escaping, and took refuge in Persia. At Teheran he lived utterly lost to all sense of his own dignity; and at the time he was residing in the low quarter of the Niguaristan, inhabited by the Berbers, he thought only of drinking arrack and smoking opium, where, completely brutalised, he still lives on a small pension granted him by the Shah of Persia.

The other sons of Kamran are effeminate men, more or less polluted by the same vices as their elder brother. Seïf ool Moolk and Saadet Mulook, after the ruin of their house, retired first into the district of Gour, and then into that of Zemindavar, in the principality of Kandahar. Nadir Mirza established himself at Bagdad. Alemguir and Ahmed Ali took refuge in India, and are the most intelligent princes of this family. The remaining brothers, Djehanguir, Djellal Eddin, Iskander, Chahab, and Zeman went to Teheran, where the three who survive owe their daily bread to the generosity of their cousin, the Shah of Persia. Mohamed Yoossoof Mirza, also their cousin, though much inclined to drunkenness, is superior to them in capacity, and is distinguished by the same qualities that won for his grandfather, Hadji Firooz Eddin, the esteem and affection of the Heratees. That prince, it will be remembered, reigned sixteen years in Herat, to the general satisfaction of the population, whom he treated in the most paternal manner. After having been vanquished by Moustapha Khan, he went to Meshed, and resided there in great retirement upon the bounty of the Persian Government. One morning a party of serbaz broke into his garden, and were proceeding to pillage it, when he went to remonstrate with them; but the simplicity of his attire so completely deceived the villains as to his identity, that they supposed him to be a servant; and to prevent him from returning to the house to give the alarm, one of them killed him on the spot with a stroke of his kandjar. The fate of his son, Malek Kassem Mirza, was not less sad. This prince was attached to the expeditionary corps which, under the command of Abbas Mirza, marched against Herat in 1833. Being detained by business at Meshed, he followed the army a few days after it had left, accompanied by only ten servants, and was attacked half-way between Meshed and Herat, by a party of Turcomans; in this murderous conflict he had the misery of seeing one of his sons fall beside him mortally wounded, and the next moment he was seized, bound, and dragged off to Khiva, where he was sold in the public market-place for a slave. Information of this fact having reached the Khan of Khiva, he purchased him immediately, and gave him the revenues of a village for his support, though he would never allow him to leave his dominions; and he died there in 1840. Mohamed Yoossoof, the son of Malek Kassem Mirza, obtained a grant of land from Assaf Dooulet, and, accompanied by some Heratees, who had attached themselves to his fortunes, he raised the little village of Singbest from the ruins in which it had lain for more than two hundred years.

Mohamed Ali, Shah of Persia, sheltered and protected all the members of the Suddozye family in the hope of one day making use of them against Herat, the possession of which he had not ceased to covet, but his successor, Nasser Eddin Shah, harassed by the intestine divisions of his kingdom, was far less taken up with the idea of extending it towards the east: but the Suddozye princes and a few Afghan chiefs still remain on the list of state pensioners; though it may now be affirmed that not one amongst them has the capacity necessary to induce the Afghans to place him on the throne of his ancestors. The influence that Russia or England may one day exercise in this part of Asia, renders anticipations of this kind very unimportant, for those powers will respectively attach to their own interests such of the Afghan chiefs as will bend with the greatest docility to their views of dominion, without considering the qualifications of the individuals whom they place at the head of the principalities. The cruelty of Yar Mohamed Khan was great; great, also, were his ambition and his avarice, which had been the source of a thousand evils to the Heratees; nevertheless they joyfully beheld him attain the sovereign power, hoping that when they were relieved of Shah Kamran, for whom contempt was the only feeling they entertained, the vizier would give them tranquillity and security; and they were not disappointed. As soon as he had proclaimed himself master of the principality, under the simple title of Vizier Saheb Kebir,* he exercised his authority with a firm hand, and introduced a great many reforms, which in his intercourse with the English he had found would be profitable to his treasury, as well as to the people; the taxes, police, customs, and all that related to them, were placed upon a fresh basis, and every one gained by these reforms. When he was firmly established he ceased to be cruel, even to those who were opposed to him, but he showed thieves and assassins no mercy. He had the tact to procure the recognition of his usurped power by his neighbours, with the greater number of whom he lived on good terms. The serdars of Herat, who up to that time had sold him their support, were reduced to complete obedience: some of the most turbulent he put down, replacing them by others from the tribe of Ali Kioozye, to which he belongs, and he eventually became absolute over the great vassals, and the nomade population under his jurisdiction. It was more by address than by severity that he obtained this result, and as no one dared to dispute with him the sovereignty he had usurped, his power was soon limited only by his will. The town of Herat, destroyed by the siege of 1838, rose by degrees from its ruins, thanks to the gold that the English had so profusely scattered around them; Yar Mohamed continued the improvements they had so happily commenced, and applied prompt remedies to the evils under which the population still suffered. He especially encouraged agriculture and commerce, placed a very light duty upon the sale of corn and the necessaries of life, and further relieved the poorer classes by setting them to work at the fortifications of the town, which were rebuilt in accordance with the plans of the English engineers. Finally, he completely checked the pillage that had been carried on, not only in the principality, but even up to the gates of Herat. The means that he employed to attain this end were so terrible that to this day, when any article is by accident dropped on the roads, or even in the fields, no one dares to take it up; the first person who finds it informs, with the utmost speed, the nearest officer of police of the fact, whose duty it is to seek out the owner, and return it to him, without putting the careless proprietor to any expense. Yar Mohamed Khan had become wealthy at this period—excessively wealthy; his rapacity,

* Grand Vizier.

without being extinguished, was a little abated, and he wished that the people, who now felt the advantages of his beneficial administration, should give him all the honour and gratitude due for it; while by throwing the blame of the previous anarchy on the weakness of Shah Kamran, in whose reign he pretended he could never realise the improvements he proposed, he contrived to render odious the memory of that unworthy though unfortunate monarch. Yar Mohamed was thus occupied in consolidating his power in Herat, when the chiefs of some distant districts, who had only nominally recognised the sovereignty of Shah Kamran, raised the standard of revolt, and he therefore resolved to strike vigorously, in order to annihilate any disposition of the kind for the future. After having confided the city to his son, the Serdar Seif Mohamed Khan, and a picked garrison, he proceeded to the district of Kaleh-noon, inhabited by the Hazarah Zeidnats; but the Serdar Kerim Dad Khan, their chief, feeling that he was not strong enough to confront the approaching danger, went to offer his submission to the Vizier, engaged to recognise his suzerainty, also to pay him a tribute in barek and horses, and gave him one of his brothers and several Hazarah chiefs as hostages for his fidelity. This happy settlement of the disturbances in Kaleh-noon enabled Yar Mohamed to turn his arms against Gour, the state of which province caused him considerable uneasiness.

This district was governed by two independent chiefs, the Serdars Moustapha and Ibrahim Khan, who, being open to more than one influence adverse to the interests of the new sovereign of Herat, now and then made a raid upon his dominions at the instigation of Kohendil Khan, Prince of Kandahar. They might have been acting in support of some discontented serdars, but on the present occasion the danger to the vizier was more imminent, for he had to unravel the plots of Seïf ool Moolk and Saadet Mulook, sons of Shah Kamran, who, when driven from the citadel of Herat, had taken refuge with Ibrahim Khan. This chief warmly embraced their cause, an alliance the more vexatious for the vizier as the country of Gour presents at every step admirable positions for an army on the defensive and is intersected by high and rugged mountains, very precipitous, and covered with forests; lying between them are beautiful valleys, inhabited by the nomade population, and in the villages which are also scattered on the steep sides of these mountains, a few men in ambuscade might easily hold a very considerable army in check. To these advantages, which enabled the fugitive princes to harass the usurper of their rights, and, in case of discomfiture, retire to a formidable position, there was added another, scarcely less important; the intrepid cousin of the vizier, Dine Mohamed Khan (who, as we have already said, married the daughter of Moustapha Khan, the other Taymooni Serdar), also consented to join their party. And we must here digress for a moment to give a brief account of his subsequent career.

After his flight from Herat, Dine Mohamed Khan soon wearied of the life that he led in the mountains of Gour, where he had been found by the messenger of Major Rawlinson when he brought him the proposal that he should march to the relief of Shah Kamran, then besieged in the citadel of Herat. He afterwards took advantage of the return of the Mohamedzyes to Kandahar to resume his active life; and when the English left that city, and Kohendil Khan proceeded there to take it from Seïf der Djing, Dine Mohamed appeared at Kandahar to offer his services to the son of Shah Shooja, who was under the protection of the British. The prince accepted them with gratitude; and in the battle which took place at Haooz Singsar, in which Seïf der Djing was defeated, Dine Mohamed distinguished himself by his accustomed bravery. With two hundred chosen men he for two hours sustained the attack of the entire army of Kohendil Khan, amounting to six thousand men; but in the end, finding himself obliged to yield, he retired to the mountains, where no one thought of disturbing him. His little band being soon destitute of everything, he proceeded to the plain of Bakooa, near the Kachrood, and placed himself in ambush on the side of the Koohi Duzd (Robber's Mountain), where he waited for a caravan of several thousand camels and mules, which was expected to pass that way; When it arrived he captured the whole, and upon this plunder maintained his troop during the winter. In the course of the two following months he completely restored his finances by pillaging other caravans, after which he returned to the mountains of Gour, where he found the sons of Kamran, with whom he made common cause.

When Yar Mohamed marched against Gour he with his usual tact began his operations by sowing dissension among his enemies, and Moustapha Khan, who supported Dine Mohamed, and Ibrahim, who took the part of the princes, quarrelled—nay, fought. In this conflict Ibrahim Khan was worsted, which led to the subjugation of the country; and the princes having lost the support of Moustapha Khan, and Ibrahim having fled to the mountains, they were obliged to retire to the district of the Serdar Akter Khan at Zemidavar, in the territory of Kandahar, where they were soon surrounded.

As to Dine Mohamed Khan, he grew tired of the harassing life he had passed for two years, and willingly gave his sanction to a reconciliation which several chiefs wished to bring about between him and the Vizier; but remarking, as he thought, a coldness in his reception by Yar Mohamed, he feared that he might be betrayed, and fled from his camp the same night. On arriving at Meshed he was kindly welcomed by Assaf Dooulet, who immediately availed himself of his acknowledged bravery by sending him with his Afghans to pacify the southern part of Khorassan, then in revolt, and the chief has since remained in the service of Persia.

Yar Mohamed had afterwards little trouble in reducing the disunited serdars of Gour. Ibrahim Khan, driven from one position to another, retired to a fortified rock in the mountain of Tchalap Dalan, which had the reputation of being impregnable; there, reduced by famine, he surrendered at discretion and swore obedience to the Vizier; but a few days after, however, he contrived to escape, and returned to the hills, where he lived for some time by pillage. This chief had about 7000 families of Taymoonis under his rule, and Yar Mohamed, after having completely devastated the country they occupied, removed them to Herat, where he established some in the city and the remainder in the suburbs; they were afterwards organized into several battalions of serbaz, and, being very brave, are now the best troops in his army. Moustapha Khan having assisted Yar Mohamed against Ibrahim Khan, the vizier spared his life, but this was not the only reason that dictated his generosity; the district inhabited by the former chieftain is the most impracticable in the country, and the difficulties that Yar Mohamed would have had to surmount in any attempt to reduce it, spoke far more in Moustapha's favour than the gratitude of the Vizier of Herat.

Having obtained these satisfactory results from his expedition, the Vizier returned to his capital and occupied himself in extending his frontier towards the north. In the commencement of 1846 he marched with his army in the direction of the Moorgab, on the banks of which river were encamped some Hazarah Zeidnats, commanded by one of the brothers of Kerim Dad Khan, of Kaleh-noon, the chief of the whole of that tribe, but these nomades decamped at the approach of the vizier, and retiring into the Persian territory, put themselves under the protection of Assaf Dooulet, who gave them the village of Kariz on the frontier of Herat. This act was not of a nature to allay the hatred felt by Yar Mohamed for the Governor of Khorassan: he did not forget it, and at a later period made him pay dearly for the vexatious opposition.

The Vizier allowed his cavalry to graze their horses in the fine pastures watered by the Moorgab, and afterwards returned to Herat to be present at the departure of his daughter Bobojane for Kabul, whose marriage with Mohamed Akbar Khan 'was,' it will be remembered, very nearly causing a serious conflict between the Vizier and the Prince of Kandahar. The latter desired nothing better than to seize this pretext for extending his territory at the expense of Yar Mohamed, but each time that he sent his troops towards the frontier of Herat, Mohamed Akbar as a devoted son-in-law, immediately made a corresponding movement towards that of Kandahar, with the army placed in observation at Ghuznee, which at once checked the ambitious aspirations of his uncle, Kohendil Khan. Nevertheless Yar Mohamed was anxious to take revenge for the depredations that had been committed by the Kandaharians, in the south of his principality, and ravaged the border villages of Kandahar. After this, and towards the middle of 1846, he marched into the Gour country, where disaffection had again manifested itself, and did not leave it till order was perfectly restored in the province. It was about this time that the Serdar Akter Khan, Alizye, attacked and beaten by Kohendil Khan, who feared his influence and his power, took refuge with Yar Mohamed, who gave him the government of the district of Gour, where he was rejoined by his tribe which had been dispersed, and it is still established there. Since that period Kohendil Khan has not dared to renew his incursions upon the Heratian territory.

Towards the close of the year 1846, the intrigues of the prime minister of the Shah of Persia, having induced his royal master to deprive Assaf Dooulet of the government of Khorassan, and the consequence of that measure having been the entire ruin of his family, one of his sons, as I have said before, raised the standard of revolt, and all Khorassan responded to his appeal. The fall of Assaf Dooulet greatly assisted the cause of Yar Mohamed, whose power increased considerably. For thirteen years the Vizier had been held in check by him; he had never permitted him to extend his rule over the small Usbek Khanats situated to the north of his dominions, and he went even so far as to counteract openly that which he more legitimately exercised over the Hazarah Zeidnats. As soon as Yar Mohamed heard that Assaf Dooulet had left for Teheran, and that he had therefore nothing to fear from him he marched once more against Kerim Dad Khan, whose submission had hitherto been only nominal. This time the Hazarah chief determined upon making open war with his suzerain; he assembled a chosen band of 12,000 of his best cavalry, and Yar Mohamed led to the attack in the open country of Kaleh-noon 8000 horse, 6000 foot, and a battery of six guns. The combat, a most sanguinary one, lasted nine hours; but the Hazarahs were at length crushed, and many chiefs lost their lives on both sides: the gallant Kerim Dad Khan, weakened by the loss of blood that streamed from many wounds, escaped with great difficulty, and was accompanied only by one single horseman of the brave men he had commanded, when he reached the Persian territory at Toorbut Sheikh Djam.

Yar Mohamed encamped upon the field of battle, and in the space of eight days collected ten thousand families of the Hazarah Zeidnats whom he removed from their native soil to that part of the district of Herat, reaching from Obeh to Gorian, where he settled them on the banks of the Herirood. By these forced immigrations of the Taymoonis and Hazarahs, the principality became more populous than it had been previously to the siege of Herat in 1838, and Yar Mohamed obtained the further advantage of keeping under his eye the most turbulent inhabitants of his dominions. He made excellent soldiers of these Eimaks and by their amalgamation with the Afghans it became almost impossible for the former to betray him.

After having installed them in their new abode, and fixed the tax they should pay at three tomaums for each tent, Yar Mohamed again took the field, and marched upon Meimana, a small independent Khanat lying north of Kaleh-noon, of which there were two chiefs, brothers, Eukmet Khan and Shere Khan, who admitted his suzerainty without hesitation. The Vizier then pushed on to the rich Khanats of Serpeul, Chibberghane, Andekhooye, and Akhtche, and their respective khans, who up to that period had nominally been vassals of the Emir of Bokhara, also submitted. From Akhtche Yar Mohamed sent an ambassador to that sovereign, and also to the Caliph of Merv, to inform them that they must with the least possible delay give up all the Heratee slaves then in their territories; he also warned them that if there was the slightest armed demonstration on their part, or on that of the Khanats which he had subjugated, he would march straight upon their capitals. Although Yar Mohamed had nothing to fear from the Shah of Persia in thus extending his dominions, he considered it politic to inform him of his march into the Usbek country, and assure him that these conquests could not but contribute to augment his power and renown, inasmuch as they were made in his name by the most humble of his vassals. Mohamed Shah having the revolt in Khorassan on his hands, and being unable to repress it, was obliged to put up with these lying protestations, and he endured what he could not prevent.

Yar Mohamed subsequently marched upon Balkh, when a courier brought him information that the gallant Kerim Dad Khan, having placed himself at the head of some fugitives of his tribe who had joined him in Khorassan, was ravaging the district of Gorian from one end to the other—his letters also brought him other news not less vexatious. Shah Pecend Khan, an independent Afghan chieftain and lord of Laush-jowaine (a fortress on the north of Lake Roustem), who was allied to the serdars of Kandahar, had at their instigation, and with the aid of some nomade Beloochees, pillaged the camps and villages in the district of Furrah and Bakooa. This untoward intelligence obliged the Vizier rapidly to retrace his steps, and move with the mass of his forces towards the quarter threatened. But, after the first five days' march, the Usbeks that he had incorporated into his army deserted, and the Khanats, which had so recently submitted, proclaimed their independence, at the same time massacring the garrisons that had been left in them. To complete his misfortunes, the cold set in with such intensity, that before he could reach Koochk a large proportion of his soldiers and four-fifths of his horses had perished; provisions suddenly failed, and hunger was added to the other miseries his army had to suffer. These difficulties, which occurred simultaneously, were certainly great, but Yar Mohamed was only three days' march from his capital; he had obtained a large sum of money in the countries through which he had passed, so that it was easy for him to repair these disasters, and from the moment of his return to Herat his activity and vigilance triumphed over them.

This success against the Usbeks naturally excited the jealousy of Persia and all the independent chiefs, his neighbours, who, dreading lest his influence and power should trench upon their own, formed a league against him; and Kandahar, obeying the impulse given by Persia, allied itself to the chiefs of Bokhara, Khulm, and Balkh, to oppose his projects and those of his ally, the Emir of Kabul. The mutual hostility of these states is the imperative result of their respective positions, and that circumstance is the cause which has for so many years prevented the union of the Afghan principalities in one kingdom. If Kabul or Herat attacks Kandahar, a diversion is made on the north by Balkh and Khulm in support of that principality; if it is on Khulm or Balkh that the central states direct an attack, then Kandahar and Persia will make a diversion in favour of the established equilibrium — the balance of power in Central Asia. Herat and Kabul have for some time reciprocally assisted each other; but it must be added that these alliances are modified and vary according to the interests that are engaged on either side. A short time before Yar Mohamed's expedition to the north, he was alarmed lest his friendly connexion with Kabul should be broken off by the death of his son-in-law Mohamed Akbar Khan; but as his widow Bobojane then became the wife of Goulam Haidar Khan, another son of Dost Mohamed's, and who also succeeded Mohamed Akbar in the post of vizier of Kabul, these fears were gradually dissipated, and, when he marched towards the south to put down the revolt of the chief of Laush-jowaine, his new son-in-law so completely overawed Kandahar that it gave him confidence in his intentions. The Vizier, however, knew by long experience that family ties are of little value in the eyes of Afghans, and that the smallest conflicting interest neutralises them completely; he therefore endeavoured, while preserving the friendship of the chiefs of Kabul, to secure the support of Persia, her sovereign having till that period been hostile to him. To attain his object he in the first instance assisted the Shah's troops that were engaged in repressing the revolt in Khorassan at the head of which were the sons of Assaf Dooulet; and in thus acting he also indulged the hatred that he felt for all the members of his family. This alliance with Persia was a fresh proof of the far-sighted character of the vizier's policy, but the friendly manifestation had very little effect upon Mohamed Shah, who detested him from his heart's core, and an opportunity of showing this feeling having presented itself, the Persian monarch did not allow it to escape him.

On the 6th of August, 1848, a messenger from the Prince Hamzeh Mirza, commander-in-chief of the Persian forces in Khorassan, brought two letters to the Shah. One of these missives came from Kohendil Khan, who declared himself the very humble vassal of the Shah of Persia, and as such requested the permission of the King of Kings to march against Herat with 15,000 men, and take it. "For a long time," said the Serdar, "the great men of that city have been constantly asking me to assist them in putting an end to the tyranny of the Vizier Yar Mohamed Khan; but I will not undertake the expedition without the authority of your majesty." The other letter was from Yar Mohamed, who expressed himself in equally devoted terms, and requested the assistance of the Shah against the hostile demonstrations of his neighbour of Kandahar. He represented, judiciously enough, that the position taken by the English near the right bank of the Indus at Dadur, near the Bolan Pass, was at so short a distance from the former city that they necessarily possessed, and could exercise whenever they pleased, a most powerful influence over the political conduct of Kohendil Khan, who had no means of releasing himself from it; also, that in furthering the designs of the Prince of Kandahar upon Herat, the Shah of Persia would be acting in direct opposition to his own interests, for the English would then be able by his means to enter Persia at any moment they imperatively intimated a wish to that effect. Mohamed Shah knew that the Vizier told the truth, for experience had long since proved that in maintaining the three principalities in Afghanistan, and upholding the independence of some of the smaller chiefs, his government could exercise a much greater ascendency over them than by uniting them under one sovereign; he could thus enter into their quarrels, and control them alternately through each other. But his antipathy to Yar Mohamed overpowered every other consideration, and he had decided on supporting Kohendil Khan when death put an end to his earthly career on the 4th of the following September, and arrested the execution of the orders he had sent to his army in favour of the Prince of Kandahar. At the time the Shah of Persia came to this unwise decision the Vizier was at Meshed, assisting Prince Hamzeh Mirza, who was besieging it. The Afghan army performed prodigies of valour in many successive assaults, but what could 8000 men do against a city the inhabitants of which had, a century before, and for two years consecutively, resisted the efforts of 60,000 Afghans, under Ahmed Shah, Suddozye, and finally obliged him to raise the siege. When the news of the death of Mohamed Shah reached Meshed, the Persian troops became demoralised, and two battalions which occupied the citadel evacuated it, and rejoined the besieging army, which, subject to daily attacks from the enemy, and starving, had very soon no other resource left than to retire into the territory of Herat, where Yar Mohamed received Prince Hamzeh Mirza most hospitably, maintaining his soldiers for many months; and when, in consequence of the recall of their commander to Teheran at the commencement of 1849, they quitted the principality, the prince presented four pieces of cannon to the Vizier in testimony of his gratitude for the treatment that he and his troops had received.

Nasser Eddin, the successor of Mohamed Shah, adopted a policy entirely different from that of his father. Towards the middle of 1849 he sent to Yar Mohamed a sword richly set with jewels, and his highest decoration, accompanied by a letter in which he stated that he considered the Vizier as his most faithful ally. The latter was not tardy in returning these professions of friendship, and in the spring of 1850 a colossal elephant, that had been presented by Yar Mohamed to his suzerain, was frequently seen promenading the streets of Teheran: in fact, the best understanding existed between Nasser Eddin and Yar Mohamed. Those who know the Vizier see in these demonstrative sympathies for Persia nothing more than an additional instance of his ability, but they remain still convinced that he will never give her his support so completely as to enable the Persians effectually to subdue the revolution in Khorassan under the Salar. That revolt is a great piece of good fortune for Yar Mohamed; he now gives the law to all the smaller chiefs around his dominions, and he is too clever not to see that the pacification of Khorassan would be a disadvantageous event for him—he therefore secretly feeds the fire, though he pretends he is endeavouring to quench it—but it is with a cupful of water.

As to Kandahar, there is less chance than ever of its receiving support from Persia; and at this time, 1850, the attention of Kohendil Khan, as well as that of the Emir of Kabul, is chiefly directed to the results that have followed the extension of territory acquired by the English at the expense of the Sikhs, and consequently their nearer approach to Afghanistan. Their present north-west frontier is the Indus, along the whole of its navigable course; and they have crossed it at two points—Peshawur on the north, and Shikapoor on the south. These are *têtes-de-pont* which command the passage of that river, and give to the Anglo-Indian government the power of exercising the greatest influence over the policy of the chiefs of Kandahar and Kabul—may Europe never have cause to repent that she has permitted those conquests which will render Great Britain and Russia all-powerful over this planet.

THE END.

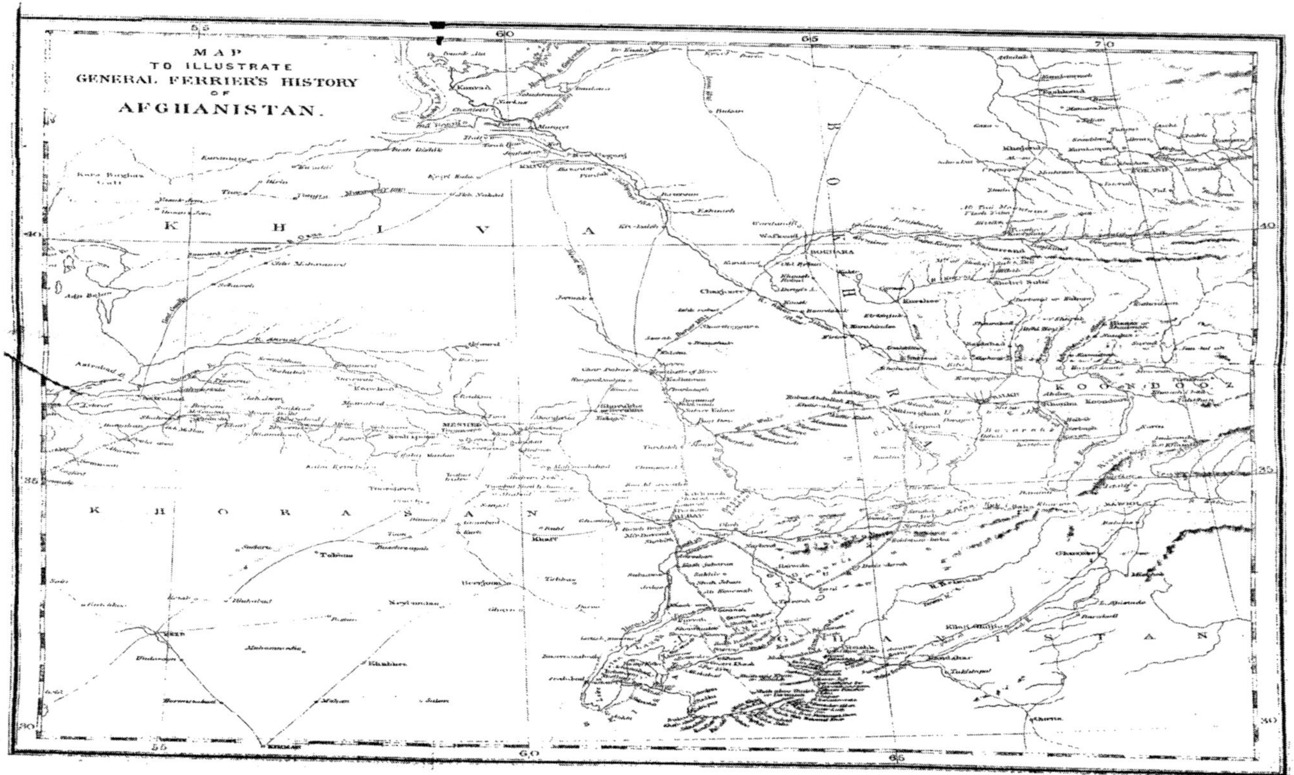
MAP
TO ILLUSTRATE
GENERAL FERRIER'S HISTORY
OF
AFGHANISTAN.
KHIVA
BOKHARA
KHORASAN
AFGHANISTAN
KOONDOOZ
BOGHARA
MESHED
KABUL
HERAT
55
60
65
70
40
35
30